Matthew Henry's Concise Commentary on the Bible

by

Matthew Henry

VOLUME 1

GENESIS TO PSALM 72

Table of Contents

Matthew Henry's

Concise

Commentary

Matthew Henry

An abridgment of the 6 volume "Matthew Henry's Commentary on the Bible".

Genesis

Genesis is a name taken from the Greek, and signifies "the book of generation or production;" it is properly so called, as containing an account of the origin of all things. There is no other history so old. There is nothing in the most ancient book which exists that contradicts it; while many things recorded by the oldest heathen writers, or to be traced in the customs of different nations, confirm what is related in the book of Genesis.

Chapter 1

Chapter Outline

Verses 1, 2

The first verse of the Bible gives us a satisfying and useful account of the origin of the earth and the heavens. The faith of humble Christians understands this better than the fancy of the most learned men. From what we see of heaven and earth, we learn the power of the great Creator. And let our make and place as men, remind us of our duty as Christians, always to keep heaven in our eye, and the earth under our feet. The Son of God, one with the Father, was with him when he made the world; nay, we are often told that the world was made by him, and nothing was made without him. Oh, what high thoughts should there be in our minds, of that great God whom we worship, and of that great Mediator in whose name we pray! And here, at the beginning of the sacred volume, we read of that Divine Spirit, whose work upon the heart of man is so often mentioned in other parts of the Bible. Observe, that at first there was nothing desirable to be seen, for the world was without form, and void; it was confusion, and emptiness. In like manner the work of grace in the soul is a new creation: and in a graceless soul, one that is not born again, there is disorder, confusion, and every evil work: it is empty of all good, for it is without God; it is dark, it is darkness itself: this is our condition by nature, till Almighty grace works a change in us.

Verses 3-5

God said, Let there be light; he willed it, and at once there was light. Oh, the power of the word of God! And in the new creation, the first thing that is wrought in the soul is light: the blessed Spirit works upon the will and affections by enlightening the understanding. Those who by sin were darkness, by grace become light in the Lord. Darkness would have been always upon fallen man, if the Son of God had not come and given us understanding, 1Jo 5:20. The light which God willed, he approved of. God divided the light from the darkness; for what fellowship has light with darkness? In heaven there is perfect light, and no darkness at all; in hell, utter darkness, and no gleam of light. The day and the night are the Lord's; let us use both to his honour, by working for him every day, and resting in him every night, meditating in his law both day and night.

Verses 6-13

The earth was emptiness, but by a word spoken, it became full of God's riches, and his they are still. Though the use of them is allowed to man, they are from God, and to his service and honour they must be used. The earth, at his command, brings forth grass, herbs, and fruits. God must have the glory of all the benefit we receive from the produce of the earth. If we have, through grace, an interest in Him who is the Fountain, we may rejoice in him when the streams of temporal mercies are dried up.

Verses 14-19

In the fourth day's work, the creation of the sun, moon, and stars is accounted for. All these are the works of God. The stars are spoken of as they appear to our eyes, without telling their number, nature, place, size, or motions; for the Scriptures were written, not to gratify curiosity, or make us astronomers, but to lead us to God, and make us saints. The lights of heaven are made to serve him; they do it faithfully, and shine in their season without fail. We are set as lights in this world to serve God; but do we in like manner answer the end of our creation? We do not: our light does not shine before God, as his lights shine before us. We burn our Master's candles, but do not mind our Master's work.

Verses 20-25

God commanded the fish and fowl to be produced. This command he himself executed. Insects, which are more numerous than the birds and beasts, and as curious, seem to have been part of this day's work. The Creator's wisdom and power are to be admired as much in an ant as in an elephant. The power of God's providence preserves all things, and fruitfulness is the effect of his blessing.

Verses 26-28

Man was made last of all the creatures: this was both an honour and a favour to him. Yet man was made the same day that the beasts were; his body was made of the same earth with theirs; and while he is in the body, he inhabits the same earth with them. God forbid that by indulging the body, and the desires of it, we should make ourselves like the beasts that perish! Man was to be a creature different from all that had been hitherto made. Flesh and spirit, heaven and earth, must be put together in him. God said, "Let us make man." Man, when he was made, was to glorify the Father, Son, and Holy Ghost. Into that great name we are baptized, for to that great name we owe our being. It is the soul of man that especially bears God's image. Man was made upright, Ec 7:29. His understanding saw Divine things clearly and truly; there were no errors or mistakes in his knowledge; his will consented at once, and in all things, to the will of God. His affections were all regular, and he had no bad appetites or passions. His thoughts were easily brought and fixed to the best subjects. Thus holy, thus happy, were our first parents in having the image of God upon them. But how is this image of God upon man defaced! May the Lord renew it upon our souls by his grace!

Verses 29, 30

Herbs and fruits must be man's food, including corn, and all the products of the earth. Let God's people cast their care upon him, and not be troubled about what they shall eat, and what they shall drink. He that feeds his birds will not starve his babes.

Verse 31

When we come to think about our works, we find, to our shame, that much has been very bad; but when God saw his work, all was very good. Good, for it was all just as the Creator would have it to be. All his works, in all places of his dominion, bless him; and therefore, bless thou the Lord, O my soul. Let us bless God for the gospel of Christ, and when we consider his almighty power, let us sinners flee from the wrath to come. If new—created unto the image of God in holiness, we shall at length enter the "new heavens and new earth, wherein dwelleth righteousness."

Chapter 2

Chapter Outline

The first sabbath.	(1–3)
Particulars about the creation.	(4–7)
The planting of the garden of Eden.	(8–14)
Man is placed in it.	(15)
God's command.	(16, 17)
The animals named, The making of woman, The Divine institution of marriage.	(18–25)

Verses 1-3

After six days, God ceased from all works of creation. In miracles, he has overruled nature, but never changed its settled course, or added to it. God did not rest as one weary, but as one well pleased. Notice the beginning of the kingdom of grace, in the sanctification, or keeping holy, of the sabbath day. The solemn observing of one day in seven as a day of holy rest and holy work, to God's honour, is the duty of all to whom God has made known his holy sabbaths. At this time none of the human race were in being but our first parents. For them the sabbath was appointed; and clearly for all succeeding generations also. The Christian sabbath, which we observe, is a seventh day, and in it we celebrate the rest of God the Son, and the finishing the work of our redemption.

Verses 4-7

Here is a name given to the Creator, "Jehovah." Where the word "LORD" is printed in capital letters in our English Bibles, in the original it is "Jehovah." Jehovah is that name of God, which denotes that he alone has his being of himself, and that he gives being to all creatures and things. Further notice is taken of plants and herbs, because they were made and appointed to be food for man. The earth did not bring forth its fruits of itself: this was done by Almighty power. Thus grace in the soul grows not of itself in nature's soil, but is the work of God. Rain also is the gift of God; it came not till the Lord God caused it. Though God works by means, yet when he pleases he can do his own work without them; and though we must not tempt God in the neglect of means, we must trust God, both in the use and in the want of means. Some way or other, God will water the plants of his own planting. Divine grace comes down like the dew, and waters the church without noise. Man was made of the small dust, such as is on the surface of the earth. The soul was not made of the earth, as the body: pity then that it should cleave to the earth, and mind earthly things. To God we must shortly give an account, how we have employed these souls; and if it be found that we have lost them, though it were to gain the world, we are undone for ever! Fools despise their own souls, by caring for their bodies before their souls.

Verses 8-14

The place fixed upon for Adam to dwell in, was not a palace, but a garden. The better we take up with plain things, and the less we seek things to gratify pride and luxury, the nearer we approach to innocency. Nature is content with a little, and that which is most natural; grace with less; but lust craves every thing, and is content with nothing. No delights can be satisfying to the soul, but those which God himself has provided and appointed for it. Eden signifies delight and pleasure. Wherever it was, it had all desirable conveniences, without any inconvenience, though no other house or garden on earth ever was so. It was adorned with every tree pleasant to the sight, and enriched with every tree that yielded fruit grateful to the taste and good for food. God, as a tender Father, desired not only Adam's profit, but his pleasure; for there is pleasure with innocency, nay there is true pleasure only in innocency. When Providence puts us in a place of plenty and pleasure, we ought to serve God with gladness of heart in the good things he gives us. Eden had two trees peculiar to itself. 1. There was the tree of life in the midst of the garden. Of this man might eat and live. Christ is now to us the Tree of life, Re 2:7; 22:2; and the Bread of life, Joh 6:48, 51. 2. There was the tree of the knowledge of good and evil, so called because there was a positive revelation of the will of God about this tree, so that by it man might know moral good and evil. What is good? It is good not to eat of this tree. What is evil? It is evil to eat of this tree. In these two trees God set before Adam good and evil, the blessing and the curse.

Verse 15

After God had formed Adam, he put him in the garden. All boasting was thereby shut out. Only he that made us can make us happy; he that is the Former of our bodies, and the Father of our spirits, and none but he, can fully provide for the happiness of both. Even in paradise itself man had to work. None of us were sent into the world to be idle. He that made our souls and bodies, has given us something to work with; and he that gave us this earth for our habitation, has made us something to work upon. The sons and heirs of heaven, while in this world, have something to do about this earth, which must have its share of their time and thoughts; and if they do it with an eye to God, they as truly serve him in it, as when they are upon their knees. Observe that the husbandman's calling is an ancient and honourable calling; it was needful even in paradise. Also, there is true pleasure in the business God calls us to, and employs us in. Adam could not have been happy if he had been idle: it is still God's law, He that will not work has no right to eat, 2Th 3:10.

Verses 16, 17

Let us never set up our own will against the holy will of God. There was not only liberty allowed to man, in taking the fruits of paradise, but everlasting life made sure to him upon his obedience. There was a trial appointed of his obedience. By transgression he would forfeit his Maker's favour, and deserve his displeasure, with all its awful effects; so that he would become liable to pain, disease, and death. Worse than that, he would lose the holy image of God, and all the comfort of his favour; and feel the torment of sinful passions, and the terror of his Maker's vengeance, which must endure for ever with his never dying soul. The forbidding to eat of the fruit of a particular tree was wisely suited to the state of our first parents. In their state of innocence, and separated from any others, what opportunity or what temptation had they to break any of the ten commandments? The event proves that the whole human race were concerned in the trial and fall of our first parents. To argue against these things is to strive against stubborn facts, as well as Divine revelation; for man is sinful, and shows by his first actions, and his conduct ever afterwards, that he is ready to do evil. He is under the Divine displeasure, exposed to sufferings and death. The Scriptures always speak of man as of this sinful character, and in this miserable state; and these things are true of men in all ages, and of all nations.

Verses 18-25

Power over the creatures was given to man, and as a proof of this he named them all. It also shows his insight into the works of God. But though he was lord of the creatures, yet nothing in this world was a help meet for man. From God are all our helpers. If we rest in God, he will work all for good. God caused deep sleep to fall on Adam; while he knows no sin, God will take care that he shall feel no pain. God, as her Father, brought the woman to the man, as his second self, and a help meet for him. That wife, who is of God's making by special grace, and of God's bringing by special providence, is likely to prove a help meet for a man. See what need there is, both of prudence and prayer in the choice of this relation, which is so near and so lasting. That had need to be well done, which is to be done for life. Our first parents needed no clothes for covering against cold or heat, for neither could hurt them: they needed none for ornament. Thus easy, thus happy, was man in his state of innocency. How good was God to him! How many favours did he load him with! How easy were the laws given to him! Yet man, being in honour, understood not his own interest, but soon became as the beasts that perish.

Chapter 3

Chapter Outline

Verses 1-5

Satan assaulted our first parents, to draw them to sin, and the temptation proved fatal to them. The tempter was the devil, in the shape and likeness of a serpent. Satan's plan was to draw our first parents to sin, and so to separate between them and their God. Thus the devil was from the beginning a murderer, and the great mischief maker. The person tempted was the woman: it was Satan's policy to enter into talk with her when she was alone. There are many temptations to which being alone gives great advantage; but the communion of saints tends very much to their strength and safety. Satan took advantage by finding her near the forbidden tree. They that would not eat the forbidden fruit, must not come near the forbidden tree. Satan tempted Eve, that by her he might tempt Adam. It is his policy to send temptations by hands we do not suspect, and by those that have most influence upon us. Satan questioned whether it were a sin or not, to eat of this tree. He did not disclose his design at first, but he put a question which seemed innocent. Those who would be safe, need to be shy of talking with the tempter. He quoted the command wrong. He spoke in a taunting way. The devil, as he is a liar, so he is a scoffer from the beginning; and scoffers are his children. It is the craft of Satan to speak of the Divine law as uncertain or unreasonable, and so to draw people to sin; it is our wisdom to keep up a firm belief of God's command, and a high respect for it. Has God said, Ye shall not lie, nor take his name in vain, nor be drunk, &c.? Yes, I am sure he has, and it is well said; and by his grace I will abide by it. It was Eve's weakness to enter into this talk with the serpent: she might have perceived by his question, that he had no good design, and should therefore have started back. Satan teaches men first to doubt, and then to deny. He promises advantage from their eating this fruit. He aims to make them discontented with their present state, as if it were not so good as it might be, and should be. No condition will of itself bring content, unless the mind be brought to it. He tempts them to seek preferment, as if they were fit to be gods. Satan ruined himself by desiring to be like the Most High, therefore he sought to infect our first parents with the same desire, that he might ruin them too. And still the devil draws people into his interest, by suggesting to them hard thoughts of God, and false hopes of advantage by sin. Let us, therefore, always think well of God as the best good, and think ill of sin as the worst evil: thus let us resist the devil, and he will flee from us.

Verses 6-8

Observe the steps of the transgression: not steps upward, but downward toward the pit. 1. She saw. A great deal of sin comes in at the eye. Let us not look on that which we are in danger of lusting after, Mt 5:28. 2. She took. It was her own act and deed. Satan may tempt, but he cannot force; may persuade us to cast ourselves down, but he cannot cast us down, Mt 4:6. 3. She did eat. When she looked perhaps she did not intend to take; or when she took, not to eat: but it ended in that. It is wisdom to stop the first motions of sin, and to leave it off before it be meddled with. 4. She gave it also to her husband with her. Those that have done ill, are willing to draw in others to do the same. 5. He did eat. In neglecting the tree of life, of which he was allowed to eat, and eating of the tree of knowledge, which was forbidden, Adam plainly showed a contempt of what God had bestowed on him, and a desire for what God did not see fit to give him. He would have what he pleased, and do what he pleased. His sin was, in one word, disobedience, Ro 5:19; disobedience to a plain, easy, and express command. He had no corrupt nature within, to betray him; but had a freedom of will, in full strength, not weakened or impaired. He turned aside quickly. He drew all his posterity into sin and ruin. Who then can say that Adam's sin had but little harm in it? When too late, Adam and Eve saw the folly of eating forbidden fruit. They saw the happiness they fell from, and the misery they were fallen into. They saw a loving God provoked, his grace and favour forfeited. See her what dishonour and trouble sin is; it makes mischief wherever it gets in, and destroys all comfort. Sooner or later it will bring shame; either the shame of true repentance, which ends in glory, or that shame and everlasting contempt, to which the wicked shall rise at the great day. See here what is commonly the folly of those that have sinned. They have more care to save their credit before men, than to obtain their pardon from God. The excuses men make to cover and lessen their sins, are vain and frivolous; like the aprons of fig-leaves, they make the matter never the better: yet we are all apt to cover our transgressions as Adam. Before they sinned, they would have welcomed God's gracious visits with humble joy; but now he was become a terror to them. No marvel that they became a terror to themselves, and full of confusion. This shows the falsehood of the tempter, and the frauds of his temptations. Satan promised they should be safe, but they cannot so much as think themselves so! Adam and Eve were now miserable comforters to each other!

Verses 9-13

Observe the startling question, Adam, where art thou? Those who by sin go astray from God, should seriously consider where they are; they are afar off from all good, in the midst of their enemies, in bondage to Satan, and in the high road to utter ruin. This lost sheep had wandered without end, if the good Shepherd had not sought after him, and told him, that where he was straying he could not be either happy or easy. If sinners will but consider where they are, they will not rest till they return to God. It is the common fault and folly of those that have done ill, when questioned about it, to acknowledge only that which is so manifest that they cannot deny it. Like Adam, we have reason to be afraid of approaching to God, if we are not covered and clothed with the righteousness of Christ. Sin appears most plainly in the glass of the commandment, therefore God set it before Adam; and in it we should see our faces. But instead of acknowledging the sin in its full extent, and taking shame to themselves, Adam and Eve excuse the sin, and lay the shame and blame on others. There is a strange proneness in those that are tempted, to say, they are tempted of God; as if our abuse of God's gifts would excuse our breaking God's laws. Those who are willing to take the pleasure and profit of sin, are backward to take the blame and shame of it. Learn hence, that Satan's temptations are all beguilings; his arguments are all deceits; his allurements are all cheats; when he speaks fair, believe him not. It is by the deceitfulness of sin the heart is hardened. See Ro 7:11; Heb 3:13. But though Satan's subtlety may draw us into sin, yet it will not justify us in sin. Though he is the tempter, we are the sinners. Let it not lessen our sorrow for sin, that we were beguiled into it; but let it increase our self-indignation, that we should suffer ourselves to be deceived by a known cheat, and a sworn enemy, who would destroy our souls.

Verses 14, 15

God passes sentence; and he begins where the sin began, with the serpent. The devil's instruments must share in the devil's punishments. Under the cover of the serpent, the devil is sentenced to be degraded and accursed of God; detested and abhorred of all mankind: also to be destroyed and ruined at last by the great Redeemer, signified by the breaking of his head. War is proclaimed between the Seed of the woman and the seed of the serpent. It is the fruit of this enmity, that there is a continual warfare between grace and corruption, in the hearts of God's people. Satan, by their corruptions, buffets them, sifts them, and seeks to devour them. Heaven and hell can never be reconciled, nor light and darkness; no more can Satan and a sanctified soul. Also, there is a continual struggle between the wicked and the godly in this world. A gracious promise is here made of Christ, as the Deliverer of fallen man from the power of Satan. Here was the drawn of the gospel day: no sooner was the wound given, than the remedy was provided and revealed. This gracious revelation of a Saviour came unasked, and unlooked for. Without a revelation of mercy, giving some hope of forgiveness, the convinced sinner would sink into despair, and be hardened. By faith in this promise, our first parents, and the patriarchs before the flood, were justified and saved. Notice is given concerning Christ. 1. His incarnation, or coming in the flesh. It speaks great encouragement to sinners, that their Saviour is the Seed of the woman, bone of our bone, Heb 2:11, 14. 2. His sufferings and death; pointed at in Satan's bruising his heel, that is, his human nature. And Christ's sufferings are continued in the sufferings of the saints for his name. The devil tempts them, persecutes and slays them; and so bruises the heel of Christ, who is afflicted in their afflictions. But while the heel is bruised on earth, the Head is in heaven. 3. His victory over Satan thereby. Christ baffled Satan's temptations, rescued souls out of his hands. By his death he gave a fatal blow to the devil's kingdom, a wound to the head of this serpent that cannot be healed. As the gospel gains ground, Satan falls.

Verses 16-19

The woman, for her sin, is condemned to a state of sorrow, and of subjection; proper punishments of that sin, in which she had sought to gratify the desire of her eye, and of the flesh, and her pride. Sin brought sorrow into the world; that made the world a vale of tears. No wonder our sorrows are multiplied, when our sins are so. He shall rule over thee, is but God's command, Wives, be subject to your own husbands. If man had not sinned, he would always have ruled with wisdom and love; if the woman had not sinned, she would always have obeyed with humility and meekness. Adam laid the blame on his wife; but though it was her fault to persuade him to eat the forbidden fruit, it was his fault to hearken to her. Thus men's frivolous pleas will, in the day of God's judgment, be turned against them. God put marks of displeasure on Adam. 1. His habitation is cursed. God gave the earth to the children of men, to be a comfortable dwelling; but it is now cursed for man's sin. Yet Adam is not himself cursed, as the serpent was, but only the ground for his sake. 2. His employments and enjoyments are imbittered to him. Labour is our duty, which we must faithfully perform; it is part of man's sentence, which idleness daringly defies. Uneasiness and weariness with labour are our just punishment, which we must patiently submit to, since they are less than our iniquity deserves. Man's food shall become unpleasant to him. Yet man is not sentenced to eat dust as the serpent, only to eat the herb of the field. 3. His life also is but short; considering how full of trouble his days are, it is in favour to him that they are few. Yet death being dreadful to nature, even when life is unpleasant, that concludes the punishment. Sin brought death into the world: if Adam had not sinned, he had not died. He gave way to temptation, but the Saviour withstood it. And how admirably the satisfaction of our Lord Jesus, by his death and sufferings, answered the sentence passed on our first parents! Did travailing pains come with sin? We read of the travail of Christ's soul, Isa 53:11; and the pains of death he was held by, are so called, Ac 2:24. Did subjection came in with sin? Christ was made under the law, Ga 4:4. Did the curse come in with sin? Christ was made a curse for us, he died a cursed death, Ga 3:13. Did thorns come in with sin? He was crowned with thorns for us. Did sweat come in with sin? He sweat for us, as it had been great drops of blood. Did sorrow come in with sin? He was a man of sorrows; his soul was, in his agony, exceeding sorrowful. Did death come in with sin? He became obedient unto death. Thus is the plaster as wide as the wound. Blessed be God for his Son our Lord Jesus Christ.

Verses 20, 21

God named the man, and called him Adam, which signifies red earth; Adam named the woman, and called her Eve, that is, life. Adam bears the name of the dying body, Eve of the living soul. Adam probably had regard to the blessing of a Redeemer, the promised Seed, in calling his wife Eve, or life; for He should be the life of all believers, and in Him all the families of the earth should be blessed. See also God's care for our first parents, notwithstanding their sin. Clothes came in with sin. Little reason have we to be proud of our clothes, which are but the badges of our shame. When God made clothes for our first parents, he made them warm and strong, but coarse and very plain; not robes of scarlet, but coats of skin. Let those that are meanly clad, learn from hence not to complain. Having food and a covering, let them be content; they are as well off as Adam and Eve. And let those that are finely clad, learn not to make the putting on of apparel their adorning. The beasts, from whose skins they were clothed, it is supposed were slain, not for man's food, but for sacrifice, to typify Christ, the great Sacrifice. Adam and Eve made for themselves aprons of fig-leaves, a covering too narrow for them to wrap themselves in, Isa 28:20. Such are all the rags of our own righteousness. But God made them coats of skin, large, strong, durable, and fit for them: such is the righteousness of Christ; therefore put ye on the Lord Jesus Christ.

Verses 22-24

God bid man go out; told him he should no longer occupy and enjoy that garden: but man liked the place, and was unwilling to leave it, therefore God made him go out. This signified the shutting out of him, and all his guilty race, from that communion with God, which was the bliss and glory of paradise. But man was only sent to till the ground out of which he was taken. He was sent to a place of toil, not to a place of torment. Our first parents were shut out from the privileges of their state of innocency, yet they were not left to despair. The way to the tree of life was shut. It was henceforward in vain for him and his to expect righteousness, life, and happiness, by the covenant of works; for the command of that covenant being broken, the curse of it is in full force: we are all undone, if we are judged by that covenant. God revealed this to Adam, not to drive him to despair, but to quicken him to look for life and happiness in the promised Seed, by whom a new and living way into the holiest is laid open for us.

Chapter 4

Chapter Outline

The birth, employment, and religion of Cain and Abel.	(1–7)
Cain murders Abel, The curse of Cain.	(8–15)
The conduct of Cain, His family.	(16–18)
Lamech and his wives, The skill of Cain's descendants.	(19–24)
The birth of another son and grandson of Adam.	(25, 26)

Verses 1-7

When Cain was born, Eve said, I have gotten a man from the Lord. Perhaps she thought that this was the promised seed. If so, she was wofully disappointed. Abel signifies vanity: when she thought she had the promised seed in Cain, whose name signifies possession, she was so taken up with him that another son was as vanity to her. Observe, each son had a calling. It is the will of God for every one to have something to do in this world. Parents ought to bring up their children to work. Give them a Bible and a calling, said good Mr. Dod, and God be with them. We may believe that God commanded Adam, after the fall, to shed the blood of innocent animals, and after their death to burn part or the whole of their bodies by fire. Thus that punishment which sinners deserve, even the death of the body, and the wrath of God, of which fire is a well-known emblem, and also the sufferings of Christ, were prefigured. Observe that the religious worship of God is no new invention. It was from the beginning; it is the good old way, Jer 6:16. The offerings of Cain and Abel were different. Cain showed a proud, unbelieving heart. Therefore he and his offering were rejected. Abel came as a sinner, and according to God's appointment, by his sacrifice expressing humility, sincerity, and believing obedience. Thus, seeking the benefit of the new covenant of mercy, through the promised Seed, his sacrifice had a token that God accepted it. Abel offered in faith, and Cain did not, Heb 11:4. In all ages there have been two sorts of worshippers, such as Cain and Abel; namely, proud, hardened despisers of the gospel method of salvation, who attempt to please God in ways of their own devising; and humble believers, who draw near to him in the way he has revealed. Cain indulged malignant anger against Abel. He harboured an evil spirit of discontent and rebellion against God. God notices all our sinful passions and discontents. There is not an angry, envious, or fretful look, that escapes his observing eye. The Lord reasoned with this rebellious man; if he came in the right way, he should be accepted. Some understand this as an intimation of mercy. "If thou doest not well, sin, that is, the sin-offering, lies at the door, and thou mayest take the benefit of it." The same word signifies sin, and a sacrifice for sin. "Though thou hast not done well, yet do not despair; the remedy is at hand." Christ, the great sin-offering, is said to stand at the door, Re 3:20. And those well deserve to perish in their sins, that will not go to the door to ask for the benefit of this sin-offering. God's acceptance of Abel's offering did not change the birthright, and make it his; why then should Cain be so angry? Sinful heats and disquiets vanish before a strict and fair inquiry into the cause.

Verses 8-15

Malice in the heart ends in murder by the hands. Cain slew Abel, his own brother, his own mother's son, whom he ought to have loved; his younger brother, whom he ought to have protected; a good brother, who had never done him any wrong. What fatal effects were these of our first parents' sin, and how must their hearts have been filled with anguish! Observe the pride, unbelief, and impenitence of Cain. He denies the crime, as if he could conceal it from God. He tries to cover a deliberate murder with a deliberate lie. Murder is a crying sin. Blood calls for blood, the blood of the murdered for the blood of the murderer. Who knows the extent and weight of a Divine curse, how far it reaches, how deep it pierces? Only in Christ are believers saved from it, and inherit the blessing. Cain was cursed from the earth. He found his punishment there where he chose his portion, and set his heart. Every creature is to us what God makes it, a comfort or a cross, a blessing or a curse. The wickedness of the wicked brings a curse upon all they do, and all they have. Cain complains not of his sin, but of his punishment. It shows great hardness of heart to be more concerned about our sufferings than our sins. God has wise and holy ends in prolonging the lives even of very wicked men. It is in vain to inquire what was the mark set upon Cain. It was doubtless known, both as a brand of infamy on Cain, and a token from God that they should not kill him. Abel, being dead, yet speaketh. He tells the heinous guilt of murder, and warns us to stifle the first risings of wrath, and teaches us that persecution must be expected by the righteous. Also, that there is a future state, and an eternal recompence to be enjoyed, through faith in Christ and his atoning sacrifice. And he tells us the excellency of faith in the atoning sacrifice and blood of the Lamb of God. Cain slew his brother, because his own works were evil, and his brother's righteous, 1Jo 3:12. In consequence of the enmity put between the Seed of the woman and the seed of the serpent, the war broke out, which has been waged ever since. In this war we are all concerned, none are neuter; our Captain has declared, He that is not with me is against me. Let us decidedly, yet in meekness, support the cause of truth and righteousness against Satan.

Verses 16-18

Cain cast off all fear of God, and attended no more on God's ordinances. Hypocritical professors, who dissemble and trifle with God, are justly left to themselves to do something grossly scandalous. So they throw off that form of godliness to which they have been a reproach, and of which they deny the power. Cain went out from the presence of the Lord, and we never find that he came into it again, to his comfort. The land Cain dwelt in was called the land of Nod, which means, 'shaking,' or 'trembling,' and so shows the restlessness and uneasiness of his own spirit, or 'the land of a vagabond:' they that depart from God cannot find rest any where else. Those on earth who looked for the heavenly city, chose to dwell in tabernacles or tents; but Cain, as not minding that city, built one on earth. Thus all who are cursed of God seek their settlement and satisfaction here below.

Verses 19-24

One of Cain's wicked race is the first recorded, as having broken the law of marriage. Hitherto, one man had but one wife at a time; but Lamech took two. Wordly things, are the only things that carnal, wicked people set their hearts upon, and are most clever and industrous about. So it was with this race of Cain. Here was a father of shepherds, and a father of musicians, but not a father of the faithful. Here is one to teach about brass and iron, but none to teach the good knowledge of the Lord: here are devices how to be rich, and how to be mighty, and how to be merry; but nothing of God, of his fear and service. Present things fill the heads of most. Lamech had enemies, whom he had provoked. He draws a comparison betwixt himself and his ancestor Cain; and flatters himself that he is much less criminal. He seems to abuse the patience of God in sparing Cain, into an encouragement to expect that he may sin unpunished.

Verses 25, 26

Our first parents were comforted in their affliction by the birth of a son, whom they called Seth, that is, 'set,' 'settled,' or 'placed;' in his seed mankind should continue to the end of time, and from him the Messiah should descend. While Cain, the head of the apostacy, is made a wanderer, Seth, from whom the true church was to come, is one fixed. In Christ and his church is the only true settlement. Seth walked in the steps of his martyred brother Abel; he was a partaker of like precious faith in the righteousness of our God and Saviour Jesus Christ, and so became a fresh witness of the grace and influence of God the Holy Spirit. God gave Adam and Eve to see the revival of religion in their family. The worshippers of God began to do more in religion; some, by an open profession of true religion, protested against the wickedness of the world around. The worse others are, the better we should be, and the more zealous. Then began the distinction between professors and profane, which has been kept up ever since, and will be, while the world stands.

Chapter 5

Chapter Outline

Verses 1-5

Adam was made in the image of God; but when fallen he begat a son in his own image, sinful and defiled, frail, wretched, and mortal, like himself. Not only a man like himself, consisting of body and soul, but a sinner like himself. This was the reverse of that Divine likeness in which Adam was made; having lost it, he could not convey it to his seed. Adam lived, in all, 930 years; and then died, according to the sentence passed upon him, "To dust thou shalt return." Though he did not die in the day he ate forbidden fruit, yet in that very day he became mortal. Then he began to die; his whole life after was but a reprieve, a forfeited, condemned life; it was a wasting, dying life. Man's life is but dying by degrees.

Verses 6-20

Concerning each of these, except Enoch, it is said, "and he died." It is well to observe the deaths of others. They all lived very long; not one of them died till he had seen almost eight hundred years, and some of them lived much longer; a great while for an immortal soul to be prisoned in a house of clay. The present life surely was not to them such a burden as it commonly is now, else they would have been weary of it. Nor was the future life so clearly revealed then, as it now under the gospel, else they would have been urgent to remove to it. All the patriarchs that lived before the flood, except Noah, were born before Adam died. From him they might receive a full account of the creation, the fall, the promise, and the Divine precepts about religious worship and a religious life. Thus God kept up in his church the knowledge of his will.

Verses 21-24

Enoch was the seventh from Adam. Godliness is walking with God: which shows reconciliation to God, for two cannot walk together except they be agreed, Am 3:3. It includes all the parts of a godly, righteous, and sober life. To walk with God, is to set God always before us, to act as always under his eye. It is constantly to care, in all things to please God, and in nothing to offend him. It is to be followers of him as dear children. The Holy Spirit, instead of saying, Enoch lived, says, Enoch walked with God. This was his constant care and work; while others lived to themselves and the world, he lived to God. It was the joy of his life. Enoch was removed to a better world. As he did not live like the rest of mankind, so he did not leave the world by death as they did. He was not found, because God had translated him, Heb 11:5. He had lived but 365 years, which, as men's ages were then, was but the midst of a man's days. God often takes those soonest whom he loves best; the time they lose on earth, is gained in heaven, to their unspeakable advantage. See how Enoch's removal is expressed: he was not, for God took him. He was not any longer in this world; he was changed, as the saints shall be, who are alive at Christ's second coming. Those who begin to walk with God when young, may expect to walk with him long, comfortably, and usefully. The true christian's steady walk in holiness, through many a year, till God takes him, will best recommend that religion which many oppose and many abuse. And walking with God well agrees with the cares, comforts, and duties of life.

Verses 25-32

Methuselah signifies, 'he dies, there is a dart,' 'a sending forth,' namely, of the deluge, which came the year that Methuselah died. He lived 969 years, the longest that any man ever lived on earth; but the longest liver must die at last. Noah signifies rest; his parents gave him that name, with a prospect of his being a great blessing to his generation. Observe his father's complaint of the calamitous state of human life, by the entrance of sin, and the curse of sin. Our whole life is spent in labour, and our time filled up with continual toil. God having cursed the ground, it is as much as some can do, with the utmost care and pains, to get a hard livelihood out comfort us." It signifies not only that desire and expectation which parents generally have about their children, that they will be comforts to them and helpers, though they often prove otherwise; but it signifies also a prospect of something more. Is Christ ours? Is heaven ours? We need better comforters under our toil and sorrow, than the dearest relations and the most promising offspring; may we seek and find comforts in Christ.

Chapter 6

Chapter Outline

The wickedness of the world which provoked God's wrath.	(1–7)
Noah finds grace.	(8–11)
Noah warned of the flood, The directions respecting the ark.	(12–21)
Noah's faith and obedience.	(22)

Verses 1-7

The most remarkable thing concerning the old world, is the destroying of it by the deluge, or flood. We are told of the abounding iniquity of that wicked world: God's just wrath, and his holy resolution to punish it. In all ages there has been a peculiar curse of God upon marriages between professors of true religion and its avowed enemies. The evil example of the ungodly party corrupts or greatly hurts the other. Family religion is put an end to, and the children are trained up according to the worldly maxims of that parent who is without the fear of God. If we profess to be the sons and daughters of the Lord Almighty, we must not marry without his consent. He will never give his blessing, if we prefer beauty, wit, wealth, or worldly honours, to faith and holiness. The Spirit of God strove with men, by sending Enoch, Noah, and perhaps others, to preach to them; by waiting to be gracious, notwithstanding their rebellions; and by exciting alarm and convictions in their consciences. But the Lord declared that his Spirit should not thus strive with men always; he would leave them to be hardened in sin, and ripened for destruction. This he determined on, because man was flesh: not only frail and feeble, but carnal and depraved; having misused the noble powers of his soul to gratify his corrupt inclinations. God sees all the wickedness that is among the children of men; it cannot be hid from him now; and if it be not repented of, it shall be made known by him shortly. The wickedness of a people is great indeed, when noted sinners are men renowned among them. Very much sin was committed in all places, by all sorts of people. Any one might see that the wickedness of man was great: but God saw that every imagination, or purpose, of the thoughts of man's heart, was only evil continually. This was the bitter root, the corrupt spring. The heart was deceitful and desperately wicked; the principles were corrupt; the habits and dispositions evil. Their designs and devices were wicked. They did evil deliberately, contriving how to do mischief. There was no good among them. God saw man's wickedness as one injured and wronged by it. He saw it as a tender father sees the folly and stubbornness of a rebellious and disobedient child, which grieves him, and makes him wish he had been childless. The words here used are remarkable; they are used after the manner of men, and do not mean that God can change, or be unhappy. Does God thus hate our sin? And shall not we be grieved to the heart for it? Oh that we may look on Him whom we have grieved, and mourn! God repented that he had made man; but we never find him repent that he redeemed man. God resolves to destroy man: the original word is very striking, 'I will wipe off man from the earth,' as dirt or filth is wiped off from a place which should be clean, and is thrown to the dunghill, the proper place for it. God speaks of man as his own creature, when he resolves upon his punishment. Those forfeit their lives who do not answer the end of their living. God speaks of resolution concerning men, after his Spirit had been long striving with them in vain. None are punished by the justice of God, but those who hate to be reformed by the grace of God.

Verses 8-11

Noah did not find favour in the eyes of men; they hated and persecuted him, because both by his life and preaching he condemned the world: but he found grace in the eyes of the Lord, and this made him more truly honourable than the men of renown. Let this be our chief desire, let us labour that we may be accepted of him. When the rest of the world was wicked, Noah kept his integrity. God's good-will towards Noah produced this good work in him. He was a just man, that is, justified before God, by faith in the promised Seed. As such he was made holy, and had right principles; and was righteous in his conversation. He was not only honest, but devout; it was his constant care to do the will of God. God looks down upon those with an eye of favour, who sincerely look up to him with an eye of faith. It is easy to be religious when religion is in fashion; but it shows strong faith and resolution, to swim against the stream, and to appear for God when no one else appears for him; Noah did so. All kinds of sin were found among men. They corrupted God's worship. Sin fills the earth with violence, and this fully justified God's resolution to destroy the world. The contagion spread. When wickedness is become general, ruin is not far off; while there is a remnant of praying people in a nation, to empty the measure as it fills, judgments may be long kept off; but when all hands are at work to pull down the fences, by sin, and none stand in the gap to make up the breach, what can be expected but a flood of wrath?

Verses 12-21

God told Noah his purpose to destroy the wicked world by water. The secret of the Lord is with them that fear him, Ps 25:14. It is with all believers, enabling them to understand and apply the declarations and warnings of the written word. God chose to do it by a flood of waters, which should drown the world. As he chooses the rod with which he corrects his children, so he chooses the sword with which he cuts off his enemies. God established his covenant with Noah. This is the first place in the Bible where the word 'covenant' is found; it seems to mean, 1. The covenant of providence; that the course of nature shall be continued to the end of time. 2. The covenant of grace; that God would be a God to Noah, and that out of his seed God would take to himself a people. God directed Noah to make an ark. This ark was like the hulk of a ship, fitted to float upon the waters. It was very large, half the size of St. Paul's cathedral, and would hold more than eighteen of the largest ships now used. God could have secured Noah without putting him to any care, or pains, or trouble; but employed him in making that which was to be the means to preserve him, for the trial of his faith and obedience. Both the providence of God, and the grace of God, own and crown the obedient and diligent. God gave Noah particular orders how to make the ark, which could not therefore but be well fitted for the purpose. God promised Noah that he and his family should be kept alive in the ark. What we do in obedience to God, we and our families are likely to have the benefit of. The piety of parents gets their children good in this life, and furthers them in the way to eternal life, if they improve it.

Verse 22

Noah's faith triumphed over all corrupt reasonings. To rear so large a building, such a one as he never saw, and to provide food for the living creatures, would require from him a great deal of care, and labour, and expense. His neighbours would laugh at him. But all such objections, Noah, by faith, got over; his obedience was ready and resolute. Having begun to build, he did not leave off till he had finished: so did he, and so must we do. He feared the deluge, and therefore prepared the ark. And in the warning given to Noah, there is a more solemn warning given to us, to flee from the wrath to come, which will sweep the world of unbelievers into the pit of destruction. Christ, the true Noah, which same shall comfort us, hath by his sufferings already prepared the ark, and kindly invites us by faith to enter in. While the day of his patience continues, let us hear and obey his voice.

Chapter 7

Chapter Outline

Noah, and his family and the living creatures, enter the ark, and the flood begins.	(1–12)
Noah shut in the ark.	(13–16)
The increase of the flood for forty days.	(17–20)
All flesh is destroyed by the flood.	(21–24)

Verses 1-12

The call to Noah is very kind, like that of a tender father to his children to come in-doors when he sees night or a storm coming. Noah did not go into the ark till God bade him, though he knew it was to be his place of refuge. It is very comfortable to see God going before us in every step we take. Noah had taken a great deal of pains to build the ark, and now he was himself kept alive in it. What we do in obedience to the command of God, and in faith, we ourselves shall certainly have the comfort of, first or last. This call to Noah reminds us of the call the gospel gives to poor sinners. Christ is an ark, in whom alone we can be safe, when death and judgment approach. The word says, "Come;" ministers say, "Come;" the Spirit says, "Come, come into the Ark." Noah was accounted righteous, not for his own righteousness, but as an heir of the righteousness which is by faith, Heb 11:7. He believed the revelation of a saviour, and sought and expected salvation through Him alone. Thus was he justified by faith, and received that Spirit whose fruit is in all goodness; but if any man have not the Spirit of Christ, he is none of his. After the hundred and twenty years, God granted seven days' longer space for repentance. But these seven days were trifled away, like all the rest. It shall be but seven days. They had only one week more, one sabbath more to improve, and to consider the things that belonged to their peace. But it is common for those who have been careless of their souls during the years of their health, when they have looked upon death at a distance, to be as careless during the days, the few days of their sickness, when they see death approaching; their hearts being hardened by the deceitfulness of sin. As Noah prepared the ark by faith in the warning given that the flood would come, so he went into it, by faith in this warning that it would come quickly. And on the day Noah was securely fixed in the ark, the fountains of the great deep were broken up. The earth had within it those waters, which, at God's command, sprang up and flooded it; and thus our bodies have in themselves those humours, which, when God pleases, become the seeds and springs of mortal diseases. The windows of heaven were opened, and the waters which were above the firmament, that is, in the air, were poured out upon the earth. The rain comes down in drops; but such rains fell then, as were never known before or since. It rained without stop or abatement, forty days and forty nights, upon the whole earth at once. As there was a peculiar exercise of the almighty power of God in causing the flood, it is vain and presumptuous to attempt explaining the method of it, by human wisdom.

Verses 13-16

The ravenous creatures were made mild and manageable; yet, when this occasion was over, they were of the same kind as before; for the ark did not alter their natures. Hypocrites in the church, who outwardly conform to the laws of that ark, are yet unchanged; and it will appear, one time or other, what kind they are after. God continued his care of Noah. God shut the door, to secure him and keep him safe in the ark; also to keep all others for ever out. In what manner this was done, God has not been pleased to make known. There is much of our gospel duty and privilege to be seen in Noah's safety in the ark. The apostle makes it a type of christian baptism, 1Pe 3:20, 21. Observe then, it is our great duty, in obedience to the gospel call, by a lively faith in Christ, to come into that way of salvation which God has provided for poor sinners. Those that come into the ark, should bring as many as they can with them, by good instructions, by persuasions, and by good examples. There is room enough in Christ for all comers. God put Adam into paradise, but did not shut him in, so he threw himself out; but when God put Noah into the ark, and so when he brings a soul to Christ, the salvation is sure: it is not in our own keeping, but in the Mediator's hand. But the door of mercy will shortly be shut against those that now make light of it. Knock now, and it shall be opened, Lu 13:25.

Verses 17-20

The flood was increasing forty days. The waters rose so high, that the tops of the highest mountains were overflowed more than twenty feet. There is no place on earth so high as to set men out of the reach of God's judgments. God's hand will find out all his enemies, Ps 21:8. When the flood thus increased, Noah's ark was lifted up, and the waters which broke down every thing else, bore up the ark. That which to unbelievers betokens death unto death, to the faithful betokens life unto life.

Verses 21-24

All the men, women, and children, that were in the world, excepting those in the ark, died. We may easily imagine what terror seized them. Our Saviour tells us, that till the very day that the flood came, they were eating and drinking, Lu 17:26, 27; they were deaf and blind to all Divine warnings. In this posture death surprised them. They were convinced of their folly when it was too late. We may suppose they tried all ways and means possible to save themselves, but all in vain. And those that are not found in Christ, the Ark, are certainly undone, undone for ever. Let us pause, and consider this tremendous judgment! Who can stand before the Lord when he is angry? The sin of sinners will be their ruin, first or last, if not repented of. The righteous God knows how to bring ruin upon the world of the ungodly, 2Pe 2:5. How tremendous will be the day of judgment and perdition of ungodly men! Happy they who are part of Christ's family, and safe with him as such; they may look forward without dismay, and rejoice that they shall triumph, when fire shall burn up the earth, and all that therein is. We are apt to suppose some favourable distinctions in our own case or character; but if we neglect, refuse, or abuse the salvation of Christ, we shall, notwithstanding such fancied advantages, be destroyed in the common ruin of an unbelieving world.

Chapter 8

Chapter Outline

Verses 1-3

The whole race of mankind, except Noah and his family, were now dead, so that God's remembering Noah, was the return of his mercy to mankind, of whom he would not make a full end. The demands of Divine justice had been answered by the ruin of sinners. God sent his wind to dry the earth, and seal up his waters. The same hand that brings the desolation, must bring the deliverance; to that hand, therefore, we must ever look. When afflictions have done the work for which they are sent, whether killing work or curing work, they will be taken away. As the earth was not drowned in a day, so it was not dried in a day. God usually works deliverance for his people gradually, that the day of small things may not be despised, nor the day of great things despaired of.

Verses 4-12

The ark rested upon a mountain, whither it was directed by the wise and gracious providence of God, that might rest the sooner. God has times and places of rest for his people after their tossing; and many times he provides for their seasonable and comfortable settlement, without their own contrivance, and quite beyond their own foresight. God had told Noah when the flood would come, yet he did not give him an account by revelation, at what times and by what steps it should go away. The knowledge of the former was necessary to his preparing the ark; but the knowledge of the latter would serve only to gratify curiosity; and concealing it from him would exercise his faith and patience. Noah sent forth a raven from the ark, which went flying about, and feeding on the carcasses that floated. Noah then sent forth a dove, which returned the first time without good news; but the second time, she brought an olive leaf in her bill, plucked off, plainly showing that trees, fruit trees, began to appear above water. Noah sent forth the dove the second time, seven days after the first, and the third time was after seven days also; probably on the sabbath day. Having kept the sabbath with his little church, he expected especial blessings from Heaven, and inquired concerning them. The dove is an emblem of a gracious soul, that, finding no solid peace of satisfaction in this deluged, defiling world, returns to Christ as to its ark, as to its Noah, its rest. The defiling world, returns to Christ as to its ark, as to its Noah, its rest. The carnal heart, like the raven, takes up with the world, and feeds on the carrion it finds there; but return thou to my rest, O my soul; to thy Noah, so the word is, Ps 116:7. And as Noah put forth his hand, and took the dove, and pulled her to him, into the ark, so Christ will save, and help, and welcome those that flee to him for rest. (Ge 8:13-19)

Verses 13-19

God consults our benefit, rather than our desires; he knows what is good for us better than we do for ourselves, and how long it is fit our restraints should continue, and desired mercies should be delayed. We would go out of the ark before the ground is dried; and perhaps, if the door, is shut, are ready to thrust off the covering, and to climb up some other way; but God's time of showing mercy is the best time. As Noah had a command to go into the ark, so, how tedious soever his confinement there was, he would wait for a command to go out of it again. We must in all our ways acknowledge God, and set him before us in all our removals. Those only go under God's protection, who follow God's direction, and submit to him.

Verses 20-22

Noah was now gone out into a desolate world, where, one might have thought, his first care would have been to build a house for himself, but he begins with an alter for God. He begins well, that begins with God. Though Noah's stock of cattle was small, and that saved at great care and pains, yet he did not grudge to serve God out of it. Serving God with our little is the way to make it more; we must never think that is wasted with which God is honoured. The first thing done in the new world was an act of worship. We are now to express our thankfulness, not by burnt-offerings, but by praise, and pious devotions and conversation. God was well pleased with what was done. But the burning flesh could no more please God, than the blood of bulls and goats, except as typical of the sacrifice of Christ, and expressing Noah's humble faith and devotedness to God. The flood washed away the race of wicked men, but it did not remove sin from man's nature, who being conceived and born in sin, thinks, devises, and loves wickedness, even from his youth, and that as much since the flood as before. But God graciously declared he never would drown the world again. While the earth remains, and man upon it, there shall be summer and winter. It is plain that this earth is not to remain always. It, and all the works in it, must shortly be burned up; and we look for new heavens and a new earth, when all these things shall be dissolved. But as long as it does remain, God's providence will cause the course of times and seasons to go on, and makes each to know its place. And on this word we depend, that thus it shall be. We see God's promises to the creatures made good, and may infer that his promises to all believers shall be so.

Chapter 9

Chapter Outline

Verses 1-3

The blessing of God is the cause of our doing well. On him we depend, to him we should be thankful. Let us not forget the advantage and pleasure we have from the labour of beasts, and which their flesh affords. Nor ought we to be less thankful for the security we enjoy from the savage and hurtful beasts, through the fear of man which God has fixed deep in them. We see the fulfilment of this promise every day, and on every side. This grant of the animals for food fully warrants the use of them, but not the abuse of them by gluttony, still less by cruelty. We ought not to pain them needlessly whilst they live, nor when we take away their lives.

Verses 4-7

The main reason of forbidding the eating of blood, doubtless was because the shedding of blood in sacrifices was to keep the worshippers in mind of the great atonement; yet it seems intended also to check cruelty, lest men, being used to shed and feed upon the blood of animals, should grow unfeeling to them, and be less shocked at the idea of shedding human blood. Man must not take away his own life. Our lives are God's, and we must only give them up when he pleases. If we in any way hasten our own death, we are accountable to God for it. When God requires the life of a man from him that took it away unjustly, the murderer cannot render that, and therefore must render his own instead. One time or other, in this world or in the next, God will discover murders, and punish those murders which are beyond man's power to punish. But there are those who are ministers of God to protect the innocent, by being a terror to evil-doers, and they must not bear the sword in vain, Ro 13:4. Wilful murder ought always to be punished with death. To this law there is a reason added. Such remains of God's image are still upon fallen man, that he who unjustly kills a man, defaces the image of God, and does dishonour to him.

Verses 8-17

As the old world was ruined, to be a monument of justice, so this world remains to this day a monument of mercy. But sin, that drowned the old world, will burn this. Articles of agreement among men are sealed, that what is promised may be the more solemn, and the doing of what is covenanted the more sure to mutual satisfaction. The seal of this covenant was the rainbow, which, it is likely, was seen in the clouds before, but was never a seal of the covenant till now it was made so. The rainbow appears when we have most reason to fear the rain prevailing; God then shows this seal of the promise, that it shall not prevail. The thicker the cloud, the brighter the bow in the cloud. Thus, as threatening afflictions abound, encouraging consolations much more abound. The rainbow is the reflection of the beams of the sun shining upon or through the drops of rain: all the glory of the seals of the covenant are derived from Christ, the Sun of righteousness. And he will shed a glory on the tears of his saints. A bow speaks terror, but this has neither string nor arrow; and a bow alone will do little hurt. It is a bow, but it is directed upward, not toward the earth; for the seals of the covenant were intended to comfort, not to terrify. As God looks upon the bow, that he may remember the covenant, so should we, that we may be mindful of the covenant with faith and thankfulness. Without revelation this gracious assurance could not be known; and without faith it can be of no use to us; and thus it is as to the still greater dangers to which all are exposed, and as to the new covenant with its blessings.

Verses 18-23

The drunkenness of Noah is recorded in the Bible, with that fairness which is found only in the Scripture, as a case and proof of human weakness and imperfection, even though he may have been surprised into the sin; and to show that the best of men cannot stand upright, unless they depend upon Divine grace, and are upheld thereby. Ham appears to have been a bad man, and probably rejoiced to find his father in an unbecoming situation. It was said of Noah, that he was perfect in his generations, ch. 6:9; but this is meant of sincerity, not of a sinless perfection. Noah, who had kept sober in drunken company, is now drunk in sober company. Let him that thinks he stands, take heed lest he fall. We have need to be very careful when we use God's good creatures plentifully, lest we use them to excess, Lu 21:34. The consequence of Noah's sin was shame. Observe here the great evil of the sin of drunkenness. It discovers men; what infirmities they have, they betray when they are drunk; and secrets are then easily got out of them. Drunken porters keep open gates. It disgraces men, and exposes them to contempt. As it shows them, so it shames them. Men say and do that when drunken, which, when sober, they would blush to think of. Notice the care of Shem and Japheth to cover their father's shame. There is a mantle of love to be thrown over the faults of all, 1Pe 4:8. Beside that, there is a robe of reverence to be thrown over the faults of parents and other superiors. The blessing of God attends on those who honour their parents, and his curse lights especially on those who dishonour them.

Verses 24-29

Noah declares a curse on Canaan, the son of Ham; perhaps this grandson of his was more guilty than the rest. A servant of servants, that is, The meanest and most despicable servant, shall he be, even to his brethren. This certainly points at the victories in after-times obtained by Israel over the Canaanites, by which they were put to the sword, or brought to pay tribute. The whole continent of Africa was peopled mostly by the descendants of Ham; and for how many ages have the better parts of that country lain under the dominion of the Romans, then of the Saracens, and now of the Turks! In what wickedness, ignorance, barbarity, slavery, and misery most of the inhabitants live!

And of the poor negroes, how many every year are sold and bought, like beasts in the market, and conveyed from one quarter of the world to do the work of beasts in another! But this in no way excuses the covetousness and barbarity of those who enrich themselves with the product of their sweat and blood. God has not commanded us to enslave negroes; and, without doubt, he will severely punish all such cruel wrongs. The fulfilment of this prophecy, which contains almost a history of the world, frees Noah from the suspicion of having uttered it from personal anger. It fully proves that the Holy Spirit took occasion from Ham's offence to reveal his secret purposes. "Blessed be the Lord God of Shem." The church should be built up and continued in the posterity of Shem; of him came the Jews, who were, for a great while, the only professing people God had in the world. Christ, who was the Lord God, in his human nature should descend from Shem; for of him, as concerning the flesh, Christ came. Noah also blesses Japheth, and, in him, the isles of the gentiles that were peopled by his seed. It speaks of the conversion of the gentiles, and the bringing of them into the church. We may read it, "God shall persuade Japheth, and being persuaded, he shall dwell in the tents of Shem." Jews and gentiles shall be united together in the gospel fold; both shall be one in Christ. Noah lived to see two worlds; but being an heir of the righteousness which is by faith, he now rests in hope, waiting to see a better than either.

Chapter 10

Chapter Outline

The sons of Noah, of Japheth, of Ham.	(1–7)
Nimrod the first monarch.	(8–14)
The descendants of Canaan, The sons of Shem.	(15–32)

Verses 1-7

This chapter shows concerning the three sons of Noah, that of them was the whole earth overspread. No nation but that of the Jews can be sure from which of these seventy it has come. The lists of names of fathers and sons were preserved of the Jews alone, for the sake of the Messiah. Many learned men, however, have, with some probability, shown which of the nations of the earth descended from each of the sons of Noah To the posterity of Japheth were allotted the isles of the gentiles; probably, the island of Britain among the rest. All places beyond the sea from Judea are called isles, Jer 25:22. That promise, Isa 42:4, The isles shall wait for his law, speaks of the conversion of the gentiles to the faith of Christ.

Verses 8-14

Nimrod was a great man in his day; he began to be mighty in the earth, Those before him were content to be upon the same level with their neighbours, and though every man bare rule in his own house, yet no man pretended any further. Nimrod was resolved to lord it over his neighbours. The spirit of the giants before the flood, who became mighty men, and men of renown, Ge 6:4, revived in him. Nimrod was a great hunter. Hunting then was the method of preventing the hurtful increase of wild beasts. This required great courage and address, and thus gave an opportunity for Nimrod to command others, and gradually attached a number of men to one leader. From such a beginning, it is likely, that Nimrod began to rule, and to force others to submit. He invaded his neighbours' rights and properties, and persecuted innocent men; endeavouring to make all his own by force and violence. He carried on his oppressions and violence in defiance of God himself. Nimrod was a great ruler. Some way or other, by arts or arms, he got into power, and so founded a monarchy, which was the terror of the mighty, and bid fair to rule all the world. Nimrod was a great builder. Observe in Nimrod the nature of ambition. It is boundless; much would have more, and still cries, Give, give. It is restless; Nimrod, when he had four cities under his command, could not be content till he had four more. It is expensive; Nimrod will rather be at the charge of rearing cities, than not have the honour of ruling them. It is daring, and will stick at nothing. Nimrod's name signifies rebellion; tyrants to men are rebels to God. The days are coming, when conquerors will no longer be spoken of with praise, as in man's partial histories, but be branded with infamy, as in the impartial records of the Bible.

Verses 15-32

The posterity of Canaan were numerous, rich, and pleasantly seated; yet Canaan was under a Divine curse, and not a curse causeless. Those that are under the curse of God, may, perhaps, thrive and prosper in this world; for we cannot know love or hatred, the blessing or the curse, by what is before us, but by what is within us. The curse of God always works really, and always terribly. Perhaps it is a secret curse, a curse to the soul, and does not work so that others can see it; or a slow curse, and does not work soon; but sinners are reserved by it for a day of wrath Canaan here has a better land than either Shem or Japheth, and yet they have a better lot, for they inherit the blessing. Abram and his seed, God's covenant people, descended from Eber, and from him were called Hebrews. How much better it is to be like Eber, the father of a family of saints and honest men, than the father of a family of hunters after power, worldly wealth, or vanities. Goodness is true greatness.

Chapter 11

Chapter Outline

Terah, father of Abram, grandfather of Lot,   (27–32)
they remove to Haran.

Verses 1-4

How soon men forget the most tremendous judgments, and go back to their former crimes! Though the desolations of the deluge were before their eyes, though they sprang from the stock of righteous Noah, yet even during his life-time, wickedness increases exceedingly. Nothing but the sanctifying grace of the Holy Spirit can remove the sinful lusts of the human will, and the depravity of the human heart. God's purpose was, that mankind should form many nations, and people all lands. In contempt of the Divine will, and against the counsel of Noah, the bulk of mankind united to build a city and a tower to prevent their separating. Idolatry was begun, and Babel became one of its chief seats. They made one another more daring and resolute. Let us learn to provoke one another to love and to good works, as sinners stir up and encourage one another to wicked works.

Verses 5-9

Here is an expression after the manner of men; The Lord came down to see the city. God is just and fair in all he does against sin and sinners, and condemns none unheard. Pious Eber is not found among this ungodly crew; for he and his are called the children of God; their souls joined not themselves to the assembly of these children of men. God suffered them to go on some way, that the works of their hands, from which they promised themselves lasting honour, might turn to their lasting reproach. God has wise and holy ends, in allowing the enemies of his glory to carry on their wicked projects a great way, and to prosper long. Observe the wisdom and mercy of God, in the methods taken for defeating this undertaking. And the mercy of God in not making the penalty equal to the offence; for he deals not with us according to our sins. The wisdom of God, in fixing upon a sure way to stop these proceedings. If they could not understand one another, they could not help one another; this would take them off from their building. God has various means, and effectual ones, to baffle and defeat the projects of proud men that set themselves against him, and particularly he divides them among themselves. Notwithstanding their union and obstinacy God was above them; for who ever hardened his heart against him, and prospered? Their language was confounded. We all suffer by it to this day: in all the pains and trouble used to learn the languages we have occasion for, we suffer for the rebellion of our ancestors at Babel. Nay, and those unhappy disputes, which are strifes of words, and arise from misunderstanding one another's words, for aught we know, are owing to this confusion of tongues. They left off to build the city. The confusion of their tongues not only unfitted them for helping one another, but they saw the hand of the Lord gone out against them. It is wisdom to leave off that which we see God fights against. God is able to blast and bring to nought all the devices and designs of Babel-builders: there is no wisdom nor counsel against the Lord. The builders departed according to their families, and the tongue they spake, to the countries and places allotted to them. The children of men never did, nor ever will, come all together again, till the great day, when the Son of man shall sit upon the throne of his glory, and all nations shall be gathered before him.

Verses 10-26

Here is a genealogy, or list of names, ending in Abram, the friend of God, and thus leading towards Christ, the promised Seed, who was the son of Abram. Nothing is left upon record but their names and ages; the Holy Ghost seeming to hasten through them to the history of Abram. How little do we know of those that are gone before us in this world, even of those that lived in the same places where we live, as we likewise know little of those who now live in distant places! We have enough to do to mind our own work. When the earth began to be peopled, men's lives began to shorten; this was the wise disposal of Providence.

Verses 27-32

Here begins the story of Abram, whose name is famous in both Testaments. Even the children of Eber had become worshippers of false gods. Those who are through grace, heirs of the land of promise, ought to remember what was the land of their birth; what was their corrupt and sinful state by nature. Abram's brethren were, Nahor, out of whose family both Isaac and Jacob had their wives; and Haran, the father of Lot, who died before his father. Children cannot be sure that they shall outlive their parents. Haran died in Ur, before the happy removal of the family out of that idolatrous country. It concerns us to hasten out of our natural state, lest death surprise us in it. We here read of Abram's departure out of Ur of the Chaldees, with his father Terah, his nephew Lot, and the rest of his family, in obedience to the call of God. This chapter leaves them about mid-way between Ur and Canaan, where they dwelt till Terah's death. Many reach to Charran, and yet fall short of Canaan; they are not far from the kingdom of God, and yet never come thither.

Chapter 12

Chapter Outline

Verses 1-3

God made choice of Abram, and singled him out from among his fellow-idolaters, that he might reserve a people for himself, among whom his true worship might be maintained till   the coming of Christ. From henceforward Abram and his seed are almost the only subject of the history in the Bible. Abram was tried whether he loved God better than all, and whether he could willingly leave all to go with God. His kindred and his father's house were a constant temptation to him, he could not continue among them without danger of being infected by them. Those who leave their sins, and turn to God, will be unspeakable gainers by the change. The command God gave to Abram, is much the same with the gospel call, for natural affection must give way to Divine grace. Sin, and all the occasions of it, must be forsaken; particularly bad company. Here are many great and precious promises. All God's precepts are attended with promises to the obedient. 1. I will make of thee a great nation. When God took Abram from his own people, he promised to make him the head of another people. 2. I will bless thee. Obedient believers shall be sure to inherit the blessing. 3. I will make thy name great. The name of obedient believers shall certainly be made great. 4. Thou shalt be a blessing. Good men are the blessings of their country. 5. I will bless them that bless thee, and curse him that curseth thee. God will take care that none are losers, by any service done for his people. 6. In thee shall all the families of the earth be blessed. Jesus Christ is the great blessing of the world, the greatest that ever the world possessed. All the true blessedness the world is now, or ever shall be possessed of, is owing to Abram and his posterity. Through them we have a Bible, a Saviour, and a gospel. They are the stock on which the Christian church is grafted.

Verses 4, 5

Abram believed that the blessing of the Almighty would make up for all he could lose or leave behind, supply all his wants, and answer and exceed all his desires; and he knew that nothing but misery would follow disobedience. Such believers, being justified by faith in Christ, have peace with God. They hold on their way to Canaan. They are not discouraged by the difficulties in their way, nor drawn aside by the delights they meet with. Those who set out for heaven must persevere to the end. What we undertake, in obedience to God's command, and in humble attendance on his providence, will certainly succeed, and end with comfort at last. Canaan was not, as other lands, a mere outward possession, but a type of heaven, and in this respect the patriarchs so earnestly prized it.

Verses 6-9

Abram found the country peopled by Canaanites, who were bad neighbours. He journeyed, going on still. Sometimes it is the lot of good men to be unsettled, and often to remove into various states. Believers must look on themselves as strangers and sojourners in this world, Heb 11:8, 13, 14. But observe how much comfort Abram had in God. When he could have little satisfaction in converse with the Canaanites whom he found there, he had abundance of pleasure in communion with that God, who brought him thither, and did not leave him. Communion with God is kept up by the word and by prayer. God reveals himself and his favours to his people by degrees; before, he had promised to show Abram this land, now, to give it to him: as grace is growing, so is comfort. It should seem, Abram understood it also as a grant of a better land, of which this was a type; for he looked for a heavenly country, Heb 11:16. As soon as Abram was got to Canaan, though he was but a stranger and sojourner there, yet he set up, and kept up, the worship of God in his family. He not only minded the ceremonial part of religion, the offering of sacrifice; but he made conscience of seeking his God, and calling on his name; that spiritual sacrifice with which God is well pleased. He preached concerning the name of the Lord; he taught his family and neighbours the knowledge of the true God, and his holy religion. The way of family worship is a good old way, no new thing, but the ancient usage of the saints. Abram was rich, and had a numerous family, was now unsettled, and in the midst of enemies; yet, wherever he pitched his tent, he built an altar: wherever we go, let us not fail to take our religion along with us.

Verses 10-20

There is no state on earth free from trials, nor any character free from blemishes. There was famine in Canaan, the glory of all lands, and unbelief, with the evils it ever brings, in Abram the father of the faithful. Perfect happiness and perfect purity dwell only in heaven. Abram, when he must for a time quit Canaan, goes to Egypt, that he might not seem to look back, and meaning to tarry there no longer than needful. There Abram dissembled his relation to Sarai, equivocated, and taught his wife and his attendants to do so too. He concealed a truth, so as in effect to deny it, and exposed thereby both his wife and the Egyptians to sin. The grace Abram was most noted for, was faith; yet he thus fell through unbelief and distrust of the Divine providence, even after God had appeared to him twice. Alas, what will become of weak faith, when strong faith is thus shaken! If God did not deliver us, many a time, out of straits and distresses which we bring ourselves into, by our own sin and folly, we should be ruined. He deals not with us according to our deserts. Those are happy chastisements that hinder us in a sinful way, and bring us to our duty, particularly to the duty of restoring what we have wrongfully taken or kept. Pharaoh's reproof of Abram was very just: What is this that thou hast done? How unbecoming a wise and good man! If those who profess religion, do that which is unfair and deceptive, especially if they say that which borders upon a lie, they must expect to hear of it; and they have reason to thank those who will tell them of it. The sending away was kind. Pharaoh was so far from any design to kill Abram, as he feared, that he took particular care of him. We often perplex ourselves with fears which are altogether groundless. Many a time we fear where no fear is. Pharaoh charged his men not to hurt Abram in any thing. It is not enough for those in authority, that they do not hurt themselves; they must keep their servants and those about them from doing hurt.

Chapter 13

Chapter Outline

God renews his promise to Abram, who removes to Hebron. (14–18)

Verses 1-4

Abram was very rich: he was very heavy, so the Hebrew word is; for riches are a burden; and they that will be rich, do but load themselves with thick clay, Hab 2:6. There is a burden of care in getting riches, fear in keeping them, temptation in using them, guilt in abusing them, sorrow in losing them, and a burden of account at last to be given up about them. Yet God in his providence sometimes makes good men rich men, and thus God's blessing made Abram rich without sorrow, Pr 10:22. Though it is hard for a rich man to get to heaven, yet in some cases it may be, Mr 10:23, 24. Nay, outward prosperity, if well managed, is an ornament to piety, and an opportunity for doing more good. Abram removed to Bethel. His altar was gone, so that he could not offer sacrifice; but he called on the name of the Lord. You may as soon find a living man without breath as one of God's people without prayer.

Verses 5-9

Riches not only afford matter for strife, and are the things most commonly striven about; but they also stir up a spirit of contention, by making people proud and covetous. Mine and thine are the great make-bates of the world. Poverty and labour, wants and wanderings, could not separate Abram and Lot; but riches did so. Bad servants often make a great deal of mischief in families and among neighbours, by their pride and passion, lying, slandering, and talebearing. What made the quarrel worse was, that the Canaanite and the Perizzite dwelt then in the land. The quarrels of professors are the reproach of religion, and give occasion to the enemies of the Lord to blaspheme. It is best to keep the peace, that it be not broken; but the next best is, if differences do happen, with all speed to quench the fire that is broken out. The attempt to stay this strife was made by Abram, although he was the elder and the greater man. Abram shows himself to be a man of cool spirit, that had the command of his passion, and knew how to turn away wrath by a soft answer. Those that would keep the peace, must never render railing for railing. And of a condescending spirit; he was willing to beseech even his inferior to be at peace. Whatever others are for, the people of God must be for peace. Abram's plea for peace was very powerful. Let the people of the land contend about trifles; but let not us fall out, who know better things, and look for a better country. Professors of religion should be most careful to avoid contention. Many profess to be for peace who will do nothing towards it: not so Abram. When God condescends to beseech us to be reconciled, we may well beseech one another. Though God had promised Abram to give this land to his seed, yet he offered an equal or better share to Lot, who had not an equal right; and he will not, under the protection of God's promise, act hardly to his kinsman. It is noble to be willing to yield for peace' sake.

Verses 10-13

Abram having offered Lot the choice, he at once accepted it. Passion and selfishness make men rude. Lot looked to the goodness of the land; therefore he doubted not that in such a fruitful soil he should certainly thrive. But what came of it? Those who, in choosing relations, callings, dwellings, or settlements, are guided and governed by the lust of the flesh, the lust of the eye, or the pride of life, cannot expect God's presence or blessing. They are commonly disappointed even in that which they principally aim at. In all our choices this principle should rule, That is best for us, which is best for our souls. Lot little considered the badness of the inhabitants. The men of Sodom were impudent, daring sinners. This was the iniquity of Sodom, pride, fulness of bread, and abundance of idleness, Eze 16:49. God often gives great plenty to great sinners. It has often been the vexatious lot of good men to live among wicked neighbours; and it must be the more grievous, if, as Lot here, they have brought it upon themselves by a wrong choice.

Verses 14-18

Those are best prepared for the visits of Divine grace, whose spirits are calm, and not ruffled with passion. God will abundantly make up in spiritual peace, what we lose for preserving neighbourly peace. When our relations are separated from us, yet God is not. Observe also the promises with which God now comforted and enriched Abram. Of two things he assures him; a good land, and a numerous issue to enjoy it. The prospects seen by faith are more rich and beautiful than those we see around us. God bade him walk through the land, not to think of fixing in it, but expect to be always unsettled, and walking through it to a better Canaan. He built an altar, in token of his thankfulness to God. When God meets us with gracious promises, he expects that we should attend him with humble praises. In outward difficulties, it is very profitable for the true believer to mediate on the glorious inheritance which the Lord has for him at the last.

Chapter 14

Chapter Outline

Verses 1-12

The wars of nations make great figure in history, but we should not have had the record of this war if Abram and Lot had not been concerned. Out of covetousness, Lot had settled in fruitful, but wicked Sodom. Its inhabitants were the most ripe for vengeance of all the descendants of Canaan. The invaders were from Chaldea and Persia, then only small kingdoms. They took Lot among the rest, and his goods. Though he was righteous, and Abram's brother's son, yet he was with the rest in this trouble. Neither our own piety, nor our relation to the favourites of Heaven, will be our security when God's judgments are abroad. Many an honest man fares the worse for his wicked neighbours: it is our wisdom to separate, or at least to distinguish ourselves from them, 2Co 6:17. So near a relation of Abram should have been a companion and a disciple of Abram. If he chose to dwell in Sodom, he must thank himself if he share in Sodom's losses. When we go out of the way of our duty, we put ourselves from under God's protection, and cannot expect that the choice made by our lusts, should end to our comfort. They took Lot's goods; it is just with God to deprive us of enjoyments, by which we suffer ourselves to be deprived of the enjoyment of him.

Verses 13-16

Abram takes this opportunity to give a real proof of his being truly friendly to Lot. We ought to be ready to succour those in distress, especially relations and friends. And though others may have been wanting in their duty to us, yet we must not neglect our duty to them. Abram rescued the captives. As we have opportunity, we must do good to all.

Verses 17-20

Melchizedek is spoken of as a king of Salem, supposed to be the place afterwards called Jerusalem, and it is generally thought that he was only a man. The words of the apostle, Heb 7:3, state only, that the sacred history has said nothing of his ancestors. The silence of the Scriptures on this, is to raise our thoughts to Him, whose generation cannot be declared. Bread and wine were suitable refreshment for the weary followers of Abram; and it is remarkable that Christ appointed the same as the memorials of his body and blood, which are meat and drink indeed to the soul. Melchizedek blessed Abram from God. He blessed God from Abram. We ought to give thanks for other's mercies as for our own. Jesus Christ, our great High Priest, is the Mediator both of our prayers and praises, and not only offers up ours, but his own for us. Abram gave him the tenth of the spoils, Heb 7:4. When we have received some great mercy from God, it is very fit we should express our thankfulness by some special act of pious charity. Jesus Christ, our great Melchisedek, is to have homage done him, and to be humbly acknowledged as our King and Priest; not only the tithe of all, but all we have, must be given up to him.

Verses 21-24

Observe the king of Sodom's grateful offer to Abram, Give me the souls, and take thou the substance. Gratitude teaches us to recompense to the utmost of our power, those that have undergone fatigues, run hazards, and been at expense for our service and benefit. Abram generously refused this offer. He accompanies his refusal with a good reason, Lest thou shouldest say, I have made Abram rich: which would reflect upon the promise promise and covenant of God, as if He would not have enriched Abraham without the spoils of Sodom. The people of God must, for their credit's sake, take heed of doing any thing that looks mean or mercenary, or that savors of covetousness and self-seeking. Abraham can trust the Possessor of Heaven and earth to provide for him.

Chapter 15

Chapter Outline

Verse 1

God assured Abram of safety and happiness; that he should for ever be safe. I am thy shield; or, I am a shield to thee, present with thee, actually caring for thee. The consideration that God himself is, and will be a shield to his people, to secure them from all evils, a shield ready to them, and a shield round about them, should silence all perplexing, tormenting fears.

Verses 2-6

Though we must never complain of God, yet we have leave to complain to him; and to state all our grievances. It is ease to a burdened spirit, to open its case to a faithful and compassionate friend. Abram's complaint is, that he had no child; that he was never likely to have any; that the want of a son was so great a trouble to him, that it took away all his comfort. If we suppose that Abram looked no further than outward comfort, this complaint was to be blamed. But if we suppose that Abram herein had reference to the promised Seed, his desire was very commendable. Till we have evidence of our interest in Christ, we should not rest satisfied; what will all avail me, if I go Christless? If we continue instant in prayer, yet pray with humble submission to the Divine will, we shall not seek in vain. God gave Abram an express promise of a son. Christians may believe in God with respect to the common concerns of this life; but the faith by which they are justified, always has respect to the person and work of Christ. Abram believed in God as promising Christ; they believe in him as having raised him from the dead, Ro 4:24. Through faith in his blood they obtain forgiveness of sins.

Verses 7-11

Assurance was given to Abram of the land of Canaan for an inheritance. God never promises more than he is able to perform, as men often do. Abram did as God commanded him. He divided the beasts in the midst, according to the ceremony used in confirming covenants, Jer 34:18, 19. Having prepared according to God's appointment, he set himself to wait for the sign God might give him. A watch must be kept upon our spiritual sacrifices. When vain thoughts, like these fowls, come down upon our sacrifices, we must drive them away, and seek to attend on God without distraction.

Verses 12-16

A deep sleep fell upon Abram; with this sleep a horror of great darkness fell upon him: a sudden change. The children of light do not always walk in the light. Several things were then foretold. 1. The suffering state of Abram's seed for a long time. They shall be strangers. The heirs of heaven are strangers on earth. They shall be servants; but Canaanites serve under a curse, the Hebrews under a blessing. They shall be suffers. Those that are blessed and beloved of God, are often sorely afflicted by wicked men. 2. The judgment of the enemies of Abram's seed. Though God may allow persecutors and oppressors to trample upon his people a great while, he will certainly reckon with them at last. 3. That great event, the deliverance of Abram's seed out of Egypt, is here foretold. 4. Their happy settlement in Canaan. They shall come hither again. The measure of sin fills gradually. Some people's measure of sin fills slowly. The knowledge of future events would seldom add to our comfort. In the most favoured families, and most happy lives, there are so many afflictions, that it is merciful in God to conceal what will befall us and ours.

Verses 17-21

The smoking furnace and the burning lamp, probably represented the Israelites' severe trials and joyful deliverance, with their gracious supports in the mean time. It is probable that this furnace and lamp, which passed between the pieces, burned and consumed them, and so completed the sacrifice, and testified God's acceptance of it. So it intimates that God's covenants with man are made by sacrifice, Ps 50:5. And we may know that he accepts our sacrifices, if he kindles in our souls pious and devout affections. The bounds of the land granted are stated. Several nations, or tribes, are spoken of, that must be cast out to make room for the seed of Abram. In this chapter we perceive in Abram faith struggling against, and triumphing over, unbelief. Wonder not, believers, if you meet with seasons of darkness and distress. But it is not the will of God that you should be cast down: fear not; for all that he was to Abram he will be to you.

Chapter 16

Chapter Outline

Sarai gives Hagar to Abram.	(1–3)
Hagar's misbehaviour to Sarai.	(4–6)
The Angel commands Hagar to return, The promise to her Birth of Ishmael.	(7–16)

Verses 1-3

Sarai, no longer expecting to have children herself, proposed to Abram to take another wife, whose children she might; her slave, whose children would be her property. This was done without asking counsel of the Lord. Unbelief worked, God's almighty power was forgotten. It was a bad example, and a source of manifold uneasiness. In every relation and situation in life there is some cross for us to bear: much of the exercise of faith consists in patiently submitting, in waiting the Lord's time, and using only those means which he appoints for the removal of the cross. Foul temptations may have very fair pretences, and be coloured with that which is very plausible. Fleshly wisdom puts us out of God's way. This would not be the case, if we would ask counsel of God by his word and by prayer, before we attempt that which is doubtful.

Verses 4-6

Abram's unhappy marriage to Hagar very soon made a great deal of mischief. We may thank ourselves for the guilt and grief that follow us, when we go out of the way of our duty. See it in this case, Passionate people often quarrel with others, for things of which they themselves must bear the blame. Sarai had given her maid to Abram, yet she cries out, My wrong be upon thee. That is never said wisely, which pride and anger put into our mouths. Those are not always in the right, who are most loud and forward in appealing to God: such rash and bold imprecations commonly speak guilt and a bad cause. Hagar forgot that she herself had first given the provocation, by despising her mistress. Those that suffer for their faults, ought to bear it patiently, 1 Pe 2:20.

Verses 7-16

Hagar was out of her place, and out of the way of her duty, and going further astray, when the Angel found her. It is a great mercy to be stopped in a sinful way, either by conscience or by providence. Whence comest thou? Consider that thou art running from duty, and the privileges thou wast blest with in Abram's tent. It is good to live in a religious family, which those ought to consider who have this advantage. Whither wilt thou go? Thou art running into sin; if Hagar return to Egypt, she will return to idol gods, and into danger in the wilderness through which she must travel. Recollecting who we are, would often teach us our duty. Inquiring whence we came, would show us our sin and folly. Considering whither we shall go, discovers our danger and misery. And those who leave their space and duty, must hasten their return, how mortifying soever it be. The declaration of the Angel, "I will," shows this Angel was the eternal Word and Son of God. Hagar could not but admire the Lord's mercy, and feel, Have I, who am so unworthy, been favoured with a gracious visit from the Lord? She was brought to a better temper, returned, and by her behaviour softened Sarai, and received more gentle treatment. Would that we were always suitably impressed with this thought, Thou God seest me!

Chapter 17

Chapter Outline

Verses 1-6

The covenant was to be accomplished in due time. The promised Seed was Christ, and Christians in him. And all who are of faith are blessed with faithful Abram, being partakers of the same covenant blessings. In token of this covenant his name was changed from Abram, "a high father," to Abraham, "the father of a multitude." All that the Christian world enjoys, it is indebted for to Abraham and his Seed.

Verses 7-14

The covenant of grace is from everlasting in the counsels of it, and to everlasting in the consequences of it. The token of the covenant was circumcision. It is here said to be the covenant which Abraham and his seed must keep. Those who will have the Lord to be to them a God, must resolve to be to him a people. Not only Abraham and Isaac, and his posterity by Isaac, were to be circumcised, but also Ishmael and the bond-servants. It sealed not only the covenant of the land of Canaan to Isaac's posterity, but of heaven, through Christ, to the whole church of God. The outward sign is for the visible church; the inward seal of the Spirit is peculiar to those whom God knows to be believers, and he alone can know them. The religious observance of this institution was required, under a very severe penalty. It is dangerous to make light of Divine institutions, and to live in the neglect of them. The covenant in question was one that involved great blessings for the world in all future ages. Even the blessedness of Abraham himself, and all the rewards conferred upon him, were for Christ's sake. Abraham was justified, as we have seen, not by his own righteousness, but by faith in the promised Messiah.

Verses 15-22

Here is the promise made to Abraham of a son by Sarai, in whom the promise made to him should be fulfilled. The assurance of this promise was the change of Sarai's name into Sarah. Sarai signifies my princess, as if her honour were confined to one family only; Sarah signifies a princess. The more favours God confers upon us, the more low we should be in our own eyes. Abraham showed great joy; he laughed, it was a laughter of delight, not of distrust. Now it was that Abraham rejoiced to see Christ's day; now he saw it and was glad, Joh 8:56. Abraham, dreading lest Ishmael should be abandoned and forsaken of God, put up a petition on his behalf. God gives us leave in prayer to be particular in making known our requests. Whatever is our care and fear, should be spread before God in prayer. It is the duty of parents to pray for their children, and the great thing we should desire is, that they may be kept in covenant with Him, and may have grace to walk before him in uprightness. Common blessings are secured to Ishmael. Outward good things are often given to those children of godly parents who are born after the flesh, for their parents' sake. Covenant blessings are reserved for Isaac, and appropriated to him.

Verses 23-27

Abraham and all his family were circumcised; so receiving the token of the covenant, and distinguishing themselves from other families that had no part nor lot in the matter. It was an implicit obedience; he did as God said unto him, and did not ask why or wherefore. He did it because God bade him. It was a speedy obedience; in the self-same day. Sincere obedience makes no delay. Not only the doctrines of revelation, but the seals of God's covenant, remind us that we are guilty, polluted sinners. They show us our need of the blood of atonement; they point to the promised Saviour, and teach us to exercise faith in him. They show us that without regeneration, and sanctification by his Spirit, and the mortification of our corrupt and carnal inclinations, we cannot be in covenant with God. But let us remember that the true circumcision is that of the heart, by the Spirit, Ro 2:28, 29. Both under the old and new dispensation, many have had the outward profession, and the outward seal, who were never sealed by the Holy Spirit of promise.

Chapter 18

Chapter Outline

The Lord appears to Abraham.	(1–8)
Sarah's unbelief reproved.	(9–15)
God reveals to Abraham the destruction of Sodom.	(16–22)
Abraham's intercession for Sodom.	(23–33)

Verses 1-8

Abraham was waiting to entertain any weary traveller, for inns were not to be met with as among us. While Abraham was thus sitting, he saw three men coming. These were three heavenly beings in human bodies. Some think they were all created angels; others, that one of them was the Son of God, the Angel of the covenant. Washing the feet is customary in those hot climates, where only sandals are worn. We should not be forgetful to entertain strangers, for thereby some have entertained angels unawares, Heb 13:2; nay, the Lord of angels himself; as we always do, when for his sake we entertain the least of his brethren. Cheerful and obliging manners in showing kindness, are great ornaments to piety. Though our condescending Lord vouchsafes not personal visits to us, yet still by his Spirit he stands at the door and knocks; when we are inclined to open, he deigns to enter; and by his gracious consolations he provides a rich feast, of which we partake with him, Re 3:20.

Verses 9-15

Where is Sarah thy wife? was asked. Note the answer, In the tent. Just at hand, in her proper place, occupied in her household concerns. There is nothing got by gadding. Those are most likely to receive comfort from God and his promises, who are in their proper place, and in the way of their duty, Lu 2:8. We are slow of heart to believe, and need line upon line to the same purport. The blessings others have from common providence, believers have from the Divine promise, which makes them very sweet, and very sure. The spiritual seed of Abraham owe their life, and joy, and hope, and all, to the promise. Sarah thinks this too good news to be true; she laughed, and therefore cannot as yet find in her heart to believe it. Sarah laughed. We might not have thought there was a difference between Sarah's laughter and Abraham's, ch. 17:17; but He who searches the heart, saw that the one sprung from unbelief, and the other from faith. She denied that she had laughed. One sin commonly brings in another, and it is not likely we shall strictly keep to truth, when we question the Divine truth. But whom the Lord loves he will rebuke, convict, silence, and bring to repentance, and if they sin before him.

Verses 16-22

The two who are supposed to have been created angels went toward Sodom. The one who is called Jehovah throughout the chapter, continued with Abraham, and would not hide from him the thing he intended to do. Though God long forbears with sinners, from which they fancy that the Lord does not see, and does not regard; yet when the day of his wrath comes, he will look toward them. The Lord will give Abraham an opportunity to intercede with him, and shows him the reason of his conduct. Consider, as a very bright part of Abraham's character and example, that he not only prayed with his family, but he was very careful to teach and rule them well. Those who expect family blessings must make conscience of family duty. Abraham did not fill their heads with matters of doubtful dispute; but he taught them to be serious and devout in the worship of God, and to be honest in their dealings with all men. Of how few may such a character be given in our days! How little care is taken by masters of families to ground those under them in the principles of religion! Do we watch from sabbath to sabbath whether they go forward or backward?

Verses 23-33

Here is the first solemn prayer upon record in the Bible; and it is a prayer for the sparing of Sodom. Abraham prayed earnestly that Sodom might be spared, if but a few righteous persons should be found in it. Come and learn from Abraham what compassion we should feel for sinners, and how earnestly we should pray for them. We see here that the effectual, fervent prayer of a righteous man avails much. Abraham, indeed, failed in his request for the whole place, but Lot was miraculously delivered. Be encouraged then to expect, by earnest prayer, the blessing of God upon your families, your friends, your neighbourhood. To this end you must not only pray, but you must live like Abraham. He knew the Judge of all the earth would do right. He does not plead that the wicked may be spared for their own sake, or because it would be severe to destroy them, but for the sake of the righteous who might be found among them. And righteousness only can be made a plea before God. How then did Christ make intercession for transgressors? Not by blaming the Divine law, nor by alleging aught in extenuation or excuse of human guilt; but by pleading HIS OWN obedience unto death.

Chapter 19

Chapter Outline

The destruction of Sodom, and the deliverance of Lot.   (1–29)

The sin and disgrace of Lot.   (30–38)

Verses 1-29

Lot was good, but there was not one more of the same character in the city. All the people of Sodom were very wicked and vile. Care was therefore taken for saving Lot and his family. Lot lingered; he trifled. Thus many who are under convictions about their spiritual state, and the necessity of a change, defer that needful work. The salvation of the most righteous men is of God's mercy, not by their own merit. We are saved by grace. God's power also must be acknowledged in bringing souls out of a sinful state If God had not been merciful to us, our lingering had been our ruin. Lot must flee for his life. He must not hanker after Sodom. Such commands as these are given to those who, through grace, are delivered out of a sinful state and condition. Return not to sin and Satan. Rest not in self and the world. Reach toward Christ and heaven, for that is escaping to the mountain, short of which we must not stop. Concerning this destruction, observe that it is a revelation of the wrath of God against sin and sinners of all ages. Let us learn from hence the evil of sin, and its hurtful nature; it leads to ruin.

Verses 30-38

See the peril of security. Lot, who kept chaste in Sodom, and was a mourner for the wickedness of the place, and a witness against it, when in the mountain, alone, and, as he thought, out of the way of temptation, is shamefully overtaken. Let him that thinks he stands high, and stands firm, take heed lest he fall. See the peril of drunkenness; it is not only a great sin itself, but lets in many sins, which bring a lasting wound and dishonour. Many a man does that, when he is drunk, which, when he is sober, he could not think of without horror. See also the peril of temptation, even from relations and friends, whom we love and esteem, and expect kindness from. We must dread a snare, wherever we are, and be always upon our guard. No excuse can be made for the daughters, nor for Lot. Scarcely any account can be given of the affair but this, The heart is deceitful above all things, and desperately wicked: who can know it? From the silence of the Scripture concerning Lot henceforward, learn that drunkenness, as it makes men forgetful, so it makes them to be forgotten.

Chapter 20

Chapter Outline

Verses 1-8

Crooked policy will not prosper: it brings ourselves and others into danger. God gives Abimelech notice of his danger of sin, and his danger of death for his sin. Every wilful sinner is a dead man, but Abimelech pleads ignorance. If our consciences witness, that, however we may have been cheated into a snare, we have not knowingly sinned against God, it will be our rejoicing in the day of evil. It is matter of comfort to those who are honest, that God knows their honesty, and will acknowledge it. It is a great mercy to be hindered from committing sin; of this God must have the glory. But if we have ignorantly done wrong, that will not excuse us, if we knowingly persist in it. He that does wrong, whoever he is, prince or peasant, shall certainly receive for the wrong which he has done, unless he repent, and, if possible, make restitution.

Verses 9-13

See here much to blame, even in the father of the faithful. Mark his distrust of God, his undue care about life, his intent to deceive. He also threw temptation in the way of others, caused affliction to them, exposed himself and Sarah to just rebukes, and yet attempted an excuse. These things are written for our warning, not for us to imitate. Even Abraham hath not whereof to glory. He cannot be justified by his works, but must be indebted for justification, to that righteousness which is upon all and unto all them that believe. We must not condemn all as hypocrites who fall into sin, if they do not continue in it. But let the unhumbled and impenitent take heed that they do not sin on, thinking that grace may abound. Abimelech, being warned of God, takes the warning; and being truly afraid of sin and its consequences, he rose early to pursue the directions given him.

Verses 14-18

We often trouble ourselves, and even are led into temptation and sin, by groundless suspicions; and find the fear of God where we expected it not. Agreements to deceive generally end in shame and sorrow; and restraints from sin, though by suffering, should be thankfully acknowledged. Though the Lord rebuke, yet he will pardon and deliver his people, and he will give them favour in the sight of those with whom they sojourn; and overrule their infirmities, when they are humbled for them, so that they shall prove useful to themselves and others.

Chapter 21

Chapter Outline

Verses 1-8

Few under the Old Testament were brought into the world with such expectations as Isaac. He was in this a type of Christ, that Seed which the holy God so long promised, and holy men so long expected. He was born according to the promise, at the set time of which God had spoken. God's promised mercies will certainly come at the time which He sets, and that is the best time. Isaac means "laughter," and there was good reason for the name, ch. 17:17; 18:13. When the Sun of comfort is risen upon the soul, it is good to remember how welcome the dawning of the day was. When Sarah received the promise, she laughed with distrust and doubt. When God gives us the mercies we began to despair of, we ought to remember with sorrow and shame our sinful distrust of his power and promise, when we were in pursuit of them. This mercy filled Sarah with joy and wonder. God's favours to his covenant people are such as surpass their own and others' thoughts and expectations: who could imagine that he should do so much for those that deserve so little, nay, for those that deserve so ill? Who would have said that God should send his Son to die for us, his Spirit to make us holy, his angels to attend us? Who would have said that such great sins should be pardoned, such mean services accepted, and such worthless worms taken into covenant? A short account of Isaac's infancy is given. God's blessing upon the nursing of children, and the preservation of them through the perils of the infant age, are to be acknowledged as signal instances of the care and tenderness of the Divine providence. See Ps 22:9, 10; Ho 11:1, 2.

Verses 9-13

Let us not overlook the manner in which this family matter instructs us not to rest in outward privileges, or in our own doings. And let us seek the blessings of the new covenant by faith in its Divine Surety. Ishmael's conduct was persecution, being done in profane contempt of the covenant and promise, and with malice against Isaac. God takes notice of what children say and do in their play; and will reckon with them, if they say or do amiss, though their parents do not. Mocking is a great sin, and very provoking to God. And the children of promise must expect to be mocked. Abraham was grieved that Ishmael should misbehave, and Sarah demand so severe a punishment. But God showed him that Isaac must be the father of the promised Seed; therefore, send Ishmael away, lest he corrupt the manners, or try to take the rights of Isaac. The covenant seed of Abraham must be a people by themselves, not mingled with those who were out of covenant: Sarah little thought of this; but God turned aright what she said.

Verses 14-21

If Hagar and Ishmael had behaved well in Abraham's family, they might have continued there; but they were justly punished. By abusing privileges, we forfeit them. Those who know not when they are well off, will be made to know the worth of mercies by the want of them. They were brought to distress in the wilderness. It is not said that the provisions were spent, or that Abraham sent them away without money. But the water was spent; and having lost their way, in that hot climate Ishmael was soon overcome with fatigue and thirst. God's readiness to help us when we are in trouble, must not slacken, but quicken our endeavours to help ourselves. The promise concerning her son is repeated, as a reason why Hagar should bestir herself to help him. It should engage our care and pains about children and young people, to consider that we know not what great use God has designed them for, and may make of them. The angel directs her to a present supply. Many who have reason to be comforted, go mourning from day to day, because they do not see the reason they have for comfort. There is a well of water near them in the covenant of grace, but they are not aware of it, till the same God that opened their eyes to see their wound, opens them to see their remedy. Paran was a wild place, fit for a wild man; such as Ishmael. Those who are born after the flesh, take up with the wilderness of this world, while the children of the promise aim at the heavenly Canaan, and cannot be at rest till they are there. Yet God was with the lad; his outward welfare was owing to this.

Verses 22-34

Abimelech felt sure that the promises of God would be fulfilled to Abraham. It is wise to connect ourselves with those who are blessed of God; and we ought to requite kindness to those who have been kind to us. Wells of water are scarce and valuable in eastern countries. Abraham took care to have his title to the well allowed, to prevent disputes in future. No more can be expected from an honest man than that he be ready to do right, as soon as he knows he has done wrong. Abraham, being now in a good neighbourhood, stayed a great while there. There he made, not only a constant practice, but an open profession of his religion. There he called on the name of the Lord, as the everlasting God; probably in the grove he planted, which was his place of prayer. Abraham kept up public worship, in which his neighbours might join. Good men should do all they can to make others so. Wherever we sojourn, we must neither neglect nor be ashamed of the worship of Jehovah.

Chapter 22

Chapter Outline

God commands Abraham to offer up Isaac.   (1, 2)

Abraham's faith and obedience to the Divine   (3–10)
command.

Another sacrifice is provided instead of   (11–14)
Isaac.

The covenant with Abraham renewed.   (15–19)

The family of Nahor.   (20–24)

Verses 1, 2

We never are secure from trials In Hebrew, to tempt, and to try, or to prove, are expressed by the same word. Every trial is indeed a temptation, and tends to show the dispositions of the heart, whether holy or unholy. But God proved Abraham, not to draw him to sin, as Satan tempts. Strong faith is often exercised with strong trials, and put upon hard services. The command to offer up his son, is given in such language as makes the trial more grievous; every word here is a sword. Observe, 1. The person to be offered: Take thy son; not thy bullocks and thy lambs. How willingly would Abraham have parted with them all to redeem Isaac! Thy son; not thy servant. Thine only son; thine only son by Sarah. Take Isaac, that son whom thou lovest. 2. The place: three days' journey off; so that Abraham might have time to consider, and might deliberately obey. 3. The manner: Offer him fro a burnt-offering; not only kill his son, his Isaac, but kill him as a sacrifice; kill him with all that solemn pomp and ceremony, with which he used to offer his burnt-offerings.

Verses 3-10

Never was any gold tried in so hot a fire. Who but Abraham would not have argued with God? Such would have been the thought of a weak heart; but Abraham knew that he had to do with a God, even Jehovah. Faith had taught him not to argue, but to obey. He is sure that what God commands is good; that what he promises cannot be broken. In matters of God, whoever consults with flesh and blood, will never offer up his Isaac to God. The good patriarch rises early, and begins his sad journey. And now he travels three days, and Isaac still is in his sight! Misery is made worse when long continued. The expression, We will come again to you, shows that Abraham expected that Isaac, being raised from the dead, would return with him. It was a very affecting question that Isaac asked him, as they were going together: "My father," said Isaac; it was a melting word, which, one would think, should strike deeper in the heart of Abraham, than his knife could in the heart of Isaac. Yet he waits for his son's question. Then Abraham, where he meant not, prophesies: "My son, God will provide a lamb for a burnt-offering." The Holy Spirit, by his mouth, seems to predict the Lamb of God, which he has provided, and which taketh away the sin of the world. Abraham lays the wood in order for his Isaac's funeral pile, and now tells him the amazing news: Isaac, thou art the lamb which God has provided! Abraham, no doubt, comforting him with the same hopes with which he himself by faith was comforted. Yet it is necessary that the sacrifice be bound. The great Sacrifice, which, in the fulness of time, was to be offered up, must be bound, and so must Isaac. This being done, Abraham takes the knife, and stretches out his hand to give the fatal blow. Here is an act of faith and obedience, which deserves to be a spectacle to God, angels, and men. God, by his providence, calls us to part with an Isaac sometimes, and we must do it with cheerful submission to his holy will, 1Sa 3:18.

Verses 11-14

It was not God's intention that Isaac should actually be sacrificed, yet nobler blood than that of animals, in due time, was to be shed for sin, even the blood of the only begotten Son of God. But in the mean while God would not in any case have human sacrifices used. Another sacrifice is provided. Reference must be had to the promised Messiah, the blessed Seed. Christ was sacrificed in our stead, as this ram instead of Isaac, and his death was our discharge. And observe, that the temple, the place of sacrifice, was afterwards built upon this same mount Moriah; and Calvary, where Christ was crucified, was near. A new name was given to that place, for the encouragement of all believers, to the end of the world, cheerfully to trust in God, and obey him. Jehovah-jireh, the Lord will provide; probably alluding to what Abraham had said, God will provide himself a lamb. The Lord will always have his eye upon his people, in their straits and distresses, that he may give them seasonable help.

Verses 15-19

There are high declarations of God's favour to Abraham in this confirmation of the covenant with him, exceeding any he had yet been blessed with. Those that are willing to part with any thing for God, shall have it made up to them with unspeakable advantage. The promise, ver. #(18), doubtless points at the Messiah, and the grace of the gospel. Hereby we know the loving-kindness of God our Saviour towards sinful man, in that he hath not withheld his Son, his only Son, from us. Hereby we perceive the love of Christ, in that he gave himself a sacrifice for our sins. Yet he lives, and calls to sinners to come to him, and partake of his blood-bought salvation. He calls to his redeemed people to rejoice in him, and to glorify him. What then shall we render for all his benefits? Let his love constrain us to live not to ourselves, but to Him who died for us, and rose again. Admiring and adoring His grace, let us devote our all to his service, who laid down his life for our salvation. Whatever is dearest to us upon earth is our Isaac. And the only way for us to find comfort in an earthly thing, is to give it by faith into the hands of God. Yet remember that Abraham was not justified by his readiness to obey, but by the infinitely more noble obedience of Jesus Christ; his faith receiving this, relying on this, rejoicing in this, disposed and made him able for such wonderful self-denial and duty. (Ge 22:20-24)

Verses 20-24

This chapter ends with some account of Nahor's family, who had settled at Haran. This seems to be given for the connexion which it had with the church of God. From thence Isaac and Jacob took wives; and before the account of those events this list is recorded. It shows that though Abraham saw his own family highly honoured with privileges, admitted into covenant, and blessed with the assurance of the promise, yet he did not look with disdain upon his relations, but was glad to hear of the increase and welfare of their families.

Chapter 23

Chapter Outline

Verses 1-13

The longest life must shortly come to a close. Blessed be God that there is a world where sin, death, vanity, and vexation cannot enter. Blessed be his name, that even death cannot part believers from union with Christ. Those whom we most love, yea, even our own bodies, which we so care for, must soon become loathsome lumps of clays, and be buried out of sight. How loose then should we be to all earthly attachments and adornments! Let us seek rather that our souls be adorned with heavenly graces. Abraham rendered honour and respect to the princes of Heth, although of the ungodly Canaanites. The religion of the Bible enjoins to pay due respect to all in authority, without flattering their persons, or countenancing their crimes if they are unworthy characters. And the noble generosity of these Canaanites shames and condemns the closeness, selfishness, and ill-humour of many that call themselves Israelites. It was not in pride that Abraham refused the gift, because he scorned to be beholden to Ephron; but in justice and in prudence. Abraham was able to pay for the field, and therefore would not take advantage of Ephron's generosity. Honesty, as well as honour, forbids us to take advantage of our neighbour's liberality, and to impose, upon those who give freely.

Verses 14-20

Prudence, as well as justice, directs us to be fair and open in our dealings; cheating bargains will not bear the light. Abraham, without fraud or delay, pays the money. He pays it at once in full, without keeping any part back; and by weight, current money with the merchant, without deceit. See how anciently money was used for the help of trade, and how honestly it should be paid when it is due. Though all the land of Canaan was Abraham by promise, yet the time of his possessing it not being come, what he had occasion for he bought and paid for. Dominion is not founded in grace. The saints' title to an eternal inheritance does not entitle them to the possessions of this world, nor justify them in doing wrong. Ephron honestly and fairly makes a good title to the land. As that which is bought, must be honestly paid for, so that which is sold, must be honestly delivered and secured. Let us manage our concerns with punctuality and exactness, in order to avoid contention. Abraham buried Sarah in cave. or vault, which was in the purchased field. It would tend to endear the land to his posterity. And it is worth noting, that a burying-place was the only piece of the land which Abraham possessed in Canaan. Those who have least of this earth, find a grave in it. This sepulchre was at the end of the field; whatever our possessions are, there is a burial-place at the end of them. It was a token of his belief and expectation of the resurrection. Abraham is contented to be still a pilgrim while he lives, but secures a place where, when he dies, his flesh may rest in hope. After all, the chief concern is, with whom we shall rise.

Chapter 24

Chapter Outline

Verses 1-9

The effect of good example, good teaching, and the worship of God in a family, will generally appear in the piety, faithfulness, prudence, and affection of the servants. To live in such families, or to have such servants, both are blessings from God which should be highly valued, and thankfully acknowledged. But no concern in life is of greater importance to ourselves, to others, or to the church of God, than marriage. It therefore ought always to be undertaken with much care and prudence, especially with reference to the will of God, and with prayer for his direction and blessing. Where good parents are not consulted and regarded, the blessing of God cannot be expected. Parents, in disposing of their children, should carefully consult the welfare of their souls, and their furtherance in the way to heaven. Observe the charge Abraham gave to a good servant, one whose conduct, faithfulness, and affection, to him and his family, he had long known. Observe also, that Abraham remembers that God had wonderfully brought him out of the land of his birth, by the call of his grace; and therefore doubts not but He will prosper his care, not to bring his son thither again. God will cause that to end in our comfort, in which we sincerely aim at his glory.

Verses 10-28

Abraham's servant devoutly acknowledged God. We have leave to be particular in recommending our affairs to the care of Divine providence. He proposes a sign, not that he intended to proceed no further, if not gratified in it; but it is a prayer that God would provide a good wife for his young master; and that was a good prayer. She should be simple, industrious, humble, cheerful, serviceable, and hospitable. Whatever may be the fashion, common sense, as well as piety, tells us, these are the proper qualifications for a wife and mother; for one who is to be a companion to her husband, the manager of domestic concerns, and trusted to form the minds of children. When the steward came to seek a wife for his master, he did not go to places of amusement and sinful pleasure, and pray that he might meet one there, but to the well of water, expecting to find one there employed aright. He prayed that God would please to make his way in this matter plain and clear before him. Our times are in God's hand; not only events themselves, but the times of them. We must take heed of being over-bold in urging what God should do, lest the event should weaken our faith, rather than strengthen it. But God owned him by making his way clear. Rebekah, in all respects, answered the characters he sought for in the woman that was to be his master's wife. When she came to the well, she went down and filled her pitcher, and came up to go home with it. She did not stand to gaze upon the strange man his camels, but minded her business, and would not have been diverted from it but by an opportunity of doing good. She did not curiously or confidently enter into discourse with him, but answered him modestly. Being satisfied that the Lord had heard his prayer, he gave the damsel some ornaments worn in eastern countries; asking at the same time respecting her kindred. On learning that she was of his master's relations, he bowed down his head and worshipped, blessing God. His words were addressed to the Lord, but being spoken in the hearing of Rebekah, she could perceive who he was, and whence he came.

Verses 29-53

The making up of the marriage between Isaac and Rebekah is told very particularly. We are to notice God's providence in the common events of human life, and in them to exercise prudence and other graces. Laban went to ask Abraham's servant in, but not till he saw the ear-ring, and bracelet upon his sister's hands. We know Laban's character, by his conduct afterwards, and may think that he would not have been so free to entertain him, if he had not hoped to be well rewarded for it. The servant was intent upon his business. Though he was come off a journey, and come to a good house, he would not eat till he had told his errand. The doing our work, and the fulfilling our trusts, either for God or man, should be preferred by us before our food: it was our Saviour's meat and drink, Joh 4:34. He tells them the charge his master had given him, with the reason of it. He relates what had happened at the well, to further the proposal, plainly showing the finger of God in it. Those events which to us seem the effect of choice, contrivance, or chance, are "appointed out" of God. This hinders not, but rather encourages the use of all proper means. They freely and cheerfully close with the proposal; and any matter is likely to be comfortable, when it proceeds from the Lord. Abraham's servant thankfully acknowledges the good success he had met with. He was a humble man, and humble men are not ashamed to own their situation in life, whatever it may be. All our temporal concerns are sweet if intermixed with godliness.

Verses 54-67

Abraham's servant, as one that chose his work before his pleasure, was for hastening home. Lingering and loitering no way become a wise and good man who is faithful to his duty. As children ought not to marry without their parents' consent, so parents ought not to marry them without their own. Rebekah consented, not only to go, but to go at once. The goodness of Rebekah's character shows there was nothing wrong in her answer, though it be not agreeable to modern customs among us. We may hope that she had such an idea of the religion and godliness in the family she was to go to, as made her willing to forget her own people and her father's house. Her friends dismiss her with suitable attendants, and with hearty good wishes. They blessed Rebekah. When our relations are entering into a new condition, we ought by prayer to commend them to the blessing and grace of God. Isaac was well employed when he met Rebekah. He went out to take the advantage of a silent evening, and a solitary place, for meditation and prayer; those divine exercises by which we converse with God and our own hearts. Holy souls love retirement; it will do us good to be often alone, if rightly employed; and we are never less alone than when alone. Observe what an affectionate son Isaac was: it was about three years since his mother died, and yet he was not, till now, comforted. See also what an affectionate husband he was to his wife. Dutiful sons promise fair to be affectionate husbands; he that fills up his first station in life with honour, is likely to do the same in those that follow.

Chapter 25

Chapter Outline

Verses 1-10

All the days, even of the best and greatest saints, are not remarkable days; some slide on silently; such were these last days of Abraham. Here is an account of Abraham's children by Keturah, and the disposition which he made of his estate. After the birth of these sons, he set his house in order, with prudence and justice. He did this while he yet lived. It is wisdom for men to do what they find to do while they live, as far as they can. Abraham lived 175 years; just one hundred years after he came to Canaan; so long he was a sojourner in a strange country. Whether our stay in this life be long or short, it matters but little, provided we leave behind us a testimony to the faithfulness and goodness of the Lord, and a good example to our families. We are told that his sons Isaac and Ishmael buried him. It seems that Abraham had himself brought them together while he lived. Let us not close the history of the life of Abraham without blessing God for such a testimony of the triumph of faith.

Verses 11-18

Ishmael had twelve sons, whose families became distinct tribes. They peopled a very large country that lay between Egypt and Assyria, called Arabia. The number and strength of this family were the fruit of the promise, made to Hagar and to Abraham, concerning Ishmael.

Verses 19-26

Isaac seems not to have been much tried, but to have spent his days in quietness. Jacob and Esau were prayed for; their parents, after being long childless, obtained them by prayer. The fulfilment of God's promise is always sure, yet it is often slow. The faith of believers is tried, their patience exercised, and mercies long waited for are more welcome when they come. Isaac and Rebekah kept in view the promise of all nations being blessed in their posterity, therefore were not only desirous of children, but anxious concerning every thing which seemed to mark their future character. In all our doubts we should inquire of the Lord by prayer. In many of our conflicts with sin and temptation, we may adopt Rebekah's words, "If it be so, why am I thus?" If a child of God, why so careless or carnal? If not a child of God, why so afraid of, or so burdened with sin?

Verses 27, 28

Esau hunted the beasts of the field with dexterity and success, till he became a conqueror, ruling over his neighbours. Jacob was a plain man, one that liked the true delights of retirement, better than all pretended pleasures. He was a stranger and a pilgrim in his spirit, and a shepherd all his days. Isaac and Rebekah had but these two children, one was the father's darling, and the other the mother's. And though godly parents must feel their affections most drawn over towards a godly child, yet they will not show partiality. Let their affections lead them to do what is just and equal to every child, or evils will arise.

Verses 29-34

We have here the bargain made between Jacob and Esau about the right, which was Esau's by birth, but Jacob's by promise. It was for a spiritual privilege; and we see Jacob's desire of the birth-right, but he sought to obtain it by crooked courses, not like his character as a plain man. He was right, that he coveted earnestly the best gifts; he was wrong, that he took advantage of his brother's need. The inheritance of their father's worldly goods did not descend to Jacob, and was not meant in this proposal. But it includeth the future possession of the land of Canaan by his children's children, and the covenant made with Abraham as to Christ the promised Seed. Believing Jacob valued these above all things; unbelieving Esau despised them. Yet although we must be of Jacob's judgment in seeking the birth-right, we ought carefully to avoid all guile, in seeking to obtain even the greatest advantages. Jacob's pottage pleased Esau's eye. "Give me some of that red;" for this he was called Edom, or Red. Gratifying the sensual appetite ruins thousands of precious souls. When men's hearts walk after their own eyes, Job 31:7, and when they serve their own bellies, they are sure to be punished. If we use ourselves to deny ourselves, we break the force of most temptations. It cannot be supposed that Esau was dying of hunger in Isaac's house. The words signify, I am going towards death; he seems to mean, I shall never live to inherit Canaan, or any of those future supposed blessings; and what signifies it who has them when I am dead and gone. This would be the language of profaneness, with which the apostle brands him, Heb 12:16; and this contempt of the birth-right is blamed, ver. #(34). It is the greatest folly to part with our interest in God, and Christ, and heaven, for the riches, honours, and pleasures of this world; it is as bad a bargain as his who sold a birth-right for a dish of pottage. Esau ate and drank, pleased his palate, satisfied his appetite, and then carelessly rose up and went his way, without any serious thought, or any regret, about the bad bargain he had made. Thus Esau despised his birth-right. By his neglect and contempt afterwards, and by justifying himself in what he had done, he put the bargain past recall. People are ruined, not so much by doing what is amiss, as by doing it and not repenting of it.

Chapter 26

Chapter Outline

Isaac, because of famine, goes to Gerar.	(1–5)
He denies his wife and is reproved by Abimelech.	(6–11)
Isaac grows rich, The Philistines' envy.	(12–17)
Isaac digs wells God blesses him.	(18–25)
Abimelech makes a covenant with Isaac.	(26–33)
Esau's wives.	(34, 35)

Verses 1-5

Isaac had been trained up in a believing dependence upon the Divine grant of the land of Canaan to him and his heirs; and now that there is a famine in the land, Isaac still cleaves to the covenant. The real worth of God's promises cannot be lessened to a believer by any cross providences that may befall him. If God engage to be with us, and we are where he would have us to be, nothing but our own unbelief and distrust can prevent our comfort. The obedience of Abraham to the Divine command, was evidence of that faith, whereby, as a sinner, he was justified before God, and the effect of that love whereby true faith works. God testifies that he approved this obedience, to encourage others, especially Isaac.

Verses 6-11

There is nothing in Isaac's denial of his wife to be imitated, nor even excused. The temptation of Isaac is the same as that which overcame his father, and that in two instances. This rendered his conduct the greater sin. The falls of those who are gone before us are so many rocks on which others have split; and the recording of them is like placing buoys to save future mariners. This Abimelech was not the same that lived in Abraham's days, but both acted rightly. The sins of professors shame them before those that are not themselves religious.

Verses 12-17

God blessed Isaac. Be it observed, for the encouragement of poor tenants who occupy other people's lands, and are honest and industrious, that God blessed him with a great increase. The Philistines envied Isaac. It is an instance of the vanity of the world; for the more men have of it, the more they are envied, and exposed to censure and injury. Also of the corruption of nature; for that is an ill principle indeed, which makes men grieve at the good of others. They made Isaac go out of their country. That wisdom which is from above, will teach us to give up our right, and to draw back from contentions. If we are wrongfully driven from one place, the Lord will make room for us in another.

Verses 18-25

Isaac met with much opposition in digging wells. Two were called Contention and Hatred. See the nature of worldly things; they make quarrels, and are occasions of strife; and what is often the lot of the most quiet and peaceable; those who avoid striving, yet cannot avoid being striven with. And what a mercy it is to have plenty of water; to have it without striving for it! The more common this mercy is, the more reason to be thankful for it. At length Isaac digged a well, for which they strove not. Those that study to be quiet, seldom fail of being so. When men are false and unkind, still God is faithful and gracious; and his time to show himself so is, when we are most disappointed by men. The same night that Isaac came weary and uneasy to Beer-sheba, God brought comforts to his soul. Those may remove with comfort who are sure of God's presence.

Verses 26-33

When a man's ways please the Lord, he maketh even his enemies to be at peace with him, Pr 16:7. Kings' hearts are in his hands, and when he pleases, he can turn them to favour his people. It is not wrong to stand upon our guard in dealing with those who have acted unfairly. But Isaac did not insist on the unkindnesses they had done him; he freely entered into friendship with them. Religion teaches us to be neighbourly, and, as much as in us lies, to live peaceable with all men. Providence smiled upon what Isaac did; God blessed his labours.

Verses 34, 35

Esau was foolish in marrying two wives together, and still more in marrying Canaanites, strangers to the blessing of Abraham, and subject to the curse of Noah. It grieved his parents that he married without their advice and consent. It grieved them that he married among those who had no religion. Children have little reason to expect God's blessing who do that which is a grief of mind to good parents.

Chapter 27

Chapter Outline

Verses 1-5

The promises of the Messiah, and of the land of Canaan, had come down to Isaac. Isaac being now about 135 years of age, and his sons about 75, and not duly considering the Divine word concerning his two sons, that the elder should serve the younger, resolved to put all the honour and power that were in the promise, upon Esau his eldest son. We are very apt to take measures rather from our own reason than from Divine revelation, and thereby often miss our way.

Verses 6-17

Rebekah knew that the blessing was intended for Jacob, and expected he would have it. But she wronged Isaac by putting a cheat on him; she wronged Jacob by tempting him to wickedness. She put a stumbling-block in Esau's way, and gave him a pretext for hatred to Jacob and to religion. All were to be blamed. It was one of those crooked measures often adopted to further the Divine promises; as if the end would justify, or excuse wrong means. Thus many have acted wrong, under the idea of being useful in promoting the cause of Christ. The answer to all such things is that which God addressed to Abraham, I am God Almighty; walk before me and be thou perfect. And it was a very rash speech of Rebekah, "Upon me be thy curse, my son." Christ has borne the curse of the law for all who take upon them the yoke of the command, the command of the gospel. But it is too daring for any creature to say, Upon me be thy curse.

Verses 18-29

Jacob, with some difficulty, gained his point, and got the blessing. This blessing is in very general terms. No mention is made of the distinguishing mercies in the covenant with Abraham. This might be owing to Isaac having Esau in his mind, though it was Jacob who was before him. He could not be ignorant how Esau had despised the best things. Moreover, his attachment to Esau, so as to disregard the mind of God, must have greatly weakened his own faith in these things. It might therefore be expected, that leanness would attend his blessing, agreeing with the state of his mind.

Verses 30-40

When Esau understood that Jacob had got the blessing, he cried with a great and exceeding bitter cry. The day is coming, when those that now make light of the blessings of the covenant, and sell their title to spiritual blessings for that which is of no value, will, in vain, ask urgently for them. Isaac, when made sensible of the deceit practised on him, trembled exceedingly. Those who follow the choice of their own affections, rather than the Divine will, get themselves into perplexity. But he soon recovers, and confirms the blessing he had given to Jacob, saying, I have blessed him, and he shall be blessed. Those who part with their wisdom and grace, their faith and a good conscience, for the honours, wealth, or pleasures of this world, however they feign a zeal for the blessing, have judged themselves unworthy of it, and their doom shall be accordingly. A common blessing was bestowed upon Esau. This he desired. Faint desires of happiness, without right choice of the end, and right use of the means, deceive many unto their own ruin. Multitudes go to hell with their mouths full of good wishes. The great difference is, that there is nothing in Esau's blessing which points at Christ; and without that, the fatness of the earth, and the plunder of the field, will stand in little stead. Thus Isaac, by faith, blessed both his sons, according as their lot should be.

Verses 41-46

Esau bore malice to Jacob on account of the blessing he had obtained. Thus he went in the way of Cain, who slew his brother, because he gained that acceptance with God of which he had rendered himself unworthy. Esau aimed to prevent Jacob or his seed from having the dominion, by taking away his life. Men may fret at God's counsels, but cannot change them. To prevent mischief, Rebekah warned Jacob of his danger, and advised him to withdraw for his safety. We must not presume too far upon the wisdom and resolution, even of the most hopeful and promising children; but care must be taken to keep them out of the way of evil. When reading this chapter, we should not fail to observe, that we must not follow even the best of men further than they act according to the law of God. We must not do evil that good may come. And though God overruled the bad actions recorded in this chapter, to fulfil his purposes, yet we see his judgment of them, in the painful consequences to all the parties concerned. It was the peculiar privilege and advantage of Jacob to convey these spiritual blessings to all nations. The Christ, the Saviour of the world, was to be born of some one family; and Jacob's was preferred to Esau's, out of the good pleasure of Almighty God, who is certainly the best judge of what is fit, and has an undoubted right to dispense his favours as he sees proper, Ro 9:12–15.

Chapter 28

Chapter Outline

Verses 1-5

Jacob had blessings promised both as to this world and that which is to come; yet goes out to a hard service. This corrected him for the fraud on his father. The blessing shall be conferred on him, yet he shall smart for the indirect course taken to obtain it. Jacob is dismissed by his father with a solemn charge. He must not take a wife of the daughters of Canaan: those who profess religion, should not marry with those that care not for religion. Also with a solemn blessing. Isaac had before blessed him unwittingly; now he does it designedly. This blessing is more full than the former; it is a gospel blessing. This promise looks as high as heaven, of which Canaan was a type. That was the better country which Jacob and the other patriarchs had in view.

Verses 6-9

Good examples impress even the profane and malicious. But Esau thought, by pleasing his parents in one thing, to atone for other wrong doings. Carnal hearts are apt to think themselves as good as they should be, because in some one matter they are not so bad as they have been.

Verses 10-15

Jacob's conduct hitherto, as recorded, was not that of one who simply feared and trusted in God. But now in trouble, obliged to flee, he looked only to God to make him to dwell in safety, and he could lie down and sleep in the open air with his head upon a stone. Any true believer would be willing to take up with Jacob's pillow, provided he might have Jacob's vision. God's time to visit his people with his comforts, is, when they are most destitute of other comforts, and other comforters. Jacob saw a ladder which reached from earth to heaven, the angels going up and coming down, and God himself at the head of it. This represents, 1. The providence of God, by which there is a constant intercourse kept up between heaven and earth. This let Jacob know that he had both a good guide and a good guard. 2. The mediation of Christ. He is this ladder; the foot on earth in his human nature, the top in heaven in his Divine nature. Christ is the Way; all God's favours come to us, and all our services go to him, by Christ, Joh 1:51. By this way, sinners draw near to the throne of grace with acceptance. By faith we perceive this way, and in prayer we approach by it. In answer to prayer we receive all needful blessings of providence and grace. We have no way of getting to heaven but by Christ. And when the soul, by faith, can see these things, then every place will become pleasant, and every prospect joyful. He will never leave us, until his last promise is accomplished in our everlasting happiness. God now spake comfortably to Jacob. He spake from the head of the ladder. All the glad tidings we receive from heaven come through Jesus Christ. The Messiah should come from Jacob. Christ is the great blessing of the world. All that are blessed, are blessed in him, and none of any family are shut out from blessedness in him, but those that shut out themselves. Jacob had to fear danger from his brother Esau; but God promises to keep him. He had a long journey before him; to an unknown country; but, Behold, I am with thee, and God promises to bring him back again to this land. He seemed to be forsaken of all his friends; but God gives him this assurance, I will not leave thee. Whom God loves, he never leaves.

Verses 16-19

God manifested himself and his favour, to Jacob, when he was asleep. The Spirit, like the wind, blows when and where it listeth, and God's grace, like the dew, tarrieth not for the sons of men. Jacob sought to improve the visit God had made him. Wherever we are, in the city or in the desert, in the house or in the field, in the shop or in the street, we may keep up our intercourse with Heaven, if it is not our own fault. But the more we see of God, the more cause we see for holy trembling before him.

Verses 20-22

Jacob made a solemn vow on this occasion. In this observe, 1. Jacob's faith. He trusts that God will be with him, and will keep him; he depends upon it. 2. Jacob's moderation in his desires. He asks not for soft clothing and dainty meat. If God give us much, we are bound to be thankful, and to use it for him; if he gives us but little, we are bound to be content, and cheerfully to enjoy him in it. 3. Jacob's piety, and his regard to God, appear in what he desired, that God would be with him, and keep him. We need desire no more to make us easy and happy. Also his resolution is, to cleave to the Lord, as his God in covenant. When we receive more than common mercy from God, we should abound in gratitude to him. The tenth is a fit proportion to be devoted to God, and employed for him; though it may be more or less, as God prospers us, 1Co 16:2. Let us then remember our Bethels, how we stand engaged by solemn vows to yield ourselves to the Lord, to take him for our God, and to devote all we have and are to his glory!

Chapter 29

Chapter Outline

Verses 1-8

Jacob proceeded cheerfully in his journey, after the sweet communion he had with God at Beth-el. Providence brought him to the field where his uncle's flocks were to be watered. What is said of the care of the shepherds for their sheep, may remind us of the tender concern which our Lord Jesus, the great Shepherd of the sheep, has for his flock the church; for he is the good Shepherd, that knows his sheep, and is known of them. The stone at the well's mouth was to secure it; water was scarce, it was not there for every one's use: but separate interests should not take us from helping one another. When all the shepherds came together with their flocks, then, like loving neighbours, they watered their flocks together. The law of kindness in the tongue has a commanding power, Pr 31:26. Jacob was civil to these strangers, and he found them civil to him.

Verses 9-14

See Rachel's humility and industry. Nobody needs to be ashamed of honest, useful labour, nor ought it to hinder any one's preferment. When Jacob understood that this was his kinswoman, he was very ready to serve her. Laban, though not the best humoured, bade him welcome, and was satisfied with the account Jacob gave of himself. While we avoid being foolishly ready to believe every thing which is told us, we must take heed of being uncharitably suspicious.

Verses 15-30

During the month that Jacob spent as a guest, he was not idle. Wherever we are, it is good to employ ourselves in some useful business. Laban was desirous that Jacob should continue with him. Inferior relations must not be imposed upon; it is our duty to reward them. Jacob made known to Laban the affection he had for his daughter Rachel. And having no wordly goods with which to endow her, he promises seven years' service Love makes long and hard services short and easy; hence we read of the labour of love, Heb 6:10. If we know how to value the happiness of heaven, the sufferings of this present time will be as nothing to us. An age of work will be but as a few days to those that love God, and long for Christ's appearing. Jacob, who had imposed upon his father, is imposed upon by Laban, his father-in-law, by a like deception. Herein, how unrighteous soever Laban was, the Lord was righteous: see Jud 1:7. Even the righteous, if they take a false step, are sometimes thus recompensed in the earth. And many who are not, like Jacob, in their marriage, disappointed in person, soon find themselves, as much to their grief, disappointed in the character. The choice of that relation ought to be made with good advice and thought on both sides. There is reason to believe that Laban's excuse was not true. His way of settling the matter made bad worse. Jacob was drawn into the disquiet of multiplying wives. He could not refuse Rachel, for he had espoused her; still less could he refuse Leah. As yet there was no express command against marrying more than one wife. It was in the patriarchs a sin of ignorance; but it will not justify the like practice now, when God's will is plainly made known by the Divine law, Le 18:18, and more fully since, by our Saviour, that one man and woman only must be joined together, 1Co 7:2.

Verses 31-35

The names Leah gave her children, expressed her respect and regard, both to God and to her husband. Reuben, or See a son, with this thought, Now will my husband love me; Levi, or joined, expecting, Now will my husband be joined unto me. Mutual affection is both the duty and comfort of the married relation; and yoke-fellows should study to recommend themselves to each other, 1Co 7:33, 34. She thankfully acknowledges the kind providence of God in hearing her. Whatever supports and comforts us under afflictions, or tends to our deliverance from them, God must be owned in it. Her fourth son she called Judah, or praise, saying, Now will I praise the Lord. This was he, of whom, as concerning the flesh, Christ came. Whatever is the matter of our rejoicing, ought to be the matter of our thanksgiving. Fresh favours should quicken us to praise God for former favours; Now will I praise the Lord more and better than I have done. All our praises must centre in Christ, both as the matter of them, and as the Mediator of them. He descended after the flesh from him whose name was "Praise," and He is our praise. Is Christ formed in my heart? Now will I praise the Lord.

Chapter 30

Chapter Outline

Verses 1-13

Rachel envied her sister: envy is grieving at the good of another, than which no sin is more hateful to God, or more hurtful to our neighbours and ourselves. She considered not that God made the difference, and that in other things she had the advantage. Let us carefully watch against all the risings and workings of this passion in our minds. Let not our eye be evil towards any of our fellow-servants, because our Master's is good. Jacob loved Rachel, and therefore reproved her for what she said amiss. Faithful reproofs show true affection. God may be to us instead of any creature; but it is sin and folly to place any creature in God's stead, and to place that confidence in any creature, which should be placed in God only. At the persuasion of Rachel, Jacob took Bilhah her handmaid to wife, that, according to the usage of those times, her children might be owned as her mistress's children. Had not Rachel's heart been influenced by evil passions, she would have thought her sister's children nearer to her, and more entitled to her care than Bilhah's. But children whom she had a right to rule, were more desirable to her than children she had more reason to love. As an early instance of her power over these children, she takes pleasure in giving them names that carry in them marks of rivalry with her sister. See what roots of bitterness envy and strife are, and what mischief they make among relations. At the persuasion of Leah, Jacob took Zilpah her handmaid to wife also. See the power of jealousy and rivalship, and admire the wisdom of the Divine appointment, which joins together one man and one woman only; for God hath called us to peace and purity.

Verses 14-24

The desire, good in itself, but often too great and irregular, of being the mother of the promised Seed, with the honour of having many children, and the reproach of being barren, were causes of this unbecoming contest between the sisters. The truth appears to be, that they were influenced by the promises of God to Abraham; whose posterity were promised the richest blessings, and from whom the Messiah was to descend.

Verses 25-43

The fourteen years being gone, Jacob was willing to depart without any provision, except God's promise. But he had in many ways a just claim on Laban's substance, and it was the will of God that he should be provided for from it. He referred his cause to God, rather than agree for stated wages with Laban, whose selfishness was very great. And it would appear that he acted honestly, when none but those of the colours fixed upon should be found among his cattle. Laban selfishly thought that his cattle would produce few different in colour from their own. Jacob's course after this agreement has been considered an instance of his policy and management. But it was done by intimation from God, and as a token of his power. The Lord will one way or another plead the cause of the oppressed, and honour those who simply trust his providence. Neither could Laban complain of Jacob, for he had nothing more than was freely agreed that he should have; nor was he injured, but greatly benefitted by Jacob's services. May all our mercies be received with thanksgiving and prayer, that coming from his bounty, they may lead to his praise.

Chapter 31

Chapter Outline

Verses 1-21

The affairs of these families are related very minutely, while (what are called) the great events of states and kingdoms at that period, are not mentioned. The Bible teaches people the common duties of life, how to serve God, how to enjoy the blessings he bestows, and to do good in the various stations and duties of life. Selfish men consider themselves robbed of all that goes past them, and covetousness will even swallow up natural affection. Men's overvaluing worldly wealth is that error which is the root of covetousness, envy, and all evil. The men of the world stand in each other's way, and every one seems to be taking away from the rest; hence discontent, envy, and discord. But there are possessions that will suffice for all; happy they who seek them in the first place. In all our removals we should have respect to the command and promise of God. If He be with us, we need not fear. The perils which surround us are so many, that nothing else can really encourage our hearts. To remember favoured seasons of communion with God, is very refreshing when in difficulties; and we should often recollect our vows, that we fail not to fulfil them.

Verses 22-35

God can put a bridle in the mouth of wicked men, to restrain their malice, though he do not change their hearts. Though they have no love to God's people, they will pretend to it, and try to make a merit of necessity. Foolish Laban! to call those things his gods which could be stolen! Enemies may steal our goods, but not our God. Here Laban lays to Jacob's charge things that he knew not. Those who commit their cause to God, are not forbidden to plead it themselves with meekness and fear. When we read of Rachel's stealing her father's images, what a scene of iniquity opens! The family of Nahor, who left the idolatrous Chaldees; is this family itself become idolatrous? It is even so. The truth seems to be, that they were like some in after-times, who sware by the Lord and by Malcham, Zep 1:5; and like others in our times, who wish to serve both God and mammon. Great numbers will acknowledge the true God in words, but their hearts and houses are the abodes of spiritual idolatry. When a man gives himself up to covetousness, like Laban, the world is his god; and he has only to reside among gross idolaters in order to become one, or at least a favourer of their abominations.

Verses 36-42

If Jacob were willingly consumed with heat in the day, and frost by night, to become the son-in-law of Laban, what should we refuse to endure, to become the sons of God? Jacob speaks of God as the God of his father; he thought himself unworthy to be regarded, but was beloved for his father's sake. He calls him the God of Abraham, and the fear of Isaac; for Abraham was dead, and gone to that world where perfect love casts out fear; but Isaac was yet alive, sanctifying the Lord in his heart, as his fear and his dread.

Verses 43-55

Laban could neither justify himself nor condemn Jacob, therefore desires to hear no more of that matter. He is not willing to own himself in fault, as he ought to have done. But he proposes a covenant of friendship between them, to which Jacob readily agrees. A heap of stones was raised, to keep up the memory of the event, writing being then not known or little used. A sacrifice of peace offerings was offered. Peace with God puts true comfort into our peace with our friends. They did eat bread together, partaking of the feast upon the sacrifice. In ancient times covenants of friendship were ratified by the parties eating and drinking together. God is judge between contending parties, and he will judge righteously; whoever do wrong, it is at their peril. They gave a new name to the place, The heap of witness. After this angry parley, they part friends. God is often better to us than our fears, and overrules the spirits of men in our favour, beyond what we could have expected; for it is not in vain to trust in him.

Chapter 32

Chapter Outline

Verses 1-8

The angels of God appeared to Jacob, to encourage him with the assurance of the Divine protection. When God designs his people for great trials, he prepares them by great comforts. While Jacob, to whom the promise belonged, had been in hard service, Esau was become a prince. Jacob sent a message, showing that he did not insist upon the birth-right. Yielding pacifies great offences, Ec 10:4. We must not refuse to speak respectfully, even to those unjustly angry with us. Jacob received an account of Esau's warlike preparations against him, and was greatly afraid. A lively sense of danger, and quickening fear arising from it, may be found united with humble confidence in God's power and promise.

Verses 9-23

Times of fear should be times of prayer: whatever causes fear, should drive us to our knees, to our God. Jacob had lately seen his guards of angels, but in this distress he applied to God, not to them; he knew they were his fellow-servants, Re 22:9. There cannot be a better pattern for true prayer than this. Here is a thankful acknowledgement of former undeserved favours; a humble confession of unworthiness; a plain statement of his fears and distress; a full reference of the whole affair to the Lord, and resting all his hopes on him. The best we can say to God in prayer, is what he has said to us. Thus he made the name of the Lord his strong tower, and could not but be safe. Jacob's fear did not make him sink into despair, nor did his prayer make him presume upon God's mercy, without the use of means. God answers prayers by teaching us to order our affairs aright. To pacify Esau, Jacob sent him a present. We must not despair of reconciling ourselves to those most angry against us.

Verses 24-32

A great while before day, Jacob being alone, more fully spread his fears before God in prayer. While thus employed, One in the likeness of a man wrestled with him. When the spirit helpeth our infirmities, and our earnest and vast desires can scarcely find words to utter them, and we still mean more than we can express, then prayer is indeed wrestling with God. However tried or discouraged, we shall prevail; and prevailing with Him in prayer, we shall prevail against all enemies that strive with us. Nothing requires more vigour and unceasing exertion than wrestling. It is an emblem of the true spirit of faith and prayer. Jacob kept his ground; though the struggle continued long, this did not shake his faith, nor silence his prayer. He will have a blessing, and had rather have all his bone put out of joint than go away without one. Those who would have the blessing of Christ, must resolve to take no denial. The fervent prayer is the effectual prayer. The Angel puts a lasting mark of honour upon him, by changing his name. Jacob signifies a supplanter. From henceforth he shall be celebrated, not for craft and artful management, but for true valour. Thou shalt be called Israel, a prince with God, a name greater than those of the great men of the earth. He is a prince indeed that is a prince with God; those are truly honourable that are mighty in prayer. Having power with God, he shall have power with men too; he shall prevail, and gain Esau's favour. Jacob gives a new name to the place. He calls it Peniel, the face of God, because there he had seen the appearance of God, and obtained the favour of God. It becomes those whom God honours, to admire his grace towards them. The Angel who wrestled with Jacob was the second Person in the sacred Trinity, who was afterwards God manifest in the flesh, and who, dwelling in human nature, is called Immanuel, Ho 12:4, 5. Jacob halted on his thigh. It might serve to keep him from being lifted up with the abundance of the revelations. The sun rose on Jacob: it is sun-rise with that soul, which has had communion with God.

Chapter 33

Chapter Outline

Verses 1-16

Jacob, having by prayer committed his case to God, went on his way. Come what will, nothing can come amiss to him whose heart is fixed, trusting in God. Jacob bowed to Esau. A humble, submissive behaviour goes far towards turning away wrath. Esau embraced Jacob. God has the hearts of all men in his hands, and can turn them when and how he pleases. It is not in vain to trust in God, and to call upon him in the day of trouble. And when a man's ways please the Lord he maketh even his enemies to be at peace with him. Esau receives Jacob as a brother, and much tenderness passes between them. Esau asks, Who are those with thee? To this common question, Jacob spoke like himself, like a man whose eyes are ever directed towards the Lord. Jacob urged Esau, though his fear was over, and he took his present. It is well when men's religion makes them generous, free-hearted, and open-handed. But Jacob declined Esau's offer to accompany him. It is not desirable to be too intimate with superior ungodly relations, who will expect us to join in their vanities, or at least to wink at them, though they blame, and perhaps mock at, our religion. Such will either be a snare to us, or offended with us. We shall venture the loss of all things, rather than endanger our souls, if we know their value; rather than renounce Christ, if we truly love him. And let Jacob's care and tender attention to his family and flocks remind us of the good Shepherd of our souls, who gathers the lambs with his arm, and carries them in his bosom, and gently leads those that are with young, Isa 40:11. As parents, teachers or pastors, we should all follow his example.

Verses 17-20

Jacob did not content himself with words of thanks for God's favour to him, but gave real thanks. Also he kept up religion, and the worship of God in his family. Where we have a tent, God must have an altar. Jacob dedicated this altar to the honour of El-elohe-Israel, God, the God of Israel; to the honour of God, the only living and true God; and to the honour of the God of Israel, as a God in covenant with him. Israel's God is Israel's glory. Blessed be his name, he is still the mighty God, the God of Israel. May we praise his name, and rejoice in his love, through our pilgrimage here on earth, and for ever in the heavenly Canaan.

Chapter 34

Chapter Outline

Verses 1-19

Young persons, especially females, are never so safe and well off as under the care of pious parents. Their own ignorance, and the flattery and artifices of designing, wicked people, who are ever laying snares for them, expose them to great danger. They are their own enemies if they desire to go abroad, especially alone, among strangers to true religion. Those parents are very wrong who do not hinder their children from needlessly exposing themselves to danger. Indulged children, like Dinah, often become a grief and shame to their families. Her pretence was, to see the daughters of the land, to see how they dressed, and how they danced, and what was fashionable among them; she went to see, yet that was not all, she went to be seen too. She went to get acquaintance with the Canaanites, and to learn their ways. See what came of Dinah's gadding. The beginning of sin is as the letting forth of water. How great a matter does a little fire kindle! We should carefully avoid all occasions of sin and approaches to it.

Verses 20-31

The Shechemites submitted to the sacred rite, only to serve a turn, to please their prince, and to enrich themselves, and it was just with God to bring punishment upon them. As nothing secures us better than true religion, so nothing exposes us more than religion only pretended to. But Simeon and Levi were most unrighteous. Those who act wickedly, under the pretext of religion, are the worst enemies of the truth, and harden the hearts of many to destruction. The crimes of others form no excuse for us. Alas! how one sin leads on to another, and, like flames of fire, spread desolation in every direction! Foolish pleasures lead to seduction; seduction produces wrath; wrath thirsts for revenge; the thirst of revenge has recourse to treachery; treachery issues in murder; and murder is followed by other lawless actions. Were we to trace the history of unlawful commerce between the sexes, we should find it, more than any other sin, ending in blood.

Chapter 35

Chapter Outline

Verses 1-5

Beth-el was forgotten. But as many as God loves, he will remind of neglected duties, one way or other, by conscience or by providences. When we have vowed a vow to God, it is best not to defer the payment of it; yet better late than never. Jacob commanded his household to prepare, not only for the journey and removal, but for religious services. Masters of families should use their authority to keep up religion in their families, Jos 24:15. They must put away strange gods. In families where there is a face of religion, and an altar to God, yet many times there is much amiss, and more strange gods than one would suppose. They must be clean, and change their garments. These were but outward ceremonies, signifying the purifying and change of the heart. What are clean clothes, and new clothes, without a clean heart, and a new heart? If Jacob had called for these idols sooner, they had parted with them sooner. Sometimes attempts for reformation succeed better than we could have thought. Jacob buried their images. We must be wholly separated from our sins, as we are from those that are dead and buried out of sight. He removed from Shechem to Beth-el. Though the Canaanites were very angry against the sons of Jacob for their barbarous usage of the Shechemites, yet they were so kept back by Divine power, that they could not take the opportunity now offered to avenge them. The way of duty is the way of safety. When we are about God's work, we are under special protection; God is with us, while we are with him; and if He be for us, who can be against us? God governs the world more by secret terrors on men's minds than we are aware of.

Verses 6-15

The comfort the saints have in holy ordinances, is not so much from Beth-el, the house of God, as from El-beth-el, the God of the house. The ordinances are empty things, if we do not meet with God in them. There Jacob buried Deborah, Rebekah's nurse. She died much lamented. Old servants in a family, that have in their time been faithful and useful, ought to be respected. God appeared to Jacob. He renewed the covenant with him. I am God Almighty, God all-sufficient, able to make good the promise in due time, and to support thee and provide for thee in the mean time. Two things are promised; that he should be the father of a great nation, and that he should be the master of a good land. These two promises had a spiritual signification, which Jacob had some notion of, though not so clear and distinct as we now have. Christ is the promised Seed, and heaven is the promised land; the former is the foundation, and the latter the top-stone, of all God's favours.

Verses 16-20

Rachel had passionately said, Give me children, or else I die; and now that she had children, she died! The death of the body is but the departure of the soul to the world of spirits. When shall we learn that it is God alone who really knows what is best for his people, and that in all worldly affairs the safest path for the Christian is to say from the heart, It is the Lord, let him do what seemeth him good. Here alone is our safety and our comfort, to know no will but his. Her dying lips called her newborn son Ben-oni, the son of my sorrow; and many a son proves to be the heaviness of her that bare him. Children are enough the sorrow of their mothers; they should, therefore, when they grow up, study to be their joy, and so, if possible, to make them some amends. But Jacob, because he would not renew the sorrowful remembrance of the mother's death every time he called his son, changed his name to Benjamin, the son of my right hand: that is, very dear to me; the support of my age, like the staff in my right hand.

Verses 21-29

What a sore affliction Reuben's sin was, is shown, "and Israel heard it." No more is said, but that is enough. Reuben thought that his father would never hear of it; but those that promise themselves secrecy in sin, are generally disappointed. The age and death of Isaac are recorded, though he died not till after Joseph was sold into Egypt. Isaac lived about forty years after he had made his will, chap. 27:2. We shall not die an hour the sooner, but much the better, for timely setting our hearts and houses in order. Particular notice is taken of the agreement of Esau and Jacob at their father's funeral, to show how God had wonderfully changed Esau's mind. It is awful to behold relations, sometimes for a little of this world's goods, disputing over the graves of their friends, while they are near going to the grave themselves.

Chapter 36

Esau and his descendants.
—The registers in this chapter show the faithfulness of God to his promise to Abraham. Esau is here called Edom, that name which kept up the remembrance of his selling his birth-right for a mess of pottage. Esau continued the same profane despiser of heavenly things. In outward prosperity and honour, the children of the covenant are often behind, and those that are out of the covenant get the start. We may suppose it a trial to the faith of God's Israel, to hear of the pomp and power

of the kings of Edom, while they were bond-slaves in Egypt; but those that look for great things from God, must be content to wait for them; God's time is the best time. Mount Seir is called the land of their possession. Canaan was at this time only the land of promise. Seir was in the possession of the Edomites. The children of this world have their all in hand, and nothing in hope, Lu 16:25; while the children of God have their all in hope, and next to nothing in hand. But, all things considered, it is beyond compare better to have Canaan in promise, than mount Seir in possession.

Chapter 37

Chapter Outline

Joseph is loved of Jacob, but hated by his brethren.	(1–4)
Joseph's dreams.	(5–11)
Jacob sends Joseph to visit his brethren, They conspire his death.	(12–22)
Joseph's brethren sell him.	(23–10)
Jacob deceived, Joseph sold to Potiphar.	(31–36)

Verses 1-4

In Joseph's history we see something of Christ, who was first humbled and then exalted. It also shows the lot of Christians, who must through many tribulations enter into the kingdom. It is a history that has none like it, for displaying the various workings of the human mind, both good and bad, and the singular providence of God in making use of them for fulfilling his purposes. Though Joseph was his father's darling, yet he was not bred up in idleness. Those do not truly love their children, who do not use them to business, and labour, and hardships. The fondling of children is with good reason called the spoiling of them. Those who are trained up to do nothing, are likely to be good for nothing. But Jacob made known his love, by dressing Joseph finer than the rest of his children. It is wrong for parents to make a difference between one child and another, unless there is great cause for it, by the children's dutifulness, or undutifulness. When parents make a difference, children soon notice it, and it leads to quarrels in families. Jacob's sons did that, when they were from under his eye, which they durst not have done at home with him; but Joseph gave his father an account of their ill conduct, that he might restrain them. Not as a tale-bearer, to sow discord, but as a faithful brother.

Verses 5-11

God gave Joseph betimes the prospect of his advancement, to support and comfort him under his long and grievous troubles. Observe, Joseph dreamed of his preferment, but he did not dream of his imprisonment. Thus many young people, when setting out in the world, think of nothing but prosperity and pleasure, and never dream of trouble. His brethren rightly interpreted the dream, though they abhorred the interpretation of it. While they committed crimes in order to defeat it, they were themselves the instruments of accomplishing it. Thus the Jews understood what Christ said of his kingdom. Determined that he should not reign over them, they consulted to put him to death; and by his crucifixion, made way for the exaltation they designed to prevent.

Verses 12-22

How readily does Joseph wait his father's orders! Those children who are best beloved by their parents, should be the most ready to obey them. See how deliberate Joseph's brethren were against him. They thought to slay him from malice aforethought, and in cold blood. Whosoever hateth his brother is a murderer, 1Jo 3:15. The sons of Jacob hated their brother because their father loved him. New occasions, as his dreams and the like, drew them on further; but this laid rankling in their hearts, till they resolved on his death. God has all hearts in his hands. Reuben had most reason to be jealous of Joseph, for he was the first-born; yet he proves his best friend. God overruled all to serve his own purpose, of making Joseph an instrument to save much people alive. Joseph was a type of Christ; for though he was the beloved Son of his Father, and hated by a wicked world, yet the Father sent him out of his bosom to visit us in great humility and love. He came from heaven to earth to seek and save us; yet then malicious plots were laid against him. His own not only received him not, but crucified him. This he submitted to, as a part of his design to redeem and save us.

Verses 23-30

They threw Joseph into a pit, to perish there with hunger and cold; so cruel were their tender mercies. They slighted him when he was in distress, and were not grieved for the affliction of Joseph, see Am 6:6; for when he was pining in the pit, they sat down to eat bread. They felt no remorse of conscience for the sin. But the wrath of man shall praise God, and the remainder of wrath he will restrain, Ps 76:10. Joseph's brethren were wonderfully restrained from murdering him, and their selling him as wonderfully turned to God's praise.

Verses 31-36

When Satan has taught men to commit one sin, he teaches them to try to conceal it with another; to hide theft and murder, with lying and false oaths: but he that covers his sin shall not prosper long. Joseph's brethren kept their own and one another's counsel for some time; but their villany came to light at last, and it is here published to the world. To grieve their father, they sent him Joseph's coat of colours; and he hastily thought, on seeing the bloody coat, that Joseph was rent in pieces. Let those that know the heart of a parent, suppose the agony of poor Jacob. His sons basely pretended to comfort him, but miserable, hypocritical comforters were they all. Had they really desired to comfort him, they might at once have done it, by telling the truth. The heart is strangely hardened by the deceitfulness of sin. Jacob refused to be comforted. Great affection to any creature prepares for so much the greater affliction, when it is taken from us, or made bitter to us: undue love commonly ends in undue grief. It is the wisdom of parents not to bring up children delicately, they know not to what hardships they may be brought before they die. From the whole of this chapter we see with wonder the ways of Providence. The malignant brothers seem to have gotten their ends; the merchants, who care not what they deal in so that they gain, have also obtained theirs; and Potiphar, having got a fine young slave, has obtained his! But God's designs are, by these means, in train for execution. This event shall end in Israel's going down to Egypt; that ends in their deliverance by Moses; that in setting up the true religion in the world; and that in the spread of it among all nations by the gospel. Thus the wrath of man shall praise the Lord, and the remainder thereof will he restrain.

Chapter 38

The profligate conduct of Judah and his family.

—This chapter gives an account of Judah and his family, and such an account it is, that it seems a wonder that of all Jacob's sons, our Lord should spring out of Judah, Heb 7:14. But God will show that his choice is of grace and not of merit, and that Christ came into the world to save sinners, even the chief. Also, that the worthiness of Christ is of himself, and not from his ancestors. How little reason had the Jews, who were so called from this Judah, to boast as they did, Joh 8:41. What awful examples the Lord proclaims in his punishments, of his utter displeasure at sin! Let us seek grace from God to avoid every appearance of sin. And let that state of humbleness to which Jesus submitted, when he came to put away sin by the sacrifice of himself, in appointing such characters as those here recorded, to be his ancestors, endear the Redeemer to our hearts.

Chapter 39

Chapter Outline

Verses 1-6

Our enemies may strip us of outward distinctions and ornaments; but wisdom and grace cannot be taken from us. They may separate us from friends, relatives, and country; but they cannot take from us the presence of the Lord. They may shut us from outward blessings, rob us of liberty, and confine us in dungeons; but they cannot shut us out from communion with God, from the throne of grace, or take from us the blessings of salvation. Joseph was blessed, wonderfully blessed, even in the house where he was a slave. God's presence with us, makes all we do prosperous. Good men are the blessings of the place where they live; good servants may be so, though mean and lightly esteemed. The prosperity of the wicked is, one way or other, for the sake of the godly. Here was a wicked family blessed for the sake of one good servant in it.

Verses 7-12

Beauty either in men or women, often proves a snare both to themselves and others. This forbids pride in it, and requires constant watchfulness against the temptation that attends it. We have great need to make a covenant with our eyes, lest the eyes infect the heart. When lust has got power, decency, and reputation, and conscience, are all sacrificed. Potiphar's wife showed that her heart was fully set to do evil. Satan, when he found he could not overcome Joseph with the troubles and the frowns of the world, for in them he still held fast his principle, assaulted him with pleasures, which have ruined more than the former. But Joseph, by the grace of God, was enabled to resist and overcome this temptation; and his escape was as great an instance of the Divine power, as the deliverance of the three children out of the fiery furnace. This sin was one which might most easily beset him. The tempter was his mistress, one whose favour would help him forward; and it was at his utmost peril if he slighted her, and made her his enemy. The time and place favoured the temptation. To all this was added frequent, constant urging. The almighty grace of God enabled Joseph to overcome this assault of the enemy. He urges what he owed both to God and his master. We are bound in honour, as well as justice and gratitude, not in any thing to wrong those who place trust in us, how secretly soever it may be done. He would not offend his God. Three arguments Joseph urges upon himself. 1. He considers who he was that was tempted. One in covenant with God, who professed religion and relation to him. 2. What the sin was to which he was tempted. Others might look upon it as a small matter; but Joseph did not so think of it. Call sin by its own name, and never lessen it. Let sins of this nature always be looked upon as great wickedness, as exceedingly sinful. 3. Against whom he was tempted to sin, against God. Sin is against God, against his nature and his dominion, against his love and his design. Those that love God, for this reason hate sin. The grace of God enabled Joseph to overcome the temptation, by avoiding the temper. He would not stay to parley with the temptation, but fled from it, as escaping for his life. If we mean not to do iniquity, let us flee as a bird from the snare, and as a roe from the hunter.

Verses 13-18

Joseph's mistress, having tried in vain to make him a guilty man, endeavoured to be avenged on him. Those that have broken the bonds of modesty, will never be held by the bonds of truth. It is no new thing for the best of men to be falsely accused of the worst of crimes, by those who themselves are the worst of criminals. It is well there is a day of discovery coming, in which all shall appear in their true characters.

Verses 19-23

Joseph's master believed the accusation. Potiphar, it is likely, chose that prison, because it was the worst; but God designed to open the way to Joseph's honour. Joseph was owned and righted by his God. He was away from all his friends and relations; he had none to help or comfort him;

but the Lord was with Joseph, and showed him mercy. Those that have a good conscience in a prison, have a good God there. God gave him favour in the sight of the keeper of the prison; he trusted him to manage the affairs of the prison. A good man will do good wherever he is, and will be a blessing even in bonds and banishment. Let us not forget, through Joseph, to look unto Jesus, who suffered being tempted, yet without sin; who was slandered, and persecuted, and imprisoned, but without cause; who by the cross ascended to the throne. May we be enabled to follow the same path in submitting and in suffering, to the same place of glory.

Chapter 40

Chapter Outline

Verses 1-19

It was not so much the prison that made the butler and baker sad, as their dreams. God has more ways than one to sadden the spirits. Joseph had compassion towards them. Let us be concerned for the sadness of our brethren's countenances. It is often a relief to those that are in trouble to be noticed. Also learn to look into the causes of our own sorrow. Is there a good reason? Is there not comfort sufficient to balance it, whatever it is? Why art thou cast down, O my soul? Joseph was careful to ascribe the glory to God. The chief butler's dream foretold his advancement. The chief baker's dream his death. It was not Joseph's fault that he brought the baker no better tidings. And thus ministers are but interpreters; they cannot make the thing otherwise than it is: if they deal faithfully, and their message prove unpleasing, it is not their fault. Joseph does not reflect upon his brethren that sold him; nor does he reflect on the wrong done him by his mistress and his master, but mildly states his own innocence. When we are called on to clear ourselves, we should carefully avoid, as much as may be, speaking ill of others. Let us be content to prove ourselves innocent, and not upbraid others with their guilt.

Verses 20-23

Joseph's interpretation of the dreams came to pass on the very day fixed. On Pharaoh's birth-day, all his servants attended him, and then the cases of these two came to be looked into. We may all profitably take notice of our birth-days, with thankfulness for the mercies of our birth, sorrow for the sinfulness of our lives, and expectation of the day of our death, as better than the day of our birth. But it seems strange that worldly people, who are so fond of living here, should rejoice at the end of one year after another of their short span of life. A Christian has cause to rejoice that he was born, also that he comes nearer to the end of his sin and sorrow, and nearer to his everlasting happiness. The chief butler remembered not Joseph, but forgot him. Joseph had deserved well   at his hands, yet he forgot him. We must not think it strange, if in this world we have hatred shown us for our love, and slights for our kindness. See how apt those who are themselves at ease are to forget others in distress. Joseph learned by his disappointment to trust in God only. We cannot expect too little from man, nor too much from God. Let us not forget the sufferings, promises, and love of our Redeemer. We blame the chief butler's ingratitude to Joseph, yet we ourselves act much more ungratefully to the Lord Jesus. Joseph had but foretold the chief butler's enlargement, but Christ wrought out ours; he mediated with the King of Kings for us; yet we forget him, though often reminded of him, and though we have promised never to forget him. Thus ill do we requite Him, like foolish people and unwise.

Chapter 41

Chapter Outline

Verses 1-8

The means of Joseph's being freed from prison were Pharaoh's dreams, as here related. Now that God no longer speaks to us in that way, it is no matter how little we either heed dreams, or tell them. The telling of foolish dreams can make no better than foolish talk. But these dreams showed that they were sent of God; when he awoke, Pharaoh's spirit was troubled.

Verses 9-32

God's time for the enlargement of his people is the fittest time. If the chief butler had got Joseph to be released from prison, it is probable he would have gone back to the land of the Hebrews. Then he had neither been so blessed himself, nor such a blessing to his family, as afterwards he proved. Joseph, when introduced to Pharaoh, gives honour to God. Pharaoh had dreamed that he stood upon the bank of the river Nile, and saw the kine, both the fat ones, and the lean ones, come out of the river. Egypt has no rain, but the plenty of the year depends upon the overflowing of the river Nile. See how many ways Providence has of dispensing its gifts; yet our dependence is still the same upon the First Cause, who makes every creature what it is to us, be it rain or river. See to what changes the comforts of this life are subject. We cannot be sure that to-morrow shall be as this day, or next year as this. We must learn how to want, as well as how to abound. Mark the goodness of God in sending the seven years of plenty before those of famine, that provision might be made. The produce of the earth is sometimes more, and sometimes less; yet, take one with another, he that gathers much, has nothing over; and he that gathers little, has no lack, Ex 16:18. And see the perishing nature of our worldly enjoyments. The great harvests of the years of plenty were quite lost, and swallowed up in the years of famine; and that which seemed very much, yet did but just serve to keep the people alive. There is bread which lasts to eternal life, which it is worth while to labour for. They that make the things of this world their good things, will find little pleasure in remembering that they have received them.

Verses 33-45

Joseph gave good advice to Pharaoh. Fair warning should always be followed by good counsel. God has in his word told us of a day of trial before us, when we shall need all the grace we can have. Now, therefore, provide accordingly. Pharaoh gave Joseph an honourable testimony. He is a man in whom the spirit of God is; and such men ought to be valued. Pharaoh puts upon Joseph marks of honour. He gave him such a name as spoke the value he had for him, Zaphnath-paaneah, "a revealer of secrets." This preferment of Joseph encourages all to trust in God. Some translate Joseph's new name, "the saviour of the world." The brightest glories, even of the upper world, are put upon Christ, the highest trust lodged in his hand, and all power given him, both in heaven and earth.

Verses 46-57

In the names of his two sons, Manasseh and Ephraim, Joseph owned the Divine providence. 1. He was made to forget his misery. 2. He was made fruitful in the land of his affliction. The seven plenteous years came, and were ended. We ought to look forward to the end of the days, both of our prosperity and of our opportunity. We must not be secure in prosperity, nor slothful in making good use of opportunity. Years of plenty will end; what thy hand finds to do, do it; and gather in gathering time. The dearth came, and the famine was not only in Egypt, but in other lands. Joseph was diligent in laying up, while the plenty lasted. He was prudent and careful in giving out, when the famine came. Joseph was engaged in useful and important labours. Yet it was in the midst of this his activity that his father Jacob said, Joseph is not! What a large portion of our troubles would be done away if we knew the whole truth! Let these events lead us to Jesus. There is a famine of the bread of life throughout the whole earth. Go to Jesus, and what he bids you, do. Attend to His voice, apply to him; he will open his treasures, and satisfy with goodness the hungry soul of every age and nation, without money and without price. But those who slight this provision must starve, and his enemies will be destroyed.

Chapter 42

Chapter Outline

Jacob sends ten sons to buy corn.   (1–6)

Joseph's treatment of his brethren.   (7–20)

Verses 1-6

Jacob saw the corn his neighbours had bought in Egypt, and brought home. It is a spur to exertion to see others supplied. Shall others get food for their souls, and shall we starve while it is to be had? Having discovered where help is to be had, we should apply for it without delay, without shrinking from labour, or grudging expense, especially as regards our never-dying souls. There is provision in Christ; but we must come to him, and seek it from him.

Verses 7-20

Joseph was hard upon his brethren, not from a spirit of revenge, but to bring them to repentance. Not seeing his brother Benjamin, he suspected that they had made away with him, and he gave them occasion to speak of their father and brother. God, in his providence, sometimes seems harsh with those he loves, and speaks roughly to those for whom yet he has great mercy in store. Joseph settled at last, that one of them should be left, and the rest go home and fetch Benjamin. It was a very encouraging word he said to them, "I fear God;" as if he had said, You may be assured I will do you no wrong; I dare not, for I know there is one higher than I. With those that fear God, we may expect fair dealing.

Verses 21-24

The office of conscience is to bring to mind things long since said and done. When the guilt of this sin of Joseph's brethren was fresh, they made light of it, and sat down to eat bread; but now, long afterward, their consciences accused them of it. See the good of afflictions; they often prove the happy means of awakening conscience, and bringing sin to our remembrance. Also, the evil of guilt as to our brethren. Conscience now reproached them for it. Whenever we think we have wrong done us, we ought to remember the wrong we have done to others. Reuben alone remembered with comfort, that he had done what he could to prevent the mischief. When we share with others in their sufferings, it will be a comfort if we have the testimony of our consciences for us, that we did not share in their evil deeds, but in our places witnessed against them. Joseph retired to weep. Though his reason directed that he should still carry himself as a stranger, because they were not as yet humbled enough, yet natural affection could not but work.

Verses 25-28

The brethren came for corn, and corn they had: not only so, but every man had his money given back. Thus Christ, like Joseph, gives out supplies without money and without price. The poorest are invited to buy. But guilty consciences are apt to take good providences in a bad sense; to put wrong meanings even upon things that make for them.

Verses 29-38

Here is the report Jacob's sons made to their father. It troubled the good man. Even the bundles of money Joseph returned, in kindness, to his father, frightened him. He laid the fault upon his sons; knowing them, he feared they had provoked the Egyptians, and wrongfully brought home their money. Jacob plainly distrusted his sons, remembering that he never saw Joseph since he had been with them. It is bad with a family, when children behave so ill that their parents know not how to trust them. Jacob gives up Joseph for gone, and Simeon and Benjamin as in danger; and concludes, All these things are against me. It proved otherwise, that all these things were for him, were working together for his good, and the good of his family. We often think that to be against us, which is really for us. We are afflicted in body, estate, name, and in our relations; and think all these things are against us, whereas they are really working for us a weight of glory. Thus does the Lord Jesus conceal himself and his favour, thus he rebukes and chastens those for whom he has purposes of love. By sharp corrections and humbling convictions he will break the stoutness and mar the pride of the heart, and bring to true repentance. Yet before sinners fully know him, or taste that he is gracious, he consults their good, and sustains their souls, to wait for him. May we do thus, never yielding to discouragement, determining to seek no other refuge, and humbling ourselves more and more under his mighty hand. In due time he will answer our petitions, and do for us more than we can expect.

Chapter 43

Chapter Outline

Jacob is persuaded to send Benjamin into Egypt.	(1–14)
Joseph's reception of his brethren, their fears.	(15–25)
Joseph makes a feast for his brethren.	(26–34)

Verses 1-14

Jacob urges his sons to go and buy a little food; now, in time of dearth, a little must suffice. Judah urges that Benjamin should go with them. It is not against the honour and duty children owe their parents, humbly to advise them, and when needful, to reason with them. Jacob saw the necessity of the case, and yielded. His prudence and justice appeared in three things. 1. He sent back the money they had found in the sack. Honesty obliges us to restore not only that which comes to us by our own fault, but that which comes to us by the mistakes of others. Though we get it by oversight, if we keep it when the oversight is discovered, it is kept by deceit. 2. He sent as much again as they took the time before; the price of corn might be risen, or they might have to pay a ransom for Simeon. 3. He sent a present of such things as the land afforded, and as were scarce in Egypt, balm, and honey, &c. Providence dispenses not its gifts to all alike. But honey and spice will never make up the want of bread-corn. The famine was sore in Canaan, yet they had balm and myrrh, &c. We may live well enough upon plain food, without dainties; but we cannot live upon dainties without plain food. Let us thank God that what is most needful and useful, generally is most cheap and common. Though men value very highly their gold and silver, and the luxuries which are counted the best fruits of every land, yet in a time of famine they willingly barter them for bread. And how little will earthly good things stand us in stead in the day of wrath! How ready should we be to renounce them all, as loss, for the excellency of the knowledge of Jesus Christ! Our way to prevail with man is by first prevailing with the Lord in fervent prayer. But, Thy will be done, should close every petition for the mercies of this life, or against the afflictions of this life.

Verses 15-25

Jacob's sons went down the second time into Egypt to buy corn. If we should ever know what a famine of the word means, let us not think it much to travel as far for spiritual food, as they did for bodily food. Joseph's steward had orders from his master to take them to his house. Even this frightened them. Those that are guilty make the worst of every thing. But the steward encouraged them. It appears, from what he said, that by his good master he was brought to the knowledge of the true God, the God of the Hebrews. Religious servants should take all fit occasions to speak of God and his providence, with reverence and seriousness.

Verses 26-34

Observe the great respect Joseph's brethren paid to him. Thus were Joseph's dreams more and more fulfilled. Joseph showed great kindness to them. He treated them nobly; but see here the early distance between Jews and gentiles. In a day of famine, it is enough to be fed; but they were feasted. Their cares and fears were now over, and they ate their bread with joy, reckoning they were upon good terms with the lord of the land. If God accept our works, our present, we have reason to be cheerful. Joseph showed special regard for Benjamin, that he might try whether his brethren would envy him. It must be our rule, to be content with what we have, and not to grieve at what others have. Thus Jesus shows those whom he loves, more and more of their need. He makes them see that he is their only refuge from destruction. He overcomes their unwillingness, and brings them to himself. Then, as he sees good, he gives them some taste of his love, and welcomes them to the provisions of his house, as an earnest of what he further intends for them.

Chapter 44

Chapter Outline

Joseph's policy to stay his brethren, and try   (1–17)
their affection for Benjamin.

Judah's supplication to Joseph.   (18–34)

Verses 1-17

Joseph tried how his brethren felt towards Benjamin. Had they envied and hated the other son of Rachel as they had hated him, and if they had the same want of feeling towards their father Jacob as heretofore, they would now have shown it. When the cup was found upon Benjamin, they would have a pretext for leaving him to be a slave. But we cannot judge what men are now, by what they have been formerly; nor what they will do, by what they have done. The steward charged them with being ungrateful, rewarding evil for good; with folly, in taking away the cup of daily use, which would soon be missed, and diligent search made for it; for so it may be read, Is not this it in which my lord drinketh, as having a particular fondness for it, and for which he would search thoroughly? Or, By which, leaving it carelessly at your table, he would make trial whether you were honest men or not? They throw themselves upon Joseph's mercy, and acknowledge the righteousness of God, perhaps thinking of the injury they had formerly done to Joseph, for which they thought God was now reckoning with them. Even in afflictions wherein we believe ourselves wronged by men, we must own that God is righteous, and finds out our sin.

Verses 18-34

Had Joseph been, as Judah supposed him, an utter stranger to the family, he could not but be wrought upon by his powerful reasonings. But neither Jacob nor Benjamin need an intercessor with Joseph; for he himself loved them. Judah's faithful cleaving to Benjamin, now, in his distress, was recompensed long afterwards by the tribe of Benjamin keeping with the tribe of Judah, when the other tribes deserted it. The apostle, when discoursing of the mediation of Christ, observes, that our Lord sprang out of Judah, Heb 7:14; and he not only made intercession for the transgressors, but he became a Surety for them, testifying therein tender concern, both for his Father and for his brethren. Jesus, the great antitype of Joseph, humbles and proves his people, even after they have had some tastes of his loving-kindness. He brings their sins to their remembrance, that they may exercise and show repentance, and feel how much they owe to his mercy.

Chapter 45

Chapter Outline

Verses 1-15

Joseph let Judah go on, and heard all he had to say. He found his brethren humbled for their sins, mindful of himself, for Judah had mentioned him twice in his speech, respectful to their father, and very tender of their brother Benjamin. Now they were ripe for the comfort he designed, by making himself known. Joseph ordered all his attendants to withdraw. Thus Christ makes himself and his loving-kindness known to his people, out of the sight and hearing of the world. Joseph shed tears of tenderness and strong affection, and with these threw off that austerity with which he had hitherto behaved toward his brethren. This represents the Divine compassion toward returning penitents. "I am Joseph, your brother." This would humble them yet more for their sin in selling him, but would encourage them to hope for kind treatment. Thus, when Christ would convince Paul, he said, I am Jesus; and when he would comfort his disciples, he said, It is I, be not afraid. When Christ manifests himself to his people, he encourages them to draw near to him with a true heart. Joseph does so, and shows them, that whatever they thought to do against him, God had brought good out of it. Sinners must grieve and be angry with themselves for their sins, though God brings good out of it, for that is no thanks to them. The agreement between all this, and the case of a sinner, on Christ's manifesting himself to his soul, is very striking. He does not, on this account, think sin a less, but a greater evil; and yet he is so armed against despair, as even to rejoice in what God hath wrought, while he trembles in thinking of the dangers and destruction from which he has escaped. Joseph promises to take care of his father and all the family. It is the duty of children, if the necessity of their parents at any time require it, to support and supply them to the utmost of their ability; this is showing piety at home, 1Ti 5:4. After Joseph had embraced Benjamin, he caressed them all, and then his brethren talked with him freely of all the affairs of their father's house. After the tokens of true reconciliation with the Lord Jesus, sweet communion with him follows.

Verses 16-24

Pharaoh was kind to Joseph, and to his relations for his sake. Egypt would make up the losses of their removal. Thus those for whom Christ intends his heavenly glory, ought not to regard the things of this world. The best of its enjoyments are but lumber; we cannot make sure of them while here, much less can we carry them away with us. Let us not set our eyes or hearts upon the world; there are better things for us in that blessed land, whither Christ, our Joseph, is gone to prepare a place. Joseph dismissed his brethren with a seasonable caution, "See that ye fall not out by the way." He knew they were too apt to be quarrelsome; and having forgiven them all, he lays this charge upon them, not to upbraid one another. This command our Lord Jesus has given to us, that we love one another, and that whatever happens, or has happened, we fall not out. For we are brethren, we have all one Father. We are all guilty, and instead of quarrelling with one another, have reason to fall out with ourselves. We are, or hope to be, forgiven of God, whom we have all offended, and, therefore, should be ready to forgive one another. We are "by the way," a way through the land of Egypt, where we have many eyes upon us, that seek advantage against us; a way that leads to the heavenly Canaan, where we hope to be for ever in perfect peace.

Verses 25-28

To hear that Joseph is alive, is too good news to be true; Jacob faints, for he believes it not. We faint, because we do not believe. At length, Jacob is convinced of the truth. Jacob was old, and did not expect to live long. He says, Let my eyes be refreshed with this sight before they are closed, and then I need no more to make me happy in this world. Behold Jesus manifesting himself as a Brother and a Friend to those who once were his despisers, his enemies. He assures them of his love and the riches of his grace. He commands them to lay aside envy, anger, malice, and strife, and to live in peace with each other. He teaches them to give up the world for him and his fulness. He supplies all that is needful to bring them home to himself, that where he is they may be also. And though, when he at last sends for his people, they may for a time feel some doubts and fears, yet the thought of seeing his glory and of being with him, will enable them to say, It is enough, I am willing to die; and I go to see, and to be with the Beloved of my soul.

Chapter 46

Chapter Outline

Verses 1-4

Even as to those events and undertakings which appear most joyful, we should seek counsel, assistance, and a blessing from the Lord. Attending on his ordinances, and receiving the pledges of his covenant love, we expect his presence, and that peace which it confers. In all removals we should be reminded of our removal out of this world. Nothing can encourage us to fear no evil when passing through the valley of the shadow of death, but the presence of Christ.

Verses 5-27

We have here a particular account of Jacob's family. Though the fulfilling of promises is always sure, yet it is often slow. It was now 215 years since God had promised Abraham to make of him a great nation, ch. 12:2; yet that branch of his seed, to which the promise was made sure, had only increased to seventy, of whom this particular account is kept, to show the power of God in making these seventy become a vast multitude.

Verses 28-34

It was justice to Pharaoh to let him know that such a family was come to settle in his dominions. If others put confidence in us, we must not be so base as to abuse it by imposing upon them. But how shall Joseph dispose of his brethren? Time was, when they were contriving to be rid of him; now he is contriving to settle them to their advantage; this is rendering good for evil. He would have them live by themselves, in the land of Goshen, which lay nearest to Canaan. Shepherds were an abomination to the Egyptians. Yet Joseph would have them not ashamed to own this as their occupation before Pharaoh. He might have procured places for them at court or in the army. But such preferments would have exposed them to the envy of the Egyptians, and might have tempted them to forget Canaan and the promise made unto their fathers. An honest calling is no disgrace, nor ought we to account it so, but rather reckon it a shame to be idle, or to have nothing to do. It is generally best for people to abide in the callings they have been bred to and used to. Whatever employment and condition God in his providence has allotted for us, let us suit ourselves to it, satisfy ourselves with it, and not mind high things. It is better to be the credit of a mean post, than the shame of a high one. If we wish to destroy our souls, or the souls of our children, then let us seek for ourselves, and for them, great things; but if not, it becomes us, having food and raiment, therewith to be content.

Chapter 47

Chapter Outline

Joseph presents his brethren to Pharaoh.	(1–6)
Jacob blesses Pharaoh.	(7–12)
Joseph's dealings with the Egyptians during the famine.	(13–26)
Jacob's age. His desire to be buried in Canaan.	(27–31)

Verses 1-6

Though Joseph was a great man, especially in Egypt, yet he owned his brethren. Let the rich and great in the world not overlook or despise poor relations. Our Lord Jesus is not ashamed to call us brethren. In answer to Pharaoh's inquiry, What is your calling? they told him that they were shepherds, adding that they were come to sojourn in the land for a time, while the famine prevailed in Canaan. Pharaoh offered to employ them as shepherds, provided they were active men. Whatever our business or employment is, we should aim to excel in it, and to prove ourselves clever and industrious.

Verses 7-12

With the gravity of old age, the piety of a true believer, and the authority of a patriarch and a prophet, Jacob besought the Lord to bestow a blessing upon Pharaoh. He acted as a man not ashamed of his religion; and who would express gratitude to the benefactor of himself and his family. We have here a very uncommon answer given to a very common question. Jacob calls his life a pilgrimage; the sojourning of a stranger in a foreign country, or his journey home to his own country. He was not at home upon earth; his habitation, his inheritance, his treasures were in heaven. He reckons his life by days; even by days life is soon reckoned, and we are not sure of the continuance of it for a day. Let us therefore number our days. His days were few. Though he had now lived one hundred and thirty years, they seemed but a few days, in comparison with the days of eternity, and the eternal state. They were evil; this is true concerning man. He is of few days and full of trouble; since his days are evil, it is well they are few. Jacob's life had been made up of evil days. Old age came sooner upon him than it had done upon some of his fathers. As the young man should not be proud of his strength or beauty, so the old man should not be proud of his age, and his hoary hairs, though others justly reverence them; for those who are accounted very old, attain not to the years of the patriarchs. The hoary head is only a crown of glory, when found in the way of righteousness. Such an answer could not fail to impress the heart of Pharaoh, by reminding him that worldly prosperity and happiness could not last long, and was not enough to satisfy. After a life of vanity and vexation, man goes down into the grave, equally from the throne as the cottage. Nothing can make us happy, but the prospect of an everlasting home in heaven, after our short and weary pilgrimage on earth.

Verses 13-26

Care being taken of Jacob and his family, which mercy was especially designed by Providence in Joseph's advancement, an account is given of the saving the kingdom of Egypt from ruin. There was no bread, and the people were ready to die. See how we depend upon God's providence. All our wealth would not keep us from starving, if rain were withheld for two or three years. See how much we are at God's mercy, and let us keep ourselves always in his love. Also see how much we smart by our own want of care. If all the Egyptians had laid up corn for themselves in the seven years of plenty, they had not been in these straits; but they regarded not the warning. Silver and gold would not feed them: they must have corn. All that a man hath will he give for his life. We cannot judge this matter by modern rules. It is plain that the Egyptians regarded Joseph as a public benefactor. The whole is consistent with Joseph's character, acting between Pharaoh and his subjects, in the fear of God. The Egyptians confessed concerning Joseph, Thou hast saved our lives. What multitudes will gratefully say to Jesus, at the last day, Thou hast saved our souls from the most tremendous destruction, and in the season of uttermost distress! The Egyptians parted with all their property, and even their liberty, for the saving of their lives: can it then be too much for us to count all but loss, and part with all, at His command, and for His sake, who will both save our souls, and give us an hundredfold, even here, in this present world? Surely if saved by Christ, we shall be willing to become his servants.

Verses 27-31

At last the time drew nigh that Israel must die. Israel, a prince with God, had power over the Angel, and prevailed, yet must die. Joseph supplied him with bread, that he might not die by famine, but that did not secure him from dying by age or sickness. He died by degrees; his candle gradually burnt down to the socket, so that he saw the time drawing nigh. It is an advantage to see the approach of death, before we feel it, that we may be quickened to do, with all our might, what our hands find to do. However, death is not far from any of us. Jacob's care, as he saw the day approach, was about his burial; not the pomp of it, but he would be buried in Canaan, because it was the land of promise. It was a type of heaven, that better country, which he declared plainly he expected, Heb 11:14. Nothing will better help to make a death-bed easy, than the certain prospect of rest in the heavenly Canaan after death. When this was done, Israel bowed himself upon the bed's head, worshipping God, as it is explained, see Heb 11:21, giving God thanks for all his favours; in feebleness thus supporting himself, expressing his willingness to leave the world. Even those who lived on Joseph's provision, and Jacob who was so dear to him, must die. But Christ Jesus gives us the true bread, that we may eat and live for ever. To Him let us come and yield ourselves, and when we draw near to death, he who supported us through life, will meet us and assure us of everlasting salvation.

Chapter 48

Chapter Outline

Joseph visits his dying father.   (1–7)

Jacob blesses Joseph's sons.   (8–22)

Verses 1-7

The death-beds of believers, with the prayers and counsels of dying persons, are suited to make serious impressions upon the young, the gay, and the prosperous: we shall do well to take children on such occasions, when it can be done properly. If the Lord please, it is very desirable to bear our dying testimony to his truth, to his faithfulness, and the pleasantness of his ways. And one would wish so to live, as to give energy and weight to our dying exhortations. All true believers are blessed at their death, but all do not depart equally full of spiritual consolations. Jacob adopted Joseph's two sons. Let them not succeed their father, in his power and grandeur in Egypt; but let them succeed in the inheritance of the promise made to Abraham. Thus the aged dying patriarch teaches these young persons to take their lot with the people of God. He appoints each of them to be the head of a tribe. Those are worthy of double honour, who, through God's grace, break through the temptations of worldly wealth and preferment, to embrace religion in disgrace and poverty. Jacob will have Ephraim and Manasseh to know, that it is better to be low, and in the church, than high, and out of it.

Verses 8-22

The two good men own God in their comforts. Joseph says, They are my sons whom God has given me. Jacob says, God hath showed me thy seed. Comforts are doubly sweet to us when we see them coming from God's hand. He not only prevents our fears, but exceeds our hopes. Jacob mentions the care the Divine providence had taken of him all his days. A great deal of hardship he had known in his time, but God kept him from the evil of his troubles. Now he was dying, he looked upon himself as redeemed from all sin and sorrow for ever. Christ, the Angel of the covenant, redeems from all evil. Deliverances from misery and dangers, by the Divine power, coming through the ransom of the blood of Christ, in Scripture are often called redemption. In blessing Joseph's sons, Jacob crossed hands. Joseph was willing to support his first-born, and would have removed his father's hands. But Jacob acted neither by mistake, nor from a partial affection to one more than the other; but from a spirit of prophecy, and by the Divine counsel. God, in bestowing blessings upon his people, gives more to some than to others, more gifts, graces, and comforts, and more of the good things of this life. He often gives most to those that are least likely. He chooses the weak things of the world; he raises the poor out of the dust. Grace observes not the order of nature, nor does God prefer those whom we think fittest to be preferred, but as it pleases him. How poor are they who have no riches but those of this world! How miserable is a death-bed to those who have no well-grounded hope of good, but dreadful apprehensions of evil, and nothing but evil for ever!

Chapter 49

Chapter Outline

Verses 1, 2

All Jacob's sons were living. His calling them together was a precept for them to unite in love, not to mingle with the Egyptians; and foretold that they should not be separated, as Abraham's sons and Isaac's were, but should all make one people. We are not to consider this address as the expression of private feelings of affection, resentment, or partiality; but as the language of the Holy Ghost, declaring the purpose of God respecting the character, circumstances, and situation of the tribes which descended from the sons of Jacob, and which may be traced in their histories.

Verses 3-7

Reuben was the first-born; but by gross sin, he forfeited the birthright. The character of Reuben is, that he was unstable as water. Men do not thrive, because they do not fix. Reuben's sin left a lasting infamy upon his family. Let us never do evil, then we need not fear being told of it. Simeon and Levi were passionate and revengeful. The murder of the Shechemites is a proof of this. Jacob protested against that barbarous act. Our soul is our honour; by its powers we are distinguished from, and raised above, the beasts that perish. We ought, from our hearts, to abhor all bloody and mischievous men. Cursed be their anger. Jacob does not curse their persons, but their lusts. I will divide them. The sentence as it respects Levi was turned into a blessing. This tribe performed an acceptable service in their zeal against the worshippers of the golden calf, Ex 32. Being set apart to God as priests, they were in that character scattered through the nation of Israel.

Verses 8-12

Judah's name signifies praise. God was praised for him, chap. 29:35, praised by him, and praised in him; therefore his brethren shall praise him. Judah should be a strong and courageous tribe. Judah is compared, not to a lion raging and ranging, but to a lion enjoying the satisfaction of his power and success, without creating vexation to others; this is to be truly great. Judah should be the royal tribe, the tribe from which Messiah the Prince should come. Shiloh, that promised Seed in whom the earth should be blessed, "that peaceable and prosperous One," or "Saviour," he shall come of Judah. Thus dying Jacob at a great distance saw Christ's day, and it was his comfort and support on his death-bed. Till Christ's coming, Judah possessed authority, but after his crucifixion this was shortened, and according to what Christ foretold, Jerusalem was destroyed, and all the poor harassed remnant of Jews were confounded together. Much which is here said concerning Judah, is to be applied to our Lord Jesus. In him there is plenty of all which is nourishing and refreshing to the soul, and which maintains and cheers the Divine life in it. He is the true Vine; wine is the appointed symbol of his blood, which is drink indeed, as shed for sinners, and applied in faith; and all the blessings of his gospel are wine and milk, without money and without price, to which every thirsty soul is welcome. Isa 55:1.

Verses 13-18

Concerning Zebulun: if prophecy says, Zebulun shall be a haven of ships, be sure Providence will so plant him. God appoints the bounds of our habitation. It is our wisdom and duty to accommodate ourselves to our lot, and to improve it; if Zebulun dwell at the heaven of the sea, let him be for a haven of ships. Concerning Issachar: he saw that the land was pleasant, yielding not only pleasant prospects, but pleasant fruits to recompense his toils. Let us, with an eye of faith, see the heavenly rest to be good, and that land of promise to be pleasant; this will make our present services easy. Dan should, by art, and policy, and surprise, gain advantages against his enemies, like a serpent biting the heel of the traveller. Jacob, almost spent, and ready to faint, relieves himself with those words, "I have waited for thy salvation, O Lord!" The salvation he waited for was Christ, the promised Seed; now that he was going to be gathered to his people, he breathes after Him to whom the gathering of the people shall be. He declared plainly that he sought heaven, the better country, Heb 11:13, 14. Now he is going to enjoy the salvation, he comforts himself that he had waited for the salvation. Christ, as our way to heaven, is to be waited on; and heaven, as our rest in Christ, is to be waited for. It is the comfort of a dying saint thus to have waited for the salvation of the Lord; for then he shall have what he has been waiting for.

Verses 19-21

Concerning Gad, Jacob alludes to his name, which signifies a troop, and foresees the character of that tribe. The cause of God and his people, though for a time it may seem to be baffled and run down, will be victorious at last. It represents the Christian's conflict. Grace in the soul is often foiled in its conflicts; troops of corruption overcome it, but the cause is God's, and grace will in the end come off conqueror, yea, more than conqueror, Ro 8:37. Asher should be a rich tribe. His inheritance bordered upon Carmel, which was fruitful to a proverb. Naphtali, is a hind let loose. We may consider it as a description of the character of this tribe. Unlike the laborious ox and ass; desirous of ease and liberty; active, but more noted for quick despatch than steady labour and perseverance. Like the suppliant who, with goodly words, craves mercy. Let not those of different tempers and gifts censure or envy one another.

Verses 22-27

The blessing of Joseph is very full. What Jacob says of him, is history as well as prophecy. Jacob reminds him of the difficulties and fiery darts of temptations he had formerly struggled through. His faith did not fail, but through his trials he bore all his burdens with firmness, and did not do anything unbecoming. All our strength for resisting temptations, and bearing afflictions, comes from God; his grace is sufficient. Joseph became the shepherd of Israel, to take care of his father and family; also the stone of Israel, their foundation and strong support. In this, as in many other things, Joseph was a remarkable type of the Good Shepherd, and tried Corner Stone of the whole church of God. Blessings are promised to Joseph's posterity, typical of the vast and everlasting blessings which come upon the spiritual seed of Christ. Jacob blessed all his sons, but especially Joseph, "who was separated from his brethren." Not only separated in Egypt, but, possessing eminent dignity, and more devoted to God. Of Benjamin it is said, He shall ravin as a wolf. Jacob was guided in what he said by the Spirit of prophecy, and not by natural affection; else he would have spoken with more tenderness of his beloved son Benjamin. Concerning him he only foresees and foretells, that his posterity should be a warlike tribe, strong and daring, and that they should enrich themselves with the spoils of their enemies; that they should be active. Blessed Paul was of this tribe, Ro 11:1; Php 3:5; he, in the morning of his day, devoured the prey as a persecutor, but in the evening divided the spoils as a preacher; he shared the blessings of Judah's Lion, and assisted in his victories.

Verses 28-33

Jacob blessed every one according to the blessings God in after-times intended to bestow upon them. He spoke about his burial-place, from a principle of faith in the promise of God, that Canaan should be the inheritance of his seed in due time. When he had finished both his blessing and his charge, and so had finished his testimony, he addressed himself to his dying work. He gathered up his feet into the bed, not only as one patiently submitting to the stroke, but as one cheerfully composing himself to rest, now that he was weary. He freely gave up his spirit into the hand of God, the Father of spirits. If God's people be our people, death will gather us to them. Under the care of the Shepherd of Israel, we shall lack nothing for body or soul. We shall remain unmoved until our work is finished; then, breathing out our souls into His hands for whose salvation we have waited, we shall depart in peace, and leave a blessing for our children after us.

Chapter 50

Chapter Outline

Verses 1-6

Though pious relatives and friends have lived to a good old age, and we are confident they are gone to glory, yet we may regret our own loss, and pay respect to their memory by lamenting them. Grace does not destroy, but it purifies, moderates, and regulates natural affection. The departed soul is out of the reach of any tokens of our affection; but it is proper to show respect to the body, of which we look for a glorious and joyful resurrection, whatever may become of its remains in this world. Thus Joseph showed his faith in God, and love to his father. He ordered the body to be embalmed, or wrapped up with spices, to preserve it. See how vile our bodies are, when the soul has forsaken them; they will in a very little time become noisome, and offensive.

Verses 7-14

Jacob's body was attended, not only by his own family, but by the great men of Egypt. Now that they were better acquainted with the Hebrews, they began to respect them. Professors of religion should endeavour by wisdom and love to remove the prejudices many have against them. Standers-by took notice of it as a grievous mourning. The death of good men is a loss to any place, and ought to be greatly lamented.

Verses 15-21

Various motives might cause the sons of Jacob to continue in Egypt, notwithstanding the prophetic vision Abraham had of their bondage there. Judging of Joseph from the general temper of human nature, they thought he would now avenge himself on those who hated and injured him without cause. Not being able to resist, or to flee away, they attempted to soften him by humbling themselves. They pleaded with him as the servants of Jacob's God. Joseph was much affected at seeing this complete fulfilment of his dreams. He directs them not to fear him, but to fear God; to humble themselves before the Lord, and to seek the Divine forgiveness. He assures them of his own kindness to them. See what an excellent spirit Joseph was of, and learn of him to render good for evil. He comforted them, and, to banish all their fears, he spake kindly to them. Broken spirits must be bound up and encouraged. Those we love and forgive, we must not only do well for, but speak kindly to.

Verses 22-26

Joseph having honoured his father, his days were long in the land, which, for the present, God had given him. When he saw his death approaching, he comforted his brethren with the assurance of their return to Canaan in due time. We must comfort others with the same comforts with which we have been comforted of God, and encourage them to rest on the promises which are our support. For a confession of his own faith, and a confirmation of theirs, he charges them to keep his remains unburied till that glorious day, when they should be settled in the land of promise. Thus Joseph, by faith in the doctrine of the resurrection, and the promise of Canaan, gave commandment concerning his bones. This would keep up their expectation of a speedy departure from Egypt, and keep Canaan continually in their minds. This would also attach Joseph's posterity to their brethren. The death, as well as the life of this eminent saint, was truly excellent; both furnish us with strong encouragement to persevere in the service of God. How happy to set our early in the heavenly race, to continue stedfastly, and to finish the course with joy! This Joseph did, this we also may do. Even when the pains of death are upon us, if we have trusted in Him upon whom the patriarchs, prophets, and apostles depended, we need not fear to say, "My flesh and my heart faileth, but God is the strength of my heart, and my portion for ever."

Exodus

The Book of Exodus relates the forming of the children of Israel into a church and a nation. We have hitherto seen true religion shown in domestic life, now, we begin to trace its effects upon the concerns of kingdoms and nations. Exodus signifies "the departure;" the chief event therein recorded is the departure of Israel from Egypt and Egyptian bondage; it plainly points out the fulfilling of several promises and prophecies to Abraham respecting his seed, and shadows forth the state of the church, in the wilderness of this world, until her arrival at the heavenly Canaan, an eternal rest.

Chapter 1

Chapter Outline

The children of Israel increase in Egypt after the death of Joseph.	(8–14)
They are oppressed, but multiply exceedingly.	(1–7)
The men-children destroyed.	(15–22)

Verses 1-7

During more than 200 years, while Abraham, Isaac, and Jacob lived at liberty, the Hebrews increased slowly; only about seventy persons went down into Egypt. There, in about the same number of years, though under cruel bondage, they became a large nation. This wonderful increase was according to the promise long before made unto the fathers. Though the performance of God's promises is sometimes slow, it is always sure.

Verses 8-14

The land of Egypt became to Israel a house of bondage. The place where we have been happy, may soon become the place of our affliction; and that may prove the greatest cross to us, of which we said, This same shall comfort us. Cease from man, and say not of any place on this side heaven, This is my rest. All that knew Joseph, loved him, and were kind to his brethren for his sake; but the best and most useful services a man does to others, are soon forgotten after his death. Our great care should be, to serve God, and to please him who is not unrighteous, whatever men are, to forget our work and labour of love. The offence of Israel is, that he prospers. There is no sight more hateful to a wicked man than the prosperity of the righteous. The Egyptians feared lest the children of Israel should join their enemies, and get them up out of the land. Wickedness is ever cowardly and unjust; it makes a man fear, where no fear is, and flee, when no one pursues him. And human wisdom often is foolishness, and very sinful. God's people had task-masters set over them, not only to burden them, but to afflict them with their burdens. They not only made them serve for Pharaoh's profit, but so that their lives became bitter. The Israelites wonderfully increased. Christianity spread most when it was persecuted: the blood of the martyrs was the seed of the church. They that take counsel against the Lord and his Israel, do but imagine a vain thing, and create greater vexation to themselves.

Verses 15-22

The Egyptians tried to destroy Israel by the murder of their children. The enmity that is in the seed of the serpent, against the Seed of the woman, makes men forget all pity. It is plain that the Hebrews were now under an uncommon blessing. And we see that the services done for God's Israel are often repaid in kind. Pharaoh gave orders to drown all the male children of the Hebrews. The enemy who, by Pharaoh, attempted to destroy the church in this its infant state, is busy to stifle the rise of serious reflections in the heart of man. Let those who would escape, be afraid of sinning, and cry directly and fervently to the Lord for assistance.

Chapter 2

Chapter Outline

Moses is born, and exposed on the river.	(1–4)
He is found, and brought up by Pharaoh's daughter.	(5–10)
Moses slays an Egyptian, and flees to Midian.	(11–15)
Moses marries the daughter of Jethro.	(16–22)
God hears the Israelites.	(23–25)

Verses 1-4

Observe the order of Providence: just at the time when Pharaoh's cruelty rose to its height by ordering the Hebrew children to be drowned, the deliverer was born. When men are contriving the ruin of the church, God is preparing for its salvation. The parents of Moses saw he was a goodly child. A lively faith can take encouragement from the least hint of the Divine favour. It is said, Heb 11:23, that the parents of Moses hid him by faith; they had the promise that Israel should be preserved, which they relied upon. Faith in God's promise quickens to the use of lawful means for obtaining mercy. Duty is ours, events are God's. Faith in God will set us above the fear of man. At three months' end, when they could not hide the infant any longer, they put him in an ark of bulrushes by the river's brink, and set his sister to watch. And if the weak affection of a mother were thus careful, what shall we think of Him, whose love, whose compassion is, as himself, boundless. Moses never had a stronger protection about him, no, not when all the Israelites were round his tent in the wilderness, than now, when he lay alone, a helpless babe upon the waves. No water, no Egyptian can hurt him. When we seem most neglected and forlorn, God is most present with us.

Verses 5-10

Come, see the place where that great man, Moses, lay, when he was a little child; it was in a bulrush basket by the river's side. Had he been left there long, he must have perished. But Providence brings Pharaoh's daughter to the place where this poor forlorn infant lay, and inclines her heart to pity it, which she dares do, when none else durst. God's care of us in our infancy ought to be often mentioned by us to his praise. Pharaoh cruelly sought to destroy Israel, but his own daughter had pity on a Hebrew child, and not only so, but, without knowing it, preserved Israel's deliverer, and provided Moses with a good nurse, even his own mother. That he should have a Hebrew nurse, the sister of Moses brought the mother into the place of a nurse. Moses was treated as the son of Pharoah's daughter. Many who, by their birth, are obscure and poor, by surprising events of Providence, are raised high in the world, to make men know that God rules.

Verses 11-15

Moses boldly owned the cause of God's people. It is plain from Heb 11. that this was done in faith, with the full purpose of leaving the honours, wealth, and pleasures of his rank among the Egyptians. By the grace of God he was a partaker of faith in Christ, which overcomes the world. He was willing, not only to risk all, but to suffer for his sake; being assured that Israel were the people of God. By special warrant from Heaven, which makes no rule for other cases, Moses slew an Egyptian, and rescued an oppressed Israelites. Also, he tried to end a dispute between two Hebrews. The reproof Moses gave, may still be of use. May we not apply it to disputants, who, by their fierce debates, divide and weaken the Christian church? They forget that they are brethren. He that did wrong quarreled with Moses. It is a sign of guilt to be angry at reproof. Men know not what they do, nor what enemies they are to themselves, when they resist and despise faithful reproofs and reprovers. Moses might have said, if this be the spirit of the Hebrews, I will go to court again, and be the son of Pharaoh's daughter. But we must take heed of being set against the ways and people of God, by the follies and peevishness of some persons that profess religion. Moses was obliged to flee into the land of Midian. God ordered this for wise and holy ends.

Verses 16-22

Moses found shelter in Midian. He was ready to help Reuel's daughters to water their flocks, although bred in learning and at court. Moses loved to be doing justice, and to act in defence of such as he saw injured, which every man ought to do, as far as it is in his power. He loved to be doing good; wherever the providence of God casts us, we should desire and try to be useful; and when we cannot do the good we would, we must be ready to do the good we can. Moses commended himself to the prince of Midian; who married one of his daughters to Moses, by whom he had a son, called Gershom, "a stranger there," that he might keep in remembrance the land in which he had been a stranger.

Verses 23-25

The Israelites' bondage in Egypt continued, though the murdering of their infants did not continue. Sometimes the Lord suffers the rod of the wicked to lie very long and very heavy on the lot of the righteous. At last they began to think of God under their troubles. It is a sign that the Lord is coming towards us with deliverance, when he inclines and enables us to cry to him for it. God heard their groaning; he made it to appear that he took notice of their complaints. He remembered his covenant, of which he is ever mindful. He considered this, and not any merit of theirs. He looked upon the children of Israel. Moses looked upon them, and pitied them; but now God looked upon them, and helped them. He had respect unto them. His eyes are now fixed upon Israel, to show himself in their behalf. God is ever thus, a very present help in trouble. Take courage then, ye who, conscious of guilt and thraldom, are looking to Him for deliverance. God in Christ Jesus is also looking upon you. A call of love is joined with a promise of the Redeemer. Come unto me, all ye that labour and are heavy laden, and I will give you rest, Mt 11:28.

Chapter 3

Chapter Outline

God appears to Moses in a burning bush.	(1–6)
God sends Moses to deliver Israel.	(7–10)
The name Jehovah.	(11–15)
The deliverance of the Israelites promised.	(16–22)

Verses 1-6

The years of the life of Moses are divided into three forties; the first forty he spent as a prince in Pharaoh's court, the second as a shepherd in Midian, the third as a king in Jeshurun. How changeable is the life of man! The first appearance of God to Moses, found him tending sheep. This seems a poor employment for a man of his parts and education, yet he rests satisfied with it; and thus learns meekness and contentment, for which he is more noted in sacred writ, than for all his learning. Satan loves to find us idle; God is pleased when he finds us employed. Being alone, is a good friend to our communion with God. To his great surprise, Moses saw a bush burning without fire to kindle it. The bush burned, and yet did not burn away; an emblem of the church in bondage in Egypt. And it fitly reminds us of the church in every age, under its severest persecutions kept by the presence of God from being destroyed. Fire is an emblem, in Scripture, of the Divine holiness and justice, also of the afflictions and trials with which God proves and purifies his people, and even of that baptism of the Holy Ghost, by which sinful affections are consumed, and the soul changed into the Divine nature and image. God gave Moses a gracious call, to which he returned a ready answer. Those that would have communion with God, must attend upon him in the ordinances wherein he is pleased to manifest himself and his glory, though it be in a bush. Putting off the shoe was a token of respect and submission. We ought to draw nigh to God with a solemn pause and preparation, carefully avoiding every thing that looks light and rude, and unbecoming his service.

God does not say, I was the God of Abraham, Isaac, and Jacob, but I am. The patriarchs still live, so many years after their bodies have been in the grave. No length of time can separate the souls of the just from their Maker. By this, God instructed Moses as to another world, and strengthened his belief of a future state. Thus it is interpreted by our Lord Jesus, who, from hence, proves that the dead are raised, Lu 20:37. Moses hid his face, as if both ashamed and afraid to look upon God. The more we see of God, and his grace, and covenant love, the more cause we shall see to worship him with reverence and godly fear.

Verses 7-10

God notices the afflictions of Israel. Their sorrows; even the secret sorrows of God's people are known to him. Their cry; God hears the cries of his afflicted people. The oppression they endured; the highest and greatest of their oppressors are not above him. God promises speedy deliverance by methods out of the common ways of providence. Those whom God, by his grace, delivers out of a spiritual Egypt, he will bring to a heavenly Canaan. (Ex 3:11-15)

Verses 11-15

Formerly Moses thought himself able to deliver Israel, and set himself to the work too hastily. Now, when the fittest person on earth for it, he knows his own weakness. This was the effect of more knowledge of God and of himself. Formerly, self-confidence mingled with strong faith and great zeal, now sinful distrust of God crept in under the garb of humility; so defective are the strongest graces and the best duties of the most eminent saints. But all objections are answered in, Certainly I will be with thee. That is enough. Two names God would now be known by. A name that denotes what he is in himself, I AM THAT I AM. This explains his name Jehovah, and signifies, 1. That he is self-existent: he has his being of himself. 2. That he is eternal and unchangeable, and always the same, yesterday, to-day, and for ever. 3. That he is incomprehensible; we cannot by searching find him out: this name checks all bold and curious inquiries concerning God. 4. That he is faithful and true to all his promises, unchangeable in his word as well as in his nature; let Israel know this, I AM hath sent me unto you. I am, and there is none else besides me. All else have their being from God, and are wholly dependent upon him. Also, here is a name that denotes what God is to his people. The Lord God of your fathers sent me unto you. Moses must revive among them the religion of their fathers, which was almost lost; and then they might expect the speedy performance of the promises made unto their fathers.

Verses 16-22

Moses' success with the elders of Israel would be good. God, who, by his grace, inclines the heart, and opens the ear, could say beforehand, They shall hearken to thy voice; for he would make them willing in this day of power. As to Pharaoh, Moses is here told that petitions and persuasions, and humble complaints, would not prevail with him; nor a mighty hand stretched out in signs and wonders. But those will certainly be broken by the power of God's hand, who will not bow to the power of his word. Pharaoh's people should furnish Israel with riches at their departure. In Pharaoh's tyranny and Israel's oppression, we see the miserable, abject state of sinners. However galling the yoke, they drudge on till the Lord sends redemption. With the invitations of the gospel, God sends the teaching of his Spirit. Thus are men made willing to seek and to strive for deliverance. Satan loses his power to hold them, they come forth with all they have and are, and apply all to the glory of God and the service of his church.

Chapter 4

Chapter Outline

Verses 1-9

Moses objects, that the people would not take his word, unless he showed them some sign. God gives him power to work miracles. But those who are now employed to deliver God's messages to men, need not the power to work miracles: their character and their doctrines are to be tried by that word of God to which they appeal. These miracles especially referred to the miracles of the Lord Jesus Christ. It belonged to Him only, to cast the power of the devil out of the soul, and to heal the soul of the leprosy of sin; and so it was for Him first to cast the devil out of the body, and to heal the leprosy of the body.

Verses 10-17

Moses continued backward to the work God designed him for; there was much of cowardice, slothfulness, and unbelief in him. We must not judge of men by the readiness of their discourse. A great deal of wisdom and true worth may be with a slow tongue. God sometimes makes choice of those as his messengers, who have the least of the advantages of art or nature, that his grace in them may appear the more glorious. Christ's disciples were no orators, till the Holy Spirit made them such. God condescends to answer the excuse of Moses. Even self-diffidence, when it hinders us from duty, or clogs us in duty, is very displeasing to the Lord. But while we blame Moses for shrinking from this dangerous service, let us ask our own hearts if we are not neglecting duties more easy, and less perilous. The tongue of Aaron, with the head and heart of Moses, would make one completely fit for this errand. God promises, I will be with thy mouth, and with his mouth. Even Aaron, who could speak well, yet could not speak to purpose, unless God gave constant teaching and help; for without the constant aid of Divine grace, the best gifts will fail.

Verses 18-23

After God had appeared in the bush, he often spake to Moses. Pharaoh had hardened his own heart against the groans and cries of the oppressed Israelites; and now God, in the way of righteous judgment, hardens his heart against the teaching of the miracles, and the terror of the plagues. But whether Pharaoh will hear, or whether he will forbear, Moses must tell him, Thus saith the Lord. He must demand a discharge for Israel, Let my son go; not only my servant, whom thou hast no right to detain, but my son. It is my son that serves me, and therefore must be spared, must be pleaded for. In case of refusal I will slay thy son, even thy first-born. As men deal with God's people, let them expect so to be dealt with.

Verses 24-31

God met Moses in anger. The Lord threatened him with death or sent sickness upon him, as the punishment of his having neglected to circumcise his son. When God discovers to us what is amiss in our lives, we must give all diligence to amend it speedily. This is the voice of every rod; it calls us to return to Him that smites us. God sent Aaron to meet Moses. The more they saw of God's bringing them together, the more pleasant their interview was. The elders of Israel met them in faith, and were ready to obey them. It often happens, that less difficulty is found than was expected, in such undertakings as are according to the will of God, and for his glory. Let us but arise and try at our proper work, the Lord will be with us and prosper us. If Israel welcomed the tidings of their deliverance, and worshipped the Lord, how should we welcome the glad tidings of redemption, embrace it in faith, and adore the Redeemer!

Chapter 5

Chapter Outline

Verses 1-9

God will own his people, though poor and despised, and will find a time to plead their cause. Pharaoh treated all he had heard with contempt. He had no knowledge of Jehovah, no fear of him, no love to him, and therefore refused to obey him. Thus Pharaoh's pride, ambition, covetousness, and political knowledge, hardened him to his own destruction. What Moses and Aaron ask is very reasonable, only to go three days' journey into the desert, and that on a good errand. We will sacrifice unto the Lord our God. Pharaoh was very unreasonable, in saying that the people were idle, and therefore talked of going to sacrifice. He thus misrepresents them, that he might have a pretence to add to their burdens. To this day we find many who are more disposed to find fault with their neighbours, for spending in the service of God a few hours spared from their wordly business, than to blame others, who give twice the time to sinful pleasures. Pharaoh's command was barbarous. Moses and Aaron themselves must get to the burdens. Persecutors take pleasure in putting contempt and hardship upon ministers. The usual tale of bricks must be made, without the usual allowance of straw to mix with the clay. Thus more work was to be laid upon the men, which, if they performed, they would be broken with labour; and if not, they would be punished.

Verses 10-23

The Egyptian task-masters were very severe. See what need we have to pray that we may be delivered from wicked men. The head-workmen justly complained to Pharaoh: but he taunted them. The malice of Satan has often represented the service and worship of God, as fit employment only for those who have nothing else to do, and the business only of the idle; whereas, it is the duty of those who are most busy in the world. Those who are diligent in doing sacrifice to the Lord, will, before God, escape the doom of the slothful servant, though with men they do not. The Israelites should have humbled themselves before God, and have taken to themselves the shame of their sin; but instead of that, they quarrel with those who were to be their deliverers. Moses returned to the Lord. He knew that what he had said and done, was by God's direction; and therefore appeals to him. When we find ourselves at any time perplexed in the way of our duty, we ought to go to God, and lay open our case before him by fervent prayer. Disappointments in our work must not drive us from our God, but still we must ponder why they are sent.

Chapter 6

Chapter Outline

God renews his promise.   (1–9)

Moses and Aaron again sent to Pharaoh.   (10–13)

The parentage of Moses and Aaron.   (14–30)

Verses 1-9

We are most likely to prosper in attempts to glorify God, and to be useful to men, when we learn by experience that we can do nothing of ourselves; when our whole dependence is placed on him, and our only expectation is from him. Moses had been expecting what God would do; but now he shall see what he will do. God would now be known by his name Jehovah, that is, a God performing what he had promised, and finishing his own work. God intended their happiness: I will take you to me for a people, a peculiar people, and I will be to you a God. More than this we need not ask, we cannot have, to make us happy. He intended his own glory: Ye shall know that I am the Lord. These good words, and comfortable words, should have revived the drooping Israelites, and have made them forget their misery; but they were so taken up with their troubles, that they did not heed God's promises. By indulging discontent and fretfulness, we deprive ourselves of the comfort we might have, both from God's word and from his providence, and go comfortless.

Verses 10-13

The faith of Moses was so feeble that he could scarcely be kept to his work. Ready obedience is always according to the strength of our faith. Though our weaknesses ought to humble us, yet they ought not to discourage us from doing our best in any service we have to do for God. When Moses repeats his baffled arguments, he is argued with no longer, but God gives him and Aaron a charge, both to the children of Israel, and to Pharaoh. God's authority is sufficient to answer all objections, and binds all to obey, without murmuring or disputing, Php 2:14.

Verses 14-30

Moses and Aaron were Israelites; raised up unto them of their brethren, as Christ also should be, who was to be the Prophet and Priest, the Redeemer and Lawgiver of the people of Israel. Moses returns to his narrative, and repeats the charge God had given him to deliver his message to Pharaoh, and his objection against it. Those who have spoken unadvisedly with their lips ought to reflect upon it with regret, as Moses seems to do here. "Uncircumcised," is used in Scripture to note the unsuitableness there may be in any thing to answer its proper purpose; as the carnal heart and depraved nature of fallen man are wholly unsuited to the services of God, and to the purposes of his glory. It is profitable to place no confidence in ourselves, all our sufficiency must be in the Lord. We never can trust ourselves too little, or our God too much. I can do nothing by myself, said the apostle, but I can do all things through Christ which strengtheneth me.

Chapter 7

Chapter Outline

Moses and Aaron encouraged.	(1–7)
The rods turned into serpents, Pharaoh's heart is hardened.	(8–13)
The river is turned into blood, The distress of the Egyptians.	(14–25)

Verses 1-7

God glorifies himself. He makes people know that he is Jehovah. Israel is made to know it by the performance of his promises to them, and the Egyptians by the pouring out of his wrath upon them. Moses, as the ambassador of Jehovah, speaking in his name, laid commands upon Pharaoh, denounced threatenings against him, and called for judgments upon him. Pharaoh, proud and great as he was, could not resist. Moses stood not in awe of Pharaoh, but made him tremble. This seems to be meant in the words, Thou shalt be a god unto Pharaoh. At length Moses is delivered from his fears. He makes no more objections, but, being strengthened in faith, goes about his work with courage, and proceeds in it with perseverance.

Verses 8-13

What men dislike, because it opposes their pride and lusts, they will not be convinced of; but it is easy to cause them to believe things they wish to be true. God always sends with his word full proofs of its Divine authority; but when men are bent to disobey, and willing to object, he often permits a snare to be laid wherein they are entangled. The magicians were cheats, trying to copy the real miracles of Moses by secret sleights or jugglings, which to a small extent they succeeded in doing, so as to deceive the bystanders, but they were at length obliged to confess they could not any longer imitate the effects of Divine power. None assist more in the destruction of sinners, than such as resist the truth by amusing men with a counterfeit resemblance of it. Satan is most to be dreaded when transformed into an angel of light.

Verses 14-25

Here is the first of the ten plagues, the turning of the water into blood. It was a dreadful plague. The sight of such vast rolling streams of blood could not but strike horror. Nothing is more common than water: so wisely has Providence ordered it, and so kindly, that what is so needful and serviceable to the comfort of human life, should be cheap and almost every where to be had; but now the Egyptians must either drink blood, or die for thirst. Egypt was a pleasant land, but the dead fish and blood now rendered it very unpleasant. It was a righteous plague, and justly sent upon the Egyptians; for Nile, the river of Egypt, was their idol. That creature which we idolize, God justly takes from us, or makes bitter to us. They had stained the river with the blood of the Hebrews' children, and now God made that river all blood. Never any thirsted after blood, but sooner or later they had enough of it. It was a significant plague; Egypt had great dependence upon their river, Zec 14:18; so that in smiting the river, they were warned of the destruction of all the produce of their country. The love of Christ to his disciples changes all their common mercies into spiritual blessings; the anger of God towards his enemies, renders their most valued advantages a curse and a misery to them. Aaron is to summon the plague by smiting the river with his rod. It was done in the sight of Pharaoh and his attendants, for God's true miracles were not performed as Satan's lying wonders; truth seeks no corners. See the almighty power of God. Every creature is that to us which he makes it to be water or blood. See what changes we may meet with in the things of this world; what is always vain, may soon become vexatious. See what mischievous work sin makes. If the things that have been our comforts prove our crosses, we must thank ourselves. It is sin that turns our waters into blood. The plague continued seven days; and in all that time Pharaoh's proud heart would not let him desire Moses to pray for the removal of it. Thus the hypocrites in heart heap up wrath. No wonder that God's anger is not turned away, but that his hand is stretched out still.

Chapter 8

Chapter Outline

Verses 1-15

Pharaoh is plagued with frogs; their vast numbers made them sore plagues to the Egyptians. God could have plagued Egypt with lions, or bears, or wolves, or with birds of prey, but he chose to do it by these despicable creatures. God, when he pleases, can arm the smallest parts of the creation against us. He thereby humbled Pharaoh. They should neither eat, nor drink, nor sleep in quiet; but wherever they were, they should be troubled by the frogs. God's curse upon a man will pursue him wherever he goes, and lie heavy upon him whatever he does. Pharaoh gave way under this plague. He promises that he will let the people go. Those who bid defiance to God and prayer, first or last, will be made to see their need of both. But when Pharaoh saw there was respite, he hardened his heart. Till the heart is renewed by the grace of God, the thoughts made by affliction do not abide; the convictions wear off, and the promises that were given are forgotten. Till the state of the air is changed, what thaws in the sun will freeze again in the shade.

Verses 16-19

These lice were produced out of the dust of the earth; out of any part of the creation God can fetch a scourge, with which to correct those who rebel against him. Even the dust of the earth obeys him. These lice were very troublesome, as well as disgraceful to the Egyptians, whose priests were obliged to take much pains that no vermin ever should be found about them. All the plagues inflicted on the Egyptians, had reference to their national crimes, or were rendered particularly severe by their customs. The magicians attempted to imitate it, but they could not. It forced them to confess, This is the finger of God! The check and restraint put upon us, must needs be from a Divine power. Sooner or later God will force even his enemies to acknowledge his own power. Pharaoh, notwithstanding this, was more and more obstinate.

Verses 20-32

Pharaoh was early at his false devotions to the river; and shall we be for more sleep and more slumber, when any service to the Lord is to be done? The Egyptians and the Hebrews were to be marked in the plague of flies. The Lord knows them that are his, and will make it appear, perhaps in this world, certainly in the other, that he has set them apart for himself. Pharaoh unwillingly entered into a treaty with Moses and Aaron. He is content they should sacrifice to their God, provided they would do it in the land of Egypt. But it would be an abomination to God, should they offer the Egyptian sacrifices; and it would be an abomination to the Egyptians, should they offer to God the objects of the worship of the Egyptians, namely, their calves or oxen. Those who would offer acceptable sacrifice to God, must separate themselves from the wicked and profane. They must also retire from the world. Israel cannot keep the feast of the Lord, either among the brick-kilns or among the flesh-pots of Egypt. And they must sacrifice as God shall command, not otherwise. Though they were in slavery to Pharaoh, yet they must obey God's commands. Pharaoh consents for them to go into the wilderness, provided they do not go so far but that he might fetch them back again. Thus, some sinners, in a pang of conviction, part with their sins, yet are loth they should go very far away; for when the fright is over, they will turn to them again. Moses promised the removal of this plague. But let not Pharaoh deal deceitfully any more. Be not deceived; God is not mocked: if we think to cheat God by a sham repentance and a false surrender of ourselves to him, we shall put a fatal cheat upon our own souls. Pharaoh returned to his hardness. Reigning lusts break through the strongest bonds, and make men presume and go from their word. Many seem in earnest, but there is some reserve, some beloved, secret sin. They are unwilling to look upon themselves as in danger of everlasting misery. They will refrain from other sins; they do much, give much, and even punish themselves much. They will leave it off sometimes, and, as it were, let their sin depart a little way; but will not make up their minds to part with all and follow Christ, bearing the cross. Rather than that, they venture all. They are sorrowful, but depart from Christ, determined to keep the world at present, and they hope for some future season, when salvation may be had without such costly sacrifices; but, at length, the poor sinner is driven away in his wickedness, and left without hope to lament his folly.

Chapter 9

Chapter Outline

Verses 1-7

God will have Israel released, Pharaoh opposes it, and the trial is, whose word shall stand. The hand of the Lord at once is upon the cattle, many of which, some of all kinds, die by a sort of murrain. This was greatly to the loss of the owners; they had made Israel poor, and now God would make them poor. The hand of God is to be seen, even in the sickness and death of cattle; for a sparrow falls not to the ground without our Father. None of the Israelites' cattle should die; the Lord shall sever. The cattle died. The Egyptians worshipped their cattle. What we make an idol of, it is just with God to remove from us. This proud tyrant and cruel oppressor deserved to be made an example by the just Judge of the universe. None who are punished according to what they deserve, can have any just cause to complain. Hardness of heart denotes that state of mind upon which neither threatenings nor promise, neither judgements nor mercies, make any abiding impression. The conscience being stupified, and the heart filled with pride and presumption, they persist in unbelief and disobedience. This state of mind is also called the stony heart. Very different is the heart of flesh, the broken and contrite heart. Sinners have none to blame but themselves, for that pride and ungodliness which abuse the bounty and patience of God. For, however the Lord hardens the hearts of men, it is always as a punishment of former sins.

Verses 8-12

When the Egyptians were not wrought upon by the death of their cattle, God sent a plague that seized their own bodies. If lesser judgments do not work, God will send greater. Sometimes God shows men their sin in their punishment. They had oppressed Israel in the furnaces, and now the ashes of the furnace are made a terror to them. The plague itself was very grievous. The magicians themselves were struck with these boils. Their power was restrained before; but they continued to withstand Moses, and to confirm Pharaoh in his unbelief, till they were forced to give way. Pharaoh continued obstinate. He had hardened his own heart, and now God justly gave him up to his own heart's lusts, permitting Satan to blind and harden him. If men shut their eyes against the light, it is just with God to close their eyes. This is the sorest judgment a man can be under out of hell.

Verses 13-21

Moses is here ordered to deliver a dreadful message to Pharaoh. Providence ordered it, that Moses should have a man of such a fierce and stubborn spirit as this Pharaoh to deal with; and every thing made it a most signal instance of the power of God has to humble and bring down the proudest of his enemies. When God's justice threatens ruin, his mercy at the same time shows a way of escape from it. God not only distinguished between Egyptians and Israelites, but between some Egyptians and others. If Pharaoh will not yield, and so prevent the judgment itself, yet those that will take warning, may take shelter. Some believed the things which were spoken, and they feared, and housed their servants and cattle, and it was their wisdom. Even among the servants of Pharaoh, some trembled at God's word; and shall not the sons of Israel dread it? But others believed not, and left their cattle in the field. Obstinate unbelief is deaf to the fairest warnings, and the wisest counsels, which leaves the blood of those that perish upon their own heads.

Verses 22-35

Woful havoc this hail made: it killed both men and cattle; the corn above ground was destroyed, and that only preserved which as yet was not come up. The land of Goshen was preserved. God causes rain or hail on one city and not on another, either in mercy or in judgment. Pharaoh humbled himself to Moses. No man could have spoken better: he owns himself wrong; he owns that the Lord is righteous; and God must be justified when he speaks, though he speaks in thunder and lightning. Yet his heart was hardened all this while. Moses pleads with God: though he had reason to think Pharaoh would repent of his repentance, and he told him so, yet he promises to be his friend. Moses went out of the city, notwithstanding the hail and lightning which kept Pharaoh and his servants within doors. Peace with God makes men thunder-proof. Pharaoh was frightened by the tremendous judgment; but when that was over, his fair promises were forgotten. Those that are not bettered by judgments and mercies, commonly become worse.

Chapter 10

Chapter Outline

Verses 1-11

The plagues of Egypt show the sinfulness of sin. They warn the children of men not to strive with their Maker. Pharaoh had pretended to humble himself; but no account was made of it, for he was not sincere therein. The plague of locusts is threatened. This should be much worse than any of that kind which had ever been known. Pharaoh's attendants persuade him to come to terms with Moses. Hereupon Pharaoh will allow the men to go, falsely pretending that this was all they desired. He swears that they shall not remove their little ones. Satan does all he can to hinder those that serve God themselves, from bringing their children to serve him. He is a sworn enemy to early piety. Whatever would put us from engaging our children in God's service, we have reason to suspect Satan in it. Nor should the young forget that the Lord's counsel is, Remember thy Creator in the days of thy youth; but Satan's counsel is, to keep children in a state of slavery to sin and to the world. Mark that the great foe of man wishes to retain him by the ties of affection, as Pharaoh would have taken hostages from the Israelites for their return, by holding their wives and children in captivity. Satan is willing to share our duty and our service with the Saviour, because the Saviour will not accept those terms.

Verses 12-20

God bids Moses stretch out his hand; locusts came at the call. An army might more easily have been resisted than this host of insects. Who then is able to stand before the great God? They covered the face of the earth, and ate up the fruit of it. Herbs grow for the service of man; yet when God pleases, insects shall plunder him, and eat the bread out of his mouth. Let our labour be, not for the habitation and meat thus exposed, but for those which endure to eternal life. Pharaoh employs Moses and Aaron to pray for him. There are those, who, in distress, seek the help of other people's prayers, but have no mind to pray for themselves. They show thereby that they have no true love to God, nor any delight in communion with him. Pharaoh desires only that this death might be taken away, not this sin. He wishes to get rid of the plague of locusts, not the plague of a hard heart, which was more dangerous. An east wind brought the locusts, a west wind carries them off. Whatever point the wind is in, it is fulfilling God's word, and turns by his counsel. The wind bloweth where it listeth, as to us; but not so as it respects God. It was also an argument for their repentance; for by this it appeared that God is ready to forgive, and swift to show mercy. If he does this upon the outward tokens of humiliation, what will he do if we are sincere! Oh that this goodness of God might lead us to repentance! Pharaoh returned to his resolution again, not to let the people go. Those who have often baffled their convictions, are justly given up to the lusts of their hearts.

Verses 21-29

The plague of darkness brought upon Egypt was a dreadful plague. It was darkness which might be felt, so thick were the fogs. It astonished and terrified. It continued three days; six nights in one; so long the most lightsome palaces were dungeons. Now Pharaoh had time to consider, if he would have improved it. Spiritual darkness is spiritual bondage; while Satan blinds men's eyes that they see not, he binds their hands and feet, that they work not for God, nor move toward heaven. They sit in darkness. It was righteous with God thus to punish. The blindness of their minds brought upon them this darkness of the air; never was mind so blinded as Pharaoh's, never was air so darkened as Egypt. Let us dread the consequences of sin; if three days of darkness were so dreadful, what will everlasting darkness be? The children of Israel, at the same time, had light in their dwellings. We must not think we share in common mercies as a matter of course, and therefore that we owe no thanks to God for them. It shows the particular favour he bears to his people. Wherever there is an Israelite indeed, though in this dark world, there is light, there is a child of light. When God made this difference between the Israelites and the Egyptians, who would not have preferred the poor cottage of an Israelite to the fine palace of an Egyptian? There is a real difference between the house of the wicked, which is under a curse, and the habitation of the just, which is blessed. Pharaoh renewed the treaty with Moses and Aaron, and consented they should take their little ones, but would have their cattle left. It is common for sinners to bargain with God Almighty; thus they try to mock him, but they deceive themselves. The terms of reconciliation with God are so fixed, that though men dispute them ever so long, they cannot possibly alter them, or bring them lower. We must come to the demand of God's will; we cannot expect he should condescend to the terms our lusts would make. With ourselves and our children, we must devote all our worldly possessions to the service of God; we know not what use he will make of any part of what we have. Pharaoh broke off the conference abruptly, and resolved to treat no more. Had he forgotten how often he had sent for Moses to ease him of his plagues? and must he now be bid to come no more? Vain malice! to threaten him with death, who was armed with such power! What will not hardness of heart, and contempt of God's word and commandments, bring men to! After this, Moses came no more till he was sent for. When men drive God's word from them, he justly gives them up to their own delusions.

Chapter 11

Chapter Outline

God's last instructions to Moses respecting   (1–3)
Pharaoh and the Egyptians.

The death of the first-born threatened.   (4–10)

Verses 1-3

A secret revelation was made to Moses while in the presence of Pharaoh, that he might give warning of the last dreadful judgment, before he went out. This was the last day of the servitude of Israel; they were about to go away. Their masters, who had abused them in their work, would have sent them away empty; but God provided that the labourers should not lose their hire, and ordered them to demand it now, at their departure, and it was given to them. God will right the injured, who in humble silence commit their cause to him; and none are losers at last by patient suffering. The Lord gave them favour in the sight of the Egyptians, by making it appear how much he favoured them. He also changed the spirit of the Egyptians toward them, and made them to be pitied of their oppressors. Those that honour God, he will honour.

Verses 4-10

The death of all the first-born in Egypt at once: this plague had been the first threatened, but is last executed. See how slow God is to wrath. The plague is foretold, the time is fixed; all their first-born should sleep the sleep of death, not silently, but so as to rouse the families at midnight. The prince was not too high to be reached by it, nor the slaves at the mill too low to be noticed. While angels slew the Egyptians, not so much as a dog should bark at any of the children of Israel. It is an earnest of the difference there shall be in the great day, between God's people and his enemies. Did men know what a difference God puts, and will put to eternity, between those that serve him and those that serve him not, religion would not seem to them an indifferent thing; nor would they act in it with so much carelessness as they do. When Moses had thus delivered his message, he went out from Pharaoh in great anger at his obstinacy; though he was the meekest of the men of the earth. The Scripture has foretold the unbelief of many who hear the gospel, that it might not be a surprise or stumbling-block to us, Ro 10:16. Let us never think the worse of the gospel of Christ for the slights men put upon it. Pharaoh was hardened, yet he was compelled to abate his stern and haughty demands, till the Israelites got full freedom. In like manner the people of God will find that every struggle against their spiritual adversary, made in the might of Jesus Christ, every attempt to overcome him by the blood of the Lamb, and every desire to attain increasing likeness and love to that Lamb, will be rewarded by increasing freedom from the enemy of souls.

Chapter 12

Chapter Outline

The beginning of the year changed, The   (1–20)
passover instituted.

Verses 1-20

The Lord makes all things new to those whom he delivers from the bondage of Satan, and takes to himself to be his people. The time when he does this is to them the beginning of a new life. God appointed that, on the night wherein they were to go out of Egypt, each family should kill a lamb, or that two or three families, if small, should kill one lamb. This lamb was to be eaten in the manner here directed, and the blood to be sprinkled on the door-posts, to mark the houses of the Israelites from those of the Egyptians. The angel of the Lord, when destroying the first-born of the Egyptians, would pass over the houses marked by the blood of the lamb: hence the name of this holy feast or ordinance. The passover was to be kept every year, both as a remembrance of Israel's preservation and deliverance out of Egypt, and as a remarkable type of Christ. Their safety and deliverance were not a reward of their own righteousness, but the gift of mercy. Of this they were reminded, and by this ordinance they were taught, that all blessings came to them through the shedding and sprinkling of blood. Observe, 1. The paschal lamb was typical. Christ is our passover, 1Co 5:7. Christ is the Lamb of God, Joh 1:29; often in the Revelation he is called the Lamb. It was to be in its prime; Christ offered up himself in the midst of his days, not when a babe at Bethlehem. It was to be without blemish; the Lord Jesus was a Lamb without spot: the judge who condemned Christ declared him innocent. It was to be set apart four days before, denoting the marking out of the Lord Jesus to be a Saviour, both in the purpose and in the promise. It was to be slain, and roasted with fire, denoting the painful sufferings of the Lord Jesus, even unto death, the death of the cross. The wrath of God is as fire, and Christ was made a curse for us. Not a bone of it must be broken, which was fulfilled in Christ, Joh 19:33, denoting the unbroken strength of the Lord Jesus. 2. The sprinkling of the blood was typical. The blood of the lamb must be sprinkled, denoting the applying of the merits of Christ's death to our souls; we must receive the atonement, Ro 5:11. Faith is the bunch of hyssop, by which we apply the promises, and the benefits of the blood of Christ laid up in them, to ourselves. It was to be sprinkled on the door-posts, denoting the open profession we are to make of faith in Christ. It was not to be sprinkled upon the threshold; which cautions us to take heed of trampling under foot the blood of the covenant. It is precious blood, and must be precious to us. The blood, thus sprinkled, was a means of preserving the Israelites from the destroying angel, who had nothing to do where the blood was. The blood of Christ is the believer's protection from the wrath of God, the curse of the law, and the damnation of hell, Ro 8:1. 3. The solemn eating of the lamb was typical of our gospel duty to Christ. The paschal lamb was not to be looked upon only, but to be fed upon. So we must by faith make Christ our own; and we must receive spiritual strength and nourishment from him, as from our food, see Joh 6:53, 55. It was all to be eaten; those who by faith feed upon Christ, must feed upon a whole Christ; they must take Christ and his yoke, Christ and his cross, as well as Christ and his crown. It was to be eaten at once, not put by till morning. To-day Christ is offered, and is to be accepted while it is called to-day, before we sleep the sleep of death. It was to be eaten with bitter herbs, in remembrance of the bitterness of their bondage in Egypt; we must feed upon Christ with sorrow and brokenness of heart, in remembrance of sin. Christ will be sweet to us, if sin be bitter. It was to be eaten standing, with their staves in their hands, as being ready to depart. When we feed upon Christ by faith, we must forsake the rule and the dominion of sin; sit loose to the world, and every thing in it; forsake all for Christ, and reckon it no bad bargain, Heb 13:13, 14. 4. The feast of unleavened bread was typical of the Christian life, 1Co 5:7, 8. Having received Christ Jesus the Lord, we must continually delight ourselves in Christ Jesus. No manner of work must be done, that is, no care admitted and indulged, which does not agree with, or would lessen this holy joy. The Jews were very strict as to the passover, so that no leaven should be found in their houses. It must be a feast kept in charity, without the leaven of malice; and in sincerity, without the leaven of hypocrisy. It was by an ordinance for ever; so long as we live we must continue feeding upon Christ, rejoicing in him always, with thankful mention of the great things he has done for us.

Verses 21-28

That night, when the first-born were to be destroyed, no Israelite must stir out of doors till called to march out of Egypt. Their safety was owing to the blood of sprinkling. If they put themselves from under the protection of that, it was at their peril. They must stay within, to wait for the salvation of the Lord; it is good to do so. In after-times they should carefully teach their children the meaning of this service. It is good for children to ask about the things of God; they that ask for the way will find it. The keeping of this solemnity every year was, 1. To look backward, that they might remember what great things God had done for them and their fathers. Old mercies, to ourselves, or to our fathers, must not be forgotten, that God may be praised, and our faith in him encouraged. 2. It was designed to look forward, as an earnest of the great sacrifice of the Lamb of God in the fulness of time. Christ our passover was sacrificed for us; his death was our life.

Verses 29-36

The Egyptians had been for three days and nights kept in anxiety and horror by the darkness; now their rest is broken by a far more terrible calamity. The plague struck their first-born, the joy and hope of their families. They had slain the Hebrews' children, now God slew theirs. It reached from the throne to the dungeon: prince and peasant stand upon the same level before God's judgments. The destroying angel entered every dwelling unmarked with blood, as the messenger of woe. He did his dreadful errand, leaving not a house in which there was not one dead. Imagine then the cry that rang through the land of Egypt, the long, loud shriek of agony that burst from every dwelling. It will be thus in that dreadful hour when the Son of man shall visit sinners with the last judgment. God's sons, his first-born, were now released. Men had better come to God's terms at first, for he will never come to theirs. Now Pharaoh's pride is abased, and he yields. God's word will stand; we get nothing by disputing, or delaying to submit. In this terror the Egyptians would purchase the favour and the speedy departure of Israel. Thus the Lord took care that their hard-earned wages should be paid, and the people provided for their journey.

Verses 37-42

The children of Israel set forward without delay. A mixed multitude went with them. Some, perhaps, willing to leave their country, laid waste by plagues; others, out of curiosity; perhaps a few out of love to them and their religion. But there were always those among the Israelites who were not Israelites. Thus there are still hypocrites in the church. This great event was 430 years from the promise made to Abraham: see Ga 3:17. So long the promise of a settlement was unfulfilled. But though God's promises are not performed quickly, they will be, in their season. This is that night of the Lord, that remarkable night, to be celebrated in all generations. The great things God does for his people, are to be not only a few days' wonder, but to be remembered throughout all ages; especially the work of our redemption by Christ. This first passover-night was a night of the Lord, much to be observed; but the last passover-night, in which Christ was betrayed and in which the first passover, with the rest of the Jewish ceremonies, was done away, was a night of the Lord, much more to be observed. Then a yoke, heavier than that of Egypt, was broken from off our necks, and a land, better than that of Canaan, set before us. It was a redemption to be celebrated in heaven, for ever and ever.

Verses 43-51

In times to come, all the congregation of Israel must keep the passover. All that share in God's mercies should join in thankful praises for them. The New Testament passover, the Lord's supper, ought not to be neglected by any. Strangers, if circumcised, might eat of the passover. Here is an early indication of favour to the gentiles. This taught the Jews that their being a nation favoured by God, entitled them to their privileges, not their descent from Abraham. Christ our passover is sacrificed for us, 1Co 5:7; his blood is the only ransom for our souls; without the shedding of it there is no remission; without the sprinkling of it there can be no salvation. Have we, by faith in him, sheltered our souls from deserved vengeance under the protection of his atoning blood? Do we keep close to him, constantly depending upon him? Do we so profess our faith in the Redeemer, and our obligations to him, that all who pass by may know to whom we belong? Do we stand prepared for his service, ready to walk in his ways, and to separate ourselves from his enemies? These are questions of vast importance to the soul; may the Lord direct our consciences honestly to answer them.

Chapter 13

Chapter Outline

Joseph's bones carried with the Israelites, (17–20)
They come to Etham.

God guideth the Israelites by a pillar of (21, 22)
cloud fire.

Verses 1-10

In remembrance of the destruction of the first-born of Egypt, both of man and of beast, and the deliverance of the Israelites out of bondage, the first-born males of the Israelites were set apart to the Lord. By this was set before them, that their lives were preserved through the ransom of the atonement, which in due time was to be made for sin. They were also to consider their lives, thus ransomed from death, as now to be consecrated to the service of God. The parents were not to look upon themselves as having any right in their first-born, till they solemnly presented them to God, and allowed his title to them. That which is, by special mercy, spared to us, should be applied to God's honour; at least, some grateful acknowledgment, in works of piety and charity, should be made. The remembrance of their coming out of Egypt must be kept up every year. The day of Christ's resurrection is to be remembered, for in it we were raised up with Christ out of death's house of bondage. The Scripture tells us not expressly what day of the year Christ rose, but it states particularly what day of the week it was; as the more valuable deliverance, it should be remembered weekly. The Israelites must keep the feast of unleavened bread. Under the gospel, we must not only remember Christ, but observe his holy supper. Do this in remembrance of him. Also care must be taken to teach children the knowledge of God. Here is an old law for catechising. It is of great use to acquaint children betimes with the histories of the Bible. And those who have God's law in their heart should have it in their mouth, and often speak of it, to affect themselves, and to teach others.

Verses 11-16

The firstlings of beast not used in sacrifice, were to be changed for others so used, or they were to be destroyed. Our souls are forfeited to God's justice, and unless ransomed by the sacrifice of Christ, will certainly perish. These institutions would continually remind them of their duty, to love and serve the Lord. In like manner, baptism and the Lord's supper, if explained and attended to, would remind us, and give us occasion to remind one another of our profession and duty.

Verses 17-20

There were two ways from Egypt to Canaan. One was only a few days' journey; the other was much further about, through the wilderness, and that was the way in which God chose to lead his people Israel. The Egyptians were to be drowned in the Red sea; the Israelites were to be humbled and proved in the wilderness. God's way is the right way, though it seems about. If we think he leads not his people the nearest way, yet we may be sure he leads them the best way, and so it will appear when we come to our journey's end. The Philistines were powerful enemies; it was needful that the Israelites should be prepared for the wars of Canaan, by passing through the difficulties of the wilderness. Thus God proportions his people's trials to their strength, 1Co 10:13. They went up in good order. They went up in five in a rank, some; in five bands, so others, which it seems rather to their faith and hope, that God would bring them to Canaan, in expectation of which they carried these bones with them while in the desert.

Verses 21, 22

The Lord went before them in a pillar, or appearance of the Divine Majesty. Christ was with the church in the wilderness, 1Co 10:9. Those whom God brings into a wilderness, he will not leave nor lose there, but will take care to lead them through it. It was great satisfaction to Moses and the pious Israelites, to be sure that they were under Divine guidance. Those who make the glory of God their end, and the word of God their rule, the Spirit of God the guide of their affections, and the providence of God the guide of their affairs, may be sure that the Lord goes before them, though they cannot see it with their eyes: we must now live by faith. When Israel marched, this pillar went before, and pointed out the place of encampment, as Divine Wisdom saw fit. It sheltered by day from the heat, and gave light by night. The Bible is a light to our feet, a lantern to our paths, with which the Saviour's love has provided us. It testifies of Christ. It is to us like the pillar to the Israelites. Listen to that voice which cries, I am the Light of the world; he that followeth me shall not walk in darkness, but shall have the Light of life, Joh 8:12. Jesus Christ alone, as shown in the Bible, and as the Holy Spirit, in answer to prayer, recommends him to the soul, is the Way, the Truth, and the Life, Joh 14:6.

Chapter 14

Chapter Outline

Verses 1-9

Pharaoh would think that all Israel was entangled in the wilderness, and so would become an easy prey. But God says, I will be honoured upon Pharaoh. All men being made for the honour of their Maker, those whom he is not honoured by, he will be honoured upon. What seems to tend to the church's ruin, is often overruled to the ruin of the church's enemies. While Pharaoh gratified his malice and revenge, he furthered the bringing to pass God's counsels concerning him. Though with the greatest reason he had let Israel go, yet now he was angry with himself for it. God makes the envy and rage of men against his people, a torment to themselves. Those who set their faces heavenward, and will live godly in Christ Jesus, must expect to be set upon by Satan's temptations and terrors. He will not tamely part with any out of his service.

Verses 10-14

There was no way open to Israel but upward, and thence their deliverance came. We may be in the way of duty, following God, and hastening toward heaven, yet may be troubled on every side. Some cried out unto the Lord; their fear led them to pray, and that was well. God brings us into straits, that he may bring us to our knees. Others cried out against Moses; fear set them murmuring as if God were not still able to work miracles. They quarrel with Moses for bringing them out of Egypt; and so were angry with God for the greatest kindness ever done them; thus gross are the absurdities of unbelief. Moses says, Fear ye not. It is always our duty and interest, when we cannot get out of troubles, yet to get above our fears; let them quicken our prayers and endeavours, but not silence our faith and hope. "Stand still," think not to save yourselves either by fighting or flying; wait God's orders, and observe them. Compose yourselves, by confidence in God, into peaceful thoughts of the great salvation God is about to work for you. If God brings his people into straits, he will find a way to bring them out.

Verses 15-20

Moses' silent prayers of faith prevailed more with God than Israel's loud outcries of fear. The pillar of cloud and fire came behind them, where they needed a guard, and it was a wall between them and their enemies. The word and providence of God have a black and dark side toward sin and sinners, but a bright and pleasant side toward the people of the Lord. He, who divided between light and darkness, Ge 1:4, allotted darkness to the Egyptians, and light to the Israelites. Such a difference there will be between the inheritance of the saints in light, and that utter darkness which will be the portion of hypocrites for ever.

Verses 21-31

The dividing the Red sea was the terror of the Canaanites, Jos 2:9; the praise and triumph of the Israelites, Ps 114:3; 106:9; 136:13. It was a type of baptism, 1Co 10:1, 2. Israel's passage through it was typical of the conversion of souls, Isa 11:15; and the Egyptians being drowned in it was typical of the final ruin of all unrepenting sinners. God showed his almighty power, by opening a passage through the waters, some miles over. God can bring his people through the greatest difficulties, and force a way where he does not find it. It was an instance of his wonderful favour to his Israel. They went through the sea, they walked upon dry land in the midst of the sea. This was done, in order to encourage God's people in all ages to trust him in the greatest straits. What cannot he do who did this? What will not he do for those that fear and love him, who did this for these murmuring, unbelieving Israelites? Then followed the just and righteous wrath of God upon his and his people's enemies. The ruin of sinners is brought on by their own rage and presumption. They might have let Israel alone, and would not; now they would flee from the face of Israel, and cannot. Men will not be convinced, till it is too late, that those who meddle with God's people, meddle to their own hurt. Moses was ordered to stretch out his hand over the sea; the waters returned, and overwhelmed all the host of the Egyptians. Pharaoh and his servants, who had hardened one another in sin, now fell together, not one escaped. The Israelites saw the Egyptians dead upon the sands. The sight very much affected them. While men see God's works, and feel the benefit, they fear him and trust in him. How well were it for us, if we were always in as good a frame as sometimes! Behold the end to which a Christian may look forward. His enemies rage, and are mighty; but while he holds fast by God, he shall pass the waves in safety guarded by that very power of his Saviour, which shall come down on every spiritual foe. The enemies of his soul whom he hath seen to-day, he shall see no more for ever.

Chapter 15

Chapter Outline

Verses 1-21

This song is the most ancient we know of. It is a holy song, to the honour of God, to exalt his name, and celebrate his praise, and his only, not in the least to magnify any man. Holiness to the Lord is in every part of it. It may be considered as typical, and prophetical of the final destruction of the enemies of the church. Happy the people whose God is the Lord. They have work to do, temptations to grapple with, and afflictions to bear, and are weak in themselves; but his grace is their strength. They are often in sorrow, but in him they have comfort; he is their song. Sin, and death, and hell threaten them, but he is, and will be their salvation. The Lord is a God of almighty power, and woe to those that strive with their Maker! He is a God of matchless perfection; he is glorious in holiness; his holiness is his glory. His holiness appears in the hatred of sin, and his wrath against obstinate sinners. It appears in the deliverance of Israel, and his faithfulness to his own promise. He is fearful in praises; that which is matter of praise to the servants of God, is very dreadful to his enemies. He is doing wonders, things out of the common course of nature; wondrous to those in whose favour they are wrought, who are so unworthy, that they had no reason to expect them. There were wonders of power and wonders of grace; in both, God was to be humbly adored.

Verses 22-27

In the wilderness of Shur the Israelites had no water. At Marah they had water, but it was bitter; so that they could not drink it. God can make bitter to us that from which we promise ourselves most, and often does so in the wilderness of this world, that our wants, and disappointments in the creature, may drive us to the Creator, in whose favour alone true comfort is to be had. In this distress the people fretted, and quarrelled with Moses. Hypocrites may show high affections, and appear earnest in religious exercises, but in the time of temptation they fall away. Even true believers, in seasons of sharp trial, will be tempted to fret, distrust, and murmur. But in every trial we should cast our care upon the Lord, and pour out our hearts before him. We shall then find that a submissive will, a peaceful conscience, and the comforts of the Holy Ghost, will render the bitterest trial tolerable, yea, pleasant. Moses did what the people had neglected to do; he cried unto the Lord. And God provided graciously for them. He directed Moses to a tree which he cast into the waters, when, at once, they were made sweet. Some make this tree typical of the cross of Christ, which sweetens the bitter waters of affliction to all the faithful, and enables them to rejoice in tribulation. But a rebellious Israelite shall fare no better than a rebellious Egyptian. The threatening is implied only, the promise is expressed. God is the great Physician. If we are kept well, it is he that keeps us; if we are made well, it is he that recovers us. He is our life and the length of our days. Let us not forget that we are kept from destruction, and delivered from our enemies, to be the Lord's servants. At Elim they had good water, and enough of it. Though God may, for a time, order his people to encamp by the bitter waters of Marah, that shall not always be their lot. Let us not faint at tribulations.

Chapter 16

Chapter Outline

The Israelites come to the wilderness of Sin. They murmur for food, God promises bread from heaven.	(1–12)
God sends quails and manna.	(13–21)
Particulars respecting the manna.	(22–31)
An omer of manna to be preserved.	(32–36)

Verses 1-12

The provisions of Israel, brought from Egypt, were spent by the middle of the second month, and they murmured. It is no new thing for the greatest kindness to be basely represented as the greatest injuries. They so far undervalue their deliverance, that they wished they had died in Egypt; and by the hand of the Lord, that is, by the plagues which cut off the Egyptians. We cannot suppose they had plenty in Egypt, nor could they fear dying for want in the wilderness, while they had flocks and herds: none talk more absurdly than murmurers. When we begin to fret, we ought to consider, that God hears all our murmurings. God promises a speedy and constant supply. He tried whether they would trust him, and rest satisfied with the bread of the day in its day. Thus he tried if they would serve him, and it appeared how ungrateful they were. When God plagued the Egyptians, it was to make them know he was their Lord; when he provided for the Israelites, it was to make them know he was their God.

Verses 13-21

At evening the quails came up, and the people caught with ease as many as they needed. The manna came down in dew. They called it "Manna, Manhu," which means, "What is this?" "It is a portion; it is that which our God has allotted us, and we will take it, and be thankful." It was pleasant food; it was wholesome food. The manna was rained from heaven; it appeared, when the dew was gone, as a small round thing, as small as the hoar frost, like coriander seed, in colour like pearls. The manna fell only six days in the week, and in double quantity on the sixth day; it bred worms and became offensive if kept more than one day, excepting on the sabbath. The people had never seen it before. It could be ground in a mill, or beaten in a mortar, and was then made into cakes and baked. It continued the forty years the Israelites were in the wilderness, wherever they went, and ceased when they arrived in Canaan. All this shows how different it was from any thing found before, or found now. They were to gather the manna every morning. We are hereby taught, 1. To be prudent and diligent in providing food for ourselves and our households; with quietness working, and eating our own bread, not the bread of idleness or deceit. God's bounty leaves room for man's duty; it did so even when manna was rained; they must not eat till they have gathered. 2. To be content with enough. Those that have most, have for themselves but food and raiment; those that have least, generally have these; so that he who gathers much has nothing over, and he who gathers little has no lack. There is not such a disproportion between one and another in the enjoyment of the things of this life, as in the mere possession of them. 3. To depend upon Providence: let them sleep quietly, though they have no bread in their tents, nor in all their camp, trusting that God, with the following day, would bring them in their daily bread. It was surer and safer in God's storehouse than their own, and would come thence sweeter and fresher. See here the folly of hoarding. The manna laid up by some, who thought themselves wiser, and better managers, than their neighbours, and who would provide lest it should fail next day, bred worms, and became good for nothing. That will prove to be most wasted, which is covetously and distrustfully spared. Such riches are corrupted, Jas 5:2, 3. The same wisdom, power, and goodness that brought food daily from above for the Israelites in the wilderness, brings food yearly out of the earth in the constant course of nature, and gives us all things richly to enjoy.

Verses 22-31

Here is mention of a seventh-day sabbath. It was known, not only before the giving of the law upon mount Sinai, but before the bringing of Israel out of Egypt, even from the beginning, Ge 2:3. The setting apart one day in seven for holy work, and, in order to that, for holy rest, was ever since God created man upon the earth, and is the most ancient of the Divine laws. Appointing them to rest on the seventh day, he took care that they should be no losers by it; and none ever will be losers by serving God. On that day they were to fetch in enough for two days, and to make it ready. This directs us to contrive family affairs, so that they may hinder us as little as possible in the work of the sabbath. Works of necessity are to be done on that day; but it is desirable to have as little as may be to do, that we may apply ourselves the more closely to prepare for the life that is to come. When they kept manna against a command, it stank; when they kept it by a command, it was sweet and good; every thing is sanctified by the word of God and prayer. On the seventh day God did not send the manna, therefore they must not expect it, nor go out to gather. This showed that it was produced by miracle.

Verses 32-36

God having provided manna to be his people's food in the wilderness, the remembrance of it was to be preserved. Eaten bread must not be forgotten. God's miracles and mercies are to be had in remembrance. The word of God is the manna by which our souls are nourished, Mt 4:4. The comforts of the Spirit are hidden manna, Re 2:17. These come from heaven, as the manna did, and are the support and comfort of the Divine life in the soul, while we are in the wilderness of this world. Christ in the word is to be applied to the soul, and the means of grace are to be used. We must every one of us gather for ourselves, and gather in the morning of our days, the morning of our opportunities; which if we let slip, it may be too late to gather. The manna must not be hoarded up, but eaten; those who have received Christ, must by faith live upon him, and not receive his grace in vain. There was manna enough for all, enough for each, and none had too much; so in Christ there is enough, but not more than we need. But those who ate manna, hungered again, died at last, and with many of them God was not well pleased; whereas they that feed on Christ by faith, shall never hunger, and shall die no more, and with them God will be for ever well pleased. Let us seek earnestly for the grace of the Holy Spirit, to turn all our knowledge of the doctrine of Christ crucified, into the spiritual nourishment of our souls by faith and love

Chapter 17

Chapter Outline

The Israelites murmur for water at Rephidim, God sendeth it out of the rock.   (1–7)

Amalek overcome, The prayers of Moses.   (8–16)

Verses 1-7

The children of Israel journeyed according to the commandment of the Lord, led by the pillar of cloud and fire, yet they came to a place where there was no water for them to drink. We may be in the way of duty, yet may meet with troubles, which Providence brings us into, for the trial of our faith, and that God may be glorified in our relief. They began to question whether God was with them or not. This is called their "tempting God," which signifies distrust of him after they had received such proofs of his power and goodness. Moses mildly answered them. It is folly to answer passion with passion; that makes bad worse. God graciously appeared to help them. How wonderful the patience and forbearance of God toward provoking sinners! That he might show his power as well as his pity, and make it a miracle of mercy, he gave them water out of a rock. God can open fountains for us where we least expect them. Those who, in this wilderness, keep to God's way, may trust him to provide for them. Also, let this direct us to depend on Christ's grace. The apostle says, that Rock was Christ, 1Co 10:4, it was a type of him. While the curse of God might justly have been executed upon our guilty souls, behold the Son of God is smitten for us. Let us ask and receive. There was a constant, abundant supply of this water. Numerous as believers are, the supply of the Spirit of Christ is enough for all. The water flowed from the rock in streams to refresh the wilderness, and attended them on their way towards Canaan; and this water flows from Christ, through the ordinances, in the barren wilderness of this world, to refresh our souls, until we come to glory. A new name was given to the place, in remembrance, not of the mercy of their supply, but of the sin of their murmuring: "Massah," Temptation, because they tempted God; "Meribah," Strife, because they chid with Moses. Sin leaves a blot upon the name.

Verses 8-16

Israel engaged with Amalek in their own necessary defence. God makes his people able, and calls them to various services for the good of his church. Joshua fights, Moses prays, both minister to Israel. The rod was held up, as the banner to encourage the soldiers. Also to God, by way of appeal to him. Moses was tired. The strongest arm will fail with being long held out; it is God only whose hand is stretched out still. We do not find that Joshua's hands were heavy in fighting, but Moses' hands were heavy in praying; the more spiritual any service is, the more apt we are to fail and flag in it. To convince Israel that the hand of Moses, whom they had been chiding, did more for their safety than their own hands, his rod than their sword, the success rises and falls as Moses lifts up or lets down his hands. The church's cause is more or less successful, as her friends are more or less strong in faith, and fervent in prayer. Moses, the man of God, is glad of help. We should not be shy, either of asking help from others, or of giving help to others. The hands of Moses being thus stayed, were steady till the going down of the sun. It was great encouragement to the people to see Joshua before them in the field of battle, and Moses above them on the hill. Christ is both to us; our Joshua, the Captain of our salvation, who fights our battles, and our Moses, who ever lives, making intercession above, that our faith fail not. Weapons formed against God's Israel cannot prosper long, and shall be broken at last. Moses must write what had been done, what Amalek had done against Israel; write their bitter hatred; write their cruel attempts; let them never be forgotten, nor what God had done for Israel in saving them from Amalek. Write what should be done; that in process of time Amalek should be totally ruined and rooted out. Amalek's destruction was typical of the destruction of all the enemies of Christ and his kingdom.

Chapter 18

Chapter Outline

Jethro brings to Moses his wife and two sons.	(1–6)
Moses entertains Jethro.	(7–12)
Jethro's counsel to Moses.	(13–27)

Verses 1-6

Jethro came to rejoice with Moses in the happiness of Israel, and to bring his wife and children to him. Moses must have his family with him, that while he ruled the church of God, he might set a good example in family government, 1Ti 3:5.

Verses 7-12

Conversation concerning God's wondrous works is good, and edifies. Jethro not only rejoiced in the honour done to his son-in-law, but in all the goodness done to Israel. Standers-by were more affected with the favours God had showed to Israel, than many were who received them. Jethro gave the glory to Israel's God. Whatever we have the joy of, God must have the praise. They joined in a sacrifice of thanksgiving. Mutual friendship is sanctified by joint worship. It is very good for relations and friends to join in the spiritual sacrifice of prayer and praise, as those that meet in Christ. This was a temperate feast; they did eat bread, manna. Jethro must see and taste that bread from heaven, and though a gentile, is welcome: the gentiles are welcomed to Christ the Bread of life.

Verses 13-27

Here is the great zeal and the toil of Moses as a magistrate. Having been employed to redeem Israel out of the house of bondage, he is a further type of Christ, that he is employed as a lawgiver and a judge among them. If the people were as quarrelsome one with another as they were with God, no doubt Moses had many causes brought before him. This business Moses was called to; it appears that he did it with great care and kindness. The meanest Israelite was welcome to bring his cause before him. Moses kept to his business from morning to night. Jethro thought it was too much for him to undertake alone; also it would make the administration of justice tiresome to the people. There may be over-doing even in well-doing. Wisdom is profitable to direct, that we may neither content ourselves with less than our duty, nor task ourselves beyond our strength. Jethro advised Moses to a better plan. Great men should not only study to be useful themselves, but contrive to make others useful. Care must be taken in the choice of the persons admitted into such a trust. They should be men of good sense, that understood business, and that would not be daunted by frowns or clamours, but abhorred the thought of a bribe. Men of piety and religion; such as fear God, who dare not to do a base thing, though they could do it secretly and securely. The fear of God will best fortify a man against temptations to injustice. Moses did not despise this advice. Those are not wise, who think themselves too wise to be counselled.

Chapter 19

Chapter Outline

Verses 1-8

Moses was called up the mountain, and was employed as the messenger of this covenant. The Maker and first Mover of the covenant, is God himself. This blessed charter was granted out of God's own free grace. The covenant here mentioned was the national covenant, by which the Israelites were a people under the government of Jehovah. It was a type of the new covenant made with true believers in Christ Jesus; but, like other types, it was only a shadow of good things to come. As a nation they broke this covenant; therefore the Lord declared that he would make a new covenant with Israel, writing his law, not upon tables of stone, but in their hearts, Jer 31:33; Heb 8:7–10. The covenant spoken of in these places as ready to vanish away, is the national covenant with Israel, which they forfeited by their sins. Unless we carefully attend to this, we shall fall into mistakes while reading the Old Testament. We must not suppose that the nation of the Jews were under the covenant of works, which knows nothing of repentance, faith in a Mediator, forgiveness of sins, or grace; nor yet that the whole nation of Israel bore the character, and possessed the privileges of true believers, as being actually sharers in the covenant of grace. They were all under a dispensation of mercy; they had outward privileges and advantages for salvation; but, like professing Christians, most rested therein, and went no further. Israel consented to the conditions. They answered as one man, All that the Lord hath spoken we will do. Oh that there had been such a heart in them! Moses, as a mediator, returned the words of the people to God. Thus Christ, the Mediator, as a Prophet, reveals God's will to us, his precepts and promises; and then, as a Priest, offers up to God our spiritual sacrifices, not only of prayer and praise, but of devout affections, and pious resolutions, the work of his own Spirit in us.

Verses 9-15

The solemn manner in which the law was delivered, was to impress the people with a right sense of the Divine majesty. Also to convince them of their own guilt, and to show that they could not stand in judgment before God by their own obedience. In the law, the sinner discovers what he ought to be, what he is, and what he wants. There he learns the nature, necessity, and glory of redemption, and of being made holy. Having been taught to flee to Christ, and to love him, the law is the rule of his obedience and faith.

Verses 16-25

Never was there such a sermon preached, before or since, as this which was preached to the church in the wilderness. It might be supposed that the terrors would have checked presumption and curiosity in the people; but the hard heart of an unawakened sinner can trifle with the most terrible threatenings and judgments. In drawing near to God, we must never forget his holiness and greatness, nor our own meanness and pollution. We cannot stand in judgment before him according to his righteous law. The convinced transgressor asks, What must I do to be saved? and he hears the voice, Believe in the Lord Jesus Christ, and thou shalt be saved. The Holy Ghost, who made the law to convince of sin, now takes of the things of Christ, and shows them to us. In the gospel we read, Christ hath redeemed us from the curse of the law, being made a curse for us. We have redemption through his blood, even the forgiveness of sins. Through him we are justified from all things, from which we could not be justified by the law of Moses. But the Divine law is binding as a rule of life. The Son of God came down from heaven, and suffered poverty, shame, agony, and death, not only to redeem us from its curse, but to bind us more closely to keep its commands.

Chapter 20

Chapter Outline

The preface to the ten commandments.	(1, 2)
The commandments of the first table.	(3–11)
Of the second table.	(12–17)
The fear of the people.	(18–21)
Idolatry again forbidden.	(22–26)

Verses 1, 2

God speaks many ways to the children of men; by conscience, by providences, by his voice, to all which we ought carefully to attend; but he never spake at any time so as he spake the TEN COMMANDMENTS. This law God had given to man before; it was written in his heart; but sin so defaced it, that it was necessary to revive the knowledge of it. The law is spiritual, and takes knowledge of the secret thoughts, desires, and dispositions of the heart. Its grand demand is love, without which outward obedience is mere hypocrisy. It requires perfect, unfailing, constant obedience; no law in the world admits disobedience to itself. Whosoever shall keep the whole law, and yet offend in one point, he is guilty of all, Jas 2:10. Whether in the heart or the conduct, in thought, word, or deed, to omit or to vary any thing, is sin, and the wages of sin is death.

Verses 3-11

The first four of the ten commandments, commonly called the FIRST table, tell our duty to God. It was fit that those should be put first, because man had a Maker to love, before he had a neighbour to love. It cannot be expected that he should be true to his brother, who is false to his God. The first commandment concerns the object of worship, JEHOVAH, and him only. The worship of creatures is here forbidden. Whatever comes short of perfect love, gratitude, reverence, or worship, breaks this commandment. Whatsoever ye do, do all the glory of God. The second commandment refers to the worship we are to render to the Lord our God. It is forbidden to make any image or picture of the Deity, in any form, or for any purpose; or to worship any creature, image, or picture. But the spiritual import of this command extends much further. All kinds of superstition are here forbidden, and the using of mere human inventions in the worship of God. The third commandment concerns the manner of worship, that it be with all possible reverence and seriousness. All false oaths are forbidden. All light appealing to God, all profane cursing, is a horrid breach of this command. It matters not whether the word of God, or sacred things, all such-like things break this commandment, and there is no profit, honour, or pleasure in them. The Lord will not hold him guiltless that taketh his name in vain. The form of the fourth commandment, "Remember," shows that it was not now first given, but was known by the people before. One day in seven is to be kept holy. Six days are allotted to worldly business, but not so as to neglect the service of God, and the care of our souls. On those days we must do all our work, and leave none to be done on the sabbath day. Christ allowed works of necessity, charity, and piety; for the sabbath was made for man, and not man for the sabbath, Mr 2:27; but all works of luxury, vanity, or self-indulgence in any form, are forbidden. Trading, paying wages, settling accounts, writing letters of business, worldly studies, trifling visits, journeys, or light conversation, are not keeping this day holy to the Lord. Sloth and indolence may be a carnal, but not a holy rest. The sabbath of the Lord should be a day of rest from worldly labour, and a rest in the service of God. The advantages from the due keeping of this holy day, were it only to the health and happiness of mankind, with the time it affords for taking care of the soul, show the excellency of this commandment. The day is blessed; men are blessed by it, and in it. The blessing and direction to keep holy are not limited to the seventh day, but are spoken of the sabbath day.

Verses 12-17

The laws of the SECOND table, that is, the last six of the ten commandments, state our duty to ourselves and to one another, and explain the great commandment, Thou shalt love thy neighbour as thyself, Lu 10:27. Godliness and honesty must go together. The fifth commandment concerns the duties we owe to our relations. Honour thy father and thy mother, includes esteem of them, shown in our conduct; obedience to their lawful commands; come when they call you, go where they send you, do what they bid you, refrain from what they forbid you; and this, as children, cheerfully, and from a principle of love. Also submission to their counsels and corrections. Endeavouring, in every thing, to comfort parents, and to make their old age easy; maintaining them if they need support, which our Saviour makes to be particularly intended in this commandment, Mt 15:4–6. Careful observers have noted a peculiar blessing in temporal things on obedient, and the reverse on disobedient children. The sixth commandment requires that we regard the life and the safety of others as we do our own. Magistrates and their officers, and witnesses testifying the truth, do not break this command. Self-defence is lawful; but much which is not deemed murder by the laws of man, is such before God. Furious passions, stirred up by anger or by drunkenness, are no excuse: more guilty is murder in duels, which is a horrible effect of a haughty, revengeful spirit. All fighting, whether for wages, for renown, or out of anger and malice, breaks this command, and the bloodshed therein is murder. To tempt men to vice and crimes which shorten life, may be included. Misconduct, such as may break the heart, or shorten the lives of parents, wives, or other relatives, is a breach of this command. This command forbids all envy, malice, hatred, or anger, all provoking or insulting language. The destruction of our own lives is here forbidden. This commandment requires a spirit of kindness, longsuffering, and forgiveness. The seventh commandment concerns chastity. We should be as much afraid of that which defiles the body, as of that which destroys it. Whatever tends to pollute the imagination, or to raise the passions, falls under this law, as impure pictures, books, conversation, or any other like matters. The eighth commandment is the law of love as it respects the property of others. The portion of worldly things allotted us, as far as it is obtained in an honest way, is the bread which God hath given us; for that we ought to be thankful, to be contented with it, and, in the use of lawful means, to trust Providence for the future. Imposing upon the ignorance, easiness, or necessity of others, and many other things, break God's law, though scarcely blamed in society. Plunderers of kingdoms though above human justice, will be included in this sentence. Defrauding the public, contracting debts without prospect of paying them, or evading payment of just debts, extravagance, all living upon charity when not needful, all squeezing the poor in their wages; these, and such things, break this command; which requires industry, frugality, and content, and to do to others, about worldly property, as we would they should do to us. The ninth commandment concerns our own and our neighbour's good name. This forbids speaking falsely on any matter, lying, equivocating, and any way devising or designing to deceive our neighbour. Speaking unjustly against our neighbour, to hurt his reputation. Bearing false witness against him, or in common conversation slandering, backbiting, and tale-bearing; making what is done amiss, worse than it is, and in any way endeavouring to raise our reputation upon the ruin of our neighbour's. How much this command is every day broken among persons of all ranks! The tenth commandment strikes at the root; Thou shalt not covet. The others forbid all desire of doing what will be an injury to our neighbour; this forbids all wrong desire of having what will gratify ourselves.

Verses 18-21

This law, which is so extensive that we cannot measure it, so spiritual that we cannot evade it, and so reasonable that we cannot find fault with it, will be the rule of the future judgment of God, as it is for the present conduct of man. If tried by this rule, we shall find our lives have been passed in transgressions. And with this holy law and an awful judgment before us, who can despise the gospel of Christ? And the knowledge of the law shows our need of repentance. In every believer's heart sin is dethroned and crucified, the law of God is written, and the image of God renewed. The Holy Spirit enables him to hate sin and flee from it, to love and keep this law in sincerity and truth; nor will he cease to repent.

Verses 22-26

Moses having entered into the thick darkness, God there spake in his hearing all that follows from hence to the end of chap. 23, which is mostly an exposition of the ten commandments. The laws in these verses relate to God's worship. The Israelites are assured of God's gracious acceptance of their devotions. Under the gospel, men are encouraged to pray every where, and wherever God's people meet in his name to worship him, he will be in the midst of them; there he will come unto them, and will bless them.

Chapter 21

Chapter Outline

Verses 1-11

The laws in this chapter relate to the fifth and sixth commandments; and though they differ from our times and customs, nor are they binding on us, yet they explain the moral law, and the rules of natural justice. The servant, in the state of servitude, was an emblem of that state of bondage to sin, Satan, and the law, which man is brought into by robbing God of his glory, by the transgression of his precepts. Likewise in being made free, he was an emblem of that liberty wherewith Christ, the Son of God, makes free from bondage his people, who are free indeed; and made so freely, without money and without price, of free grace.

Verses 12-21

God, who by his providence gives and maintains life, by his law protects it. A wilful murderer shall be taken even from God's altar. But God provided cities of refuge to protect those whose unhappiness it was, and not their fault, to cause the death of another; for such as by accident, when a man is doing a lawful act, without intent of hurt, happens to kill another. Let children hear the sentence of God's word upon the ungrateful and disobedient; and remember that God will certainly requite it, if they have ever cursed their parents, even in their hearts, or have lifted up their hands against them, except they repent, and flee for refuge to the Saviour. And let parents hence learn to be very careful in training up their children, setting them a good example, especially in the government of their passions, and in praying for them; taking heed not to provoke them to wrath. Through poverty the Israelites sometimes sold themselves or their children; magistrates sold some persons for their crimes, and creditors were in some cases allowed to sell their debtors who could not pay. But "man-stealing," the object of which is to force another into slavery, is ranked in the New Testament with the greatest crimes. Care is here taken, that satisfaction be made for hurt done to a person, though death do not follow. The gospel teaches masters to forbear, and to moderate threatenings, Eph 6:9, considering with Job, What shall I do, when God riseth up? Job 31:13, 14.

Verses 22-36

The cases here mentioned give rules of justice then, and still in use, for deciding similar matters. We are taught by these laws, that we must be very careful to do no wrong, either directly or indirectly. If we have done wrong, we must be very willing to make it good, and be desirous that nobody may lose by us.

Chapter 22

Judicial laws.

—The people of God should ever be ready to show mildness and mercy, according to the spirit of these laws. We must answer to God, not only for what we do maliciously, but for what we do heedlessly. Therefore, when we have done harm to our neighbour, we should make restitution, though not compelled by law. Let these scriptures lead our souls to remember, that if the grace of God has indeed appeared to us, then it has taught us, and enabled us so to conduct ourselves by its holy power, that denying ungodliness and wordly lusts, we should live soberly, righteously, and godly in this present world, Tit 2:12. And the grace of God teaches us, that as the Lord is our portion, there is enough in him to satisfy all the desires of our souls.

Chapter 23

Chapter Outline

Laws against falsehood and injustice.	(1–9)
The year of rest, The sabbath, The three festivals.	(10–19)
God promises to conduct the Israelites to Canaan.	(20–33)

Verses 1-9

In the law of Moses are very plain marks of sound moral feeling, and of true political wisdom. Every thing in it is suited to the desired and avowed object, the worship of one only God, and the separation of Israel from the pagan world. Neither parties, friends, witnesses, nor common opinions, must move us to lessen great faults, to aggravate small ones, excuse offenders, accuse the innocent, or misrepresent any thing.

Verses 10-19

Every seventh year the land was to rest. They must not plough or sow it; what the earth produced of itself, should be eaten, and not laid up. This law seems to have been intended to teach dependence on Providence, and God's faithfulness in sending the larger increase while they kept his appointments. It was also typical of the heavenly rest, when all earthly labours, cares, and interests shall cease for ever. All respect to the gods of the heathen is strictly forbidden. Since idolatry was a sin to which the Israelites leaned, they must blot out the remembrance of the gods of the heathen. Solemn religious attendance on God, in the place which he should choose, is strictly required. They must come together before the Lord. What a good Master do we serve, who has made it our duty to rejoice before him! Let us devote with pleasure to the service of God that portion of our time which he requires, and count his sabbaths and ordinances to be a feast unto our souls. They were not to come empty-handed; so now, we must not come to worship God empty-hearted; our souls must be filled with holy desires toward him, and dedications of ourselves to him; for with such sacrifices God is well pleased.

Verses 20-33

It is here promised that they should be guided and kept in their way through the wilderness to the land of promise, Behold, I send an angel before thee, mine angel. The precept joined with this promise is, that they be obedient to this angel whom God would send before them. Christ is the Angel of Jehovah; this is plainly taught by St. Paul, 1Co 10:9. They should have a comfortable settlement in the land of Canaan. How reasonable are the conditions of this promise; that they should serve the only true God; not the gods of the nations, which are no gods at all. How rich are the particulars of this promise! The comfort of their food, the continuance of their health, the increase of their wealth, the prolonging their lives to old age. Thus hath godliness the promise of the life that now is. It is promised that they should subdue their enemies. Hosts of hornets made way for the hosts of Israel; such mean creatures can God use for chastising his people's enemies. In real kindness to the church, its enemies are subdued by little and little; thus we are kept on our guard, and in continual dependence on God. Corruptions are driven out of the hearts of God's people, not all at once, but by little and little. The precept with this promise is, that they should not make friendship with idolaters. Those that would keep from bad courses, must keep from bad company. It is dangerous to live in a bad neighbourhood; others' sins will be our snares. Our greatest danger is from those who would make us sin against God.

Chapter 24

Chapter Outline

Verses 1-8

A solemn covenant was made between God and Israel. Very solemn it was, typifying the covenant of grace between God and believers, through Christ. As soon as God separated to himself a peculiar people, he governed them by a written word, as he has done ever since. God's covenants and commands are so just in themselves, and so much for our good, that the more we think of them, and the more plainly and fully they are set before us, the more reason we may see to comply with them. The blood of the sacrifice was sprinkled on the altar, on the book, and on the people. Neither their persons, their moral obedience, nor religious services, would meet with acceptance from a holy God, except through the shedding and sprinkling' of blood. Also the blessings granted unto them were all of mercy; and the Lord would deal with them in kindness. Thus the sinner, by faith in the blood of Christ, renders willing and acceptable obedience. (Ex 24:9-11)

Verses 9-11

The elders saw the God of Israel; they had some glimpse of his glory, though whatever they saw, it was something of which no image or picture could be made, yet enough to satisfy them that God was with them of a truth. Nothing is described but what was under his feet. The sapphires are the pavement under his feet; let us put all the wealth of this world under our feet, and not in our hearts. Thus the believer sees in the face of Jesus Christ, far clearer discoveries of the glorious justice and holiness of God, than ever he saw under terrifying convictions; and through the Saviour, holds communion with a holy God.

Verses 12-18

A cloud covered the mount six days; a token of God's special presence there. Moses was sure that he who called him up would protect him. Even those glorious attributes of God which are most terrible to the wicked, the saints with humble reverence rejoice in. And through faith in the atoning Sacrifice, we hope for greater honour than Moses ever enjoyed on earth. Now we see through a glass darkly, but when he shall appear, then face to face. This vision of God will continue with equal, if not increasing brightness of joy; not for a few days only, but through eternity.

Chapter 25

Chapter Outline

What the Israelites were to offer for making the tabernacle.	(1–9)
The ark.	(10–22)
The table, with its furniture.	(23–30)
The candlestick.	(31–40)

Verses 1-9

God chose the people of Israel to be a peculiar people to himself, above all people, and he himself would be their King. He ordered a royal palace to be set up among them for himself, called a sanctuary, or holy place, or habitation. There he showed his presence among them. And because in the wilderness they dwelt in tents, this royal palace was ordered to be a tabernacle, that it might move with them. The people were to furnish Moses with the materials, by their own free will. The best use we can make of our worldly wealth, is to honour God with it in works of piety and charity.

We should ask, not only, What must we do? but, What may we do for God? Whatever they gave, they must give it cheerfully, not grudgingly, for God loves a cheerful giver, 2Co 9:7. What is laid out in the service of God, we must reckon well bestowed; and whatsoever is done in God's service, must be done by his direction. (Ex 25:10-22)

Verses 10-22

The ark was a chest, overlaid with gold, in which the two tables of the law were to be kept. These tables are called the testimony; God in them testified his will. This law was a testimony to the Israelites, to direct them in their duty, and would be a testimony against them, if they transgressed. This ark was placed in the holy of holies; the blood of the sacrifices was sprinkled, and the incense burned, before it, by the high priest; and above it appeared the visible glory, which was the symbol of the Divine presence. This was a type of Christ in his sinless nature, which saw no corruption, in personal union with his Divine nature, atoning for our sins against it, by his death. The cherubim of gold looked one towards another, and both looked downward toward the ark. It denotes the angels' attendance on the Redeemer, their readiness to do his will, their presence in the assemblies of saints, and their desire to look into the mysteries of the gospel. It was covered with a covering of gold, called the mercy-seat. God is said to dwell, or sit between the cherubim, on the mercy-seat. There he would give his law, and hear supplicants, as a prince on his throne.

Verses 23-30

A table was to be made of wood, overlaid with gold, to stand in the outer tabernacle, to be always furnished with the shew-bread. This table, with the articles on it, and its use, seems to typify the communion which the Lord holds with his redeemed people in his ordinances, the provisions of his house, the feasts they are favoured with. Also the food for their souls, which they always find when they hunger after it; and the delight he takes in their persons and services, as presented before him in Christ.

Verses 31-40

The candlestick represents the light of God's word and Spirit, in and through Christ Jesus, afforded in this dark world to his believing people, to direct their worship and obedience, and to afford them consolations. The church is still dark, as the tabernacle was, in comparison with what it will be in heaven; but the word of God is a light shining in a dark place, 2Pe 1:19, and a dark place indeed the world would be without it. In ver. #(40) is an express caution to Moses. Nothing was left to his own fancy, or to that of the workmen, or the people; but the will of God must be observed in every particular. Christ's instruction to his disciples, Mt 28:20, is like this, Observe all things whatsoever I have commanded you. Let us remember that we are the temples of the Holy Ghost, that we have the law of God in our hearts, that we are to live a life of communion with God, feast on his ordinances, and are the light of the world, if indeed we are followers of Christ. May the Lord help us to try ourselves by this view of religion, and to walk according thereto.

Chapter 26

Chapter Outline

Verses 1-6

God manifested his presence among the Israelites in a tabernacle or tent, because of their condition in the wilderness. God suits the tokens of his favour, and the gifts of his grace, to his people's state and wants. The curtains of the tabernacle were to be very rich. They were to be embroidered with cherubim, signifying that the angels of God pitch their tents round about the church, Ps 34:7. (Ex 26:7-14)

Verses 7-14

The curtains of meaner materials, being made both longer and broader, covered the others, and were defended by coverings of skins. The whole represents the person and doctrine of Christ, and the church of true Christians, and all heavenly things, which outwardly are mean, but inwardly, and in the sight of God, are glorious and precious.

Verses 15-30

The sockets of silver each weighed about 115 pounds; they were placed in rows on the ground. In every pair of these sockets, a strong board of shittim-wood, covered with plates of gold, was fitted by mortises and tenons. Thus walls were formed for the two sides, and for the west end. The wall was further held together by bars, which passed through rings of gold. Over this the curtains were spread. Though movable, it was strong and firm. The materials were very costly. In all this it was a type of the church of God, built upon the foundation of the apostles and prophets, Jesus Christ himself being the chief Corner-stone, Eph 2:20, 21.

Verses 31-37

A vail, or curtain, separated the holy place from the most holy place. It was hung upon pillars. This vail was for a partition between the holy place and the most holy; which forbade any to look into the holiest of all. The apostle tells what was the meaning of this vail, Heb 9:8. That the ceremonial law could not make the comers thereunto perfect, nor would the observance of it bring men to heaven; the way into the holiest of all was not made manifest, while the first tabernacle was standing. Life and immortality lay hidden till they were brought to light by the gospel; which was signified by the rending of this vail at the death of Christ, Mt 27:51. We have now boldness to enter into the holiest, in all acts of worship, by the blood of Jesus; yet such as obliges us to holy reverence. Another vail was for the outer door of the tabernacle. This vail was all the defence the tabernacle had. God takes care of his church on earth. A curtain shall be, if God please to make it so, as strong a defence to his house, as gates of brass and bars of iron. With this typical description of Christ and his church before us, what is our judgment of these matters? Do we see any glory in the person of Christ? any excellence in his character? any thing precious in his salvation? or any wisdom in the doctrine of the cross? Will our religion bear examination? and are we more careful to approve our hearts to God than our characters toward men?

Chapter 27

Chapter Outline

Verses 1-8

In the court before the tabernacle, where the people attended, was an altar, to which they must bring their sacrifices, and on which their priests must offer them to God. It was of wood overlaid with brass. A grate of brass was let into the hollow of the altar, about the middle of which the fire was kept, and the sacrifice burnt. It was made of net-work like a sieve, and hung hollow, that the ashes might fall through. This brazen altar was a type of Christ dying to make atonement for our sins. The wood had been consumed by the fire from heaven, if it had not been secured by the brass: nor could the human nature of Christ have borne the wrath of God, if it had not been supported by Divine power.

Verses 9-19

The tabernacle was enclosed in a court, about sixty yards long and thirty broad, formed by curtains hung upon brazen pillars, fixed in brazen sockets. Within this enclosure the priests and Levites offered the sacrifices, and thither the Jewish people were admitted. These distinctions represented the difference between the visible nominal church, and the true spiritual church, which alone has access to God, and communion with him.

Verses 20, 21

The pure oil signified the gifts and graces of the Spirit, which all believers receive from Christ, the good Olive, and without which our light cannot shine before men. The priests were to light the lamps, and tend them. It is the work of ministers, by preaching and expounding the Scriptures, which are as a lamp, to enlighten the church, God's tabernacle upon earth. Blessed be God, this light is not now confined to the Jewish tabernacle, but is a light to lighten the gentiles, and for salvation unto the ends of the earth.

Chapter 28

Chapter Outline

Verses 1-5

Hitherto the heads of families were the priests, and offered sacrifices; but now this office was confined to the family of Aaron only; and so continued till the gospel dispensation. The holy garments not only distinguished the priests from the people, but were emblems of that holy conduct which should ever be the glory and beauty, the mark of the ministers of religion, without which their persons and ministrations will be had in contempt. They also typified the glory of the Divine majesty, and the beauty of complete holiness, which rendered Jesus Christ the great High Priest. But our adorning under the gospel, is not to be of gold and costly array, but the garments of salvation, the robe of righteousness.

Verses 6-14

This richly-wrought ephod was the outmost garment of the high priest; plain linen ephods were worn by the inferior priests. It was a short coat without sleeves, fastened close to the body with a girdle. The shoulder-pieces were buttoned together with precious stones set in gold, one on each shoulder, on which were engraven the names of the children of Israel. Thus Christ, our High Priest, presents his people before the Lord for a memorial. As Christ's coat had no seam, but was woven from the top throughout, so it was with the ephod. The golden bells on this ephod, by their preciousness and pleasant sound, well represent the good profession that the saints make, and the pomegranates the fruit they bring forth.

Verses 15-30

The chief ornament of the high priest, was the breastplate, a rich piece of cloth, curiously worked. The name of each tribe was graven in a precious stone, fixed in the breastplate, to signify how precious, in God's sight, believers are, and how honourable. How small and poor soever the tribe was, it was as a precious stone in the breastplate of the high priest; thus are all the saints dear to Christ, however men esteem them. The high priest had the names of the tribes, both on his shoulders and on his breast, which reminds us of the power and the love with which our Lord Jesus pleads for those that are his. He not only bears them up in his arms with almighty strength, but he carries them in his bosom with tender affection. What comfort is this to us in all our addresses to God! The Urim and Thummim, by which the will of God was made known in doubtful cases, were put in this breastplate. Urim and Thummim signify light and integrity. There are many conjectures what these were; the most probable opinion seems to be, that they were the twelve precious stones in the high priest's breastplate. Now, Christ is our Oracle. By him God, in these last days, makes known himself and his mind to us, Heb 1:1, 2; Joh 1:18. He is the true Light, the faithful Witness, the Truth itself, and from him we receive the Spirit of Truth, who leads into all truth.

Verses 31-39

The robe of the ephod was under the ephod, and reached down to the knees, without sleeves. Aaron must minister in the garments appointed. We must serve the Lord with holy fear, as those who know they deserve to die. A golden plate was fixed on Aaron's forehead, engraven with "Holiness to the Lord." Aaron was hereby reminded that God is holy, and that his priests must be holy, devoted to the Lord. This must appear in their forehead, in open profession of their relation to God. It must be engraven like the engravings of a signet; deep and durable; not painted so as to be washed off, but firm and lasting; such must our holiness to the Lord be. Christ is our High Priest; through him sins are forgiven to us, and not laid to our charge. Our persons, our doings, are pleasing to God upon the account of Christ, and not otherwise.

Verses 40-43

The priest's garments typify the righteousness of Christ. If we appear not before God in that, we shall bear our iniquity, and die. Blessed is he, therefore, that watcheth, and keepeth his garments, Re 16:15. And blessed be God that we have a High Priest, appointed of God, and set apart for his work; furnished for his high office by the glory of his Divine majesty, and the beauty of perfect holiness. Happy are we, if by the law spiritually understood, we see that such a High Priest became us; that we cannot draw near to a holy God, or be accepted, but by him. There is no light, no wisdom, no perfection, but from him; no glory, no beauty, but in being like unto him. Let us take encouragement from the power, love, and compassion of our High Priest, to draw near with boldness to the throne of grace, that we may obtain mercy, and find grace to help in time of need.

Chapter 29

Chapter Outline

Verses 1-37

Aaron and his sons were to be set apart for the priest's office, with ceremony and solemnity. Our Lord Jesus is the great High Priest of our profession, called of God to be so; anointed with the Spirit, whence he is called Messiah, the Christ; clothed with glory and beauty; sanctified by his own blood; made perfect, or consecrated through sufferings, Heb 2:10. All believers are spiritual priests, to offer spiritual sacrifices, 1Pe 2:5, washed in the blood of Christ, and so made to our God priests, Re 1:5, 6. They also are clothed with the beauty of holiness, and have received the anointing, 1Jo 2:27. The Spirit of God is called the finger of God, (Lu 11:20, compared with Mt 12:28,) and by him the merit of Christ is applied to our souls. This consecration signifies the admission of a sinner into the spiritual priesthood, to offer spiritual sacrifices, acceptable to God through Jesus Christ.

Verses 38-46

A lamb was to be offered upon the altar every morning, and a lamb every evening. This typified the continual intercession which Christ ever lives to make for his church. Though he offered himself but once for all, that one offering thus becomes a continual offering. This also teaches us to offer to God the spiritual sacrifices of prayer and praise every day, morning and evening. Our daily devotions are the most needful of our daily works, and the most pleasant of our daily comforts. Prayer-time must be kept up as duly as meal-time. Those starve their own souls, who keep not up constant attendance on the throne of grace; constancy in religion brings in the comfort of it.

Chapter 30

Chapter Outline

Verses 1-10

The altar of incense represented the Son of God in his human nature, and the incense burned thereon typified his pleading for his people. The continual intercession of Christ was represented by the daily burning of incense thereon, morning and evening. Once every year the blood of the atonement was to be applied to it, denoting that the intercession of Christ has all its virtue from his sufferings on earth, and that we need no other sacrifice or intercessor but Christ alone.

Verses 11-16

The tribute was half a shekel, about fifteen pence of our money. The rich were not to give more, nor the poor less; the souls of the rich and poor are alike precious, and God is no respecter of persons, Ac 10:34; Job 34:19. In other offerings men were to give according to their wordly ability; but this, which was the ransom of the soul, must be alike for all. The souls of all are of equal value, equally in danger, and all equally need a ransom. The money raised was to be used in the service of the tabernacle. Those who have the benefit, must not grudge the necessary charges of God's public worship. Money cannot make atonement for the soul, but it may be used for the honour of Him who has made the atonement, and for the maintenance of the gospel by which the atonement is applied.

Verses 17-21

A large vessel of brass, holding water, was to be set near the door of the tabernacle. Aaron and his sons must wash their hands and feet at this laver, every time they went in to minister. This was to teach them purity in all their services, and to dread the pollution of sin. They must not only wash and be made clean, when first made priests, but must wash and be kept clean, whenever they went to minister. It teaches us daily to attend upon God, daily to renew our repentance for sin, and our looking to the blood of Christ for remission; for in many things we daily offend.

Verses 22-38

Directions are here given for making the holy anointing oil, and the incense to be used in the service of the tabernacle. To show the excellency of holiness, there was this spiced oil in the tabernacle, which was grateful to the sight and to the smell. Christ's name is as ointment poured forth, So 1:3, and the good name of Christians is like precious ointment, Ec 7:1. The incense burned upon the golden altar was prepared of sweet spices. When it was used, it was to be beaten very small; thus it pleased the Lord to bruise the Redeemer, when he offered himself for a sacrifice of a sweet-smelling savour. The like should not be made for any common use. Thus God would keep in the people's minds reverence for his own services, and teach us not to profane or abuse any thing whereby God makes himself known. It is a great affront to God to jest with sacred things, and to make sport with his word and ordinances. It is most dangerous and fatal to use professions of the gospel of Christ to forward wordly interests.

Chapter 31

Chapter Outline

Bezaleel and Aholiab are appointed and   (1–11)
qualified for the work of the tabernacle.

The observance of the sabbath.   (12–17)

Moses receives the tables of the law.   (18)

Verses 1-11

The Israelites, who had been masons and bricklayers in Egypt, were not qualified for curious workmanship; but the Spirit who gave the apostles utterance in divers tongues, miraculously gave Bezaleel and Aholiab the skill that was wanting. The honour which comes from God, is always attended with a work to be done; to be employed for God is high honour. Those whom God calls to any service, he will find or make fit for it. The Lord gives different gifts to different persons; let each mind his proper work, diligently remembering that whatever wisdom any one possesses, the Lord put it in the heart, to do his commandments.

Verses 12-17

Orders were now given that a tabernacle should be set up for the service of God. But they must not think that the nature of the work, and the haste that was required, would justify them in working at it on sabbath days. The Hebrew word /shabath/ signifies rest, or ceasing from labour. The thing signified by the sabbath is that rest in glory which remains for the people of God; therefore the moral obligation of the sabbath must continue, till time is swallowed up in eternity.

Verse 18

The law was written in tables of stone, to show how lasting it is: to denote likewise the hardness of our hearts; one might more easily write on stone, than write any thing good on our corrupt natural hearts. It was written with the finger of God; by his will and power. God only can write his law in the heart: he gives a heart of flesh; then, by his Spirit, which is the finger of God, writes his will in the heart, 2Co 3:3.

Chapter 32

Chapter Outline

The people cause Aaron to make a golden   (1–6)
calf.

Verses 1-6

While Moses was in the mount, receiving the law from God, the people made a tumultuous address to Aaron. This giddy multitude were weary of waiting for the return of Moses. Weariness in waiting betrays to many temptations. The Lord must be waited for till he comes, and waited for though he tarry. Let their readiness to part with their ear-rings to make an idol, shame our niggardliness in the service of the true God. They did not draw back on account of the cost of their idolatry; and shall we grudge the expenses of religion? Aaron produced the shape of an ox or calf, giving it some finish with a graving tool. They offered sacrifice to this idol. Having set up an image before them, and so changed the truth of God into a lie, their sacrifices were abomination. Had they not, only a few days before, in this very place, heard the voice of the Lord God speaking to them out of the midst of the fire, Thou shalt not make to thyself any graven image? Had they not themselves solemnly entered into covenant with God, that they would do all he had said to them, and would be obedient? ch. 24:7. Yet before they stirred from the place where this covenant had been solemnly made, they brake an express command, in defiance of an express threatening. It plainly shows, that the law was no more able to make holy, than it was to justify; by it is the knowledge of sin, but not the cure of sin. Aaron was set apart by the Divine appointment to the office of the priesthood; but he, who had once shamed himself so far as to build an altar to a golden calf, must own himself unworthy of the honour of attending at the altar of God, and indebted to free grace alone for it. Thus pride and boasting were silenced.

Verses 7-14

God says to Moses, that the Israelites had corrupted themselves. Sin is the corruption of the sinner, and it is a self-corruption; every man is tempted when he is drawn aside of his own lust. They had turned aside out of the way. Sin is a departing from the way of duty into a by-path. They soon forgot God's works. He sees what they cannot discover, nor is any wickedness of the world hid from him. We could not bear to see the thousandth part of that evil which God sees every day. God expresses the greatness of his just displeasure, after the manner of men who would have prayer of Moses could save them from ruin; thus he was a type of Christ, by whose mediation alone, God would reconcile the world to himself. Moses pleads God's glory. The glorifying God's name, as it ought to be our first petition, and it is so in the Lord's prayer, so it ought to be our great plea. And God's promises are to be our pleas in prayer; for what he has promised he is able to perform. See the power of prayer. In answer to the prayers of Moses, God showed his purpose of sparing the people, as he had before seemed determined on their destruction; which change of the outward discovery of his purpose, is called repenting of the evil.

Verses 15-20

What a change it is, to come down from the mount of communion with God, to converse with a wicked world. In God we see nothing but what is pure and pleasing; in the world nothing but what is sinful and provoking. That it might appear an idol is nothing in the world, Moses ground the calf to dust. Mixing this powder with their drink, signified that the backslider in heart should be filled with his own ways.

Verses 21-29

Never did any wise man make a more frivolous and foolish excuse than that of Aaron. We must never be drawn into sin by any thing man can say or do to us; for men can but tempt us to sin, they cannot force us. The approach of Moses turned the dancing into trembling. They were exposed to shame by their sin. The course Moses took to roll away this reproach, was, not by concealing the sin, or putting any false colour upon it, but by punishing it. The Levites were to slay the ringleaders in this wickedness; yet none were executed but those who openly stood forth. Those are marked for ruin who persist in sin: those who in the morning were shouting and dancing, before night were dying. Such sudden changes do the judgments of the Lord sometimes make with sinners that are secure and jovial in their sin.

Verses 30-35

Moses calls it a great sin. The work of ministers is to show people the greatness of their sins. The great evil of sin appears in the price of pardon. Moses pleads with God for mercy; he came not to make excuses, but to make atonement. We are not to suppose that Moses means that he would be willing to perish for ever, for the people's sake. We are to love our neighbour as ourselves, and not more than ourselves. But having that mind which was in Christ, he was willing to lay down his life in the most painful manner, if he might thereby preserve the people. Moses could not wholly turn away the wrath of God; which shows that the law of Moses was not able to reconcile men to God, and to perfect our peace with him. In Christ alone, God so pardons sin as to remember it no more. From this history we see, that no unhumbled, carnal heart, can long endure the holy precepts, the humbling truths, and the spiritual worship of God. But a god, a priest, a worship, a doctrine, and a sacrifice, suited to the carnal mind, will ever meet with abundance of worshippers. The very gospel itself may be so perverted as to suit a worldly taste. Well is it for us, that the Prophet like unto Moses, but who is beyond compare more powerful and merciful, has made atonement for our souls, and now intercedes in our behalf. Let us rejoice in his grace.

Chapter 33

Chapter Outline

Verses 1-6

Those whom God pardons, must be made to know what their sin deserved. "Let them go forward as they are;" this was very expressive of God's displeasure. Though he promises to make good his covenant with Abraham, in giving them Canaan, yet he denies them the tokens of his presence they had been blessed with. The people mourned for their sin. Of all the bitter fruits and consequences of sin, true penitents most lament, and dread most, God's departure from them. Canaan itself would be no pleasant land without the Lord's presence. Those who parted with ornaments to maintain sin, could do no less than lay aside ornaments, in token of sorrow and shame for it.

Verses 7-11

Moses took the tabernacle, and pitched it without the camp. This seems to have been a temporary building, set up for worship, and at which he judged disputes among the people. The people looked after him; they were very desirous to be at peace with God, and concerned to know what would come to pass. The cloudy pillar which had withdrawn from the camp when it was polluted with idolatry, now returned. If our hearts go forth toward God to meet him, he will graciously come to meet us.

Verses 12-23

Moses is very earnest with God. Thus, by the intercession of Christ, we are not only saved from ruin, but become entitled to everlasting happiness. Observe here how he pleads. We find grace in God's sight, if we find grace in our hearts to guide and quicken us in the way of our duty. Moses speaks as one who dreaded the thought of going forward without the Lord's presence. God's gracious promises, and mercy towards us, should not only encourage our faith, but also excite our fervency in prayer. Observe how he speeds. See, in a type, Christ's intercession, which he ever lives to make for all that come to God by him; and that it is not by any thing in those for whom he intercedes. Moses then entreats a sight of God's glory, and is heard in that also. A full discovery of the glory of God, would overwhelm even Moses himself. Man is mean, and unworthy of it; weak, and could not bear it; guilty, and could not but dread it. The merciful display which is made in Christ Jesus, alone can be borne by us. The Lord granted that which would abundantly satisfy. God's goodness is his glory; and he will have us to know him by the glory of his mercy, more than by the glory of his majesty. Upon the rock there was a fit place for Moses to view the goodness and glory of God. The rock in Horeb was typical of Christ the Rock; the Rock of refuge, salvation, and strength. Happy are they who stand upon this Rock. The cleft may be an emblem of Christ, as smitten, crucified, wounded, and slain. What follows, denotes the imperfect knowledge of God in the present state, even as revealed in Christ; for this, when compared with the heavenly sight of him. is but like seeing a man that is gone by, whose back only is to be seen. God in Christ, as he is, even the fullest and brightest displays of his glory, grace, and goodness, are reserved to another state.

Chapter 34

Chapter Outline

Verses 1-4

When God made man in his own image, the moral law was written in his heart, by the finger of God, without outward means. But since the covenant then made with man was broken, the Lord has used the ministry of men, both in writing the law in the Scriptures, and in writing it in the heart. When God was reconciled to the Israelites, he ordered the tables to be renewed, and wrote his law in them. Even under the gospel of peace by Christ, the moral law continues to bind believers. Though Christ has redeemed us from the curse of the law, yet not from the commands of it. The first and the best evidence of the pardon of sin, and peace with God, is the writing the law in the heart.

Verses 5-9

The Lord descended by some open token of his presence and manifestation of his glory in a cloud, and thence proclaimed his NAME; that is, the perfections and character which are denoted by the name JEHOVAH. The Lord God is merciful; ready to forgive the sinner, and to relieve the needy. Gracious; kind, and ready to bestow undeserved benefits. Long-suffering; slow to anger, giving time for repentance, only punishing when it is needful. He is abundant in goodness and truth; even sinners receive the riches of his bounty abundantly, though they abuse them. All he reveals is infallible truth, all he promises is in faithfulness. Keeping mercy for thousands; he continually shows mercy to sinners, and has treasures, which cannot be exhausted, to the end of time. Forgiving iniquity, and transgression, and sin; his mercy and goodness reach to the full and free forgiveness of sin. And will by no means clear the guilty; the holiness and justice of God are part of his goodness and love towards all his creatures. In Christ's sufferings, the Divine holiness and justice are fully shown, and the evil of sin is made known. God's forgiving mercy is always attended by his converting, sanctifying grace. None are pardoned but those who repent and forsake the allowed practice of every sin; nor shall any escape, who abuse, neglect, or despise this great salvation.

Moses bowed down, and worshipped reverently. Every perfection in the name of God, the believer may plead with Him for the forgiveness of his sins, the making holy of his heart, and the enlargement of the Redeemer's kingdom.

Verses 10-17

The Israelites are commanded to destroy every monument of idolatry, however curious or costly; to refuse all alliance, friendship, or marriage with idolaters, and all idolatrous feasts; and they were reminded not with idolaters, and all idolatrous feats; and they were reminded not to repeat the crime of making molten images. Jealously is called the rage of a man, Pr 6:34; but in God it is holy and just displeasure. Those cannot worship God aright, who do not worship him only.

Verses 18-27

Once a week they must rest, even in ploughing time, and in harvest. All worldly business must give way to that holy rest; even harvest work will prosper the better, for the religious observance of the sabbath day in harvest time. We must show that we prefer our communion with God, and our duty to him, before the business or the joy of harvest. Thrice a year they must appear before the Lord God, the God of Israel. Canaan was a desirable land, and the neighbouring nations were greedy; yet God says, They shall not desire it. Let us check all sinful desires against God and his glory, in our hearts, and then trust him to check all sinful desires in the hearts of others against us. The way of duty is the way of safety. Those who venture for him never lose by him. Three feasts are here mentioned: 1. The Passover, in remembrance of the deliverance out of Egypt. 2. The feast of weeks, or the feast of Pentecost; added to it is the law of the first-fruits. 3. The feast of in-gathering, or the feast of Tabernacles. Moses is to write these words, that the people might know them better. We can never be enough thankful to God for the written word. God would make a covenant with Israel, in Moses as a mediator. Thus the covenant of grace is made with believers through Christ.

Verses 28-35

Near and spiritual communion with God improves the graces of a renewed and holy character. Serious godliness puts a lustre upon a man's countenance, such as commands esteem and affection. The vail which Moses put on, marked the obscurity of that dispensation, compared with the gospel dispensation of the New Testament. It was also an emblem of the natural vail on the hearts of men respecting spiritual things. Also the vail that was and is upon the nation of Israel, which can only be taken away by the Spirit of the Lord showing to them Christ, as the end of the law for righteousness to every one that believeth. Fear and unbelief would put the vail before us, they would hinder our free approach to the mercy-seat above. We should spread our wants, temporal and spiritual, fully before our heavenly Father; we should tell him our hinderances, struggles, trails, and temptations; we should acknowledge our offences.

Chapter 35

Chapter Outline

Verses 1-3

The mild and easy yoke of Christ has made our sabbath duties more delightful, and our sabbath restraints less irksome, than those of the Jews; but we are the more guilty by neglecting them. Surely God's wisdom in giving us the sabbath, with all the mercy of its purposes, are sinfully disregarded. Is it nothing to pour contempt upon the blessed day, which a bounteous God has given to us for our growth in grace with the church below, and to prepare us for happiness with the church above?

Verses 4-19

The tabernacle was to be dedicated to the honour of God, and used in his service; and therefore what was brought for it, was an offering to the Lord. The rule is, Whosoever is of a willing heart, let him bring. All that were skilful must work. God dispenses his gifts; and as every man hath received, so he must minister, 1Pe 4:10. Those that were rich, must bring in materials to work on; those that were skilful, must serve the tabernacle with their skill: as they needed one another, so the tabernacle needed them both, 1Co 12:7–21.

Verses 20-29

Without a willing mind, costly offerings would be abhorred; with it, the smallest will be accepted. Our hearts are willing, when we cheerfully assist in promoting the cause of God. Those who are diligent and contented in employments considered mean, are as much accepted of God as those engaged in splendid services. The women who spun the goats' hair were wise-hearted, because they did it heartily to the Lord. Thus the labourer, mechanic, or servant who attends to his work in the faith and fear of God, may be as wise, for his place, as the most useful minister, and he equally accepted of the Lord. Our wisdom and duty consist in giving God the glory and use of our talents, be they many or few.

Verses 30-35

Here is the Divine appointment of the master-workmen, that there might be no strife for the office, and that all who were employed in the work might take direction from, and give account to them. Those whom God called by name to his service, he filled with the Spirit of God. Skill, even in worldly employments, is God's gift, and comes from above. But many are ready enough in cutting out work for other people, and can tell what this man or that man should do; but the burdens they bind on others, they themselves will not touch with one of their fingers. Such will fall under the character of slothful servants. These men were not only to devise and to work themselves, but they were to teach others. Those that rule should teach; and those to whom God has given knowledge, should be willing to make it known for the benefit of others.

Chapter 36

The making of the tabernacle, The liberality of the people restrained.
—The readiness and zeal with which these builders set about their work, the exactness with which they performed it, and the faithfulness with which they objected to receive more contributions, are worthy of our imitation. Thus should we serve God, and our superiors also, in all things lawful. Thus should all who are in public trusts abhor filthy lucre, and avoid all occasions and temptations to covetousness. Where have we the representation of God's love towards us, that we by love dwell in him and he in us, save in Emmanuel? Mt 1:23. This is the sum of the ministry of reconciliation, 2Co 5:18, 19. This was the design of the "tabernacle of witness," a visible testimony of the love of God to the race of men, however they were fallen from their first state. And this love was shown by Christ's taking up his abode on earth; by the Word being made flesh, Joh 1:14, wherein, as the original expresses it, he did tabernacle among us.

Chapter 37

The making of the ark, and the furniture of the tabernacle.
—In the furniture of the tabernacle were emblems of a spiritual and acceptable service. The incense represented the prayers of the saints. The sacrifice of the alter represented the Lamb of God that taketh away the sins of the world. The golden pot with manna, or bread from heaven, the flesh of Jesus Christ, which he gave for the life of the world. The candlestick, with its lights, the teaching and enlightening of the Holy Spirit. The shew-bread represented that provision for those who hunger and thirst after righteousness, which the gospel, the ordinances and the sacraments of the house of prayer, abundantly bestow. The exactness of the workmen to their rule, should be followed by us; seeking for the influences of the Holy Spirit, that we may rejoice in and glorify God while in this world, and at length be with him for ever.

Chapter 38

Chapter Outline

The brazen altar and laver.   (1–8)

The court.   (9–20)

The offerings of the people.   (21–31)

Verses 1-8

In all ages of the church there have been some persons more devoted to God, more constant in their attendance upon his ordinances, and more willing to part even with lawful things, for his sake, than others. Some women, devoted to God and zealous for the tabernacle worship, expressed zeal by parting with their mirrors, which were polished plates of brass. Before the invention of looking-glasses, these served the same purposes. (Ex 38:9-20)

Verses 9-20

The walls of the court being of curtains only, intimated that the state of the Jewish church itself was movable and changeable; and in due time to be taken down and folded up, when the place of the tent should be enlarged, and its cords lengthened, to make room for the Gentile world.

Verses 21-31

The foundation of massy pieces of silver showed the solidity and purity of the truth upon which the church is founded. Let us regard the Lord Jesus Christ while reading of the furniture of the tabernacle. While looking at the altar of burnt-offering, let us see Jesus. In him, his righteousness, and salvation, is a full and sufficient offering for sin. In the laver of regeneration, by his Holy Spirit, let our souls be washed, and they shall be clean; and as the people offered willingly, so may our souls be made willing. Let us be ready to part with any thing, and count all but loss to win Christ.

Chapter 39

Chapter Outline

The priests' garments.   (1–31)

The tabernacle completed.   (32–43)

Verses 1-31

The priests' garments were rich and splendid. The church in its infancy was thus taught by shadows of good things to come; but the substance is Christ, and the grace of the gospel. Christ is our great High Priest. When he undertook the work of our redemption, he put on the clothes of service, he arrayed himself with the gifts and graces of the Spirit, girded himself with resolution to go through the undertaking, took charge of all God's spiritual Israel, laid them near his heart, engraved them on the palms of his hands, and presented them to his Father. And he crowned himself with holiness to the Lord, consecrating his whole undertaking to the honour of his Father's holiness. True believers are spiritual priests. The clean linen with which all their clothes of service must be made, is the righteousness of saints, Re 19:8.

Verses 32-43

The tabernacle was a type or emblem of Jesus Christ. As the Most High dwelt visibly within the sanctuary, even on the ark, so did he reside in the human nature and tabernacle of his dear Son; in Christ dwelt all the fulness of the Godhead bodily, Col 2:9. The tabernacle was a symbol of every real Christian. In the soul of every true follower of the Saviour the Father dwells, the object of his worship, and the author of his blessings. The tabernacle also typified the church of the Redeemer. The meanest and the mightiest are alike dear to the Father's love, freely exercised through faith in Christ. The tabernacle was a type and emblem of the heavenly temple, Re 21:3. What, then, will be the splendour of His appearance, when the cloud shall be withdrawn, and his faithful worshippers shall see him as he is!

Chapter 40

Chapter Outline

The tabernacle is to be set up, Aaron and his sons to be sanctified.	(1–15)
Moses performs all as directed.	(16–33)
The glory of the Lord fills the tabernacle.	(34–38)

Verses 1-15

When a new year begins, we should seek to serve God better than the year before. In half a year the tabernacle was completed. When the hearts of numbers are earnest in a good cause, much may be done in a short time; and when the commandments of God are continually attended to, as the rule of working, all will be done well. The high-priesthood was in the family of Aaron till Christ came, and in Him, the substance of all these shadows, it continues for ever.

Verses 16-33

When the tabernacle and the furniture of it were prepared, they did not put off rearing it till they came to Canaan; but, in obedience to the will of God, they set it up in the midst of their camp. Those who are unsettled in the world, must not think that this will excuse want of religion; as if it were enough to begin to serve God when they begin to be settled in the world. No; a tabernacle for God is very needful, even in a wilderness, especially as we may be in another world before we come to fix in this. And we may justly fear lest we should deceive ourselves with a form of godliness.

The thought that so few entered Canaan, should warn young persons especially, not to put off the care of their souls.

Verses 34-38

The cloud covered the tabernacle even in the clearest day; it was not a cloud which the sun scatters. This cloud was a token of God's presence to be seen day and night, by all Israel, that they might never again question, Is the Lord among us, or is he not? It guided the camp of Israel through the wilderness. While the cloud rested on the tabernacle, they rested; when it removed, they followed it. The glory of the Lord filled the tabernacle. In light and fire the Shechinah made itself visible: God is Light; our God is a consuming Fire. Yet so dazzling was the light, and so dreadful the fire, that Moses was not able to enter into the tent of the congregation, till the splendour was abated. But what Moses could not do, our Lord Jesus has done, whom God caused to draw near; and who has invited us to come boldly, even to the mercy-seat. Being taught by the Holy Spirit to follow the example of Christ, as well as to depend upon him, to attend his ordinances, and obey his precepts, we shall be kept from losing our way, and be led in the midst of the paths of judgment, till we come to heaven, the habitation of his holiness. BLESSED BE GOD FOR JESUS CHRIST!

Leviticus

God ordained divers kinds of oblations and sacrifices, to assure his people of the forgiveness of their offences, if they offered them in true faith and obedience. Also he appointed the priests and Levites, their apparel, offices, conduct, and portion. He showed what feasts they should observe, and at what times. He declared by these sacrifices and ceremonies, that the reward of sin is death, and that without the blood of Christ, the innocent Lamb of God, there can be no forgiveness of sins.

Chapter 1

Chapter Outline

The offerings.   (1, 2)

From the herds.   (3–9)

From the flocks, and of fowls.   (10–17)

Verses 1, 2

The offering of sacrifices was an ordinance of true religion, from the fall of man unto the coming of Christ. But till the Israelites were in the wilderness, no very particular regulations seem to have been appointed. The general design of these laws is plain. The sacrifices typified Christ; they also shadowed out the believer's duty, character, privilege, and communion with God. There is scarcely any thing spoken of the Lord Jesus in Scripture which has not also a reference to his people. This book begins with the laws concerning sacrifices; the most ancient were the burnt-offerings, about which God here gives Moses directions. It is taken for granted that the people would be willing to bring offerings to the Lord. The very light of nature directs man, some way or other, to do honour to his Maker, as his Lord. Immediately after the fall, sacrifices were ordained.

Verses 3-9

In the due performance of the Levitical ordinances, the mysteries of the spiritual world are represented by corresponding natural objects; and future events are exhibited in these rites. Without this, the whole will seem unmeaning ceremonies. There is in these things a type of the sufferings of the Son of God, who was to be a sacrifice for the sins of the whole world? The burning body of an animal was but a faint representation of that everlasting misery, which we all have deserved; and which our blessed Lord bore in his body and in his soul, when he died under the load of our iniquities. Observe, 1. The beast to be offered must be without blemish. This signified the strength and purity that were in Christ, and the holy life that should be in his people. 2. The owner must offer it of his own free will. What is done in religion, so as to please God, must be done by love. Christ willingly offered himself for us. 3. It must be offered at the door of the tabernacle, where the brazen altar of burnt-offerings stood, which sanctified the gift: he must offer it at the door, as one unworthy to enter, and acknowledging that a sinner can have no communion with God, but by sacrifice. 4. The offerer must put his hand upon the head of his offering, signifying thereby, his desire and hope that it might be accepted from him, to make atonement for him. 5. The sacrifice was to be killed before the Lord, in an orderly manner, and to honour God. It signified also, that in Christians the flesh must be crucified with its corrupt affections and lust. 6. The priests were to sprinkle the blood upon the altar; for the blood being the life, that was it which made atonement. This signified the pacifying and purifying of our consciences, by the sprinkling of the blood of Jesus Christ upon them by faith. 7. The beast was to be divided into several pieces, and then to be burned upon the altar. The burning of the sacrifice signified the sharp sufferings of Christ, and the devout affections with which, as a holy fire, Christians must offer up themselves, their whole spirit, soul, and body, unto God. 8. This is said to be an offering of a sweet savour. As an act of obedience to a Divine command, and a type of Christ, this was well-pleasing to God; and the spiritual sacrifices of Christians are acceptable to God, through Christ, 1Pe 2:5.

Verses 10-17

Those who could not offer a bullock, were to bring a sheep or a goat; and those who were not able to do that, were accepted of God, if they brought a turtle-dove, or a pigeon. Those creatures were chosen for sacrifice which were mild, and gentle, and harmless; to show the innocence and meekness that were in Christ, and that should be in Christians. The offering of the poor was as typical of Christ's atonement as the more costly sacrifices, and expressed as fully repentance, faith, and devotedness to God. We have no excuse, if we refuse the pleasant and reasonable service now required. But we can no more offer the sacrifice of a broken heart, or of praise and thanksgiving, than an Israelite could offer a bullock or a goat, except as God hath first given to us. The more we do in the Lord's service, the greater are our obligations to him, for the will, for the ability, and opportunity. In many things God leaves us to fix what shall be spent in his service, whether of our time or our substance; yet where God's providence has put much into a man's power, scanty offerings will not be accepted, for they are not proper expressions of a willing mind. Let us be devoted in body and soul to his service, whatever he may call us to give, venture, do, or suffer for his sake.

Chapter 2

Chapter Outline

Verses 1-11

Meat-offerings may typify Christ, as presented to God for us, and as being the Bread of life to our souls; but they rather seem to denote our obligation to God for the blessings of providence, and those good works which are acceptable to God. The term "meat" was, and still is, properly given to any kind of provision, and the greater part of this offering was to be eaten for food, not burned. These meat-offerings are mentioned after the burnt-offerings: without an interest in the sacrifice of Christ, and devotedness of heart to God, such services cannot be accepted. Leaven is the emblem of pride, malice, and hypocrisy, and honey of sensual pleasure. The former are directly opposed to the graces of humility, love, and sincerity, which God approves; the latter takes men from the exercises of devotion, and the practice of good works. Christ, in his character and sacrifice, was wholly free from the things denoted by leaven; and his suffering life and agonizing death were the very opposites to worldly pleasure. His people are called to follow, and to be like him.

Verses 12-16

Salt is required in all the offerings. God hereby intimates to them that their sacrifices, in themselves, were unsavoury. All religious services must be seasoned with grace. Christianity is the salt of the earth. Directions are given about offering their first-fruits at harvest. If a man, with a thankful sense of God's goodness in giving him a plentiful crop, was disposed to present an offering to God, let him bring the first ripe and full ears. Whatever was brought to God must be the best in its kind, though it were but green ears of corn. Oil and frankincense must be put upon it. Wisdom and humility soften and sweeten the spirits and services of young people, and their green ears of corn shall be acceptable. God takes delight in the first ripe fruits of the Spirit, and the expressions of early piety and devotion. Holy love to God is the fire by which all our offerings must be made. The frankincense denotes the mediation and intercession of Christ, by which our services are accepted. Blessed be God that we have the substance, of which these observances were but shadows. There is that excellency in Christ, and in his work as Mediator, which no types and shadows can fully represent. And our dependence thereon must be so entire, that we must never lose sight of it in any thing we do, if we would be accepted of God.

Chapter 3

Chapter Outline

The peace-offering of the herd.   (1–5)

The peace-offering of the flock.   (6–17)

Verses 1-5

The peace-offerings had regard to God as the giver of all good things. These were divided between the altar, the priest, and the owner. They were called peace-offering, because in them God and his people did, as it were, feast together, in token of friendship. The peace-offerings were offered by way of supplication. If a man were in pursuit of any mercy, he would add a peace-offering to his prayer for it. Christ is our Peace, our Peace-offering; for through him alone it is that we can obtain an answer of peace to our prayers. Or, the peace-offering was offered by way of thanksgiving for some mercy received. We must offer to God the sacrifice of praise continually, by Christ our Peace; and then this shall please the Lord better than an ox or bullock.

Verses 6-17

Here is a law that they should eat neither fat nor blood. As for the fat, it means the fat of the inwards, the suet. The blood was forbidden for the same reason; because it was God's part of every sacrifice. God would not permit the blood that made atonement to be used as a common thing, Heb 10:29; nor will he allow us, though we have the comfort of the atonement made, to claim for ourselves any share in the honour of making it. This taught the Jews to observe distinction between common and sacred things; it kept them separate from idolaters. It would impress them more deeply with the belief of some important mystery in the shedding of the blood and the burning the fat of their solemn sacrifices. Christ, as the Prince of peace, "made peace with the blood of his cross." Through him the believer is reconciled to God; and having the peace of God in his heart, he is disposed to follow peace with all men. May the Lord multiply grace, mercy, and peace, to all who desire to bear the Christian character.

Chapter 4

Chapter Outline

Verses 1-12

Burnt-offerings, meat-offerings, and peace-offerings, had been offered before the giving of the law upon mount Sinai; and in these the patriarchs had respect to sin, to make atonement for it. But the Jews were now put into a way of making atonement for sin, more particularly by sacrifice, as a shadow of good things to come; yet the substance is Christ, and that one offering of himself, by which he put away sin. The sins for which the sin-offerings were appointed are supposed to be open acts. They are supposed to be sins of commission, things which ought not to have been done. Omissions are sins, and must come into judgment: yet what had been omitted at one time, might be done at another; but a sin committed was past recall. They are supposed to be sins committed through ignorance. The law begins with the case of the anointed priest. It is evident that God never had any infallible priest in his church upon earth, when even the high priest was liable to fall into sins of ignorance. All pretensions to act without error are sure marks of Antichrist. The beast was to be carried without the camp, and there burned to ashes. This was a sign of the duty of repentance, which is the putting away sin as a detestable thing, which our soul hates. The sin-offering is called sin. What they did to that, we must do to our sins; the body of sin must be destroyed, Ro 6:6. The apostle applies the carrying this sacrifice without the camp to Christ, Heb 13:11–13.

Verses 13-21

If the leaders of the people, through mistake, caused them to err, an offering must be brought, that wrath might not come upon the whole congregation. When sacrifices were offered, the persons, on whose behalf they were devoted, were to lay their hands on the heads of the victims, and to confess their sins. The elders were to do so, when the sacrifices were offered for the whole congregation. The load of sin was supposed then to be borne by the guiltless animal. When the offering is completed, it is said, atonement is made, and the sin shall be forgiven. The saving of churches and kingdoms from ruin, is owing to the satisfaction and mediation of Christ.

Verses 22-26

Those who have power to call others to account, are themselves accountable to the Ruler of rulers. The sin of the ruler, committed through ignorance, must come to his knowledge, either by the check of his own conscience, or by the reproof of his friends; both which even the best and greatest, not only should submit to, but be thankful for. That which I see not, teach thou me, and, Show me wherein I have erred, are prayers we should put up to God every day; that if, through ignorance, we fall into sin, we may not through ignorance abide in it.

Verses 27-35

Here is the law of the sin-offering for a common person. To be able to plead, when charged with sin, that we did it ignorantly, and through the surprise of temptation, will not bring us off, if we have no interest in that great plea, Christ hath died. The sins of ignorance committed by a common person, needed a sacrifice; the greatest are not above, the meanest are not below Divine justice. None, if offenders, were overlooked. Here rich and poor meet together; they are alike sinners, and welcome to Christ. From all these laws concerning the sin-offerings, we may learn to hate sin, and to watch against it; and to value Christ, the great and true Sin-offering, whose blood cleanses from all sin, which it was not possible that the blood of bulls and of goats should take away. For us to err, with the Bible in our hands, is the effect of pride, sloth, and carelessness. We need to use frequent self-examination, with serious study of the Scriptures, and earnest prayer for the convincing influences of God the Holy Spirit; that we may detect our sins of ignorance, repent, and obtain forgiveness through the blood of Christ.

Chapter 5

Chapter Outline

Concerning various trespasses.   (1–13)

Concerning trespasses against the Lord.   (14–19)

Verses 1-13

The offences here noticed are, 1. A man's concealing the truth, when he was sworn as a witness to speak the truth, the whole truth, and nothing but the truth. If, in such a case, for fear of offending one that has been his friend, or may be his enemy, a man refuses to give evidence, or gives it but in part, he shall bear his iniquity. And that is a heavy burden, which, if some course be not taken to get it removed, will sink a man to hell. Let all that are called at any time to be witnesses, think of this law, and be free and open in their evidence, and take heed of prevaricating. An oath of the Lord is a sacred thing, not to be trifled with. 2. A man's touching any thing that was ceremonially unclean. Though his touching the unclean thing only made him ceremonially defiled, yet neglecting to wash himself according to the law, was either carelessness or contempt, and contracted moral guilt. As soon as God, by his Spirit, convinces our consciences of any sin or duty, we must follow the conviction, as not ashamed to own our former mistake. 3. Rash swearing, that a man will do or not do such a thing. As if the performance of his oath afterward prove unlawful, or what cannot be done. Wisdom and watchfulness beforehand would prevent these difficulties. In these cases the offender must confess his sin, and bring his offering; but the offering was not accepted, unless accompanied with confession and humble prayer for pardon. The confession must be particular; that he hath sinned in that thing. Deceit lies in generals; many will own they have sinned, for that all must own; but their sins in any one particular they are unwilling to allow. The way to be assured of pardon, and armed against sin for the future, is to confess the exact truth. If any were very poor, they might bring some flour, and that should be accepted. Thus the expense of the sin-offering was brought lower than any other, to teach that no man's poverty shall ever bar the way of his pardon. If the sinner brought two doves, one was to be offered for a sin-offering, and the other for a burnt-offering. We must first see that our peace be made with God, and then we may expect that our services for his glory will be accepted by him. To show the loathsomeness of sin, the flour, when offered, must not be made grateful to the taste by oil, or to the smell by frankincense. God, by these sacrifices, spoke comfort to those who had offended, that they might not despair, nor pine away in their sins. Likewise caution not to offend any more, remembering how expensive and troublesome it was to make atonement.

Verses 14-19

Here are offerings to atone for trespasses against a neighbour. If a man put to his own use unwittingly, any thing dedicated to God, he was to bring this sacrifice. We are to be jealous over ourselves, to ask pardon for the sin, and make satisfaction for the wrong, which we do but suspect ourselves guilty of. The law of God is so very broad, the occasions of sin in this guilty of. The law of God is so very broad, the occasions of sin in this world are so numerous, and we are so prone to evil, that we need to fear always, and to pray always, that we may be kept from sin. Also we should look before us at every step. The true Christian daily pleads guilty before God, and seeks forgiveness through the blood of Christ. And the gospel salvation is so free, that the poorest is not shut out; and so full, that the most burdened conscience may find relief from it. Yet the evil of sin is so displayed as to cause every pardoned sinner to abhor and dread it.

Chapter 6

Chapter Outline

Verses 1-7

Though all the instances relate to our neighbour, yet it is called a trespass against the Lord. Though the person injured be mean, and even despicable, yet the injury reflects upon that God who has made the command of loving our neighbour next to that of loving himself. Human laws make a difference as to punishments; but all methods of doing wrong to others, are alike violations of the Divine law, even keeping what is found, when the owner can be discovered. Frauds are generally accompanied with lies, often with false oaths. If the offender would escape the vengeance of God, he must make ample restitution, according to his power, and seek forgiveness by faith in that one Offering which taketh away the sin of the world. The trespasses here mentioned, still are trespasses against the law of Christ, which insists as much upon justice and truth, as the law of nature, or the law of Moses.

Verses 8-13

The daily sacrifice of a lamb is chiefly referred to. The priest must take care of the fire upon the altar. The first fire upon the altar came from heaven, ch. 9:24; by keeping that up continually, all their sacrifices might be said to be consumed with the fire from heaven, in token of God's acceptance. Thus should the fire of our holy affections, the exercise of our faith and love, of prayer and praise, be without ceasing.

Verses 14-23

The law of the burnt-offerings put upon the priests a great deal of care and work; the flesh was wholly burnt, and the priests had nothing but the skin. But most of the meat-offering was their own. It is God's will that his ministers should be provided with what is needful.

Verses 24-30

The blood of the sin-offering was to be washed out of the clothes on which it should happen to be sprinkled, which signified the regard we ought to have to the blood of Christ, not counting it a common thing. The vessel in which the flesh of the sin-offering was boiled must be broken, if it were an earthen one; but if a brazen one, well washed. This showed that the defilement was not wholly taken away by the offering; but the blood of Christ thoroughly cleanses from all sin. All these rules set forth the polluting nature of sin, and the removal of guilt from the sinner to the sacrifice. Behold and wonder at Christ's love, in that he was content to be made a sin-offering for us, and so to procure our pardon for continual sins and failings. He that knew no sin was made sin (that is, a sin-offering) for us, 2Co 5:21. Hence we have pardon, and not only pardon, but power also, against sin, Ro 8:3.

Chapter 7

Chapter Outline

Verses 1-10

In the sin-offering and the trespass-offering, the sacrifice was divided between the altar and the priest; the offerer had no share, as he had in the peace-offerings. The former expressed repentance and sorrow for sin, therefore it was more proper to fast than feast; the peace-offerings denoted communion with a reconciled God in Christ, the joy and gratitude of a pardoned sinner, and the privileges of a true believer.

Verses 11-27

As to the peace-offerings, in the expression of their sense of mercy, God left them more at liberty, than in the expression of their sense of sin; that their sacrifices, being free-will offerings, might be the more acceptable, while, by obliging them to bring the sacrifices of atonement, God shows the necessity of the great Propitiation. The main reason why blood was forbidden of old, was because the Lord had appointed blood for an atonement. This use, being figurative, had its end in Christ, who by his death and blood-shedding caused the sacrifices to cease. Therefore this law is not now in force on believers.

Verses 28-34

The priest who offered, was to have the breast and the right shoulder. When the sacrifice was killed, the offerer himself must present God's part of it; that he might signify his cheerfully giving it up to God. He was with his own hands to lift it up, in token of his regard to God as the God of heaven; and then to wave it to and fro, in token of his regard to God as the Lord of the whole earth. Be persuaded and encouraged to feed and feast upon Christ, our Peace-offering. This blessed

Peace-offering is not for the priests only, for saints of the highest rank and greatest eminence, but for the common people also. Take heed of delay. Many think to repent and return to God when they are dying and dropping into hell; but they should eat the peace-offering, and eat it now. Stay not till the day of the Lord's patience be run out, for eating the third day will not be accepted, nor will catching at Christ when thou art gone to hell! (Le 7:35-38)

Verses 35-38

Solemn acts of religious worship are not things which we may do or not do at our pleasure; it is at our peril if we omit them. An observance of the laws of Christ cannot be less necessary than of the laws of Moses.

Chapter 8

Chapter Outline

Verses 1-13

The consecration of Aaron and his sons had been delayed until the tabernacle had been prepared, and the laws of the sacrifices given. Aaron and his sons were washed with water, to signify that they ought to purify themselves from all sinful dispositions, and ever after to keep themselves pure. Christ washes those from their sins in his own blood whom he makes kings and priests to our God, Re 1:5, 6; and those that draw near to God must be washed in pure water, Heb 10:22. The anointing of Aaron was to typify the anointing of Christ with the Spirit, which was not given by measure to him. All believers have received the anointing.

Verses 14-36

In these types we see our great High Priest, even Christ Jesus, solemnly appointed, anointed, and invested with his sacred office, by his own blood, and the influences of his Holy Spirit. He sanctifies the ordinances of religion, to the benefit of his people and the honour of God the Father; who for his sake accepts our worship, though it is polluted with sin. We may also rejoice, that he is a merciful and faithful High Priest, full of compassion to the feeble-minded and tempest-tossed soul. All true Christians are consecrated to be spiritual priests. We should seriously ask ourselves, whether in our daily walk we study to maintain this character? and abound in spiritual sacrifices, acceptable to God through Christ? If so, still there is no cause for boasting. Let us not despise our fellow-sinners; but remembering what we have done, and how we are saved, let us seek and pray for their salvation.

Chapter 9

Chapter Outline

Verses 1-21

These many sacrifices, which were all done away by the death of Christ, teach us that our best services need washing in his blood, and that the guilt of our best sacrifices needs to be done away by one more pure and more noble than they. Let us be thankful that we have such a High Priest. The priests had not a day's respite from service allowed. God's spiritual priests have constant work, which the duty of every day requires; they that would give up their account with joy, must redeem time. The glory of God appeared in the sight of the people, and owned what they had done. We are not now to expect such appearances, but God draws nigh to those who draw nigh to him, and the offerings of faith are acceptable to him; though the sacrifices being spiritual, the tokens of the acceptance are spiritual likewise. When Aaron had done all that was to be done about the sacrifices, he lifted up his hands towards the people, and blessed them. Aaron could but crave a blessing, God alone can command it.

Verses 22-24

When the solemnity was finished, and the blessing pronounced, God testified his acceptance. There came a fire out from before the Lord, and consumed the sacrifice. This fire might justly have fastened upon the people, and have consumed them for their sins; but its consuming the sacrifice signified God's acceptance of it, as an atonement for the sinner. This also was a figure of good things to come. The Spirit descended upon the apostles in fire. And the descent of this holy fire into our souls, to kindle in them pious and devout affections toward God, and such a holy zeal as burns up the flesh and the lusts of it, is a certain token of God's gracious acceptance of our persons and performances. Nothing goes to God, but what comes from him. We must have grace, that holy fire, from the God of grace, else we cannot serve him acceptably, Heb 12:28. The people were affected with this discovery of God's glory and grace. They received it with the highest joy; triumphing in the assurance given them that they had God nigh unto them. And with the lowest reverence; humbly adoring the majesty of that God, who vouchsafed thus to manifest himself to them. That is a sinful fear of God, which drives us from him; a gracious fear makes us bow before him.

Chapter 10

Chapter Outline

Verses 1, 2

Next to Moses and Aaron, none were more likely to be honourable in Israel than Nadab and Abihu. There is reason to think that they were puffed up with pride, and that they were heated with wine. While the people were prostrate before the Lord, adoring his presence and glory, they rushed into the tabernacle to burn incense, though not at the appointed time; both together, instead of one alone, and with fire not taken from the altar. If it had been done through ignorance, they had been allowed to bring a sin-offering. But the soul that doeth presumptuously, and in contempt of God's majesty and justice, that soul shall be cut off. The wages of sin is death. They died in the very act of their sin. The sin and punishment of these priests showed the imperfection of that priesthood from the very beginning, and that it could not shelter any from the fire of God's wrath, otherwise than as it was typical of Christ's priesthood.

Verses 3-7

The most quieting considerations under affliction are fetched from the word of God. What was it that God spake? Though Aaron's heart must have been filled with anguish and dismay, yet with silent submission he revered the justice of the stroke. When God corrects us or ours for sin, it is our duty to accept the punishment, and say, It is the Lord, let him do what seemeth him good. Whenever we worship God, we come nigh unto him, as spiritual priests. This ought to make us very serious in all acts of devotion. It concerns us all, when we come nigh to God, to do every religious exercise, as those who believe that the God with whom we have to do, is a holy God. He will take vengeance on those that profane his sacred name by trifling with him.

Verses 8-11

Do not drink wine or strong drink. During the time they ministered, the priests were forbidden it. It is required of gospel ministers, that they be not given to wine, 1Ti 3:3. It is, Lest ye die; die when ye are in drink. The danger of death, to which we are continually exposed, should engage all to be sober.

Verses 12-20

Afflictions should rather quicken us to our duty, than take us from it. But our unfitness for duty, when it is natural and not sinful, will have great allowances made for it; God will have mercy, and not sacrifice. Let us profit by the solemn warning this history conveys. When professing worshippers come with zeal without knowledge, carnal affections, earthly, light, vain, trifling thoughts, the devices of will-worship, instead of the offering of soul and spirit; then the incense is kindled by a flame which never came down from heaven, which the Spirit of a holy God never sent within their hearts.

Chapter 11

What animals were clean and unclean.
—These laws seem to have been intended, 1. As a test of the people's obedience, as Adam was forbidden to eat of the tree of knowledge; and to teach them self-denial, and the government of their appetites. 2. To keep the Israelites distinct from other nations. Many also of these forbidden animals were objects of superstition and idolatry to the heathen. 3. The people were taught to make distinctions between the holy and unholy in their companions and intimate connexions. 4. The law forbad, not only the eating of the unclean beasts, but the touching of them. Those who would be kept from any sin, must be careful to avoid all temptations to it, or coming near it. The exceptions are very minute, and all were designed to call forth constant care and exactness in their obedience; and to teach us to obey. Whilst we enjoy our Christian liberty, and are free from such burdensome observances, we must be careful not to abuse our liberty. For the Lord hath redeemed and called his people, that they may be holy, even as he is holy. We must come out, and be separate from the world; we must leave the company of the ungodly, and all needless connexions with those who are dead in sin; we must be zealous of good works devoted followers of God, and companions of his people.

Chapter 12

Ceremonial purification.
—After the laws concerning clean and unclean food, come the laws concerning clean and unclean persons. Man imparts his depraved nature to his offspring, so that, excepting as the atonement of Christ and the sanctification of the Spirit prevent, the original blessing, "Increase and multiply," Ge 1:28, is become to the fallen race a direful curse, and communicates sin and misery. Let those women who have received mercy from God in child-bearing, with all thankfulness own God's goodness to them; and this shall please the Lord better than sacrifices.

Chapter 13

Chapter Outline

Verses 1-17

The plague of leprosy was an uncleanness, rather than a disease. Christ is said to cleanse lepers, not to cure them. Common as the leprosy was among the Hebrews, during and after their residence in Egypt, we have no reason to believe that it was known among them before. Their distressed state and employment in that land must have rendered them liable to disease. But it was a plague often inflicted immediately by the hand of God. Miriam's leprosy, and Gehazi's, and king Uzziah's, were punishments of particular sins; no marvel there was care taken to distinguish it from a common distemper. The judgment of it was referred to the priests. And it was a figure of the moral pollutions of men's minds by sin, which is the leprosy of the soul, defiling to the conscience, and from which Christ alone can cleanse. The priest could only convict the leper, (by the law is the knowledge of sin,) but Christ can cure the sinner, he can take away sin. It is a work of great importance, but of great difficulty, to judge of our spiritual state. We all have cause to suspect ourselves, being conscious of sores and spots; but whether clean or unclean is the question. As there were certain marks by which to know it was leprosy, so there are marks of such as are in the gall of bitterness. The priest must take time in making his judgment. This teaches all, both ministers and people, not to be hasty in censures, nor to judge anything before the time. If some men's sins go before unto judgment, the sins of others follow after, and so do men's good works. If the person suspected were found to be clean, yet he must wash his clothes, because there had been ground for the suspicion. We have need to be washed in the blood of Christ from our spots, though not leprosy spots; for who can say, I am pure from sin?

Verses 18-44

The priest is told what judgment to make, if there were any appearance of a leprosy in old sores; and such is the danger of those who having escaped the pollutions of the world are again entangled therein. Or, in a burn by accident, ver. #(24). The burning of strife and contention often occasions the rising and breaking out of that corruption, which proves that men are unclean. Human life lies exposed to many grievances. With what troops of diseases are we beset on every side; and thy all entered by sin! If the constitution be healthy, and the body lively and easy, we are bound to glorify God with our bodies. Particular note was taken of the leprosy, if in the head. If the leprosy of sin has seized the head; if the judgment be corrupted, and wicked principles, which support wicked practices, are embraced, it is utter uncleanness, from which few are cleansed. Soundness in the faith keeps leprosy from the head.

Verses 45, 46

When the priest had pronounced the leper unclean, it put a stop to his business in the world, cut him off from his friends and relations, and ruined all the comfort he could have in the world. He must humble himself under the mighty hand of God, not insisting upon his cleanness, when the priest had pronounced him unclean, but accepting the punishment. Thus must we take to ourselves the shame that belongs to us, and with broken hearts call ourselves "Unclean, unclean;" heart unclean, life unclean; unclean by original corruption, unclean by actual transgression; unclean, therefore deserving to be for ever shut out from communion with God, and all hope of happiness in him; unclean, therefore undone, if infinite mercy do not interpose. The leper must warn others to take heed of coming near him. He must then be shut out of the camp, and afterward, when they came to Canaan, be shut out of the city, town, or village where he lived, and dwell with none but those that were lepers like himself. This typified the purity which ought to be in the gospel church.

Verses 47-59

The garment suspected to be tainted with leprosy was not to be burned immediately. If, upon search, it was found that there was a leprous spot, it must be burned, or at least that part of it. If it proved to be free, it must be washed, and then might be used. This also sets forth the great evil there is in sin. It not only defiles the sinner's conscience, but it brings a stain upon all he has and all that he does. And those who make their clothes servants to their pride and lust, may see them thereby tainted with leprosy. But the robes of righteousness never fret, nor are moth-eaten.

Chapter 14

Chapter Outline

Verses 1-9

The priests could not cleanse the lepers; but when the Lord removed the plague, various rules were to be observed in admitting them again to the ordinances of God, and the society of his people. They represent many duties and exercises of truly repenting sinners, and the duties of ministers respecting them. If we apply this to the spiritual leprosy of sin, it intimates that when we withdraw from those who walk disorderly, we must not count them as enemies, but admonish them as brethren. And also that when God by his grace has brought to repentance, they ought with tenderness and joy, and sincere affection, to be received again. Care should always be taken that sinners may not be encouraged, nor penitents discouraged. If it were found that the leprosy was healed, the priest must declare it with the particular solemnities here described. The two birds, one killed, and the other dipped in the blood of the bird that was killed, and then let loose, may signify Christ shedding his blood for sinners, and rising and ascending into heaven. The priest having pronounced the leper clean from the disease, he must make himself clean from all remains of it. Thus those who have comfort of the remission of their sins, must with care and caution cleanse themselves from sins; for every one that has this hope in him, will be concerned to purify himself.

Verses 10-32

The cleansed leper was to be presented to the Lord, with his offerings. When God has restored us to enjoy public worship again, after sickness, distance, or otherwise, we should testify our thanksgiving by our diligent use of the liberty. And both we and our offerings must be presented before the Lord, by the Priest that made us clean, even our Lord Jesus. Beside the usual rites of the trespass-offering, some of the blood, and some of the oil, was to be put upon him that was to be cleansed. Wherever the blood of Christ is applied for justification, the oil of the Spirit is applied for sanctification; these two cannot be separated. We have here the gracious provision the law made for poor lepers. The poor are as welcome to God's altar as the rich. But though a meaner sacrifice was accepted from the poor, yet the same ceremony was used for the rich; their souls are as precious, and Christ and his gospel are the same to both. Even for the poor one lamb was necessary. No sinner could be saved, had it not been for the Lamb that was slain, and hath redeemed us to God with his blood.

Verses 33-53

The leprosy in a house is unaccountable to us, as well as the leprosy in a garment; but now sin, where that reigns in a house, is a plague there, as it is in a heart. Masters of families should be aware, and afraid of the first appearance of sin in their families, and put it away, whatever it is. If the leprosy is got into the house, the infected part must be taken out. If it remain in the house, the whole must be pulled down. The owner had better be without a dwelling, than live in one that was infected. The leprosy of sin ruins families and churches. Thus sin is so interwoven with the human body, that it must be taken down by death.

Verses 54-57

When that God who is rich in mercy, for his great love wherewith he loved us, even when we were dead in sins, hath quickened us by his grace, Eph 2:4, 5, we shall manifest the change by repenting, and forsaking former sins. Let us follow after holiness, and let us compassionate other poor lepers, and desire, seek, and pray for their cleansing.

Chapter 15

Laws concerning ceremonial uncleanness.

—We need not be curious in explaining these laws; but have reason to be thankful that we need fear no defilement, except that of sin, nor need ceremonial and burdensome purifications. These laws remind us that God sees all things, even those which escape the notice of men. The great gospel duties of faith and repentance are here signified, and the great gospel privileges of the application of Christ's blood to our souls for our justification, and his grace for our sanctification.

Chapter 16

Chapter Outline

Verses 1-14

Without entering into particulars of the sacrifices on the great day of atonement, we may notice that it was to be a statute for ever, till that dispensation be at an end. As long as we are continually sinning, we continually need the atonement. The law of afflicting our souls for sin, is a statue which will continue in force till we arrive where all tears, even those of repentance, will be wiped from our eyes. The apostle observes it as a proof that the sacrifices could not take away sin, and cleanse the conscience from it, that in them there was a remembrance made of sin every year, upon the day of atonement, Heb 10:1, 3. The repeating the sacrifices, showed there was in them but a feeble effort toward making atonement; this could be done only by offering up the body of Christ once for all; and that sacrifice needed not to be repeated. (Le 16:15-34)

Verses 15-34

Here are typified the two great gospel privileges, of the remission of sin, and access to God, both of which we owe to our Lord Jesus. See the expiation of guilt. Christ is both the Maker and the Matter of the atonement; for he is the Priest, the High Priest, that makes reconciliation for the sins of the people. And as Christ is the High Priest, so he is the Sacrifice with which atonement is made; for he is all in all in our reconciliation to God. Thus he was figured by the two goats. The slain goat was a type of Christ dying for our sins; the scape-goat a type of Christ rising again for our justification. The atonement is said to be completed by putting the sins of Israel upon the head of the goat, which was sent away into a wilderness, a land not inhabited; and the sending away of the goat represented the free and full remission of their sins. He shall bear upon him all their iniquities. Thus Christ, the Lamb of God, takes away the sin of the world, by taking it upon himself, Joh 1:29. The entrance into heaven, which Christ made for us, was typified by the high priest's entrance into the most holy place. See Heb 9:7. The high priest was to come out again; but our Lord Jesus ever lives, making intercession, and always appears in the presence of God for us. Here are typified the two great gospel duties of faith and repentance. By faith we put our hands upon the head of the offering; relying on Christ as the Lord our Righteousness, pleading his satisfaction, as that which alone is able to atone for our sins, and procure us a pardon. By repentance we afflict our souls; not only fasting for a time from the delights of the body, but inwardly sorrowing for sin, and living a life of self-denial, assuring ourselves, that if we confess our sins, God is faithful and just to forgive us our sins, and to cleanse us from all unrighteousness. By the atonement we obtain rest for our souls, and all the glorious liberties of the children of God. Sinner, get the blood of Christ effectually applied to thy soul, or else thou canst never look God in the face with any comfort or acceptance. Take this blood of Christ, apply it by faith, and see how it atones with God.

Chapter 17

Chapter Outline

All sacrifices to be offered at the tabernacle.	(1–9)
Eating of blood, or of animals which died a natural death, forbidden.	(10–16)

Verses 1-9

All the cattle killed by the Israelites, while in the wilderness, were to be presented before the door of the tabernacle, and the flesh to be returned to the offerer, to be eaten as a peace-offering, according to the law. When they entered Canaan, this only continued in respect of sacrifices. The spiritual sacrifices we are now to offer, are not confined to any one place. We have now no temple or altar that sanctifies the gift; nor does the gospel unity rest only in one place, but in one heart, and the unity of the Spirit. Christ is our Altar, and the true Tabernacle; in him God dwells among men. It is in him that our sacrifices are acceptable to God, and in him only. To set up other mediators, or other altars, or other expiatory sacrifices, is, in effect, to set up other gods. And though God will graciously accept our family offerings, we must not therefore neglect attending at the tabernacle.

Verses 10-16

Here is a confirmation of the law against eating blood. They must eat no blood. But this law was ceremonial, and is now no longer in force; the coming of the substance does away the shadow. The blood of beasts is no longer the ransom, but Christ's blood only; therefore there is not now the reason for abstaining there then was. The blood is now allowed for the nourishment of our bodies; it is no longer appointed to make an atonement for the soul. Now the blood of Christ makes atonement really and effectually; to that, therefore, we must have regard, and not consider it as a common thing, or treat it with indifference.

Chapter 18

Unlawful marriages and fleshly lusts.

—Here is a law against all conformity to the corrupt usages of the heathen. Also laws against incest, against brutal lusts, and barbarous idolatries; and the enforcement of these laws from the ruin of the Canaanites. God here gives moral precepts. Close and constant adherence to God's ordinances is the most effectual preservative from gross sin. The grace of God only will secure us; that grace is to be expected only in the use of the means of grace. Nor does He ever leave any to their hearts' lusts, till they have left him and his services.

Chapter 19

laws.

—There are some ceremonial precepts in this chapter, but most of these precepts are binding on us, for they are explanations of the ten commandments. It is required that Israel be a holy people, because the God of Israel is a holy God, ver. #(2). To teach real separation from the world and the flesh, and entire devotedness to God. This is now the law of Christ; may the Lord bring every thought within us into obedience to it! Children are to be obedient to their parents, ver. #(3). The fear here required includes inward reverence and esteem, outward respect and obedience, care to please them and to make them easy. God only is to be worshipped, ver. #(4). Turn not from the true God to false ones, from the God who will make you holy and happy, to those that will deceive you, and make you for ever miserable. Turn not your eyes to them, much less your heart. They should leave the gleanings of their harvest and vintage for the poor, ver. #(9). Works of piety must be always attended with works of charity, according to our ability. We must not be covetous, griping, and greedy of every thing we can lay claim to, nor insist upon our right in all things. We are to be honest and true in all our dealings, ver. #(11). Whatever we have in the world, we must see that we get it honestly, for we cannot be truly rich, or long rich, with that which is not so. Reverence to the sacred name of God must be shown, ver. #(12). We must not detain what belongs to another, particularly the wages of the hireling, ver. #(13). We must be tender of the credit and safety of those that cannot help themselves, ver. #(14). Do no hurt to any, because they are unwilling or unable to avenge themselves. We ought to take heed of doing any thing which may occasion our weak brother to fall. The fear of God should keep us from doing wrong things, though they will not expose us to men's anger. Judges, and all in authority, are commanded to give judgment without partiality, ver. #(15). To be a tale-bearer, and to sow discord among neighbours, is as bad an office as a man can put himself into. We are to rebuke our neighbour in love, ver. #(17). Rather rebuke him than hate him, for an injury done to thyself. We incur guilt by not reproving; it is hating our brother. We should say, I will do him the kindness to tell him of his faults. We are to put off all malice, and to put on brotherly love, ver. #(18). We often wrong ourselves, but we soon forgive ourselves those wrongs, and they do not at all lessen our love to ourselves; in like manner we should love our neighbour. We must in many cases deny ourselves for the good of our neighbour. Ver. #(31): For Christians to have their fortunes told, to use spells and charms, or the like, is a sad affront to God. They must be grossly ignorant who ask, "What harm is there in these things?" Here is a charge to young people to show respect to the aged, ver. #(32). Religion teaches good manners, and obliges us to honour those to whom honour is due. A charge was given to the Israelites to be very tender of strangers, ver. #(33). Strangers, and the widows and fatherless, are God's particular care. It is at our peril, if we do them any wrong. Strangers shall be welcome to God's grace; we should do what we can to recommend religion to them. Justice in weights and measures is commanded, ver. #(35). We must make conscience of obeying God's precepts. We are not to pick and choose our duty, but must aim at standing complete in all the will of God. And the nearer our lives and tempers are to the precepts of God's law, the happier shall we be, and the happier shall we make all around us, and the better shall we adorn the gospel.

Chapter 20

Chapter Outline

Verses 1-9

Are we shocked at the unnatural cruelty of the ancient idolaters in sacrificing their children? We may justly be so. But are there not very many parents, who, by bad teaching and wicked examples, and by the mysteries of iniquity which they show their children, devote them to the service of Satan, and forward their everlasting ruin, in a manner even more to be lamented? What an account must such parents render to God, and what a meeting will they have with their children at the day of judgment! On the other hand, let children remember that he who cursed father or mother was surely put to death. This law Christ confirmed. Laws which were made before are repeated, and penalties annexed to them. If men will not avoid evil practices, because the law has made these practices sin, and it is right that we go on that principle, surely they should avoid them when the law has made them death, from a principle of self-preservation. In the midst of these laws comes in a general charge, Sanctify yourselves, and be ye holy. It is the Lord that sanctifies, and his work will be done, though it be difficult. Yet his grace is so far from doing away our endeavours, that it strongly encourages them. Work out your salvation, for it is God that worketh in you.

Verses 10-27

These verses repeat what had been said before, but it was needful there should be line upon line. What praises we owe to God that he has taught the evil of sin, and the sure way of deliverance from it! May we have grace to adorn the doctrine of God our Saviour in all things; may we have no fellowship with unfruitful works of darkness, but reprove them.

Chapter 21

Laws concerning the priests.

—As these priests were types of Christ, so all ministers must be followers of him, that their example may teach others to imitate the Saviour. Without blemish, and separate from sinners, He executed his priestly office on earth. What manner of persons then should his ministers be! But all are, if Christians, spiritual priests; the minister especially is called to set a good example, that the people may follow it. Our bodily infirmities, blessed be God, cannot now shut us out from his service, from these privileges, or from his heavenly glory. Many a healthful, beautiful soul is lodged in a feeble, deformed body. And those who may not be suited for the work of the ministry, may serve God with comfort in other duties in his church.

Chapter 22

Laws concerning the priests and sacrifices.

—In this chapter we have divers laws concerning the priests and sacrifices, all for preserving the honour of the sanctuary. Let us recollect with gratitude that our great High Priest cannot be hindered by any thing from the discharge of his office. Let us also remember, that the Lord requires us to reverence his name, his truths, his ordinances, and commandments. Let us beware of hypocrisy, and examine ourselves concerning our sinful defilements, seeking to be purified from them in the blood of Christ, and by his sanctifying Spirit. Whoever attempts to expiate his own sin, or draws near in the pride of self-righteousness, puts as great an affront on Christ, as he who comes to the Lord's table from the gratification of sinful lusts. Nor can the minister who loves the souls of the people, suffer them to continue in this dangerous delusion. He must call upon them, not only to repent of their sins, and forsake them; but to put their whole trust in the atonement of Christ, by faith in his name, for pardon and acceptance with God; thus only will the Lord make them holy, as his own people.

Chapter 23

Chapter Outline

The feast of Tabernacles.   (33–44)

Verses 1-3

In this chapter we have the institution of holy times; many of which have been mentioned before. Though the yearly feasts were made more remarkable by general attendance at the sanctuary, yet these must not be observed more than the sabbath. On that day they must withdraw from all business of the world. It is a sabbath of rest, typifying spiritual rest from sin, and rest in God. God's sabbaths are to be religiously observed in every private house, by every family apart, as well as by families together, in holy assemblies. The sabbath of the Lord in our dwellings will be their beauty, strength, and safety; it will sanctify, build up, and glorify them.

Verses 4-14

The feast of the Passover was to continue seven days; not idle days, spent in sport, as many that are called Christians spend their holy-days. Offerings were made to the Lord at his altar; and the people were taught to employ their time in prayer, and praise, and godly meditation. The sheaf of first-fruits was typical of the Lord Jesus, who is risen from the dead as the First-fruits of them that slept. Our Lord Jesus rose from the dead on the very day that the first-fruits were offered. We are taught by this law to honour the Lord with our substance, and with the first-fruits of all our increase, Pr 3:9. They were not to eat of their new corn, till God's part was offered to him out of it; and we must always begin with God: begin every day with him, begin every meal with him, begin every affair and business with him; seek first the kingdom of God.

Verses 15-22

The feast of Weeks was held in remembrance of the giving of the law, fifty days after the departure from Egypt; and looked forward to the outpouring of the Holy Ghost, fifty days after Christ our Passover was sacrificed for us. On that day the apostles presented the first-fruits of the Christian church to God. To the institution of the feast of Pentecost, is added a repetition of that law, by which they were required to leave the gleanings of their fields. Those who are truly sensible of the mercy they received from God, will show mercy to the poor without grudging.

Verses 23-32

the blowing of trumpets represented the preaching of the gospel, by which men are called to repent of sin, and to accept the salvation of Christ, which was signified by the day of atonement. Also it invited to rejoice in God, and become strangers and pilgrims on earth, which was denoted by the feast of Tabernacles, observed in the same month. At the beginning of the year, they were called by this sound of trumpet to shake off spiritual drowsiness, to search and try their ways, and to amend them. The day of atonement was the ninth day after this; thus they were awakened to prepare for that day, by sincere and serious repentance, that it might indeed be to them a day of atonement. The humbling of our souls for sin, and the making our peace with God, is work that requires the whole man, and the closest application of mind. On that day God spake peace to his people, and to his saints; therefore they must lay aside all their wordly business, that they might the more clearly hear that voice of joy and gladness.

Verses 33-44

In the feast of Tabernacles there was a remembrance of their dwelling in tents, or booths, in the wilderness, as well as their fathers dwelling in tents in Canaan; to remind them of their origin and their deliverance. Christ's tabernacling on earth in human nature, might also be prefigured. And it represents the believer's life on earth: a stranger and pilgrim here below, his home and heart are above with his Saviour. They would the more value the comforts and conveniences of their own houses, when they had been seven days dwelling in the booths. It is good for those who have ease and plenty, sometimes to learn what it is to endure hardness. The joy of harvest ought to be improved for the furtherance of our joy in God. The earth is the Lord's, and the fullness thereof; therefore whatever we have the comfort of, he must have the glory of, especially when any mercy is perfected. God appointed these feasts, "Beside the sabbaths and your free-will offerings." Calls to extraordinary services will not excuse from constant and stated ones.

Chapter 24

Chapter Outline

Verses 1-9

The loaves of bread typify Christ as the Bread of life, and the food of the souls of his people. He is the Light of his church, the Light of the world; in and through his word this light shines. By this light we discern the food prepared for our souls; and we should daily, but especially from sabbath to sabbath, feed thereon in our hearts with thanksgiving. And as the loaves were left in the sanctuary, so should we abide with God till he dismiss us.

Verses 10-23

This offender was the son of an Egyptian father, and an Israelitish mother. The notice of his parents shows the common ill effect of mixed marriages. A standing law for the stoning of blasphemers was made upon this occasion. Great stress is laid upon this law. It extends to the strangers among them, as well as to those born in the land. Strangers, as well as native Israelites, should be entitled to the benefit of the law, so as not to suffer wrong; and should be liable to the penalty of this law, in case they did wrong. If those who profane the name of God escape punishment from men, yet the Lord our God will not suffer them to escape his righteous judgments. What enmity against God must be in the heart of man, when blasphemies against God proceed out of his mouth. If he that despised Moses' law, died without mercy, of what punishment will they be worthy, who despise and abuse the gospel of the Son of God! Let us watch against anger, do no evil, avoid all connexions with wicked people, and reverence that holy name which sinners blaspheme.

Chapter 25

Chapter Outline

Verses 1-7

All labour was to cease in the seventh year, as much as daily labour on the seventh day. These statues tell us to beware of covetousness, for a man's life consists not in the abundance of his possessions. We are to exercise willing dependence on God's providence for our support; to consider ourselves the Lord's tenants or stewards, and to use our possessions accordingly. This year of rest typified the spiritual rest which all believers enter into through Christ. Through Him we are eased of the burden of wordly care and labour, both being sanctified and sweetened to us; and we are enabled and encouraged to live by faith.

Verses 8-22

The word "jubilee" signifies a peculiarly animated sound of the silver trumpets. This sound was to be made on the evening of the great day of atonement; for the proclamation of gospel liberty and salvation results from the sacrifice of the Redeemer. It was provided that the lands should not be sold away from their families. They could only be disposed of, as it were, by leases till the year of jubilee, and then returned to the owner or his heir. This tended to preserve their tribes and families distinct, till the coming of the Messiah. The liberty every man was born to, if sold or forfeited, should return at the year of jubilee. This was typical of redemption by Christ from the slavery of sin and Satan, and of being brought again to the liberty of the children of God. All bargains ought to be made by this rule, "Ye shall not oppress one another," not take advantage of one another's ignorance or necessity, "but thou shalt fear thy God." The fear of God reigning in the heart, would restrain from doing wrong to our neighbour in word or deed. Assurance was given that they should be great gainers, by observing these years of rest. If we are careful to do our duty, we may trust God with our comfort. This was a miracle for an encouragement to all neither sowed or reaped. This was a miracle for an encouragement to all God's people, in all ages, to trust him in the way of duty. There is nothing lost by faith and self-denial in obedience. Some asked, What shall we eat the seventh year? Thus many Christians anticipate evils, questioning what they shall do, and fearing to proceed in the way of duty. But we have no right to anticipate evils, so as to distress ourselves about them. To carnal minds we may appear to act absurdly, but the path of duty is ever the path of safety.

Verses 23-34

If the land were not redeemed before the year of jubilee, it then returned to him that sold or mortgaged it. This was a figure of the free grace of God in Christ; by which, and not by any price or merit of our own, we are restored to the favour of God. Houses in walled cities were more the fruits of their own industry than land in the country, which was the direct gift of God's bounty; therefore if a man sold a house in a city, he might redeem it only within a year after the sale. This encouraged strangers and proselytes to come and settle among them.

Verses 35-38

Poverty and decay are great grievances, and very common; the poor ye have always with you. Thou shalt relieve him; by sympathy, pitying the poor; by service, doing for them; and by supply, giving to them according to their necessity, and thine ability. Poor debtors must not be oppressed. Observe the arguments here used against extortion: "Fear thy God." Relieve the poor, "that they may live with thee;" for they may be serviceable to thee. The rich can as ill spare the poor, as the poor can the rich. It becomes those that have received mercy to show mercy.

Verses 39-55

A native Israelite, if sold for debt, or for a crime, was to serve but six years, and to go out the seventh. If he sold himself, through poverty, both his work and his usage must be such as were fitting for a son of Abraham. Masters are required to give to their servants that which is just and equal, Col 4:1. At the year of jubilee the servant should go out free, he and his children, and should return to his own family. This typified redemption from the service of sin and Satan, by the grace of God in Christ, whose truth makes us free, Joh 8:32. We cannot ransom our fellow-sinners, but we may point out Christ to them; while by his grace our lives may adorn his gospel, express our love, show our gratitude, and glorify his holy name.

Chapter 26

Chapter Outline

Verses 1-13

This chapter contains a general enforcement of all the laws given by Moses; by promises of reward in case of obedience, on the one hand; and threatenings of punishment for disobedience, on the other. While Israel maintained a national regard to God's worship, sabbaths, and sanctuary, and did not turn aside to idolatry, the Lord engaged to continue to them temporal mercies and religious advantages. These great and precious promises, though they relate chiefly to the life which now is, were typical of the spiritual blessings made sure by the covenant of grace to all believers, through Christ. 1. Plenty and abundance of the fruits of the earth. Every good and perfect gift must be expected from above, from the Father of lights. 2. Peace under the Divine protection. Those dwell in safety, that dwell in God. 3. Victory and success in their wars. It is all one with the Lord to save by many or by few. 4. The increase of their people. The gospel church shall be fruitful. 5. The favour of God, which is the fountain of all Good. 6. Tokens of his presence in and by his ordinances. The way to have God's ordinances fixed among us, is to cleave closely to them. 7. The grace of the covenant. All covenant blessings are summed up in the covenant relation, I will be your God, and ye shall be my people; and they are all grounded upon their redemption. Having purchased them, God would own them, and never cast them off till they cast him off. (Le 26:14-39)

Verses 14-39

After God has set the blessing before them which would make them a happy people if they would be obedient, he here sets the curse before them, the evils which would make them miserable, if they were disobedient. Two things would bring ruin. 1. A contempt of God's commandments. They that reject the precept, will come at last to renounce the covenant. 2. A contempt of his corrections. If they will not learn obedience by the things they suffer, God himself would be against them; and this is the root and cause of all their misery. And also, The whole creation would be at war with them. All God's sore judgments would be sent against them. The threatenings here are very particular, they were prophecies, and He that foresaw all their rebellions, knew they would prove so. TEMPORAL judgments are threatened. Those who will not be parted from their sins by the commands of God, shall be parted from them by judgments. Those wedded to their lusts, will have enough of them. SPIRITUAL judgments are threatened, which should seize the mind. They should find no acceptance with God. A guilty conscience would be their continual terror. It is righteous with God to leave those to despair of pardon, who presume to sin; and it is owing to free grace, if we are not left to pine away in the iniquity we were born in, and have lived in.

Verses 40-46

Among the Israelites, persons were not always prosperous or afflicted according to their obedience or disobedience. But national prosperity was the effect of national obedience, and national judgments were brought on by national wickedness. Israel was under a peculiar covenant. National wickedness will end in the ruin of any people, especially where the word of God and the light of the gospel are enjoyed. Sooner or later, sin will be the ruin, as well as the reproach, of every people. Oh that, being humbled for our sins, we might avert the rising storm before it bursts upon us! God grant that we may, in this our day, consider the things which belong to our eternal peace.

Chapter 27

Chapter Outline

Verses 1-13

Zeal for the service of God disposed the Israelites, on some occasions, to dedicate themselves or their children to the service of the Lord, in his house for life. Some persons who thus dedicated themselves might be employed as assistants; in general they were to be redeemed for a value. It is good to be zealously affected and liberally disposed for the Lord's service; but the matter should be well weighed, and prudence should direct as to what we do; else rash vows and hesitation in doing them will dishonour God, and trouble our own minds.

Verses 14-25

Our houses, lands, cattle, and all our substance, must be used to the glory of God. It is acceptable to him that a portion be given to support his worship, and to promote his cause. But God would not approve such a degree of zeal as ruined a man's family.

Verses 26-33

Things or persons devoted, are distinguished from things or persons that were only sanctified. Devoted things were most holy to the Lord, and could neither be taken back nor applied to other purposes. Whatever productions they had the benefit, God must be honoured with the tenth of, if it could be applied. Thus they acknowledge God to be the Owner of their land, the Giver of its fruits, and themselves to be his tenants, and dependants upon him. Thus they gave him thanks for the plenty they enjoyed, and besought his favour in the continuance of it. We are taught to honour the Lord with our substance.

Verse 34

The last verse seems to have reference to this whole book. Many of the precepts in it are moral, and always binding; others are ceremonial, and peculiar to the Jewish nation; yet they have a spiritual meaning, and so teach us; for unto us, by these institutions, is the gospel preached, as well as unto them, Heb 4:2. The doctrine of reconciliation to God by a Mediator, is not clouded with the smoke of burning sacrifice, but cleared by the knowledge of Christ and him crucified. We are under the sweet and easy institutions of the gospel, which pronounces those true worshippers, who worship the Father in spirit and truth, by Christ only, and in his name. Yet, let us not think, because we are not tied to the ceremonial rites and oblations, that a little care, time, and expense, will serve to honour God with. Having boldness to enter into the holiest by the blood of Jesus, let us draw near with a true heart, and in full assurance of faith, worshipping God with the more cheerfulness and humble confidence, still saying, BLESSED BE GOD FOR JESUS CHRIST.

Numbers

This book is called NUMBERS from the several numberings of the people contained in it. It extends from the giving of the law at Sinai, till their arrival in the plains of Jordan. An account is given of their murmuring and unbelief, for which they were sentenced to wander in the wilderness nearly forty years; also some laws, both, moral and ceremonial. Their trials greatly tended to distinguish the wicked and hypocrites from the faithful and true servants of God, who served him with a pure heart.

Chapter 1

Chapter Outline

The numbering of the Israelites.   (1–43)

The number of the people.   (44–46)

The Levites not numbered with the rest.   (47–54)

Verses 1-43

The people were numbered to show God's faithfulness in thus increasing the seed of Jacob, that they might be the better trained for the wars and conquest of Canaan, and to ascertain their families in order to the division of the land. It is said of each tribe, that those were numbered who were able to go forth to war; they had wars before them, though now they met with no opposition. Let the believer be prepared to withstand the enemies of his soul, though all may appear to be peace.

Verses 44-46

We have here the sum total. How much was required to maintain all these in the wilderness! They were all provided for by God every day. When we observe the faithfulness of God, however unlikely the performance of his promise may appear, we may take courage as to those which yet remain to be fulfilled to the church of God.

Verses 47-54

Care is here taken to distinguish the tribe of Levi, which, in the matter of the golden calf, had distinguished itself. Singular services shall be recompensed by singular honours. It was to the honour of the Levites, that to them was committed the care of the tabernacle and its treasures, in their camps and in their marches. It was for the honour of the holy things that none should see them, or touch them, but those who were called of God to the service. We all are unfit and unworthy to have fellowship with God, till called by his grace into the fellowship of his Son Jesus Christ our Lord; and so, being the spiritual seed of that great High Priest, we are made priests to our God. Great care must be taken to prevent sin, for preventing sin is preventing wrath. Being a holy tribe, they were not reckoned among other Israelites. They that minister about holy things, should neither entangle themselves, nor be entangled, in worldly affairs. And let every believer seek to do what the Lord has commanded.

Chapter 2

The order of the tribes in their tents.

—The tribes were to encamp about the tabernacle, which was to be in the midst of them. It was a token of God's gracious presence. Yet they were to pitch their tents afar off, in reverence to the sanctuary. The children of Israel put themselves in their posts, without murmuring or disputing; and as it was their safety, so it was their beauty. It is our duty and interest to be contented with the place allotted to us, and to endeavour to occupy it in a proper manner, without envying or murmuring; without ambition or covetousness. Thus the gospel church ought to be compact, according to the Scripture model, every one knowing and keeping his place; and then all that wish well to the church rejoice, beholding their order, Col 2:5.

Chapter 3

Chapter Outline

The sons of Aaron, The Levites taken instead of the first-born.	(1–13)
The Levites numbered by their families, Their duties.	(14–39)
The first-born are numbered.	(40–51)

Verses 1-13

There was much work belonging to the priests' office, and there were now only Aaron and his two sons to do it; God appoints the Levites to attend them. Those whom God finds work for, he will find help for. The Levites were taken instead of the first-born. When He that made us, saves us, as the first-born of Israel were saved, we are laid under further obligations to serve him faithfully. God's right to us by redemption, confirms the right he has to us by creation.

Verses 14-39

The Levites were in three classes, according to the sons of Levi; Gershon, Kohath, and Merari; and these were subdivided into families. The posterity of Moses were not at all honoured or privileged, but stood upon the level with other Levites; thus it was plain, that Moses did not seek the advancement of his own family, or to secure any honours to it. The tribe of Levi was by much the least of all the tribes. God's chosen are but a little flock in comparison with the world.

Verses 40-51

The number of the first-born, and that of the Levites, came near to each other. Known unto God are all his works beforehand; there is an exact proportion between them, and so it will appear, when they are compared together. The small number of first-born, over and above the number of the Levites, were to be redeemed, and the redemption-money given to Aaron. The church is called the church of the first-born, which is redeemed, not as they were, with silver and gold; but, being devoted by sin to the justice of God, is ransomed with the precious blood of the Son of God. All men are the Lord's by creation, and all true christians are his by redemption. Each should know his own post and duty; nor can any service required by such a Master be rightly accounted mean or hard.

Chapter 4

Chapter Outline

The Levites' service.	(1–3)
The duties of the Kohathites.	(4–20)
The duties of the Gershonites and Merarites.	(21–33)
The numbers of the serviceable Levites.	(34–49)

Verses 1-3

The middle-aged men of the tribe of Levi, all from thirty years old to fifty, were to be employed in the service of the tabernacle. The service of God requires the best of our strength, and the prime portion of our time, which cannot be better spent than to the honour of Him who is the First and Best. And the service of God should be done when we are most lively and active. Those do not consider this who put off repentance to old age, and so leave the best work to be done in the worst time.

Verses 4-20

The Kohathites were to carry the holy things of the tabernacle. All the holy things were to be covered; not only for security and respect, but to keep them from being seen. This not only marked the reverence due to holy things, but the mystery of the things signified by those types, and the darkness of the dispensation. But now, through Christ, the case is altered, and we are encouraged to come boldly to the throne of grace.

Verses 21-33

We have here the charge of the other two families of the Levites, which, though not so honourable as the first, yet was necessary, and to be done regularly. All the things were delivered them by name. It intimates the care God takes of his church and every member of it. The death of the saints is represented as the taking down of the tabernacle, 2Co 5:1, and the putting it off, 2Pe 1:14. All shall be raised up in the great day, when these vile bodies shall be made like the glorious body of Jesus Christ, and so shall be for ever with the Lord.

Verses 34-49

God so ordered it, that though the Merarites were the fewest in number, yet they should have most able men among them; for whatever service God calls men to, he will furnish them for it, give strength in proportion to the work, and grace sufficient. The least of the tribes had many more able men than the Levites: those who engage in the service of this world, are many more than those devoted to the service of God. May our souls be wholly devoted to his service.

Chapter 5

Chapter Outline

Verses 1-10

The camp was to be cleansed. The purity of the church must be kept as carefully as the peace and order of it. Every polluted Israelite must be separated. The wisdom from above is first pure, then peaceable. The greater profession of religion any house or family makes, the more they are obliged to put away iniquity far from them. If a man overreach or defraud his brother in any matter, it is a trespass against the Lord, who strictly charges and commands us to do justly. What is to be done when a man's awakened conscience charges him with guilt of this kind, though done long ago? He must confess his sin, confess it to God, confess it to his neighbour, and take shame to himself; though it go against him to own himself in a lie, yet he must do it. Satisfaction must be made for the offence done to God, as well as for the loss sustained by the neighbour; restitution in that case is not enough without faith and repentance. While that which is wrongly gotten is knowingly kept, the guilt remains on the conscience, and is not done away by sacrifice or offering, prayers or tears; for it is the same act of sin persisted in. This is the doctrine of right reason, and of the word of God. It detects hypocrites, and directs the tender conscience to proper conduct, which, springing from faith in Christ, will make way for inward peace.

Verses 11-31

This law would make the women of Israel watch against giving cause for suspicion. On the other hand, it would hinder the cruel treatment such suspicions might occasion. It would also hinder the guilty from escaping, and the innocent from coming under just suspicion. When no proof could be brought, the wife was called on to make this solemn appeal to a heart-searching God. No woman, if she were guilty, could say "Amen" to the adjuration, and drink the water after it, unless she disbelieved the truth of God, or defied his justice. The water is called the bitter water, because it caused the curse. Thus sin is called an evil and a bitter thing. Let all that meddle with forbidden pleasures, know that they will be bitterness in the latter end. From the whole learn, 1. Secret sins are known to God, and sometimes are strangely brought to light in this life; and that there is a day coming when God will, by Christ, judge the secrets of men according to the gospel, Ro 2:16. 2 In particular, Whoremongers and adulterers God will surely judge. Though we have not now the waters of jealousy, yet we have God's word, which ought to be as great a terror. Sensual lusts will end in bitterness. 3. God will manifest the innocency of the innocent. The same providence is for good to some, and for hurt to others. And it will answer the purposes which God intends.

Chapter 6

Chapter Outline

The law concerning the Nazarites.   (1–21)

The form of blessing the people.   (22–27)

Verses 1-21

The word Nazarite signifies separation. Some were appointed of God, before their birth, to be Nazarites all their days, as Samson and John the Baptist. But, in general, it was a vow of separation from the world and devotedness to the services of religion, for a limited time, and under certain rules, which any person might make if they pleased. A Nazarite is spoken of as well known; but his obligation is brought to a greater certainty than before. That the fancies of superstitious men might not multiply the restraints endlessly, God gives them rules. They must not drink wine or strong drink, nor eat grapes. Those who separate themselves to God, must not gratify the desires of the body, but keep it under. Let all Christians be very moderate in the use of wine and strong drink; for if the love of these once gets the mastery of a man, he becomes an easy prey to Satan. The Nazarites were to eat nothing that came of the vine; this may teach the utmost care to avoid sin, and all that borders upon it, and leads to it, or may be a temptation to us. They must not cut their hair. They must neither poll their heads, nor shave their beards; this was the mark of Samson being a Nazarite. This signified neglect of the body, and of the ease and ornament of it. Those who separate themselves to God, must keep their consciences pure from dead works, and not touch unclean things. All the days of their separation they must be holy to the Lord. This was the meaning of those outward observances, and without this they were of no account. No penalty or sacrifice was appointed for those who wilfully broke their vow of being Nazarites; they must answer another day for such profane trifling with the Lord their God; but those were to be relieved who did not sin wilfully. There is nothing in Scripture that bears the least resemblance to the religious orders of the church of Rome, except these Nazarites. But mark the difference, or rather how completely opposed! The religious of that church are forbidden to marry; but no such restriction is laid upon the Nazarites. They are commanded to abstain from meats; but the Nazarites might eat any food allowed other Israelites. They are not generally forbidden wine, not even on their fasting days; but the Nazarites might not have wine at any time. Their vow is lasting, even to the end of their lives; the Nazarites' vow was only for a limited time, at their own will; and in certain cases not unless allowed by husbands or parents. Such a thorough difference there is between rules of man's invention and those directed in Scripture, Let us not forget that the Lord Jesus is not only our Surety, but also our example. For his sake we must renounce worldly pleasures, abstain from fleshy lusts, be separate from sinners, make open profession of our faith, moderate natural affections, be spiritually-minded, and devoted to God's service, and desirous to be an example all around us. (Nu 6:22-27)

Verses 22-27

The priests were solemnly to bless the people in the name of the Lord. To be under the almighty protection of God our Saviour; to enjoy his favour as the smile of a loving Father, or as the cheering beams of the sun; while he mercifully forgives our sins, supplies our wants, consoles the heart, and prepares us by his grace for eternal glory; these things form the substance of this blessing, and the sum total of all blessings. In so rich a list of mercies worldly joys are not worthy to be mentioned. Here is a form of prayer. The name Jehovah is three times repeated. The Jews think there is some mystery; and we know what it is, the New Testament having explained it. There we are directed to expect the blessing from the grace of our Lord Jesus Christ, the love of the Father, and the communion of the Holy Ghost, 2Co 13:14; each of which Persons is Jehovah, and yet they are not three Lords, but one Lord.

Chapter 7

Chapter Outline

Verses 1-9

The offering of the princes to the service of the tabernacle was not made till it was fully set up. Necessary observances must always take place of free-will offerings. The more any are advanced, the greater opportunity they have of serving God and their generation. No sooner was the tabernacle set up, than provision is made for the removal of it. Even when but just settled in the world, we must be preparing for changes and removes, especially for the great change.

Verses 10-89

The princes and great men were most forward in the service of God. Here is an example to those in authority, and of the highest rank; they ought to use their honour and power, their estate and interest, to promote religion and the service of God in the places where they live. Though it was a time of joy and rejoicing, yet still, in the midst of their sacrifices, we find a sin-offering. As, in our best services, we are conscious that there is sin, there should be repentance, even in our most joyful services. In all approaches to God we must by faith look to Christ as the Sin-offering. They brought their offerings each on a day. God's work should not be done confusedly, or in a hurry; take time, and we shall have done the sooner, or, at least, we shall have done the better. If services are to be done for twelve days together, we must not call it a task and a burden. All their offerings were the same; all the tribes of Israel had an equal share in the altar, and an equal interest in the sacrifices offered upon it. He who now spake to Moses, as the Shechinah or Divine Majesty, from between the Cherubim, was the Eternal Word, the second Person in the Trinity; for all God's communion with man is by his Son, by whom he made the world, and rules the church, who is the same yesterday, to-day, and for ever.

Chapter 8

Chapter Outline

The lamps of the sanctuary.   (1–4)

Consecration of the Levites, and their   (5–26)
service.

Verses 1-4

Aaron himself lighted the lamps, thus representing his Divine Master. The Scripture is a light shining in a dark place, 2Pe 1:19. A dark place even the church would be without it; as the tabernacle, which had no window, would have been without the lamps. The work of ministers is to light these lamps, by expounding and applying the word of God. Jesus Christ is the only Light of our dark, sinful world; and by his atonement, by his word and the Holy Spirit, he diffuses light around.

Verses 5-26

Here we have directions for the solemn ordination of the Levites. All Israel must know that they took not this honour to themselves, but were called of God to it; nor was it enough that they were distinguished from others. All who are employed for God, must be dedicated to him, according to the employment. Christians must be baptized, ministers must be ordained; we must first give ourselves unto the Lord, and then our services. The Levites must be cleansed. They must be clean that bear the vessels of the Lord. Moses must sprinkle the water of purifying upon them. This signifies the application of the blood of Christ to our souls by faith, that we may be fit to serve the living God. God declares his acceptance of them. All who expect to share in the privileges of the tabernacle, must resolve to do the service of the tabernacle. As, on the one hand, none of God's creatures are his necessary servants, he needs not the service of any of them; so none are merely honorary servants, to do nothing. All whom God owns, he employs; angels themselves have their services.

Chapter 9

Chapter Outline

Of the Passover.   (1–14)

The removals of the Israelites.   (15–23)

Verses 1-14

God gave particular orders for the keeping of this passover, and, for aught that appears, after this, they kept no passover till they came to Canaan, Jos 5:10. It early showed that the ceremonial institutions were not to continue always, as so soon after they were appointed, some were suffered to sleep for many years. But the ordinance of the Lord's Supper was not thus set aside in the first days of the Christian church, although those were days of greater difficulty and distress than Israel knew in the wilderness; nay, in the times of persecution, the Lord's Supper was celebrated more frequently than afterward. Israelites in the wilderness could not forget the deliverance out of Egypt. There was danger of this when they came to Canaan. Instructions were given concerning those who were ceremonially unclean, when they were to eat the passover. Those whose minds and consciences are defiled by sin, are unfit for communion with God, and cannot partake with comfort of the gospel passover, till they are cleansed by true repentance and faith. Observe with what trouble and concern these men complained that they were kept back from offering to the Lord. It should be a trouble to us, when by any occasion we are kept back from the solemnities of a sabbath or a sacrament. Observe the deliberation of Moses in resolving this case. Ministers must ask counsel of God's mouth, not determine according to their own fancy or affection, but according to the word of God to the best of their knowledge. And if, in difficult cases, time is taken to spread the matter before God by humble, believing prayer, the Holy Spirit assuredly will direct in the good and right way. God gave directions in this case, and in other similar cases, explanatory of the law of the passover. As those who, against their minds, are forced to absent themselves from God's ordinances, may expect the favours of God's grace under their affliction, so those who, of choice, absent themselves, may expect God's wrath for their sin. Be not deceived: God is not mocked.

Verses 15-23

This cloud was appointed to be the visible sign and symbol of God's presence with Israel. Thus we are taught to see God always near us, both night and day. As long as the cloud rested on the tabernacle, so long they continued in the same place. There is no time lost, while we are waiting God's time. When the cloud was taken up, they removed, however comfortably they were encamped. We are kept at uncertainty concerning the time of our putting off the earthly house of this tabernacle, that we may be always ready to remove at the command of the Lord. It is very safe and pleasant going when we see God before us, and resting where he appoints us to rest. The leading of this cloud is spoken of as signifying the guidance of the blessed Spirit. We are not now to expect such tokens of the Divine presence and guidance; but the promise is sure to all God's spiritual Israel, that he will guide them by his counsel. Ps 73:24, even unto death, Ps 48:14. All the children of God shall be led by the Spirit of God, Ro 8:14. He will direct the paths of those who in all their ways acknowledge him, Pr 3:6. At the commandment of the Lord, our hearts should always move and rest, saying, Father, thy will be done; dispose of me and mine as thou pleasest. What thou wilt, and where thou wilt; only let me be thine, and always in the way of my duty. In applying general precepts to particular circumstances, there should be good counsel and fervent prayer. When any undertaking is evidently wrong, or doubtfully right, and yet the mind leans that way, in such a case "the moving of the cloud," as men sometimes miscall it, is generally no more than a temptation Satan is permitted to propose; and men fancy they are following the Lord, when they are following their own wayward inclinations. The record of his mercy will conduct us with unerring truth, through Christ, to everlasting peace. Follow the pillar of the cloud and of fire. Lay the BIBLE to heart, and receive with meekness the ingrafted word, which is able to save your souls.

Chapter 10

Chapter Outline

Verses 1-10

Here are directions concerning the public notices to be given the people by sound of trumpet. Their laws in every case were to be Divine, therefore, even in this matter Moses is directed. These trumpets typify the preached gospel. It sounds an alarm to sinners, calls them to repent, proclaims liberty to the captives and slaves of Satan, and collects the worshippers of God. It directs and encourages their heavenly journey; stirs them up to combat against the world and sin, encouraging them with the assurance of victory. It leads their attention to the sacrifice of Christ, and shows the Lord's presence for their protection. It is also necessary that the gospel trumpet give a distinct sound, according to the persons addressed, or the end proposed; whether to convince, humble, console, exhort, reprove, or teach. The sounding of the trumpet of the gospel is God's ordinance, and demands the attention of all to whom it is sent. (Nu 10:11-28)

Verses 11-28

After the Israelites had continued nearly a year at mount Sinai, and all was settled respecting their future worship, they began their march to Canaan. True religion begins with the knowledge of the holy law of God, and humiliation for sin, but we must go on towards perfection, in acquaintance with Christ and his gospel, and those effectual encouragements, motives, and assistances to holiness, which it proposes. They took their journey according to the commandment of the Lord, De 1:6–8, and as the cloud led them. Those who give themselves to the direction of God's word and Spirit, steer a steady course, even when they seem bewildered. While they are sure they cannot lose their God and Guide, they need not fear losing their way. They went out of the wilderness of Sinai, and rested in the wilderness of Paran. All our removes in this world are but from one wilderness to another. The changes we think will be for the better do not always prove so. We shall never be at rest, never at home, till we come to heaven, but all will be well there.

Verses 29-32

Moses invites his kindred to go to Canaan. Those that are bound for the heavenly Canaan, should ask and encourage their friends to go with them: we shall have none the less of the joys of heaven, for others coming to share with us. It is good having fellowship with those who have fellowship with God. But the things of this world, which are seen, draw strongly from the pursuit of the things of the other world, which are not seen. Moses urges that Hobab might be serviceable to them. Not to show where they must encamp, nor what way they must march, the cloud was to direct that; but to show the conveniences of the place they marched through, and encamped in. It well consists with our trust in God's providence, to use the help of our friends.

Verses 33-36

Their going out and coming in, gives an example to us to begin and end every day's journey and every day's work with prayer. Here is Moses's prayer when the ark set forward, "Rise up, and let thine enemies be scattered." There are those in the world who are enemies to God and haters of him; secret and open enemies; enemies to his truths, his laws, his ordinances, his people. But for the scattering and defeating of God's enemies, there needs no more than God's arising. Observe also the prayer of Moses when the ark rested, that God would cause his people to rest. The welfare and happiness of the Israel of God, consist in the continual presence of God among them. Their safety is not in their numbers, but in the favour of God, and his gracious return to them, and resting with them. Upon this account, Happy art thou, O Israel! who is like unto thee, O people! God will go before them, to find them resting-places by the way. His promise is, and their prayers are, that he will never leave them nor forsake them.

Chapter 11

Chapter Outline

Verses 1-3

Here is the people's sin; they complained. See the sinfulness of sin, which takes occasion from the commandment to be provoking. The weakness of the law discovered sin, but could not destroy it; checked, but could not conquer it. They complained. Those who are of a discontented spirit, will always find something to quarrel or fret about, though the circumstances of their outward condition be ever so favourable. The Lord heard it, though Moses did not. God knows the secret frettings and murmurings of the heart, though concealed from men. What he noticed, he was much displeased with, and he chastised them for this sin. The fire of their wrath against God burned in their minds; justly did the fire of God's wrath fasten on their bodies; but God's judgments came on them gradually, that they might take warning. It appeared that God delights not in punishing; when he begins, he is soon prevailed with to let it fall.

Verses 4-9

Man, having forsaken his proper rest, feels uneasy and wretched, though prosperous. They were weary of the provision God had made for them, although wholesome food and nourishing. It cost no money or care, and the labour of gathering it was very little indeed; yet they talked of Egypt's cheapness, and the fish they ate there freely; as if that cost them nothing, when they paid dearly for it with hard service! While they lived on manna, they seemed exempt from the curse sin has brought on man, that in the sweat of his face he should eat bread; yet they speak of it with scorn. Peevish, discontented minds will find fault with that which has no fault in it, but that it is too good for them. Those who might be happy, often make themselves miserable by discontent. They could not be satisfied unless they had flesh to eat. It is evidence of the dominion of the carnal mind, when we want to have the delights and satisfaction of sense. We should not indulge in any desire which we cannot in faith turn into prayer, as we cannot when we ask meat for our lust. What is lawful of itself becomes evil, when God does not allot it to us, yet we desire it.

Verses 10-15

The provocation was very great; yet Moses expressed himself otherwise than became him. He undervalued the honour God had put upon him. He magnified his own performances, while he had the Divine wisdom to direct him, and Almighty power to dispense rewards and punishments. He speaks distrustfully of the Divine grace. Had the work been much less he could not have gone through it in his own strength; but had it been much greater, through God strengthening him, he might have done it. Let us pray, Lord, lead us not into temptation.

Verses 16-23

Moses is to choose such as he knew to be elders, that is, wise and experienced men. God promises to qualify them. If they were not found fit for the employ, they should be made fit. Even the discontented people shall be gratified too, that every mouth may be stopped. See here, I. The vanity of all the delights of sense; they will cloy, but they will not satisfy. Spiritual pleasures alone will satisfy and last. As the world passes away, so do the lusts of it. 2. What brutish sins gluttony and drunkenness are! they make that to hurt the body which should be its health. Moses objects. Even true and great believers sometimes find it hard to trust God under the discouragements of second causes, and against hope to believe in hope. God here brings Moses to this point, The Lord God is Almighty; and puts the proof upon the issue, Thou shalt see whether my word shall come to pass or not. If he speaks, it is done.

Verses 24-30

We have here the fulfilment of God's word to Moses, that he should have help in the government of Israel. He gave of his Spirit to the seventy elders. They discoursed to the people of the things of God, so that all who heard them might say, that God was with them of a truth. Two of the elders, Eldad and Medad, went not out unto the tabernacle, as the rest, being sensible of their own weakness and unworthiness. But the Spirit of God found them in the camp, and there they exercised their gift of praying, preaching, and praising God; they spake as moved by the Holy Ghost. The Spirit of God is not confined to the tabernacle, but, like the wind, blows where He listeth. And they that humble themselves shall be exalted; and those who are most fit for government, are least ambitious of it. Joshua does not desire that they should be punished, but only restrained for the future. This motion he made out of zeal for what he thought to be the unity of the church. He would have them silenced, lest they should occasion a schism, or should rival Moses; but Moses was not afraid of any such effects from that Spirit which God had put upon them. Shall we reject those whom Christ has owned, or restrain any from doing good, because they are not in every thing of our mind? Moses wishes all the Lord's people were prophets, that he would put his Spirit upon all of them. Let the testimony of Moses be believed by those who desire to be in power; that government is a burden. It is a burden of care and trouble to those who make conscience of the duty of it; and to those who do not, it will prove a heavier burden in the day of account. Let the example of Moses be followed by those in power; let them not despise the advice and assistance of others, but desire it, and be thankful for it. If all the present number of the Lord's people were rendered prophets, or ministers, by the Spirit of Christ, though not all agreed in outward matters, there is work enough for all, in calling sinners to repentance, and faith in our Lord Jesus.

Verses 31-35

God performed his promise to the people, in giving them flesh. How much more diligent men are in collecting the meat that perishes, than in labouring for meat which endures to everlasting life! We are quick-sighted in the affairs of time; but stupidity blinds us as to the concerns of eternity. To pursue worldly advantages, we need no arguments; but when we are to secure the true riches, then we are all forgetfulness. Those who are under the power of a carnal mind, will have their lusts fulfilled, though it be to the certain damage and ruin of their precious souls. They paid dearly for their feasts. God often grants the desires of sinners in wrath, while he denies the desires of his own people in love. What we unduly desire, if we obtain it, we have reason to fear, will be some way or other a grief and cross to us. And what multitudes there are in all places, who shorten their lives by excess of one kind or other! Let us seek for those pleasures which satisfy, but never surfeit; and which will endure for evermore.

Chapter 12

Chapter Outline

God rebukes the murmuring of Aaron and Miriam.   (1–9)

Miriam struck with leprosy, and healed at the prayer of Moses.   (10–16)

Verses 1-9

The patience of Moses was tried in his own family, as well as by the people. The pretence was, that he had married a foreign wife; but probably their pride was hurt, and their envy stirred up, by his superior authority. Opposition from our near relations, and from religious friends, is most painful. But this is to be looked for, and it will be well if in such circumstances we can preserve the gentleness and meekness of Moses. Moses was thus fitted to the work he was called to. God not only cleared Moses, but praised him. Moses had the spirit of prophecy in a way which set him far above all other prophets; yet he that is least in the kingdom of heaven, is greater than he; and our Lord Jesus infinitely excels him, Heb 3:1. Let Miriam and Aaron consider whom it was they insulted. We have reason to be afraid of saying or doing any thing against the servants of God. And those are presumptuous indeed who are not afraid to speak evil of dignities, 2Pe 2:10. The removal of God's presence is the surest and saddest token of God's displeasure. Woe to us, if he depart! he never departs, till by sin and folly we drive him from us.

Verses 10-16

The cloud departed, and Miriam became leprous. When God goes, evil comes: expect no good when God departs. Her foul tongue, as Bishop Hall says, was justly punished with a foul face. Aaron, as priest, was judge of the leprosy. He could not pronounce her leprous without trembling, knowing himself to be equally guilty. But if she was thus punished for speaking against Moses, what will become of those who sin against Christ? Aaron, who joined his sister in speaking against Moses, is forced for himself and his sister, to beseech him, and to speak highly of him whom he had so lately blamed. Those who trample upon the saints and servants of God, will one day be glad to make court to them. It is well when rebukes produce confession of sin and repentance. Such offenders, though corrected and disgraced, shall be pardoned. Moses made it appear, that he forgave the injury done him. To this pattern of Moses, and that of our Saviour, who said, "Father, forgive them," we must conform. A reason is given for Miriam's being put out of the camp for seven days; because thus she ought to accept the punishment of her sin. When under the tokens of God's displeasure for sin, it becomes us to take shame to ourselves. This hindered the people's progress in their march forward towards Canaan. Many things oppose us, but nothing so hinders us in the way to heaven, as sin.

Chapter 13

Chapter Outline

Verses 1-20

A memorable and melancholy history is related in this and the following chapter, of the turning back of Israel from the borders of Canaan, and the sentencing them to wander and perish in the wilderness, for their unbelief and murmuring. It appears, De 1:22, that the motion to search out the land came from the people. They had a better opinion of their own policy than of God's wisdom. Thus we ruin ourselves by believing the reports and representations of sense rather than Divine revelation. We walk by sight not by faith. Moses gave the spies this charge, Be of good courage. It was not only a great undertaking they were put upon, which required good management and resolution; but a great trust was reposed in them, which required that they should be faithful. Courage in such circumstances can only spring from strong faith, which Caleb and Joshua alone possessed.

Verses 21-25

The searchers of the land brought a bunch of grapes with them, and other fruits, as proofs of the goodness of the country; which was to Israel both the earnest and the specimen of all the fruits of Canaan. Such are the present comforts we have in communion with God, foretastes of the fulness of joy we expect in the heavenly Canaan. We may see by them what heaven is.

Verses 26-33

We may wonder that the people of Israel staid forty days for the return of their spies, when they were ready to enter Canaan, under all the assurances of success they could have from the Divine power, and the miracles that had hitherto attended them. But they distrusted God's power and promise. How much we stand in our own light by our unbelief! At length the messengers returned; but the greater part discouraged the people from going forward to Canaan. Justly are the Israelites left to this temptation, for putting confidence in the judgment of men, when they had the word of God to trust in. Though they had found the land as good as God had said, yet they would not believe it to be as sure as he had said, but despaired of having it, though Eternal Truth had engaged it to them. This was the representation of the evil spies. Caleb, however, encouraged them to go forward, though seconded by Joshua only. He does not say, Let us go up and conquer it; but, Let us go and possess it. Difficulties that are in the way of salvation, dwindle and vanish before a lively, active faith in the power and promise of God. All things are possible, if they are promised, to him that believes; but carnal sense and carnal professors are not to be trusted. Unbelief overlooks the promises and power of God, magnifies every danger and difficulty, and fills the heart with discouragement. May the Lord help us to believe! we shall then find all things possible.

Chapter 14

Chapter Outline

The people murmur at the account of the spies.	(1–4)
Joshua and Caleb labour to still the people.	(5–10)
The Divine threatenings, The intercession of Moses.	(11–19)
The murmurers forbidden to enter the promised land.	(20–35)
Death of the evil spies.	(36–39)
Defeat of the people, who now would invade the land.	(40–45)

Verses 1-4

Those who do not trust God, continually vex themselves. The sorrow of the world worketh death. The Israelites murmured against Moses and Aaron, and in them reproached the Lord. They look back with causeless discontent. See the madness of unbridled passions, which makes men prodigal of what nature accounts most dear, life itself. They wish rather to die criminals under God's justice, than to live conquerors in his favour. At last they resolve, that, instead of going forward to Canaan, they would go back to Egypt. Those who walk not in God's counsels, seek their own ruin. Could they expect that God's cloud would lead them, or his manna attend them? Suppose the difficulties of conquering Canaan were as they imagined, those of returning to Egypt were much greater. We complain of our place and lot, and we would change; but is there any place or condition in this world, that has not something in it to make us uneasy, if we are disposed to be so? The way to better our condition, is to get our spirits in a better frame. See the folly of turning from the ways of God. But men run on the certain fatal consequences of a sinful course.

Verses 5-10

Moses and Aaron were astonished to see a people throw away their own mercies. Caleb and Joshua assured the people of the goodness of the land. They made nothing of the difficulties in the way of their gaining it. If men were convinced of the desirableness of the gains of religion, they would not stick at the services of it. Though the Canaanites dwell in walled cities, their defence was departed from them. The other spies took notice of their strength, but these of their wickedness. No people can be safe, when they have provoked God to leave them. Though Israel dwell in tents, they are fortified. While we have the presence of God with us, we need not fear the most powerful force against us. Sinners are ruined by their own rebellion. But those who, like Caleb and Joshua, faithfully expose themselves for God, are sure to be taken under his special protection, and shall be hid from the rage of men, either under heaven or in heaven. (Nu 14:11-19)

Verses 11-19

Moses made humble intercession for Israel. Herein he was a type of Christ, who prayed for those that despitefully used him. The pardon of a nation's sin, is the turning away the nation's punishment; and for that Moses is here so earnest. Moses argued that, consistently with God's character, in his abundant mercies, he could forgive them.

Verses 20-35

The Lord granted the prayer of Moses so far as not at once to destroy the congregation. But disbelief of the promise forbids the benefit. Those who despise the pleasant land shall be shut out of it. The promise of God should be fulfilled to their children. They wished to die in the wilderness; God made their sin their ruin, took them at their word, and their carcases fell in the wilderness. They were made to groan under the burden of their own sin, which was too heavy for them to bear. Ye shall know my breach of promise, both the causes of it, that it is procured by your sin, for God never leaves any till they first leave him; and the consequences of it, that will produce your ruin. But your little ones, now under twenty years old, which ye, in your unbelief, said should be a prey, them will I bring in. God will let them know that he can put a difference between the guilty and the innocent, and cut them off without touching their children. Thus God would not utterly take away his loving kindness.

Verses 36-39

Here is the sudden death of the ten evil spies. They sinned in bringing a slander upon the land of promise. Those greatly provoke God, who misrepresent religion, raise dislike in men's minds toward it, or give opportunity to those to do so, who seek occasion. Justly are murmurers made mourners. If they had mourned for the sin, when they were faithfully reproved, the sentence had been prevented; but as they mourned for the judgment only, it did them no service. There is in hell such mourning as this; but tears will not quench the flames, nor cool the tongue.

Verses 40-45

Some of the Israelites were now earnest to go forward toward Canaan. But it came too late. If men would but be as earnest for heaven while their day of grace lasts, as they will be when it is over, how well would it be for them! That which has been duty in its season, when mistimed, may be turned into sin. Those who are out of the way of their duty, are not under God's protection, and go at their peril. God bade them go, and they would not; he forbade them, and they would go. Thus is the carnal mind enmity against God. They had distrusted God's strength; they now presume upon their own without his. And the expedition fails accordingly; now the sentence began to be executed, that their carcases should fall in the wilderness. That affair can never end well, which begins with sin. The way to obtain peace with our friends, and success against our enemies, is, to have God, as our Friend, and to keep in his love. Let us take warning from the fate of Israel, lest we perish after the same example of unbelief. Let us go forth, depending on God's mercy, power, promise, and truth; he will be with us, and bring our souls to everlasting rest.

Chapter 15

Chapter Outline

Verses 1-21

Full instructions are given about the meat-offerings and drink-offerings. The beginning of this law is very encouraging, When ye come into the land of your habitation which I give unto you. This was a plain intimation that God would secure the promised land to their seed. It was requisite, since the sacrifices of acknowledgment were intended as the food of God's table, that there should be a constant supply of bread, oil, and wine, whatever the flesh-meat was. And the intent of this law is to direct the proportions of the meat-offering and drink-offering. Natives and strangers are placed on a level in this as in other like matters. It was a happy forewarning of the calling of the Gentiles, and of their admission into the church. If the law made so little difference between Jew and Gentile, much less would the gospel, which broke down the partition-wall, and reconciled both to God.

Verses 22-29

Though ignorance will in a degree excuse, it will not justify those who might have known their Lord's will, yet did it not. David prayed to be cleansed from his secret faults, those sins which he himself was not aware of. Sins committed ignorantly, shall be forgiven through Christ the great Sacrifice, who, when he offered up himself once for all upon the cross, seemed to explain one part of the intention of his offering, in that prayer, Father, forgive them, for they know not what they do. It looked favourably upon the Gentiles, that this law of atoning for sins of ignorance, is expressly made to extend to those who were strangers to Israel.

Verses 30-36

Those are to be reckoned presumptuous sinners, who sin designedly against God's will and glory. Sins thus committed are exceedingly sinful. He that thus breaks the commandment reproaches the Lord. He also despises the word of the Lord. Presumptuous sinners despise it, thinking themselves too great, too good, and too wise, to be ruled by it. A particular instance of presumption in the sin of sabbath-breaking is related. The offence was gathering sticks on the sabbath day, to make a fire, whereas the people were to bake and seethe what they had occasion for, the day before, Ex 16:23. This was done as an affront both to the law and to the Lawgiver. God is jealous for the honour of his sabbaths, and will not hold him guiltless who profanes them, whatever men may do. God intended this punishment for a warning to all, to make conscience of keeping holy the sabbath. And we may be assured that no command was ever given for the punishment of sin, which, at the judgment day, shall not prove to have come from perfect love and justice. The right of God to a day of devotion to himself, will be disputed and denied only by such as listen to the pride and unbelief of their hearts, rather than to the teaching of the Spirit of truth and life. Wherein consists the difference between him who was detected gathering sticks in the wilderness on the day of God, and the man who turns his back upon the blessings of sabbath appointments, and the promises of sabbath mercies, to use his time, his cares, and his soul, in heaping up riches; and waste his hours, his property, and his strength in sinful pleasure? Wealth may come by the unhallowed effort, but it will not come alone; it will have its awful reward. Sinful pursuits lead to ruin.

Verses 37-41

The people are ordered by the Lord to make fringes on the borders of their garments. The Jews were distinguished from their neighbours in their dress, as well as in their diet, and thus taught not to be conformed to the way of the heathen in other things. They proclaimed themselves Jews wherever they were, as not ashamed of God and his law. The fringes were not appointed for trimming and adorning their clothes, but to stir up their minds by way of remembrance, 2Pe 3:1. If they were tempted to sin, the fringe would warn them not to break God's commandments. We should use every means of refreshing our memories with the truths and precepts of God's word, to strengthen and quicken our obedience, and arm our minds against temptation. Be holy unto your God; cleansed from sin, and sincerely devoted to his service; and that great reason for all the commandments is again and again repeated, "I am the Lord your God."

Chapter 16

Chapter Outline

The rebellion of Korah, Dathan, and Abiram Korah contends for the priesthood.	(1–11)
Disobedience of Dathan and Abiram.	(12–15)
The glory of the Lord appears, The intercession of Moses and Aaron.	(16–22)
The earth swallows up Dathan and Abiram.	(23–34)
The company of Korah consumed.	(35–40)
The people murmur A plague sent.	(41–50)

Verses 1-11

Pride and ambition occasion a great deal of mischief both in churches and states. The rebels quarrel with the settlement of the priesthood upon Aaron and his family. Small reason they had to boast of the people's purity, or of God's favour, as the people had been so often and so lately polluted with sin, and were now under the marks of God's displeasure. They unjustly charge Moses and Aaron with taking honour to themselves; whereas they were called of God to it. See here, 1. What spirit levellers are of; those who resist the powers God has set over them. 2. What usage they have been serviceable. Moses sought instruction from God. The heart of the wise studies to answer, and asks counsel of God. Moses shows their privileges as Levites, and convicts them of the sin of undervaluing these privileges. It will help to keep us from envying those above us, duly to consider how many there are below us.

Verses 12-15

Moses summoned Dathan and Abiram to bring their complaints; but they would not obey. They bring very false charges against Moses. Those often fall under the heaviest censures, who in truth deserve the highest praise. Moses, though the meekest man, yet, finding God reproached in him, was very wroth; he could not bear to see the people ruining themselves. He appeals to God as to his own integrity. He bade them appear with Aaron next morning, at the time of offering the morning incense. Korah undertook thus to appear. Proud ambitious men, while projecting their own advancement, often hurry on their own shameful fall.

Verses 16-22

The same glory of the Lord that appeared to place Aaron in his office at first, Le 9:23, now appeared to confirm him in it; and to confound those who set up against him. Nothing is more terrible to those who are conscious of guilt, than the appearance of the Divine glory. See how dangerous it is to have fellowship with sinners, and to partake with them. Though the people had treacherously deserted them, yet Moses and Aaron approved themselves faithful shepherds of Israel. If others fail in their duty to us, that does not take away the obligations we are under to seek their welfare. Their prayer was a pleading prayer, and it proved a prevailing one.

Verses 23-34

The seventy elders of Israel attend Moses. It is our duty to do what we can to countenance and support lawful authority when it is opposed. And those who would not perish with sinners, must come out from among them, and be separate. It was in answer to the prayer of Moses, that God stirred up the hearts of the congregation to remove for their own safety. Grace to separate from evil-doers is one of the things that accompany salvation. God, in justice, left the rebels to the obstinacy and hardness of their own hearts. Moses, by Divine direction, when all Israel were waiting the event, declares that if the rebels die a common death, he will be content to be called and counted an imposter. As soon as Moses had spoken the word, God caused the earth to open and swallow them all up. The children perished with their parents; in which, though we cannot tell how bad they might be to deserve it, or how good God might be otherwise to them; yet of this we are sure, that Infinite Justice did them no wrong. It was altogether miraculous. God has, when he pleases, strange punishments for the workers of iniquity. It was very significant. Considering how the earth is still in like manner loaded with the weight of man's sins, we have reason to wonder that it does not now sink under its load. The ruin of others should be our warning. Could we, by faith, hear the outcries of those that are gone down to the bottomless pit, we should give more diligence than we do to escape for our lives, lest we also come into their condemnation.

Verses 35-40

A fire went out from the Lord, and consumed the two hundred and fifty men that offered incense, while Aaron, who stood with them, was preserved alive. God is jealous of the honour of his own institutions, and will not have them invaded. The sacrifice of the wicked is an abomination to the Lord. The censers are devoted, and, as all devoted things, must be made serviceable to the glory of God. This covering of the altar would remind the children of Israel of this event, that others might hear and fear, and do no more presumptuously. They brought destruction on themselves both in body and soul. Thus all who break the law and neglect the gospel choose and love death.

Verses 41-50

The gaping earth was scarcely closed, before the same sins are again committed, and all these warnings slighted. They called the rebels the people of the Lord; and find fault with Divine justice. The obstinacy of Israel notwithstanding the terrors of God's law, as given on mount Sinai, and the terrors of his judgments, shows how necessary the grace of God is to change men's hearts and lives. Love will do what fear cannot. Moses and Aaron interceded with God for mercy, knowing how great the provocation was. Aaron went, and burned incense between the living and the dead, not to purify the air, but to pacify an offended God. As one tender of the life of every Israelite, Aaron made all possible speed. We must render good for evil. Observe especially, that Aaron was a type of Christ. There is an infection of sin in the world, which only the cross and intercession of Jesus Christ can stay and remove. He enters the defiled and dying camp. He stands between the dead and the living; between the eternal Judge and the souls under condemnation. We must have redemption through His blood, even the remission of sins. We admire the ready devotion of Aaron: shall we not bless and praise the unspeakable grace and love which filled the Saviour's heart, when he placed himself in our stead, and bought us with his life? Greatly indeed hath God commended his love towards us, in that while we were yet sinners, Christ died for us, Ro 5:8.

Chapter 17

Chapter Outline

Twelve rods laid up before the Lord.   (1–7)

Aaron's rod buds, and is kept for a   (8–13)
memorial.

Verses 1-7

It is an instance of the grace of God, that, having wrought divers miracles to punish sin, he would work one more to prevent it. Twelve rods or staves were to be brought in. It is probable that they were the staves which the princes used as ensigns of their authority; old dry staves, that had no sap in them. They were to expect that the rod of the tribe, or prince, whom God chose to the priesthood, should bud and blossom. Moses did not object that the matter was sufficiently settled already; he did not undertake to determine it; but left the case before the Lord.

Verses 8-13

While all the other rods remained as they were. Aaron's rod became a living branch. In some places there were buds, in others blossoms, in others fruit, at the same time; all this was miraculous. Thus Aaron was manifested to be under the special blessing of Heaven. Fruitfulness is the best evidence of a Divine call; and the plants of God's setting, and the boughs cut off them, will flourish.

This rod was preserved, to take away the murmurings of the people, that they might not die. The design of God, in all his providences, and in the memorials of them, is to take away sin. Christ was manifested to take away sin. Christ is expressly called a rod out of the stem of Jesse: little prospect was there, according to human views, that he should ever flourish. But the dry rod revived and blossomed to the confusion of his adversaries. The people cry, Behold, we die, we perish, we all perish! This was the language of a repining people, quarrelling with the judgments of God, which by their own pride and obstinacy they brought upon themselves. It is very wicked to fret against God when we are in affliction, and in our distress thus to trespass yet more. If we die, if we perish, it is of ourselves, and the blame will be upon our own heads. When God judges, he will overcome, and will oblige the most obstinate gainsayers to confess their folly. And how great are our mercies, that we have a clearer and a better dispensation, established upon better promises!

Chapter 18

Chapter Outline

Verses 1-7

The people complained of their difficulty and peril in drawing near to God. God here gives them to understand, that the priests should come near for them. Aaron would see reason not to be proud of his preferment, when he considered the great care and charge upon him. Be not high-minded, but fear. The greater the trust of work and power that is committed to us, the greater danger there is of betraying that trust. This is a good reason why we should neither envy others' honours, nor desire high places.

Verses 8-19

All believers are spiritual priests, and God has promised to take care of them. Godliness has the promise of the life that now is. And from the provision here made for the priests, the apostle shows that it is the duty of christian churches to maintain their ministers. Scandalous maintenance makes scandalous ministers. The priests were to be wholly devoted to their ministry, not diverted from it, or disturbed in it, by worldly care or business. Also, that they might be examples of living by faith, not only in God's providence, but in his ordinances. The best should be offered for the first-fruits unto the Lord. Those who think to save, by putting God off with the refuse, deceive themselves, for God is not mocked.

Verses 20-32

As Israel was a people not to be numbered among the nations, so Levi was a tribe to be distinguished from the rest. Those who have God for their Inheritance and their Portion for ever, ought to look with holy contempt and indifference upon the possessions of this world. The Levites were to give God his dues out of their tithes, as well as the Israelites out of their increase. See, in ver. #(31), the way to have comfort in all our worldly possessions, so as to bear no sin by reason of them. 1. We must be sure that what we have is got honestly and in the service of God. That meat is best eaten which is first earned; but if any will not work, neither shall he eat, 2Th 3:10. 2. We must be sure that God has his dues out of it. We have the comfort of our substance, when we have honoured the Lord with it. Ye shall bear no sin by reason of it, when ye have heaved the best from it. We should give alms of such things as we have, that all may be holy and comfortable to us.

Chapter 19

Chapter Outline

Verses 1-10

The heifer was to be wholly burned. This typified the painful sufferings of our Lord Jesus, both in soul and body, as a sacrifice made by fire, to satisfy God's justice for man's sin. These ashes are said to be laid up as a purification for sin, because, though they were only to purify from ceremonial uncleanness, yet they were a type of that purification for sin which our Lord Jesus made by his death. The blood of Christ is laid up for us in the word and sacraments, as a fountain of merit, to which by faith we may have constant recourse, for cleansing our consciences.

Verses 11-22

Why did the law make a corpse a defiling thing? Because death is the wages of sin, which entered into the world by it, and reigns by the power of it. The law could not conquer death, nor abolish it, as the gospel does, by bringing life and immortality to light, and so introducing a better hope. As the ashes of the heifer signified the merit of Christ, so the running water signified the power and grace of the blessed Spirit, who is compared to rivers of living water; and it is by his work that the righteousness of Christ is applied to us for our cleansing. Those who promise themselves benefit by the righteousness of Christ, while they submit not to the grace and influence of the Holy Spirit, do but deceive themselves; we cannot be purified by the ashes, otherwise than in the running water. What use could there be in these appointments, if they do not refer to the doctrines concerning the sacrifice of Christ? But comparing them with the New Testament, the knowledge to be got from them is evident. The true state of fallen man is shown in these institutions. Here we learn the defiling nature of sin, and are warned to avoid evil communications.

Chapter 20

Chapter Outline

Verses 1-13

After thirty-eight years' tedious abode in the wilderness, the armies of Israel advanced towards Canaan again. There was no water for the congregation. We live in a wanting world, and wherever we are, must expect to meet with something to put us out. It is a great mercy to have plenty of water, a mercy which, if we found the want of, we should more own the worth of. Hereupon they murmured against Moses and Aaron. They spake the same absurd and brutish language their fathers had done. It made their crime the worse, that they had smarted so long for the discontent and distrusts of their fathers, yet they venture in the same steps. Moses must again, in God's name, command water out of a rock for them; God is as able as ever to supply his people with what is needful for them. But Moses and Aaron acted wrong. They took much of the glory of this work of wonder to themselves; "Must we fetch water?" As if it were done by some power or worthiness of their own. They were to speak to the rock, but they smote it. Therefore it is charged upon them, that they did not sanctify God, that is, they did not give to him alone that glory of this miracle which was due unto his name. And being provoked by the people, Moses spake unadvisedly with his lips. The same pride of man would still usurp the office of the appointed Mediator; and become to ourselves wisdom, righteousness, and sanctification, and redemption. Such a state of sinful independence, such a rebellion of the soul against its Saviour, the voice of God condemns in every page of the gospel.

Verses 14-21

The nearest way to Canaan from the place where Israel encamped, was through the country of Edom. The ambassadors who were sent returned with a denial. The Edomites feared to receive damage by the Israelites. And had this numerous army been under any other discipline than that of the righteous God himself, there might have been cause for this jealousy. But Esau hated Jacob because of the blessing; and now the hatred revived, when the blessing was about to be inherited. We must not think it strange, if reasonable requests be denied by unreasonable men, and if those whom God favours be affronted by men.

Verses 22-29

God bids Aaron prepare to die. There is something of displeasure in these orders. Aaron must not enter Canaan, because he had failed in his duty at the waters of strife. There is much of mercy in them. Aaron, though he dies for his transgression, dies with ease, and in honour. He is gathered to his people, as one who dies in the arms of Divine grace. There is much significancy in these orders. Aaron must not enter Canaan, to show that the Levitical priesthood could make nothing perfect; that must be done by bringing in a better hope. Aaron submits, and dies in the method and manner appointed; and, for aught that appears, with as much cheerfulness as if he had been going to bed. It was a great satisfaction to Aaron to see his son, who was dear to him, preferred; and his office preserved and secured: especially, to see in this a figure of Christ's everlasting priesthood. A good man would desire, if it were the will of God, not to outlive his usefulness. Why should we covet to continue any longer in this world, than while we may do some service in it for God and our generation?

Chapter 21

Chapter Outline

The Canaanites of Arad destroyed.	(1–3)
The people murmuring, are plagued with fiery serpents, They repenting, are healed through the brazen serpent.	(4–9)
Further journeys of the Israelites.	(10–20)
Sihon and Og overcome, Their land possessed.	(21–35)

Verses 1-3

Before the people began their march round the country of Edom, the king of Arad, a Canaanite, who inhabited the southern part of the country, attacked them in the wilderness, and took some prisoners. This was to lead the Israelites to look more thoroughly to the Lord.

Verses 4-9

The children of Israel were wearied by a long march round the land of Edom. They speak discontentedly of what God had done for them, and distrustfully of what he would do. What will they be pleased with, whom manna will not please? Let not the contempt which some cast on the word of God, make us value it less. It is the bread of life, substantial bread, and will nourish those who by faith feed upon it, to eternal life, whoever may call it light bread. We see the righteous judgment God brought upon them for murmuring. He sent fiery serpents among them, which bit or stung many to death. It is to be feared that they would not have owned the sin, if they had not felt the smart; but they relent under the rod. And God made a wonderful provision for their relief. The Jews themselves say it was not the sight of the brazen serpent that cured; but in looking up to it, they looked up to God as the Lord that healed them. There was much gospel in this. Our Saviour declared, Joh 3:14, 15, that as Moses lifted up the serpent in the wilderness, so the Son of man must be lifted up, that whatsoever believeth in him, should not perish. Compare their disease and ours. Sin bites like a serpent, and stings like an adder. Compare the application of their remedy and ours. They looked and lived, and we, if we believe, shall not perish. It is by faith that we look unto Jesus, Heb 12:2. Whosoever looked, however desperate his case, or feeble his sight, or distant his place, was certainly and perfectly cured. The Lord can relieve us from dangers and distresses, by means which human reason never would have devised. Oh that the venom of the old serpent, inflaming men's passions, and causing them to commit sins which end in their eternal destruction, were as sensibly felt, and the danger as plainly seen, as the Israelites felt pain from the bite of the fiery serpents, and feared the death which followed! Then none would shut their eyes to Christ, or turn from his gospel. Then a crucified Saviour would be so valued, that all things else would be accounted loss for him; then, without delay, and with earnestness and simplicity, all would apply to him in the appointed way, crying, Lord, save us; we perish! Nor would any abuse the freeness of Christ's salvation, while they reckoned the price which it cost him.

Verses 10-20

We have here the removes of the children of Israel, till they came to the plains of Moab, from whence they passed over Jordan into Canaan. The end of their pilgrimage was near. "They set forward." It were well if we did thus; and the nearer we come to heaven, were so much the more active and abundant in the work of the Lord. The wonderful success God granted to his people, is here spoken of, and, among the rest, their actions on the river Arnon, at Vaheb in Suphah, and other places on that river. In every stage of our lives, nay, in every step, we should notice what God has wrought for us; what he did at such a time, and what in such a place, ought to be distinctly remembered. God blessed his people with a supply of water. When we come to heaven, we shall remove to the well of life, the fountain of living waters. They received it with joy and thankfulness, which made the mercy doubly sweet. With joy must we draw water out of the wells of salvation, Isa 12:3. As the brazen serpent was a figure of Christ, who is lifted up for our cure, so is this well a figure of the Spirit, who is poured forth for our comfort, and from whom flow to us rivers of living waters, Joh 7:38, 39. Does this well spring up in our souls? If so, we should take the comfort to ourselves, and give the glory to God. God promised to give water, but they must open the ground. God's favours must be expected in the use of such means as are within our power, but still the power is only of God.

Verses 21-35

Sihon went with his forces against Israel, out of his own borders, without provocation, and so ran upon his own ruin. The enemies of God's church often perish by the counsels they think most wisely taken. Og, king of Bashan, instead of being warned by the fate of his neighbours, to make peace with Israel, makes war with them, which proves in like manner his destruction. Wicked men do their utmost to secure themselves and their possessions against the judgments of God; but all in vain, when the day comes on which they must fall. God gave Israel success, while Moses was with them, that he might see the beginning of the glorious work, though he must not live to see it finished. This was, in comparison, but as the day of small things, yet it was an earnest of great things. We must prepare for fresh conflicts and enemies. We must make no peace or truce with the powers of darkness, nor even treat with them; nor should we expect any pause in our contest. But, trusting in God, and obeying his commands, we shall be more than conquerors over every enemy.

Chapter 22

Chapter Outline

Balak's fear of Israel, He sends for Balaam.   (1–14)

Balaam goes to Balak.   (15–21)

The opposition to Balaam by the way.   (22–35)

Balaam and Balak meet.   (36–41)

Verses 1-14

The king of Moab formed a plan to get the people of Israel cursed; that is, to set God against them, who had hitherto fought for them. He had a false notion, that if he could get some prophet to pray for evil upon them, and to pronounce a blessing upon himself and his forces, that then he should be able to deal with them. None had so great a reputation as Balaam; and Balak will employ him, though he send a great way for him. It is not known whether the Lord had ever spoken to Balaam, or by him, before this; though it is probable he had, and it is certain he did afterwards. Yet we have abundant proof that he lived and died a wicked man, an enemy to God and his people. And the curse shall not come upon us if there is not a cause, even though men utter it. To prevail with Balaam, they took the wages of unrighteousness, but God laid restraint upon Balaam, forbidding him to curse Israel. Balaam was no stranger to Israel's cause; so that he ought to have answered the messengers at once, that he would never curse a people whom God had blessed; but he takes a night's time to consider what he should do. When we parley with temptations, we are in great danger of being overcome. Balaam was not faithful in returning God's answer to the messengers. Those are a fair mark for Satan's temptation, who lessen Divine restraints; as if to go against God's law were only to go without his leave. The messengers also are not faithful in returning Balaam's answer to Balak. Thus many are abused by the flatteries of those about them, and are prevented from seeing their own faults and follies.

Verses 15-21

A second embassy was sent to Balaam. It were well for us, if we were as earnest and constant in prosecuting a good work, notwithstanding disappointments. Balak laid a bait, not only for Balaam's covetousness, but for his pride and ambition. How earnestly should we beg of God daily to mortify such desires in us! Thus sinners stick at no pains, spare no cost, and care not how low they stoop, to gratify their luxury, or their malice. Shall we then be unwilling to do what is right? God forbid! Balaam's convictions charged him to keep to the command of God; nor could any man have spoken better. But many call God theirs, who are not his, not truly because not only his. There is no judging men by their words; God knows the heart. Balaam's corruptions at the same time inclined him to go contrary to the command. He seemed to refuse the temptation; but he expressed no abhorrence of it. He had a strong desire to accept the offer, and hoped that God might give him leave to go. He had already been told what the will of God was. It is a certain evidence of the ruling of corruption in the heart, to beg leave to sin. God gave Balaam up to his own heart's lusts. As God sometimes denies the prayers of his people in love, so sometimes he grants the desires of the wicked in wrath.

Verses 22-35

We must not think, that because God does not always by his providence restrain men from sin, therefore he approves of it, or that it is not hateful to him. The holy angels oppose sin, and perhaps are employed in preventing it more than we are aware. This angel was an adversary to Balaam, because Balaam counted him his adversary; those are really our best friends, and we ought so to reckon them, who stop our progress in sinful ways. Balaam has notice of God's displeasure by the ass. It is common for those whose hearts are fully set in them to do evil, to push on violently, through the difficulties Providence lays in their way. The Lord opened the mouth of the ass. This was a great miracle wrought by the power of God. He who made man speak, could, when he pleased, make the ass to speak with man's voice. The ass complained of Balaam's cruelty. The righteous God does not allow the meanest or weakest to be abused; but they shall be able to speak in their own defence, or he will some way or other speak for them. Balaam at length has his eyes opened. God has many ways to bring down the hard and unhumbled heart. When our eyes are opened, we shall see the danger of sinful ways, and how much it was for our advantage to be crossed. Balaam seemed to relent; I have sinned; but it does not appear that he was sensible of this wickedness of his heart, or willing to own it. If he finds he cannot go forward, he will be content, since there is no remedy, to go back. Thus many leave their sins, only because their sins have left them. The angel declared that he should not only be unable to curse Israel, but should be forced to bless them: this would be more for the glory of God, and to his own confusion, than if he had turned back.

Verses 36-41

Balak has now nothing to complain of, but that Balaam did not come sooner. Balaam bids Balak not depend too much upon him. He seems to speak with vexation; but is really as desirous to please Balak, as ever he had pretended to be to please God. See what need we have to pray every day, Our Father which art in heaven, lead us not into temptation. Let us be jealous over our own hearts, seeing how far men may go in the knowledge of God, and yet come short of Divine grace.

Chapter 23

Chapter Outline

Balak's sacrifice, Balaam pronounces a   (1–10)
blessing instead of a curse.

Balak's   disappointment,   and   second   (11–30)
sacrifice, Balaam again blesses Israel.

Verses 1-10

With the camps of Israel full in view, Balaam ordered seven altars to be built, and a bullock and a ram to be offered on each. Oh the sottishness of superstition, to imagine that God will be at man's beck! The curse is turned into a blessing, by the overruling power of God, in love to Israel. God designed to serve his own glory by Balaam, and therefore met him. If God put a word into the mouth of Balaam, who would have defied God and Israel, surely he will not be wanting to those who desire to glorify God, and to edify his people; it shall be given what they should speak. He who opened the mouth of the ass, caused the mouth of this wicked man to speak words as contrary to the desire of his heart, as those of the ass were to the powers of the brute. The miracle was as great in the one case as in the other. Balaam pronounces Israel safe. He owns he could do no more than God suffered him to do. He pronounces them happy in their distinction from the rest of the nations. Happy in their numbers, which made them both honourable and formidable. Happy in their last end. Death is the end of all men; even the righteous must die, and it is good for us to think of this with regard to ourselves, as Balaam does here, speaking of his own death. He pronounces the righteous truly blessed, not only while they live, but when they die; which makes their death even more desirable than life itself. But there are many who desire to die the death of the righteous, but do not endeavour to live the life of the righteous; gladly would they have an end like theirs, but not a way like theirs. They would be saints in heaven, but not saints on earth. This saying of Balaam's is only a wish, not a prayer; it is a vain wish, being only a wish for the end, without any care for the means. Many seek to quiet their consciences with the promise of future amendment, or take up with some false hope, while they neglect the only way of salvation, by which a sinner can be righteous before God.

Verses 11-30

Balak was angry with Balaam. Thus a confession of God's overruling power is extorted from a wicked prophet, to the confusion of a wicked prince. A second time the curse is turned into a blessing; and this blessing is both larger and stronger than the former. Men change their minds, and break their words; but God never changes his mind, and therefore never recalls his promise. And when in Scripture he is said to repent, it does not mean any change of his mind; but only a change of his way. There was sin in Jacob, and God saw it; but there was not such as might provoke him to give them up to ruin. If the Lord sees that we trust in his mercy, and accept of his salvation; that we indulge no secret lust, and continue not in rebellion, but endeavour to serve and glorify him; we may be sure that he looks upon us as accepted in Christ, that our sins are all pardoned. Oh the wonders of providence and grace, the wonders of redeeming love, of pardoning mercy, of the new-creating Spirit! Balak had no hope of ruining Israel, and Balaam showed that he had more reason to fear being ruined by them. Since Balaam cannot say what he would have him, Balak wished him to say nothing. But though there are many devices in man's heart, God's counsels shall stand. Yet they resolve to make another attempt, though they had no promise on which to build their hopes. Let us, who have a promise that the vision at the end shall speak and not lie, continue earnest in prayer, Lu 18:1.

Chapter 24

Chapter Outline

Verses 1-9

Now Balaam spake not his own sense, but the language of the Spirit that came upon him. Many have their eyes open who have not their hearts open; are enlightened, but not sanctified. That knowledge which puffs men up with pride, will but serve to light them to hell, whither many go with their eyes open. The blessing is nearly the same as those given before. He admires in Israel, their beauty. The righteous, doubtless, is more excellent than his neighbour. Their fruitfulness and increase. Their honour and advancement. Their power and victory. He looks back upon what had been done for them. Their power and victory. He looks back upon what had been done for them. Their courage and security. The righteous are bold as a lion, not when assaulting others, but when at rest, because God maketh them to dwell in safety. Their influence upon their neighbours. God takes what is done to them, whether good or evil, as done to himself. (Nu 24:10-14)

Verses 10-14

This vain attempt to curse Israel is ended. Balak broke out into a rage against Balaam, and expressed great vexation. Balaam has a very full excuse; God restrained him from saying what he would have said, and constrained him to say what he would not have uttered.

Verses 15-25

Under the powerful influence of the Spirit of prophecy, Balaam foretold the future prosperity and extensive dominion of Israel. Balaam boasts that his eyes are open. The prophets were in old times called seers. He had heard the words of God, which many do who neither heed them, nor hear God in them. He knew the knowledge of the Most High. A man may be full of the knowledge of God, yet utterly destitute of the grace of God. He calls God the Most High and the Almighty. No man could seem to express a greater respect to God; yet he had no true fear of him, love to him, nor faith in him; so far a man may go toward heaven, and yet come short of it at last. Here is Balaam's prophecy concerning Him who should be the crown and glory of his people Israel; who is David in the type; but our Lord Jesus, the promised Messiah, is chiefly pointed at, and of him it is an illustrious prophecy. Balaam, a wicked man, shall see Christ, but shall not see him nigh; not see him as Job, who saw him as his Redeemer, and saw him for himself. When he comes in the clouds, every eye shall see him; but many will see him, as the rich man in hell saw Abraham, afar off. He shall come out of Jacob, and Israel, as a Star and a Sceptre; the former denoting his glory and lustre; the latter his power and authority. Christ shall be King, not only of Jacob and Israel, but of all the world; so that all shall be either governed by his golden sceptre, or dashed in pieces by his iron rod. Balaam prophesied concerning the Amalekites and Kenites, part of whose country he had now in view. Even a nest in a rock will not be a lasting security. Here is a prophecy that looks as far forward as to the Greeks and Romans. He acknowledges all the revolutions of states and kingdoms to be the Lord's doing. These events will make such desolations, that scarcely any will escape. They that live then, will be as brands plucked out of the fire. May God fit us for the worst of times! Thus Balaam, instead of cursing the church, curses Amalek the first, and Rome the last enemy of the church. Not Rome pagan only, but Rome papal also; antichrist and all the antichristian powers. Let us ask ourselves, Do we in knowledge, experience, or profession, excel Balaam? No readiness of speech, even in preaching or prayer, no gifts of knowledge or prophecy, are in themselves different from, or superior to the boasted gifts of him who loved the wages of unrighteousness, and died the enemy of God. Simple dependence on the Redeemer's atoning blood and sanctifying grace, cheerful submission to the Divine will, constant endeavours to glorify God and benefit his people, these are less splendid, but far more excellent gifts, and always accompany salvation. No boasting hypocrite ever possessed these; yet the feeblest believer has something of them, and is daily praying for more of them.

Chapter 25

Chapter Outline

Verses 1-5

The friendship of the wicked is more dangerous than their enmity; for none can prevail against God's people if they are not overcome by their inbred lusts; nor can any enchantment hurt them, but the enticements of worldly interests and pleasures. Here is the sin of Israel, to which they are enticed by the daughters of Moab and Midian. Those are our worst enemies who draw us to sin, for that is the greatest mischief any man can do us. Israel's sin did that which all Balaam's enchantments could not do; it set God against them. Diseases are the fruits of God's anger, and the just punishments of prevailing sins; one infection follows the other. Ringleaders in sin ought to be made examples of justice.

Verses 6-15

Phinehas, in the courage of zeal and faith, executed vengeance on Zimri and Cozbi. This act can never be an example for private revenge, or religious persecution, or for irregular public vengeance.

Verses 16-18

We read not that any Midianites died of the plague; God punished them with the sword of an enemy, not with the rod of a father. We must set ourselves against whatever is an occasion of sin to us, Mt 5:29, 30. Whatever draws us to sin, should be a vexation to us, as a thorn in the flesh. And none will be more surely and severely punished than those who, after Satan's example, and with his subtlety, tempt others to sin.

Chapter 26

Chapter Outline

Numbering of Israel in the plains of Moab.	(1–51)
The division of the land.	(52–56)
Number of the Levites.	(57–62)
None remaining of the first numbering.	(63–65)

Verses 1-51

Moses did not number the people but when God commanded him. We have here the families registered, as well as the tribes. The total was nearly the same as when numbered at mount Sinai. Notice is here taken of the children of Korah; they died not, as the children of Dathan and Abiram; they seem not to have joined even their own father in rebellion. If we partake not of the sins of sinners, we shall not partake of their plagues. (Nu 26:52-56)

Verses 52-56

In distributing these tribes, the general rule of equity is prescribed; that to many should be given more, and to fewer less. Though it seems left to the prudence of their prince, the matter at last must be settled by the providence of God, with which all must be satisfied.

Verses 57-62

Levi was God's tribe; therefore it was not numbered with the rest, but alone. It came not under the sentence, that none of them should enter Canaan excepting Caleb and Joshua.

Verses 63-65

The execution of the sentence passed on the murmurers, chap. 14:29, is observable. There was not one man numbered now, who was numbered then, but Caleb and Joshua. Here appeared the righteousness of God, and his faithfulness to his threatenings. Especially observe the truth of God, in performing his promise to Caleb and Joshua. Death makes awful havoc of the human species, and causes surprising changes in families and nations; yet all is appointed in perfect wisdom, justice, and truth, by the Lord himself. This should stir us up to think upon the hateful nature of sin, the cause of all these devastations. We should renew our repentance, seek forgiveness, value the salvation of Christ, remember how frail we are, prepare for the summons of death, and fill up our days in serving our generation according to the will of God.

Chapter 27

Chapter Outline

The daughters of Zelophehad apply for an inheritance, The law of inheritances.	(1–11)
Moses warned of his death.	(12–14)
Joshua appointed to succeed Moses.	(15–23)

Verses 1-11

The five daughters of Zelophehad considered themselves as left destitute, having neither father nor brother to inherit any land. Their believing expectation that the word of the Lord would be performed in due season, and their desire of an interest in the promised inheritance; and the modest, candid manner in which they asked, without secret murmurs or discontents, are a good example. They ask for a possession in the land of Canaan. Herein they discovered, 1. Strong faith in the power and promise of God, concerning the giving of the land of Canaan to Israel. 2. And earnest desire of a place and name in the land of promise, which was a type of heaven. 3. Respect and honour for their father, whose name was dear to them now he was gone. He never had done any thing that might bar his children's claim. It is a comfort to parents when they come to die, if though they have smarted for their own sin, yet they are not conscious of any of those iniquities which

God will visit on their children. God himself gives judgment. He takes notice of the affairs, not only of nations, but of private families, and orders them according to his will. The petition is granted. Those who seek an inheritance in the land of promise, shall have what they seek for, and other things shall be added to them.

Verses 12-14

Moses must die, but he shall have the satisfaction of seeing the land of promise. This sight of Canaan signified his believing prospect of the better country, that is, the heavenly. Moses must die, but death does not cut him off; it only brings him to rest with the holy patriarchs. It is but to die as they died, having lived as they lived; and as their end was peace, why should we fear any evil in the passage of that dark valley? (Nu 27:15-23)

Verses 15-23

Envious spirits do not love their successors; but Moses was not one of these. We should concern ourselves, both in our prayers and in our endeavours, for the rising generation, that religion may be maintained and advanced, when we are in our graves. God appoints a successor, even Joshua; who had signalized himself by his courage in fighting Amalek, his humility in ministering to Moses, and his faith and sincerity in witnessing against the report of the evil spies. This man God appoints to succeed Moses; a man in whom is the Spirit, the Spirit of grace. He is a good man, fearing God and hating covetousness, and acting from principle. He has the spirit of government; he is fit to do the work and discharge the trusts of his place. He has a spirit of conduct and courage; he had also the Spirit of prophecy. That man is not fully qualified for any service in the church of Christ, who is destitute of the graces and gifts of the Holy Spirit, whatever human abilities he may possess. And in Joshua's succession we are reminded "that the law was given by Moses," who by reason of our transgression could not bring us to heaven; but "grace and truth came by Jesus Christ," for the salvation of every believer.

Chapter 28

Chapter Outline

Offerings, The daily sacrifice.	(1–8)
The offering on the sabbath and new moons.	(9–15)
Offerings at the passover, and on the day of first-fruits.	(16–31)

Verses 1-8

God saw fit now to repeat the law of sacrifices. This was a new generation of men; and they were concerned to keep their peace with God when at war with their enemies. The daily sacrifice is called a continual burnt-offering; when we are bid to pray always, at least every morning and evening we should offer up solemn prayers and praises to God. Nothing is added here but that the wine poured out in the drink-offering is to be strong wine, to teach us to serve God with the best we have. It was a figure of the blood of Christ, the memorial of which is still left to the church in wine; and of the blood of the martyrs, which was poured out as a drink-offering on the sacrifice and service of our faith, Php 2:17.

Verses 9-15

Every sabbath day, beside the two lambs offered for the daily burnt-offering, there must be two more offered. This teaches us to double our devotions on sabbath days, for so the duty of the day requires. The sabbath rest is to be observed, in order more closely to apply ourselves to the sabbath work, which ought to fill up the sabbath time. The offerings in the new moons showed thankfulness for the renewing of earthly blessings: when we rejoice in the gifts of providence, we must make the sacrifice of Christ, that great gift of special grace, the fountain and spring-head of our joy. And the worship performed in the new moons is made typical of gospel solemnities, Isa 66:23. As the moon borrows light from the sun, and is renewed by its influences; so the church borrows her light from Jesus Christ, who is the Sun of righteousness, renewing the state of the church, especially under the gospel. (Nu 28:16-31)

Verses 16-31

By the sacrifices enjoined in this chapter, we are reminded of the continued power of the sacrifice of Christ, and of our continual need to depend thereon. No hurrying employments, or perilous situations, or prosperous circumstances, should cause slackness in our religious exercises; but should rather stir us up to greater diligence in seeking help from, or giving thanks to the Lord. And all is to be accompanied with repentance, faith is the Lord Jesus, and love to him, and to produce true holiness in our conduct towards all men; otherwise God will abhor our most solemn services and abundant devotions. And Christ is able to supply the wants of every day, every week, every month, every year, every ordinance, every case.

Chapter 29

Chapter Outline

The offering at the feats of trumpets, and on the day of atonement.	(1–11)
Offerings at the feast of tabernacles.	(12–40)

Verses 1-11

There were more sacred solemnities in the seventh month than in any other. It was the space between harvest and seed-time. The more leisure we have from the pressing occupations of this life, the more time we should spend in the immediate service of God. The blowing of the trumpets was appointed, Le 22:24. Here they are directed what sacrifices to offer on that day. Those who would know the mind of God in the Scriptures, must compare one part with another. The latter discoveries of Divine light explain what was dark, and supply what was wanting, in the former, that the man of God may be perfect.

Verses 12-40

Soon after the day of atonement, the day in which men were to afflict their souls, followed the feast of Tabernacles, in which they were to rejoice before the Lord. Their days of rejoicing were to be days of sacrifices. A disposition to be cheerful does us good, when it encourages our hearts in the duties of God's service. All the days of dwelling in booths they must offer sacrifices; while we are here in a tabernacle state, it is our interest, as well as our duty, constantly to keep up communion with God. The sacrifices for each of the seven days are appointed. Every day there must be a sin-offering, as in the other feasts. Our burnt-offerings of praise cannot be accepted of God, unless we have an interest in the great sacrifice which Christ offered, when he made himself a Sin-offering for us. And no extraordinary services should put aside stated devotions. Every thing here reminds us of our sinfulness. The life that we live in the flesh must be by the faith of the Son of God; until we go to be with him, to behold his glory, and praise his mercy, who hath loved us and washed us from our sins in his own blood. To whom be honour and glory for ever. Amen.

Chapter 30

Chapter Outline

Vows to be kept.	(1, 2)
The cases wherein vows might be released.	(3–16)

Verses 1, 2

No man can be bound by his own promise to do what he is already, by the Divine precept, forbidden to do. In other matters the command is, that he shall not break his words, through he may change his mind.

Verses 3-16

Two cases of vows are determined. The case of a daughter in her father's house. When her vow comes to his knowledge, it is in his power either to confirm it or do it away. The law is plain in the case of a wife. If her husband allows her vow, though only by silence, it stands. If he disallows it, her obligation to her husband takes place of it; for to him she ought to be in subjection, as unto the

Lord. The Divine law consults the good order of families. It is fit that every man should bear rule in his own house, and have his wife and children in subjection; rather than that this great rule should be broken, or any encouragement be given to inferior relations to break those bonds asunder, God releases the obligation even of a solemn vow. So much does religion secure the welfare of all societies; and in it the families of the earth have a blessing.

Chapter 31

Verses 1-6

All who, without commission from God, dare to execute private revenge, and who, from ambition, covetousness, or resentment, wage war and desolate kingdoms, must one day answer for it. But if God, instead of sending an earthquake, a pestilence, or a famine, be pleased to authorize and command any people to avenge his cause, such a commission surely is just and right. The Israelites could show such a commission, though no persons now can do so. Their wars were begun and carried on expressly by Divine direction, and they were enabled to conquer by miracles. Unless it can be proved that the wicked Canaanites did not deserve their doom, objectors only prove their dislike to God, and their love to his enemies. Man makes light of the evil of sin, but God abhors it.

This explains the terrible executions of the nations which had filled the measure of their sins.

Verses 7-12

The Israelites slew the Kings of Midian. They slew Balaam. God's overruling providence brought him thither, and their just vengeance found him. Had he himself rightly believed what he had said of the happy state of Israel, he would not have thus herded with the enemies of Israel. The Midianites' wicked wiles were Balaam's projects: it was just that he should perish with them, Ho 4:5. They took the women and children captives. They burnt their cities and castles, and returned to the camp.

Verses 13-18

The sword of war should spare women and children; but the sword of justice should know no distinction, but that of guilty or not guilty. This war was the execution of a righteous sentence upon a guilty nation, in which the women were the worst criminals. The female children were spared, who, being brought up among the Israelites, would not tempt them to idolatry. The whole history shows the hatefulness of sin, and the guilt of tempting others; it teaches us to avoid all occasions of evil, and to give no quarter to inward lusts. The women and children were not kept for sinful purposes, but for slaves, a custom every where practised in former times, as to captives. In the course of providence, when famine and plagues visit a nation for sin, children suffer in the common calamity. In this case parents are punished in their children; and for children dying before actual sin, full provision is made as to their eternal happiness, by the mercy of God in Christ.

Verses 19-24

The Israelites had to purify themselves according to the law, and to abide without the camp seven days, though they had not contracted any moral guilt, the war being just and lawful, and commanded by God. Thus God would preserve in their minds a dread and detestation of shedding blood. The spoil had been used by Midianites, and being now come into the possession of Israelites, it was fit that it should be purified.

Verses 25-47

Whatever we have, God justly claims a part. Out of the people's share God required one in fifty, but out of the soldiers' share only one in five hundred. The less opportunity we have of honouring God with personal services, the more should we give in money or value.

Verses 48-54

The success of the Israelites had been very remarkable, so small a company overcoming such multitudes, but it was still more wonderful that not one was slain or missing. They presented the gold they found among the spoils, as an offering to the Lord. Thus they confessed, that instead of claiming a reward for their service, they needed forgiveness of much that had been amiss, and desired to be thankful for the preservation of their lives, which might justly have been taken away.

Chapter 32

Chapter Outline

The tribes of Reuben and Gad request an inheritance on the east of Jordan.	(1–5)
Moses reproves the Reubenites and Gadites.	(6–15)
They explain their views, Moses consents.	(16–27)
They take possession of the land to the east of Jordan.	(28–42)

Verses 1-5

Here is a proposal made by the Reubenites and Gadites, that the land lately conquered might be allotted to them. Two things common in the world might lead these tribes to make this choice; the lust of the eye, and the pride of life. There was much amiss in the principle they went upon; they consulted their own private convenience more than the public good. Thus to the present time, many seek their own things more than the things of Jesus Christ; and are led by worldly interests and advantages to take up short of the heavenly Canaan.

Verses 6-15

The proposal showed disregard to the land of Canaan, distrust of the Lord's promise, and unwillingness to encounter the difficulties and dangers of conquering and driving out the inhabitants of that land. Moses is wroth with them. It will becomes any of God's Israel to sit down unconcerned about the difficult and perilous concerns of their brethren, whether public or personal. He reminds them of the fatal consequences of the unbelief and faint-heartedness of their fathers, when they were, as themselves, just ready to enter Canaan. If men considered as they ought what would be the end of sin, they would be afraid of the beginning of it.

Verses 16-27

Here is the good effect of plain dealing. Moses, by showing their sin, and the danger of it, brought them to their duty, without murmuring or disputing. All men ought to consider the interests of others as well as their own; the law of love requires us to labour, venture, or suffer for each other as there may be occasion. They propose that their men of war should go ready armed before the children of Israel into the land of Canaan, and that they should not return till the conquest of Canaan was ended. Moses grants their request, but he warns them of the danger of breaking their word. If you fail, you sin against the Lord, and not against your brethren only; God will certainly reckon with you for it. Be sure your sin will find you out. Sin will surely find out the sinner sooner or later. It concerns us now to find our sins out, that we may repent of them, and forsake them, lest they find us out to our ruin.

Verses 28-42

Concerning the settlement of these tribes, observe, that they built the cities, that is, repaired them. They changed the names of them; probably they were idolatrous, therefore they should be forgotten. A spirit of selfishness, of seeking our own, not the things of Christ, when each one ought to assist others, is as dangerous as it is common. It is impossible to be sincere in the faith, sensible of the goodness of God, constrained by the love of Christ, sanctified by the power of the Holy Ghost, and yet be indifferent to the progress of religion, and the spiritual success of others, through love of ease, or fear of conflict. Let then your light so shine before men, that they may see your good works, and glorify your Father which is in heaven.

Chapter 33

Chapter Outline

Encampments of the Israelites.   (1–49)

The Canaanites to be destroyed.   (50–56)

Verses 1-49

This is a brief review of the travels of the children of Israel through the wilderness. It is a memorable history. In their travels towards Canaan they were continually on the remove. Such is our state in this world; we have here no continuing city, and all our removes in this world are but from one part a desert to another. They were led to and fro, forward and backward, yet were all the while under the direction of the pillar of cloud and fire. God led them about, yet led them the right way. The way God takes in bringing his people to himself is always the best way, though it does not always seem to us the nearest way. Former events are mentioned. Thus we ought to keep in mind the providences of God concerning us and families, us and our land, and the many instances of that Divine care which has led us, and fed us, and kept us all our days hitherto. Few periods of our lives can be thought upon, without reminding us of the Lord's goodness, and our own ingratitude and disobedience: his kindness leaves us without excuse for our sins. We could not wish to travel over again the stages we have passed, unless we could hope, by the grace of God, to shun the sins we then committed, and to embrace such opportunities of doing good as we have let slip. Soon will our wanderings end, and our eternal state be fixed beyond recall; how important then is the present moment! Happy are those whom the Lord now guides with his counsel, and will at length receive to his glory. To this happiness the gospel calls us. Behold now is the accepted time, now is the day of salvation. Let sinners seize the opportunity, and flee for refuge to the hope set before them. Let us redeem our time, to glorify God and serve our generation; and he will carry us safely through all, to his eternal kingdom.

Verses 50-56

Now that they were to pass over Jordan, they were entering again into temptation to follow idols; and they are threatened that, if they spared either the idols or the idolaters, their sin would certainly be their punishment. They would foster vipers in their own bosoms. The remnant of the Canaanites, if they made any peace with them, though but for a time, would be pricks in their eyes, and thorns in their sides. We must expect trouble and affliction from whatever sin we indulge; that which we are willing should tempt us, will vex us. It was intended that the Canaanites should be put out of the land; but if the Israelites learned their wicked ways, they also would be put out. Let us hear this and fear. If we do not drive out sin, sin will drive us out. If we are not the death of our lusts, our lusts will be the death of our souls.

Chapter 34

Chapter Outline

The bounds of the promised land. (1–15)

Those appointed to divide the land. (16–29)

Verses 1-15

Canaan was of small extent; as it is here bounded, it is but about 160 miles in length, and about 50 in breadth; yet this was the country promised to the father of the faithful, and the possession of the seed of Israel. This was that little spot of ground, in which alone, for many ages, God was known. This was the vineyard of the Lord, the garden enclosed; but as it is with gardens and vineyards, the narrowness of the space was made up by the fruitfulness of the soil. Though the earth is the Lord's, and the fulness thereof, yet few know him, and serve him; but those few are happy, because fruitful to God. Also, see how little a share of the world God gives to his own people. Those who have their portion in heaven, have reason to be content with a small pittance of this earth. Yet a little that a righteous man has, having it from the love of God, and with his blessing, is far better and more comfortable than the riches of many wicked. (Nu 34:16-29)

Verses 16-29

God here appoints men to divide the land to them. So sure must they feel of victory and success while God fought for them, that the persons are named who should be intrusted with the dividing of the land.

Chapter 35

Chapter Outline

The cities of the Levites. (1–8)

The cities of refuge, The laws about murder. (9–34)

Verses 1-8

The cities of the priests and Levites were not only to accommodate them, but to place them, as religious teachers, in several parts of the land. For though the typical service of the tabernacle or temple was only in one place, the preaching of the word of God, and prayer and praise, were not thus confined. These cities were to be given out of each tribe. Each thus made a grateful acknowledgement to God. Each tribe had the benefit of the Levites dwelling amongst them, to teach them the knowledge of the Lord; thus no parts of the country were left to sit in darkness. The gospel provides that he who is taught in the word, should communicate to him that teaches, in all good things, Ga 6:6. We are to free God's ministers from distracting cares, and to leave them at leisure for the duties of their station; so that they may be wholly employed therein, and avail themselves of every opportunity, by acts of kindness, to gain the good-will of the people, and to draw their attention.

Verses 9-34

To show plainly the abhorrence of murder, and to provide the more effectually for the punishment of the murderer, the nearest relation of the deceased, under the title of avenger of blood, (or the redeemer of blood,) in notorious cases, might pursue, and execute vengeance. A distinction is made, not between sudden anger and malice aforethought, both which are the crime of murder; but between intentionally striking a man with any weapon likely to cause death, and an unintentional blow. In the latter case alone, the city of refuge afforded protection. Murder in all its forms, and under all disguises, pollutes a land. Alas! that so many murders, under the name of duels, prize-fights, &c. should pass unpunished. There were six cities of refuge; one or other might be reached in less than a day's journey from any part of the land. To these, man-slayers might flee for refuge, and be safe, till they had a fair trial. If acquitted from the charge, they were protected from the avenger of blood; yet they must continue within the bounds of the city till the death of the high priest. Thus we are reminded that the death of the great High Priest is the only means whereby sins are pardoned, and sinners set at liberty. These cities are plainly alluded to, both in the Old and New Testament, we cannot doubt the typical character of their appointment. Turn ye to the strong hold, ye prisoners of hope, saith the voice of mercy, Zec 9:12, alluding to the city of refuge. St. Paul describes the strong consolation of fleeing for refuge to the hope set before us, in a passage always applied to the gracious appointment of the cities of refuge, Heb 6:18. The rich mercies of salvation, through Christ, prefigured by these cities, demand our regard. 1. Did the ancient city rear its towers of safety on high? See Christ raised up on the cross; and is he not exalted at the right hand of his Father, to be a Prince and a Saviour, to give repentance and remission of sins? 2. Does not the highway of salvation, resemble the smooth and plain path to the city of refuge? Survey the path that leads to the Redeemer. Is there any stumbling-block to be found therein, except that which an evil heart of unbelief supplies for its own fall? 3. Waymarks were set up pointing to the city. And is it not the office of the ministers of the gospel to direct sinners to Him? 4. The gate of the city stood open night and day. Has not Christ declared, Him that cometh unto me I will in nowise cast out? 5. The city of refuge afforded support to every one who entered its walls. Those who have reached the refuge, may live by faith on Him whose flesh is meat indeed, and whose blood is drink indeed. 6. The city was a refuge for all. In the gospel there is no respect of persons. That soul lives not which deserves not Divine wrath; that soul lives not which may not in simple faith hope for salvation and life eternal, through the Son of God.

Chapter 36

Chapter Outline

Verses 1-4

The heads of the tribe of Manasseh represent the evil which might follow, if the daughters of Zelophehad should marry into any other tribes. They sought to preserve the Divine appointment of inheritances, and that contests and quarrels should not rise among those who should come afterwards. It is the wisdom and duty of those who have estates in the world, to settle them, and to dispose of them, so that no strife and contention may arise. (Nu 36:5-12)

Verses 5-12

Those who consult the oracles of God, concerning the making of their heavenly inheritance sure, shall not only be directed what to do, but their inquiries shall be graciously accepted. God would not have one tribe enriched at the expense of another. Each tribe was to keep to its own inheritance. The daughters of Zelophehad submitted to this appointment. How could they fail to marry well, when God himself directed them? Let the people of God learn how suitable and proper it is, like the daughters of Israel, to be united only to their own people. Ought not every true believer Israel, to be united only to their own people. Ought not every true believer in Jesus, to be very attentive in the near and tender relations of life, to be united only to such as are united to the Lord? All our intentions and inclinations ought to be subjected to the will of God, when that is made known to us, and especially in contracting marriage. Although the word of God allows affection and preference in this important relation, it does not sanction that foolish, ungovernable, and idolatrous passion, which cares not what may be the end; but in defiance of authority, determines upon self-gratification. All such conduct, however disguised, is against common sense, the interests of society, the happiness of the marriage relation, and, what is still more evil, against the religion of Christ.

Verse 13

These are the judgments the Lord commanded in the plains of Moab. Most of them related to the settlement in Canaan, into which the Israelites were now entering. Whatever new condition God, by his providence, brings us into, we must beg him to teach us the duties of it, and to enable us to do them, that we may do the work of the day in its day, the duty of a place in its place.

Deuteronomy

This book repeats much of the history and of the laws contained in the three foregoing books: Moses delivered it to Israel a little before his death, both by word of mouth, that it might affect, and by writing, that it might abide. The men of that generation to which the law was first given were all dead, and a new generation was sprung up, to whom God would have it repeated by Moses himself, now they were going to possess the land of Canaan. The wonderful love of God to his church is set forth in this book; how he ever preserved his church for his own mercies sake, and would still have his name called upon among them. Such are the general outlines of this book, the whole of which shows Moses' love for Israel, and marks him an eminent type of the Lord Jesus Christ. Let us apply the exhortations and persuasions to our own consciences, to excite our minds to a believing, grateful obedience to the commands of God.

Chapter 1

Chapter Outline

The words Moses spake to Israel in the plains of Moab, The promise of Canaan.	(1–8)
Judges provided for the people.	(9–18)
Of the sending the spies—God's anger for their unbelief and disobedience.	(19–46)

Verses 1-8

Moses spake to the people all the Lord had given him in commandment. Horeb was but eleven days distant from Kadesh-barnea. This was to remind them that their own bad conduct had occasioned their tedious wanderings; that they might the more readily understand the advantages of obedience. They must now go forward. Though God brings his people into trouble and affliction, he knows when they have been tried long enough. When God commands us to go forward in our Christian course, he sets the heavenly Canaan before us for our encouragement.

Verses 9-18

Moses reminds the people of the happy constitution of their government, which might make them all safe and easy, if it was not their own fault. He owns the fulfilment of God's promise to Abraham, and prays for the further accomplishment of it. We are not straitened in the power and goodness of God; why should we be straitened in our own faith and hope? Good laws were given to the Israelites, and good men were to see to the execution of them, which showed God's goodness to them, and the care of Moses.

Verses 19-46

Moses reminds the Israelites of their march from Horeb to Kadesh-barnea, through that great and terrible wilderness. He shows how near they were to a happy settlement in Canaan. It will aggravate the eternal ruin of hypocrites, that they were not far from the kingdom of God. As if it were not enough that they were sure of their God before them, they would send men before them. Never any looked into the Holy Land, but they must own it to be a good land. And was there any cause to distrust this God? An unbelieving heart was at the bottom of all this. All disobedience to God's laws, and distrust of his power and goodness, flow from disbelief of his word, as all true obedience springs from faith. It is profitable for us to divide our past lives into distinct periods; to give thanks to God for the mercies we have received in each, to confess and seek the forgiveness of all the sins we can remember; and thus to renew our acceptance of God's salvation, and our surrender of ourselves to his service. Our own plans seldom avail to good purpose; while courage in the exercise of faith, and in the path of duty, enables the believer to follow the Lord fully, to disregard all that opposes, to triumph over all opposition, and to take firm hold upon the promised blessings.

Chapter 2

Chapter Outline

The Edomites to be spared.	(1–7)
The Moabites and Ammonites to be spared.	(8–23)
The Amorites to be destroyed.	(24–37)

Verses 1-7

Only a short account of the long stay of Israel in the wilderness is given. God not only chastised them for their murmuring and unbelief, but prepared them for Canaan; by humbling them for sin, teaching them to mortify their lusts, to follow God, and to comfort themselves in him. Though Israel may be long kept waiting for deliverance and enlargement, it will come at last. Before God brought Israel to destroy their enemies in Canaan, he taught them to forgive their enemies in Edom. They must not, under pretence of God's covenant and conduct, think to seize all they could lay hands on. Dominion is not founded in grace. God's Israel shall be well placed, but must not expect to be placed alone in the midst of the earth. Religion must never be made a cloak for injustice. Scorn to be beholden to Edomites, when thou hast an all-sufficient God to depend upon. Use what thou hast, use it cheerfully. Thou hast experienced the care of the Divine providence, never use any crooked methods for thy supply. All this is equally to be applied to the experience of the believer.

Verses 8-23

We have the origin of the Moabites, Edomites, and Ammonites. Moses also gives an instance older than any of these; the Caphtorims drove the Avims out of their country. These revolutions show what uncertain things wordly possessions are. It was so of old, and ever will be so. Families decline, and from them estates are transferred to families that increase; so little continuance is there in these things. This is recorded to encourage the children of Israel. If the providence of God has done this for Moabites and Ammonites, much more would his promise do it for Israel, his peculiar people. Cautions are given not to meddle with Moabites and Ammonites. Even wicked men must not be wronged. God gives and preserves outward blessings to wicked men; these are not the best things, he has better in store for his own children.

Verses 24-37

God tried his people, by forbidding them to meddle with the rich countries of Moab and Ammon. He gives them possession of the country of the Amorites. If we keep from what God forbids, we shall not lose by our obedience. The earth is the Lord's and the fulness thereof; and he gives it to whom he pleases; but when there is no express direction, none can plead his grant for such proceedings. Though God assured the Israelites that the land should be their own, yet they must contend with the enemy. What God gives we must endeavour to get. What a new world did Israel now come into! Much more joyful will the change be, which holy souls will experience, when they remove out of the wilderness of this world to the better country, that is, the heavenly, to the city that has foundations. Let us, by reflecting upon God's dealings with his people Israel, be led to meditate upon our years spent in vanity, through our transgressions. But happy are those whom Jesus has delivered from the wrath to come. To whom he hath given the earnest of his Spirit in their hearts. Their inheritance cannot be affected by revolutions of kingdoms, or changes in earthly possessions.

Chapter 3

Chapter Outline

Verses 1-11

Og was very powerful, but he did not take warning by the ruin of Sihon, and desire conditions of peace. He trusted his own strength, and so was hardened to his destruction. Those not awakened by the judgments of God on others, ripen for the like judgments on themselves.

Verses 12-20

This country was settled on the Reubenites, Gadites, and half the tribe of Manasseh: see Nu 32. Moses repeats the condition of the grant to which they agreed. When at rest, we should desire to see our brethren at rest too, and should be ready to do what we can towards it; for we are not born for ourselves, but are members one of another.

Verses 21-29

Moses encouraged Joshua, who was to succeed him. Thus the aged and experienced in the service of God, should do all they can to strengthen the hands of those who are young, and setting out in religion. Consider what God has done, what God has promised. If God be for us, who can be against us, so as to prevail? We reproach our Leader if we follow him trembling. Moses prayed, that, if it were God's will, he might go before Israel, over Jordan into Canaan. We should never allow any desires in our hearts, which we cannot in faith offer up to God by prayer. God's answer to this prayer had a mixture of mercy and judgment. God sees it good to deny many things we desire. He may accept our prayers, yet not grant us the very things we pray for. It God does not by his providence give us what we desire, yet if by his grace he makes us content without, it comes to much the same. Let it suffice thee to have God for thy Father, and heaven for thy portion, though thou hast not every thing thou wouldst have in the world. God promised Moses a sight of Canaan from the top of Pisgah. Though he should not have the possession of it, he should have the prospect of it. Even great believers, in this present state, see heaven but at a distance. God provided him a successor. It is a comfort to the friends of the church of Christ, to see God's work likely to be carried on by others, when they are silent in the dust. And if we have the earnest and prospect of heaven, let these suffice us; let us submit to the Lord's will, and speak no more to Him of matters which he sees good to refuse us.

Chapter 4

Chapter Outline

Verses 1-23

The power and love of God to Israel are here made the ground and reason of a number of cautions and serious warnings; and although there is much reference to their national covenant, yet all may be applied to those who live under the gospel. What are laws made for but to be observed and obeyed? Our obedience as individuals cannot merit salvation; but it is the only evidence that we are partakers of the gift of God, which is eternal life through Jesus Christ, Considering how many temptations we are compassed with, and what corrupt desires we have in our bosoms, we have great need to keep our hearts with all diligence. Those cannot walk aright, who walk carelessly.

Moses charges particularly to take heed of the sin of idolatry. He shows how weak the temptation would be to those who thought aright; for these pretended gods, the sun, moon, and stars, were only blessings which the Lord their God had imparted to all nations. It is absurd to worship them; shall we serve those that were made to serve us? Take heed lest ye forget the covenant of the Lord your God. We must take heed lest at any time we forget our religion. Care, caution, and watchfulness, are helps against a bad memory.

Verses 24-40

Moses urged the greatness, glory, and goodness of God. Did we consider what a God he is with whom we have to do, we should surely make conscience of our duty to him, and not dare to sin against him. Shall we forsake a merciful God, who will never forsake us, if we are faithful unto him? Whither can we go? Let us be held to our duty by the bonds of love, and prevailed with by the mercies of God to cleave to him. Moses urged God's authority over them, and their obligations to him. In keeping God's commandments they would act wisely for themselves. The fear of the Lord, that is wisdom. Those who enjoy the benefit of Divine light and laws, ought to support their character for wisdom and honour, that God may be glorified thereby. Those who call upon God, shall certainly find him within call, ready to give an answer of peace to every prayer of faith. All these statutes and judgments of the Divine law are just and righteous, above the statutes and judgments of any of the nations. What they saw at mount Sinai, gave an earnest of the day of judgment, in which the Lord Jesus shall be revealed in flaming fire. They must also remember what they heard at mount Sinai. God manifests himself in the works of the creation, without speech or language, yet their voice is heard, Ps 19:1, 3; but to Israel he made himself known by speech and language, condescending to their weakness. The rise of this nation was quite different from the origin of all other nations. See the reasons of free grace; we are not beloved for our own sakes, but for Christ's sake. Moses urged the certain benefit and advantage of obedience. This argument he had begun with, ver. #(1), That ye may live, and go in and possess the land; and this he concludes with, ver. #(40), That it may go well with thee, and with thy children after thee. He reminds them that their prosperity would depend upon their piety. Apostacy from God would undoubtedly be the ruin of their nation. He foresees their revolt from God to idols. Those, and those only, shall find God to their comfort, who seek him with all their heart. Afflictions engage and quicken us to seek God; and, by the grace of God working with them, many are thus brought back to their right mind. When these things are come upon thee, turn to the Lord thy God, for thou seest what comes of turning from him. Let all the arguments be laid together, and then say, if religion has not reason on its side. None cast off the government of their God, but those who first abandon the understanding of a man.

Verses 41-49

Here is the introduction to another discourse, or sermon, Moses preached to Israel, which we have in the following chapters. He sets the law before them, as the rule they were to work by, the way they were to walk in. He sets it before them, as the glass in which they were to see their natural face, that, looking into this perfect law of liberty, they might continue therein. These are the laws, given when Israel was newly come out of Egypt; and they were now repeated. Moses gave these laws in charge, while they encamped over against Beth-peor, an idol place of the Moabites. Their present triumphs were a powerful argument for obedience. And we should understand our own situation as sinners, and the nature of that gracious covenant to which we are invited. Therein greater things are shown to us than ever Israel saw from mount Sinai; greater mercies are given to us than they experienced in the wilderness, or in Canaan. One speaks to us, who is of infinitely greater dignity than Moses; who bare our sins upon the cross; and pleads with us by His dying love.

Chapter 5

Chapter Outline

Verses 1-5

Moses demands attention. When we hear the word of God we must learn it; and what we have learned we must put in practice, for that is the end of hearing and learning; not to fill our heads with notions, or our mouths with talk, but to direct our affections and conduct.

Verses 6-22

There is some variation here from Ex 20 as between the Lord's prayer in Mt 6 and Lu 11. It is more necessary that we tie ourselves to the things, than to the words unalterably. The original reason for hallowing the sabbath, taken from God's resting from the work of creation on the seventh day, is not here mentioned. Though this ever remains in force, it is not the only reason. Here it is taken from Israel's deliverance out of Egypt; for that was typical of our redemption by Jesus Christ, in remembrance of which the Christian sabbath was to be observed. In the resurrection of Christ we were brought into the glorious liberty of the children of God, with a mighty hand, and an outstretched arm. How sweet is it to a soul truly distressed under the terrors of a broken law, to hear the mild and soul-reviving language of the gospel!

Verses 23-33

Moses refers to the consternation caused by the terror with which the law was given. God's appearances have always been terrible to man, ever since the fall; but Christ, having taken away sin, invites us to come boldly to the throne of grace. They were in a good mind, under the strong convictions of the word they heard. Many have their consciences startled by the law who have them not purified; fair promises are extorted from them, but no good principles are fixed and rooted in them. God commended what they said. He desires the welfare and salvation of poor sinners. He has given abundant proof that he does so; he gives us time and space to repent. He has sent his Son to redeem us, promised his Spirit to those who pray for him, and has declared that he has no pleasure in the ruin of sinners. It would be well with many, if there were always such a heart in them, as there seems to be sometimes; when they are under conviction of sin, or the rebukes of providence, or when they come to look death in the face. The only way to be happy, is to be holy. Say to the righteous, It shall be well with them. Let believers make it more and more their study and delight, to do as the Lord God hath commanded.

Chapter 6

Chapter Outline

A persuasive to obedience.	(1–3)
An exhortation to obedience.	(4, 5)
Obedience taught.	(6–16)
General precepts, Instructions to be given to their children.	(17–25)

Verses 1-3

In this and the like passages, the "commandments" seem to denote the moral law, the "statues" the ceremonial law, and the "judgments" the law by which the judges decided. Moses taught the people all that, and that only, which God commanded him to teach. Thus Christ's ministers are to teach his churches all he has commanded, neither more nor less, Mt 28:20. The fear of God in the heart will be the most powerful principle of obedience. It is highly desirable that not we only, but our children, and our children's children, may fear the Lord. Religion and righteousness advance and secure the prosperity of any people.

Verses 4, 5

Here is a brief summary of religion, containing the first principles of faith and obedience. Jehovah our God is the only living and true God; he only is God, and he is but One God. Let us not desire to have any other. The three-fold mention of the Divine names, and the plural number of the word translated God, seem plainly to intimate a Trinity of persons, even in this express declaration of the unity of the Godhead. Happy those who have this one Lord for their God. It is better to have one fountain than a thousand cisterns; one all-sufficient God than a thousand insufficient friends. This is the first and great commandment of God's law, that we love him; and that we do all parts of our duty to him from a principle of love; My son, give me thine heart. We are to love God with all our heart, and soul, and might. That is, 1. With a sincere love; not in word and tongue only, but inwardly in truth. 2. With a strong love. He that is our All, must have our all, and none but he. 3. With a superlative love; we must love God above any creature whatever, and love nothing but what we love for him. 4. With an intelligent love. To love him with all the heart, and with all the understanding, we must see good cause to love him. 5. With an entire love; he is ONE, our hearts must be united in his love. Oh that this love of God may be shed abroad in our hearts!

Verses 6-16

Here are means for maintaining and keeping up religion in our hearts and houses. 1. Meditation. God's words must be laid up in our hearts, that our thoughts may be daily employed about them. 2. The religious education of children. Often repeat these things to them. Be careful and exact in teaching thy children. Teach these truths to all who are any way under thy care. 3. Pious discourse. Thou shalt talk of these things with due reverence and seriousness, for the benefit not only of thy children, but of thy servants, thy friends and companions. Take all occasions to discourse with those about thee, not of matters of doubtful disputation, but of the plain truths and laws of God, and the things that belong to our peace. 4. Frequent reading of the word. God appointed them to write sentences of the law upon their walls, and in scrolls of parchment to be worn about their wrists. This seems to have been binding in the letter of it to the Jews, as it is to us in the intent of it; which is, that we should by all means make the word of God familiar to us; that we may have it ready to use upon all occasions, to restrain us from sin, and direct us in duty. We must never be ashamed to own our religion, nor to own ourselves under its check and government. Here is a caution not to forget God in a day of prosperity and plenty. When they came easily by the gift, they would be apt to grow secure, and unmindful of the Giver. Therefore be careful, when thou liest safe and soft, lest thou forget the Lord. When the world smiles, we are apt to make court to it, and expect our happiness in it, and so we forget Him who is our only portion and rest. There is need of great care and caution at such a time. Then beware; being warned of your danger, stand upon your guard. Thou shalt not tempt the Lord thy God; neither by despairing of his power and goodness, while we keep in the way of our duty; nor by presuming upon it, when we turn aside out of that way.

Verses 17-25

Moses gives charge to keep God's commandments. Negligence will ruin us; but we cannot be saved without diligence. It is our interest, as well as our duty, to be religious. It will be our life. Godliness has the promise of the continuance and comfort of the life that now is, as far as it is for God's glory. It will be our righteousness. It is only through the Mediator we can be righteous before God. The knowledge of the spirituality and excellency of the holy law of God, is suited to show sinful man his need of a Saviour, and to prepare his heart to welcome a free salvation. The gospel honours the law, not only in the perfect obedience of the Son of God, the Lord Jesus Christ; but in that it is a plan for bringing back apostate rebels and enemies, by repentance, faith, forgiveness, and renewing grace, to love God above all things, even in this world; and in the world above, to love him perfectly, even as angels love him.

Chapter 7

Chapter Outline

Intercourse with the Canaanites forbidden. (1–11)

Promises if they were obedient. (12–26)

Verses 1-11

Here is a strict caution against all friendship and fellowship with idols and idolaters. Those who are in communion with God, must have no communication with the unfruitful works of darkness. Limiting the orders to destroy, to the nations here mentioned, plainly shows that after ages were not to draw this into a precedent. A proper understanding of the evil of sin, and of the mystery of a crucified Saviour, will enable us to perceive the justice of God in all his punishments, temporal and eternal. We must deal decidedly with our lusts that war against our souls; let us not show them any mercy, but mortify, and crucify, and utterly destroy them. Thousands in the world that now is, have been undone by ungodly marriages; for there is more likelihood that the good will be perverted, than that the bad will be converted. Those who, in choosing yoke-fellows, keep not within the bounds of a profession of religion, cannot promise themselves helps meet for them.

Verses 12-26

We are in danger of having fellowship with the works of darkness if we take pleasure in fellowship with those who do such works. Whatever brings us into a snare, brings us under a curse. Let us be constant to our duty, and we cannot question the constancy of God's mercy. Diseases are God's servants; they go where he sends them, and do what he bids them. It is therefore good for the health of our bodies, thoroughly to mortify the sin of our souls; which is our rule of duty. Yet sin is never totally destroyed in this world; and it actually prevails in us much more than it would do, if we were watchful and diligent. In all this the Lord acts according to the counsel of his own will; but that counsel being hid from us, forms no excuse for our sloth and negligence, of which it is in no degree the cause. We must not think, that because the deliverance of the church, and the destruction of the enemies of the soul, are not done immediately, therefore they will never be done. God will do his own work in his own method and time; and we may be sure that they are always the best. Thus corruption is driven out of the hearts of believers by little and little. The work of sanctification is carried on gradually; but at length there will be a complete victory. Pride, security, and other sins that are common effects of prosperity, are enemies more dangerous than beasts of the field, and more apt to increase upon us.

Chapter 8

Chapter Outline

Exhortations and cautions, enforced by the   (1–9)
Lord's former dealings with Israel, and his
promises.

Exhortations and cautions further enforced.   (10–20)

Verses 1-9

Obedience must be, 1. Careful, observe to do; 2. Universal, to do all the commandments; and 3. From a good principle, with a regard to God as the Lord, and their God, and with a holy fear of him. To engage them to this obedience. Moses directs them to look back. It is good to remember all the ways, both of God's providence and grace, by which he has led us through this wilderness, that we may cheerfully serve him and trust in him. They must remember the straits they were sometimes brought into, for mortifying their pride, and manifesting their perverseness; to prove them, that they and others might know all that was in their heart, and that all might see that God chose them, not for any thing in them which might recommend them to his favour. They must remember the miraculous supplies of food and raiment granted them. Let none of God's children distrust their Father, nor take any sinful course for the supply of their necessities. Some way or other, God will provide for them in the way of duty and honest diligence, and verily they shall be fed. It may be applied spiritually; the word of God is the food of the soul. Christ is the word of God; by him we live. They must also remember the rebukes they had been under, and not without need. This use we should make of all our afflictions; by them let us be quickened to our duty. Moses also directs them to look forward to Canaan. Look which way we will, both to look back and to look forward, to Canaan. Look which way we will, both to look back and to look forward will furnish us with arguments for obedience. Moses saw in that land a type of the better country. The gospel church is the New Testament Canaan, watered with the Spirit in his gifts and graces, planted with trees of righteousness, bearing fruits of righteousness. Heaven is the good land, in which nothing is wanting, and where is fulness of joy.

Verses 10-20

Moses directs to the duty of a prosperous condition. Let them always remember their Benefactor. In everything we must give thanks. Moses arms them against the temptations of a prosperous condition. When men possess large estates, or are engaged in profitable business, they find the temptation to pride, forgetfulness of God, and carnal-mindedness, very strong; and they are anxious and troubled about many things. In this the believing poor have the advantage; they more easily perceive their supplies coming from the Lord in answer to the prayer of faith; and, strange as it may seem, they find less difficulty in simply trusting him for daily bread. They taste a sweetness therein, which is generally unknown to the rich, while they are also freed from many of their temptations. Forget not God's former dealings with thee. Here is the great secret of Divine Providence. Infinite wisdom and goodness are the source of all the changes and trials believers experience. Israel had many bitter trials, but it was "to do them good." Pride is natural to the human heart. Would one suppose that such a people, after their slavery at the brick-kilns, should need the thorns of the wilderness to humble them? But such is man! And they were proved that they might be humbled. None of us live a single week without giving proofs of our weakness, folly, and depravity. To broken-hearted souls alone the Saviour is precious indeed. Nothing can render the most suitable outward and inward trials effectual, but the power of the Spirit of God. See here how God's giving and our getting are reconciled, and apply it to spiritual wealth. All God's gifts are in pursuance of his promises. Moses repeats the warning he had often given of the fatal consequences of forsaking God. Those who follow others in sin, will follow them to destruction. If we do as sinners do, we must expect to fare as sinners fare.

Chapter 9

Chapter Outline

Verses 1-6

Moses represents the strength of the enemies they were now to encounter. This was to drive them to God, and engage their hope in him. He assures them of victory, by the presence of God with them. He cautions them not to have the least thought of their own righteousness, as if that procured this favour at God's hand. In Christ we have both righteousness and strength; in Him we must glory, not in ourselves, nor in any sufficiency of our own. It is for the wickedness of these nations that God drives them out. All whom God rejects, are rejected for their own wickedness; but none whom he accepts are accepted for their own righteousness. Thus boasting is for ever done away: see Eph 2:9, 11, 12.

Verses 7-29

That the Israelites might have no pretence to think that God brought them to Canaan for their righteousness, Moses shows what a miracle of mercy it was, that they had not been destroyed in the wilderness. It is good for us often to remember against ourselves, with sorrow and shame, our former sins; that we may see how much we are indebted to free grace, and may humbly own that we never merited any thing but wrath and the curse at God's hand. For so strong is our propensity to pride, that it will creep in under one pretence or another. We are ready to fancy that our righteousness has got for us the special favour of the Lord, though in reality our wickedness is more plain than our weakness. But when the secret history of every man's life shall be brought forth at the day of judgment, all the world will be proved guilty before God. At present, One pleads for us before the mercy-seat, who not only fasted, but died upon the cross for our sins; through whom we may approach, though self-condemned sinners, and beseech for undeserved mercy and for eternal life, as the gift of God in Him. Let us refer all the victory, all the glory, and all the praise, to Him who alone bringeth salvation.

Chapter 10

Chapter Outline

Verses 1-11

Moses reminded the Israelites of God's great mercy to them, notwithstanding their provocations. There were four things in and by which the Lord showed himself reconciled to Israel. God gave them his law. Thus God has intrusted us with Bibles, sabbaths, and sacraments, as tokens of his presence and favour. God led them forward toward Canaan. He appointed a standing ministry among them for holy things. And now, under the gospel, when the pouring forth of the Spirit is more plentiful and powerful, the succession is kept up by the Spirit's work on men's hearts, qualifying and making some willing for that work in every age. God accepted Moses as an advocate or intercessor for them, and therefore appointed him to be their prince and leader. Moses was a type of Christ, who ever lives, pleading for us, and has all power in heaven and in earth.

Verses 12-22

We are here taught our duty to God in our principles and our practices. We must fear the Lord our God. We must love him, and delight in communion with him. We must walk in the ways in which he has appointed us to walk. We must serve him with all our heart and soul. What we do in his service we must do cheerfully, and with good will. We must keep his commandments. There is true honour and pleasure in obedience. We must give honour to God; and to him we must cleave, as one we love and delight in, trust in, and from whom we have great expectations. We are here taught our duty to our neighbour. God's common gifts to mankind oblige us to honour all men. And those who have themselves been in distress, and have found mercy with God, should be ready to show kindness to those who are in the like distress. We are here taught our duty to ourselves. Circumcise your hearts. Cast away all corrupt affections and inclinations, which hinder you from fearing and loving God. By nature we do not love God. This is original sin, the source whence our wickedness proceeds; and the carnal mind is enmity against God, for it is not subject to the law of God, neither indeed can be; so then they that are in the flesh cannot please God, Ro 8:5–9. Let us, without delay or reserve, come and cleave to our reconciled God in Jesus Christ, that we may love, serve, and obey him acceptably, and be daily changed into his image, from glory to glory, by the Spirit of the Lord. Consider the greatness and glory of God; and his goodness and grace; these persuade us to our duty. Blessed Spirit! Oh for thy purifying, persevering, and renewing influences, that being called out of the state of strangers, such as our fathers were, we may be found among the number of the children of God, and that our lot may be among the saints.

Chapter 11

Chapter Outline

Verses 1-7

Observe the connexion of these two; Thou shalt love the Lord, and keep his charge. Love will work in obedience, and that only is acceptable obedience which flows from a principle of love, 1Jo 5:3. Moses recounts some of the great and terrible works of God which their eyes had seen. What our eyes have seen, especially in our early days, should affect us, and make us better long afterwards.

Verses 8-17

Moses sets before them, for the future, life and death, the blessing and the curse, according as they did or did not keep God's commandment. Sin tends to shorten the days of all men, and to shorten the days of a people's prosperity. God will bless them with an abundance of all good things, if they would love him and serve him. Godliness has the promise of the life that now is; but the favour of God shall put gladness into the heart, more than the increase of corn, and wine, and oil. Revolt from God to idols would certainly be their ruin. Take heed that your hearts be not deceived. All who forsake God to set their affection upon any creature, will find themselves wretchedly deceived, to their own destruction; and this will make it worse, that it was for want of taking heed.

Verses 18-25

Let all be directed by the three rules here given. 1. Let our hearts be filled with the word of God. There will not be good practices in the life, unless there be good thoughts, good affections, and good principles in the heart. 2. Let our eyes be fixed upon the word of God, having constant regard to it as the guide of our way, as the rule of our work, Ps 119:30. 3. Let our tongues be employed about the word of God. Nor will any thing do more to cause prosperity, and keeping up religion in a nation, than the good education of children.

Verses 26-32

Moses sums up all the arguments for obedience in two words, the blessing and the curse. He charged the people to choose which they would have. Moses then appointed a public and solemn proclamation of the blessing and curse, to be made upon the two mountains of Gerizim and Ebal. We have broken the law, and are under its curse, without remedy from ourselves. In mercy, the gospel again sets before us a blessing and a curse. A blessing, if we obey the call to repentance, to faith in Christ, and newness of heart and life through him; an awful curse, if we neglect so great salvation. Let us thankfully welcome these glad tidings of great joy; and let us not harden our hearts, but hear this voice of God while it is called to-day, and while he invites us to come to him upon a mercy-seat. Let us be diligent to make our calling and election sure.

Chapter 12

Chapter Outline

Monuments of idolatry to be destroyed.   (1–4)

The place of God's service to be kept.   (5–32)

Verses 1-4

Moses comes to the statutes he had to give in charge to Israel; and begins with such as relate to the worship of God. The Israelites are charged not to bring the rites and usages of idolaters into the worship of God; not under colour of making it better. We cannot serve God and mammon; nor worship the true God and idols; nor depend upon Christ Jesus and upon superstitious or self-righteous confidences.

Verses 5-32

The command to bring ALL the sacrifices to the door of the tabernacle, was now explained with reference to the promised land. As to moral service, then, as now, men might pray and worship every where, as they did in their synagogues. The place which God would choose, is said to be the place where he would put his name. It was to be his habitation, where, as King of Israel, he would be found by all who reverently sought him. Now, under the gospel, we have no temple or altar that sanctifies the gift but Christ only: and as to the places of worship, the prophets foretold that in every place the spiritual incense should be offered, Mal 1:11. Our Saviour declared, that those are accepted as true worshippers, who worship God in sincerity and truth, without regard either to this mountain or Jerusalem, Joh 4:21. And a devout Israelite might honour God, keep up communion with him, and obtain mercy from him, though he had no opportunity of bringing a sacrifice to his altar. Work for God should be done with holy joy and cheerfulness. Even children and servants must rejoice before God; the services of religion are to be a pleasure, and not a task or drudgery. It is the duty of people to be kind to their ministers, who teach them well, and set them good examples. As long as we live, we need their assistance, till we come to that world where ordinances will not be needed. Whether we eat or drink, or whatever we do, we are commanded to do all to the glory of God. And we must do all in the name of the Lord Jesus Christ, giving thanks to the Father through him. They must not even inquire into the modes and forms of idolatrous worship. What good would it do them to know those depths of Satan? And our inward satisfaction will be more and more, as we abound in love and good works, which spring from faith and the in-dwelling Spirit of Christ.

Chapter 13

Chapter Outline

Verses 1-5

Moses had cautioned against the peril that might arise from the Canaanites. Here he cautions against the rise of idolatry among themselves. It is needful for us to be well acquainted with the truths and precepts of the Bible; for we may expect to be proved by temptations of evil under the appearance of good, of error in the guise of truth; nor can any thing rightly oppose such temptations, but the plain, express testimony of God's word to the contrary. And it would be a proof of sincere affection for God, that, notwithstanding specious pretences, they should not be wrought upon the forsake God, and follow other gods to serve them.

Verses 6-11

It is the policy of Satan to try to lead us to evil by those whom we love, whom we least suspect of any ill design, and whom we are desirous to please, and apt to conform to. The enticement here is supposed to come from a brother or child, who are near by nature; from a wife or friend, who are near by choice, and are to us as our souls. But it is our duty to prefer God and religion, before the nearest and dearest friends we have in the world. We must not, to please our friends, break God's law. Thou shalt not consent to him, nor go with him, not for company, or curiosity, not to gain his affections. It is a general rule, If sinners entice thee, consent thou not, Pr 1:10. And we must not hinder the course of God's justice.

Verses 12-18

Here is the case of a city revolting from the God of Israel, and serving other gods. The crime is supposed to be committed by one of the cities of Israel. Even when they were ordered to preserve their religion by force, yet they were not allowed to bring others to it by fire and sword. Spiritual judgments under the Christian dispensation are more terrible than the execution of criminals; we have not less cause than the Israelites had, to fear the Divine wrath. Let us then fear the spiritual idolatry of covetousness, and the love of worldly pleasure; and be careful not to countenance them in our families, by our example or by the education of our children. May the Lord write his law and truth in our hearts, there set up his throne, and shed abroad his love!

Chapter 14

Chapter Outline

Verses 1-21

Moses tells the people of Israel how God had given them three distinguishing privileges, which were their honour, and figures of those spiritual blessings in heavenly things, with which God has in Christ blessed us. Here is election; "The Lord hath chosen thee." He did not choose them because they were by their own acts a peculiar people to him above other nations, but he chose them that they might be so by his grace; and thus were believers chosen, Eph 1:4. Here is adoption; "Ye are the children of the Lord your God;" not because God needed children, but because they were orphans, and needed a father. Every spiritual Israelite is indeed a child of God, a partaker of his nature and favour. Here is sanctification; "Thou art a holy people." God's people are required to be holy, and if they are holy, they are indebted to the grace God which makes them so. Those whom God chooses to be his children, he will form to be a holy people, and zealous of good works. They must be careful to avoid every thing which might disgrace their profession, in the sight of those who watch for their halting. Our heavenly Father forbids nothing but for our welfare. Do thyself no harm; do not ruin thy health, thy reputation, thy domestic comforts, thy peace of mind. Especially do not murder thy soul. Do not be the vile slave of thy appetites and passions. Do not render all around thee miserable, and thyself wretched; but aim at that which is most excellent and useful. The laws which regarded many sorts of flesh as unclean, were to keep them from mingling with their idolatrous neighbours. It is plain in the gospel, that these laws are now done away. But let us ask our own hearts, Are we of the children of the Lord our God? Are we separate from the ungodly world, in being set apart to God's glory, the purchase of Christ's blood? Are we subjects of the work of the Holy Ghost? Lord, teach us from these precepts how pure and holy all thy people ought to live!

Verses 22-29

A second portion from the produce of their land was required. The whole appointment evidently was against the covetousness, distrust, and selfishness of the human heart. It promoted friendliness, liberality, and cheerfulness, and raised a fund for the relief of the poor. They were taught that their worldly portion was most comfortably enjoyed, when shared with their brethren who were in want.

If we thus serve God, and do good with what we have, it is promised that the Lord our God will bless us in all the works of our land. The blessing of God is all to our outward prosperity; and without that blessing, the work of our hands will bring nothing to pass. The blessing descends upon the working hand. Expect not that God should bless thee in thy idleness and love of ease. And it descends upon the giving hand. He who thus scatters, certainly increases; and to be free and generous in the support of religion, and any good work, is the surest and safest way of thriving.

Chapter 15

Chapter Outline

Verses 1-11

This year of release typified the grace of the gospel, in which is proclaimed the acceptable year of the Lord; and by which we obtain the release of our debts, that is, the pardon of our sins. The law is spiritual, and lays restraints upon the thoughts of the heart. We mistake, if we think thoughts are free from God's knowledge and check. That is a wicked heart indeed, which raises evil thoughts from the good law of God, as theirs did, who, because God had obliged them to the charity of forgiving, denied the charity of giving. Those who would keep from the act of sin, must keep out of their minds the very thought of sin. It is a dreadful thing to have the cry of the poor justly against us. Grudge not a kindness to thy brother; distrust not the providence of God. What thou doest, do freely, for God loves a cheerful giver, 2Co 9:7.

Verses 12-18

Here the law concerning Hebrew servants is repeated. There is an addition, requiring the masters to put some small stock into their servants' hands to set up with for themselves, when sent out of their servitude, wherein they had received no wages. We may expect family blessings, the springs of family prosperity, when we make conscience of our duty to our family relations. We are to remember that we are debtors to Divine justice, and have nothing to pay with. That we are slaves, poor, and perishing. But the Lord Jesus Christ, by becoming poor, and by shedding his blood, has made a full and free provision for the payment of our debts, the ransom of our souls, and the supply of all our wants. When the gospel is clearly preached, the acceptable year of the Lord is proclaimed; the year of release of our debts, of the deliverance of our souls, and of obtaining rest in him. And as faith in Christ and love to him prevail, they will triumph over the selfishness of the heart, and over the unkindness of the world, doing away the excuses that rise from unbelief, distrust, and covetousness.

Verses 19-23

Here is a direction what to do with the firstlings. We are not now limited as the Israelites were; we make no difference between a first calf, or lamb, and the rest. Let us then look to the gospel meaning of this law, devoting ourselves and the first of our time and strength to God; and using all our comforts and enjoyments to his praise, and under the direction of his law, as we have them all by his gift.

Chapter 16

Chapter Outline

The yearly feasts.	(1–17)
Of judges, Groves and images forbidden.	(18–22)

Verses 1-17

The laws for the three yearly feasts are here repeated; that of the Passover, that of the Pentecost, that of Tabernacles; and the general law concerning the people's attendance. Never should a believer forget his low estate of guilt and misery, his deliverance, and the price it cost the Redeemer; that gratitude and joy in the Lord may be mingled with sorrow for sin, and patience under the tribulations in his way to the kingdom of heaven. They must rejoice in their receivings from God, and in their returns of service and sacrifice to him; our duty must be our delight, as well as our enjoyment. If those who were under the law must rejoice before God, much more we that are under the grace of the gospel; which makes it our duty to rejoice evermore, to rejoice in the Lord always. When we rejoice in God ourselves, we should do what we can to assist others also to rejoice in him, by comforting the mourners, and supplying those who are in want. All who make God their joy, may rejoice in hope, for He is faithful that has promised.

Verses 18-22

Care is taken for the due administration of justice. All personal regards must be laid aside, so that right is done to all, and wrong to none. Care is taken to prevent following the idolatrous customs of the heathen. Nothing belies God more, or tends more to corrupt the minds of men, than representing and worshipping, by an image, that God, who is an almighty and eternal Spirit, present every where. Alas! even in gospel days, and under a better dispensation, established upon better promises, there is a tendency to set up idols, under one form or another, in the human heart.

Chapter 17

Chapter Outline

Verses 1-7

No creature which had any blemish was to be offered in sacrifice to God. We are thus called to remember the perfect, pure, and spotless sacrifice of Christ, and reminded to serve God with the best of our abilities, time, and possession, or our pretended obedience will be hateful to him. So great a punishment as death, so remarkable a death as stoning, must be inflicted on the Jewish idolater. Let all who in our day set up idols in their hearts, remember how God punished this crime in Israel.

Verses 8-13

Courts of judgment were to be set up in every city. Though their judgment had not the Divine authority of an oracle, it was the judgment of wise, prudent, experienced men, and had the advantage of a Divine promise.

Verses 14-20

God himself was in a particular manner Israel's King; and if they set another over them, it was necessary that he should choose the person. Accordingly, when the people desired a king, they applied to Samuel, a prophet of the Lord. In all cases, God's choice, if we can but know it, should direct, determine, and overrule ours. Laws are given for the prince that should be elected. He must carefully avoid every thing that would turn him from God and religion. Riches, honours, and pleasures, are three great hinderances of godliness, (the lusts of the flesh, the lusts of the eye, and the pride of life,) especially to those in high stations; against these the king is here warned. The king must carefully study the law of God, and make that his rule; and having a copy of the Scriptures of his own writing, must read therein all the days of his life. It is not enough to have Bibles, but we must use them, use them daily, as long as we live. Christ's scholars never learn above their Bibles, but will have constant occasion for them, till they come to that world where knowledge and love will be made perfect. The king's writing and reading were as nothing, if he did not practise what he wrote and read. And those who fear God and keep his commandments, will fare the better for it even in this world.

Chapter 18

Chapter Outline

Verses 1-8

Care is taken that the priests entangle not themselves with the affairs of this life, nor enrich themselves with the wealth of this world; they have better things to mind. Care is likewise taken that they want not the comforts and conveniences of this life. The people must provide for them. He that has the benefit of solemn religious assemblies, ought to give help for the comfortable support of those that minister in such assemblies.

Verses 9-14

Was it possible that a people so blessed with Divine institutions, should ever be in any danger of making those their teachers whom God had made their captives? They were in danger; therefore, after many like cautions, they are charged not to do after the abominations of the nations of Canaan. All reckoning of lucky or unlucky days, all charms for diseases, all amulets or spells to prevent evil, fortune-telling, &c. are here forbidden. These are so wicked as to be a chief cause of the rooting out of the Canaanites. It is amazing to think that there should be any pretenders of this kind in such a land, and day of light, as we live in. They are mere impostors who blind and cheat their followers.

Verses 15-22

It is here promised concerning Christ, that there should come a Prophet, great above all the prophets; by whom God would make known himself and his will to the children of men, more fully and clearly than he had ever done before. He is the Light of the world, Joh 8:12. He is the World by whom God speaks to us, Joh 1:1; Heb 1:2. In his birth he should be one of their nation. In his resurrection he should be raised up at Jerusalem, and from thence his doctrine should go forth to all the world. Thus God, having raised up his Son Christ Jesus, sent him to bless us. He should be like unto Moses, only above him. This prophet is come, even JESUS; and is "He that should come," and we are to look for no other. The view of God which he gives, will not terrify or overwhelm, but encourages us. He speaks with fatherly affection and Divine authority united. Whoever refuses to listen to Jesus Christ, shall find it is at his peril; the same that is the Prophet is to be his Judge, Joh 12:48. Woe then to those who refuse to hearken to His voice, to accept His salvation, or yield obedience to His sway! But happy they who trust in Him, and obey Him. He will lead them in the paths of safety and peace, until He brings them to the land of perfect light, purity, and happiness. Here is a caution against false prophets. It highly concerns us to have a right touchstone wherewith to try the word we hear, that we may know what that word is which the Lord has not spoken. Whatever is against the plain sense of the written word, or which gives countenance or encouragement to sin, we may be sure is not that which the Lord has spoken.

Chapter 19

Chapter Outline

Verses 1-13

Here is the law settled between the blood of the murdered, and the blood of the murderer; provision is made, that the cities of refuge should be a protection, so that a man should not die for that as a crime, which was not his willing act. In Christ, the Lord our Righteousness, refuge is provided for those who by faith flee unto him. But there is no refuge in Jesus Christ for presumptuous sinners, who go on still in their trespasses. Those who flee to Christ from their sins, shall be safe in him, but not those who expect to be sheltered by him in their sins.

Verse 14

Direction is given to fix landmarks in Canaan. It is the will of God that every one should know his own; and that means should be used to hinder the doing and suffering of wrong. This, without doubt, is a moral precept, and still binding. Let every man be content with his own lot, and be just to his neighbours in all things.

Verses 15-21

Sentence should never be passed upon the testimony of one witness alone. A false witness should suffer the same punishment which he sought to have inflicted upon the person he accused. Nor could any law be more just. Let all Christians not only be cautious in bearing witness in public, but be careful not to join in private slanders; and let all whose consciences accuse them of crime, without delay flee for refuge to the hope set before them in Jesus Christ.

Chapter 20

Chapter Outline

Verses 1-9

In the wars wherein Israel engaged according to the will of God, they might expect the Divine assistance. The Lord was to be their only confidence. In these respects they were types of the Christian's warfare. Those unwilling to fight, must be sent away. The unwillingness might arise from a man's outward condition. God would not be served by men forced against their will. Thy people shall be willing, Ps 110:3. In running the Christian race, and fighting the good fight of faith, we must lay aside all that would make us unwilling. If a man's unwillingness rose from weakness and fear, he had leave to return from the war. The reason here given is, lest his brethren's heart fail as well as his heart. We must take heed that we fear not with the fear of them that are afraid, Isa 8:12.

Verses 10-12

The Israelites are here directed about the nations on whom they made war. Let this show God's grace in dealing with sinners. He proclaims peace, and beseeches them to be reconciled. Let it also show us our duty in dealing with our brethren. Whoever are for war, we must be for peace. Of the cities given to Israel, none of their inhabitants must be left. Since it could not be expected that they should be cured of their idolatry, they would hurt Israel. These regulations are not the rules of our conduct, but Christ's law of love. The horrors of war must fill the feeling heart with anguish upon every recollection; and are proofs of the wickedness of man, the power of Satan, and the just vengeance of God, who thus scourges a guilty world. But how dreadful their case who are engaged in unequal conflict with their Maker, who will not submit to render him the easy tribute of worship and praise! Certain ruin awaits them. Let neither the number nor the power of the enemies of our souls dismay us; nor let even our own weakness cause us to tremble or to faint. The Lord will save us; but in this war let none engage whose hearts are fond of the world, or afraid of the cross and the conflict. Care is here taken that in besieging cities the fruit-trees should not be destroyed. God is a better friend to man than he is to himself; and God's law consults our interests and comforts; while our own appetites and passions, which we indulge, are enemies to our welfare. Many of the Divine precepts restrain us from destroying that which is for our life and food. The Jews understand this as forbidding all wilful waste upon any account whatsoever. Every creature of God is good; as nothing is to be refused, so nothing is to be abused. We may live to want what we carelessly waste.

Chapter 21

Chapter Outline

Verses 1-9

If a murderer could not be found out, great solemnity is provided for putting away the guilt from the land, as an expression of dread and detesting of that sin. The providence of God has often wonderfully brought to light these hidden works of darkness, and the sin of the guilty has often strangely found them out. The dread of murder should be deeply impressed upon every heart, and all should join in detecting and punishing those who are guilty. The elders were to profess that they had not been any way aiding or abetting the sin. The priests were to pray to God for the country and nation, that God would be merciful. We must empty that measure by our prayers, which others are filling by their sins. All would be taught by this solemnity, to use the utmost care and diligence to prevent, discover, and punish murder. We may all learn from hence to take heed of partaking in other men's sins. And we have fellowship with the unfruitful works of darkness, if we do not reprove them.

Verses 10-14

By this law a soldier was allowed to marry his captive, if he pleased. This might take place upon some occasions; but the law does not show any approval of it. It also intimates how binding the laws of justice and honour are in marriage; which is a sacred engagement.

Verses 15-17

This law restrains men from disinheriting their eldest sons without just cause. The principle in this case as to children, is still binding to parents; they must give children their right without partiality.

Verses 18-21

Observe how the criminal is here described. He is a stubborn and rebellious son. No child was to fare the worse for weakness of capacity, slowness, or dulness, but for wilfulness and obstinacy. Nothing draws men into all manner of wickedness, and hardens them in it more certainly and fatally, than drunkenness. When men take to drinking, they forget the law of honouring parents. His own father and mother must complain of him to the elders of the city. Children who forget their duty, must thank themselves, and not blame their parents, if they are regarded with less and less affection. He must be publicly stoned to death by the men of his city. Disobedience to a parent's authority must be very evil, when such a punishment was ordered; nor is it less provoking to God now, though it escapes punishment in this world. But when young people early become slaves to sensual appetites, the heart soon grows hard, and the conscience callous; and we can expect nothing but rebellion and destruction.

Verses 22, 23

By the law of Moses, the touch of a dead body was defiling, therefore dead bodies must not be left hanging, as that would defile the land. There is one reason here which has reference to Christ; "He that is hanged is accursed of God;" that is, it is the highest degree of disgrace and reproach. Those who see a man thus hanging between heaven and earth, will conclude him abandoned of both, and unworthy of either. Moses, by the Spirit, uses this phrase of being accursed of God, when he means no more than being treated most disgracefully, that it might afterward be applied to the death of Christ, and might show that in it he underwent the curse of the law for us; which proves his love, and encourages to faith in him.

Chapter 22

Chapter Outline

Of humanity towards brethren.	(1–4)
Various precepts.	(5–12)
Against impurity.	(13–30)

Verses 1-4

If we duly regard the golden rule of "doing to others as we would they should do unto us," many particular precepts might be omitted. We can have no property in any thing that we find. Religion teaches us to be neighbourly, and to be ready to do all good offices to all men. We know not how soon we may have occasion for help.

Verses 5-12

God's providence extends itself to the smallest affairs, and his precepts do so, that even in them we may be in the fear of the Lord, as we are under his eye and care. Yet the tendency of these laws, which seem little, is such, that being found among the things of God's law, they are to be accounted great things. If we would prove ourselves to be God's people, we must have respect to his will and to his glory, and not to the vain fashions of the world. Even in putting on our garments, as in eating or in drinking, all must be done with a serious regard to preserve our own and others' purity in heart and actions. Our eye should be single, our heart simple, and our behaviour all of a piece.

Verses 13-30

These and the like regulations might be needful then, and yet it is not necessary that we should curiously examine respecting them. The laws relate to the seventh commandment, laying a restraint upon fleshly lusts which war against the soul.

Chapter 23

Chapter Outline

Who are shut out from the congregation.	(1–8)
Cleanliness enjoined.	(15–25)
Of fugitive servants, Usury, and other precepts.	(9–14)

Verses 1-8

We ought to value the privileges of God's people, both for ourselves and for our children, above all other advantages. No personal blemishes, no crimes of our forefathers, no difference of nation, shuts us out under the Christian dispensation. But an unsound heart will deprive us of blessings; and a bad example, or an unsuitable marriage, may shut our children from them.

Verses 9-14

The camp of the Lord must have nothing offensive in it. If there must be this care taken to preserve the body clean, much more should we be careful to keep the mind pure.

Verses 15-25

It is honourable to shelter and protect the weak, provided they are not wicked. Proselytes and converts to the truth, should be treated with particular tenderness, that they may have no temptation to return to the world. We cannot honour God with our substance, unless it be honestly and honourably come by. It must not only be considered what we give, but how we got it. Where the borrower gets, or hopes to get, it is just that the lender should share the gain; but to him that borrows for necessary food, pity must be showed. That which is gone out of thy lips, as a solemn and deliberate vow, must not be recalled, but thou shalt keep and perform it punctually and fully. They were allowed to pluck and eat of the corn or grapes that grew by the road side; only they must not carry any away. This law intimated what great plenty of corn and wine they should have in Canaan. It provided for the support of poor travellers, and teaches us to be kind to such, teaches us to be ready to distribute, and not to think every thing lost that is given away. Yet it forbids us to abuse the kindness of friends, or to take advantage of what is allowed. Faithfulness to their engagements should mark the people of God; and they should never encroach upon others.

Chapter 24

Chapter Outline

Verses 1-4

Where the providence of God, or his own wrong choice in marriage, has allotted to a Christian a trial instead of a help meet; he will from his heart prefer bearing the cross, to such relief as tends to sin, confusion, and misery. Divine grace will sanctify this cross, support under it, and teach so to behave, as will gradually render it more tolerable.

Verses 5-13

It is of great consequence that love be kept up between husband and wife; that they carefully avoid every thing which might make them strange one to another. Man-stealing was a capital crime, which could not be settled, as other thefts, by restitution. The laws concerning leprosy must be carefully observed. Thus all who feel their consciences under guilt and wrath, must not cover it, or endeavour to shake off their convictions; but by repentance, and prayer, and humble confession, take the way to peace and pardon. Some orders are given about pledges for money lent. This teaches us to consult the comfort and subsistence of others, as much as our own advantage. Let the poor debtor sleep in his own raiment, and praise God for thy kindness to him. Poor debtors ought to feel more than commonly they do, the goodness of creditors who do not take all the advantage of the law against them, nor should this ever be looked upon as weakness.

Verses 14-22

It is not hard to prove that purity, piety, justice, mercy, fair conduct, kindness to the poor and destitute, consideration for them, and generosity of spirit, are pleasing to God, and becoming in his redeemed people. The difficulty is to attend to them in our daily walk and conversation.

Chapter 25

Chapter Outline

Verses 1-3

Every punishment should be with solemnity, that those who see it may be filled with dread, and be warned not to offend in like manner. And though the criminals must be shamed as well as put to pain, for their warning and disgrace, yet care should be taken that they do not appear totally vile. Happy those who are chastened of the Lord to humble them, that they should not be condemned with the world to destruction.

Verse 4

This is a charge to husbandmen. It teaches us to make much of the animals that serve us. But we must learn, not only to be just, but kind to all who are employed for the good of our better part, our souls, 1Co 9:9.

Verses 5-12

The custom here regulated seems to have been in the Jewish law in order to keep inheritances distinct; now it is unlawful.

Verses 13-16

Dishonest gain always brings a curse on men's property, families, and souls. Happy those who judge themselves, repent of and forsake their sins, and put away evil things, that they may not be condemned of the Lord.

Verses 17-19

Let every persecutor and injurer of God's people take warning from the case of the Amalekites. The longer it is before judgement comes, the more dreadful will it be at last. Amalek may remind us of the foes of our souls. May we be enabled to slay all our lusts, all the corruptions both within and without, all the powers of darkness and of the world, which oppose our way to the blessed Saviour.

Chapter 26

Chapter Outline

Verses 1-11

When God has made good his promises to us, he expects we should own it to the honour of his faithfulness. And our creature comforts are doubly sweet, when we see them flowing from the fountain of the promise. The person who offered his first-fruits, must remember and own the mean origin of that nation, of which he was a member. A Syrian ready to perish was my father. Jacob is here called a Syrian. Their nation in its infancy sojourned in Egypt as strangers, they served there as slaves. They were a poor, despised, oppressed people in Egypt; and though become rich and great, had no reason to be proud, secure, or forgetful of God. He must thankfully acknowledge God's great goodness to Israel. The comfort we have in our own enjoyments, should lead us to be thankful for our share in public peace and plenty; and with present mercies we should bless the Lord for the former mercies we remember, and the further mercies we expect and hope for. He must offer his basket of first-fruits. Whatever good thing God gives us, it is his will that we make the most comfortable use we can of it, tracing the streams to the Fountain of all consolation.

Verses 12-15

How should the earth yield its increase, or, if it does, what comfort can we take in it, unless therewith our God gives us his blessing? All this represented the covenant relation between a reconciled God and every true believer, and the privileges and duties belonging to it. We must be watchful, and show that according to the covenant of grace in Christ Jesus, the Lord is our God, and we are his people, waiting in his appointed way for the performance of his gracious promises.

Verses 16-19

Moses here enforces the precepts. They are God's laws, therefore thou shalt do them, to that end were they given thee; do them, and dispute them not; do them, and draw not back; do them, not carelessly and hypocritically, but with thy heart and soul, thy whole heart and thy whole soul. We forswear ourselves, and break the most sacred engagement, if, when we have taken the Lord to be our God, we do not make conscience of obeying his commands. We are elected to obedience, 1Pe 1:2; chosen that we should be holy, Eph 1:4; purified a peculiar people, that we might not only do good works, but be zealous in them, Tit 2:14. Holiness is true honour, and the only way to everlasting honour.

Chapter 27

Chapter Outline

Verses 1-10

As soon as they were come into Canaan, they must set up a monument, on which they must write the words of this law. They must set up an altar. The word and prayer must go together. Though they might not, of their own heads, set up any altar besides that at the tabernacle; yet, by the appointment of God, they might, upon special occasion. This altar must be made of unhewn stones, such as they found upon the field. Christ, our Altar, is a stone cut out of the mountain without hands, refused by the builders, as having no form or comeliness, but accepted of God the Father, and made the Head of the corner. In the Old Testament the words of the law are written, with the curse annexed; which would overcome us with horror, if we had not, in the New Testament, an altar erected close by, which gives consolation. Blessed be God, the printed copies of the Scriptures among us, do away the necessity of such methods as were presented to Israel. The end of the gospel ministry is, and the end of preachers ought to be, to make the word of God as plain as possible. Yet, unless the Spirit of God prosper such labours with Divine power, we shall not, even by these means, be made wise unto salvation: for this blessing we should therefore daily and earnestly pray.

Verses 11-26

The six tribes appointed for blessing, were all children of the free women, for to such the promise belongs, Ga 4:31. Levi is here among the rest. Ministers should apply to themselves the blessing and curse they preach to others, and by faith set their own Amen to it. And they must not only allure people to their duty with the promises of a blessing, but awe them with the threatenings of a curse, by declaring that a curse would be upon those who do such things. To each of the curses the people were to say, Amen. It professed their faith, that these, and the like curses, were real declarations of the wrath of God against the ungodliness and unrighteousness of men, not one jot of which shall fall to the ground. It was acknowledging the equity of these curses. Those who do such things deserve to fall, and lie under the curse. Lest those who were guilty of other sins, not here mentioned, should think themselves safe from the curse, the last reaches all. Not only those who do the evil which the law forbids, but those also who omit the good which the law requires. Without the atoning blood of Christ, sinners can neither have communion with a holy God, nor do any thing acceptable to him; his righteous law condemns every one who, at any time, or in any thing, transgresses it. Under its awful curse we remain as transgressors, until the redemption of Christ is applied to our hearts. Wherever the grace of God brings salvation, it teaches the believer to deny ungodliness and wordly lusts, to live soberly, righteously, and godly in this present world, consenting to, and delighting in the words of God's law, after the inward man. In this holy walk, true peace and solid joy are to be found.

Chapter 28

Chapter Outline

Verses 1-14

This chapter is a very large exposition of two words, the blessing and the curse. They are real things and have real effects. The blessings are here put before the curses. God is slow to anger, but swift to show mercy. It is his delight to bless. It is better that we should be drawn to what is good by a child-like hope of God's favour, than that we be frightened to it by a slavish fear of his wrath. The blessing is promised, upon condition that they diligently hearken to the voice of God. Let them keep up religion, the form and power of it, in their families and nation, then the providence of God would prosper all their outward concerns.

Verses 15-44

If we do not keep God's commandments, we not only come short of the blessing promised, but we lay ourselves under the curse, which includes all misery, as the blessing all happiness. Observe the justice of this curse. It is not a curse causeless, or for some light cause. The extent and power of this curse. Wherever the sinner goes, the curse of God follows; wherever he is, it rests upon him. Whatever he has is under a curse. All his enjoyments are made bitter; he cannot take any true comfort in them, for the wrath of God mixes itself with them. Many judgments are here stated, which would be the fruits of the curse, and with which God would punish the people of the Jews, for their apostacy and disobedience. We may observe the fulfilling of these threatenings in their present state. To complete their misery, it is threatened that by these troubles they should be bereaved of all comfort and hope, and left to utter despair. Those who walk by sight, and not by faith, are in danger of losing reason itself, when every thing about them looks frightful.

Verses 45-68

If God inflicts vengeance, what miseries his curse can bring upon mankind, even in this present world! Yet these are but the beginning of sorrows to those under the curse of God. What then will be the misery of that world where their worm dieth not, and their fire is not quenched! Observe what is here said of the wrath of God, which should come and remain upon the Israelites for their sins. It is amazing to think that a people so long the favourites of Heaven, should be so cast off;

and yet that a people so scattered in all nations should be kept distinct, and not mixed with others. If they would not serve God with cheerfulness, they should be compelled to serve their enemies. We may justly expect from God, that if we do not fear his fearful name, we shall feel his fearful plagues; for one way or other God will be feared. The destruction threatened is described. They have, indeed, been plucked from off the land, ver. #(63). Not only by the Babylonish captivity, and when Jerusalem was destroyed by the Romans; but afterwards, when they were forbidden to set foot in Jerusalem. They should have no rest; no rest of body, ver. 65, but be continually on the remove, either in hope of gain, or fear of persecution. No rest of the mind, which is much worse. They have been banished from city to city, from country to country; recalled, and banished again. These events, compared with the favour shown to Israel in ancient times, and with the prophecies about them, should not only excite astonishment, but turn unto us for a testimony, assuring us of the truth of Scripture. And when the other prophecies of their conversion to Christ shall come to pass, the whole will be a sign and a wonder to all the nations of the earth, and the forerunner of a general spread of true christianity. The fulfilling of these prophecies upon the Jewish nation, delivered more than three thousand years ago, shows that Moses spake by the Spirit of God; who not only foresees the ruin of sinners, but warns of it, that they may prevent it by a true and timely repentance, or else be left without excuse. And let us be thankful that Christ hath redeemed us from the curse of the law, by being made a curse for us, and bearing in his own person all that punishment which our sins merit, and which we must otherwise have endured for ever. To this Refuge and salvation let sinners flee; therein let believers rejoice, and serve their reconciled God with gladness of heart, for the abundance of his spiritual blessings.

Chapter 29

Chapter Outline

Moses calls Israel's mercies to remembrance.	(1–9)
The Divine wrath on those who flatter themselves in their wickedness.	(10–21)
The ruin of the Jewish nation.	(22–28)
Secret things belong unto God.	(29)

Verses 1-9

Both former mercies, and fresh mercies, should be thought on by us as motives to obedience. The hearing ear, and seeing eye, and the understanding heart, are the gift of God. All that have them, have them from him. God gives not only food and raiment, but wealth and large possessions, to many to whom he does not give grace. Many enjoy the gifts, who have not hearts to perceive the Giver, nor the true design and use of the gifts. We are bound, in gratitude and interest, as well as in duty and faithfulness, to keep the words of the covenant.

Verses 10-21

The national covenant made with Israel, not only typified the covenant of grace made with true believers, but also represented the outward dispensation of the gospel. Those who have been enabled to consent to the Lord's new covenant of mercy and grace in Jesus Christ, and to give up themselves to be his people, should embrace every opportunity of renewing their open profession of relation to him, and their obligation to him, as the God of salvation, walking according thereto. The sinner is described as one whose heart turns away from his God; there the mischief begins, in the evil heart of unbelief, which inclines men to depart from the living God to dead idols. Even to this sin men are now tempted, when drawn aside by their own lusts and fancies. Such men are roots that bear gall and wormwood. They are weeds which, if let alone, overspread the whole field. Satan may for a time disguise this bitter morsel, so that thou shalt not have the natural taste of it, but at the last day, if not before, the true taste shall be discerned. Notice the sinner's security in sin. Though he hears the words of the curse, yet even then he thinks himself safe from the wrath of God. There is scarcely a threatening in all the book of God more dreadful than this. Oh that presumptuous sinners would read it, and tremble! for it is a real declaration of the wrath of God, against ungodliness and unrighteousness of man.

Verses 22-28

Idolatry would be the ruin of their nation. It is no new thing for God to bring desolating judgments on a people near to him in profession. He never does this without good reason. It concerns us to seek for the reason, that we may give glory to God, and take warning to ourselves. Thus the law of Moses leaves sinners under the curse, and rooted out of the Lord's land; but the grace of Christ toward penitent, believing sinners, plants them again in their land; and they shall no more be pulled up, being kept by the power of God.

Verse 29

Moses ends his prophecy of the Jews' rejection, just as St. Paul ends his discourse on the same subject, when it began to be fulfilled, Ro 11:33. We are forbidden curiously to inquire into the secret counsels of God, and to determine concerning them. But we are directed and encouraged, diligently to seek into that which God has made known. He has kept back nothing that is profitable for us, but only that of which it is good for us to be ignorant. The end of all Divine revelation is, not to furnish curious subjects of speculation and discourse, but that we may do all the words of this law, and be blessed in our deed. This, the Bible plainly reveals; further than this, man cannot profitably go. By this light he may live and die comfortably, and be happy for ever.

Chapter 30

Chapter Outline

Verses 1-10

In this chapter is a plain intimation of the mercy God has in store for Israel in the latter days. This passage refers to the prophetic warnings of the last two chapters, which have been mainly fulfilled in the destruction of Jerusalem by the Romans, and in their dispersion to the present day; and there can be no doubt that the prophetic promise contained in these verses yet remain to come to pass. The Jewish nation shall in some future period, perhaps not very distant, be converted to the faith of Christ; and, many think, again settled in the land of Canaan. The language here used is in a great measure absolute promises; not merely a conditional engagement, but declaring an event assuredly to take place. For the Lord himself here engages to "circumcise their hearts;" and when regenerating grace has removed corrupt nature, and Divine love has supplanted the love of sin, they certainly will reflect, repent, return to God, and obey him; and he will rejoice in doing them good. The change that will be wrought upon them will not be only outward, or consisting in mere opinions; it will reach to their souls. It will produce in them an utter hatred of all sin, and a fervent love to God, as their reconciled God in Christ Jesus; they will love him with all their hearts, and with all their soul. They are very far from this state of mind at present, but so were the murderers of the Lord Jesus, on the day of Pentecost; who yet in one hour were converted unto God. So shall it be in the day of God's power; a nation shall be born in a day; the Lord will hasten it in his time. As a conditional promise this passage belongs to all persons and all people, not to Israel only; it assures us that the greatest sinners, if they repent and are converted, shall have their sins pardoned, and be restored to God's favour.

Verses 11-14

The law is not too high for thee. It is not only known afar off; it is not confined to men of learning. It is written in thy books, made plain, so that he who runs may read it. It is in thy mouth, in the tongue commonly used by thee, in which thou mayest hear it read, and talk of it among thy children. It is delivered so that it is level to the understanding of the meanest. This is especially true of the gospel of Christ, to which the apostle applies it. But the word is nigh us, and Christ in that word; so that if we believe with the heart, that the promises of the Messiah are fulfilled in our Lord Jesus, and confess them with our mouth, we then have Christ with us.

Verses 15-20

What could be said more moving, and more likely to make deep and lasting impressions? Every man wishes to obtain life and good, and to escape death and evil; he desires happiness, and dreads misery. So great is the compassion of the Lord, that he has favoured men, by his word, with such a knowledge of good and evil as will make them for ever happy, if it be not their own fault. Let us hear the sum of the whole matter. If they and theirs would love God, and serve him, they should live and be happy. If they or theirs should turn from God, desert his service, and worship other gods, that would certainly be their ruin. There never was, since the fall of man, more than one way to heaven; which is marked out in both Testaments, though not with equal clearness. Moses meant that same way of acceptance, which Paul more plainly described; and Paul's words mean the same obedience, on which Moses more fully treated. In both Testaments the good and right way is brought near, and plainly revealed to us.

Chapter 31

Chapter Outline

Moses encourages the people, and Joshua.	(1–8)
The law to be read every seventh year.	(9–13)
The Israelites' apostacy foretold, A song given to be witness against them.	(14–22)
The law delivered to the Levites.	(22–30)

Verses 1-8

Moses assures Israel of the constant presence of God with them. This is applied by the apostle to all God's spiritual Israel, to encourage their faith and hope; unto us is this gospel preached, as well as unto them; he will never fail thee, nor forsake thee, Heb 13:5. Moses commends Joshua to them for a leader; one whose wisdom, and courage, and affection they had long known; one whom God had appointed to be their leader; and therefore would own and bless. Joshua is well pleased to be admonished by Moses to be strong and of good courage. Those shall speed well, who have God with them; therefore they ought to be of good courage. Through God let us do valiantly, for through him we shall do victoriously; if we resist the devil, he will flee from us.

Verses 9-13

Though we read the word in private, we must not think it needless to hear it read in public. This solemn reading of the law must be done in the year of release. The year of release was typical of gospel grace, which is called the acceptable year of the Lord; for our pardon and liberty by Christ, engage us to keep his commandments. It must be read to all Israel, men, women, children, and to the strangers. It is the will of God that all people should acquaint themselves with his word. It is a rule to all, therefore should be read to all. Whoever has read of the pains taken by many persons to get scraps of the Scriptures, when a whole copy could not be obtained, or safely possessed, will see how thankful we should be for the thousands of copies amongst us. They will also understand the very different situation in which the Israelites were placed for many ages. But the heart of man is so careless, that all will be found too little, to keep up a knowledge of the truths, precepts, and worship of God.

Verses 14-22

Moses and Joshua attended the Divine Majesty at the door of the tabernacle. Moses is told again that he must shortly die; even those who are most ready and willing to die, need to be often reminded of its coming. The Lord tells Moses, that, after his death, the covenant he had taken so much pains to make between Israel and their God, would certainly be broken. Israel would forsake Him; then God would forsake Israel. Justly does he cast those off who so unjustly cast him off. Moses is directed to deliver them a song, which should remain a standing testimony for God, as faithful to them in giving them warning, and against them, as persons false to themselves in not taking the warning. The word of God is a discerner of the thoughts and intents of men's hearts, and meets them by reproofs and correction. Ministers who preach the word, know not the imaginations of men; but God, whose word it is, knows perfectly.

Verses 23-30

The solemn delivery of the book of the law to the Levites, to be deposited in, or rather by the side, of the ark, is again related. The song which follows in the next chapter is delivered to Moses, and by him to the people. He wrote it first, as the Holy Spirit taught him; and then spake it in the hearing of all the people. Moses tells them plainly, I know that after my death ye will utterly corrupt yourselves. Many a sad thought, no doubt, it occasioned to this good man; but his comfort was, that he had done his duty, and that God would be glorified in their dispersion, if not in their settlement, for the foundation of God stands sure.

Chapter 32

Chapter Outline

The exhortation with which the song was delivered.   (44–47)

Moses to go up mount Nebo to die.   (48–52)

Verses 1, 2

Moses begins with a solemn appeal to heaven and earth, concerning the truth and importance of what he was about to say. His doctrine is the gospel, the speech of God, the doctrine of Christ; the doctrine of grace and mercy through him, and of life and salvation by him.

Verses 3-6

"He is a Rock." This is the first time God is called so in Scripture. The expression denotes that the Divine power, faithfulness, and love, as revealed in Christ and the gospel, form a foundation which cannot be changed or moved, on which we may build our hopes of happiness. And under his protection we may find refuge from all our enemies, and in all our troubles; as the rocks in those countries sheltered from the burning rays of the sun, and from tempests, or were fortresses from the enemy. "His work is perfect:" that of redemption and salvation, in which there is a display of all the Divine perfection, complete in all its parts. All God's dealings with his creatures are regulated by wisdom which cannot err, and perfect justice. He is indeed just and right; he takes care that none shall lose by him. A high charge is exhibited against Israel. Even God's children have their spots, while in this imperfect state; for if we say we have no sin, no spot, we deceive ourselves. But the sin of Israel was not habitual, notorious, unrepented sin; which is a certain mark of the children of Satan. They were fools to forsake their mercies for lying vanities. All wilful sinners, especially sinners in Israel, are unwise and ungrateful.

Verses 7-14

Moses gives particular instances of God's kindness and concern for them. The eagle's care for her young is a beautiful emblem of Christ's love, who came between Divine justice and our guilty souls, and bare our sins in his own body on the tree. And by the preached gospel, and the influences of the Holy Spirit, He stirs up and prevails upon sinners to leave Satan's bondage. In ver. #(13, 14), are emblems of the conquest believers have over their spiritual enemies, sin, Satan, and the world, in and through Christ. Also of their safety and triumph in him; of their happy frames of soul, when they are above the world, and the things of it. This will be the blessed case of spiritual Israel in every sense in the latter day.

Verses 15-18

Here are two instances of the wickedness of Israel, each was apostacy from God. These people were called Jeshurun, "an upright people," so some; "a seeing people," so others: but they soon lost the reputation both of their knowledge and of their righteousness. They indulged their appetites, as if they had nothing to do but to make provision for the flesh to fulfil the lusts of it. Those who make a god of themselves, and a god of their bellies, in pride and wantonness, and cannot bear to be told of it, thereby forsake God, and show they esteem him lightly. There is but one way of a sinner's acceptance and sanctification, however different modes of irreligion, or false religion, may show that favourable regard for other ways, which is often miscalled candid. How mad are idolaters, who forsake the Rock of salvation, to run themselves upon the rock of perdition!

Verses 19-25

The revolt of Israel was described in the foregoing verses, and here follow the resolves of Divine justice as to them. We deceive ourselves, if we think that God will be mocked by a faithless people. Sin makes us hateful in the sight of the holy God. See what mischief sin does, and reckon those to be fools that mock at it.

Verses 26-38

The idolatry and rebellions of Israel deserved, and the justice of God seemed to demand, that they should be rooted out. But He spared Israel, and continues them still to be living witnesses of the truth of the Bible, and to silence unbelievers. They are preserved for wise and holy purposes and the prophecies give us some idea what those purposes are. The Lord will never disgrace the throne of his glory. It is great wisdom, and will help much to the return of sinners to God, seriously to consider their latter end, or the future state. It is here meant particularly of what God foretold by Moses, about this people in the latter days; but it may be applied generally. Oh that men would consider the happiness they will lose, and the misery they will certainly plunge into, if they go on in their trespasses! What will be in the end thereof? Jer 5:31. For the Lord will in due time bring down the enemies of the church, in displeasure against their wickedness. When sinners deem themselves most secure, they suddenly fall into destruction. And God's time to appear for the deliverance of his people, is when things are at the worst with them. But those who trust to any rock but God, will find it fail them when they most need it. The rejection of the Messiah by the Jewish nation, is the continuance of their ancient idolatry, apostacy, and rebellion. They shall be brought to humble themselves before the Lord, to repent of their sins, and to trust in their long-rejected Mediator for salvation. Then he will deliver them, and make their prosperity great.

Verses 39-43

This conclusion of the song speaks, 1. Glory to God. No escape can be made from his power. 2. It speaks terror to his enemies. Terror indeed to those who hate him. The wrath of God is here revealed from heaven against them. 3. It speaks comfort to his own people. The song concludes with words of joy. Whatever judgments are brought upon sinners, it shall go well with the people of God.

Verses 44-47

Here is the solemn delivery of this song to Israel, with a charge to mind all the good words Moses had said unto them. It is not a trifle, but a matter of life and death: mind it, and you are made for ever; neglect it, and you are for ever undone. Oh that men were fully persuaded that religion is their life, even the life of their souls!

Verses 48-52

Now Moses had done his work, why should he desire to live a day longer? God reminds him of the sin of which he had been guilty, for which he was kept from entering Canaan. It is good for the best of men to die repenting the infirmities of which they are conscious. But those may die with comfort and ease, whenever God calls for them, notwithstanding the sins they remember against themselves, who have a believing prospect, and a well-grounded hope of eternal life beyond death.

Chapter 33

Chapter Outline

The glorious majesty of God.	(1–5)
The blessings of the twelve tribes.	(6–23)
Strength to believers.	(24, 25)
The excellency of Israel.	(26–29)

Verses 1-5

To all his precepts, warnings, and prophecies, Moses added a solemn blessing. He begins with a description of the glorious appearances of God, in giving the law. His law works like fire. If received, it is melting, warming, purifying, and burns up the dross of corruption; if rejected, it hardens, sears, pains, and destroys. The Holy Spirit came down in cloven tongues, as of fire; for the gospel also is a fiery law. The law of God written in the heart, is a certain proof of the love of God shed abroad there: we must reckon His law one of the gifts of his grace.

Verses 6-23

The order in which the tribes are here blessed, is not the same as is observed elsewhere. The blessing of Judah may refer to the whole tribe in general, or to David as a type of Christ. Moses largely blesses the tribe of Levi. Acceptance with God is what we should all aim at, and desire, in all our devotions, whether men accept us or not, 2Co 5:9. This prayer is a prophecy, that God will keep up a ministry in his church to the end of time. The tribe of Benjamin had their inheritance close to mount Zion. To be situated near the ordinances, is a precious gift from the Lord, a privilege not to be exchanged for any worldly advantage, or indulgence. We should thankfully receive the earthly blessings sent to us, through the successive seasons. But those good gifts which come down from the Father of lights, through the rising of the Sun of righteousness, and the pouring out of his Spirit like the rain which makes fruitful, are infinitely more precious, as the tokens of his special love. The precious things here prayed for, are figures of spiritual blessing in heavenly things by Christ, the gifts, graces, and comforts of the Spirit. When Moses prays for the good will of Him that dwelt in the bush, he refers to the covenant, on which all our hopes of God's favour must be founded. The providence of God appoints men's habitations, and wisely disposes men to different employments for the public good. Whatever our place and business are, it is our wisdom and duty to apply thereto; and it is happiness to be well pleased therewith. We should not only invite others to the service of God, but abound in it. The blessing of Naphtali. The favour of God is the only favour satisfying to the soul. Those are happy indeed, who have the favour of God; and those shall have it, who reckon that in having it they have enough, and desire no more.

Verses 24, 25

All shall be sanctified to true believers; if their way be rough, their feet shall be shod with the preparation of the gospel of peace. As thy days, so shall thy strength be. The "day" is often in Scripture put for the events of the day; it is a promise that God would graciously and constantly support under trials and troubles, whatever they were. It is a promise sure to all the spiritual seed of Abraham. Have they work allotted? They shall have strength to do it. Have they burdens appointed? They shall have strength, and never be tempted above what they are able to bear.

Verses 26-29

None had such a God as Israel. There is no people like the Israel of God. What is here said of the church of Israel is to be applied to the spiritual church. Never were people so well seated and sheltered. Those who make God their habitation, shall have all the comforts and benefits of a habitation in him, Ps 91:1. Never were people so well supported and borne up. How low soever the people of God are at any time brought, everlasting arms are underneath them, to keep the spirit from sinking, from fainting, and their faith from failing. Divine grace is sufficient for them, 2Co 12:9. Never were people so well commanded. Thus believers are more than conquerors over their spiritual enemies, through Christ that loved them. Never were people so well secured and protected. Israel shall dwell in safety alone. All who keep close to God, shall be kept safe by him. Never were people so well provided for. Every true Israelite looks with faith to the better country, the heavenly Canaan, which is filled with better things than corn and wine. Never were people so well helped. If in danger of any harm, or in want of any good, they had an eternal God to go to. Nothing could hurt those whom God helped, nor was it possible the people should perish who were saved by the Lord. Never were people so well armed. Those in whose hearts is the excellency of holiness, are defended by the whole armour of God, Eph 6. Never were people so well assured of victory over their enemies. Thus shall the God of peace tread Satan under the feet of all believers, and shall do it shortly, Ro 16:20. May God help us to seek and to set our affections on the things above; and to turn our souls from earthly perishing objects; that we may not have our lot with Israel's foes in the regions of darkness and despair, but with the Israel of God, in the realms of love and eternal happiness.

Chapter 34

Chapter Outline

Verses 1-4

Moses seemed unwilling to leave his work; but that being finished, he manifested no unwillingness to die. God had declared that he should not enter Canaan. But the Lord also promised that Moses should have a view of it, and showed him all that good land. Such a sight believers now have, through grace, of the bliss and glory of their future state. Sometimes God reserves the brightest discoveries of his grace to his people to support their dying moments. Those may leave this world with cheerfulness, who die in the faith of Christ, and in the hope of heaven.

Verses 5-8

Moses obeyed this command of God as willingly as any other, though it seemed harder. In this he resembled our Lord Jesus Christ. But he died in honour, in peace, and in the most easy manner; the Saviour died upon the disgraceful and torturing cross. Moses died very easily; he died "at the mouth of the Lord," according to the will of God. The servants of the Lord, when they have done all their other work, must die at last, and be willing to go home, whenever their Master sends for them, Ac 21:13. The place of his burial was not known. If the soul be at rest with God, it is of little consequence where the body rests. There was no decay in the strength of his body, nor in the vigour and activity of his mind; his understanding was as clear, and his memory as strong as ever. This was the reward of his services, the effect of his extraordinary meekness. There was solemn mourning for him. Yet how great soever our losses have been, we must not give ourselves up to sorrow. If we hope to go to heaven rejoicing, why should we go to the grave mourning?

Verses 9-12

Moses brought Israel to the borders of Canaan, and then died and left them. This signifies that the law made nothing perfect, Heb 7:19 It brings men into a wilderness of conviction, but not into the Canaan of rest and settled peace. That honour was reserved for Joshua, our Lord Jesus, of whom Joshua was a type, (and the name is the same,) to do that for us which the law could not do, Ro 8:3. Through him we enter into the spiritual rest of conscience, and eternal rest in heaven. Moses was greater than any other prophet of the Old Testament. But our Lord Jesus went beyond him, far more than the other prophets came short of him. And see a strong resemblance between the redeemer of the children of Israel and the Redeemer of mankind. Moses was sent by God, to deliver the Israelites form a cruel bondage; he led them out, and conquered their enemies. He became not only their deliverer, but their lawgiver; not only their lawgiver, but their judge; and, finally, leads them to the border of the land of promise. Our blessed Saviour came to rescue us out of the slavery of the devil, and to restore us to liberty and happiness. He came to confirm every moral precept of the first lawgiver; and to write them, not on tables of stone, but on fleshly tables of the heart. He came to be our Judge also, inasmuch as he hath appointed a day when he will judge all the secrets of men, and reward or punish accordingly. This greatness of Christ above Moses, is a reason why Christians should be obedient and faithful to the holy religion by which they profess to be Christ's followers. God, by his grace, make us all so!

Joshua

Here is the history of Israel's passing into the land of Canaan, conquering and dividing it, under the command of Joshua, and their history until his death. The power and truth of God in fulfilling his promises to Israel, and in executing his justly threatened vengeance on the Canaanites, are wonderfully displayed. This should teach us to regard the tremendous curses denounced in the word of God against impenitent sinners, and to seek refuge in Christ Jesus.

Chapter 1

Chapter Outline

The Lord appoints Joshua to succeed Moses.	(1–4)
God promises to assist Joshua.	(5–9)
Preparation to pass over Jordan.	(10–15)
The people promise to obey Joshua.	(16–18)

Verses 1-4

Joshua had attended upon Moses. He who was called to honour, had been long used to business. Our Lord Jesus took upon him the form of a servant. Joshua was trained up under command. Those are fittest to rule, who have learned to obey. The removal of useful men should quicken survivors to be the more diligent in doing good. Arise, go over Jordan. At this place and at this time the banks were overflowed. Joshua had no bridge or boats, and yet he must believe that God, having ordered the people over, would open a way.

Verses 5-9

Joshua is to make the law of God his rule. He is charged to meditate therein day and night, that he might understand it. Whatever affairs of this world we have to mind, we must not neglect the one thing needful. All his orders to the people, and his judgments, must be according to the law of God. Joshua must himself be under command; no man's dignity or dominion sets him above the law of God. He is to encourage himself with the promise and presence of God. Let not the sense of thine own infirmities dishearten thee; God is all-sufficient. I have commanded, called, and commissioned thee to do it, and will be sure to bear thee out in it. When we are in the way of duty, we have reason to be strong and very bold. Our Lord Jesus, as Joshua here, was borne up under his sufferings by a regard to the will ofGod, and the commandment from his Father.

Verses 10-15

Joshua says to the people, Ye shall pass over Jordan, and shall possess the land; because God had said so to him. We honour the truth of God, when we stagger not at the promise of God. The two tribes and a half were to go over Jordan with their brethren. When God, by his providence, has given us rest, we ought to consider what service we may do to our brethren.

Verses 16-18

The people of Israel engage to obey Joshua; All that thou commandest us to do we will readily do, without murmuring or disputing, and whithersoever thou sendest us we will go. The best we can ask of God for our magistrats, is, that they may have the presence of God; that will make them blessings to us, so that in seeking this for them, we consult our own interest. May we be enabled to enlist under the banner of the Captain of our salvation, to be obedient to his commands, and to fight the good fight of faith, with all that trust in and love his name, against all who oppose his authority; for whoever refuses to obey him must be destroyed.

Chapter 2

Chapter Outline

Verses 1-7

Faith in God's promises ought not to do away, but to encourage our diligence in the use of proper means. The providence of God directed the spies to the house of Rahab. God knew where there was one that would be true to them, though they did not. Rahab appears to have been an innkeeper; and if she had formerly been one of bad life, which is doubtful, she had left her evil courses. That which seems to us most accidental, is often overruled by the Divine providence to serve great ends. It was by faith that Rahab received those with peace, against whom her king and country had war. We are sure this was a good work; it is so spoken of by the apostle, Jas 2:25; and she did it by faith, such a faith as set her above the fear of man. Those only are true believers, who find in their hearts to venture for God; they take his people for their people, and cast in their lot among them. The spies were led by the special providence of God, and Rahab entertained them out of regard to Israel and Israel's God, and not for lucre or for any evil purpose. Though excuses may be offered for the guilt of Rahab's falsehood, it seems best to admit nothing which tends to explain it away. Her views of the Divine law must have been very dim: a falsehood like this, told by those who enjoy the light of revelation, whatever the motive, would deserve heavy censure.

Verses 8-21

Rahab had heard of the miracles the Lord wrought for Israel. She believed that his promises would certainly be fulfilled, and his threatenings take effect; and that there was no way of escape but by submitting to him, and joining with his people. The conduct of Rahab proved that she had the real principle of Divine faith. Observe the promises the spies made to her. The goodness of God is often expressed by his kindness and truth, Ps 117:2; in both these we must be followers of him. Those who will be conscientious in keeping promises, are cautious in making them. The spies make needful conditions. The scarlet cord, like the blood upon the doorpost at the passover, recalls to remembrance the sinner's security under the atoning blood of Christ; and that we are to flee thereto for refuge from the wrath of a justly offended God. The same cord Rahab used for the saving of these Israelites, was to be used for her own safety. What we serve and honour God with, we may expect he will bless, and make useful to us.

Verses 22-24

The report the spies brought was encouraging. All the people of the country faint because of Israel; they have neither wisdom to yield, nor courage to fight. Those terrors of conscience, and that sense of Divine wrath, which dismay the ungodly, but bring not to repentance, are fearful forebodings of approaching destruction. But grace yet abounds to the chief of sinners. Let them, without delay, flee to Christ, and all shall be well.

Chapter 3

Chapter Outline

The Israelites come to Jordan.	(1–6)
The Lord encourages joshua—Joshua encourages the people.	(7–13)
The Israelites pass through Jordan on dry land.	(14–17)

Verses 1-6

The Israelites came to Jordan in faith, having been told that they should pass it. In the way of duty, let us proceed as far as we can, and depend on the Lord. Joshua led them. Particular notice is taken of his early rising, as afterwards upon other occasions, which shows how little he sought his own ease. Those who would bring great things to pass, must rise early. Love not sleep, lest thou come to poverty. All in public stations should always attend to the duty of their place. The people were to follow the ark. Thus must we walk after the rule of the word, and the direction of the Spirit, in everything; so shall peace be upon us as upon the Israel of God; but we must follow our ministers only as they follow Christ. All their way through the wilderness was an untrodden path, but most so this through Jordan. While we are here, we must expect and prepare to pass ways that we have not passed before; but in the path of duty we may proceed with boldness and cheerfulness. Whether we are called to suffer poverty, pain, labour, persecution, reproach, or death, we are following the Author and Finisher of our faith; nor can we set our feet in any dangerous or difficult spot, through our whole journey, but faith will there see the prints of the Redeemer's feet, who trod that very path to glory above, and bids us follow him, that where he is, we may be also. They were to sanctify themselves. Would we experience the effects of God's love and power, we must put away sin, and be careful not to grieve the Holy Spirit of God.

Verses 7-13

The waters of Jordan shall be cut off. This must be done in such a way as never was done, but in the dividing of the Red sea. That miracle is here repeated; God has the same power to finish the salvation of his people, as to begin it; the WORD of the Lord was as truly with Joshua as with Moses. God's appearances for his people ought to encourage faith and hope. God's work is perfect, he will keep his people. Jordan's flood cannot keep out Israel, Canaan's force cannot turn them out again.

Verses 14-17

Jordan overflowed all its banks. This magnified the power of God, and his kindness to Israel. Although those who oppose the salvation of God's people have all advantages, yet God can and will conquer. This passage over Jordan, as an entrance to Canaan, after their long, weary wanderings in the wilderness, shadowed out the believer's passage through death to heaven, after he has finished his wanderings in this sinful world. Jesus, typified by the ark, hath gone before, and he crossed the river when it most flooded the country around. Let us treasure up experiences of His faithful and tender care, that they may help our faith and hope in the last conflict.

Chapter 4

Chapter Outline

Verses 1-9

The works of the Lord are so worthy of remembrance, and the heart of man is so prone to forget them, that various methods are needful to refresh our memories, for the glory of God, our advantage, and that of our children. God gave orders for preparing this memorial.

Verses 10-19

The priests with the ark did not stir till ordered to move. Let none be weary of waiting, while they have the tokens of God's presence with them, even the ark of the covenant, though it be in the depths of adversity. Notice is taken of the honour put upon Joshua. Those are feared in the best manner, and to the best purpose, who make it appear that God is with them, and that they set him before them.

Verses 20-24

It is the duty of parents to tell their children betimes of the words and works of God, that they may be trained up in the way they should go. In all the instruction parents give their children, they should teach them to fear God. Serious godliness is the best learning. Are we not called, as much as the Israelites, to praise the loving-kindness of our God? Shall we not raise a pillar to our God, who has brought us through dangers and distresses in so wonderful a way? For hitherto the Lord hath helped us, as much as he did his saints of old. How great the stupidity and ingratitude of men, who perceive not His hand, and will not acknowledge his goodness, in their frequent deliverances!

Chapter 5

Chapter Outline

The Canaanites are afraid, Circumcision renewed.	(1–9)
The passover at Gilgal, The manna ceases.	(10–12)
The Captain of the Lord's host appears to Joshua.	(13–15)

Verses 1-9

How dreadful is their case, who see the wrath of God advancing towards them, without being able to turn it aside, or escape it! Such will be the horrible situation of the wicked; nor can words express the anguish of their feelings, or the greatness of their terror. Oh that they would now take warning, and before it be too late, flee for refuge to lay hold upon that hope set before them in the gospel! God impressed these fears on the Canaanites, and dispirited them. This gave a short rest to the Israelites, and circumcision rolled away the reproach of Egypt. They were hereby owned to be the free-born children of God, having the seal of the covenant. When God glorifies himself in perfecting the salvation of his people, he not only silences all enemies, but rolls back their reproaches upon themselves.

Verses 10-12

A solemn passover was kept, at the time appointed by the law, in the plains of Jericho, in defiance of the Canaanites round about them. It was a performance of the promise, that when they went up to keep the feasts, their land should be under the special protection of the Divine providence, Ex 34:24. Notice is taken of the ceasing of the manna as soon as they had eaten the old corn of the land. For as it came just when they needed, so it continued as long as they needed it. This teaches us not to expect supplies by miracles, when they may be had in a common way. The word and ordinances of God are spiritual manna, with which God nourishes his people in this wilderness. Though often forfeited, yet they are continued while we are here; but when we come to the heavenly Canaan, this manna will cease, for we shall no longer need it.

Verses 13-15

We read not of any appearance of God's glory to Joshua till now. There appeared to him one as a man to be noticed. This Man was the Son of God, the eternal Word. Joshua gave him Divine honours: he received them, which a created angel would not have done, and he is called Jehovah, chap. 6:2. To Abraham he appeared as a traveller; to Joshua as a man of war. Christ will be to his people what their faith needs. Christ had his sword drawn, which encouraged Joshua to carry on the war with vigour. Christ's sword drawn in his hand, denotes how ready he is for the defence and salvation of his people. His sword turns every way. Joshua will know whether he is a friend or a foe. The cause between the Israelites and Canaanites, between Christ and Beelzebub, will not admit of any man's refusing to take one part or the other, as he may do in worldly contests. Joshua's inquiry shows an earnest desire to know the will of Christ, and a cheerful readiness and resolution to do it. All true Christians must fight under Christ's banner, and they will conquer by his presence and assistance.

Chapter 6

Chapter Outline

Verses 1-5

Jericho resolves Israel shall not be its master. It shut itself up, being strongly fortified both by art and nature. Thus were they foolish, and their hearts hardened to their destruction; the miserable case of all that strengthen themselves against the Almighty. God resolves Israel shall be its master, and that quickly. No warlike preparations were to be made. By the uncommon method of besieging the city, the Lord honoured the ark, as the symbol of his presence, and showed that all the victories were from him. The faith and patience of the people were proved and increased.

Verses 6-16

Wherever the ark went, the people attended it. God's ministers, by the trumpet of the everlasting gospel, which proclaims liberty and victory, must encourage the followers of Christ in their spiritual warfare. As promised deliverances must be expected in God's way, so they must be expected in his time. At last the people were to shout: they did so, and the walls fell. This was a shout of faith; they believed the walls of Jericho would fall. It was a shout of prayer; they cry to Heaven for help, and help came.

Verses 17-27

Jericho was to be a solemn and awful sacrifice to the justice of God, upon those who had filled up the measure of their sins. So He appoints, from whom, as creatures, they received their lives, and to whom, as sinners, they had forfeited them. Rahab perished not with them that believed not, Heb 11:31. All her kindred were saved with her; thus faith in Christ brings salvation to the house, Ac 16:31. She, and they with her, were plucked as brands from the burning. With Rahab, or with the men of Jericho; our portion must be assigned, as we posses or disregard the sign of salvation; even faith in Christ, which worketh by love. Let us remember what depends upon our choice, and let us choose accordingly. God shows the weight of a Divine curse; where it rests there is no getting from under it; for it brings ruin without remedy.

Chapter 7

Chapter Outline

The Israelites smitten at Ai.	(1–5)
Joshua's humiliation and prayer.	(6–9)
God instructs Joshua what to do.	(10–5)
Achan is detected, He is destroyed.	(16–26)

Verses 1-5

Achan took some of the spoil of Jericho. The love of the world is that root of bitterness, which of all others is most hardly rooted up. We should take heed of sin ourselves, lest by it many be defiled or disquieted, Heb 12:15; and take heed of having fellowship with sinners, lest we share their guilt. It concerns us to watch over one another to prevent sin, because others' sins may be to our damage. The easy conquest of Jericho excited contempt of the enemy, and a disposition to expect the Lord to do all for them without their using proper means. Thus men abuse the doctrines of Divine grace, and the promises of God, into excuses for their own sloth and self-indulgence. We are to work out our own salvation, though it is God that works in us. It was a dear victory to the Canaanites, whereby Israel was awakened and reformed, and reconciled to their God, and the people of Canaan hardened to their own ruin.

Verses 6-9

Joshua's concern for the honour of God, more than even for the fate of Israel, was the language of the Spirit of adoption. He pleaded with God. He laments their defeat, as he feared it would reflect on God's wisdom and power, his goodness and faithfulness. We cannot at any time urge a better plea than this, Lord, what wilt thou do for thy great name? Let God be glorified in all, and then welcome his whole will.

Verses 10-15

God awakens Joshua to inquiry, by telling him that when this accursed thing was put away, all would be well. Times of danger and trouble should be times of reformation. We should look at home, into our own hearts, into our own houses, and make diligent search to find out if there be not some accursed thing there, which God sees and abhors; some secret lust, some unlawful gain, some undue withholding from God or from others. We cannot prosper, until the accursed thing be destroyed out of our hearts, and put out of our habitations and our families, and forsaken in our lives. When the sin of sinners finds them out, God is to be acknowledged. With a certain and unerring judgment, the righteous God does and will distinguish between the innocent and the guilty; so that though the righteous are of the same tribe, and family, and household with the wicked, yet they never shall be treated as the wicked.

Verses 16-26

See the folly of those that promise themselves secrecy in sin. The righteous God has many ways of bringing to light the hidden works of darkness. See also, how much it is our concern, when God is contending with us, to find out the cause that troubles us. We must pray with holy Job, Lord, show me wherefore thou contendest with me. Achan's sin began in the eye. He saw these fine things, as Eve saw the forbidden fruit. See what comes of suffering the heart to walk after the eyes, and what need we have to make this covenant with our eyes, that if they wander they shall be sure to weep for it. It proceeded out of the heart. They that would be kept from sinful actions, must mortify and check in themselves sinful desires, particularly the desire of worldly wealth. Had Achan looked upon these things with an eye of faith, he would have seen they were accursed things, and would have dreaded them; but looking on them with an eye of sense only, he saw them as goodly things, and coveted them. When he had committed the sin, he tried to hide it. As soon as he had got this plunder, it became his burden, and he dared not to use his ill-gotten treasure. So differently do objects of temptation appear at a distance, to what they do when they have been gotten. See the deceitfulness of sin; that which is pleasing in the commission, is bitter in the reflection. See how they will be deceived that rob God. Sin is a very troublesome thing, not only to a sinner himself, but to all about him. The righteous God will certainly recompense tribulation to them that trouble his people. Achan perished not alone in his sin. They lose their own, who grasp at more than their own. His sons and daughters were put to death with him. It is probable that they helped to hide the things; they must have known of them. What fatal consequences follow, even in this world, to the sinner himself, and to all belonging him! One sinner destroys much good. What, then, will be the wrath to come? Let us flee from it to Christ Jesus as the sinner's Friend. There are circumstances in the confession of Achan, marking the progress of sin, from its first entrance into the heart to its being done, which may serve as the history of almost every offence against the law of God, and the sacrifice of Jesus Christ.

Chapter 8

Chapter Outline

Verses 1, 2

When we have faithfully put away sin, that accursed thing which separates between us and God, then, and not till then, we may look to hear from God to our comfort; and God's directing us how to go on in our Christian work and warfare, is a good evidence of his being reconciled to us. God encouraged Joshua to proceed. At Ai the spoil was not to be destroyed as at Jericho, therefore there was no danger of the people's committing such a trespass. Achan, who caught at forbidden spoil, lost that, and life, and all; but the rest of the people, who kept themselves from the accursed thing, were quickly rewarded for their obedience. The way to have the comfort of what God allows us, is, to keep from what he forbids us. No man shall lose by self-denial.

Verses 3-22

Observe Joshua's conduct and prudence. Those that would maintain their spiritual conflicts must not love their ease. Probably he went into the valley alone, to pray to God for a blessing, and he did not seek in vain. He never drew back till the work was done. Those that have stretched out their hands against their spiritual enemies, must never draw them back.

Verses 23-29

God, the righteous Judge, had sentenced the Canaanites for their wickedness; the Israelites only executed his doom. None of their conduct can be drawn into an example for others. Especial reason no doubt there was for this severity to the king of Ai; it is likely he had been notoriously wicked and vile, and a blasphemer of the God of Israel.

Verses 30-35

As soon as Joshua got to the mountains Ebal and Gerizim, without delay, and without caring for the unsettled state of Israel, or their enemies, he confirmed the covenant of the Lord with his people, as appointed, De 11; 27. We must not think to defer covenanting with God till we are settled in the world; nor must any business put us from minding and pursuing the one thing needful. The way to prosper is to begin with God, Mt 6:33. They built an altar, and offered sacrifice to God, in token of their dedicating themselves to God, as living sacrifices to his honour, in and by a Mediator. By Christ's sacrifice of himself for us, we have peace with God. It is a great mercy to any people to have the law of God in writing, and it is fit that the written law should be in a known tongue, that it may be seen and read of all men.

Chapter 9

Chapter Outline

Verses 1, 2

Hitherto the Canaanites had defended themselves, but here they consult to attack Israel. Their minds were blinded, and their hearts hardened to their destruction. Though often at enmity with each other, yet they united against Israel. Oh that Israel would learn of Canaanites, to sacrifice private interests to the public welfare, and to lay aside all quarrels among themselves, that they may unite against the enemies of God's kingdom! (Jos 9:3-13)

Verses 3-13

Other people heard these tidings, and were driven thereby to make war upon Israel; but the Gibeonites were led to make peace with them. Thus the discovery of the glory and the grace of God in the gospel, is to some a savour of life unto life, but to others a savour of death unto death, 2Co 2:16. The same sun softens wax and hardens clay. The falsehood of the Gibeonites cannot be justified. We must not do evil that good may themselves to the God of Israel, we have reason to think Joshua would have been directed by the oracle of God to spare their lives. But when they had once said, "We are come from a far country," they were led to say it made of skins, and their clothes: one lie brings on another, and that a third, and so on. The way of that sin is especially down-hill. Yet their faith and prudence are to be commended. In submitting to Israel they submitted to the God of Israel, which implied forsaking their idolatries. And how can we do better than cast ourselves upon the mercy of a God of all goodness? The way to avoid judgment is to meet it by repentance.

Let us do like these Gibeonites, seek peace with God in the rags of abasement, and godly sorrow; so our sin shall not be our ruin. Let us be servants to Jesus, our blessed Joshua, and we shall live.

Verses 14-21

The Israelites, having examined the provisions of the Gibeonites, hastily concluded that they confirmed their account. We make more haste than good speed, when we stay not to take God with us, and do not consult him by the word and prayer. The fraud was soon found out. A lying tongue is but for a moment. Had the oath been in itself unlawful, it would not have been binding; for no obligation can render it our duty to commit a sin. But it was not unlawful to spare the Canaanites who submitted, and left idolatry, desiring only that their lives might be spared. A citizen of Zion swears to his own hurt, and changes not, Ps 15:4. Joshua and the princes, when they found that they had been deceived, did not apply to Eleazar the high priest to be freed from their engagement, much less did they pretend that no faith is to be kept with those to whom they had sworn. Let this convince us how we ought to keep our promises, and make good our bargains; and what conscience we ought to make of our words.

Verses 22-27

The Gibeonites do not justify their lie, but plead that they did it to save their lives. And the fear was not merely of the power of man; one might flee from that to the Divine protection; but of the power of God himself, which they saw engaged against them. Joshua sentences them to perpetual bondage. They must be servants, but any work becomes honourable, when it is done for the house of the Lord, and the offices thereof. Let us, in like manner, submit to our Lord Jesus, saying, We are in thy hand, do unto us as seemeth good and right unto thee, only save our souls; and we shall not repent it. If He appoints us to bear his cross, and serve him, that shall be neither shame nor grief to us, while the meanest office in God's service will entitle us to a dwelling in the house of the Lord all the days of our life. And in coming to the Saviour, we do not proceed upon a peradventure. We are invited to draw nigh, and are assured that him that cometh to Him, he will in nowise cast out. Even those things which sound harsh, and are humbling, and form sharp trials of our sincerity, will prove of real advantage.

Chapter 10

Chapter Outline

Five kings war against Gibeon.	(1–6)
Joshua succours Gibeon, The sun and moon stand still.	(7–14)
The kings are taken, their armies defeated, and they are put to death.	(15–27)

Seven other kings defeated and slain.   (28–43)

Verses 1-6

When sinners leave the service of Satan and the friendship of the world, that they make peace with God and join Israel, they must not marvel if the world hate them, if their former friends become foes. By such methods Satan discourages many who are convinced of their danger, and almost persuaded to be Christians, but fear the cross. These things should quicken us to apply to God for protection, help, and deliverance.

Verses 7-14

The meanest and most feeble, who have just begun to trust the Lord, are as much entitled to be protected as those who have long and faithfully been his servants. It is our duty to defend the afflicted, who, like the Gibeonites, are brought into trouble on our account, or for the sake of the gospel. Joshua would not forsake his new vassals. How much less shall our true Joshua fail those who trust in Him! We may be wanting in our trust, but our trust never can want success. Yet God's promises are not to slacken and do away, but to quicken and encourage our endeavours. Notice the great faith of Joshua, and the power of God answering it by the miraculous staying of the sun, that the day of Israel's victories might be made longer. Joshua acted on this occasion by impulse on his mind from the Spirit of God. It was not necessary that Joshua should speak, or the miracle be recorded, according to the modern terms of astronomy. The sun appeared to the Israelites over Gibeon, and the moon over the valley of Ajalon, and there they appeared to be stopped on their course for one whole day. Is any thing too hard for the Lord? forms a sufficient answer to ten thousand difficulties, which objectors have in every age started against the truth of God as revealed in his written word. Proclamation was hereby made to the neighbouring nations, Behold the works of the Lord, and say, What nation is there so great as Israel, who has God so nigh unto them?

Verses 15-27

None moved his tongue against any of the children of Israel. This shows their perfect safety. The kings were called to an account, as rebels against the Israel of God. Refuges of lies will but secure for God's judgment. God punished the abominable wickedness of these kings, the measure of whose iniquity was now full. And by this public act of justice, done upon these ringleaders of the Canaanites in sin, he would possess his people with the greater dread and detestation of the sins of the nations that God cast out from before them. Here is a type and figure of Christ's victories over the powers of darkness, and of believers' victories through him. In our spiritual conflicts we must not be satisfied with obtaining some important victory. We must pursue our scattered enemies, searching out the remains of sin as they rise up in our hearts, and thus pursue the conquest. In so doing, the Lord will afford light until the warfare be accomplished.

Verses 28-43

Joshua made speed in taking these cities. See what a great deal of work may be done in a little time, if we will be diligent, and improve our opportunities. God here showed his hatred of the idolatries and other abominations of which the Canaanites had been guilty, and shows us how great the provocation was, by the greatness of the destruction brought upon them. Here also was typified the destruction of all the enemies of the Lord Jesus, who, having slighted the riches of his grace, must for ever feel the weight of his wrath. The Lord fought for Israel. They could not have gotten the victory, if God had not undertaken the battle. We conquer when God fights for us; if he be for us, who can be against us?

Chapter 11

Chapter Outline

Verses 1-9

The wonders God wrought for the Israelites were to encourage them to act vigorously themselves. Thus the war against Satan's kingdom, carried on by preaching the gospel, was at first forwarded by miracles; but being fully proved to be of God, we are now left to the Divine grace in the usual course, in the use of the sword of the Spirit. God encouraged Joshua. Fresh dangers and difficulties make it necessary to seek fresh supports from the word of God, which we have nigh unto us for use in every time of need. God proportions our trials to our strength, and our strength to our trials. Joshua's obedience in destroying the horses and chariots, shows his self-denial in compliance with God's command. The possession of things on which the carnal heart is prone to depend, is hurtful to the life of faith, and the walk with God; therefore it is better to be without worldly advantages, than to have the soul endangered by them. (Jos 11:10-14)

Verses 10-14

The Canaanites filled up the measure of their iniquity, and were, as a judgment, left to the pride, obstinacy, and enmity of their hearts, and to the power of Satan; all restraints being withdrawn, while the dispensations of Providence tended to drive them to despair. They brought on themselves the vengeance they justly merited, of which the Israelites were to be executioners, by the command the Lord gave to Moses.

Verses 15-23

Never let the sons of Anak be a terror to the Israel of God, for their day to fall will come. The land rested from war. It ended not in a peace with the Canaanites, that was forbidden, but in a peace from them. There is a rest, a rest from war, remaining for the people of God, into which they shall enter, when their warfare is accomplished. That which was now done, is compared with what had been said to Moses. God's word and his works, if viewed together, will be found mutually to set each other forth. If we make conscience of our duty, we need not question the performance of the promise. But the believer must never put off his armour, or expect lasting peace, till he closes his eyes in death; nay, as his strength and usefulness increase, he may expect more heavy trials; yet the Lord will not permit any enemies to assault the believer till he has prepared him for the battle. Christ Jesus ever lives to plead for his people, and their faith shall not fail, however Satan may be permitted to assault them. And however tedious, sharp, and difficult the believer's warfare, his patience in tribulation may be encouraged by the joyfulness of hope; for he will, ere long, rest from sin and from sorrow in the Canaan above.

Chapter 12

Chapter Outline

Verses 1-6

Fresh mercies must not drown the remembrance of former mercies, nor must the glory of the present instruments of good to the church diminish the just honour of those who went before them, since God is the same who wrought by both. Moses gave to one part of Israel a very rich and fruitful country, but it was on the outside of Jordan. Joshua gave to all Israel the holy land, within Jordan. So the law has given to some few of God's spiritual Israel worldly blessings, earnests of good things to come; but our Lord Jesus, the true Joshua, provided for all the children of promise spiritual blessings, and the heavenly Canaan.

Verses 7-24

We have here the limits of the country Joshua conquered. A list is given of the kings subdued by Israel: thirty-one in all. This shows how fruitful Canaan then was, in which so many chose to throng together. This was the land God appointed for Israel; yet in our day it is one of the most barren and unprofitable countries in the world. Such is the effect of the curse it lies under, since its possessors rejected Christ and his gospel, as was foretold by Moses, De 29:23. The vengeance of a righteous God, inflicted on all these kings and their subjects, for their wickedness, should make us dread and hate sin. The fruitful land bestowed on his chosen people, should fill our hearts with hope and confidence in his mercy, and with humble gratitude.

Chapter 13

Chapter Outline

Verses 1-6

At this chapter begins the account of the dividing of the land of Canaan among the tribes of Israel by lot; a narrative showing the performance of the promise made to the fathers, that this land should be given to the seed of Jacob. We are not to pass over these chapters of hard names as useless. Where God has a mouth to speak, and a hand to write, we should find an ear to hear, and an eye to read; and may God give us a heart to profit! Joshua is supposed to have been about one hundred years old at this time. It is good for those who are old and stricken in years to be put in remembrance of their being so. God considers the frame of his people, and would not have them burdened with work above their strength. And all people, especially old people, should set to do that quickly which must be done before they die, lest death prevent them, Ec 9:10. God promise that he would make the Israelites masters of all the countries yet unsubdued, through Joshua was old, and not able to do it; old, and not likely to live to see it done. Whatever becomes of us, and however we may be laid aside as despised, broken vessels, God will do his own work in his own time. We must work out our salvation, then God will work in us, and work with us; we must resist our spiritual enemies, then God will tread them under our feet; we must go forth to our Christian work and warfare, then God will go forth before us.

Verses 7-33

The land must be divided among the tribes. It is the will of God that every man should know his own, and not take that which is another's. The world must be governed, not by force, but right. Wherever our habitation is placed, and in whatever honest way our portion is assigned, we should consider them as allotted of God; we should be thankful for, and use them as such, while every prudent method should be used to prevent disputes about property, both at present and in future. Joshua must be herein a type of Christ, who has not only conquered the gates of hell for us, but has opened to us the gates of heaven, and having purchased the eternal inheritance for all believers, will put them in possession of it. Here is a general description of the country given to the two tribes and a half, by Moses. Israel must know their own, and keep to it; and may not, under pretence of their being God's peculiar people, encroach on their neighbours. Twice in this chapter it is noticed, that to the tribe of Levi Moses gave no inheritance: see Nu 18:20. Their maintenance must be brought out of all the tribes. The ministers of the Lord should show themselves indifferent about worldly interests, and the people should take care they want nothing suitable. And happy are those who have the Lord God of Israel for their inheritance, though little of this world falls to their lot. His providences will supply their wants, his consolations will support their souls, till they gain heavenly joy and everlasting pleasures.

Chapter 14

Chapter Outline

The nine tribes and a half to have their inheritance.   (1–5)

Caleb obtains Hebron.   (6–15)

Verses 1-5

The Israelites must occupy the new conquests. Canaan would have been subdued in vain, if it had not been inhabited. Yet every man might not go and settle where he pleased. God shall choose our inheritance for us. Let us survey our heritage of present mercy, our prospect for the land of promise, eternal in the heavens. Is God any respecter of persons? Is it not better that our place, as to earthly good or sorrow, should be determined by the infinite wisdom of our heavenly Father, than by our own ignorance? Should not those for whom the great mystery of godliness was exhibited, those whose redemption was purchased by Jesus Christ, thankfully refer their earthly concerns to his appointment?

Verses 6-15

Caleb's request is, "Give me this mountain," or Hebron, because it was formerly in God's promise to him, and he would let Israel knows how much he valued the promise. Those who live by faith value that which is given by God's promise, far above what is given by his providence only. It was now in the Anakims' possession, and Caleb would let Israel know how little he feared the enemy, and that he would encourage them to push on their conquests. Caleb answered to his name, which signifies "all heart." Hebron was settled on Caleb and his heirs, because he wholly followed the Lord God of Israel. Happy are we if we follow him. Singular piety shall be crowned with singular favour.

Chapter 15

Chapter Outline

The borders of the lot of Judah.   (1–12)

Caleb's portion, His daughter's blessing.   (13–19)

The cities of Judah.   (20–63)

Verses 1-12

Joshua allotted to Judah, Ephraim, and the half of Manasseh, their inheritances before they left Gilgal. Afterwards removing to Shiloh, another survey was made, and the other tribes had their portion assigned. In due time all God's people are settled.

Verses 13-19

Achsah obtained some land by Caleb's free grant. He gave her a south land. Land indeed, but a south land, dry and apt to be parched. She obtained more, on her request, and he gave the upper and the nether springs. Those who understand it but of one field, watered both with the rain of heaven, and the springs that issued out of the earth, countenance the allusion commonly made to this, when we pray for spiritual and heavenly blessings which relate to our souls, as blessings of the upper springs, and those which relate to the body and the life that now is, as blessings of the nether springs. All the blessings, both of the upper and the nether springs, belong to the children of God. As related to Christ, they have them freely given of the Father, for the lot of their inheritance.

Verses 20-63

Here is a list of the cities of Judah. But we do not here find Bethlehem, afterwards the city of David, and ennobled by the birth of our Lord Jesus in it. That city, which, at the best, was but little among the thousands of Judah, Mic 5:2, except that it was thus honoured, was now so little as not to be accounted one of the cities.

Chapter 16

The sons of Joseph.
—This and the following chapter should not be separated. They give the lots of Ephraim and Manasseh, the children of Joseph, who, next to Judah, were to have the post of honour, and therefore had the first and best portion in the northern part of Canaan, as Judah in the southern part. God's people now, as of old, suffer his enemies to remain. Blessed Lord, when will all our enemies be subdued? 1Co 15:26. Do thou drive them all out; thou alone canst do it. These settled boundaries may remind us, that our situation and provision in this life, as well as our future inheritance, are appointed by the only wise and righteous God, and we should be content with our portion, since he knows what is best for us, and all we have is more than we deserve.

Chapter 17

Chapter Outline

The lot of Manasseh.   (1–6)

Verses 1-6

Manasseh was but half of the tribe of Joseph, yet it was divided into two parts. The daughters of Zelophehad now reaped the benefit of their pious zeal and prudent forecast. Those who take care in the wilderness of this world, to make sure to themselves a place in the inheritance of the saints in light, will have the comfort of it in the other world; while those who neglect it now, will lose it for ever. Lord, teach us here to believe and obey, and give us an inheritance among thy saints, in glory everlasting.

Verses 7-13

There was great communication between Manasseh and Ephraim. Though each tribe had its inheritance, yet they should intermix one with another, to do good offices one to another, as became those, who, though of different tribes, were all one Israel, and were bound to love as brethren. But they suffered the Canaanites to live among them, against the command of God, to serve their own ends.

Verses 14-18

Joshua, as a public person, had no more regard to his own tribe than to any other, but would govern without favour or affection; wherein he has left a good example to all in public trusts. Joshua tells them, that what was fallen to their share would be a sufficient lot for them, if they would but work and fight. Men excuse themselves from labour by any pretence; and nothing serves the purpose better than having rich and powerful relations, able to provide for them; and they are apt to desire a partial and unfaithful disposal of what is intrusted to those they think able to give such help. But there is more real kindness in pointing out the advantages within reach, and in encouraging men to make the best of them, than in granting indulgences to sloth and extravagance. True religion gives no countenance to these evils. The rule is, They shall not eat who will not work; and many of our "cannots" are only the language of idleness, which magnifies every difficulty and danger. This is especially the case in our spiritual work and warfare. Without Christ we can do nothing, but we are apt to sit still and attempt nothing. if we belong to Him, he will stir us up to our best endeavours, and to cry to him for help. Then our coast will be enlarged, 1Ch 4:9, 10, and complainings silenced, or rather, turned into joyful thanksgivings.

Chapter 18

Chapter Outline

The tabernacle set up at Shiloh.   (1)

The remainder of the land described and   (2–10)
divided.

The boundaries of Benjamin.   (11–28)

Verse 1

Shiloh was in the lot of Ephraim, the tribe to which Joshua belonged, and it was proper that the tabernacle should be near the residence of the chief governor. The name of this city is the same as that by which Jacob prophesied of the Messiah, Ge 49:10. It is supposed by some that the city was thus called, when it was chosen for the resting-place of the ark, which typified our great Peace-maker, and the way by him to a reconciled God.

Verses 2-10

After a year or more, Joshua blamed their slackness, and told them how to proceed. God, by his grace, has given us a title to a good land, the heavenly Canaan, but we are slack to take possession of it; we enter not into that rest, as we might by faith, and hope, and holy joy. How long shall it be thus with us? How long shall we thus stand in our own light, and forsake our own mercies for lying vanities? Joshua stirs the Israelites up to take possession of their lots. He is ready to do his part, if they will do theirs.

Verses 11-28

The boundaries of each portion were distinctly drawn, and the inheritance of each tribe settled. All contests and selfish claims were prevented by the wise appointment of God, who allotted the hill and the valley, the corn and pasture, the brooks and rivers, the towns and cities. Is the lot of any servant of Christ cast in affliction and sorrow? It is the Lord; let him do what seemeth him good. Are we in prosperity and peace? It is from above. Be humbled when you compare the gift with your own unworthiness. Forget not Him that gave the good, and always be ready to resign it at his command.

Chapter 19

Chapter Outline

The lot of Simeon.   (1–9)

The lot of Zebulun.   (10–16)

The lot of Issachar, Asher, Naphtali, and   (17–51)
Dan.

Verses 1-9

The men of Judah did not oppose taking away the cities within their border, when convinced that they had more than was right. If a true believer has obtained an unintended and improper advantage in any thing, he will give it up without murmuring. Love seeketh not her own, and doth not behave unseemly; it will induce those in whom it richly dwells, to part with their own to supply what is lacking to their brethren.

Verses 10-16

In the division to each tribe of Israel, the prophetic blessings of Jacob were fulfilled. They chose for themselves, or it was divided to them by lot, in the manner and places that he foresaw. So sure a rule to go by is the word of prophecy: we see by it what to believe, and it proves beyond all dispute the things that are of God.

Verses 17-51

Joshua waited till all the tribes were settled, before he asked any provision for himself. He was content to be unfixed, till he saw them all placed, and herein is an example to all in public places, to prefer the common welfare before private advantage. Those who labour most to do good to others, seek an inheritance in the Canaan above: but it will be soon enough to enter thereon, when they have done all the service to their brethren of which they are capable. Nor can any thing more effectually assure them of their title to it, than endeavouring to bring others to desire, to seek, and to obtain it. Our Lord Jesus came and dwelt on earth, not in pomp but poverty, providing rest for man, yet himself not having where to lay his head; for Christ pleased not himself. Nor would he enter upon his inheritance, till by his obedience to death he secured the eternal inheritance for all his people; nor will he account his own glory completed, till every ransomed sinner is put in possession of his heavenly rest.

Chapter 20

Chapter Outline

The law concerning the cities of refuge.   (1–6)
The cities appointed as refuges.   (7–9)

Verses 1-6

When the Israelites were settled in their promised inheritance, they were reminded to set apart the cities of refuge, whose use and typical meaning have been explained, Nu 35; De 19. God's spiritual Israel have, and shall have in Christ and heaven, not only rest to repose in, but refuge to secure themselves in. These cities were designed to typify the relief which the gospel provides for penitent sinners, and their protection from the curse of the law and the wrath of God, in our Lord Jesus, to whom believers flee for refuge, Heb 6:18.

Verses 7-9

These cities, as those also on the other side Jordan, stood so that a man might in half a day reach one of them from any part of the country. God is ever a Refuge at hand. They were all Levites' cities. It was kindness to the poor fugitive, that when he might not go up to the house of the Lord, yet he had the servants of God with him, to instruct him, and pray for him, and to help to make up the want of public ordinances. Some observe a significance in the names of these cities with application to Christ our Refuge. Kedesh signifies holy, and our Refuge is the holy Jesus. Shechem, a shoulder, and the government is upon his shoulder. Hebron, fellowship, and believers are called into the fellowship of Christ Jesus our Lord. Bezer, a fortification, for he is a strong hold to all those that trust in him. Ramoth, high or exalted, for Him hath God exalted with his own right hand. Golan, joy or exultation, for in Him all the saints are justified, and shall glory.

Chapter 21

Chapter Outline

Cities for the Levites.	(1–8)
The cities allotted to the Levites.	(9–42)
God gave the land and rest to the Israelites, according to his promise.	(43–45)

Verses 1-8

The Levites waited till the other tribes were provided for, before they preferred their claim to Joshua. They build their claim upon a very good foundation; not their own merits or services, but the Divine precept. The maintenance of ministers is not a thing left merely to the will of the people, that they may let them starve if they please; they which preach the gospel should live by the gospel, and should live comfortably. (Jos 21:9-42)

Verses 9-42

By mixing the Levites with the other tribes, they were made to see that the eyes of all Israel were upon them, and therefore it was their concern to walk so that their ministry might not be blamed. Every tribe had its share of Levites' cities. Thus did God graciously provide for keeping up religion among them, and that they might have the word in all parts of the land. Yet, blessed be God, we have the gospel more diffused amongst us. (Jos 21:43-45)

Verses 43-45

God promised to give to the seed of Abraham the land of Canaan for a possession, and now they possessed it, and dwelt therein. And the promise of the heavenly Canaan is as sure to all God's spiritual Israel; for it is the promise of Him that cannot lie. There stood not a man before them. The after-prevalence of the Canaanites was the effect of Israel's slothfulness, and the punishment of their sinful inclination to the idolatries and abominations of the heathen whom they harboured and indulged. There failed not aught of any good thing, which the Lord had spoken to the house of Israel. In due season all his promises will be accomplished; then will his people acknowledge that the Lord has exceeded their largest expectations, and made them more than conquerors, and brought them to their desired rest.

Chapter 22

Chapter Outline

Verses 1-9

Joshua dismisses the tribes with good counsel. Those who have the commandment have it in vain, unless they do the commandment; and it will not be done aright unless we take diligent heed. In particular to love the Lord our God, as the best of beings, and the best of friends; and as far as that principle rules in the heart, there will be constant care and endeavour to walk in his ways, even those that are narrow and up-hill. In every instance to keep his commandments. At all times, and in all conditions, with purpose of heart to cleave unto the Lord, and to serve him and his kingdom among men, with all our heart, and with all our soul. This good counsel is given to all; may God give us grace to take it!

Verses 10-20

Here is the care of the separated tribes to keep their hold of Canaan's religion. At first sight it seemed a design to set up an altar against the altar at Shiloh. God is jealous for his own institutions; we should be so too, and afraid of every thing that looks like, or leads to idolatry. Corruptions in religion are best dealt with at first. But their prudence in following up this zealous resolution is no less commendable. Many an unhappy strife would be prevented, or soon made up, by inquiries into the matter of the offence. The remembrance of great sins committed formerly, should engage us to stand on our guard against the beginnings of sin; for the way of sin is down-hill. We are all concerned to reprove our neighbour when he does amiss, lest we suffer sin upon him, Le 19:17. The offer made that they should be welcome to come to the land where the Lord's tabernacle was, and settle there, was in the spirit of true Israelites.

Verses 21-29

The tribes took the reproofs of their brethren in good part. With solemnity and meekness they proceeded to give all the satisfaction in their power. Reverence of God is expressed in the form of their appeal. This brief confession of faith would remove their brethren's suspicion that they intended to worship other gods. Let us always speak of God with seriousness, and mention his name with a solemn pause. Those who make appeals to Heaven with a careless "God knows," take his name in vain: it is very unlike this. They express great confidence of their own uprightness in the matter of their appeal. "God knows it," for he is perfectly acquainted with the thoughts and intents of the heart. In every thing we do in religion, it highly concerns us to approve ourselves to God, remembering that he knows the heart. And if our sincerity be known to God, we should study likewise to let others know it by its fruits, especially those who, though they mistake us, show zeal for the glory of God. They disdained the design of which they were suspected to be guilty, and fully explained their true intent in building this altar. Those who have found the comfort and benefit of God's ordinances, cannot but desire to preserve them to their seed, and to use all possible care that their children may be looked upon as having a part in him. Christ is the great Altar that sanctifies every gift; the best evidence of our interest in him is the work of his Spirit in our hearts.

Verses 30-34

It is well that there was on both sides a disposition to peace, as there was a zeal for God; for quarrels about religion, for want of wisdom and love, often prove the most fierce and difficult to be made up. Proud and peevish spirits, when they have passed any unjust blame on their brethren, though full evidence be brought of its unfairness, can by no means be persuaded to withdraw it. But Israel was not so prejudiced. They looked upon their brethren's innocence as a token of God's presence. Our brethren's zeal for the power of godliness, and faith and love, notwithstanding the fears of their breaking the unity of the church, are things of which we should be very glad to be satisfied. The altar was called ED, a witness. It was a witness of their care to keep their religion pure and entire, and would witness against their descendants, if they should turn from following after the Lord. Happy will it be when all professed Christians learn to copy the example of Israel, to unite zeal and steady adherence to the cause of truth, with candour, meekness, and readiness to understand each other, to explain and to be satisfied with the explanations of their brethren. May the Lord increase the number of those who endeavour to keep the unity of the Spirit in the bond of peace! may increasing grace and consolation be with all who love Jesus Christ in sincerity!

Chapter 23

Chapter Outline

Joshua's exhortation before his death.   (1–10)

Joshua warns the people of idolatry.   (11–16)

Verses 1-10

Joshua was old and dying, let them observe what he said now. He put them in mind of the great things God had done for them in his days. He exhorted them to be very courageous. Keep with care, do with diligence, and regard with sincerity what is written. Also, very cautiously to endeavour that the heathen idolatry may be forgotten, so that it may never be revived. It is sad that among Christians the names of the heathen gods are so commonly used, and made so familiar as they are. Joshua exhorts them to be very constant. There might be many things amiss among them, but they had not forsaken the Lord their God; the way to make people better, is to make the best of them.

Verses 11-16

Would we cleave to the Lord, we must always stand upon our guard, for many a soul is lost through carelessness. Love the Lord your God, and you will not leave him. Has God been thus true to you? Be not you false to him. He is faithful that has promised, Heb 10:23. The experience of every Christian witnesses the same truth. Conflicts may have been severe and long, trials great and many; but at the last he will acknowledge that goodness and mercy followed him all the days of his life. Joshua states the fatal consequences of going back; know for a certainty it will be your ruin. The first step would be, friendship with idolaters; the next would be, marrying with them; the end of that would be, serving their gods. Thus the way of sin is down-hill, and those who have fellowship with sinners, cannot avoid having fellowship with sin. He describes the destruction he warns them of. The goodness of the heavenly Canaan, and the free and sure grant God has made of it, will add to the misery of those who shall for ever be shut out from it. Nothing will make them see how wretched they are, so much, as to see how happy they might have been. Let us watch and pray against temptation. Let us trust in God's faithfulness, love, and power; let us plead his promises, and cleave to his commandments, then we shall be happy in life, in death, and for ever.

Chapter 24

Chapter Outline

God's benefits to their fathers.   (1–14)

Joshua renews the covenant between the   (15–28)
people and God.

Joshua's death, Joseph's bones buried, The   (29–33)
state of Israel.

Verses 1-14

We must never think our work for God done, till our life is done. If he lengthen out our days beyond what we expected, like those of Joshua, it is because he has some further service for us to do. He who aims at the same mind which was in Christ Jesus, will glory in bearing the last testimony to his Saviour's goodness, and in telling to all around, the obligations with which the unmerited goodness of God has bound him. The assembly came together in a solemn religious manner. Joshua spake to them in God's name, and as from him. His sermon consists of doctrine and application. The doctrinal part is a history of the great things God had done for his people, and for their fathers before them. The application of this history of God's mercies to them, is an exhortation to fear and serve God, in gratitude for his favour, and that it might be continued.

Verses 15-28

It is essential that the service of God's people be performed with a willing mind. For LOVE is the only genuine principle whence all acceptable service of God can spring. The Father seeks only such to worship him, as worship him in spirit and in truth. The carnal mind of man is enmity against God, therefore, is not capable of such spiritual worship. Hence the necessity of being born again. But numbers rest in mere forms, as tasks imposed upon them. Joshua puts them to their choice; but not as if it were indifferent whether they served God or not. Choose you whom ye will serve, now the matter is laid plainly before you. He resolves to do this, whatever others did. Those that are bound for heaven, must be willing to swim against the stream. They must not do as the most do, but as the best do. And no one can behave himself as he ought in any station, who does not deeply consider his religious duties in family relations. The Israelites agree with Joshua, being influenced by the example of a man who had been so great a blessing to them; We also will serve the Lord. See how much good great men do, by their influence, if zealous in religion. Joshua brings them to express full purpose of heart to cleave to the Lord. They must come off from all confidence in their own sufficiency, else their purposes would be in vain. The service of God being made their deliberate choice, Joshua binds them to it by a solemn covenant. He set up a monument of it. In this affecting manner Joshua took his last leave of them; if they perished, their blood would be upon their own heads. Though the house of God, the Lord's table, and even the walls and trees before which we have uttered our solemn purposes of serving him, would bear witness against us if we deny him, yet we may trust in him, that he will put his fear into our hearts, that we shall not depart from him. God alone can give grace, yet he blesses our endeavours to engage men to his service.

Verses 29-33

Joseph died in Egypt, but gave commandment concerning his bones, that they should not rest in their grave till Israel had rest in the land of promise. Notice also the death and burial of Joshua, and of Eleazar the chief priest. The most useful men, having served their generation, according to the will of God, one after another, fall asleep and see corruption. But Jesus, having spent and ended his life on earth more effectually than either Joshua or Joseph, rose from the dead, and saw no corruption. And the redeemed of the Lord shall inherit the kingdom he prepared for them from the foundation of the world. They will say in admiration of the grace of Jesus, Unto him that loved us, and washed us from our sins in his own blood, and hath made us kings and priests unto God and his Father, to him be glory and dominion for ever and ever. Amen.

Judges

The book of Judges is the history of Israel during the government of the Judges, who were occasional deliverers, raised up by God to rescue Israel from their oppressors, to reform the state of religion, and to administer justice to the people. The state of God's people does not appear in this book so prosperous, nor their character so religious, as might have been expected; but there were many believers among them, and the tabernacle service was attended to. The history exemplifies the frequent warnings and predictions of Moses, and should have close attention. The whole is full of important instruction.

Chapter 1

Chapter Outline

Verses 1-8

The Israelites were convinced that the war against the Canaanites was to be continued; but they were in doubt as to the manner in which it was to be carried on after the death of Joshua. In these respects they inquired of the Lord. God appoints service according to the strength he has given. From those who are most able, most work is expected. Judah was first in dignity, and must be first in duty. Judah's service will not avail unless God give success; but God will not give the success, unless Judah applies to the service. Judah was the most considerable of all the tribes, and Simeon the least; yet Judah begs Simeon's friendship, and prays for aid from him. It becomes Israelites to help one another against Canaanites; and all Christians, even those of different tribes, should strengthen one another. Those who thus help one another in love, have reason to hope that God will graciously help both. Adoni-bezek was taken prisoner. This prince had been a severe tyrant. The Israelites, doubtless under the Divine direction, made him suffer what he had done to others; and his own conscience confessed that he was justly treated as he had treated others. Thus the righteous God sometimes, in his providence, makes the punishment answer the sin.

Verses 9-20

The Canaanites had iron chariots; but Israel had God on their side, whose chariots are thousands of angels, Ps 68:17. Yet they suffered their fears to prevail against their faith. About Caleb we read in Jos 15:16–19. The Kenites had settled in the land. Israel let them fix where they pleased, being a quiet, contented people. They that molested none, were molested by none. Blessed are the meek, for they shall inherit the earth.

Verses 21-36

The people of Israel were very careless of their duty and interest. Owing to slothfulness and cowardice, they would not be at the pains to complete their conquests. It was also owing to their covetousness: they were willing to let the Canaanites live among them, that they might make advantage of them. They had not the dread and detestation of idolatry they ought to have had. The same unbelief that kept their fathers forty years out of Canaan, kept them now out of the full possession of it. Distrust of the power and promise of God deprived them of advantages, and brought them into troubles. Thus many a believer who begins well is hindered. His graces languish, his lusts revive, Satan plies him with suitable temptations, the world recovers its hold; he brings guilt into his conscience, anguish into his heart, discredit on his character, and reproach on the gospel. Though he may have sharp rebukes, and be so recovered that he does not perish, yet he will have deeply to lament his folly through his remaining days; and upon his dying bed to mourn over the opportunities of glorifying God and serving the church he has lost. We can have no fellowship with the enemies of God within us or around us, but to our hurt; therefore our only wisdom is to maintain unceasing war against them.

Chapter 2

Chapter Outline

The angel of the Lord rebukes the people.   (1–5)

The wickedness of the new generation after   (6–23)
Joshua.

Verses 1-5

It was the great Angel of the covenant, the Word, the Son of God, who spake with Divine authority as Jehovah, and now called them to account for their disobedience. God sets forth what he had done for Israel, and what he had promised. Those who throw off communion with God, and have fellowship with the unfruitful works of darkness, know not what they do now, and will have nothing to say for themselves in the day of account shortly. They must expect to suffer for this their folly. Those deceive themselves who expect advantages from friendship with God's enemies. God often makes men's sin their punishment; and thorns and snares are in the way of the froward, who will walk contrary to God. The people wept, crying out against their own folly and ingratitude. They trembled at the word, and not without cause. It is a wonder sinners can ever read the Bible with dry eyes. Had they kept close to God and their duty, no voice but that of singing had been heard in their congregation; but by their sin and folly they made other work for themselves, and nothing is to be heard but the voice of weeping. The worship of God, in its own nature, is joy, praise, and thanksgiving; our sins alone render weeping needful. It is pleasing to see men weep for their sins; but our tears, prayers, and even amendment, cannot atone for sin.

Verses 6-23

We have a general idea of the course of things in Israel, during the time of the Judges. The nation made themselves as mean and miserable by forsaking God, as they would have been great and happy if they had continued faithful to him. Their punishment answered to the evil they had done. They served the gods of the nations round about them, even the meanest, and God made them serve the princes of the nations round about them, even the meanest. Those who have found God true to his promises, may be sure that he will be as true to his threatenings. He might in justice have abandoned them, but he could not for pity do it. The Lord was with the judges when he raised them up, and so they became saviours. In the days of the greatest distress of the church, there shall be some whom God will find or make fit to help it. The Israelites were not thoroughly reformed; so mad were they upon their idols, and so obstinately bent to backslide. Thus those who have forsaken the good ways of God, which they have once known and professed, commonly grow most daring and desperate in sin, and have their hearts hardened. Their punishment was, that the Canaanites were spared, and so they were beaten with their own rod. Men cherish and indulge their corrupt appetites and passions; therefore God justly leaves them to themselves, under the power of their sins, which will be their ruin. God has told us how deceitful and desperately wicked our hearts are, but we are not willing to believe it, until by making bold with temptation we find it true by sad experience. We need to examine how matters stand with ourselves, and to pray without ceasing, that we may be rooted and grounded in love, and that Christ may dwell in our hearts by faith. Let us declare war against every sin, and follow after holiness all our days.

Chapter 3

Chapter Outline

Verses 1-7

As the Israelites were a type of the church on earth, they were not to be idle and slothful. The Lord was pleased to try them by the remains of the devoted nations they spared. Temptations and trials detect the wickedness of the hearts of sinners; and strengthen he graces of believers in their daily conflict with Satan, sin, and this evil world. They must live in this world, but they are not of it, and are forbidden to conform to it. This marks the difference between the followers of Christ and mere professors. The friendship of the world is more fatal than its enmity; the latter can only kill the body, but the former murders many precious souls.

Verses 8-11

The first judge was Othniel: even in Joshua's time Othniel began to be famous. Soon after Israel's settlement in Canaan their purity began to be corrupted, and their peace disturbed. But affliction makes those cry to God who before would scarcely speak to him. God returned in mercy to them for their deliverance. The Spirit of the Lord came upon Othniel. The Spirit of wisdom and courage to qualify him for the service, and the Spirit of power to excite him to it. He first judged Israel, reproved and reformed them, and then went to war. Let sin at home be conquered, that worst of enemies, then enemies abroad will be more easily dealt with. Thus let Christ be our Judge and Lawgiver, then he will save us.

Verses 12-30

When Israel sins again, God raises up a new oppressor. The Israelites did ill, and the Moabites did worse; yet because God punishes the sins of his own people in this world, Israel is weakened, and Moab strengthened against them. If lesser troubles do not do the work, God will send greater. When Israel prays again, God raises up Ehud. As a judge, or minister of Divine justice, Ehud put to death Eglon, the king of Moab, and thus executed the judgments of God upon him as an enemy to God and Israel. But the law of being subject to principalities and powers in all things lawful, is the rule of our conduct. No such commissions are now given; to pretend to them is to blaspheme God. Notice Ehud's address to Eglon. What message from God but a message of vengeance can a proud rebel expect? Such a message is contained in the word of God; his ministers are boldly to declare it, without fearing the frown, or respecting the persons of sinners. But, blessed be God, they have to deliver a message of mercy and of free salvation; the message of vengeance belongs only to those who neglect the offers of grace. The consequence of this victory was, that the land had rest eighty years. It was a great while for the land to rest; yet what is that to the saints' everlasting rest in the heavenly Canaan.

Verse 31

The side of the country which lay south-west, was infested by the Philistines. God raised up Shamgar to deliver them; having neither sword nor spear, he took an ox-goad, the instrument next at hand. God can make those serviceable to his glory and to his church's good, whose birth, education, and employment, are mean and obscure. It is no matter what the weapon is, if God directs and strengthens the arm. Often he works by unlikely means, that the excellency of the power may appear to be of God.

Chapter 4

Chapter Outline

Verses 1-3

The land had rest for eighty years, which should have confirmed them in their religion; but it made them secure, and indulge their lusts. Thus the prosperity of fools destroys them. Jabin and his general Sisera, mightily oppressed Israel. This enemy was nearer than any of the former. Israel cried unto the Lord, when distress drove them to him, and they saw no other way of relief. Those who slight God in prosperity, will find themselves under a necessity of seeking him in trouble.

Verses 4-9

Deborah was a prophetess; one instructed in Divine knowledge by the inspiration of the Spirit of God. She judged Israel as God's mouth to them; correcting abuses, and redressing grievances. By God's direction, she ordered Barak to raise an army, and engage Jabin's forces. Barak insisted much upon her presence. Deborah promised to go with him. She would not send him where she would not go herself. Those who in God's name call others to their duty, should be ready to assist them in it. Barak values the satisfaction of his mind, and the good success of his enterprise, more than mere honour.

Verses 10-16

Siser's confidence was chiefly in his chariots. But if we have ground to hope that God goes before us, we may go on with courage and cheerfulness. Be not dismayed at the difficulties thou meetest with in resisting Satan, in serving God, or suffering for him; for is not the Lord gone before thee? Follow him then fully. Barak went down, though upon the plain the iron chariots would have advantage against him: he quitted the mountain in dependence on the Divine power; for in the Lord alone is the salvation of his people, Jer 3:23. He was not deceived in his confidence. When God goes before us in our spiritual conflicts, we must bestir ourselves; and when, by his grace, he gives us some success against the enemies of our souls, we must improve it by watchfulness and resolution.

Verses 17-24

Sisera's chariots had been his pride and his confidence. Thus are those disappointed who rest on the creature; like a broken reed, it not only breaks under them, but pierces them with many sorrows. The idol may quickly become a burden, Isa 46:1; what we were sick for, God can make us sick of. It is probable that Jael really intended kindness to Sisera; but by a Divine impulse she was afterwards led to consider him as the determined enemy of the Lord and of his people, and to destroy him. All our connexions with God's enemies must be broken off, if we would have the Lord for our God, and his people for our people. He that had thought to have destroyed Israel with his many iron chariots, is himself destroyed with one iron nail. Thus the weak things of the world confound the mighty. The Israelites would have prevented much mischief, if they had sooner destroyed the Canaanites, as God commanded and enabled them: but better be wise late, and buy wisdom by experience, than never be wise.

Chapter 5

Chapter Outline

Verses 1-5

No time should be lost in returning thanks to the Lord for his mercies; for our praises are most acceptable, pleasant, and profitable, when they flow from a full heart. By this, love and gratitude would be more excited and more deeply fixed in the hearts of believers; the events would be more known and longer remembered. Whatever Deborah, Barak, or the army had done, the Lord must have all the praise. The will, the power, and the success were all from Him.

Verses 6-11

Deborah describes the distressed state of Israel under the tyranny of Jabin, that their salvation might appear more gracious. She shows what brought this misery upon them. It was their idolatry. They chose new gods, with new names. But under all these images, Satan was worshipped. Deborah was a mother to Israel, by diligently promoting the salvation of their souls. She calls on those who shared the advantages of this great salvation, to offer up thanks to God for it. Let such as are restored, not only to their liberty as other Israelites, but to their rank, speak God's praises. This is the Lord's doing. In these acts of his, justice was executed on his enemies. In times of persecution, God's ordinances, the walls of salvation, whence the waters of life are drawn, are resorted to at the hazard of the lives of those who attend them. At all times Satan will endeavour to hinder the believer from drawing near to the throne of grace. Notice God's kindness to his trembling people. It is the glory of God to protect those who are most exposed, and to help the weakest. Let us notice the benefit we have from the public peace, the inhabitants of villages especially, and give God the praise.

Verses 12-23

Deborah called on her own soul to be in earnest. He that will set the hearts of other men on fire with the love of Christ, must himself burn with love. Praising God is a work we should awake to, and awake ourselves unto. She notices who fought against Israel, who fought for them, and who kept away. Who fought against them. They were obstinate enemies to God's people, therefore the more dangerous. Who fought for them. The several tribes that helped are here spoken of with honour; for though God is above all to be glorified, those who are employed must have their due praise, to encourage others. But the whole creation is at war with those to whom God is an enemy. The river of Kishon fought against their enemies. At most times it was shallow, yet now, probably by the great rain that fell, it was so swelled, and the stream so deep and strong, that those who attempted to pass, were drowned. Deborah's own soul fought against them. When the soul is employed in holy exercises, and heart-work is made of them, through the grace of God, the strength of our spiritual enemies will be trodden down, and will fall before us. She observes who kept away, and did not side with Israel, as might have been expected. Thus many are kept from doing their duty by the fear of trouble, the love of ease, and undue affection to their worldly business and advantage. Narrow, selfish spirits care not what becomes of God's church, so that they can but get, keep, and save money. All seek their own, Php 2:21. A little will serve those for a pretence to stay at home, who have no mind to engage in needful services, because there is difficulty and danger in them. But we cannot keep away from the contest between the Lord and his enemies; and if we do not actively endeavour to promote his cause in this wicked world, we shall fall under the curse against the workers of iniquity. Though He needs no human help, yet he is pleased to accept the services of those who improve their talents to advance his cause. He requires every man to do so.

Verses 24-31

Jael had a special blessing. Those whose lot is cast in the tent, in a low and narrow sphere, if they serve God according to the powers he has given them, shall not lose their reward. The mother of Sisera looked for his return, not in the least fearing his success. Let us take heed of indulging eager desires towards any temporal good, particularly toward that which cherishes vain-glory, for that was what she here doted on. What a picture does she present of an ungodly and sensual heart! How shameful and childish these wishes of an aged mother and her attendants for her son! And thus does God often bring ruin on his enemies when they are most puffed up. Deborah concludes with a prayer to God for the destruction of all his foes, and for the comfort of all his friends. Such shall be the honour, and joy of all who love God in sincerity, they shall shine for ever as the sun in the firmament.

Chapter 6

Chapter Outline

Israel oppressed by Midianites. (1–6)

Israel rebuked by a prophet. (7–10)

Verses 1-6

Israel's sin was renewed, and Israel's troubles were repeated. Let all that sin expect to suffer. The Israelites hid themselves in dens and caves; such was the effect of a guilty conscience. Sin dispirits men. The invaders left no food for Israel, except what was taken into the caves. They prepared that for Baal with which God should have been served, now God justly sends an enemy to take it away in the season thereof.

Verses 7-10

They cried to God for a deliverer, and he sent them a prophet to teach them. When God furnishes a land with faithful ministers, it is a token that he has mercy in store for it. He charges them with rebellion against the Lord; he intends to bring them to repentance. Repentance is real when the sinfulness of sin, as disobedience to God, is chiefly lamented.

Verses 11-24

Gideon was a man of a brave, active spirit, yet in obscurity through the times: he is here stirred up to undertake something great. It was very sure that the Lord was with him, when his Angel was with him. Gideon was weak in faith, which made it hard to reconcile the assurances of the presence of God with the distress to which Israel was brought. The Angel answered his objections. He told him to appear and act as Israel's deliverer, there needed no more. Bishop Hall says, While God calls Gideon valiant, he makes him so. God delights to advance the humble. Gideon desires to have his faith confirmed. Now, under the influences of the Spirit, we are not to expect signs before our eyes such as Gideon here desired, but must earnestly pray to God, that if we have found grace in his sight, he would show us a sign in our heart, by the powerful working of his Spirit there, The Angel turned the meat into an offering made by fire; showing that he was not a man who needed meat, but the Son of God, who was to be served and honoured by sacrifice, and who in the fulness of time was to make himself a sacrifice. Hereby a sign was given to Gideon, that he had found grace in God's sight. Ever since man has by sin exposed himself to God's wrath and curse, a message from heaven has been a terror to him, as he scarcely dares to expect good tidings thence. In this world, it is very awful to have any converse with that world of spirits to which we are so much strangers. Gideon's courage failed him. But God spoke peace to him.

Verses 25-32

See the power of God's grace, that he could raise up a reformer; and the kindness of his grace, that he would raise up a deliverer, out of the family of a leader in idolatry. Gideon must not think it enough not to worship at that altar; he must throw it down, and offer sacrifice on another. It was needful he should make peace with God, before he made war on Midian. Till sin be pardoned through the great Sacrifice, no good is to be expected. God, who has all hearts in his hands, influenced Joash to appear for his son against the advocates for Baal, though he had joined formerly in the worship of Baal. Let us do our duty, and trust God with our safety. Here is a challenge to Baal, to do either good or evil; the result convinced his worshippers of their folly, in praying to one to help them that could not avenge himself.

Verses 33-40

These signs are truly miraculous, and very significant. Gideon and his men were going to fight the Midianites; could God distinguish between a small fleece of Israel, and the vast floor of Midian? Gideon is made to know that God could do so. Is Gideon desirous that the dew of Divine grace might come down upon himself in particular? He sees the fleece wet with dew to assure him of it. Does he desire that God will be as the dew to all Israel? Behold, all the ground is wet. What cause we sinners of the Gentiles have, to bless the Lord that the dew of heavenly blessings, once confined to Israel, is now sent to all the inhabitants of the earth! Yet still the means of grace are in different measures, according to the purposes of God. In the same congregation, one man's soul is like Gideon's moistened fleece, another like the dry ground.

Chapter 7

Chapter Outline

Verses 1-8

God provides that the praise of victory may be wholly to himself, by appointing only three hundred men to be employed. Activity and prudence go with dependence upon God for help in our lawful undertakings. When the Lord sees that men would overlook him, and through unbelief, would shrink from perilous services, or that through pride they would vaunt themselves against him, he will set them aside, and do his work by other instruments. Pretences will be found by many, for deserting the cause and escaping the cross. But though a religious society may thus be made fewer in numbers, yet it will gain as to purity, and may expect an increased blessing from the Lord. God chooses to employ such as are not only well affected, but zealously affected in a good thing. They grudged not at the liberty of the others who were dismissed. In doing the duties required by God, we must not regard the forwardness or backwardness of others, nor what they do, but what God looks for at our hands. He is a rare person who can endure that others should excel him in gifts or blessings, or in liberty; so that we may say, it is by the special grace of God that we regard what God says to us, and not look to men what they do.

Verses 9-15

The dream seemed to have little meaning in it; but the interpretation evidently proved the whole to be from the Lord, and discovered that the name of Gideon had filled the Midianites with terror. Gideon took this as a sure pledge of success; without delay he worshipped and praised God, and returned with confidence to his three hundred men. Wherever we are, we may speak to God, and worship him. God must have the praise of that which encourages our faith. And his providence must be acknowledged in events, though small and seemingly accidental.

Verses 16-22

This method of defeating the Midianites may be alluded to, as exemplifying the destruction of the devil's kingdom in the world, by the preaching of the everlasting gospel, the sounding that trumpet, and the holding forth that light out of earthen vessels, for such are the ministers of the gospel, 2Co 4:6, 7. God chose the foolish things of the world to confound the wise, a barley-cake to overthrow the tents of Midian, that the excellency of the power might be of God only. The gospel is a sword, not in the hand, but in the mouth: the sword of the Lord and of Gideon; of God and Jesus Christ, of Him that sits on the throne and the Lamb. The wicked are often led to avenge the cause of God upon each other, under the power of their delusions, and the fury of their passions. See also how God often makes the enemies of the church instruments to destroy one another; it is a pity that the church's friends should ever act like them.

Verses 23-25

Two chief commanders of the host of Midian were taken and slain by the men of Ephraim. It were to be wished that we all did as these did, and that where help is needed, that it were willingly and readily performed by another. And that if there were any excellent and profitable matter begun, we were willing to have fellow-labourers to the finishing and perfecting the same, and not, as often, hinder one another.

Chapter 8

Chapter Outline

Verses 1-3

Those who will not attempt or venture any thing in the cause of God, will be the most ready to censure and quarrel with such as are of a more zealous and enterprising spirit. And those who are the most backward to difficult services, will be the most angry not to have the credit of them. Gideon stands here as a great example of self-denial; and shows us that envy is best removed by humility. The Ephraimites had given vent to their passion in very wrong freedom of speech, a certain sign of a weak cause: reason runs low when chiding flies high.

Verses 4-12

Gideon's men were faint, yet pursuing; fatigued with what they had done, yet eager to do more against their enemies. It is many a time the true Christian's case, fainting, and yet pursuing. The world knows but little of the persevering and successful struggle the real believer maintains with his sinful heart. But he betakes himself to that Divine strength, in the faith of which he began his conflict, and by the supply of which alone he can finish it in triumph.

Verses 13-17

The active servants of the Lord meet with more dangerous opposition from false professors than from open enemies; but they must not care for the behaviour of those who are Israelites in name, but Midianites in heart. They must pursue the enemies of their souls, and of the cause of God, though they are ready to faint through inward conflicts and outward hardships. And they shall be enabled to persevere. The less men help, and the more they seek to hinder, the more will the Lord assist. Gideon's warning being slighted, the punishment was just. Many are taught with the briers and thorns of affliction, who would not learn otherwise.

Verses 18-21

The kings of Midian must be reckoned with. As they confessed themselves guilty of murder, Gideon acted as the avenger of blood, being the next of kin to the persons slain. Little did they think to have heard of this so long after; but murder seldom goes unpunished in this life. Sins long forgotten by man, must be accounted for to God. What poor consolation in death from the hope of suffering less pain, and of dying with less disgrace than some others! yet many are more anxious on these accounts, than concerning the future judgment, and what will follow.

Verses 22-28

Gideon refused the government the people offered him. No good man can be pleased with any honour done to himself, which belongs only to God. Gideon thought to keep up the remembrance of this victory by an ephod, made of the choicest of the spoils. But probably this ephod had, as usual, a teraphim annexed to it, and Gideon intended this for an oracle to be consulted. Many are led into false ways by one false step of a good man. It became a snare to Gideon himself, and it proved the ruin of the family. How soon will ornaments which feed the lust of the eye, and form the pride of life, as well as tend to the indulgences of the flesh, bring shame on those who are fond of them!

Verses 29-35

As soon as Gideon was dead, who kept the people to the worship of the God of Israel, they found themselves under no restraint; then they went after Baalim, and showed no kindness to the family of Gideon. No wonder if those who forget their God, forget their friends. Yet conscious of our own ingratitude to the Lord, and observing that of mankind in general, we should learn to be patient under any unkind returns we meet with for our poor services, and resolve, after the Divine example, not to be overcome of evil, but to overcome evil with good.

Chapter 9

Chapter Outline

Abimelech murders his brethren, and is made king.	(1–6)
Jotham rebukes the Shechemites.	(7–21)
The Shechemites conspire against Abimelech.	(22–29)
Abimelech destroys Shechem.	(30–49)
Abimelech slain.	(50–57)

Verses 1-6

The men of Shechem chose Abimelech king. God was not consulted whether they should have any king, much less who it should be. If parents could see what their children would do, and what they are to suffer, their joy in them often would be turned into sorrow: we may be thankful that we cannot know what shall happen. Above all, we should fear and watch against sin; for our evil conduct may produce fatal effects upon our families, after we are in our graves.

Verses 7-21

There was no occasion for the trees to choose a king, they are all the trees of the Lord which he has planted. Nor was there any occasion for Israel to set a king over them, for the Lord was their King. Those who bear fruit for the public good, are justly respected and honoured by all that are wise, more than those who merely make a figure. All these fruit-trees gave much the same reason for their refusal to be promoted over the trees; or, as the margin reads it, to go up and down for the trees. To rule, involves a man in a great deal both of toil and care. Those who are preferred to public trust and power, must forego all private interests and advantages, for the good of others. And those advanced to honour and dignity, are in great danger of losing their fruitfulness. For which reason, they that desire to do good, are afraid of being too great. Jotham compares Abimelech to the bramble or thistle, a worthless plant, whose end is to be burned. Such a one was Abimelech.

Verses 22-29

Abimelech is seated in the throne his father refused. But how long does this glory last? Stay but three years, and see the bramble withered and burned. The prosperity of the wicked is short and fickle. The Shechemites are plagued by no other hand than Abimelech's. They raised him unjustly to the throne; they first feel the weight of his sceptre.

Verses 30-49

Abimelech intended to punish the Schechemites for slighting him now, but God punished them for their serving him formerly in the murder of Gideon's sons. When God uses men as instruments in his hand to do his work, he means one thing, and they another. That, which they hoped would have been for their welfare, proved a snare and a trap, as those will certainly find, who run to idols for shelter; such will prove a refuge of lies. (Jdg 9:50-57)

Verses 50-57

The Shechemites were ruined by Abimelech; now he is reckoned with, who was their leader in villany. Evil pursues sinners, and sometimes overtakes them, when not only at ease, but triumphant. Though wickedness may prosper a while, it will not prosper always. The history of mankind, if truly told, would greatly resemble that of this chapter. The records of what are called splendid events present to us such contests for power. Such scenes, though praised of men, fully explain the Scripture doctrine of the deceitfulness and desperate wickedness of the human heart, the force of men's lust, and the effect of Satan's influence. Lord, thou has given us thy word of truth and righteousness, O pour upon us thy spirit of purity, peace, and love, and write thy holy law in our hearts.

Chapter 10

Chapter Outline

Tola and Jair judge Israel.	(1–5)
The Philistines and Ammonites oppress Israel.	(6–9)

Israel's repentance.   (10–18)

Verses 1-5

Quiet and peaceable reigns, though the best to live in, yield least variety of matter to be spoken of. Such were the days of Tola and Jair. They were humble, active, and useful men, rulers appointed of God.

Verses 6-9

Now the threatening was fulfilled, that the Israelites should have no power to stand before their enemies, Le 26:17, 37. By their evil ways and their evil doings they procured this to themselves.

Verses 10-18

God is able to multiply men's punishments according to the numbers of their sins and idols. But there is hope when sinners cry to the Lord for help, and lament their ungodliness as well as their more open transgressions. It is necessary, in true repentance, that there be a full conviction that those things cannot help us which we have set in competition with God. They acknowledged what they deserved, yet prayed to God not to deal with them according to their deserts. We must submit to God's justice, with a hope in his mercy. True repentance is not only for sin, but from sin. As the disobedience and misery of a child are a grief to a tender father, so the provocations of God's people are a grief to him. From him mercy never can be sought in vain. Let then the trembling sinner, and the almost despairing backslider, cease from debating about God's secret purposes, or from expecting to find hope from former experiences. Let them cast themselves on the mercy of God our Saviour, humble themselves under his hand, seek deliverance from the powers of darkness, separate themselves from sin, and from occasions of it, use the means of grace diligently, and wait the Lord's time, and so they shall certainly rejoice in his mercy.

Chapter 11

Chapter Outline

Jephtah and the Gileadites.   (1–11)

He attempts to make peace.   (12–28)

Jephthah's vow. He vanquishes the   (29–40)
Ammonites.

Verses 1-11

Men ought not to be blamed for their parentage, so long as they by their personal merits roll away any reproach. God had forgiven Israel, therefore Jephthah will forgive. He speaks not with confidence of his success, knowing how justly God might suffer the Ammonites to prevail for the further punishment of Israel. Nor does he speak with any confidence at all in himself. If he succeed, it is the Lord delivers them into his hand; he thereby reminds his countrymen to look up to God as the Giver of victory. The same question as here, in fact, is put to those who desire salvation by Christ. If he save you, will ye be willing that he shall rule you? On no other terms will he save you. If he make you happy, shall he make you holy? If he be your helper, shall he be your Head? Jephthah, to obtain a little worldly honour, was willing to expose his life: shall we be discouraged in our Christian warfare by the difficulties we may meet with, when Christ has promised a crown of life to him that overcometh?

Verses 12-28

One instance of the honour and respect we owe to God, as our God, is, rightly to employ what he gives us to possess. Receive it from him, use it for him, and part with it when he calls for it. The whole of this message shows that Jephthah was well acquainted with the books of Moses. His argument was clear, and his demand reasonable. Those who possess the most courageous faith, will be the most disposed for peace, and the readiest to make advances to obtain; but rapacity and ambition often cloak their designs under a plea of equity, and render peaceful endeavours of no avail.

Verses 29-40

Several important lessons are to be learned from Jephthah's vow. 1. There may be remainders of distrust and doubting, even in the hearts of true and great believers. 2. Our vows to God should not be as a purchase of the favour we desire, but to express gratitude to him. 3. We need to be very well-advised in making vows, lest we entangle ourselves. 4. What we have solemnly vowed to God, we must perform, if it be possible and lawful, though it be difficult and grievous to us. 5. It well becomes children, obediently and cheerfully to submit to their parents in the Lord. It is hard to say what Jephthah did in performance of his vow; but it is thought that he did not offer his daughter as a burnt-offering. Such a sacrifice would have been an abomination to the Lord; it is supposed she was obliged to remain unmarried, and apart from her family. Concerning this and some other such passages in the sacred history, about which learned men are divided and in doubt, we need not perplex ourselves; what is necessary to our salvation, thanks be to God, is plain enough. If the reader recollects the promise of Christ concerning the teaching of the Holy Spirit, and places himself under this heavenly Teacher, the Holy Ghost will guide to all truth in every passage, so far as it is needful to be understood.

Chapter 12

Chapter Outline

Verses 1-7

The Ephraimites had the same quarrel with Jephthah as with Gideon. Pride was at the bottom of the quarrel; only by that comes contention. It is ill to fasten names of reproach upon persons or countries, as is common, especially upon those under outward disadvantages. It often occasions quarrels that prove of ill consequence, as it did here. No contentions are so bitter as those between brethren or rivals for honour. What need we have to watch and pray against evil tempers! May the Lord incline all his people to follow after things which make for peace!

Verses 8-15

We have here a short account of three more of the judges of Israel. The happiest life of individuals, and the happiest state of society, is that which affords the fewest remarkable events. To live in credit and quiet, to be peacefully useful to those around us, to possess a clear conscience; but, above all, and without which nothing can avail, to enjoy communion with God our Saviour while we live, and to die at peace with God and man, form the substance of all that a wise man can desire.

Chapter 13

Chapter Outline

Verses 1-7

Israel did evil: then God delivered them again into the hands of the Philistines. When Israel was in this distress, Samson was born. His parents had been long childless. Many eminent persons were born of such mothers. Mercies long waited for, often prove signal mercies; and by them others may be encouraged to continue their hope in God's mercy. The angel notices her affliction. God often sends comfort to his people very seasonably, when they feel their troubles most. This deliverer of Israel must be devoted to God. Manoah's wife was satisfied that the messenger was of God. She gave her husband a particular account, both of the promise and of the precept. Husbands and wives should tell each other their experiences of communion with God, and their improvements in acquaintance with him, that they may help each other in the way that is holy.

Verses 8-14

Blessed are those who have not seen, and yet, as Manoah, have believed. Good men are more careful and desirous to know the duty to be done by them, than to know the events concerning them: duty is ours, events are God's. God will guide those by his counsel, who desire to know their duty, and apply to him to teach them. Pious parents, especially, will beg Divine assistance. The angel repeats the directions he had before given. There is need of much care for the right ordering both of ourselves and our children, that we may be duly separate from the world, and living sacrifices to the Lord.

Verses 15-23

What Manoah asked for instruction in his duty, he was readily told; but what he asked to gratify his curiosity, was denied. God has in his word given full directions concerning our duty, but never designed to answer other questionings. There are secret things which belong not to us, of which we must be quite contented to be ignorant, while in this world. The name of our Lord is wonderful and secret; but by his wonderful works he makes himself known as far as is needful for us. Prayer is the ascent of the soul to God. But without Christ in the heart by faith, our services are offensive smoke; in him, acceptable flame. We may apply this to Christ's sacrifice of himself for us; he ascended in the flame of his own offering, for by his own blood he entered in once into the holy place, Heb 9:12. In Manoah's reflections there is great fear; We shall surely die. In his wife's reflection there is great faith. As a help meet for him, she encouraged him. Let believers who have had communion with God in the word and prayer, to whom he has graciously manifested himself, and who have had reason to think God has accepted their works, take encouragement from thence in a cloudy and dark day. God would not have done what he has done for my soul, if he had designed to forsake me, and leave me to perish at last; for his work is perfect. Learn to reason as Manoah's wife; If God designed me to perish under his wrath, he would not give me tokens of his favour.

Verses 24, 25

The Spirit of the Lord began to move Samson when a youth. This was evidence that the Lord blessed him. Where God gives his blessing, he gives his Spirit to qualify for the blessing. Those are blessed indeed in whom the Spirit of grace begins to work in the days of their childhood. Samson drank no wine or strong drink, yet excelled in strength and courage, for he had the Spirit of God moving him; therefore be not drunk with wine, but be filled with the Spirit.

Chapter 14

Chapter Outline

Verses 1-4

As far as Samson's marriage was a common case, it was weak and foolish of him to set his affections upon a daughter of the Philistines. Shall one, not only an Israelite, but a Nazarite, devoted to the Lord, covet to become one with a worshipper of Dagon? It does not appear that he had any reason to think her wise or virtuous, or any way likely to be a help meet for him; but he saw something in her agreeable to his fancy. He that, in the choice of a wife, is only guided by his eye, and governed by his fancy, must afterwards thank himself if he find a Philistine in his arms. Yet it was well done not to proceed till Samson had made his parents acquainted with the matter. Children ought not to marry, nor to move towards it, without the advice and consent of their parents. Samson's parents did well to dissuade him from yoking himself unequally with unbelievers. It seems that it pleased God to leave Samson to follow his own inclinations, intending to bring out good from his conduct; and his parents consented, because he was bent upon it. However, his example is not recorded for us to do likewise.

Verses 5-9

By enabling him to kill a lion, God let Samson know what he could do in the strength of the Spirit of the Lord, that he might never be afraid to look the greatest difficulties in the face. He was alone in the vineyards, whither he had rambled. Young people consider not how they exposed themselves to the roaring lion that seeks to devour, when they wander from their prudent, pious parents. Nor do men consider what lions lurk in the vineyards, the vineyards of red wines. Our Lord Jesus having conquered Satan, that roaring lion, believers, like Samson, find honey in the carcass abundant strength and satisfaction, enough for themselves, and for all their friends.

Verses 10-20

Samson's riddle literally meant no more than that he had got honey, for food and for pleasure, from the lion, which in its strength and fury was ready to devour him. But the victory of Christ over Satan, by means of his humiliation, agonies, and death, and the exaltation that followed to him, with the glory thence to the Father, and spiritual advantages to his people, seem directly alluded to. And even death, that devouring monster, being robbed of his sting, and stripped of his horror, forwards the soul to the realms of bliss. In these and other senses, out of the eater comes forth meat, and out of the strong, sweetness. Samson's companions obliged his wife to get the explanation from him. A worldly wife, or a worldly friend, is to a godly man as an enemy in the camp, who will watch every opportunity to betray him. No union can be comfortable or lasting, where secrets cannot be intrusted, without danger of being divulged. Satan, in his temptations, could not do us the mischief he does, if he did not plough with the heifer of our corrupt nature. His chief advantage against us arises from his correspondence with our deceitful hearts and inbred lusts. This proved an occasion of weaning Samson from his new relations. It were well for us, if the unkindness we meet with from the world, and our disappointments in it, obliged us by faith and prayer to return to our heavenly Father's house, and to rest there. See how little confidence is to be put in man. Whatever pretence of friendship may be made, a real Philistine will soon be weary of a true Israelite.

Chapter 15

Chapter Outline

Samson is denied his wife, He smites the Philistines.	(1–8)
Samson kills a thousand of the Philistines with a jaw-bone.	(9–17)
His distress from thirst.	(18–20)

Verses 1-8

When there are differences between relations, let those be reckoned the wisest and best, who are most forward to forgive or forget, and most willing to stoop and yield for the sake of peace. In the means which Samson employed, we must look at the power of God supplying them, and making them successful, to mortify the pride and punish the wickedness of the Philistines. The Philistines threatened Samson's wife that they would burn her and her father's house. She, to save herself and oblige her countrymen, betrayed her husband; and the very thing that she feared, and by sin sought to avoid, came upon her! She, and her father's house, were burnt with fire, and by her countrymen, whom she thought to oblige by the wrong she did to her husband. The mischief we seek to escape by any unlawful practices, we often pull down upon our own heads.

Verses 9-17

Sin dispirits men, it hides from their eyes the things that belong to their peace. The Israelites blamed Samson for what he had done against the Philistines, as if he had done them a great injury. Thus our Lord Jesus did many good works, and for those the Jews were ready to stone him. When the Spirit of the Lord came upon Samson, his cords were loosed: where the Spirit of the Lord is, there is liberty, and those are free indeed who are thus set free. Thus Christ triumphed over the powers of darkness that shouted against him, as if they had him in their power. Samson made great destruction among the Philistines. To take the bone of an ass for this, was to do wonders by the foolish things of the world, that the excellency of the power might be of God, not of man. This victory was not in the weapon, was not in the arm; but it was in the Spirit of God, which moved the weapon by the arm. We can do all things through Him that strengtheneth us. Seest thou a poor Christian, who is enabled to overcome a temptation by weak, feeble counsel, there is the Philistine vanquished by a sorry jaw-bone.

Verses 18-20

So little notice did the men of Judah take of their deliverer, that he was ready to perish for want of a draught of water. Thus are the greatest slights often put upon those who do the greatest services. Samson prayed to God in this distress. Those that forget to attend God their praises, may be compelled to attend him with their prayers. Past experiences of God's power and goodness, are excellent pleas in prayer for further mercy. He pleads his being exposed to God's enemies; our best pleas are taken from God's glory. The Lord sent him seasonable relief. The place of this action was, from the jaw-bone, called Lehi. And in the place thus called, God caused a fountain suddenly and seasonably to open, close by Samson. We should be more thankful for the mercy of water, did we consider how ill we can spare it. Israel submitted to him whom they had betrayed. God was with him; henceforward they were directed by him as their judge.

Chapter 16

Chapter Outline

Verses 1-3

Hitherto Samson's character has appeared glorious, though uncommon. In this chapter we find him behaving in so wicked a manner, that many question whether or not he were a godly man. But the apostle has determined this, Heb 11:32. By adverting to the doctrines and examples of Scripture, the artifices of Satan, the deceitfulness of the human heart, and the methods in which the Lord frequently deals with his people, we may learn useful lessons from this history, at which some needlessly stumble, while others cavil and object. The peculiar time in which Samson lived may account for many things, which, if done in our time, and without the special appointment of Heaven, would be highly criminal. And there might have been in him many exercises of piety, which, if recorded, would have reflected a different light upon his character. Observe Samson's danger. Oh that all who indulge their sensual appetites in drunkenness, or any fleshly lusts, would see themselves thus surrounded, way-laid, and marked for ruin by their spiritual enemies! The faster they sleep, the more secure they feel, the greater their danger. We hope it was with a pious resolution not to return to his sin, that he rose under a fear of the danger he was in. Can I be safe under this guilt? It was bad that he lay down without such checks; but it would have been worse, if he had laid still under them.

Verses 4-17

Samson had been more than once brought into mischief and danger by the love of women, yet he would not take warning, but is again taken in the same snare, and this third time is fatal. Licentiousness is one of the things that take away the heart. This is a deep pit into which many have fallen; but from which few have escaped, and those by a miracle of mercy, with the loss of reputation and usefulness, of almost all, except their souls. The anguish of the suffering is ten thousand times greater than all the pleasures of the sin.

Verses 18-21

See the fatal effects of false security. Satan ruins men by flattering them into a good opinion of their own safety, and so bringing them to mind nothing, and fear nothing; and then he robs them of their strength and honour, and leads them captive at his will. When we sleep our spiritual enemies do not. Samson's eyes were the inlets of his sin, (ver. #(1),) and now his punishment began there. Now the Philistines blinded him, he had time to remember how his own lust had before blinded him. The best way to preserve the eyes, is, to turn them away from beholding vanity. Take warning by his fall, carefully to watch against all fleshly lusts; for all our glory is gone, and our defence departed from us, when our separation to God, as spiritual Nazarites, is profaned.

Verses 22-24

Samson's afflictions were the means of bringing him to deep repentance. By the loss of his bodily sight the eyes of his understanding were opened; and by depriving him of bodily strength, the Lord was pleased to renew his spiritual strength. The Lord permits some few to wander wide and sink deep, yet he recovers them at last, and marking his displeasure at sin in their severe temporal sufferings, preserves them from sinking into the pit of destruction. Hypocrites may abuse these examples, and infidels mock at them, but true Christians will thereby be rendered more humble, watchful, and circumspect; more simple in their dependence on the Lord, more fervent in prayer to be kept from falling, and in praise for being preserved; and, if they fall, they will be kept from sinking into despair.

Verses 25-31

Nothing fills up the sins of any person or people faster than mocking and misusing the servants of God, even thought it is by their own folly that they are brought low. God put it into Samson's heart, as a public person, thus to avenge on them God's quarrel, Israel's, and his own. That strength which he had lost by sin, he recovers by prayer. That it was not from passion or personal revenge, but from holy zeal for the glory of God and Israel, appears from God's accepting and answering the prayer. The house was pulled down, not by the natural strength of Samson, but by the almighty power of God. In his case it was right he should avenge the cause of God and Israel. Nor is he to be accused of self-murder. He sought not his own death, but Israel's deliverance, and the destruction of their enemies. Thus Samson died in bonds, and among the Philistines, as an awful rebuke for his sins; but he died repentant. The effects of his death typified those of the death of Christ, who, of his own will, laid down his life among transgressors, and thus overturned the foundation of Satan's kingdom, and provided for the deliverance of his people. Great as was the sin of Samson, and justly as he deserved the judgments he brought upon himself, he found mercy of the Lord at last; and every penitent shall obtain mercy, who flees for refuge to that Saviour whose blood cleanses from all sin. But here is nothing to encourage any to indulge sin, from a hope they shall at last repent and be saved.

Chapter 17

Chapter Outline

The beginning of idolatry in Israel, Micah and his mother.   (1–6)

Micah hires a Levite to be his priest.   (7–13)

Verses 1-6

What is related in this, and the rest of the chapters to the end of this book, was done soon after the death of Joshua: see chap. Jud 20:28. That it might appear how happy the nation was under the Judges, here is showed how unhappy they were when there was no Judge. The love of money made Micah so undutiful to his mother as to rob her, and made her so unkind to her son, as to curse him. Outward losses drive good people to their prayers, but bad people to their curses. This woman's silver was her god, before it was made into a graven or a molten image. Micah and his mother agreed to turn their money into a god, and set up idol worship in their family. See the cause of this corruption. Every man did that which was right in his own eyes, and then they soon did that which was evil in the sight of the Lord.

Verses 7-13

Micah thought it was a sign of God's favour to him and his images, that a Levite should come to his door. Thus those who please themselves with their own delusions, if Providence unexpectedly bring any thing to their hands that further them in their evil way, are apt from thence to think that God is pleased with them.

Chapter 18

The Danites seek to enlarge their inheritance, and rob Micah.

—The Danites determined to take Micah's gods with them. Oh the folly of these Danites! How could they imagine those gods should protect them, that could not keep themselves from being stolen! To take them for their own use, was a double crime; it showed they neither feared God, nor regarded man, but were lost both to godliness and honesty. What a folly was it for Micah to call those his gods, which he had made, when He only is to be worshipped by us as God, that made us! That is put in God's place, which we are concerned about, as if our all were bound up in it. If people will walk in the name of their false gods, much more should we love and serve the true God!

Chapter 19

The wickedness of the men of Gibeah.

—The three remaining chapters of this book contain a very sad history of the wickedness of the men of Gibeah, in Benjamin. The righteous Lord permits sinners to execute just vengeance on one another, and if the scene here described is horrible, what will the discoveries of the day of judgment be! Let each of us consider how to escape from the wrath to come, how to mortify the sins of our own hearts, to resist Satan's temptations, and to avoid the pollutions there are in the world.

Chapter 20

The tribe of Benjamin nearly extirpated.

—The Israelites' abhorrence of the crime committed at Gibeah, and their resolution to punish the criminals, were right; but they formed their resolves with too much haste and self-confidence. The eternal ruin of souls will be worse, and more fearful, than these desolations of a tribe.

Chapter 21

The Israelites lament for the Benjamites.

—Israel lamented for the Benjamites, and were perplexed by the oath they had taken, not to give their daughters to them in marriage. Men are more zealous to support their own authority than that of God. They would have acted better if they had repented of their rash oaths, brought sin-offerings, and sought forgiveness in the appointed way, rather than attempt to avoid the guilt of perjury by actions quite as wrong. That men can advise others to acts of treachery or violence, out of a sense of duty, forms a strong proof of the blindness of the human mind when left to itself, and of the fatal effects of a conscience under ignorance and error.

Ruth

We find in this book excellent examples of faith, piety, patience, humility, industry, and loving-kindness, in the common events of life. Also we see the special care which God's providence take of our smallest concerns, encouraging us to full trust therein. We may view this book as a beautiful, because natural representation of human life; as a curious detail of important facts; and as a part of the plan of redemption.

Chapter 1

Chapter Outline

Elimelech and his sons die in the land of Moab. (1–5)

Naomi returns home. (6–14)

Orpah stays behind, but Ruth goes with Naomi. (15–18)

They come to Bethlehem. (19–22)

Verses 1-5

Elimelech's care to provide for his family, was not to be blamed; but his removal into the country of Moab could not be justified. And the removal ended in the wasting of his family. It is folly to think of escaping that cross, which, being laid in our way, we ought to take up. Changing our place seldom is mending it. Those who bring young people into bad acquaintance, and take them out of the way of public ordinances, thought they may think them well-principled, and armed against temptation, know not what will be the end. It does not appear that the women the sons of Elimelech married, were proselyted to the Jewish religion. Earthly trials or enjoyments are of short continuance. Death continually removes those of every age and situation, and mars all our outward comforts: we cannot too strongly prefer those advantages which shall last for ever.

Verses 6-14

Naomi began to think of returning, after the death of her two sons. When death comes into a family, it ought to reform what is amiss there. Earth is made bitter to us, that heaven may be made dear. Naomi seems to have been a person of faith and piety. She dismissed her daughters-in-law with prayer. It is very proper for friends, when they part, to part with them thus part in love. Did Naomi do well, to discourage her daughters from going with her, when she might save them from the idolatry of Moab, and bring them to the faith and worship of the God of Israel? Naomi, no doubt, desired to do that; but if they went with her, she would not have them to go upon her account. Those that take upon them a profession of religion only to oblige their friends, or for the sake of company, will be converts of small value. If they did come with her, she would have them make it their deliberate choice, and sit down first and count the cost, as it concerns those to do who make a profession of religion. And more desire "rest in the house of a husband," or some wordly settlement or earthly satisfaction, than the rest to which Christ invites our souls; therefore when tried they will depart from Christ, though perhaps with some sorrow.

Verses 15-18

See Ruth's resolution, and her good affection to Naomi. Orpah was loth to part from her; yet she did not love her well enough to leave Moab for her sake. Thus, many have a value and affection for Christ, yet come short of salvation by him, because they will not forsake other things for him. They love him, yet leave him, because they do not love him enough, but love other things better. Ruth is an example of the grace of God, inclining the soul to choose the better part. Naomi could desire no more than the solemn declaration Ruth made. See the power of resolution; it silences temptation. Those that go in religious ways without a stedfast mind, stand like a door half open, which invites a thief; but resolution shuts and bolts the door, resists the devil and forces him to flee.

Verses 19-22

Naomi and Ruth came to Bethlehem. Afflictions will make great and surprising changes in a little time. May God, by his grace, fit us for all such changes, especially the great change!, Naomi signifies "pleasant," or "amiable;" Mara, "bitter," or "bitterness." She was now a woman of a sorrowful spirit. She had come home empty, poor, a widow and childless. But there is a fulness for believers of which they never can be emptied; a good part which shall not be taken from those who have it. The cup of affliction is a "bitter" cup, but she owns that the affliction came from God. It well becomes us to have our hearts humbled under humbling providences. It is not affliction itself, but affliction rightly borne, that does us good.

Chapter 2

Chapter Outline

Ruth gleans in the field of Boaz. (1–3)

The kindness of Boaz to Ruth. (4–16)

Ruth returns to her mother-in-law. (17–23)

Verses 1-3

Observe Ruth's humility. When Providence had made her poor, she cheerfully stoops to her lot. High spirits will rather starve than stoop; not so Ruth. Nay, it is her own proposal. She speaks humbly in her expectation of leave to glean. We may not demand kindness as a debt, but ask, and take it as a favour, though in a small matter. Ruth also was an example of industry. She loved not to eat the bread of idleness. This is an example to young people. Diligence promises well, both for this world and the other. We must not be shy of any honest employment. No labour is a reproach. Sin is a thing below us, but we must not think any thing else so, to which Providence call us. She was an example of regard to her mother, and of trust in Providence. God wisely orders what seem to us small events; and those that appear altogether uncertain, still are directed to serve his own glory, and the good of his people.

Verses 4-16

The pious and kind language between Boaz and his reapers shows that there were godly persons in Israel. Such language as this is seldom heard in our field; too often, on the contrary, what is immoral and corrupt. A stranger would form a very different opinion of our land, from that which Ruth would form of Israel from the converse and conduct of Boaz and his reapers. But true religion will teach a man to behave aright in all states and conditions; it will form kind masters and faithful servants, and cause harmony in families. True religion will cause mutual love and kindness among persons of different ranks. It had these effects on Boaz and his men. When he came to them he prayed for them. They did not, as soon as he was out of hearing curse him, as some ill-natured servants that hate their master's eye, but they returned his courtesy. Things are likely to go on well where there is such good-will as this between masters and servants. They expressed their kindness to each other by praying one for another. Boaz inquired concerning the stranger he saw, and ordered her to be well treated. Masters must take care, not only that they do no hurt themselves, but that they suffer not their servants and those under them to do wrong. Ruth humbly owned herself unworthy of favours, seeing she was born and brought up a heathen. It well becomes us all to think humbly of ourselves, esteeming others better than ourselves. And let us, in the kindness of Boaz to Ruth, note the kindness of the Lord Jesus Christ to poor sinners.

Verses 17-23

It encourages industry, that in all labour, even that of gleaning, there is profit. Ruth was pleased with what she gained by her own industry, and was careful to secure it. Let us thus take care that we lose not those things which we have wrought, which we have gained for our souls' good, 2Jo 1:8. Parents should examine their children, as Naomi did, not to frighten or discourage them, so as to make them hate home, or tempt them to tell a lie; but to commend them if they have done well, and with mildness to reprove and caution them if they have done otherwise. It is a good question for us to ask ourselves every night, Where have I gleaned to-day? What improvement have I made in knowledge and grace? What have I done that will turn to a good account? When the Lord deals bountifully with us, let us not be found in any other field, nor seeking for happiness and satisfaction in the creature. We lose Divine favours, if we slight them. Ruth dutifully observed her mother's directions. And when the harvest was ended, she kept her aged mother company at home. Dinah went out to see the daughters of the land; her vanity ended in disgrace, Ge 34. Ruth kept at home, and helped to maintain her mother, and went out on no other errand than to get provision for her; her humility and industry ended in preferment.

Chapter 3

Chapter Outline

Verses 1-5

The married state should be a rest, as much as any thing upon earth can be so, as it ought to fix the affections and form a connexion for life. Therefore it should be engaged in with great seriousness, with earnest prayers for direction, for the blessing of God, and with regard to his precepts. Parents should carefully advise their children in this important concern, that it may be well with them as to their souls. Be it always remembered, That is best for us which is best for our souls. The course Naomi advised appears strange to us; but it was according to the laws and usages of Israel. If the proposed measure had borne the appearance of evil, Naomi would not have advised it. Law and custom gave Ruth, who was now proselyted to the true religion, a legal claim upon Boaz. It was customary for widows to assert this claim, De 25:5–10. But this is not recorded for imitation in other times, and is not to be judged by modern rules. And if there had been any evil in it, Ruth was a woman of too much virtue and too much sense to have listened to it.

Verses 6-13

What in one age or nation would be improper, is not always so in another age or another nation. Being a judge of Israel, Boaz would tell Ruth what she should do; also whether he had the right of redemption, and what methods must be taken, and what rites used, in order to accomplishing her marriage with him or another person. The conduct of Boaz calls for the highest praise. He attempted not to take advantage of Ruth; he did not disdain her as a poor, destitute stranger, nor suspect her of any ill intentions. He spoke honourably of her as a virtuous woman, made her a promise, and as soon as the morning arrived, sent her away with a present to her mother-in-law. Boaz made his promise conditional, for there was a kinsman nearer than he, to whom the right of redemption belonged.

Verses 14-18

Ruth had done all that was fit for her to do, she must patiently wait the event. Boaz, having undertaken this matter, would be sure to manage it well. Much more reason have true believers to cast their care on God, because he has promised to care for them. Our strength is to sit still, Isa 30:7. This narrative may encourage us to lay ourselves by faith at the feet of Christ: He is our near Kinsman; having taken our nature upon him. He has the right to redeem. Let us seek to receive from him his directions: Lord, what wilt thou have me to do? Ac 9:6. He will never blame us as doing this unseasonably. And let us earnestly desire and seek the same rest for our children and friends, that it may be well with them also.

Chapter 4

Chapter Outline

Verses 1-8

This matter depended on the laws given by Moses about inheritances, and doubtless the whole was settled in the regular and legal manner. This kinsman, when he heard the conditions of the bargain, refused it. In like manner many are shy of the great redemption; they are not willing to espouse religion; they have heard well of it, and have nothing to say against it; they will give it their good word, but they are willing to part with it, and cannot be bound to it, for fear of marring their own inheritance in this world. The right was resigned to Boaz. Fair and open dealing in all matters of contract and trade, is what all must make conscience of, who would approve themselves true Israelites, without guile. Honesty will be found the best policy.

Verses 9-12

Men are ready to seize opportunities for increasing their estates, but few know the value of godliness. Such are the wise men of this world, whom the Lord charges with folly. They attend not to the concerns of their souls, but reject the salvation of Christ, for fear of marring their inheritance. But God did Boaz the honour to bring him into the line of the Messiah, while the kinsman, who was afraid of lessening himself, and marring his inheritance, has his name, family, and inheritance forgotten.

Verses 13-22

Ruth bore a son, through whom thousands and myriads were born to God; and in being the lineal ancestor of Christ, she was instrumental in the happiness of all that shall be saved by him; even of us Gentiles, as well as those of Jewish descent. She was a witness for God to the Gentile world, that he had not utterly forsaken them, but that in due time they should become one with his chosen people, and partake of his salvation. Prayer to God attended the marriage, and praise to him attended the birth of the child. What a pity it is that pious language should not be more used among Christians, or that it should be let fall into formality! Here is the descent of David from Ruth. And the period came when Bethlehem-Judah displayed greater wonders than those in the history of

Ruth, when the outcast babe of another forlorn female of the same race appeared, controlling the counsels of the Roman master of the world, and drawing princes and wise men from the east, with treasures of gold, and frankincense, and myrrh to his feet. His name shall endure for ever, and all nations shall call Him blessed. In that Seed shall all the nations of the earth be blessed.

1 Samuel

In this book we have an account of Eli, and the wickedness of his sons; also of Samuel, his character and actions. Then of the advancement of Saul to be the king of Israel, and his ill behaviour, until his death made way for David's succession to the throne, who was an eminent type of Christ. David's patience, modesty, constancy, persecution by open enemies and feigned friends, are a pattern and example to the church, and to every member of it. Many things in this book encourage the faith, hope, and patience of the suffering believer. It contains also many useful cautions and awful warnings.

Chapter 1

Chapter Outline

Elkanah and his family.	(1–8)
Hannah's prayer.	(9–18)
Samuel, Hannah presents him to the Lord.	(19–28)

Verses 1-8

Elkanah kept up his attendance at God's altar, notwithstanding the unhappy differences in his family. If the devotions of a family prevail not to put an end to its divisions, yet let not the divisions put a stop to the devotions. To abate our just love to any relation for the sake of any infirmity which they cannot help, and which is their affliction, is to make God's providence quarrel with his precept, and very unkindly to add affliction to the afflicted. It is evidence of a base disposition, to delight in grieving those who are of a sorrowful spirit, and in putting those out of humour who are apt to fret and be uneasy. We ought to bear one another's burdens, not add to them. Hannah could not bear the provocation. Those who are of a fretful spirit, and are apt to lay provocations too much to heart, are enemies to themselves, and strip themselves of many comforts both of life and godliness. We ought to notice comforts, to keep us from grieving for crosses. We should look at that which is for us, as well as what is against us.

Verses 9-18

Hannah mingled tears with her prayers; she considered the mercy of our God, who knows the troubled soul. God gives us leave, in prayer, not only to ask good things in general, but to mention that special good thing we most need and desire. She spoke softly, none could hear her. Hereby she testified her belief of God's knowledge of the heart and its desires. Eli was high priest, and judge in Israel. It ill becomes us to be rash and hasty in censures of others, and to think people guilty of bad things while the matter is doubtful and unproved. Hannah did not retort the charge, and upbraid Eli with the wicked conduct of his own sons. When we are at any time unjustly censured, we have need to set a double watch before the door of our lips, that we do not return censure for censure. Hannah thought it enough to clear herself, and so must we. Eli was willing to acknowledge his mistake. Hannah went away with satisfaction of mind. She had herself by prayer committed her case to God, and Eli had prayed for her. Prayer is heart's ease to a gracious soul. Prayer will smooth the countenance; it should do so. None will long remain miserable, who use aright the privilege of going to the mercy-seat of a reconciled God in Christ Jesus.

Verses 19-28

Elkanah and his family had a journey before them, and a family of children to take with them, yet they would not move till they had worshipped God together. Prayer and provender do not hinder a journey. When men are in such haste to set out upon journeys, or to engage in business, that they have not time to worship God, they are likely to proceed without his presence and blessing. Hannah, though she felt a warm regard for the courts of God's house, begged to stay at home. God will have mercy, and not sacrifice. Those who are detained from public ordinances, by the nursing and tending of little children, may take comfort from this instance, and believe, that if they do that duty in a right spirit, God will graciously accept them therein. Hannah presented her child to the Lord with a grateful acknowledgment of his goodness in answer to prayer. Whatever we give to God, it is what we have first asked and received from him. All our gifts to him were first his gifts to us. The child Samuel early showed true piety. Little children should be taught to worship God when very young. Their parents should teach them in it, bring them to it, and put them on doing it as well as they can; God will graciously accept them, and will teach them to do better.

Chapter 2

Chapter Outline

Verses 1-10

Hannah's heart rejoiced, not in Samuel, but in the Lord. She looks beyond the gift, and praises the Giver. She rejoiced in the salvation of the Lord, and in expectation of His coming, who is the whole salvation of his people. The strong are soon weakened, and the weak are soon strengthened, when God pleases. Are we poor? God made us poor, which is a good reason why we should be content, and make up our minds to our condition. Are we rich? God made us rich, which is a good reason why we should be thankful, and serve him cheerfully, and do good with the abundance he gives us. He respects not man's wisdom or fancied excellences, but chooses those whom the world accounts foolish, teaching them to feel their guilt, and to value his free and precious salvation. This prophecy looks to the kingdom of Christ, that kingdom of grace, of which Hannah speaks, after having spoken largely of the kingdom of providence. And here is the first time that we meet with the name MESSIAH, or his Anointed. The subjects of Christ's kingdom will be safe, and the enemies of it will be ruined; for the Anointed, the Lord Christ, is able to save, and to destroy.

Verses 11-26

Samuel, being devoted to the Lord in a special manner, was from a child employed about the sanctuary in the services he was capable of. As he did this with a pious disposition of mind, it was called ministering unto the Lord. He received a blessing from the Lord. Those young people who serve God as well as they can, he will enable to improve, that they may serve him better. Eli shunned trouble and exertion. This led him to indulge his children, without using parental authority to restrain and correct them when young. He winked at the abuses in the service of the sanctuary till they became customs, and led to abominations; and his sons, who should have taught those that engaged in the service of the sanctuary what was good, solicited them to wickedness. Their offence was committed even in offering the sacrifices for sins, which typified the atonement of the Saviour! Sins against the remedy, the atonement itself, are most dangerous, they tread under foot the blood of the covenant. Eli's reproof was far too mild and gentle. In general, none are more abandoned than the degenerate children of godly persons, when they break through restraints.

Verses 27-36

Those who allow their children in any evil way, and do not use their authority to restrain and punish them, in effect honour them more than God. Let Eli's example excite parents earnestly to strive against the beginnings of wickedness, and to train up their children in the nurture and admonition of the Lord. In the midst of the sentence against the house of Eli, mercy is promised to Israel. God's work shall never fall to the ground for want of hands to carry it on. Christ is that merciful and faithful High Priest, whom God raised up when the Levitical priesthood was thrown off, who in all things did his Father's mind, and for whom God will build a sure house, build it on a rock, so that hell cannot prevail against it.

Chapter 3

Chapter Outline

The word of the Lord first revealed to Samuel. (1–10)

God tells Samuel the destruction of Eli's house. (11–18)

Samuel established to be a prophet. (19–21)

Verses 1-10

The call which Divine grace designs shall be made effectual; will be repeated till it is so, till we come to the call. Eli, perceiving that it was the voice of God that Samuel heard, instructed him what to say. Though it was a disgrace to Eli, for God's call to be directed to Samuel, yet he told him how to meet it. Thus the elder should do their utmost to assist and improve the younger that are rising up. Let us never fail to teach those who are coming after us, even such as will soon be preferred before us, Joh 1:30. Good words should be put into children's mouths betimes, by which they may be prepared to learn Divine things, and be trained up to regard them.

Verses 11-18

What a great deal of guilt and corruption is there in us, concerning which we may say, It is the iniquity which our own heart knoweth; we are conscious to ourselves of it! Those who do not restrain the sins of others, when it is in their power to do it, make themselves partakers of the guilt, and will be charged as joining in it. In his remarkable answer to this awful sentence, Eli acknowledged that the Lord had a right to do as he saw good, being assured that he would do nothing wrong. The meekness, patience, and humility contained in those words, show that he was truly repentant; he accepted the punishment of his sin.

Verses 19-21

All increase in wisdom and grace, is owing to the presence of God with us. God will graciously repeat his visits to those who receive them aright. Early piety will be the greatest honour of young people. Those who honour God he will honour. Let young people consider the piety of Samuel, and from him they will learn to remember their Creator in the days of their youth. Young children are capable of religion. Samuel is a proof that their waiting upon the Lord will be pleasing to him. He is a pattern of all those amiable tempers, which are the brightest ornament of youth, and a sure source of happiness.

Chapter 4

Chapter Outline

Verses 1-9

Israel is smitten before the Philistines. Sin, the accursed thing, was in the camp, and gave their enemies all the advantage they could wish for. They own the hand of God in their trouble; but, instead of submitting, they speak angrily, as not aware of any just provocation they had given him. The foolishness of man perverts his way, and then his heart frets against the Lord, Pr 19:3, and finds fault with him. They supposed that they could oblige God to appear for them, by bringing the ark into their camp. Those who have gone back in the life of religion, sometimes discover great fondness for the outward observances of it, as if those would save them; and as if the ark, God's throne, in the camp, would bring them to heaven, though the world and the flesh are on the throne in the heart.

Verses 10, 11

The taking of the ark was a great judgment upon Israel, and a certain token of God's displeasure. Let none think to shelter themselves from the wrath of God, under the cloak of outward profession.

Verses 12-18

The defeat of the army was very grievous to Eli as a judge; the tidings of the death of his two sons, to whom he had been so indulgent, and who, as he had reason to fear, died impenitent, touched him as a father; yet there was a greater concern on his spirit. And when the messenger concluded his story with, "The ark of God is taken," he is struck to the heart, and died immediately. A man may die miserably, yet not die eternally; may come to an untimely end, yet the end be peace.

Verses 19-22

The wife of Phinehas seems to have been a person of piety. Her dying regret was for the loss of the ark, and the departure of the glory from Israel. What is any earthly joy to her that feels herself dying? No joy but that which is spiritual and divine, will stand in any stead then; death is too serious a thing to admit the relish of any earthly joy. What is it to one that is lamenting the loss of the ark? What pleasure can we take in our creature comforts and enjoyments, if we want God's word and ordinances; especially if we want the comfort of his gracious presence, and the light of his countenance? If God go, the glory goes, and all good goes. Woe unto us if he depart! But though the glory is withdrawn from one sinful nation, city, or village after another, yet it shall never depart altogether, but shines forth in one place when eclipsed in another.

Chapter 5

Chapter Outline

Dagon is broken before the ark.   (1–5)

The Philistine smitten.   (6–12)

Verses 1-5

See the ark's triumph over Dagon. Thus the kingdom of Satan will certainly fall before the kingdom of Christ, error before truth, profaneness before godliness, and corruption before grace in the hearts of the faithful. When the interests of religion seem to be ready to sink, even then we may be confident that the day of their triumph will come. When Christ, the true Ark of the covenant, really enters the heart of fallen man, which is indeed Satan's temple, all idols will fall, every endeavour to set them up again will be vain, sin will be forsaken, and unrighteous gain restored; the Lord will claim and possess the throne. But pride, self-love, and worldly lusts, though dethroned and crucified, still remain within us, like the stump of Dagon. Let us watch and pray that they may not prevail. Let us seek to have them more entirely destroyed.

Verses 6-12

The hand of the Lord was heavy upon the Philistines; he not only convinced them of their folly, but severely chastised their insolence. Yet they would not renounce Dagon; and instead of seeking God's mercy, they desired to get clear of his ark. Carnal hearts, when they smart under the judgments of God, would rather, if it were possible, put him far from them, than enter into covenant or communion with him, and seek him for their friend. But their devices to escape the Divine judgments only increase them. Those that fight against God will soon have enough of it.

Chapter 6

Chapter Outline

The Philistines consult how to send back the ark.	(1–9)
They bring it to Bethshemesh.	(10–18)
The people smitten for looking into the ark.	(19–21)

Verses 1-9

Seven months the Philistines were punished with the presence of the ark; so long it was a plague to them, because they would not send it home sooner. Sinners lengthen out their own miseries by refusing to part with their sins. The Israelites made no effort to recover the ark. Alas! where shall we find concern for religion prevail above all other matters? In times of public calamity we fear for ourselves, for our families, and for our country; but who cares for the ark of God? We are favoured with the gospel, but it is treated with neglect or contempt. We need not wonder if it should be taken from us; to many persons this, though the heavies of calamities, would occasion no grief. There are multitudes whom any profession would please as well as that of Christianity. But there are those who value the house, the word, and the ministry of God above their richest possessions, who dread the loss of these blessings more than death. How willing bad men are to shift off their convictions, and when they are in trouble, to believe it is a chance that happens; and that the rod has no voice which they should hear or heed!

Verses 10-18

These two kine knew their owner, their great Owner, whom Hophin and Phinehas knew not. God's providence takes notice even of brute creatures, and serves its own purposes by them. When the reapers saw the ark, they rejoiced; their joy for that was greater than the joy of harvest. The return of the ark, and the revival of holy ordinances, after days of restraint and trouble, are matters of great joy.

Verses 19-21

It is a great affront to God, for vain men to pry into, and meddle with the secret things which belong not to them, De 29:29; Col 2:18. Man was ruined by desiring forbidden knowledge. God will not suffer his ark to be profaned. Be not deceived, God is not mocked. Those that will not fear his goodness, and reverently use the tokens of his grace, shall be made to feel his justice. The number smitten is expressed in an unusual manner in the original, and it is probable that it means 1170. They desire to be rid of the ark. Foolish men run from one extreme to the other. They should rather have asked, How may we have peace with God, and recover his favor? Mic 6:6, 7. Thus, when the word of God works with terror on sinners' consciences, they, instead of taking the blame and shame to themselves, quarrel with the word, and put that from them. Many stifle their convictions, and put salvation away from them.

Chapter 7

Chapter Outline

Verses 1-4

God will find a resting-place for his ark; if some thrust it from them, the hearts of others shall be inclined to receive it. It is no new thing for God's ark to be in a private house. Christ and his apostles preached from house to house, when they could not have public places. Twenty years passed before the house of Israel cared for the want of the ark. During this time the prophet Samuel laboured to revive true religion. The few words used are very expressive; and this was one of the most effectual revivals of religion which ever took place in Israel.

Verses 5, 6

Israel drew water and poured it out before the Lord; signifying their humiliation and sorrow for sin. They pour out their hearts in repentance before the Lord. They were free and full in their confession, and fixed in their resolution to cast away from them all their wrong doings. They made a public confession, We have sinned against the Lord; thus giving glory to God, and taking shame to themselves. And if we thus confess our sins, we shall find our God faithful and just to forgive us our sins.

Verses 7-12

The Philistines invaded Israel. When sinners begin to repent and reform, they must expect that Satan will muster all his force against them, and set his instruments at work to the utmost, to oppose and discourage them. The Israelites earnestly beg Samuel to pray for them. Oh what a comfort it is to all believers, that our great Intercessor above never ceases, is never silent! for he always appears in the presence of God for us. Samuel's sacrifice, without his prayer, had been an empty shadow. God gave a gracious answer. And Samuel erected a memorial of this victory, to the glory of God, and to encourage Israel. Through successive generations, the church of God has had cause to set up Eben-ezers for renewed deliverances; neither outward persecutions nor inward corruptions have prevailed against her, because "hitherto the Lord hath helped her:" and he will help, even to the end of the world.

Verses 13-17

In this great revival of true religion, the ark was neither removed to Shiloh, nor placed with the tabernacle any where else. This disregard to the Levitical institutions showed that their typical meaning formed their chief use; and when that was overlooked, they became a lifeless service, not to be compared with repentance, faith, and the love of God and man.

Chapter 8

Chapter Outline

The evil government of Samuel's sons.	(1–3)
The Israelites ask for a king.	(4–9)
The manner of a king.	(10–22)

Verses 1-3

It does not appear that Samuel's sons were so profane and vicious as Eli's sons; but they were corrupt judges, they turned aside after lucre. Samuel took no bribes, but his sons did, and then they perverted judgment. What added to the grievance of the people was, that they were threatened by an invasion from Nahash, king of the Ammonites.

Verses 4-9

Samuel was displeased; he could patiently bear what reflected on himself, and his own family; but it displeased him when they said, Give us a king to judge us, because that reflected upon God. It drove him to his knees. When any thing disturbs us, it is our interest, as well as our duty, to show our trouble before God. Samuel is to tell them that they shall have a king. Not that God was pleased with their request, but as sometimes he opposes us from loving-kindness, so at other times he gratifies us in wrath; he did so here. God knows how to bring glory to himself, and serves his own wise purposes, even by men's foolish counsels.

Verses 10-22

If they would have a king to rule them, as the eastern kings ruled their subjects, they would find the yoke exceedingly heavy. Those that submit to the government of the world and the flesh, are told plainly, what hard masters they are, and what tyranny the dominion of sin is. The law of God and the manner of men widely differ from each other; the former should be our rule in the several relations of life; the latter should be the measure of our expectations from others. These would be their grievances, and, when they complained to God, he would not hear them. When we bring ourselves into distress by our own wrong desires and projects, we justly forfeit the comfort of prayer, and the benefit of Divine aid. The people were obstinate and urgent in their demand. Sudden resolves and hasty desires make work for long and leisurely repentance. Our wisdom is, to be thankful for the advantages, and patient under the disadvantages of the government we may live under; and to pray continually for our rulers, that they may govern us in the fear of God, and that we may live under them in all godliness and honesty. And it is a hopeful symptom when our desires of worldly objects can brook delay; and when we can refer the time and manner of their being granted to God's providence.

Chapter 9

Chapter Outline

Verses 1-10

Saul readily went to seek his father's asses. His obedience to his father was praise-worthy. His servant proposed, that since they were now at Ramah, they should call on Samuel, and take his advice. Wherever we are, we should use our opportunities of acquainting ourselves with those who are wise and good. Many will consult a man of God, if he comes in their way, that would not go a step out of their way to get wisdom. We sensibly feel worldly losses, and bestow much pains to make them up; but how little do we attempt, and how soon are we weary, in seeking the salvation of our souls! If ministers could tell men how to secure their property, or to get wealth, they would be more consulted and honoured than they now are, though employed in teaching them how to escape eternal misery, and to obtain eternal life. Most people would rather be told their fortune than their duty. Samuel needed not their money, nor would he have denied his advice, if they had not brought it; but they gave it to him as a token of respect, and of the value they put upon his office, and according to the general usage of those times, always to bring a present to those in authority.

Verses 11-17

The very maid-servants of the city could direct to the prophet. They had heard of the sacrifice, and could tell of the necessity for Samuel's presence. It is no small benefit to live in religious and holy places. And we should always be ready to help those who are seeking after God's prophets. Though God had, in displeasure, granted Israel's request for a king, yet he sends them a man to be captain over them, to save them out of the hand of the Philistines. He does it, listening graciously to their cry.

Verses 18-27

Samuel, that good prophet, was so far from envying Saul, or bearing him any ill-will, that he was the first and most forward to do him honour. Both that evening and early the next morning, Samuel communed with Saul upon the flat roof of the house. We may suppose Samuel now convinced Saul that he was the person God had fixed upon for the government, and of his own willingness to resign. How different are the purposes of the Lord for us, from our intentions for ourselves! Perhaps Saul was the only one who ever went out to seek asses, and literally found a kingdom; but many have set out and moved their dwellings to seek riches and pleasures, who have been guided to places where they found salvation for their souls. Thus they have met with those who addressed them as if aware of the secrets of their lives and hearts, and have been led seriously to regard the word of the Lord. If this has been our case, though our worldly plans have not prospered, let us not care for that; the Lord has given us, or has prepared us for, what is far better.

Chapter 10

Chapter Outline

Verses 1-8

The sacred anointing, then used, pointed at the great Messiah, or Anointed One, the King of the church, and High Priest of our profession, who was anointed with the oil of the Spirit, not by measure, but without measure, and above all the priests and princes of the Jewish church. For Saul's further satisfaction, Samuel gives him some signs which should come to pass the same day. The first place he directs him to, was the sepulchre of one of his ancestors; there he must be reminded of his own mortality, and now that he had a crown before him, must think of his grave, in which all his honour would be laid in the dust. From the time of Samuel there appears to have been schools, or places where pious young men were brought up in the knowledge of Divine things. Saul should find himself strongly moved to join with them, and should be turned into another man from what he had been. The Spirit of God changes men, wonderfully transforms them. Saul, by praising God in the communion of saints, became another man, but it may be questioned if he became a new man.

Verses 9-16

The signs Samuel had given Saul, came to pass punctually; he found that God had given him another heart, another disposition of mind. Yet let not an outward show of devotion, and a sudden change for the present, be too much relied on; Saul among the prophets was Saul still. His being anointed was kept private. He leaves it to God to carry on his own work by Samuel, and sits still, to see how the matter will fall.

Verses 17-27

Samuel tells the people, Ye have this day rejected your God. So little fond was Saul now of that power, which soon after, when he possessed it, he could not think of parting with, that he hid himself. It is good to be conscious of our unworthiness and insufficiency for the services to which we are called; but men should not go into the contrary extreme, by refusing the employments to which the Lord and the church call them. The greater part of the people treated the matter with indifference. Saul modestly went home to his own house, but was attended by a band of men whose hearts God disposed to support his authority. If the heart bend at any time the right way, it is because He has touched it. One touch is enough when it is Divine. Others despised him. Thus differently are men affected to our exalted Redeemer. There is a remnant who submit to him, and follow him wherever he goes; they are those whose hearts God has touched, whom he has made willing. But there are others who despise him, who ask, How shall this man save us? They are offended in him, and they will be punished.

Chapter 11

Chapter Outline

Jabesh-gilead delivered.

(1–11)

Saul confirmed in his kingdom.

(12–15)

Verses 1-11

The first fruit of Saul's government was the rescue of Jabesh-gilead from the Ammonites. To save their lives, men will part with liberty, and even consent to have their eyes put out; is it then no wisdom to part with that sin which is as dear to us as our right eye, rather than to be cast into hell-fire? See the faith and confidence of Saul, and, grounded thereon, his courage and resolution. See also his activity in this business. When the Spirit of the Lord comes upon men, it will make them expert, even without experience. When zeal for the glory of God, and love for the brethren, urge men to earnest efforts, and when God is pleased to help, great effects may speedily be produced.

Verses 12-15

They now honoured Saul whom they had despised; and if an enemy be made a friend, that is more to our advantage than to have him slain. The once despised Saviour will at length be acknowledged by all as the Lord's own anointed king. As yet, upon his mercy-seat, he receives the submission of rebels, and even pleads their cause; but shortly, from his righteous tribunal, he will condemn all who persist in opposing him.

Chapter 12

Chapter Outline

Samuel testifies his integrity.

(1–5)

Samuel reproves the people.

(6–15)

Thunder sent in harvest time.

(16–25)

Verses 1-5

Samuel not only cleared his own character, but set an example before Saul, while he showed the people their ingratitude to God and to himself. There is a just debt which all men to their own good name, especially men in public stations, which is, to guard it against unjust blame and suspicions, that they may finish their course with honour, as well as with joy. And that we have in our places lived honestly, will be our comfort, under any slights and contempt that may be put upon us.

Verses 6-15

The work of ministers is to reason with people; not only to exhort and direct, but to persuade, to convince men's judgments, and so to gain their wills and affections. Samuel reasons of the righteous acts of the Lord. Those who follow God faithfully, he will enable to continue following him. Disobedience would certainly be the ruin of Israel. We mistake if we think that we can escape God's justice, by trying to shake off his dominion. If we resolve that God shall not rule us, yet he will judge us.

Verses 16-25

At Samuel's word, God sent thunder and rain, at a season of the year when, in that country, the like was not seen. This was to convince them they had done wickedly in asking a king; not only by its coming at an unusual time, in wheat harvest, and on a clear day, but by the prophet's giving notice of it before. He showed their folly in desiring a king to save them, rather than God, or Samuel; promising themselves more from an arm of flesh, than from the arm of God, or from the power of prayer. Could their prince command such forces as the prophet could do by his prayers? It startled them very much. Some will not be brought to see their sins by any gentler methods than storms and thunders. They entreat Samuel to pray for them. Now they see their need of him whom shortly before they slighted. Thus many who will not have Christ to reign over them, would yet be glad to have him intercede for them, to turn away the wrath of God. Samuel aims to confirm the people in their religion. Whatever we make a god of, we shall find it deceive us. Creatures in their own places are good; but when put in God's place, they are vain things. We sin if we restrain prayer, and in particular if we cease praying for the church. They only asked him to pray for them; but he promises to do more, to teach them. He urges that they were bound in gratitude to serve God, considering what great things he had done for them; and that they were bound in interest to serve him, considering what he would do against them, if they should still do wickedly. Thus, as a faithful watchman, he gave them warning, and so delivered his own soul. If we consider what great things the Lord hath done for us, especially in the great work of redemption, we can neither want motive, encouragement, nor assistance in serving him.

Chapter 13

Chapter Outline

Verses 1-7

Saul reigned one year, and nothing particular happened; but in his second year the events recorded in this chapter took place. For above a year he gave the Philistine time to prepare for war, and to weaken and to disarm the Israelites. When men are lifted up in self-sufficiency, they are often led into folly. The chief advantages of the enemies of the church are derived from the misconduct of its professed friends. When Saul at length sounded an alarm, the people, dissatisfied with his management, or terrified by the power of the enemy, did not come to him, or speedily deserted him.

Verses 8-14

Saul broke the order expressly given by Samuel, see ch. 1Sa 10:8, as to what should be done in cases of extremity. Saul offered sacrifice without Samuel, and did it himself, though he was neither priest nor prophet. When charged with disobedience, he justified himself in what he had done, and gave no sign of repentance for it. He would have this act of disobedience pass for an instance of his prudence, and as a proof of his piety. Men destitute of inward piety, often lay great stress on the outward performances of religion. Samuel charges Saul with being an enemy to himself. Those that disobey the commandments of God, do foolishly for themselves. Sin is folly, and the greatest sinners are the greatest fools. Our disposition to obey or disobey God, will often be proved by our behaviour in things which appear small. Men see nothing but Saul's outward act, which seems small; but God saw that he did this with unbelief and distrust of his providence, with contempt of his authority and justice, and with rebellion against the light of his own conscience. Blessed Saviour, may we never, like Saul, bring our poor offerings, or fancied peace-offerings, without looking to thy precious, thy all-sufficient sacrifice! Thou only, O Lord, canst make, or hast made, our peace in the blood of the cross.

Verses 15-23

See how politic the Philistines were when they had power; they not only prevented the people of Israel from making weapons of war, but obliged them to depend upon their enemies, even for instruments of husbandry. How impolitic Saul was, who did not, in the beginning of his reign, set himself to redress this. Want of true sense always accompanies want of grace. Sins which appear to us very little, have dangerous consequences. Miserable is a guilty, defenceless nation; much more those who are destitute of the whole armour of God.

Chapter 14

Chapter Outline

Verses 1-15

Saul seems to have been quite at a loss, and unable to help himself. Those can never think themselves safe who see themselves out of God's protection. Now he sent for a priest and the ark. He hopes to make up matters with the Almighty by a partial reformation, as many do whose hearts are unhumbled and unchanged. Many love to have ministers who prophesy smooth things to them. Jonathan felt a Divine impulse and impression, putting him upon this bold adventure. God will direct the steps of those that acknowledge him in all their ways, and seek to him for direction, with full purpose of heart to follow his guidance. Sometimes we find most comfort in that which is least our own doing, and into which we have been led by the unexpected but well-observed turns of Divine providence. There was trembling in the host. It is called a trembling of God, signifying, not only a great trembling they could not resist, nor reason themselves out of, but that it came at once from the hand of God. He that made the heart, knows how to make it tremble.

Verses 16-23

The Philistines were, by the power of God, set against one another. The more evident it was that God did all, the more reason Saul had to inquire whether God would give him leave to do any thing. But he was in such haste to fight a fallen enemy, that he would not stay to end his devotions, nor hear what answer God would give him. He that believeth, will not make such haste, nor reckon any business so urgent, as not to allow time to take God with him.

Verses 24-35

Saul's severe order was very unwise; if it gained time, it lost strength for the pursuit. Such is the nature of our bodies, that daily work cannot be done without daily bread, which therefore our Father in heaven graciously gives. Saul was turning aside from God, and now he begins to build altars, being then most zealous, as many are, for the form of godliness when he was denying the power of it.

Verses 36-46

If God turns away our prayer, we have reason to suspect it is for some sin harboured in our hearts, which we should find out, that we may put it away, and put it to death. We should always first suspect and examine ourselves; but an unhumbled heart suspects every other person, and looks every where but at home for the sinful cause of calamity. Jonathan was discovered to be the offender. Those most indulgent to their own sins are most severe upon others; those who most disregard God's authority, are most impatient when their own commands are slighted. Such as cast abroad curses, endanger themselves and their families. What do we observe in the whole of Saul's behaviour on this occasion, but an impetuous, proud, malignant, impious disposition? And do we not in every instance perceive that man, left to himself, betrays the depravity of his nature, and is enslaved to the basest tempers.

Verses 47-52

Here is a general account of Saul's court and camp. He had little reason to be proud of his royal dignity, nor had any of his neighbours cause to envy him, for he had but little enjoyment after he took the kingdom. And often men's earthly glory makes a blaze just before the dark night of disgrace and woe comes on them.

Chapter 15

Chapter Outline

Verses 1-9

The sentence of condemnation against the Amalekites had gone forth long before, Ex 17:14; De 25:19, but they had been spared till they filled up the measure of their sins. We are sure that the righteous Lord does no injustice to any. The remembering the kindness of the ancestors of the Kenites, in favour to them, at the time God was punishing the injuries done by the ancestors of the Amalekites, tended to clear the righteousness of God in this dispensation. It is dangerous to be found in the company of God's enemies, and it is our duty and interest to come out from among them, lest we share in their sins and plagues, Re 18:4. As the commandment had been express, and a test of Saul's obedience, his conduct evidently was the effect of a proud, rebellious spirit. He destroyed only the refuse, that was good for little. That which was now destroyed was sacrificed to the justice of God.

Verses 10-23

Repentance in God is not a change of mind, as it is in us, but a change of method. The change was in Saul; "He is turned back from following me." Hereby he made God his enemy. Samuel spent a whole night in pleading for Saul. The rejection of sinners is the grief of believers: God delights not in their death, nor should we. Saul boasts to Samuel of his obedience. Thus sinners think, by justifying themselves, to escape being judged of the Lord. The noise the cattle made, like the rust of the silver, Jas 5:3, witnessed against him. Many boast of obedience to the command of God; but what means then their indulgence of the flesh, their love of the world, their angry and unkind spirit, and their neglect of holy duties, which witness against them? See of what evil covetousness is the root; and see what is the sinfulness of sin, and notice that in it which above any thing else makes it evil in the sight of the Lord; it is disobedience: "Thou didst not obey the voice of the Lord." Carnal, deceitful hearts, like Saul, think to excuse themselves from God's commandments by what pleases themselves. It is hard to convince the children of disobedience. But humble, sincere, and conscientious obedience to the will of God, is more pleasing and acceptable to him than all burnt-offering and sacrifices. God is more glorified and self more denied, by obedience than by sacrifice. It is much easier to bring a bullock or lamb to be burned upon the altar, than to bring every high thought into obedience to God, and to make our will subject to his will. Those are unfit and unworthy to rule over men, who are not willing that God should rule over them.

Verses 24-31

There were several signs of hypocrisy in Saul's repentance. 1. He besought Samuel only, and seemed most anxious to stand right in his opinion, and to gain his favour. 2. He excuses his fault, even when confessing it; that is never the way of a true penitent. 3. All his care was to save his credit, and preserve his interest in the people. Men are fickle and alter their minds, feeble and cannot effect their purposes; something happens they could not foresee, by which their measures are broken; but with God it is not so. The Strength of Israel will not lie.

Verses 32-35

Many think the bitterness of death is past when it is not gone by; they put that evil day far from them, which is very near. Samuel calls Agag to account for his own sins. He followed the example of his ancestors' cruelty, justly therefore is all the righteous blood shed by Amalek required. Saul seems unconcerned at the token of God's displeasure which he lay under, yet Samuel mourns day and night for him. Jerusalem was carnally secure while Christ wept over it. Do we desire to do the whole will of God? Turn to him, not in form and appearance, but with sincerity.

Chapter 16

Chapter Outline

Samuel sent to Bethlehem to Jesse.	(1–5)
David is anointed.	(6–13)
Saul troubled with an evil spirit, is quieted by David.	(14–23)

Verses 1-5

It appears that Saul was grown very wicked. Of what would he not be guilty, who durst think to kill Samuel? The elders of Bethlehem trembled at Samuel's coming. It becomes us to stand in awe of God's messengers, and to tremble at his word. His answer was, I come peaceably, for I come to sacrifice. When our Lord Jesus came into the world, though men had reason to fear that his errand was to condemn the world, yet he gave full assurance that he came peaceably, for he came to sacrifice, and he brought his offering with him; A body hast thou prepared me. Let us sanctify ourselves, and depend upon His sacrifice.

Verses 6-13

It was strange that Samuel, who had been so disappointed in Saul, whose countenance and stature recommended him, should judge of another man by that rule. We can tell how men look, but God can tell what they are. He judges of men by the heart. We often form a mistaken judgment of characters; but the Lord values only the faith, fear, and love, which are planted in the heart, beyond human discernment. And God does not favour our children according to our fond partiality, but often most honours and blesses those who have been least regarded. David at length was pitched upon. He was the youngest of the sons of Jesse; his name signifies Beloved; he was a type of God's beloved Son. It should seem, David was least set by of all the sons of Jesse. But the Spirit of the Lord came upon David from that day forward. His anointing was not an empty ceremony, a Divine power went with that instituted sign; he found himself advanced in wisdom and courage, with all the qualifications of a prince, though not advanced in his outward circumstances. This would satisfy him that his election was of God. The best evidence of our being predestinated to the kingdom of glory, is, our being sealed with the Spirit of promise, and experience of a work of grace in our hearts.

Verses 14-23

Saul is made a terror to himself. The Spirit of the Lord departed from him. If God and his grace do not rule us, sin and Satan will have possession of us. The devil, by the Divine permission, troubled and terrified Saul, by the corrupt humours of his body, and passions of his mind. He grew fretful, peevish, and discontented, and at times a madman. It is a pity that music, which may be serviceable to the good temper of the mind, should ever be abused, to support vanity and luxury, and made an occasion of drawing the heart from God and serious things. That is driving away the good Spirit, not the evil spirit. Music, diversions, company, or business, have for a time often been employed to quiet the wounded conscience; but nothing can effect a real cure but the blood of Christ, applied in faith, and the sanctifying Spirit sealing the pardon, by his holy comforts. All other plans to dispel religious melancholy are sure to add to distress, either in this world or the next.

Chapter 17

Chapter Outline

and goes to meet him.   (40–47)

He kills Goliath.   (48–58)

Verses 1-11

Men so entirely depend upon God in all things, that when he withdraws his help, the most valiant and resolute cannot find their hearts or hands, as daily experience shows.

Verses 12-30

Jesse little thought of sending his son to the army at that critical juncture; but the wise God orders actions and affairs, so as to serve his designs. In times of general formality and lukewarmness, every degree of zeal which implies readiness to go further, or to venture more in the cause of God than others, will be blamed as pride and ambition, and by none more than by near relations, like Eliab, or negligent superiors. It was a trial of David's meekness, patience, and constancy. He had right and reason on his side, and did not render railing for railing; with a soft answer he turned away his brother's wrath. This conquest of his own passion was more honourable than that of Goliath. Those who undertake great and public services, must not think it strange if they are spoken ill of, and opposed by those from whom they expect support and assistance. They must humbly go on with their work, in the face not only of enemies' threats, but of friends' slights and suspicions.

Verses 31-39

A shepherd lad, come the same morning from keeping sheep, had more courage than all the mighty men of Israel. Thus God often sends good words to his Israel, and does great things for them, by the weak and foolish things of the world. As he had answered his brother's passion with meekness, so David answered Saul's fear with faith. When David kept sheep, he proved himself very careful and tender of his flock. This reminds us of Christ, the good Shepherd, who not only ventured, but laid down his life for the sheep. Our experience ought to encourage us to trust in God, and be bold in the way of duty. He that has delivered, does and will continue to do so. David gained leave to fight the Philistine. Not being used to such armour as Saul put upon him, he was not satisfied to go in that manner; this was from the Lord, that it might more plainly appear he fought and conquered in faith, and that the victory was from Him who works by the feeblest and most despised means and instruments. It is not to be inquired how excellent any thing is, but how proper. Let Saul's coat be ever so rich, and his armour ever so strong, what is David the better if they fit him not? But faith, prayer, truth, and righteousness; the whole armour of God, and the mind that was in Christ; are equally needful for all the servants of the Lord, whatever may be their work.

Verses 40-47

The security and presumption of fools destroy them. Nothing can excel the humility, faith, and piety which appear in David's words. He expressed his assured expectation of success; he gloried in his mean appearance and arms, that the victory might be ascribed to the Lord alone.

Verses 48-58

See how frail and uncertain life is, even when a man thinks himself best fortified; how quickly, how easily, and by how small a matter, the passage may be opened for life to go out, and death to enter! Let not the strong man glory in his strength, nor the armed man in his armour. God resists the proud, and pours contempt on those who defy him and his people. No one ever hardened his heart against God and prospered. The history is recorded, that all may exert themselves for the honour of God, and the support of his cause, with bold and unshaken reliance on him. There is one conflict in which all the followers of the Lamb are, and must be engaged; one enemy, more formidable than Goliath, still challenges the armies of Israel. But "resist the devil, and he will flee from you." Go forth to battle with the faith of David, and the powers of darkness shall not stand against you. But how often is the Christian foiled through an evil heart of unbelief!

Chapter 18

Chapter Outline

Jonathan's friendship for David.   (1–5)

Saul seeks to kill David.   (6–11)

Saul's fear of David.   (12–30)

Verses 1-5

The friendship of David and Jonathan was the effect of Divine grace, which produces in true believers one heart and one soul, and causes them to love each other. This union of souls is from partaking in the Spirit of Christ. Where God unites hearts, carnal matters are too weak to separate them. Those who love Christ as their own souls, will be willing to join themselves to him in an everlasting covenant. It was certainly a great proof of the power of God's grace in David, that he was able to bear all this respect and honour, without being lifted up above measure.

Verses 6-11

David's troubles not only immediately follow his triumphs, but arise from them; such is the vanity of that which seems greatest in this world. It is a sign that the Spirit of God is departed from men, if, like Saul, they are peevish, envious, suspicious, and ill-natured. Compare David, with his harp in his hand, aiming to serve Saul, and Saul, with his javelin in his hand, aiming to slay David; and observe the sweetness and usefulness of God's persecuted people, and the barbarity of their persecutors. But David's safety must be ascribed to God's providence.

Verses 12-30

For a long time David was kept in continual apprehension of falling by the hand of Saul, yet he persevered in meek and respectful behaviour towards his persecutor. How uncommon is such prudence and discretion, especially under insults and provocations! Let us inquire if we imitate this part of the exemplary character before us. Are we behaving wisely in all our ways? Is there no sinful omission, no rashness of spirit, nothing wrong in our conduct? Opposition and perverseness in others, will not excuse wrong tempers in us, but should increase our care, and attention to the duties of our station. Consider Him that endured contradiction of sinners against himself, lest ye be weary and faint in your minds, Heb 12:3. If David magnified the honour of being son-in-law to king Saul, how should we magnify the honour of being sons to the King of kings!

Chapter 19

Chapter Outline

Verses 1-10

How forcible are right words! Saul was, for a time, convinced of the unreasonableness of his enmity to David; but he continued his malice against David. So incurable is the hatred of the seed of the serpent against that of the woman; so deceitful and desperately wicked is the heart of man without the grace of God, Jer 17:9.

Verses 11-24

Michal's stratagem to gain time till David got to a distance was allowable, but her falsehood had not even the plea of necessity to excuse it, and manifests that she was not influenced by the same spirit of piety which had dictated Jonathan's language to Saul. In flying to Samuel, David made God his refuge. Samuel, as a prophet, was best able to advise him what to do in this day of distress. He met with little rest or satisfaction in Saul's court, therefore went to seek it in Samuel's church. What little pleasure is to be had in this world, those have who live a life of communion with God; to that David returned in the time of trouble. So impatient was Saul after David's blood, so restless against him, that although baffled by one providence after another, he could not see that David was under the special protection of God. And when God will take this way to protect David, even Saul prophesies. Many have great gifts, yet no grace; they may prophesy in Christ's name, yet are disowned by him. Let us daily seek for renewing grace, which shall be in us as a well of water springing up into everlasting life. Let us cleave to truth and holiness with full purpose of heart. In every danger and trouble, let us seek protection, comfort, and direction in God's ordinances.

Chapter 20

Chapter Outline

Verses 1-10

The trials David met with, prepared him for future advancement. Thus the Lord deals with those whom he prepares unto glory. He does not put them into immediate possession of the kingdom, but leads them to it through much tribulation, which he makes the means of fitting them for it. Let them not murmur at his gracious appointment, nor distrust his care; but let them look forward with joyful expectation to the crown which is laid up for them. Sometimes it appears to us that there is but a step between us and death; at all times it may be so, and we should prepare for the event. But though dangers appear most threatening, we cannot die till the purpose of God concerning us is accomplished; nor till we have served our generation according to his will, if we are believers. Jonathan generously offers David his services. This is true friendship. Thus Christ testifies his love to us, Ask, and it shall be done for you; and we must testify our love to him, by keeping his commandments.

Verses 11-23

Jonathan faithfully promises that he would let David know how he found his father affected towards him. It will be kindness to ourselves and to ours, to secure an interest in those whom God favours, and to make his friends ours. True friendship rests on a firm basis, and is able to silence ambition, self-love, and undue regard for others. But who can fully understand the love of Jesus, who gave himself as a sacrifice for rebellious, polluted sinners! how great then ought to be the force and effects of our love to him, to his cause, and his people!

Verses 24-34

None were more constant than David in attending holy duties; nor had he been absent, but self-preservation obliged him to withdraw. In great peril present opportunities for Divine ordinances may be waved. But it is bad for us, except in case of necessity, to omit any opportunity of statedly attending on them. Jonathan did wisely and well for himself and family, to secure an interest in David, yet for this he is blamed. It is good to take God's people for our people. It will prove to our advantage at last, however it may now be thought against our interest. Saul was outrageous. What savage beasts, and worse, does anger make men!

Verses 35-42

The separation of two such faithful friends was grievous to both, but David's case was the more deplorable, for David was leaving all his comforts, even those of God's sanctuary. Christians need not sorrow, as men without hope; but being one with Christ, they are one with each other, and will meet in his presence ere long, to part no more; to meet where all tears shall be wiped from their eyes.

Chapter 21

Chapter Outline

David with Ahimelech.   (1–9)

David at Gath feigns himself mad.   (10–15)

Verses 1-9

David, in distress, fled to the tabernacle of God. It is great comfort in a day of trouble, that we have a God to go to, to whom we may open our cases, and from whom we may ask and expect direction. David told Ahimelech a gross untruth. What shall we say to this? The Scripture does not conceal it, and we dare not justify it; it was ill done, and proved of bad consequence; for it occasioned the death of the priests of the Lord. David thought upon it afterward with regret. David had great faith and courage, yet both failed him; he fell thus foully through fear and cowardice, and owing to the weakness of his faith. Had he trusted God aright, he would not have used such a sorry, sinful shift for his own preservation. It is written, not for us to do the like, no, not in the greatest straits, but for our warning. David asked of Ahimelech bread and a sword. Ahimelech supposed they might eat the shew-bread. The Son of David taught from it, that mercy is to be preferred to sacrifice; that ritual observances must give way to moral duties. Doeg set his foot as far within the tabernacle as David did. We little know with what hearts people come to the house of God, nor what use they will make of pretended devotion. If many come in simplicity of heart to serve their God, others come to observe their teachers and to prove accusers. Only God and the event can distinguish between a David and a Doeg, when both are in the tabernacle. (1Sa 21:10-15)

Verses 10-15

God's persecuted people have often found better usage from Philistines than from Israelites. David had reason to put confidence in Achish, yet he began to be afraid. His conduct was degrading, and discovered wavering in his faith and courage. The more simply we depend on God, and obey him, the more comfortably and surely we shall walk through this troublesome world.

Chapter 22

Chapter Outline

Verses 1-5

See what weak instruments God sometimes uses, to bring about his own purposes. The Son of David is ready to receive distressed souls, who will be commanded by him. He receives all who come unto Him, however vile and miserable; he changes them into a holy people, and employs them in his service: those who would reign with him must be contented first to suffer with and for him. Observe with what tender concern David provided for his aged parents. The first thing he does is to find them a quiet habitation, whatever became of himself. Let children learn to honour their parents, in every thing consulting their ease and satisfaction. Though highly preferred, and much employed, let them not forget their aged parents. The steps of a good man are ordered by the Lord. And the Lord will preserve his people for their appointed work, however they may be hated and exposed.

Verses 6-19

See the nature of jealous malice and its pitiful arts. Saul looks upon all about him as his enemies, because they do not just say as he says. In Ahimelech's answer to Saul we have the language of conscious innocence. But what wickedness will not the evil spirit hurry men to when he gets the dominion! Saul alleges that which was utterly false and unproved. But the most bloody tyrants have found instruments of their cruelty as barbarous as themselves. Doeg, having murdered the priests, went to the city, Nob, and put all to the sword there. Nothing so vile but those may do it, who have provoked God to give them up to their hearts' lusts. Yet this was the accomplishment of the threatenings against the house of Eli. Though Saul was unrighteous in doing this, yet God was righteous in permitting it. No word of God shall fall to the ground.

Verses 20-23

David greatly lamented the calamity. It is great trouble to a good man to find himself any way the cause of evil to others. He must have been much pained, when he considered that his falsehood was one cause of this fatal event. David speaks with assurance of his own safety, and promises that Abiathar should have his protection. With the Son of David, all who are his may be sure they shall be in safeguard, Ps 91:1. In the hurry and distraction David was continually in, he found time for communion with God, and found comfort in it.

Chapter 23

Chapter Outline

Verses 1-6

When princes persecute God's people, let them expect vexation on all sides. The way for any country to be quiet, is to let God's church be quiet in it: if Saul fight against David, the Philistines fight against his country. David considered himself the protector of the land. Thus did the Saviour Jesus, and left us an example. Those are unlike David, who sullenly decline to do good, if they are not rewarded for services.

Verses 7-13

Well might David complain of his enemies, that they rewarded him evil for good, and that for his love they were his adversaries. Christ was used thus basely. David applied to his great Protector for direction. No sooner was the ephod brought him than he made use of it. We have the Scriptures in our hands, let us take advice from them in doubtful cases. Say, Bring hither the Bible. David's address to God is very solemn, also very particular. God allows us to be so in our addresses to him; Lord, direct me in this matter, about which I am now at a loss. God knows not only what will be, but what would be, if it were not hindered; therefore he knows how to deliver the godly out of temptation, and how to render to every man according to his works.

Verses 14-18

David made no attempt against Saul; he kept God's way, waited God's time, and was content to secure himself in woods and wildernesses. Let it make us think the worse of this world, which often gives such bad treatment to its best men: let it make us long for that kingdom where goodness shall for ever be in glory, and holiness in honour. We find Jonathan comforting David. As a pious friend, he directed him to God, the Foundation of his comfort. As a self-denying friend, he takes pleasure in the prospect of David's advancement to the throne. As a constant friend, he renewed his friendship with him. Our covenant with God should be often renewed, and therein our communion with him kept up. If the converse of one friend, at one meeting, gives comfort and strengthens our hearts, what may not be expected from the continual supports and powerful love of the Saviour of sinners, the covenanted Friend of believers!

Verses 19-29

In the midst of his wickedness, Saul affected to speak the language of piety. Such expressions, without suitable effects, can only amuse or deceive those who hear, and those who use them. This mountain was an emblem of the Divine Providence coming between David and the destroyer. Let us not be dismayed at the prospect of future difficulties, but stay ourselves upon Him who is wonderful in counsel and excellent in working. Sooner than his promise shall fail, he will commission Philistines to effect our escape, at the very moment when our case appears most desperate. God requires entire dependence on him, If ye will not believe, surely ye shall not be established, Isa 7:9.

Chapter 24

Chapter Outline

David spares Saul's life.	(1–7)
David shows his innocence.	(8–15)
Saul acknowledges his fault.	(16–22)

Verses 1-7

God delivered Saul into David's hand. It was an opportunity given to David to exercise faith and patience. He had a promise of the kingdom, but no command to slay the king. He reasons strongly, both with himself and with his men, against doing Saul any hurt. Sin is a thing which it becomes us to startle at, and to resist temptations thereto. He not only would not do this bad thing himself, but he would not suffer those about him to do it. Thus he rendered good for evil, to him from whom he received evil for good; and was herein an example to all who are called Christians, not to be overcome of evil, but to overcome evil with good.

Verses 8-15

David was falsely charged with seeking Saul's hurt; he shows Saul that God's providence had given him opportunity to do it. And it was upon a good principle that he refused to do it. He declares his fixed resolution never to be his own avenger. If men wrong us, God will right us, at farthest, in the judgment of the great day.

Verses 16-22

Saul speaks as quite overcome with David's kindness. Many mourn for their sins, who do not truly repent of them; weep bitterly for them, yet continue in love and in league with them. Now God made good to David that word on which he had caused him to hope, that he would bring forth his righteousness as the light, Ps 37:6. Those who take care to keep a good conscience, may leave it to God to secure them the credit of it. Sooner or later, God will force even those who are of the synagogue of Satan to know and to own those whom he has loved. They parted in peace. Saul went home convinced, but not converted; ashamed of his envy to David, yet retaining in his breast that root of bitterness; vexed that when at last he had found David, he could not find in his heart to destroy him, as he had designed. Malice often seems dead when it is only asleep, and will revive with double force. Yet, whether the Lord bind men's hands, or affect their hearts, so that they do not hurt us, the deliverance is equally from him; it is an evidence of his love, and an earnest of our salvation, and should make us thankful.

Chapter 25

Chapter Outline

Verse 1

All Israel lamented Samuel, and they had reason. He prayed daily for them. Those have hard hearts, who can bury faithful ministers without grief; who do not feel their loss of those who have prayed for them, and taught them the way of the Lord.

Verses 2-11

We should not have heard of Nabal, if nothing had passed between him and David. Observe his name, Nabal, "A fool;" so it signifies. Riches make men look great in the eye of the world; but to one that takes right views, Nabal looked very mean. He had no honour or honesty; he was churlish, cross, and ill-humoured; evil in his doings, hard and oppressive; a man that cared not what fraud and violence he used in getting and saving. What little reason have we to value the wealth of this world, when so great a churl as Nabal abounds, and so good a man as David suffers want!, David pleaded the kindness Nabal's shepherds had received. Considering that David's men were in distress and debt, and discontented, and the scarcity of provisions, it was by good management that they were kept from plundering. Nabal went into a passion, as covetous men are apt to do, when asked for any thing, thinking thus to cover one sin with another; and, by abusing the poor, to excuse themselves from relieving them. But God will not thus be mocked. Let this help us to bear reproaches and misrepresentations with patience and cheerfulness, and make us easy under them; it has often been the lot of the excellent ones of the earth. Nabal insists much on the property he had in the provisions of his table. May he not do what he will with his own? We mistake, if we think we are absolute lords of what we have, and may do what we please with it. No; we are but stewards, and must use it as we are directed, remembering it is not our own, but His who intrusted us with it.

Verses 12-17

God is kind to the evil and unthankful, and why may not we be so? David determined to destroy Nabal, and all that belonged to him. Is this thy voice, O David? Has he been so long in the school of affliction, where he should have learned patience, and yet is so passionate? He at other times was calm and considerate, but is put into such a heat by a few hard words, that he seeks to destroy a whole family. What are the best of men, when God leaves them to themselves, that they may know what is in their hearts? What need to pray, Lord, lead us not into temptation!

Verses 18-31

By a present Abigail atoned for Nabal's denial of David's request. Her behaviour was very submissive. Yielding pacifies great offences. She puts herself in the place of a penitent, and of a petitioner. She could not excuse her husband's conduct. She depends not upon her own reasonings, but on God's grace, to soften David, and expects that grace would work powerfully. She says that it was below him to take vengeance on so weak and despicable an enemy as Nabal, who, as he would do him no kindness, so he could do him no hurt. She foretells the glorious end of David's present troubles. God will preserve thy life; therefore it becomes not thee unjustly and unnecessarily to take away the lives of any, especially of the people of thy God and Saviour. Abigail keeps this argument for the last, as very powerful with so good a man; that the less he indulged his passion, the more he consulted his peace and the repose of his own conscience. Many have done that in a heat, which they have a thousand times wished undone again. The sweetness of revenge is soon turned into bitterness. When tempted to sin, we should consider how it will appear when we think upon it afterwards.

Verses 32-39

David gives God thanks for sending him this happy check in a sinful way. Whoever meet us with counsel, direction, comfort, caution, or seasonable reproof, we must see God sending them. We ought to be very thankful for those happy providences which are the means of keeping us from sinning. Most people think it enough, if they take reproof patiently; but few will take it thankfully, and commend those who give it, and accept it as a favour. The nearer we are to committing sin, the greater is the mercy of a seasonable restraint. Sinners are often most secure when most in danger. He was very drunk. A sign he was Nabal, a fool, that could not use plenty without abusing it; who could not be pleasant with his friends without making a beast of himself. There is not a surer sign that a man has but little wisdom, nor a surer way to destroy the little he has, than drinking to excess. Next morning, how he is changed! His heart overnight merry with wine, next morning heavy as a stone; so deceitful are carnal pleasures, so soon passes the laughter of the fool; the end of that mirth is heaviness. Drunkards are sad, when they reflect upon their own folly. About ten days after, the Lord smote Nabal, that he died. David blessed God that he had been kept from killing Nabal.

Worldly sorrow, mortified pride, and an affrighted conscience, sometimes end the joys of the sensualist, and separate the covetous man from his wealth; but, whatever the weapon, the Lord smites men with death when it pleases him.

Verses 39-44

Abigail believed that David would be king over Israel, and greatly esteemed his pious and excellent character. She deemed his proposal of marriage honourable, and advantageous to her, notwithstanding his present difficulties. With great humility, and doubtless agreeably to the customs of those times, she consented, being willing to share his trails. Thus those who join themselves to Christ, must be willing now to suffer with him, believing that hereafter they shall reign with him.

Chapter 26

Chapter Outline

Saul goes after David, who again spares Saul's life.	(1–12)
David exhorts Saul.	(13–20)
Saul acknowledges his sin.	(21–25)

Verses 1-12

How soon do unholy hearts lose the good impressions convictions have made upon them! How helpless were Saul and all his men! All as though disarmed and chained, yet nothing is done to them; they are only asleep. How easily can God weaken the strongest, befool the wisest, and baffle the most watchful! David still resolved to wait till God thought fit to avenge him on Saul. He will by no means force his way to the promised crown by any wrong methods. The temptation was very strong; but if he yielded, he would sin against God, therefore he resisted the temptation, and trusted God with the event.

Verses 13-20

David reasoned seriously and affectionately with Saul. Those who forbid our attendance on God's ordinances, do what they can to estrange us from God, and to make us heathens. We are to reckon that which exposes us to sin the greatest injury that can be done us. If the Lord stirred thee up against me, either in displeasure to me, taking this way to punish me for my sins against him, or in displeasure to thee, if it be the effect of that evil spirit from the Lord which troubles thee; let Him accept an offering from us both. Let us join in seeking peace, and to be reconciled with God by sacrifice.

Verses 21-25

Saul repeated his good words and good wishes. But he showed no evidence of true repentance towards God. David and Saul parted to meet no more. No reconciliation among men is firm, which is not founded in an cemented by peace with God through Jesus Christ. In sinning against God, men play the fool, and err exceedingly. Many obtain a passing view of these truths, who hate and close their eyes against the light. Fair professions do not entitle those to confidence who have long sinned against the light, yet the confessions of obstinate sinners may satisfy us that we are in the right way, and encourage us to persevere, expecting our recompence from the Lord alone.

Chapter 27

Chapter Outline

David retires to Gath.   (1–7)

David deceives Achish.   (8–12)

Verses 1-7

Unbelief is a sin that easily besets even good men, when without are fightings, and within are fears; and it is a hard matter to get over them. Lord, increase our faith! We may blush to think that the word of a Philistine should go further than the word of an Israelite, and that the city of Gath should be a place of refuge for a good man, when the cities of Israel refuse him a safe abode. David gained a comfortable settlement, not only at a distance from Gath, but bordering upon Israel, where he might keep up a correspondence with his own countrymen.

Verses 8-12

While David was in the land of the Philistines, he attacked some remains of the devoted nations. The people whom he cut off were long before doomed to destruction. It is often wisdom to shun public notice, but we must in no situation be idle. We must always try to do somewhat in the cause of God. This expedition David hid from Achish. But an equivocation which serves the purpose of a lie, is as like to it as a hypocrite is to a profane person, it is only better in appearance, therefore more dangerous. Yet, though believers often manifest imperfections, they can never be prevailed upon to renounce the service of God, and to unite interests with his enemies, or finally to become the servants of sin and Satan. But what a train of evils follow from unbelief! When we forget the Lord's past mercies, and his gracious assurances, we shall be overwhelmed with desponding fears, and probably be led to adopt some dishonourable method to get rid of our troubles. Nothing can so effectually establish us in holy tempers and practices, and preserve us from perplexities, as firm, unshaken dependence upon the promises of God in Christ Jesus.

Chapter 28

Chapter Outline

Verses 1-6

David could not refuse Achish without danger. If he promised assistance, and then stood neuter, or went over to the Israelites, he would behave with ingratitude and treachery. If he fought against Israel, he would sin greatly. It seemed impossible that he should get out of this difficulty with a clear conscience; but his evasive answer, intended to gain time, was not consistent with the character of an Israelite indeed. Troubles are terrors to the children of disobedience. In his distress, Saul inquired of the Lord. He did not seek in faith, but with a double, unstable mind. Saul had put the law in force against those that had familiar spirits, Ex 22:18. Many seem zealous against, sin, when they are any way hurt by it, who have no concern for the glory of God, nor any dislike of sin as sin. Many seem enemies to sin in others, while they indulge it in themselves. Saul will drive the devil out of his kingdom, yet harbours him in his heart by envy and malice. How foolish to consult those whom, according to God's law, he had endeavoured to root out!

Verses 7-19

When we go from the plain path of duty, every thing draws us further aside, and increases our perplexity and temptation. Saul desires the woman to bring one from the dead, with whom he wished to speak; this was expressly forbidden, De 18:11. All real or pretended witchcraft or conjuration, is a malicious or an ignorant attempt to gain knowledge or help from some creature, when it cannot be had from the Lord in the path of duty. While Samuel was living, we never read of Saul's going to advise with him in any difficulties; it had been well for him if he had. But now he is dead, "Bring me up Samuel." Many who despise and persecute God's saints and ministers when living, would be glad to have them again, when they are gone. The whole shows that it was no human fraud or trick. Though the woman could not cause Samuel's being sent, yet Saul's inquiry might be the occasion of it. The woman's surprise and terror proved that it was an unusual and unexpected appearance. Saul had despised Samuel's solemn warnings in his lifetime, yet now that he hoped, as in defiance of God, to obtain some counsel and encouragement from him, might not God permit the soul of his departed prophet to appear to Saul, to confirm his former sentence, and denounce his doom? The expression, "Thou and thy sons shall be with me," means no more than that they shall be in the eternal world. There appears much solemnity in God's permitting the soul of a departed prophet to come as a witness from heaven, to confirm the word he had spoken on earth.

Verses 20-25

Those that expect any good counsel or comfort, otherwise than from God, and in the way of his institutions, will be as wretchedly disappointed as Saul. Though terrified even to despair, he was not humbled. He confessed not his sins, offered no sacrifices, and presented no supplications. He does not seem to have cared about his sons or his people, or to have attempted any escape; but in sullen despair he rushed upon his doom. God sets up a few such beacons, to warn men not to stifle convictions, or despise his word. But while one repenting thought remains, let no sinner suppose himself in this case. Let him humble himself before God, determined to live and die beseeching his favour, and he will succeed.

Chapter 29

Chapter Outline

David objected to by the Philistines.   (1–5)

He is dismissed by Achish.   (6–11)

Verses 1-5

David waited with a secret hope that the Lord would help him out of his difficulty. But he seems to have been influenced too much by the fear of man, in consenting to attend Achish. It is hard to come near to the brink of sin, and not to fall in. God inclined the princes of the Philistines to oppose David's being employed in the battle. Thus their dislike befriended him, when no friend could do him such a kindness.

Verses 6-11

David scarcely ever had a greater deliverance than when dismissed from such insnaring service. God's people should always behave themselves so, as, if possible, to get the good word of all they have dealings with: and it is due to those who have acted well, to speak well of them.

Chapter 30

Chapter Outline

Ziklag spoiled by the Amalekites.   (1–6)

David overtakes the Amalekites.   (7–15)

Verses 1-6

When we go abroad in the way of our duty, we may comfortably hope that God will take care of our families in our absence, but not otherwise. If, when we come off a journey, we find our abode in peace, and not laid waste, as David here found his, let the Lord be praised for it. David's men murmured against him. Great faith must expect such severe trials. But, observe, that David was brought thus low, only just before he was raised to the throne. When things are at the worst with the church and people of God, then they begin to mend. David encouraged himself in the Lord his God. His men fretted at their loss, the soul of the people was bitter; their own discontent and impatience added to the affliction and misery. But David bore it better, though he had more reason than any of them to lament it. They gave liberty to their passions, but he set his graces to work; and while they dispirited each other, he, by encouraging himself in God, kept his spirit calm. Those who have taken the Lord for their God, may take encouragement from him in the worst times.

Verses 7-15

If in all our ways, even when, as in this case, there can be no doubt they are just, we acknowledge God, we may expect that he will direct our steps, as he did those of David. David, in tenderness to his men, would by no means urge them beyond their strength. The Son of David thus considers the frames of his followers, who are not all alike strong and vigorous in their spiritual pursuits and conflicts; but, where we are weak, there he is kind; nay more, there he is strong, 2Co 12:9, 10. A poor Egyptian lad, scarcely alive, is made the means of a great deal of good to David. Justly did Providence make this poor servant, who was basely used by his master, an instrument in the destruction of the Amalekites; for God hears the cry of the oppressed. Those are unworthy the name of true Israelites, who shut up their compassion from persons in distress. We should neither do an injury nor deny a kindness to any man; some time or other it may be in the power of the lowest to return a kindness or an injury.

Verses 16-20

Sinners are nearest to ruin, when they cry, Peace and safety, and put the evil day far from them. Nor does any thing give our spiritual enemies more advantage than sensuality and indulgence. Eating and drinking, and dancing, have been the soft and pleasant way in which many have gone down to the congregation of the dead. The spoil was recovered, and brought off; nothing was lost, but a great deal gained.

Verses 21-31

What God gives us, he designs we should do good with. In distributing the spoil, David was just and kind. Those are men of Belial indeed, who delight in putting hardships upon their brethren, and care not who is starved, so that they may be fed to the full. David was generous and kind to all his friends. Those who consider the Lord as the Giver of their abundance, will dispose of it with fairness and liberality.

Chapter 31

Chapter Outline

Saul's defeat and death.   (1–7)

Saul's body rescued by the men of   (8–13)
Jabesh-gilead.

Verses 1-7

We cannot judge of the spiritual or eternal state of any by the manner of their death; for in that, there is one event to the righteous and to the wicked. Saul, when sorely wounded, and unable to resist or to flee, expressed no concern about his never-dying soul; but only desired that the Philistines might not insult over him, or put him to pain, and he became his own murderer. As it is the grand deceit of the devil, to persuade sinners, under great difficulties, to fly to this last act of desperation, it is well to fortify the mind against it, by a serious consideration of its sinfulness before God, and its miserable consequences in society. But our security is not in ourselves. Let us seek protection from Him who keepeth Israel. Let us watch and pray; and take unto us the whole armour of God, that we may be able to withstand in the evil day, and having done all, to stand.

Verses 8-13

The Scripture makes no mention what became of the souls of Saul and his sons, after they were dead; but of their bodies only: secret things belong not to us. It is of little consequence by what means we die, or what is done with our dead bodies. If our souls are saved, our bodies will be raised incorruptible and glorious; but not to fear His wrath, who is able to destroy both body and soul in hell, is the extreme of folly and wickedness. How useless is the respect of fellow-creatures to those who are suffering the wrath of God! While pompous funerals, grand monuments, and he praises of men, honour the memory of the deceased, the soul may be suffering in the regions of darkness and despair! Let us seek that honour which cometh from God only.

2 Samuel

This book is the history of the reign of king David. It relates his victories, the growth of the prosperity of Israel, and his reformation of the state of religion. With these events are recorded the grievous sins he committed, and the family as well as public troubles with which he was punished. We here meet with many things worthy of imitation, and many that are written for our warning. The history of king David is given in Scripture with much faithfulness, and from it he appears, to those who fairly balance his many virtues and excellent qualities against his faults, to have been a great and good man.

Chapter 1

Chapter Outline

Tidings brought to David of the death of Saul.	(1–10)
The Amalekite is put to death.	(11–16)
David's lamentation for Saul and Jonathan.	(17–27)

Verses 1-10

The blow which opened David's way to the throne was given about the time he had been sorely distressed. Those who commit their concerns to the Lord, will quietly abide his will. It shows that he desired not Saul's death, and he was not impatient to come to the throne.

Verses 11-16

David was sincere in his mourning for Saul; and all with him humbled themselves under the hand of God, laid so heavily upon Israel by this defeat. The man who brought the tidings, David put to death, as a murderer of his prince. David herein did not do unjustly; the Amalekite confessed the crime. If he did as he said, he deserved to die for treason; and his lying to David, if indeed it were a lie, proved, as sooner or later that sin will prove, lying against himself. Hereby David showed himself zealous for public justice, without regard to his own private interest.

Verses 17-27

Kasheth, or "the bow," probably was the title of this mournful, funeral song. David does not commend Saul for what he was not; and says nothing of his piety or goodness. Jonathan was a dutiful son, Saul an affectionate father, therefore dear to each other. David had reason to say, that Jonathan's love to him was wonderful. Next to the love between Christ and his people, that affection which springs form it, produces the strongest friendship. The trouble of the Lord's people, and triumphs of his enemies, will always grieve true believers, whatever advantages they may obtain by them.

Chapter 2

Chapter Outline

Verses 1-7

After the death of Saul, many went to David at Ziklag, 1Ch 12:22, but he trusted in God who promised him the kingdom, to give it in his own time and manner. Yet assurance of hope in God's promise, will quicken pious endeavours. If I be chosen to the crown of life, it does not follow, Then I will do nothing; but, Then I will do all that God directs me. This good use David made of his election, and so will all whom God has chosen. In all our journeys and removes, it is comfortable to see God going before us; and we may do so, if by faith and prayer we set Him before us. God, according to the promise, directed David's path. David rose gradually: thus the kingdom of the Messiah, the Son of David, is set up by degrees; he is Lord of all, but we see not yet all things put under him.

Verses 8-17

The nation in general refused David. By this the Lord trained up his servant for future honour and usefulness; and the tendency of true godliness was shown in his behaviour while passing through various difficulties. David was herein a type of Christ, whom Israel would not submit to, though anointed of the Father to be a Prince and a Saviour to them. Abner meant, Let the young men fight before us, when he said, Let them play before us: fools thus make a mock at sin. But he is unworthy the name of a man, that can thus trifle with human blood.

Verses 18-24

Death often comes by ways we least suspect. We are often betrayed by the accomplishments we are proud of! Asahel's swiftness, which he presumed so much upon, did him no service, but hastened his end.

Verses 25-32

Abner appeals to Joab concerning the miserable consequences of a civil war. Those who make light of such unnatural contests, will find that they are bitterness to all concerned. How easy it is for men to use reason, when it makes for them, who would not use it, if it made against them! See how the issue of things alter men's minds! The same thing which looked pleasant in the morning, at night looked dismal. Those who are most forward to enter into contention, will repent before they have done with it, and had better leave it off before it be meddled with, as Solomon advises. This is true of every sin, oh that men would consider it in time, that it will be bitterness in the latter end! Asahel's funeral is here mentioned. Distinctions are made between the dust of some and that of others; but in the resurrection no difference will be made, but between the godly and ungodly, which will remain for ever.

Chapter 3

Chapter Outline

Verses 1-6

The length of this war tried the faith and patience of David, and made his settlement at last the more welcome. The contest between grace and corruption in the hearts of believers, may fitly be compared to this warfare. There is a long war between them, the flesh lusting against the spirit, and the spirit against the flesh; but as the work of holiness is carried on, corruption, like the house of Saul, grows weaker and weaker; while grace, like the house of David, grows stronger and stronger.

Verses 7-21

Many, like Abner, are not above committing base crimes, who are too proud to bear reproof, or even the suspicion of being guilty. While men go on in sin, and apparently without concern, they are often conscious that they are fighting against God. Many mean to serve their own purposes; and will betray those who trust them, when they can get any advantage. Yet the Lord serves his own designs, even by those who are thus actuated by revenge, ambition, or lust; but as they intend not to honour him, in the end they will be thrown aside with contempt. There was real generosity both to Michal and to the memory of Saul, in David's receiving the former, remembering probably how once he owed his life to her affection, and knowing that she was separated from him partly by her father's authority. Let no man set his heart on that which he is not entitled to. If any disagreement has separated husband and wife, as they expect the blessing of God, let them be reconciled, and live together in love.

Verses 22-39

Judgments are prepared for such scorners as Abner; but Joab, in what he did, acted wickedly. David laid Abner's murder deeply to heart, and in many ways expressed his detestation of it. The guilt of blood brings a curse upon families: if men do not avenge it, God will. It is a sad thing to die like a fool, as they do that any way shorten their own days, and those who make no provision for another world. Who would be fond of power, when a man may have the name of it, and must be accountable for it, yet is hampered in the use of it? David ought to have done his duty, and then trusted God with the issue. Carnal policy spared Joab. The Son of David may long delay, but never fails to punish impenitent sinners. He who now reigns upon the throne of David, has a kingdom of a nobler kind. Whatever He doeth, is noticed by all his willing people, and is pleasing to them.

Chapter 4

Chapter Outline

Ishbosheth murdered.   (1–7)

David puts to death the murderers.   (8–12)

Verses 1-7

See how Ishbosheth was murdered! When those difficulties dispirit us, which should sharpen our endeavours, we betray both our heavenly crowns and our earthly lives. Love not sleep, lest thou come to poverty and ruin. The idle soul is an easy prey to the destroyer. We know not when and where death will meet us. When we lie down to sleep, we are not sure that we may not sleep the sleep of death before we awake; nor do we know from what hand the death-blow may come.

Verses 8-12

A person may be glad to obtain his just wishes, and yet really regret the means by which he receives them. He may be sorry for the death of a person by which he is a gainer. These men shed innocent blood, from the basest motives. David justly executed vengeance upon them. He would not be beholden to any to help him by unlawful practices. God had helped him over many a difficulty, and through many a danger, therefore he depended upon him to crown and complete his own work. He speaks of his redemption from all adversity, as a thing done; though he had many storms yet before him, he knew that He who had delivered, would deliver.

Chapter 5

Chapter Outline

David king over all Israel.   (1–5)

He takes the strong-hold of Zion.   (6–10)

David's kingdom established.   (11–16)

He defeats the Philistines.   (17–25)

Verses 1-5

David was anointed king a third time. His advances were gradual, that his faith might be tried, and that he might gain experience. Thus his kingdom typified that of the Messiah, which was to come to its height by degrees. Thus Jesus became our Brother, took upon him our nature, dwelt in it that he might become our Prince and Saviour: thus the humbled sinner takes encouragement from the endearing relation, applies for his salvation, submits to his authority, and craves his protection.

Verses 6-10

The enemies of God's people are often very confident of their own strength, and most secure when their day to fall draws nigh. But the pride and insolence of the Jebusites animated David, and the Lord God of hosts was with him. Thus in the day of God's power, Satan's strong-hold, the human heart, is changed into a habitation of God through the Spirit, and into a throne on which the Son of David rules, and brings every thought into obedience to himself. May He thus come, and claim, and cleanse, each of our hearts; and, destroying every idol, may he reign there for ever!

Verses 11-16

David's house was not the worse, nor the less fit to be dedicated to God, for being built by the sons of the stranger. It is prophesied of the gospel church, The sons of strangers shall build up thy walls, and their kings shall minister unto thee, Isa 60:10. David's government was rooted and built up. David was established king; so is the Son of David, and all who, through him, are made to our God kings and priests. Never had the nation of Israel appeared so great as it began now to be. Many have the favour and love of God, yet do not perceive it, and so want the comfort of it; but to be exalted to that, and to perceive it, is happiness. David owned it was for his people's sake God had done great things for him; that he might be a blessing to them, and that they might be happy under him.

Verses 17-25

The Philistines considered not that David had the presence of God with him, which Saul had forfeited and lost. The kingdom of the Messiah, as soon as it was set up in the world, was thus attacked by the powers of darkness. The heathen raged, and the kings of the earth set themselves to oppose it; but all in vain, Ps 2:1, &c. The destruction will turn, as this did, upon Satan's own kingdom. David owns dependence on God for victory; and refers himself to the good pleasure of God, Wilt thou do it? The assurance God has given us of victory over our spiritual enemies, should encourage us in our spiritual conflicts. David waited till God moved; he stirred then, but not till then. He was trained up in dependence on God and his providence. God performed his promise, and David failed not to improve his advantages. When the kingdom of the Messiah was to be set up, the apostles, who were to beat down the devil's kingdom, must not attempt any thing till they received the promise of the Spirit; who came with a sound from heaven, as of a rushing, mighty wind, Ac 2:2.

Chapter 6

Chapter Outline

Verses 1-5

God is present with the souls of his people, when they want the outward tokens of his presence; but now David is settled in the throne, the honour of the ark begins to revive. Let us learn hence, to think and to speak highly of God; and to think and speak honourably of holy ordinances, which are to us as the ark was unto Israel, the tokens of God's presence, Mt 28:20. Christ is our Ark; in and by him God manifests his favour, and accepts our prayers and praises. The ark especially typified Christ and his mediation, in which the name of Jehovah and all his glories are displayed. The priests should have carried the ark upon their shoulders. Philistines may carry the ark in a cart without suffering for it; but if Israelites do so, it is at their peril, because this was not what God appointed.

Verses 6-11

Uzzah was struck dead for touching the ark. God saw presumption and irreverence in Uzzah's heart. Familiarity, even with that which is most awful, is apt to breed contempt. If it were so great a crime for one to lay hold on the ark of the covenant who had no right to do so, what is it for those to lay claim to the privileges of the covenant that come not up to the terms of it? Obed-edom opened his doors without fear, knowing the ark was a savour of death unto death to those only who treated it wrong. The same hand that punished Uzzah's proud presumption, rewarded Obed-edom's humble boldness. Let none think the worse of the gospel for the judgments on those that reject it, but consider the blessings it brings to all who receive it. Let masters of families be encouraged to keep up religion in their families. It is good to live in a family that entertains the ark, for all about it will fare the better.

Verses 12-19

It became evident, that happy was the man who had the ark near him. Christ is indeed a Stone of stumbling, and a Rock of offence, to those that are disobedient; but to those that believe, he is a Corner-stone, elect, precious, 1Pe 2:6–8. Let us be religious. Is the ark a blessing to others' houses? We may have it, and the blessing of it, without fetching it away from our neighbours. David, at first setting out, offered sacrifices to God. We are likely to speed in our enterprises, when we begin with God, and give diligence to seek peace with him. And we are so unworthy, and our services are so defiled, that all our joy in God must be connected with repentance and faith in the Redeemer's atoning blood. David attended with high expressions of joy. We ought to serve God with our whole body and soul, and with every endowment and power we possess. On this occasion David laid aside his royal robes, and put on a plain linen dress. David prayed with and for the people, and as a prophet, solemnly blessed them in the name of the Lord.

Verses 20-23

David returned to bless his household, to pray with them, and for them, and to offer up family thanksgiving for this national mercy. It is angels' work to worship God, surely that cannot lower the greatest of men. But even the palaces of princes are not free from family troubles. Exercises of religion appear mean in the eyes of those who have little or no religion themselves. If we can approve ourselves to God in what we do in religion, and do it as before the Lord, we need not heed reproach. Piety will have its praise: let us not be indifferent in it, nor afraid or ashamed to own it. David was contented to justify himself, and he did not further reprove or blame Michal's insolence; but God punished her. Those that honour God, he will honour; but those that despise him, and his servants and service, shall be lightly esteemed.

Chapter 7

Chapter Outline

David's care for the ark.	(1–3)
God's covenant with David.	(4–17)
His prayer and thanksgiving.	(18–29)

Verses 1-3

David being at rest in his palace, considered how he might best employ his leisure and prosperity in the service of God. He formed a design to build a temple for the ark. Nathan here did not speak as a prophet, but as a godly man, encouraging David by his private judgment. We ought to do all we can to encourage and promote the good purposes and designs of others, and, as we have opportunity, to forward a good work.

Verses 4-17

Blessings are promised to the family and posterity of David. These promises relate to Solomon, David's immediate successor, and the royal line of Judah. But they also relate to Christ, who is often called David and the Son of David. To him God gave all power in heaven and earth, with authority to execute judgment. He was to build the gospel temple, a house for God's name; the spiritual temple of true believers, to be a habitation of God through the Spirit. The establishing of his house, his throne, and his kingdom for ever, can be applied to no other than to Christ and his kingdom: David's house and kingdom long since came to an end. The committing iniquity cannot be applied to the Messiah himself, but to his spiritual seed; true believers have infirmities, for which they must expect to be corrected, though they are not cast off.

Verses 18-29

David's prayer is full of the breathings of devout affection toward God. He had low thoughts of his own merits. All we have, must be looked upon as Divine gifts. He speaks very highly and honourably of the Lord's favours to him. Considering what the character and condition of man is, we may be amazed that God should deal with him as he does. The promise of Christ includes all; if the Lord God be ours, what more can we ask, or think of? Eph 3:20. He knows us better than we know ourselves; therefore let us be satisfied with what he has done for us. What can we say more for ourselves in our prayers, than God has said for us in his promises? David ascribes all to the free grace of God. Both the great things He had done for him, and the great things He had made known to him. All was for his word's sake, that is, for the sake of Christ the eternal Word. Many, when they go to pray, have their hearts to seek, but David's heart was found, that is, it was fixed; gathered in from its wanderings, entirely engaged to the duty, and employed in it. That prayer which is from the tongue only, will not please God; it must be found in the heart; that must be lifted up and poured out before God. He builds his faith, and hopes to speed, upon the sureness of God's promise. David prays for the performance of the promise. With God, saying and doing are not two things, as they often are with men; God will do as he hath said. The promises of God are not made to us by name, as to David, but they belong to all who believe in Jesus Christ, and plead them in his name.

Chapter 8

Chapter Outline

Verses 1-8

David subdued the Philistines. They had long been troublesome to Israel. And after the long and frequent struggles the saints have with the powers of darkness, like Israel with the Philistines, the Son of David shall tread them all under foot, and make the saints more than conquerors. He smote the Moabites, and made them tributaries to Israel. Two parts he destroyed, the third part he spared. The line that was to keep alive, though it was but one, is ordered to be a full line. Let the line of mercy be stretched to the utmost. He smote the Syrians. In all these wars David was protected, for this in his psalms he often gives glory to God.

Verses 9-14

All the precious things David was master of, were dedicated things; they were designed for building the temple. The idols of gold David destroyed, 2Sa 5:21, but the vessels of gold he dedicated. Thus, in the conquest of a soul by the grace of the Son of David, what stands in opposition to God must be destroyed, every lust must be mortified and crucified, but what may glorify him must be dedicated; thus the property of it is altered. God employs his servants in various ways; some, as David, in spiritual battles; others, as Solomon, in spiritual buildings; and one prepares work for the other, that God may have the glory of all.

Verses 15-18

David neither did wrong, nor denied or delayed right to any. This speaks his close application to business; also his readiness to admit all addresses and appeals made to him. He had no respect of persons in judgment. Herein he was a type of Christ. To Him let us submit, his friendship let us seek, his service let us count our pleasure, diligently attending to the work he assigns to each of us. David made his sons chief rulers; but all believers, Christ's spiritual seed, are better preferred, for they are made kings and priests to our God, Re 1:6.

Chapter 9

Chapter Outline

David sends for Mephibosheth.   (1–8)

And provides for him.   (9–13)

Verses 1-8

Amidst numerous affairs we are apt to forget the gratitude we owe, and the engagements we are under, not only to our friends, but to God himself. Yet persons of real godliness will have no rest till they have discharged them. And the most proper objects of kindness and charity, frequently will not be found without inquiry. Jonathan was David's sworn friend, therefore he shows kindness to his son Mephibosheth. God is faithful to us; let us not be unfaithful to one another. If Providence has raised us, and our friends and their families are brought low, we must look upon that as giving us the fairer opportunity of being kind to them.

Verses 9-13

As David was a type of Christ, his Lord and Son, his Root and Offspring, let his kindness to Mephibosheth remind us of the kindness and love of God our Saviour to fallen man, to whom he was under no obligation, as David was to Jonathan. The Son of God seeks this lost and ruined race, who sought not after him. He comes to seek and to save them!

Chapter 10

Chapter Outline

Verses 1-5

Nahash had been an enemy to Israel, yet had showed kindness to David. David therefore resolves gratefully to return it. If a Pharisee gives alms in pride, though God will not reward it, yet he that receives the alms ought to return thanks for it. Those who bear ill-will to their neighbours, are resolved not to believe that their neighbours bear any good-will to them. There is nothing so well meant, but it may be ill interpreted, and is wont to be so, by men who love nobody but themselves. The best men must not think it strange if they are thus misrepresented. Charity thinketh no evil. According to the usages of those days and countries, Hanun treated David's ambassadors in the most contemptuous manner. David showed much concern for his servants. Let us learn not to lay unjust reproaches to heart; they will wear off, and turn only to the shame of those who utter or do them; while the reputation wrongfully hurt in a little time grows again, as these beards did. God will bring forth thy righteousness as the light, therefore wait patiently for him, Ps 37:6, 7.

Verses 6-14

They that are at war with the Son of David, not only give the provocation, but begin the war. God has forces to send against those that set his wrath at defiance, Isa 5:19, which will convince them that none ever hardened his heart against God, and prospered. Christ's soldiers should strengthen one another's hands in their spiritual warfare. Let nothing be wanting in us, whatever the success be. When we make conscience of doing our duty, we may, with satisfaction, leave the event with God, assuredly hoping for his salvation in his own way and time.

Verses 15-19

Here is a new attempt of the Syrians. Even the baffled cause will make head as long as there is any life in it; the enemies of the Son of David do so. But now the promise made to Abraham, Ge 15:18, and repeated to Joshua, Jos 1:4, that the borders of Israel should extend to the river Euphrates, was performed. Learn hence, that it is dangerous to help those who have God against them; for when they fall, their helpers will fall with them.

Chapter 11

Chapter Outline

Verses 1-5

Observe the occasions of David's sin; what led to it. 1. Neglect of his business. He tarried at Jerusalem. When we are out of the way of our duty, we are in temptation. 2. Love of ease: idleness gives great advantage to the tempter. 3. A wandering eye. He had not, like Job, made a covenant with his eyes, or, at this time, he had forgotten it. And observe the steps of the sin. See how the way of sin is down-hill; when men begin to do evil, they cannot soon stop. Observe the aggravations of the sin. How could David rebuke or punish that in others, of which he was conscious that he himself was guilty?

Verses 6-13

Giving way to sin hardens the heart, and provokes the departure of the Holy Spirit. Robbing a man of his reason, is worse than robbing him of his money; and drawing him into sin, is worse than drawing him into any wordly trouble whatever.

Verses 14-27

Adulteries often occasion murders, and one wickedness is sought to be covered by another. The beginnings of sin are much to be dreaded; for who knows where they will end? Can a real believer ever tread this path? Can such a person be indeed a child of God? Though grace be not lost in such an awful case, the assurance and consolation of it must be suspended. All David's life, spirituality, and comfort in religion, we may be sure were lost. No man in such a case can have evidence to be satisfied that he is a believer. The higher a man's confidence is, who has sunk in wickedness, the greater his presumption and hypocrisy. Let not any one who resembles David in nothing but his transgressions, bolster up his confidence with this example. Let him follow David in his humiliation, repentance, and his other eminent graces, before he thinks himself only a backslider, and not a hypocrite. Let no opposer of the truth say, These are the fruits of faith! No; they are the effects of corrupt nature. Let us all watch against the beginnings of self-indulgence, and keep at the utmost distance from all evil. But with the Lord there is mercy and plenteous redemption. He will cast out no humble, penitent believer; nor will he suffer Satan to pluck his sheep out of his hand. Yet the Lord will recover his people, in such a way as will mark his abhorrence of their crimes, to hinder all who regard his word from abusing the encouragements of his mercy.

Chapter 12

Chapter Outline

Nathan's parable—David confesses his sin.	(1–14)
The birth of Solomon.	(15–25)
David's severity to the Ammonites.	(26–31)

Verses 1-14

God will not suffer his people to lie still in sin. By this parable Nathan drew from David a sentence against himself. Great need there is of prudence in giving reproofs. In his application, he was faithful. He says in plain terms, Thou art the man. God shows how much he hates sin, even in his own people; and wherever he finds it, he will not let it go unpunished. David says not a word to excuse himself or make light of his sin, but freely owns it. When David said, I have sinned, and Nathan perceived that he was a true penitent, he assured him his sin was forgiven. Thou shalt not die: that is, not die eternally, nor be for ever put away from God, as thou wouldest have been, if thou hadst not put away the sin. Though thou shalt all thy days be chastened of the Lord, yet thou shalt not be condemned with the world. There is this great evil in the sins of those who profess religion and relation to God, that they furnish the enemies of God and religion with matter for reproach and blasphemy. And it appears from David's case, that even where pardon is obtained, the Lord will visit the transgression of his people with the rod, and their iniquity with stripes. For one momentary gratification of a vile lust, David had to endure many days and years of extreme distress.

Verses 15-25

David now penned the 51st Psalm, in which, though he had been assured that his sin was pardoned, he prays earnestly for pardon, and greatly laments his sin. He was willing to bear the shame of it, to have it ever before him, to be continually upbraided with it. God gives us leave to be earnest with him in prayer for particular blessings, from trust in his power and general mercy, though we have no particular promise to build upon. David patiently submitted to the will of God in the death of one child, and God made up the loss to his advantage, in the birth of another. The way to have creature comforts continued or restored, or the loss made up some other way, is cheerfully to resign them to God. God, by his grace, particularly owned and favoured that son, and ordered him to be called Jedidiah, Beloved of the Lord. Our prayers for our children are graciously and as fully answered when some of them die in their infancy, for they are well taken care of, and when others live, "beloved of the Lord."

Verses 26-31

To be thus severe in putting the children of Ammon to slavery was a sign that David's heart was not yet made soft by repentance, at the time when this took place. We shall be most compassionate, kind, and forgiving to others, when we most feel our need of the Lord's forgiving love, and taste the sweetness of it in our own souls.

Chapter 13

Chapter Outline

Ammon's violence to his sister.	(1–20)
Absalom murders his brother Ammon.	(21–29)
David's grief, Absalom flees to Geshur.	(30–39)

Verses 1-20

From henceforward David was followed with one trouble after another. Adultery and murder were David's sins, the like sins among his children were the beginnings of his punishment: he was too indulgent to his children. Thus David might trace the sins of his children to his own misconduct, which must have made the anguish of the chastisement worse. Let no one ever expect good treatment from those who are capable of attempting their seduction; but it is better to suffer the greatest wrong than to commit the least sin.

Verses 21-29

Observe the aggravations of Absalom's sin: he would have Ammon slain, when least fit to go out of the world. He engaged his servants in the guilt. Those servants are ill-taught who obey wicked masters, against God's commands. Indulged children always prove crosses to godly parents, whose foolish love leads them to neglect their duty to God.

Verses 30-39

Jonadab was as guilty of Ammon's death, as of his sin; such false friends do they prove, who counsel us to do wickedly. Instead of loathing Absalom as a murderer, David, after a time, longed to go forth to him. This was David's infirmity: God saw something in his heart that made a difference, else we should have thought that he, as much as Eli, honoured his sons more than God.

Chapter 14

Chapter Outline

Verses 1-20

We may notice here, how this widow pleads God's mercy, and his clemency toward poor guilty sinners. The state of sinners is a state of banishment from God. God pardons none to the dishonour of his law and justice, nor any who are impenitent; nor to the encouragement of crimes, or the hurt of others.

Verses 21-24

David was inclined to favour Absalom, yet, for the honour of his justice, he could not do it but upon application made for him, which may show the methods of Divine grace. It is true that God has thoughts of compassion toward poor sinners, not willing that any should perish; yet he is only reconciled to them through a Mediator, who pleads on their behalf. God was in Christ reconciling the world to himself, and Christ came to this land of our banishment, to bring us to God.

Verses 25-27

Nothing is said of Absalom's wisdom and piety. All here said of him is, that he was very handsome. A poor commendation for a man that had nothing else in him valuable. Many a polluted, deformed soul dwells in a fair and comely body. And we read that he had a very fine head of hair. It was a burden to him, but he would not cut it as long as he could bear the weight. That which feeds and gratifies pride, is not complained of, though uneasy. May the Lord grant us the beauty of holiness, and the adorning of a meek and quiet spirit! Only those who fear God are truly happy.

Verses 28-33

By his insolent carriage toward Joab, Absalom brought Joab to plead for him. By his insolent message to the king, he gained his wishes. When parents and rulers countenance such characters, they will soon suffer the most fatal effects. But did the compassion of a father prevail to reconcile him to an impenitent son, and shall penitent sinners question the compassion of Him who is the Father of mercies?

Chapter 15

Chapter Outline

Verses 1-6

David allows Absalom's pomp. Those parents know not what they do, who indulge a proud humour in their children: many young people are ruined by pride. And those commonly are most eager for authority who least understand its duties.

Verses 7-12

See how willing tender parents are to believe the best concerning their children. But how easy and how wicked is it, for children to take advantage of good parents, and to deceive them with the show of religion! The principal men of Jerusalem joined Absalom's feast upon his sacrifice. Pious persons are glad to see others appear religious, and this gives occasion for deceptions. The policy of wicked men, and the subtlety of Satan, are exerted to draw good persons to countenance base designs.

Verses 13-23

David determined to quit Jerusalem. He took this resolve, as a penitent submitting to the rod. Before unrighteous Absalom he could justify himself, and stand out; but before the righteous God he must condemn himself, and yield to his judgments. Thus he accepts the punishment of his sin. And good men, when they themselves suffer, are anxious that others should not be led to suffer with them. He compelled none; those whose hearts were with Absalom, to Absalom let them go, and so shall their doom be. Thus Christ enlists none but willing followers. David cannot bear to think that Ittai, a stranger and an exile, a proselyte and a new convert, who ought to be encouraged and made easy, should meet with hard usage. But such value has Ittai for David's wisdom and goodness, that he will not leave him. He is a friend indeed, who loves at all times, and will adhere to us in adversity. Let us cleave to the Son of David, with full purpose of heart, and neither life nor death shall separate us from his love.

Verses 24-30

David is very careful for the safety of the ark. It is right to be more concerned for the church's prosperity than our own; to prefer the success of the gospel above our own wealth, credit, ease, and safety. Observe with what satisfaction and submission David speaks of the Divine disposal. It is our interest, as well as our duty, cheerfully to acquiesce in the will of God, whatever befalls us. Let us see God's hand in all events; and that we may not be afraid of what shall be, let us see all events in God's hand. David's sin was ever before him, Ps 51:3; but never so plain, nor ever appearing so black as now. He never wept thus when Saul hunted him, but a wounded conscience makes troubles lie heavy, Ps 38:4.

Verses 31-37

David prays not against Ahithophel's person, but against his counsel. He prayed this, in firm belief that God has all hearts in his hand, and tongues also. But we must second our prayers with endeavours, and David did so, else we tempt God. But we do not find wisdom and simplicity so united in any mere man, that we can perceive nothing which needs forgiveness. Yet, when the Son of David was treated with all possible treachery and cruelty, his wisdom, meekness, candour, and patience, were perfect. Him let us follow, cleave to, and serve, in life and in death.

Chapter 16

Chapter Outline

Ziba's falsehood.	(1–4)
David cursed by Shimei.	(5–14)
Ahithophel's counsel.	(15–23)

Verses 1-4

Ziba belied Mephibosheth. Great men ought always to be jealous of flatterers, and to be careful that they hear both sides.

Verses 5-14

David bore Shimei's curses much better than Ziba's flatteries; by these he was brought to pass a wrong judgment on another, by those to pass a right judgment on himself: the world's smiles are more dangerous than its frowns. Once and again David spared Saul's life, while Saul sought his. But innocence is no defence against malice and falsehood; nor are we to think it strange, if we are charged with that which we have been most careful to keep ourselves from. It is well for us, that men are not to be our judges, but He whose judgment is according to truth. See how patient David was under this abuse. Let this remind us of Christ, who prayed for those who reviled and crucified him. A humble spirit will turn reproaches into reproofs, and get good from them, instead of being provoked by them. David the hand of God in it, and comforts himself that God would bring good out of his affliction. We may depend upon God to repay, not only our services, but our sufferings.

Verses 15-23

The wisest counsellors of that age were Ahithophel and Hushai: Absalom thinks himself sure of success, when he has both; on them he relies, and consults not the ark, though he had that with him. But miserable counsellors were they both. Hushai would never counsel him to do wisely. Ahithophel counselled him to do wickedly; and so did as effectually betray him, as he did, who was designedly false to him: for they that advise men to sin, certainly advise them to their hurt. After all, honesty is the best policy, and will be found so in the long run. Ahithophel gave wicked counsel to Absalom; to render himself so hateful to his father, that he would never be reconciled to him; this cursed policy was of the devil. How desperately wicked is the human heart!

Chapter 17

Chapter Outline

Ahithophel's counsel overthrown.   (1–21)

He hangs himself, Absalom pursues David.   (22–29)

Verses 1-21

Here was a wonderful effect of Divine Providence blinding Absalom's mind and influencing his heart, that he could not rest in Ahithophel's counsel, and that he should desire Hushai's advice. But there is no contending with that God who can arm a man against himself, and destroy him by his own mistakes and passions. Ahithophel's former counsel was followed, for God intended to correct David; but his latter counsel was not followed, for God meant not to destroy him. He can overrule all counsels. Whatever wisdom or help any man employs or affords, the success is from God alone, who will not let his people perish.

Verses 22-29

Ahithophel hanged himself for vexation that his counsel was not followed. That will break a proud man's heart which will not break a humble man's sleep. He thought himself in danger, concluding, that, because his counsel was not followed, Absalom's cause would fail; and to prevent a possible public execution, he does justice upon himself. Thus the breath is stopped, and the head laid low, from which nothing could be expected but mischief. Absalom chased his father. But observe how God sometimes makes up to his people that comfort from strangers, which they are disappointed of in their own families. Our King needs not our help; but he assures us, that what we do for the least of his brethren, who are sick, poor, and destitute, shall be accepted and recompensed as if done to himself

Chapter 18

Chapter Outline

Absalom's army defeated.   (1–8)

He is slain.   (9–18)

David's over-sorrow.   (19–33)

Verses 1-8

How does David render good for evil! Absalom would have only David smitten; David would have only Absalom spared. This seems to be a resemblance of man's wickedness towards God, and God's mercy to man, of which it is hard to say which is most amazing. Now the Israelites see what it is to take counsel against the Lord and his anointed.

Verses 9-18

Let young people look upon Absalom, hanging on a tree, accursed, forsaken of heaven and earth; there let them read the Lord's abhorrence of rebellion against parents. Nothing can preserve men from misery and contempt, but heavenly wisdom and the grace of God.

Verses 19-33

By directing David to give God thanks for his victory, Ahimaaz prepared him for the news of his son's death. The more our hearts are fixed and enlarged, in thanksgiving to God for our mercies, the better disposed we shall be to bear with patience the afflictions mixed with them. Some think David's wish arose from concern about Absalom's everlasting state; but he rather seems to have spoken without due thought. He is to be blamed for showing so great fondness for a graceless son. Also for quarrelling with Divine justice. And for opposing the justice of the nation, which, as king, he had to administer, and which ought to be preferred before natural affection. The best men are not always in a good frame; we are apt to over-grieve for what we over-loved. But while we learn from this example to watch and pray against sinful indulgence, or neglect of our children, may we not, in David, perceive a shadow of the Saviour's love, who wept over, prayed for, and even suffered death for mankind, though vile rebels and enemies.

Chapter 19

Chapter Outline

Joab causes David to cease mourning.   (1–8)

David returns to Jordan.   (9–15)

Verses 1-8

To continue to lament for so bad a son as Absalom, was very unwise, and very unworthy. Joab censures David, but not with proper respect and deference to his sovereign. A plain case may be fairly pleaded with those above us, and they may be reproved for what they do amiss, but it must not be with rudeness and insolence. Yet David took the reproof and the counsel, prudently and mildly. Timely giving way, usually prevents the ill effects of mistaken measures.

Verses 9-15

God's providence, by the priests' persuasions and Amasa's interest, brought the people to resolve the recall of the king. David stirred not till he received this invitation. Our Lord Jesus will rule in those that invite him to the throne in their hearts, and not till he is invited. He first bows the heart, and makes it willing in the day of his power, then rules in the midst of his enemies, Ps 110:2, 3.

Verses 16-23

Those who now slight and abuse the Son of David, would be glad to make their peace when he shall come in his glory; but it will be too late. Shimei lost no time. His abuse had been personal, and with the usual right feeling of good men, David could more easily forgive it.

Verses 24-30

David recalls the forfeiture of Mephibosheth's estate; and he expressed joy for the king's return. A good man contentedly bears his own losses, while he sees Israel in peace, and the Son of David exalted.

Verses 31-39

Barzillai thought he had done himself honour in doing the king any service. Thus, when the saints shall be called to inherit the kingdom, they will be amazed at the recompence being so very far beyond the service, Mt 25:37. A good man would not go any where to be burdensome; or, will rather be so to his own house than to another's. It is good for all, but especially becomes old people, to think and speak much of dying. The grave is ready for me, let me go and get ready for it.

Verses 40-43

The men of Israel though themselves despised, and the fiercer words of the men of Judah produced very bad effects. Much evil might be avoided, if men would watch against pride, and remember that a soft answer turneth away wrath. Though we have right and reason on our side, if we speak it with fierceness, God is displeased.

Chapter 20

Chapter Outline

Verses 1-3

One trial arises after another for our good, till we reach the place where sin and sorrow are for ever done away. Angry disputers misunderstand or misconstrue one another's words; proud men will have every thing their own way, or wholly refuse their assistance. The favour of the many is not to be depended upon; and what have others to expect, when Hosanna to the Son of David was soon changed to Crucify him, crucify him?

Verses 4-13

Joab barbarously murdered Amasa. The more plot there is in a sin, the worse it is. Joab contentedly sacrificed the interest both of the king and the kingdom to his personal revenge. But one would wonder with what face a murderer could pursue a traitor; and how, under such a load of guilt, he had courage to enter upon danger: his conscience was seared.

Verses 14-22

Justly is that place attacked, which dares to harbour a traitor; nor will the heart fare better which indulges rebellious lusts, that will not have Christ to reign over them. A discreet woman, by her prudent management, satisfied Joab, and yet saved the city. Wisdom is not confined to rank or sex; it consists not in deep knowledge; but in understanding how to act as matters arise, that troubles may be turned away and benefits secured. A great deal of mischief would be prevented, if contending parties would understand one another. Let both sides be undeceived. The single condition of peace is, the surrender of the traitor. It is so in God's dealing with the soul, when besieged by conviction and distress; sin is the traitor; the beloved lust is the rebel: part with that, cast away the transgression, and all shall be well. There is no peace on any other terms.

Verses 23-26

Here is the state of David's court, after his restoration. It is well when able men are appointed to discharge public duties; let all seek to perform those duties, as faithful servants to the Son of David.

Chapter 21

Chapter Outline

Verses 1-9

Every affliction arises from sin, and should lead us to repent and humble ourselves before God; but some troubles especially show that they are sent to bring sin to remembrance. God's judgments often look a great way back, which requires us to do so, when we are under his rebukes. It is not for us to object against the people's smarting for the sin of their king; perhaps they helped him. Nor against this generation suffering for the sin of the last. God often visits the sins of the fathers upon the children, and he gives no account of any matters. Time does not wear out the guilt of sin; nor can we build hopes of escape upon the delay of judgments. If we cannot understand all the reasons of Providence in this matter, still we have no right to demand that God should acquaint us with those reasons. It must be right, because it is the will of God, and in the end it will be proved to be so. Money is no satisfaction for blood. It should seem, Saul's posterity trod in his steps, for it is called a bloody house. It was the spirit of the family, therefore they are justly reckoned with for his sin, as well as for their own. The Gibeonites did not require this out of malice against Saul or his family. It was not to gratify any revenge, but for the public good. They were put to death at the beginning of harvest; they were thus sacrificed to turn away the wrath of Almighty God, who had withheld the harvest-mercies for some years past, and to obtain his favour in the present harvest. In vain do we expect mercy from God, unless we do justice upon our sins. Executions must not be thought cruel, which are for the public welfare.

Verses 10-14

That a guilty land should enjoy many years of plenty, calls for gratitude; and we need not wonder misused abundance should be punished with scarcity; yet how few are disposed to ask of the Lord concerning the sinful cause, while numbers search for the second causes by which he is pleased to work! But the Lord will plead the cause of those who cannot or will not avenge themselves; and the prayers of the poor are of great power. When God sent rain to water the earth, these bodies were buried, for then it appeared that God was entreated for the land. When justice is done on earth, vengeance from heaven ceases. God is pacified, and is entreated for us through Christ, who was hanged on a tree, and so made a curse for us, to do away our guilt, though he was himself guiltless.

Verses 15-22

These events seem to have taken place towards the end of David's reign. David fainted, but he did not flee, and God sent help in the time of need. In spiritual conflicts, even strong saints sometimes wax faint; then Satan attacks them furiously; but those who stand their ground and resist him, shall be relieved and made more than conquerors. Death is a Christian's last enemy, and a son of Anak; but through Him that triumphed for us, believers shall be more than conquerors at last, even over that enemy.

Chapter 22

David's psalm of thanksgiving.
—This chapter is a psalm of praise; we find it afterwards nearly as Ps 18. They that trust God in the way of duty, shall find him a present help in their greatest dangers: David did so. Remarkable preservations should be particularly mentioned in our praises. We shall never be delivered from all enemies till we get to heaven. God will preserve all his people, 2Ti 4:18. Those who receive signal mercies from God, ought to give him the glory. In the day that God delivered David, he sang this song. While the mercy is fresh, and we are most affected with it, let the thank-offering be brought, to be kindled with the fire of that affection. All his joys and hopes close, as all our hopes should do, in the great Redeemer.

Chapter 23

Chapter Outline

Verses 1-7

These words of David are very worthy of regard. Let those who have had long experience of God's goodness, and the pleasantness of heavenly wisdom, when they come to finish their course, bear their testimony to the truth of the promise. David avows his Divine inspiration, that the Spirit of God spake by him. He, and other holy men, spake and wrote as they were moved by the Holy

Ghost. In many things he had his own neglect and wrong conduct to blame. But David comforted himself that the Lord had made with him an everlasting covenant. By this he principally intended the covenant of mercy and peace, which the Lord made with him as a sinner, who believed in the promised Saviour, who embraced the promised blessing, who yielded up himself to the Lord, to be his redeemed servant. Believers shall for ever enjoy covenant blessings; and God the Father, Son, and Holy Ghost, shall be for ever glorified in their salvation. Thus pardon, righteousness, grace, and eternal life, are secured as the gift of God through Jesus Christ. There is an infinite fulness of grace and all blessings treasured up in Christ, for those who seek his salvation. This covenant was all David's salvation, he so well knew the holy law of God and the extent of his own sinfulness, that he perceived what was needful for his own case in this salvation. It was therefore all his desire. In comparison, all earthly objects lost their attractions; he was willing to give them up, or to die and leave them, that he might enjoy full happiness, Ps 73:24–28. Still the power of evil, and the weakness of his faith, hope, and love, were his grief and burden. Doubtless he would have allowed that his own slackness and want of care were the cause; but the hope that he should soon be made perfect in glory, encouraged him in his dying moments.

Verses 8-39

David once earnestly longed for the water at the well of Bethlehem. It seems to be an instance of weakness. He was thirsty; with the water of that well he had often refreshed himself when a youth, and it was without due thought that he desired it. Were his valiant men so forward to expose themselves, upon the least hint of their prince's mind, and so eager to please him, and shall not we long to approve ourselves to our Lord Jesus, by ready compliance with his will, as shown us by his word, Spirit, and providence? But David poured out the water as a drink-offering to the Lord. Thus he would cross his own foolish fancy, and punish himself for indulging it, and show that he had sober thoughts to correct his rash ones, and knew how to deny himself. Did David look upon that water as very precious which was got at the hazard of these men's blood, and shall not we much more value those benefits for purchasing which our blessed Saviour shed his blood? Let all beware of neglecting so great salvation.

Chapter 24

Chapter Outline

David numbers the people.	(1–9)
He chooses the pestilence.	(10–15)
The staying the pestilence.	(16, 17)
David's sacrifice, The plague removed.	(18–25)

Verses 1-9

For the people's sin David was left to act wrong, and in his chastisement they received punishment. This example throws light upon God's government of the world, and furnishes a useful lesson. The pride of David's heart, was his sin in numbering of the people. He thought thereby to appear the more formidable, trusting in an arm of flesh more than he should have done, and though he had written so much of trusting in God only. God judges not of sin as we do. What appears to us harmless, or, at least, but a small offence, may be a great sin in the eye of God, who discerns the thoughts and intents of the heart. Even ungodly men can discern evil tempers and wrong conduct in believers, of which they themselves often remain unconscious. But God seldom allows those whom he loves the pleasures they sinfully covet.

Verses 10-15

It is well, when a man has sinned, if he has a heart within to smite him for it. If we confess our sins, we may pray in faith that God would forgive them, and take away, by pardoning mercy, that sin which we cast away by sincere repentance. What we make the matter of our pride, it is just in God to take from us, or make bitter to us, and make it our punishment. This must be such a punishment as the people have a large share in, for though it was David's sin that opened the sluice, the sins of the people all contributed to the flood. In this difficulty, David chose a judgment which came immediately from God, whose mercies he knew to be very great, rather than from men, who would have triumphed in the miseries of Israel, and have been thereby hardened in their idolatry. He chose the pestilence; he and his family would be as much exposed to it as the poorest Israelite; and he would continue for a shorter time under the Divine rebuke, however severe it was. The rapid destruction by the pestilence shows how easily God can bring down the proudest sinners, and how much we owe daily to the Divine patience.

Verses 16, 17

Perhaps there was more wickedness, especially more pride, and that was the sin now chastised, in Jerusalem than elsewhere, therefore the hand of the destroyer is stretched out upon that city; but the Lord repented him of the evil, changed not his mind, but his way. In the very place where Abraham was stayed from slaying his son, this angel, by a like countermand, was stayed from destroying Jerusalem. It is for the sake of the great Sacrifice, that our forfeited lives are preserved from the destroying angel. And in David is the spirit of a true shepherd of the people, offering himself as a sacrifice to God, for the salvation of his subjects.

Verses 18-25

God's encouraging us to offer to him spiritual sacrifices, is an evidence of his reconciling us to himself. David purchased the ground to build the altar. God hates robbery for burnt-offering. Those know not what religion is, who chiefly care to make it cheap and easy to themselves, and who are best pleased with that which costs them least pains or money. For what have we our substance, but to honour God with it; and how can it be better bestowed? See the building of the altar, and the offering proper sacrifices upon it. Burnt-offerings to the glory of God's justice; peace-offerings to the glory of his mercy. Christ is our Altar, our Sacrifice; in him alone we may expect to escape his wrath, and to find favour with God. Death is destroying all around, in so many forms, and so suddenly, that it is madness not to expect and prepare for the close of life.

1 Kings

The history now before us accounts for the affairs of the kingdoms of Judah and Israel, yet with special regard to the kingdom of God among them; for it is a sacred history. It is earlier as to time, teaches much more, and is more interesting than any common histories.

Chapter 1

Chapter Outline

Verses 1-4

We have David sinking under infirmities. He was chastised for his recent sins, and felt the effects of his former toils and hardships.

Verses 5-10

Indulgent parents are often chastised with disobedient children, who are anxious to possess their estates. No worldly wisdom, nor experience, nor sacredness of character, can insure the continuance in any former course of those who remain under the power of self-love. But we may well wonder by what arts Joab and Abiathar could be drawn aside.

Verses 11-31

Observe Nathan's address to Bathsheba. Let me give thee counsel how to save thy own life, and the life of thy son. Such as this is the counsel Christ's ministers give us in his name, to give all diligence, not only that no man take our crown, Re 3:11, but that we save our lives, even the lives of our souls. David made a solemn declaration of his firm cleaving to his former resolution, that Solomon should be his successor. Even the recollection of the distresses from which the Lord redeemed him, increased his comfort, inspired his hopes, and animated him to his duty, under the decays of nature and the approach of death.

Verses 32-53

The people expressed great joy and satisfaction in the elevation of Solomon. Every true Israelite rejoices in the exaltation of the Son of David. Combinations formed upon evil principles will soon be dissolved, when self-interest calls another way. How can those who do evil deeds expect to have good tidings? Adonijah had despised Solomon, but soon dreaded him. We see here, as in a glass, Jesus, the Son of David and the Son of God, exalted to the throne of glory, notwithstanding all his enemies. His kingdom is far greater than that of his father David, and therein all the true people of God cordially rejoice. The prosperity of his cause is vexation and terror to his enemies. No horns of the altar, nor forms of godliness, nor pretences to religion, can profit those who will not submit to His authority, and accept of his salvation; and if their submission be hypocritical, they shall perish without remedy.

Chapter 2

Chapter Outline

Verses 1-4

David's charge to Solomon is, to keep the charge of the Lord. The authority of a dying father is much, but nothing to that of a living God. God promised David that the Messiah should come from his descendants, and that promise was absolute; but the promise, that there should not fail of them a man on the throne of Israel, was conditional; if he walks before God in sincerity, with zeal and resolution: in order hereunto, he must take heed to his way. (1Ki 2:5-11)

Verses 5-11

These dying counsels concerning Joab and Shimei, did not come from personal anger, but for the security of Solomon's throne, which was the murders he had committed, but would readily repeat them to carry any purpose; though long reprieved, he shall be reckoned with at last. Time does not wear out the guilt of any sin, particularly of murder. Concerning Shimei, Hold him not guiltless; do not think him any true friend to thee, or thy government, or fit to be trusted; he has no less malice now than he had then. David's dying sentiments are recorded, as delivered under the influence of the Holy Ghost, 2Sa 23:1-7. The Lord discovered to him the offices and the salvation of that glorious personage, the Messiah, whose coming he then foretold, and from whom he derived all his comforts and expectations. That passage gives a decided proof that David died under the influence of the Holy Ghost, in the exercise of faith and hope.

Verses 12-25

Solomon received Bathsheba with all the respect that was owing to a mother; but let none be asked for that which they ought not to grant. It ill becomes a good man to prefer a bad request, or to appear in a bad cause. According to eastern customs it was plain that Adonijah sought to be king, by his asking for Abishag as his wife, and Solomon could not be safe while he lived. Ambitious, turbulent spirits commonly prepare death for themselves. Many a head has been lost by catching at a crown.

Verses 26-34

Solomon's words to Abiathar, and his silence, imply that some recent conspiracies had been entered into. Those that show kindness to God's people shall have it remembered to their advantage. For this reason Solomon spares Abiathar's life, but dismisses him from his offices. In case of such sins as the blood of beasts would atone for, the altar was a refuge, but not in Joab's case. Solomon looks upward to God as the Author of peace, and forward to eternity as the perfection of it. The Lord of peace himself gives us that peace which is everlasting.

Verses 35-46

The old malignity remains in the unconverted heart, and a watchful eye should be kept on those who, like Shimei, have manifested their enmity, but have given no evidence of repentance. No engagements or dangers will restrain worldly men; they go on, though they forfeit their lives and souls. Let us remember, God will not accommodate his judgment to us. His eye is over us; and let us strive to walk as in his presence. Let our every act, word, and thought, be governed by this great truth, that the hour is quickly coming when the smallest circumstances of our lives shall be brought to light, and our eternal state be fixed by a righteous and unerring God. Thus Solomon's throne was established in peace, as the type of the Redeemer's kingdom of peace and righteousness. And it is a comfort, in reference to the enmity of the church's enemies, that, how much soever they rage, it is a vain thing they imagine. Christ's throne is established, and they cannot shake it.

Chapter 3

Chapter Outline

Solomon's marriage.	(1–4)
His vision, His prayer for wisdom.	(5–15)
The judgment of Solomon.	(16–28)

Verses 1-4

He that loved the Lord, should, for his sake, have fixed his love upon one of the Lord's people. Solomon was a wise man, a rich man, a great man; yet the brightest praise of him, is that which is the character of all the saints, even the poorest, "He loved the Lord." Where God sows plentifully, he expects to reap accordingly; and those that truly love God and his worship, will not grudge the expenses of their religion. We must never think that wasted which is laid out in the service of God.

Verses 5-15

Solomon's dream was not a common one. While his bodily powers were locked up in sleep, the powers of his soul were strengthened; he was enabled to receive the Divine vision, and to make a suitable choice. God, in like manner, puts us in the ready way to be happy, by assuring us we shall have what we need, and pray for. Solomon's making such a choice when asleep, and the powers of reason least active, showed it came from the grace of God. Having a humble sense of his own wants and weakness, he pleads, Lord, I am but a little child. The more wise and considerate men are, the better acquainted they are with their own weakness, and the more jealous of themselves. Solomon begs of God to give him wisdom. We must pray for it, Jas 1:5, that it may help us in our particular calling, and the various occasions we have. Those are accepted of God, who prefer spiritual blessings to earthly good. It was a prevailing prayer, and prevailed for more than he asked. God gave him wisdom, such as no other prince was ever blessed with; and also gave him riches and honour. If we make sure of wisdom and grace, these will bring outward prosperity with them, or sweeten the want of it. The way to get spiritual blessings, is to wrestle with God in prayer for them. The way to get earthly blessings, is to refer ourselves to God concerning them. Solomon has wisdom given him, because he did ask it, and wealth, because he did not.

Verses 16-28

An instance of Solomon's wisdom is given. Notice the difficulty of the case. To find out the true mother, he could not try which the child loved best, and therefore tried which loved the child best: the mother's sincerity will be tried, when the child is in danger. Let parents show their love to their children, especially by taking care of their souls, and snatching them as brands out of the burning. By this and other instances of the wisdom with which God endued him, Solomon had great reputation among his people. This was better to him than weapons of war; for this he was both feared and loved.

Chapter 4

Chapter Outline

Verses 1-19

In the choice of the great officers of Solomon's court, no doubt, his wisdom appeared. Several are the same that were in his father's time. A plan was settled by which no part of the country was exhausted to supply his court, though each sent its portion.

Verses 20-28

Never did the crown of Israel shine so bright, as when Solomon wore it. He had peace on all sides. Herein, his kingdom was a type of the Messiah's; for to Him it is promised that he shall have the heathen for his inheritance, and that princes shall worship him. The spiritual peace, and joy, and holy security, of all the faithful subjects of the Lord Jesus, were typified by that of Israel. The kingdom of God is not, as Solomon's was, meat and drink, but, what is infinitely better, righteousness, and peace, and joy in the Holy Ghost. The vast number of his attendants, and the great resort to him, are shown by the provision daily made. Herein Christ far outdoes Solomon, that he feeds all his subjects, not with the bread that perishes, but with that which endures to eternal life.

Verses 29-34

Solomon's wisdom was more his glory than his wealth. He had what is here called largeness of heart, for the heart is often put for the powers of the mind. He had the gift of utterance, as well as wisdom. It is very desirable, that those who have large gifts of any kind, should have large hearts to use them for the good of others. What treasures of wisdom and knowledge are lost! But every sort of knowledge that is needful for salvation is to be found in the holy Scriptures. There came persons from all parts, who were more eager after knowledge than their neighbours, to hear the wisdom of Solomon. Solomon was herein a type of Christ, in whom are hid all treasures of wisdom and knowledge; and hid for us, for he is made of God to us, wisdom. Christ's fame shall spread through all the earth, and men of all nations shall come to him, learn of him, and take upon them his easy yoke, and find rest for their souls.

Chapter 5

Chapter Outline

Solomon's agreement with Hiram.   (1–9)
Solomon's workmen for the temple.   (10–18)

Verses 1-9

Here is Solomon's design to build a temple. There is no adversary, no Satan, so the word is; no instrument of Satan to oppose it, or to divert from it. Satan does all he can, to hinder temple work.

When there is no evil abroad, then let us be ready and active in that which is good, and get forward. Let God's promises quicken our endeavours. And all outward skill and advantages should be made serviceable to the interests of Christ's kingdom. It Tyre supplies Israel with craftsmen, Israel will supply Tyre with corn, Eze 27:17. Thus, by the wise disposal of Providence, one country has need of another, and is benefitted by another, that there may be dependence on one another, to the glory of God.

Verses 10-18

The temple was chiefly built by the riches and labour of Gentiles, which typified their being called into the church. Solomon commanded, and they brought costly stones for the foundation. Christ, who is laid for a Foundation, is a chosen and precious Stone. We should lay our foundation firm, and bestow most pains on that part of our religion which lies out of the sight of men. And happy those who, as lively stones, are built up a spiritual house, for a habitation of God through the Spirit. Who among us will build in the house of the Lord?

Chapter 6

Chapter Outline

Verses 1-10

The temple is called the house of the Lord, because it was directed and modelled by him, and was to be employed in his service. This gave it the beauty of holiness, that it was the house of the Lord, which was far beyond all other beauties. It was to be the temple of the God of peace, therefore no iron tool must be heard; quietness and silence suit and help religious exercises. God's work should be done with much care and little noise. Clamour and violence often hinder, but never further the work of God. Thus the kingdom of God in the heart of man grows up in silence, Mr 5:27.

Verses 11-14

None employ themselves for God, without having his eye upon them. But God plainly let Solomon know that all the charge for building this temple, would neither excuse from obedience to the law of God, nor shelter from his judgments, in case of disobedience.

Verses 15-38

See what was typified by this temple. 1. Christ is the true Temple. In him dwells all the fulness of the Godhead; in him meet all God's spiritual Israel; through him we have access with confidence to God. 2. Every believer is a living temple, in whom the Spirit of God dwells, 1Co 3:16. This living temple is built upon Christ as its Foundation, and will be perfect in due time. 3. The gospel church is the mystical temple. It grows to a holy temple in the Lord, enriched and beautified with the gifts and graces of the Spirit. This temple is built firm, upon a Rock. 4. Heaven is the everlasting temple. There the church will be fixed. All that shall be stones in that building, must, in the present state of preparation, be fitted and made ready for it. Let sinners come to Jesus as the living Foundation, that they may be built on him, a part of this spiritual house, consecrated in body and soul to the glory of God.

Chapter 7

Chapter Outline

Solomon's buildings.	(1–12)
Furniture of the temple.	(13–47)
Vessels of gold.	(48–51)

Verses 1-12

All Solomon's buildings, though beautiful, were intended for use. Solomon began with the temple; he built for God first, and then his other buildings. The surest foundations of lasting prosperity are laid in early piety. He was thirteen years building his house, yet he built the temple in little more than seven years; not that he was more exact, but less eager in building his own house, than in building God's. We ought to prefer God's honour before our own ease and satisfaction.

Verses 13-47

The two brazen pillars in the porch of the temple, some think, were to teach those that came to worship, to depend upon God only, for strength and establishment in all their religious exercises. "Jachin," God will fix this roving mind. It is good that the heart be established with grace. "Boaz," In him is our strength, who works in us both to will and to do. Spiritual strength and stability are found at the door of God's temple, where we must wait for the gifts of grace, in use of the means of grace. Spiritual priests and spiritual sacrifices must be washed in the laver of Christ's blood, and of regeneration. We must wash often, for we daily contract pollution. There are full means provided for our cleansing; so that if we have our lot for ever among the unclean it will be our own fault.

Let us bless God for the fountain opened by the sacrifice of Christ for sin and for uncleanness.

Verses 48-51

Christ is now the Temple and the Builder; the Altar and the Sacrifice; the Light of our souls, and the Bread of life; able to supply all the wants of all that have applied or shall apply to him. Outward images cannot represent, words cannot express, the heart cannot conceive, his preciousness or his love. Let us come to him, and wash away our sins in his blood; let us seek for the purifying grace of his Spirit; let us maintain communion with the Father through his intercession, and yield up ourselves and all we have to his service. Being strengthened by him, we shall be accepted, useful, and happy.

Chapter 8

Chapter Outline

Verses 1-11

The bringing in the ark, is the end which must crown the work: this was done with great solemnity. The ark was fixed in the place appointed for its rest in the inner part of the house, whence they expected God to speak to them, even in the most holy place. The staves of the ark were drawn out, so as to direct the high priest to the mercy-seat over the ark, when he went in, once a year, to sprinkle the blood there; so that they continued of use, though there was no longer occasion to carry it by them. The glory of God appearing in a cloud may signify, 1. The darkness of that dispensation, in comparison with the light of the gospel, by which, with open face, we behold, as in a glass, the glory of the Lord. 2. The darkness of our present state, in comparison with the sight of God, which will be the happiness of heaven, where the Divine glory is unveiled.

Verses 12-21

Solomon encouraged the priests, who were much astonished at the dark cloud. The dark dispensations of Providence should quicken us in fleeing for refuge to the hope of the gospel. Nothing can more reconcile us to them, than to consider what God has said, and to compare his word and works together. Whatever good we do, we must look on it as the performance of God's promise to us, not of our promises to him.

Verses 22-53

In this excellent prayer, Solomon does as we should do in every prayer; he gives glory to God. Fresh experiences of the truth of God's promises call for larger praises. He sues for grace and favour from God. The experiences we have of God's performing his promises, should encourage us to depend upon them, and to plead them with him; and those who expect further mercies, must be thankful for former mercies. God's promises must be the guide of our desires, and the ground of our hopes and expectations in prayer. The sacrifices, the incense, and the whole service of the temple, were all typical of the Redeemer's offices, oblation, and intercession. The temple, therefore, was continually to be remembered. Under one word, "forgive," Solomon expressed all that he could ask in behalf of his people. For, as all misery springs from sin, forgiveness of sin prepares the way for the removal of every evil, and the receiving of every good. Without it, no deliverance can prove a blessing. In addition to the teaching of the word of God, Solomon entreated the Lord himself to teach the people to profit by all, even by their chastisements. They shall know every man the plague of his own heart, what it is that pains him; and shall spread their hands in prayer toward this house; whether the trouble be of body or mind, they shall represent it before God. Inward burdens seem especially meant. Sin is the plague of our own hearts; our in-dwelling corruptions are our spiritual diseases: every true Israelite endeavours to know these, that he may mortify them, and watch against the risings of them. These drive him to his knees; lamenting these, he spreads forth his hands in prayer. After many particulars, Solomon concludes with the general request, that God would hearken to his praying people. No place, now, under the gospel, can add to the prayers made in or towards it. The substance is Christ; whatever we ask in his name, it shall be given us. In this manner the Israel of God is established and sanctified, the backslider is recovered and healed. In this manner the stranger is brought nigh, the mourner is comforted, the name of God is glorified. Sin is the cause of all our troubles; repentance and forgiveness lead to all human happiness.

Verses 54-61

Never was a congregation dismissed with what was more likely to affect them, and to abide with them. What Solomon asks for in this prayer, is still granted in the intercession of Christ, of which his supplication was a type. We shall receive grace sufficient, suitable, and seasonable, in every time of need. No human heart is of itself willing to obey the gospel call to repentance, faith, and newness of life, walking in all the commandments of the Lord, yet Solomon exhorts the people to be perfect. This is the scriptural method, it is our duty to obey the command of the law and the call of the gospel, seeing we have broken the law. When our hearts are inclined thereto, feeling our sinfulness and weakness, we pray for Divine assistance; thus are we made able to serve God through Jesus Christ.

Verses 62-66

Solomon offered a great sacrifice. He kept the feast of tabernacles, as it seems, after the feast of dedication. Thus should we go home, rejoicing, from holy ordinances, thankful for God's Goodness

Chapter 9

Chapter Outline

Verses 1-9

God warned Solomon, now he had newly built and dedicated the temple, that he and his people might not be high-minded, but fear. After all the services we can perform, we stand upon the same terms with the Lord as before. Nothing can purchase for us liberty to sin, nor would the true believer desire such a licence. He would rather be chastened of the Lord, than be allowed to go on with ease and prosperity in sin.

Verses 10-14

Solomon gave Hiram twenty cities. Hiram did not like them. If Solomon would gratify him, let it be in his own element, by becoming his partner in trade, as he did. See how the providence of God suits this earth to the various tempers of men, and the dispositions of men to the earth, and all for the good of mankind in general.

Verses 15-28

Here is a further account of Solomon's greatness. He began at the right end, for he built God's house first, and finished that before he began his own; then God blessed him, and he prospered in all his other buildings. Let piety begin, and profit follow; leave pleasure to the last. Whatever pains we take for the glory of God, and to profit others, we are likely to have the advantage. Canaan, the holy land, the glory of all lands, had no gold in it; which shows that the best produce is that which is for the present support of life, our own and others; such things did Canaan produce. Solomon got much by his merchandise, and yet has directed us to a better trade, within reach of the poorest. Wisdom is better than the merchandise of silver, and the gain thereof than fine gold, Pr 3:14.

Chapter 10

Chapter Outline

Verses 1-13

The queen of Sheba came to Solomon to hear his wisdom, thereby to improve her own. Our Saviour mentions her inquiries after God, by Solomon, as showing the stupidity of those who inquire not after God, by our Lord Jesus Christ. By waiting and prayer, by diligently searching the Scriptures, by consulting wise and experienced Christians, and by practising what we have learned, we shall be delivered from difficulties. Solomon's wisdom made more impression upon the queen of Sheba than all his prosperity and grandeur. There is a spiritual excellence in heavenly things, and in consistent Christians, to which no reports can do justice. Here the truth exceeded; and all who, through grace, are brought to commune with God, will say the one half was not told them of the pleasures and the advantages of wisdom's ways. Glorified saints, much more, will say of heaven, that the thousandth part was not told them, 1Co 2:9. She pronounced them happy that constantly attended Solomon. With much more reason may we say of Christ's servants, Blessed are they that dwell in his house; they will be still praising him. She made a noble present to Solomon. What we present to Christ, he needs not, but will have us do so to express our gratitude. The believer who has been with Jesus, will return to his station, discharge his duties with readiness, and from better motives; looking forward to the day when, being absent from the body, he shall be present with the Lord.

Verses 14-29

Solomon increased his wealth. Silver was nothing accounted of. Such is the nature of worldly wealth, plenty of it makes it the less valuable; much more should the enjoyment of spiritual riches lessen our esteem of all earthly possessions. If gold in abundance makes silver to be despised, shall not wisdom, and grace, and the foretastes of heaven, which are far better than gold, make gold to be lightly esteemed? See in Solomon's greatness the performance of God's promise, and let it encourage us to seek first the righteousness of God's kingdom. This was he, who, having tasted all earthly enjoyments, wrote a book, to show the vanity of all worldly things, the vexation of spirit that attends them, and the folly of setting our hearts upon them: and to recommend serious godliness, as that which will do unspeakably more to make us happy, that all the wealth and power he was master of; and, through the grace of God, it is within our reach.

Chapter 11

Chapter Outline

Solomon's wives and concubines, His idolatry.	(1–8)
God's anger.	(9–13)
Solomon's adversaries.	(14–25)

Verses 1-8

There is not a more melancholy and astonishing instance of human depravity in the sacred Scriptures, than that here recorded. Solomon became a public worshipper of abominable idols! Probably he by degrees gave way to pride and luxury, and thus lost his relish for true wisdom. Nothing forms in itself a security against the deceitfulness and depravity of the human heart. Nor will old age cure the heart of any evil propensity. If our sinful passions are not crucified and mortified by the grace of God, they never will die of themselves, but will last even when opportunities to gratify them are taken away. Let him that thinks he stands, take heed lest he fall. We see how weak we are of ourselves, without the grace of God; let us therefore live in constant dependence on that grace. Let us watch and be sober: ours is a dangerous warfare, and in an enemy's country, while our worst foes are the traitors in our own hearts. (1Ki 11:9-13)

Verses 9-13

The Lord told Solomon, it is likely by a prophet, what he must expect for his apostacy. Though we have reason to hope that he repented, and found mercy, yet the Holy Ghost did not expressly record it, but left it doubtful, as a warning to others not to sin. The guilt may be taken away, but not the reproach; that will remain. Thus it must remain uncertain to us till the day of judgment, whether or not Solomon was left to suffer the everlasting displeasure of an offended God.

Verses 14-25

While Solomon kept close to God and to his duty, there was no enemy to give him uneasiness; but here we have an account of two. If against us, he can make us fear even the least, and the very grasshopper shall be a burden. Though they were moved by principles of ambition or revenge, God used them to correct Solomon.

Verses 26-40

In telling the reason why God rent the kingdom from the house of Solomon, Ahijah warned Jeroboam to take heed of sinning away his preferment. Yet the house of David must be supported; out of it the Messiah would arise. Solomon sought to kill his successor. Had not he taught others, that whatever devices are in men's hearts, the counsel of the Lord shall stand? Yet he himself thinks to defeat that counsel. Jeroboam withdrew into Egypt, and was content to live in exile and obscurity for awhile, being sure of a kingdom at last. Shall not we be content, who have a better kingdom in reserve?

Verses 41-43

Solomon's reign was as long as his father's, but his life was not so. Sin shortened his days. If the world, with all its advantages, could satisfy the soul, and afford real joy, Solomon would have found it so. But he was disappointed in all, and to warn us, has left this record of all earthly enjoyments, "Vanity and vexation of spirit." The New Testament declares that one greater than Solomon is come to reign over us, and to possess the throne of his father David. May we not see something of Christ's excellency faintly represented to us in this figure?

Chapter 12

Chapter Outline

Rehoboam's accession, The people's petition, His rough answer.	(1–15)
Ten tribes revolt.	(16–24)
Jeroboam's idolatry.	(25–33)

Verses 1-15

The tribes complained not to Rehoboam of his father's idolatry, and revolt from God. That which was the greatest grievance, was none to them; so careless were they in matters of religion, if they might live at ease, and pay no taxes. Factious spirits will never want something to complain of. And when we see the Scripture account of Solomon's reign; the peace, wealth, and prosperity Israel then enjoyed; we cannot doubt but that their charges were false, or far beyond the truth. Rehoboam answered the people according to the counsel of the young men. Never was man more blinded by pride, and desire of arbitrary power, than which nothing is more fatal. God's counsels were hereby fulfilled. He left Rehoboam to his own folly, and hid from his eyes the things which belonged to his peace, that the kingdom might be rent from him. God serves his own wise and righteous purposes by the imprudences and sins of men. Those that lose the kingdom of heaven, throw it away, as Rehoboam, by wilfulness and folly.

Verses 16-24

The people speak unbecomingly of David. How soon are good men, and their good services to the public, forgotten ! These considerations should reconcile us to our losses and troubles, that God is the Author of them, and our brethren the instruments: let us not meditate revenge. Rehoboam and his people hearkened to the word of the Lord. When we know God's mind, we must submit, how much soever it crosses our own mind. If we secure the favour of God, not all the universe can hurt us.

Verses 25-33

Jeroboam distrusted the providence of God; he would contrive ways and means, and sinful ones too, for his own safety. A practical disbelief of God's all-sufficiency is at the bottom of all our departures from him. Though it is probable he meant his worship for Jehovah the God of Israel, it was contrary to the Divine law, and dishonourable to the Divine majesty to be thus represented. The people might be less shocked at worshipping the God of Israel under an image, than if they had at once been asked to worship Baal; but it made way for that idolatry. Blessed Lord, give us grace to reverence thy temple, thine ordinances, thine house of prayer, thy sabbaths, and never more, like Jeroboam, to set up in our hearts any idol of abomination. Be thou to us every thing precious; do thou reign and rule in our hearts, the hope of glory.

Chapter 13

Chapter Outline

Verses 1-10

In threatening the altar, the prophet threatens the founder and worshippers. Idolatrous worship will not continue, but the word of the Lord will endure for ever. The prediction plainly declared that the family of David would continue, and support true religion, when the ten tribes would not be able to resist them. If God, in justice, harden the hearts of sinners, so that the hand they have stretched out in sin they cannot pull in again by repentance, that is a spiritual judgment, represented by this, and much more dreadful. Jeroboam looked for help, not from his calves, but from God only, from his power, and his favour. The time may come when those that hate the preaching, would be glad of the prayers of faithful ministers. Jeroboam does not desire the prophet to pray that his sin might be pardoned, and his heart changed, but only that his hand might be restored. He seemed affected for the present with both the judgment and the mercy, but the impression wore off. God forbade his messenger to eat or drink in Bethel, to show his detestation of their idolatry and apostacy from God, and to teach us not to have fellowship with the works of darkness. Those have not learned self-denial, who cannot forbear one forbidden meal.

Verses 11-22

The old prophet's conduct proves that he was not really a godly man. When the change took place under Jeroboam, he preferred his ease and interest to his religion. He took a very bad method to bring the good prophet back. It was all a lie. Believers are most in danger of being drawn from their duty by plausible pretences of holiness. We may wonder that the wicked prophet went unpunished, while the holy man of God was suddenly and severely punished. What shall we make of this? The judgments of God are beyond our power to fathom; and there is a judgment to come. Nothing can excuse any act of wilful disobedience. This shows what they must expect who hearken to the great deceiver. They that yield to him as a tempter, will be terrified by him as a tormentor. Those whom he now fawns upon, he will afterwards fly upon; and whom he draws into sin, he will try to drive to despair.

Verses 23-34

God is displeased at the sins of his own people; and no man shall be protected in disobedience, by his office, his nearness to God, or any services he has done for him. God warns all whom he employs, strictly to observe their orders. We cannot judge of men by their sufferings, nor of sins by present punishments; with some, the flesh is destroyed, that the spirit may be saved; with others, the flesh is pampered, that the soul may ripen for hell. Jeroboam returned not from his evil way. He promised himself that the calves would secure the crown to his family, but they lost it, and sunk his family. Those betray themselves who think to support themselves by any sin whatever. Let us dread prospering in sinful ways; pray to be kept from every delusion and temptation, and to be enabled to walk with self-denying perseverance in the way of God's commands.

Chapter 14

Chapter Outline

Abijah being sick, his mother consults Ahijah.	(1–6)
The destruction of Jeroboam's house.	(7–20)
Rehoboam's wicked reign.	(21–31)

Verses 1-6

"At that time," when Jeroboam did evil, his child sickened. When sickness comes into our families, we should inquire whether there may not be some particular sin harboured in our houses, which the affliction is sent to convince us of, and reclaim us from. It had been more pious if he had desired to know wherefore God contended with him; had begged the prophet's prayers, and cast away his idols from him; but most people would rather be told their fortune, than their faults or their duty. He sent to Ahijah, because he had told him he should be king. Those who by sin disqualify themselves for comfort, yet expect that their ministers, because they are good men, should speak peace and comfort to them, greatly wrong themselves and their ministers. He sent his wife in disguise, that the prophet might only answer her question concerning her son. Thus some people would limit their ministers to smooth things, and care not for having the whole counsel of God declared to them, lest it should prophesy no good concerning them, but evil. But she shall know, at the first word, what she has to trust to. Tidings of a portion with hypocrites will be heavy tidings. God will judge men according to what they are, not by what they seem to be.

Verses 7-20

Whether we keep an account of God's mercies to us or not, he does; and he will set them in order before us, if we are ungrateful, to our greater confusion. Ahijah foretells the speedy death of the child then sick, in mercy to him. He only in the house of Jeroboam had affection for the true worship of God, and disliked the worship of the calves. To show the power and sovereignty of his grace, God saves some out of the worst families, in whom there is some good thing towards the Lord God of Israel. The righteous are removed from the evil to come in this world, to the good to come in a better world. It is often a bad sign for a family, when the best in it are buried out of it. Yet their death never can be a loss to themselves. It was a present affliction to the family and kingdom, by which both ought to have been instructed. God also tells the judgments which should come upon the people of Israel, for conforming to the worship Jeroboam established. After they left the house of David, the government never continued long in one family, but one undermined and destroyed another. Families and kingdoms are ruined by sin. If great men do wickedly, they draw many others, both into the guilt and punishment. The condemnation of those will be severest, who must answer, not only for their own sins, but for sins others have been drawn into, and kept in, by them.

Verses 21-31

Here is no good said of Rehoboam, and much said to the disadvantage of his subjects. The abounding of the worst crimes, of the worst of the heathen, in Jerusalem, the city the Lord had chosen for his temple and his worship, shows that nothing can mend the hearts of fallen men but the sanctifying grace of the Holy Spirit. On this alone may we depend; for this let us daily pray, in behalf of ourselves and all around us. The splendour of their temple, the pomp of their priesthood, and all the advantages with which their religion was attended, could not prevail to keep them close to it; nothing less than the pouring out the Spirit will keep God's Israel in their allegiance to him. Sin exposes, makes poor, and weakens any people. Shishak, king of Egypt, came and took away the treasures. Sin makes the gold become dim, changes the most fine gold, and turns it into brass.

Chapter 15

Chapter Outline

Verses 1-8

Abijam's heart was not perfect with the Lord his God; he wanted sincerity; he began well, but he fell off, and walked in all the sins of his father, following his bad example, though he had seen the bad consequences of it. David's family was continued as a lamp in Jerusalem, to maintain the true worship of God there, when the light of Divine truth was extinguished in all other places. The Lord has still taken care of his cause, while those who ought to have been serviceable thereto have lived and perished in their sins. The Son of David will still continue a light to his church, to establish it in truth and righteousness to the end of time. There are two kinds of fulfilling the law, one legal, the other by the gospel. Legal is, when men do all things required in the law, and that by themselves. None ever thus fulfilled the law but Christ, and Adam before his fall. The gospel manner of fulfilling the law is, to believe in Christ who fulfilled the law for us, and to endeavour in the whole man to obey God in all his precepts. And this is accepted of God, as to all those that are in Christ. Thus David and others are said to fulfil the law.

Verses 9-24

Asa did what was right in the eyes of the Lord. That is right indeed which is so in God's eyes. Asa's times were times of reformation. He removed that which was evil; there reformation begins, and a great deal he found to do. When Asa found idolatry in the court, he rooted it out thence. Reformation must begin at home. Asa honours and respects his mother; he loves her well, but he loves God better. Those that have power are happy when thus they have hearts to use it well. We must not only cease to do evil, but learn to do well; not only cast away the idols of our iniquity, but dedicate ourselves and our all to God's honour and glory. Asa was cordially devoted to the service of God, his sins not arising from presumption. But his league with Benhadad arose from unbelief. Even true believers find it hard, in times of urgent danger, to trust in the Lord with all their heart. Unbelief makes way for carnal policy, and thus for one sin after another. Unbelief has often led Christians to call in the help of the Lord's enemies in their contests with their brethren; and some who once shone brightly, have thus been covered with a dark cloud towards the end of their days.

Verses 25-34

During the single reign of Asa in Judah, the government of Israel was in six or seven different hands. Observe the ruin of the family of Jeroboam; no word of God shall fall to the ground. Divine threatenings are not designed merely to terrify. Ungodly men execute the just judgments of God upon each other. But in the midst of dreadful sins and this apparent confusion, the Lord carries on his own plan: when it is fully completed, the glorious justice, wisdom, truth, and mercy therein displayed, shall be admired and adored through all the ages of eternity.

Chapter 16

Chapter Outline

Verses 1-14

This chapter relates wholly to the kingdom of Israel, and the revolutions of that kingdom. God calls Israel his people still, though wretchedly corrupted. Jehu foretells the same destruction to come upon Baasha's family, which that king had been employed to bring upon the family of Jeroboam. Those who resemble others in their sins, may expect to resemble them in the plagues they suffer, especially those who seem zealous against such sins in others as they allow in themselves. Baasha himself dies in peace, and is buried with honour. Herein plainly appears that there are punishments after death, which are most to be dreaded. Let Elah be a warning to drunkards, who know not but death may surprise them. Death easily comes upon men when they are drunk. Besides the diseases which men bring themselves into by drinking, when in that state, men are easily overcome by an enemy, and liable to bad accidents. Death comes terribly upon men in such a state, finding them in the act of sin, and unfitted for any act of devotion; that day comes upon them unawares. The word of God was fulfilled, and the sins of Baasha and Elah were reckoned for, with which they provoked God. Their idols are called their vanities, for idols cannot profit nor help; miserable are those whose gods are vanities.

Verses 15-28

When men forsake God, they will be left to plague one another. Proud aspiring men ruin one another. Omri struggled with Tibni some years. Though we do not always understand the rules by which God governs nations and individuals in his providence, we may learn useful lessons from the history before us. When tyrants succeed each other, and massacres, conspiracies, and civil wars, we may be sure the Lord has a controversy with the people for their sins; they are loudly called to repent and reform. Omri made himself infamous by his wickedness. Many wicked men have been men of might and renown; have built cities, and their names are found in history; but they have no name in the book of life.

Verses 29-34

Ahab did evil above all that reigned before him, and did it with a particular enmity both against Jehovah and Israel. He was not satisfied with breaking the second commandment by image-worship, he broke the first by worshipping other gods: making light of lesser sins makes way for greater. Marriages with daring offenders also imbolden in wickedness, and hurry men on to the greatest excesses. One of Ahab's subjects, following the example of his presumption, ventured to build Jericho. Like Achan, he meddled with the accursed thing; turned that to his own use, which was devoted to God's honour: he began to build, in defiance of the curse well devoted to God's honour: he began to build, in defiance of the curse well known in Israel; but none ever hardened his heart against God, and prospered. Let the reading of this chapter cause us to mark the dreadful end of all the workers of iniquity. And what does the history of all ungodly men furnish, what ever rank or situation they move in, but sad examples of the same?

Chapter 17

Chapter Outline

Verses 1-7

God wonderfully suits men to the work he designs them for. The times were fit for an Elijah; an Elijah was fit for them. The Spirit of the Lord knows how to fit men for the occasions. Elijah let Ahab know that God was displeased with the idolaters, and would chastise them by the want of rain, which it was not in the power of the gods they served to bestow. Elijah was commanded to hide himself. If Providence calls us to solitude and retirement, it becomes us to go: when we cannot be useful, we must be patient; and when we cannot work for God, we must sit still quietly for him. The ravens were appointed to bring him meat, and did so. Let those who have but from hand to mouth, learn to live upon Providence, and trust it for the bread of the day, in the day. God could have sent angels to minister to him; but he chose to show that he can serve his own purposes by the meanest creatures, as effectually as by the mightiest. Elijah seems to have continued thus above a year. The natural supply of water, which came by common providence, failed; but the miraculous supply of food, made sure to him by promise, failed not. If the heavens fail, the earth fails of course; such are all our creature-comforts: we lose them when we most need them, like brooks in summer. But there is a river which makes glad the city of God, that never runs dry, a well of water that springs up to eternal life. Lord, give us that living water! (1Ki 17:8-16)

Verses 8-16

Many widows were in Israel in the days of Elias, and some, it is likely, would have bidden him welcome to their houses; yet he is sent to honour and bless with his presence a city of Sidon, a Gentile city, and so becomes the first prophet of the Gentiles. Jezebel was Elijah's greatest enemy; yet, to show her how powerless was her malice, God will find a hiding-place for him even in her own country. The person appointed to entertain Elijah is not one of the rich or great men of Sidon; but a poor widow woman, in want, and desolate, is made both able and willing to sustain him. It is God's way, and it is his glory, to make use of, and put honour upon, the weak and foolish things of the world. O woman, great was thy faith; one has not found the like, no not in Israel. She took the prophet's word, that she should not lose by it. Those who can venture upon the promise of God, will make no difficulty to expose and empty themselves in his service, by giving him his part first. Surely the increase of this widow's faith, so as to enable her thus readily to deny herself, and to depend upon the Divine promise, was as great a miracle in the kingdom of grace, as the increase of her meal and oil in the kingdom of providence. Happy are all who can thus, against hope, believe and obey in hope. One poor meal's meat this poor widow gave the prophet; in recompence of it, she and her son did eat above two years, in a time of famine. To have food from God's special favour, and in such good company as Elijah, made it more than doubly sweet. It is promised to those who trust in God, that they shall not be ashamed in evil time; in days of famine they shall be satisfied.

Verses 17-24

Neither faith nor obedience shut out afflictions and death. The child being dead, the mother spake to the prophet, rather to give vent to her sorrow, than in hope of relief. When God removes our comforts from us, he remembers our sins against us, perhaps the sins of our youth, though long since past. When God remembers our sins against us, he designs to teach us to remember them against ourselves, and to repent of them. Elijah's prayer was doubtless directed by the Holy Spirit. The child revived. See the power of prayer, and the power of Him who hears prayer.

Chapter 18

Chapter Outline

Elijah sends Ahab notice of his coming.	(1–16)
Elijah meets Ahab.	(17–20)
Elijah's trial of the false prophets.	(21–40)
Elijah, by prayer, obtains rain.	(41–46)

Verses 1-16

The severest judgments, of themselves, will not humble or change the hearts of sinners; nothing, except the blood of Jesus Christ, can atone for the guilt of sin; nothing, except the sanctifying Spirit of God, can purge away its pollution. The priests and the Levites were gone to Judah and Jerusalem, 2Ch 11:13, 14, but instead of them God raised up prophets, who read and expounded the word. They probably were from the schools of the prophets, first set up by Samuel. They had not the spirit of prophecy as Elijah, but taught the people to keep close to the God of Israel. These Jezebel sought to destroy. The few that escaped death were forced to hide themselves. God has his remnant among all sorts, high and low; and that faith, fear, and love of his name, which are the fruits of the Holy Spirit, will be accepted through the Redeemer. See how wonderfully God raises up friends for his ministers and people, for their shelter in difficult times. Bread and water were now scarce, yet Obadiah will find enough for God's prophets, to keep them alive. Ahab's care was not to lose all the beasts; but he took no care about his soul, not to lose that. He took pains to seek grass, but none to seek the favour of God; fencing against the effect, but not inquiring how to remove the cause.

But it bodes well with a people, when God calls his ministers to stand forth, and show themselves. And we may the better endure the bread of affliction, while our eyes see our teachers.

Verses 17-20

One may guess how people stand affected to God, by observing how they stand affected to his people and ministers. It has been the lot of the best and most useful men, like Elijah, to be called and counted the troublers of the land. But those who cause God's judgments do the mischief, not he that foretells them, and warns the nation to repent.

Verses 21-40

Many of the people wavered in their judgment, and varied in their practice. Elijah called upon them to determine whether Jehovah or Baal was the self-existent, supreme God, the Creator, Governor, and Judge of the world, and to follow him alone. It is dangerous to halt between the service of God and the service of sin, the dominion of Christ and the dominion of our lusts. If Jesus be the only Saviour, let us cleave to him alone for every thing; if the Bible be the world of God, let us reverence and receive the whole of it, and submit our understanding to the Divine teaching it contains. Elijah proposed to bring the matter to a trial. Baal had all the outward advantages, but the event encourages all God's witnesses and advocates never to fear the face of man. The God that answers by fire, let him be God: the atonement was to be made by sacrifice, before the judgment could be removed in mercy. The God therefore that has power to pardon sin, and to signify it by consuming the sin-offering, must needs be the God that can relieve from the calamity. God never required his worshippers to honour him in the manner of the worshippers of Baal; but the service of the devil, though sometimes it pleases and pampers the body, yet, in other things, really is cruel to it, as in envy and drunkenness. God requires that we mortify our lusts and corruptions; but bodily penances and severities are no pleasure to him. Who has required these things at your hands? A few words uttered in assured faith, and with fervent affection for the glory of God, and love to the souls of men, or thirstings after the Lord's image and his favour, form the effectual, fervent prayer of the righteous man, which availeth much. Elijah sought not his own glory, but that of God, for the good of the people. The people are all agreed, convinced, and satisfied; Jehovah, he is the God. Some, we hope, had their hearts turned, but most of them were convinced only, not converted. Blessed are they that have not seen what these saw, yet have believed, and have been wrought upon by it, more than they that saw it.

Verses 41-46

Israel, being so far reformed as to acknowledge the Lord to be God, and to consent to the execution of Baal's prophets, was so far accepted, that God poured out blessing upon the land. Elijah long continued praying. Though the answer of our fervent and believing supplications does not come quickly, we must continue earnest in prayer, and not faint or give over. A little cloud at length appeared, which soon overspread the heavens, and watered the earth. Great blessings often arise from small beginnings, showers of plenty from a cloud of span long. Let us never despise the day of small things, but hope and wait for great things from it. From what small beginnings have great matters arisen! It is thus in all the gracious proceedings of God with the soul. Scarcely to be perceived are the first workings of his Spirit in the heart, which grow up at last to the wonder of men, and applause of angels. Elijah hastened Ahab home, and attended him. God will strengthen his people for every service to which his commandments and providence call them. The awful displays of Divine justice and holiness dismay the sinner, extort confessions, and dispose to outward obedience while the impression lasts; but the view of these, with mercy, love, and truth in Christ Jesus, is needful to draw the soul to self-abasement, trust, and love. The Holy Spirit employs both in the conversion of sinners; when sinners are impressed with Divine truths, they should be exhorted to set about the duties to which the Saviour calls his disciples.

Chapter 19

Chapter Outline

Elijah flees to the wilderness.	(1–8)
God manifests himself to Elijah.	(9–13)
God's answer to Elijah.	(14–18)
The call of Elisha.	(19–21)

Verses 1-8

Jezebel sent Elijah a threatening message. Carnal hearts are hardened and enraged against God, by that which should convince and conquer them. Great faith is not always alike strong. He might be serviceable to Israel at this time, and had all reason to depend upon God's protection, while doing God's work; yet he flees. His was not the deliberate desire of grace, as Paul's, to depart and be with Christ. God thus left Elijah to himself, to show that when he was bold and strong, it was in the Lord, and the power of his might; but of himself he was no better than his fathers. God knows what he designs us for, though we do not, what services, what trials, and he will take care that we are furnished with grace sufficient.

Verses 9-13

The question God put, What doest thou here, Elijah? is a reproof. It concerns us often to ask whether we are in our place, and in the way of our duty. Am I where I should be? whither God calls me, where my business lies, and where I may be useful? He complained of the people, and their obstinacy in sin; I only am left. Despair of success hinders many a good enterprise. Did Elijah come hither to meet with God? he shall find that God will meet him. The wind, and earthquake, and fire, did not make him cover his face, but the still voice did. Gracious souls are more affected by the tender mercies of the Lord, than by his terrors. The mild voice of Him who speaks from the cross, or the mercy-seat, is accompanied with peculiar power in taking possession of the heart.

Verses 14-18

God repeated the question, What doest thou here? Then he complained of his discouragement; and whither should God's prophets go with their complaints of that kind, but to their Master? The Lord gave him an answer. He declares that the wicked house of Ahab shall be rooted out, that the people of Israel shall be punished for their sins; and he shows that Elijah was not left alone as he had supposed, and also that a helper should at once be raised up for him. Thus all his complaints are answered and provided for. God's faithful ones are often his hidden ones, Ps 83:3, and the visible church is scarcely to be seen: the wheat is lost in chaff, and the gold in dross, till the sifting, refining, separating day comes. The Lord knows them that are his, though we do not; he sees in secret. When we come to heaven we shall miss many whom we thought to have met there; we shall meet many whom we little thought to have met there. God's love often proves larger than man's charity, and far more extended.

Verses 19-21

Elijah found Elisha by Divine direction, not in the schools of the prophets, but in the field; not reading, or praying, or sacrificing, but ploughing. Idleness is no man's honour, nor is husbandry any man's disgrace. An honest calling in the world, does not put us out of the way of our heavenly calling, any more than it did Elisha. His heart was touched by the Holy Spirit, and he was ready to leave all to attend Elijah. It is in a day of power that Christ's subjects are made willing; nor would any come to Christ unless they were thus drawn. It was a discouraging time for prophets to set out in. A man that had consulted with flesh and blood, would not be fond of Elijah's mantle; yet Elisha cheerfully leaves all to accompany him. When the Saviour said to one and to another, Follow me, the dearest friends and most profitable occupations were cheerfully left, and the most arduous duties done from love to his name. May we, in like manner, feel the energy of his grace working in us mightily, and by unreserved submission at once, may we make our calling and election sure.

Chapter 20

Chapter Outline

Benhadad besieges Samaria.	(1–11)
Benhadad's defeat.	(12–21)
The Syrians again defeated.	(22–30)
Ahab makes peace with Benhadad.	(31–43)

Verses 1-11

Benhadad sent Ahab a very insolent demand. Ahab sent a very disgraceful submission; sin brings men into such straits, by putting them out of the Divine protection. If God do not rule us, our enemies shall: guilt dispirits men, and makes them cowards. Ahab became desperate. Men will part with their most pleasant things, those they most love, to save their lives; yet they lose their souls rather than part with any pleasure or interest to prevent it. Here is one of the wisest sayings that ever Ahab spake, and it is a good lesson to all. It is folly to boast of any day to come, since we know not what it may bring forth. Apply it to our spiritual conflicts. Peter fell by self-confidence. Happy is the man who is never off his watch.

Verses 12-21

The proud Syrians were beaten, and the despised Israelites were conquerors. The orders of the proud, drunken king disordered his troops, and prevented them from attacking the Israelites. Those that are most secure, are commonly least courageous. Ahab slew the Syrians with a great slaughter. God often makes one wicked man a scourge to another.

Verses 22-30

Those about Benhadad advised him to change his ground. They take it for granted that it was not Israel, but Israel's gods, that beat them; but they speak very ignorantly of Jehovah. They supposed that Israel had many gods, to whom they ascribed limited power within a certain district; thus vain were the Gentiles in their imaginations concerning God. The greatest wisdom in worldly concerns is often united with the most contemptible folly in the things of God.

Verses 31-43

This encouragement sinners have to repent and humble themselves before God; Have we not heard, that the God of Israel is a merciful God? Have we not found him so? That is gospel repentance, which flows from an apprehension of the mercy of God, in Christ; there is forgiveness with him. What a change is here! The most haughty in prosperity often are most abject in adversity; an evil spirit will thus affect a man in both these conditions. There are those on whom, like Ahab, success is ill bestowed; they know not how to serve either God or their generation, or even their own true interests with their prosperity: Let favour be showed to the wicked, yet will he not learn righteousness. The prophet designed to reprove Ahab by a parable. If a good prophet were punished for sparing his friend and God's when God said, Smite, of much sorer punishment should a wicked king be thought worthy, who spared his enemy and God's, when God said, Smite. Ahab went to his house, heavy and displeased, not truly penitent, or seeking to undo what he had done amiss; every way out of humour, notwithstanding his victory. Alas! many that hear the glad tidings of Christ, are busy and there till the day of salvation is gone.

Chapter 21

Chapter Outline

Verses 1-4

Naboth, perhaps, had been pleased that he had a vineyard situated so near the palace, but the situation proved fatal to him; many a man's possessions have been his snare, and his neighbourhood to greatness, of bad consequence. Discontent is a sin that is its own punishment, and makes men torment themselves. It is a sin that is its own parent; it arises not from the condition, but from the mind: as we find Paul contented in a prison, so Ahab was discontented in a palace. He had all the delights of Canaan, that pleasant land, at command; the wealth of a kingdom, the pleasures of a court, and the honours and powers of a throne; yet all avails him nothing without Naboth's vineyard. Wrong desires expose men to continual vexations, and those that are disposed to fret, however well off, may always find something or other to fret at.

Verses 5-16

When, instead of a help meet, a man has an agent for Satan, in the form of an artful, unprincipled, yet beloved wife, fatal effects may be expected. Never were more wicked orders given by any prince, than those Jezebel sent to the rulers of Jezreel. Naboth must be murdered under colour of religion. There is no wickedness so vile, so horrid, but religion has sometimes been made a cover for it. Also, it must be done under colour of justice, and with the formalities of legal process. Let us, from this sad story, be amazed at the wickedness of the wicked, and the power of Satan in the children of disobedience. Let us commit the keeping of our lives and comforts to God, for innocence will not always be our security; and let us rejoice in the knowledge that all will be set to rights in the great day.

Verses 17-29

Blessed Paul complains that he was sold under sin, Ro 7:14, as a poor captive against his will; but Ahab was willing, he sold himself to sin; of choice, and as his own act and deed, he loved the dominion of sin. Jezebel his wife stirred him up to do wickedly. Ahab is reproved, and his sin set before his eyes, by Elijah. That man's condition is very miserable, who has made the word of God his enemy; and very desperate, who reckons the ministers of that word his enemies, because they tell him the truth. Ahab put on the garb and guise of a penitent, yet his heart was unhumbled and unchanged. Ahab's repentance was only what might be seen of men; it was outward only. Let this encourage all that truly repent, and unfeignedly believe the holy gospel, that if a pretending partial penitent shall go to his house reprieved, doubtless, a sincere believing penitent shall go to his house justified.

Chapter 22

Chapter Outline

Verses 1-14

The same easiness of temper, which betrays some godly persons into friendship with the declared enemies of religion, renders it very dangerous to them. They will be drawn to wink at and countenance such conduct and conversation as they ought to protest against with abhorrence. Whithersoever a good man goes, he ought to take his religion with him, and not be ashamed to own it when he is with those who have no regard for it. Jehoshaphat had not left behind him, at Jerusalem, his affection and reverence for the word of the Lord, but avowed it, and endeavoured to bring it into Ahab's court. And Ahab's prophets, to please Jehoshaphat, made use of the name of Jehovah: to please Ahab, they said, Go up. But the false prophets cannot so mimic the true, but that he who has spiritual senses exercised, can discern the fallacy. One faithful prophet of the Lord was worth them all. Wordly men have in all ages been alike absurd in their views of religion. They would have the preacher fit his doctrine to the fashion of the times, and the taste of the hearers, and yet to add. Thus saith the Lord, to words that men would put into their mouths. They are ready to cry out against a man as rude and foolish, who scruples thus to try to secure his own interests, and to deceive others.

Verses 15-28

The greatest kindness we can do to one that is going in a dangerous way, is, to tell him of his danger. To leave the hardened criminal without excuse, and to give a useful lesson to others, Micaiah related his vision. This matter is represented after the manner of men: we are not to imagine that God is ever put upon new counsels; or that he needs to consult with angels, or any creature, about the methods he should take; or that he is the author of sin, or the cause of any man's telling or believing a lie. Micaiah returned not the blow of Zedekiah, yet, since he boasted of the Spirit, as those commonly do that know least of the Holy Spirit's operations, the true prophet left him to be convinced of his error by the event. Those that will not have their mistakes set right in time, by the word of God, will be undeceived, when it is too late, by the judgments of God. We should be ashamed of what we call trials, were we to consider what the servants of God have endured. Yet it will be well, if freedom from trouble prove not more hurtful to us; we are more easily allured and bribed into unfaithfulness and conformity to the world, than driven to them.

Verses 29-40

Ahab basely intended to betray Johoshaphat to danger, that he might secure himself. See what they get that join with wicked men. How can it be expected that he should be true to his friend, who has been false to his God! He had said in compliment to Ahab, I am as thou art, and now he was indeed taken for him. Those that associate with evil-doers, are in danger of sharing in their plagues. By Jehoshaphat's deliverance, God let him know, that though he was displeased with him, yet he had not deserted him. God is a friend that will not fail us when other friends do. Let no man think to hide himself from God's judgment. God directed the arrow to hit Ahab; those cannot escape with life, whom God has doomed to death. Ahab lived long enough to see part of Micaiah's prophecy accomplished. He had time to feel himself die; with what horror must he have thought upon the wickedness he had committed!

Verses 41-50

Jehoshaphat's reign appears to have been one of the best, both as to piety and prosperity. He pleased God, and God blessed him.

Verses 51-53

Ahaziah's reign was very short, not two years; some sinners God makes quick work with. A very bad character is given of him; he listened not to instruction, took no warning, but followed the example of his wicked father, and the counsel of his more wicked mother, Jezebel, who was still living. Miserable are the children who not only derive a sinful nature from their parents, but are taught by them to increase it; and most unhappy parents are they, that help to damn their children's souls. Hardened sinners rush forward, unawed and unmoved, in the ways from which others before them have been driven into everlasting misery.

2 Kings

Chapter Outline

Verses 1-8

When Ahaziah rebelled against the Lord, Moab revolted from him. Sin weakens and impoverishes us. Man's revolt from God is often punished by the rebellion of those who owe subjection to him. Ahaziah fell through a lattice, or railing. Wherever we go, there is but a step between us and death. A man's house is his castle, but not to secure him against God's judgments. The whole creation, which groans under the burden of man's sin, will, at length, sink and break under the weight like this lattice. He is never safe that has God for his enemy. Those that will not inquire of the word of God for their comfort, shall hear it to their terror, whether they will or no.

Verses 9-18

Elijah called for fire from heaven, to consume the haughty, daring sinners; not to secure himself, but to prove his mission, and to reveal the wrath of God from heaven, against the ungodliness and unrighteousness of men. Elijah did this by a Divine impulse, yet our Saviour would not allow the disciples to do the like, Lu 9:54. The dispensation of the Spirit and of grace by no means allowed it. Elijah was concerned for God's glory, those for their own reputation. The Lord judges men's practices by their principles, and his judgment is according to truth. The third captain humbled himself, and cast himself upon the mercy of God and Elijah. There is nothing to be got by contending with God; and those are wise for themselves, who learn submission from the fatal end of obstinacy in others. The courage of faith has often struck terror into the heart of the proudest sinner. So thunderstruck is Ahaziah with the prophet's words, that neither he, nor any about him, offer him violence. Who can harm those whom God shelters? Many who think to prosper in sin, are called hence like Ahaziah, when they do not expect it. All warns us to seek the Lord while he may be found.

Chapter 2

Chapter Outline

Elisha heals the waters of Jericho, Those   (19–25)
that mocked Elisha destroyed.

Verses 1-8

The Lord had let Elijah know that his time was at hand. He therefore went to the different schools of the prophets to give them his last exhortations and blessing. The removal of Elijah was a type and figure of the ascension of Christ, and the opening of the kingdom of heaven to all believers. Elisha had long followed Elijah, and he would not leave him now when he hoped for the parting blessing. Let not those who follow Christ come short by tiring at last. The waters of Jordan, of old, yielded to the ark; now, to the prophet's mantle, as a token of God's presence. When God will take up his faithful ones to heaven, death is the Jordan which they must pass through, and they find a way through it. The death of Christ has divided those waters, that the ransomed of the Lord may pass over. O death, where is thy sting, thy hurt, thy terror!

Verses 9-12

That fulness, from whence prophets and apostles had all their supply, still exists as of old, and we are told to ask large supplies from it. Diligent attendance upon Elijah, particularly in his last hours, would be proper means for Elisha to obtain much of his spirit. The comforts of departing saints, and their experiences, help both to gild our comforts and to strengthen our resolutions. Elijah is carried to heaven in a fiery chariot. Many questions might be asked about this, which could not be answered. Let it suffice that we are told, what his Lord, when he came, found him doing. He was engaged in serious discourse, encouraging and directing Elisha about the kingdom of God among men. We mistake, if we think preparation for heaven is carried on only by contemplation and acts of devotion. The chariot and horses appeared like fire, something very glorious, not for burning, but brightness. By the manner in which Elijah and Enoch were taken from this world, God gave a glimpse of the eternal life brought to light by the gospel, of the glory reserved for the bodies of the saints, and of the opening of the kingdom of heaven to all believers. It was also a figure of Christ's ascension. Though Elijah was gone triumphantly to heaven, yet this world could ill spare him. Surely their hearts are hard, who feel not, when God, by taking away faithful, useful men, calls for weeping and mourning. Elijah was to Israel, by his counsels, reproofs, and prayers, better than the strongest force of chariot and horse, and kept off the judgments of God. Christ bequeathed to his disciples his precious gospel, like Elijah's mantle; the token of the Divine power being exerted to overturn the empire of Satan, and to set up the kingdom of God in the world. The same gospel remains with us, though the miraculous powers are withdrawn, and it has Divine strength for the conversion and salvation of sinners.

Verses 13-18

Elijah left his mantle to Elisha; as a token of the descent of the Spirit upon him; it was more than if he had left him thousands of gold and silver. Elisha took it up, not as a sacred relic to be worshipped, but as a significant garment to be worn. Now that Elijah was taken to heaven, Elisha inquired, 1. After God; when our creature-comforts are removed, we have a God to go to, who lives for ever. 2. After the God that Elijah served, and honoured, and pleaded for. The Lord God of the holy prophets is the same yesterday, to-day, and for ever; but what will it avail us to have the mantles of those that are gone, their places, their books, if we have not their spirit, their God? See Elisha's dividing the river; God's people need not fear at last passing through the Jordan of death as on dry ground. The sons of the prophets made a needless search for Elijah. Wise men may yield to that, for the sake of peace, and the good opinion of others, which yet their judgment is against, as needless and fruitless. Traversing hills and valleys will never bring us to Elijah, but following the example of his holy faith and zeal will, in due time.

Verses 19-25

Observe the miracle of healing the waters. Prophets should make every place to which they come better for them, endeavouring to sweeten bitter spirits, and to make barren souls fruitful, by the word of God, which is like the salt cast into the water by Elisha. It was an apt emblem of the effect produced by the grace of God on the sinful heart of man. Whole families, towns, and cities, sometimes have a new appearance through the preaching of the gospel; wickedness and evil have been changed into fruitfulness in the works of righteousness, which are, through Christ, to the praise and glory of God. Here is a curse on the youths of Bethel, enough to destroy them; it was not a curse causeless, for it was Elisha's character, as God's prophet, that they abused. They bade him "go up," reflecting on the taking up of Elijah into heaven. The prophet acted by Divine impulse. If the Holy Spirit had not directed Elisha's solemn curse, the providence of God would not have followed it with judgment. The Lord must be glorified as a righteous God who hates sin, and will reckon for it. Let young persons be afraid of speaking wicked words, for God notices what they say. Let them not mock at any for defects in mind or body; especially it is at their peril, if they scoff at any for well doing. Let parents that would have comfort in their children, train them up well, and do their utmost betimes to drive out the foolishness that is bound up in their hearts. And what will be the anguish of those parents, at the day of judgment, who witness the everlasting condemnation of their offspring, occasioned by their own bad example, carelessness, or wicked teaching!

Chapter 3

Chapter Outline

Verses 1-5

Jehoram took warning by God's judgment, and put away the image of Baal, yet he maintained the worship of the calves. Those do not truly repent or reform, who only part with the sins they lose by, but continue to love the sins that they think to gain by.

Verses 6-19

The king of Israel laments their distress, and the danger they were in. He called these kings together, yet he charges it upon Providence. Thus the foolishness of man perverteth his way, and then his heart fretteth against the Lord, Pr 19:3. It was well that Jehoshaphat inquired of the Lord now, but it had been much better if he had done it before he engaged in this war. Good men sometimes neglect their duty, till necessity and affliction drive them to it. Wicked people often fare the better for the friendship and society of the godly. To try their faith and obedience, Elisha bids them make the valley full of pits to receive water. Those who expect God's blessings, must dig pools for the rain to fill, as in the valley of Baca, and thus make even that a well, Ps 84:6. We need not inquire whence the water came. God is not tied to second causes. They that sincerely seek for the dew of God's grace, shall have it, and by it be made more than conquerors.

Verses 20-27

It is a blessing to be favoured with the company of those who have power with God, and can prevail by their prayers. A kingdom may be upheld and prosper, in consequence of the fervent prayers of those who are dear to God. May we place our highest regard upon such as are most precious in his account. When sinners are saying Peace, peace, destruction comes upon them: despair will follow their mad presumption. In Satan's service and at his suggestion, such horrid deeds have been done, as cause the natural feelings of the heart to shudder; like the king of Moab's sacrificing his son. It is well not to urge the worst of men to extremities; we should rather leave them to the judgment of God.

Chapter 4

Chapter Outline

Elisha multiplies the widow's oil.	(1–7)
The Shunammite obtains a son.	(8–17)
The Shunammite's son restored to life.	(18–37)
The miracle of healing the pottage, and of feeding the sons of the prophets.	(38–44)

Verses 1-7

Elisha's miracles were acts of real charity: Christ's were so; not only great wonders, but great favours to those for whom they were wrought. God magnifies his goodness with his power. Elisha readily received a poor widow's complaint. Those that leave their families under a load of debt, know not what trouble they cause. It is the duty of all who profess to follow the Lord, while they trust to God for daily bread, not to tempt him by carelessness or extravagance, nor to contract debts; for nothing tends more to bring reproach upon the gospel, or distresses their families more when they are gone. Elisha put the widow in a way to pay her debt, and to maintain herself and her family. This was done by miracle, but so as to show what is the best method to assist those who are in distress, which is, to help them to improve by their own industry what little they have. The oil, sent by miracle, continued flowing as long as she had empty vessels to receive it. We are never straitened in God, or in the riches of his grace; all our straitness is in ourselves. It is our faith that fails, not his promise. He gives more than we ask: were there more vessels, there is enough in God to fill them; enough for all, enough for each; and the Redeemer's all-sufficiency will only be stayed from the supplying the wants of sinners and saving their souls, when no more apply to him for salvation. The widow must pay her debt with the money she received for her oil. Though her creditors were too hard with her, yet they must be paid, even before she made any provision for her children. It is one of the main laws of the Christian religion, that we pay every just debt, and give every one his own, though we leave ever so little for ourselves; and this, not of constraint, but for conscience' sake. Those who bear an honest mind, cannot with pleasure eat their daily bread, unless it be their own bread. She and her children must live upon the rest; that is, upon the money received for the oil, with which they must put themselves into a way to get an honest livelihood. We cannot now expect miracles, yet we may expect mercies, if we wait on God, and seek to him. Let widows in particular depend upon him. He that has all hearts in his hand, can, without a miracle, send as effectual a supply.

Verses 8-17

Elisha was well thought of by the king of Israel for his late services; a good man can take as much pleasure in serving others, as in raising himself. But the Shunammite needed not any good offices of this kind. It is a happiness to dwell among our own people, that love and respect us, and to whom we are able to do good. It would be well with many, if they did but know when they are really well off. The Lord sees the secret wish which is suppressed in obedience to his will, and he will hear the prayers of his servants in behalf of their benefactors, by sending unasked-for and unexpected mercies; nor must the professions of men of God be supposed to be delusive like those of men of the world.

Verses 18-37

Here is the sudden death of the child. All the mother's tenderness cannot keep alive a child of promise, a child of prayer, one given in love. But how admirably does the prudent, pious mother, guard her lips under this sudden affliction! Not one peevish word escapes from her. Such confidence had she of God's goodness, that she was ready to believe that he would restore what he had now taken away. O woman, great is thy faith! He that wrought it, would not disappoint it. The sorrowful mother begged leave of her husband to go to the prophet at once. She had not thought it enough to have Elisha's help sometimes in her own family, but, though a woman of rank, attended on public worship. It well becomes the men of God, to inquire about the welfare of their friends and their families. The answer was, It is well. All well, and yet the child dead in the house! Yes! All is well that God does; all is well with them that are gone, if they are gone to heaven; and all well with us that stay behind, if, by the affliction, we are furthered in our way thither. When any creature-comfort is taken from us, it is well if we can say, through grace, that we did not set our hearts too much upon it; for if we did, we have reason to fear it was given in anger, and taken away in wrath. Elisha cried unto God in faith; and the beloved son was restored alive to his mother. Those who would convey spiritual life to dead souls, must feel deeply for their case, and labour fervently in prayer for them. Though the minister cannot give Divine life to his fellow-sinners, he must use every means, with as much earnestness as if he could do so.

Verses 38-44

There was a famine of bread, but not of hearing the word of God, for Elisha had the sons of the prophets sitting before him, to hear his wisdom. Elisha made hurtful food to become safe and wholesome. If a mess of pottage be all our dinner, remember that this great prophet had no better for himself and his guests. The table often becomes a snare, and that which should be for our welfare, proves a trap: this is a good reason why we should not feed ourselves without fear. When we are receiving the supports and comforts of life, we must keep up an expectation of death, and a fear of sin. We must acknowledge God's goodness in making our food wholesome and nourishing; I am the Lord that healeth thee. Elisha also made a little food go a great way. Having freely received, he freely gave. God has promised his church, that he will abundantly bless her provision, and satisfy her poor with bread, Ps 132:15; whom he feeds, he fills; and what he blesses, comes to much. Christ's feeding his hearers was a miracle far beyond this, but both teach us that those who wait upon God in the way of duty, may hope to be supplied by Divine Providence.

Chapter 5

Chapter Outline

Verses 1-8

Though the Syrians were idolaters, and oppressed God's people, yet the deliverance of which Naaman had been the means, is here ascribed to the Lord. Such is the correct language of Scripture, while those who write common history, plainly show that God is not in all their thoughts. No man's greatness, or honour, can place him our of the reach of the sorest calamities of human life: there is many a sickly, crazy body under rich and gay clothing. Every man has some but or other, something that blemishes and diminishes him, some allay to his grandeur, some damp to his joy. This little maid, though only a girl, could give an account of the famous prophet the Israelites had among them. Children should be early told of the wondrous works of God, that, wherever they go, they may talk of them. As became a good servant, she desired the health and welfare of her master, though she was a captive, a servant by force; much more should servants by choice, seek their masters' good. Servants may be blessings to the families where they are, by telling what they know of the glory of God, and the honour of his prophets. Naaman did not despise what she told, because of her meanness. It would be well if men were as sensible of the burden of sin as they are of bodily disease. And when they seek the blessings which the Lord sends in answer to the prayers of his faithful people, they will find nothing can be had, except they come as beggars for a free gift, not as lords to demand or purchase.

Verses 9-14

Elisha knew Naaman to be a proud man, and he would let him know, that before the great God all men stand upon the same level. All God's commands make trial of men's spirits, especially those which direct a sinner how to apply for the blessings of salvation. See in Naaman the folly of pride; a cure will not content him, unless he be cured with pomp and parade. He scorns to be healed, unless he be humoured. The way by which a sinner is received and made holy, through the blood, and by the Spirit of Christ, through faith alone in his name, does not sufficiently humour or employ self, to please the sinner's heart. Human wisdom thinks it can supply wiser and better methods of cleansing. Observe, masters should be willing to hear reason. As we should be deaf to the counsel of the ungodly, though given by great and respected names, so we are to have our ears open to good advice, though brought by those below us. Wouldst thou not do any thing? When diseased sinners are content to do any thing, to submit to any thing, to part with any thing, for a cure, then, and not till then, is there any hope of them. The methods for the healing of the leprosy of sin, are so plain, that we are without excuse if we do not observe them. It is but, Believe, and be saved; Repent, and be pardoned; Wash, and be clean. The believer applies for salvation, not neglecting, altering, or adding to the Saviour's directions; he is thus made clean from guilt, while others, who neglect them, live and die in the leprosy of sin.

Verses 15-19

The mercy of the cure affected Naaman more than the miracle. Those are best able to speak of the power of Divine grace, who themselves experience it. He also shows himself grateful to Elisha the prophet. Elijah refused any recompence, not because he thought it unlawful, for he received presents from others, but to show this new convert that the servants of the God of Israel looked upon worldly wealth with a holy contempt. The whole work was from God, in such a manner, that the prophet would not give counsel when he had no directions from the Lord. It is not well violently to oppose the lesser mistakes which unite with men's first convictions; we cannot bring men forward any faster than the Lord prepares them to receive instruction. Yet as to us, if, in covenanting with God, we desire to reserve any known sin, to continue to indulge ourselves in it, that is a breach of his covenant. Those who truly hate evil, will make conscience of abstaining from all appearances of evil.

Verses 20-27

Naaman, a Syrian, a courtier, a soldier, had many servants, and we read how wise and good they were. Elisha, a holy prophet, a man of God, has but one servant, and he proves a base liar. The love of money, that root of all evil, was at the bottom of Gehazi's sin. He thought to impose upon the prophet, but soon found that the Spirit of prophecy could not be deceived, and that it was in vain to lie to the Holy Ghost. It is folly to presume upon sin, in hopes of secrecy. When thou goest aside into any by-path, does not thy own conscience go with thee? Does not the eye of God go with thee? He that covers his sin, shall not prosper; particularly, a lying tongue is but for a moment. All the foolish hopes and contrivances of carnal worldlings are open before God. It is not a time to increase our wealth, when we can only do it in such ways as are dishonourable to God and religion, or injurious to others. Gehazi was punished. If he will have Naaman's money, he shall have his disease with it. What was Gehazi profited, though he gained two talents, when thereby he lost his health, his honour, his peace, his service, and, if repentance prevented not, his soul for ever? Let us beware of hypocrisy and covetousness, and dread the curse of spiritual leprosy remaining on our souls.

Chapter 6

Chapter Outline

Verses 1-7

There is that pleasantness in the converse of servants of God, which can make those who listen to them forget the pain and the weariness of labour. Even the sons of the prophets must not be unwilling to labour. Let no man think an honest employment a burden or a disgrace. And labour of the head, is as hard, and very often harder, than labour with the hands. We ought to be careful of that which is borrowed, as of our own, because we must do as we would be done by. This man was so respecting the axe-head. And to those who have an honest mind, the sorest grievance of poverty is, not so much their own want and disgrace, as being rendered unable to pay just debts.

But the Lord cares for his people in their smallest concerns. And God's grace can thus raise the stony iron heart, which is sunk into the mud of this world, and raise up affections, naturally earthly.

Verses 8-12

The king of Israel regarded the warnings Elisha gave him, of danger from the Syrians, but would not heed the warnings of danger from his sins. Such warnings are little heeded by most; they would save themselves from death, but will not from hell. Nothing that is done, said, or thought, by any person, in any place, at any time, is out of God's knowledge.

Verses 13-23

What Elisha said to his servant is spoken to all the faithful servants of God, when without are fightings, and within are fears. Fear not, with that fear which has torment and amazement; for they that are with us, to protect us, are more than they that are against us, to destroy us. The eyes of his body were open, and with them he saw the danger. Lord, open the eyes of our faith, that with them we may see thy protecting hand. The clearer sight we have of the sovereignty and power of Heaven, the less we shall fear the troubles of earth. Satan, the god of this world, blinds men's eyes, and so deludes them unto their own ruin; but when God enlightens their eyes, they see themselves in the midst of their enemies, captives to Satan, and in danger of hell, though, before, they thought their condition good. When Elisha had the Syrians at his mercy, he made it appear that he was influenced by Divine goodness as well as Divine power. Let us not be overcome of evil, but overcome evil with good. The Syrians saw it was to no purpose to try to assault so great and so good a man.

Verses 24-33

Learn to value plenty, and to be thankful for it; see how contemptible money is, when in time of famine it is so freely parted with for any thing that is eatable! The language of Jehoram to the woman may be the language of despair. See the word of God fulfilled; among the threatenings of God's judgments upon Israel for their sins, this was one, that they should eat the flesh of their own children, De 28:53–57. The truth and the awful justice of God were displayed in this horrible transaction. Alas! what miseries sin has brought upon the world! But the foolishness of man perverts his way, and then his heart frets against the Lord. The king swears the death of Elisha. Wicked men will blame any one as the cause of their troubles, rather than themselves, and will not leave their sins. If rending the clothes, without a broken and contrite heart, would avail, if wearing sackcloth, without being renewed in the spirit of their mind, would serve, they would not stand out against the Lord. May the whole word of God increase in us reverent fear and holy hope, that we may be stedfast and immovable, always abounding in the work of the Lord, knowing that our labour is not in vain in the Lord.

Chapter 7

Chapter Outline

Verses 1, 2

Man's extremity is God's opportunity of making his own power to be glorious: his time to appear for his people is when their strength is gone. Unbelief is a sin by which men greatly dishonour and displease God, and deprive themselves of the favours he designed for them. Such will be the portion of those that believe not the promise of eternal life; they shall see it at a distance, but shall never taste of it. But no temporal deliverances and mercies will in the end profit sinners, unless they are led to repentance by the goodness of God.

Verses 3-11

God can, when he pleases, make the stoutest heart to tremble; and as for those who will not fear God, he can make them fear at the shaking of a leaf. Providence ordered it, that the lepers came as soon as the Syrians were fled. Their consciences told them that mischief would befall them, if they took care of themselves only. Natural humanity, and fear of punishment, are powerful checks on the selfishness of the ungodly. These feelings tend to preserve order and kindness in the world; but they who have found the unsearchable riches of Christ, will not long delay to report the good tidings to others. From love to him, not from selfish feelings, they will gladly share their earthly good things with their brethren.

Verses 12-20

Here see the wants of Israel supplied in a way they little thought of, which should encourage us to depend upon the power and goodness of God in our greatest straits. God's promise may be safely relied on, for no word of his shall fall to the ground. The nobleman that questioned the truth of Elisha's word, saw the plenty, to silence and shame his unbelief, and therein saw his own folly; but he did not eat of the plenty he saw. Justly do those find the world's promises fail them, who think that the promises of God will disappoint them. Learn how deeply God resents distrust of his power, providence, and promise: how uncertain life is, and the enjoyments of it: how certain God's threatenings are, and how sure to come on the guilty. May God help us to inquire whether we are exposed to his threatenings, or interested in his promises.

Chapter 8

Chapter Outline

Verses 1-6

The kindness of the good Shunammite to Elisha, was rewarded by the care taken of her in famine. It is well to foresee an evil, and wisdom, when we foresee it, to hide ourselves if we lawfully may do so. When the famine was over, she returned out of the land of the Philistines; that was no proper place for an Israelite, any longer than there was necessity for it. Time was when she dwelt so securely among her own people, that she had no occasion to be spoken for to the king; but there is much uncertainty in this life, so that things or persons may fail us which we most depend upon, and those befriend us which we think we shall never need. Sometimes events, small in themselves, prove of consequence, as here; for they made the king ready to believe Gehazi's narrative, when thus confirmed. It made him ready to grant her request, and to support a life which was given once and again by miracle.

Verses 7-15

Among other changes of men's minds by affliction, it often gives other thoughts of God's ministers, and teaches to value the counsels and prayers of those whom they have hated and despised. It was not in Hazael's countenance that Elisha read what he would do, but God revealed it to him, and it fetched tears from his eyes: the more foresight men have, the more grief they are liable to. It is possible for a man, under the convictions and restraints of natural conscience, to express great abhorrence of a sin, yet afterwards to be reconciled to it. Those that are little and low in the world, cannot imagine how strong the temptations of power and prosperity are, which, if ever they arrive at, they will find how deceitful their hearts are, how much worse than they suspected. The devil ruins men, by saying they shall certainly recover and do well, so rocking them asleep in security. Hazael's false account was an injury to the king, who lost the benefit of the prophet's warning to prepare for death, and an injury to Elisha, who would be counted a false prophet. It is not certain that Hazael murdered his master, or if he caused his death it may have been without any design. But he was a dissembler, and afterwards proved a persecutor to Israel.

Verses 16-24

A general idea is given of Jehoram's badness. His father, no doubt, had him taught the true knowledge of the Lord, but did ill to marry him to the daughter of Ahab; no good could come of union with an idolatrous family.

Verses 25-29

Names do not make natures, but it was bad for Jehoshaphat's family to borrow names from Ahab's. Ahaziah's relation to Ahab's family was the occasion of his wickedness and of his fall. When men choose wives for themselves, let them remember they are choosing mothers for their children. Providence so ordered it, that Ahaziah might be cut off with the house of Ahab, when the measure of their iniquity was full. Those who partake with sinners in their sin, must expect to partake with them in their plagues. May all the changes, troubles, and wickedness of the world, make us more earnest to obtain an interest in the salvation of Christ.

Chapter 9

Chapter Outline

Verses 1-10

In these and the like events, we must acknowledge the secret working of God, disposing men to fulfil his purposes respecting them. Jehu was anointed king over Israel, by the Lord's special choice. The Lord still had a remnant of his people, and would yet preserve his worship among them. Of this Jehu was reminded. He was commanded to destroy the house of Ahab, and, as far as he acted in obedience to God, and upon right principles, he needed not to regard reproach or opposition. The murder of God's prophets is strongly noticed. Jezebel persisted in idolatry and enmity to Jehovah and his servants, and her iniquity was now full.

Verses 11-15

Those who faithfully deliver the Lord's message to sinners, have in all ages been treated as madmen. Their judgment, speech, and conduct are contrary to those of other men; they endure much in pursuit of objects, and are influenced by motives, into which the others cannot enter. But above all, the charge is brought by the worldly and ungodly of all sorts, who are mad indeed; while the principles and practice of the devoted servants of God, prove to be wise and reasonable. Some faith in the word of God, seems to have animated Jehu to this undertaking.

Verses 16-29

Jehu was a man of eager spirit. The wisdom of God is seen in the choice of those employed in his work. But it is not for any man's reputation to be known by his fury. He that has rule over his own spirit, is better than the mighty. Joram met Jehu in the portion of Naboth. The circumstances of events are sometimes ordered by Divine Providence to make the punishment answer to the sin, as face answers to face in a glass. The way of sin can never be the way of peace, Isa 57:21. What peace can sinners have with God? No peace so long as sin is persisted in; but when it is repented of and forsaken, there is peace. Joram died as a criminal, under the sentence of the law. Ahaziah was joined with the house of Ahab. He was one of them; he had made himself so by sin. It is dangerous to join evil-doers; we shall be entangled in guilt and misery by it.

Verses 30-37

Instead of hiding herself, as one afraid of Divine vengeance, Jezebel mocked at fear. See how a heart, hardened against God, will brave it out to the last. There is not a surer presage of ruin, than an unhumbled heart under humbling providences. Let those look at Jezebel's conduct and fate, who use arts to seduce others to commit wickedness, and to draw them aside from the ways of truth and righteousness. Jehu called for aid against Jezebel. When reformation-work is on foot, it is time to ask, Who sides with it? Her attendants delivered her up. Thus she was put to death. See the end of pride and cruelty, and say, The Lord is righteous. When we pamper our bodies, let us think how vile they are; shortly they will be a feast for worms under ground, or beasts above ground. May we all flee from that wrath which is revealed from heaven, against all ungodliness and unrighteousness of men.

Chapter 10

Chapter Outline

Verses 1-14

In the most awful events, though attended by the basest crimes of man, the truth and justice of God are to be noticed; and he never did nor can command any thing unjust or unreasonable. Jehu destroyed all that remained of the house of Ahab; all who had been partners in his wickedness. When we think upon the sufferings and miseries of mankind, when we look forward to the resurrection and last judgment, and think upon the vast number of the wicked waiting their awful sentence of everlasting fire; when the whole sum of death and misery has been considered, the solemn question occurs, Who slew all these? The answer is, SIN. Shall we then harbour sin in our bosoms, and seek for happiness from that which is the cause of all misery?

Verses 15-28

Is thine heart right? This is a question we should often put to ourselves. I make a fair profession, have gained a reputation among men, but, is my heart right? Am I sincere with God? Jehonadab owned Jehu in the work, both of revenge and of reformation. An upright heart approves itself to God, and seeks no more than his acceptance; but if we aim at the applause of men, we are upon a false foundation. Whether Jehu looked any further we cannot judge. The law of God was express, that idolaters were to be put to death. Thus idolatry was abolished for the present out of Israel. May we desire that it be rooted out of our hearts.

Verses 29-36

It is justly questionable whether Jehu acted from a good principle, and whether he did not take some false steps in doing it; yet no services done for God shall go unrewarded. But true conversion is not only from gross sin, but from all sin; not only from false gods, but from false worships. True conversion is not only from wasteful sins, but from gainful sins; not only from sins which hurt our worldly interests, but from those that support and befriend them; in forsaking which is the great trial whether we can deny ourselves and trust God. Jehu showed great care and zeal for rooting out a false religion, but in the true religion he cared not, took no heed to please God and do his duty. Those that are heedless, it is to be feared, are graceless. The people were also careless, therefore it is not strange that in those days the Lord began to cut Israel short. They were short in their duty to God, therefore God cut them short in their extent, wealth, and power.

Chapter 11

Chapter Outline

Athaliah usurps the government of Judah, Jehoash made king.	(1–12)
Athaliah put to death.	(13–16)
The worship of the Lord restored.	(17–21)

Verses 1-12

Athaliah destroyed all she knew to be akin to the crown. Jehoash, one of the king's sons, was hid. Now was the promise made to David bound up in one life only, and yet it did not fail. Thus to the Son of David, the Lord, according to his promise, will secure a spiritual seed, hidden sometimes, and unseen, but hidden in God's pavilion, and unhurt. Six years Athaliah tyrannized. Then the king was brought forward. A child indeed, but he had a good guardian, and, what was better, a good God to go to With such joy and satisfaction must the kingdom of Christ be welcomed into our hearts, when his throne is set up there, and Satan the usurper is cast out. Say, Let the King, even Jesus, live, for ever live and reign in my soul, and in all the world.

Verses 13-16

Athaliah hastened her own destruction. She herself was the greatest traitor, and yet was first and loudest in crying, Treason, treason! The most guilty are commonly the most forward to reproach others.

Verses 17-21

King and people would cleave most firmly to each other, when both had joined themselves to the Lord. It is well with a people, when all the changes that pass over them help to revive, strengthen, and advance the interests of religion among them. Covenants are of use, both to remind us of, and bind us to, the duties already binding on us. They immediately abolished idolatry; and, pursuant to the covenant with one another, they expressed mutual readiness to help each other. The people rejoiced, and Jerusalem was quiet. The way for people to be joyful and at peace, is to engage fully in the service of God; for the voice of joy and thanksgiving is in the dwellings of the righteous, but there is no peace for the wicked.

Chapter 12

Chapter Outline

Jehoash orders the repair of the temple.   (1–16)

He is slain by his servants.   (17–21)

Verses 1-16

It is a great mercy to young people, especially to all young men of rank, like Jehoash, to have those about them who will instruct them to do what is right in the sight of the Lord; and they do wisely and well for themselves, when willing to be counselled and ruled. The temple was out of repair; Jehoash orders the repair of the temple. The king was zealous. God requires those who have power, to use it for the support of religion, the redress of grievances, and repairing of decays. The king employed the priests to manage, as most likely to be hearty in the work. But nothing was done effectually till the twenty-third year of his reign. Another method was therefore taken. When public distributions are made faithfully, public contributions will be made cheerfully. While they were getting all they could for the repair of the temple, they did not break in upon the stated maintenance of the priests. Let not the servants of the temple be starved, under colour of repairing the breaches of it. Those that were intrusted did the business carefully and faithfully. They did not lay it out in ornaments for the temple, till the other work was completed; hence we may learn, in all our expenses, to prefer that which is most needful, and, in dealing for the public, to deal as we would for ourselves.

Verses 17-21

Let us review the character of Jehoash, and consider what we may learn from it. When we see what a sad conclusion there was to so promising a beginning, it ought to make us seek into our spiritual declinings. If we know any thing of Christ as the foundation of our faith and hope, let us desire to know nothing but Christ. May the work of the blessed Spirit on our souls be manifest; may we see, feel, and be earnest, in seeking after Jesus in all his fulness, suitableness, and grace, that our souls may be brought over from dead works to serve the living and true God.

Chapter 13

Chapter Outline

Verses 1-9

It was the ancient honour of Israel that they were a praying people. Jehoahaz, their king, in his distress, besought the Lord; applied himself for help, but not to the calves; what help could they give him? He sought the Lord. See how swift God is to show mercy; how ready to hear prayer; how willing to find a reason to be gracious; else he would not look so far back as the ancient covenant Israel had so often broken, and forfeited. Let this invite and engage us for ever to him; and encourage even those who have forsaken him, to return and repent; for there is forgiveness with him, that he may be feared. And if the Lord answer the mere cry of distress for temporal relief, much more will he regard the prayer of faith for spiritual blessings.

Verses 10-19

Jehoash, the king, came to Elisha, to receive his dying counsel and blessing. It may turn much to our spiritual advantage, to attend the sick-beds and death-beds of good men, that we may be encouraged in religion by the living comforts they have from it in a dying hour. Elisha assured the king of his success; yet he must look up to God for direction and strength; must reckon his own hands not enough, but go on, in dependence upon Divine aid. The trembling hands of the dying prophet, as they signified the power of God, gave this arrow more force than the hands of the king in his full strength. By contemning the sign, the king lost the thing signified, to the grief of the dying prophet. It is a trouble to good men, to see those to whom they wish well, forsake their own mercies, and to see them lose advantages against spiritual enemies.

Verses 20-25

God has many ways to chastise a provoking people. Trouble comes sometimes from that point whence we least feared it. The mention of this invasion on the death of Elisha, shows that the removal of God's faithful prophets is a presage of coming judgments. His dead body was a means of giving life to another dead body. This miracle was a confirmation of his prophecies. And it may have reference to Christ, by whose death and burial, the grave is made a safe and happy passage to life to all believers. Jehoash was successful against the Syrians, just as often as he had struck the ground with the arrows, then a stop was put to his victories. Many have repented, when too late, of distrusts and the straitness of their desires.

Chapter 14

Chapter Outline

Amaziah's good reign.	(1–7)
Amaziah provokes Jehoash king of Israel, and is overcome.	(8–14)
He is slain by conspirators.	(15–22)
Wicked reign of Jeroboam II.	(23–29)

Verses 1-7

Amaziah began well, but did not go on so. It is not enough to do that which our pious predecessors did, merely to keep up the common usage, but we must do it as they did, from the same principle of faith and devotion, and with the same sincerity and resolution.

Verses 8-14

For some time after the division of the kingdoms, Judah suffered much from the enmity of Israel. After Asa's time, it suffered more by the friendship of Israel, and by the alliance made with them. Now we meet with hostility between them again. How may a humble man smile to hear two proud and scornful men set their wits on work, to vilify and undervalue one another! Unholy success excites pride; pride excites contentions. The effects of pride in others, are insufferable to those who are proud themselves. These are the sources of trouble and sin in private life; but when they arise between princes, they become the misery of their whole kingdoms. Jehoash shows Amaziah the folly of his challenge; Thine heart has lifted thee up. The root of all sin is in the heart, thence it flows. It is not Providence, the event, the occasion, whatever it is, that makes men proud, secure, discontented, or the like, but their own hearts do it. (2Ki 14:15-22)

Verses 15-22

Amaziah survived his conqueror fifteen years. He was slain by his own subjects. Azariah, or Uzziah, seems to have been very young when his father was slain. Though the years of his reign are reckoned from that event, he was not fully made king till eleven years afterwards.

Verses 23-29

God raised up the prophet Jonah, and by him declared the purposes of his favour to Israel. It is a sign that God has not cast off his people, if he continues faithful ministers among them. Two reasons are given why God blessed them with those victories: 1. Because the distress was very great, which made them objects of his compassion. 2. Because the decree was not yet gone forth for their destruction. Many prophets there had been in Israel, but none left prophecies in writing till this age, and their prophecies are part of the Bible. Hosea began to prophesy in the reign of this Jeroboam. At the same time Amos prophesied; soon after Micah, then Isaiah, in the days of Ahaz and Hezekiah. Thus God, in the darkest and most degenerate ages of the church, raised up some to be burning and shining lights in it; to their own age, by their preaching and living, and a few by their writings, to reflect light upon us in the last times.

Chapter 15

Chapter Outline

Reign of Azariah, or Uzziah, king of Judah.	(1–7)
The latter kings of Israel.	(8–31)
Jotham, king of Judah.	(32–38)

Verses 1-7

Uzziah did for the most part that which was right. It was happy for the kingdom that a good reign was a long one.

Verses 8-31

This history shows Israel in confusion. Though Judah was not without troubles, yet that kingdom was happy, compared with the state of Israel. The imperfections of true believers are very different from the allowed wickedness of ungodly men. Such is human nature, such are our hearts, if left to themselves, deceitful above all things, and desperately wicked. We have reason to be thankful for restraints, for being kept out of temptation, and should beg of God to renew a right spirit within us.

Verses 32-38

Jotham showed great respect to the temple. If magistrates cannot do all they would, for the suppressing of vice and profaneness, let them do the more to support and advance piety and virtue.

Chapter 16

Chapter Outline

Verses 1-9

Few and evil were the days of Ahaz. Those whose hearts condemn them, will go any where in a day of distress, rather than to God. The sin was its own punishment. It is common for those who bring themselves into straits by one sin, to try to help themselves out by another.

Verses 10-16

God's altar had hitherto been kept in its place, and in use; but Ahaz put another in the room of it. The natural regard of the mind of man to some sort of religion, is not easily extinguished; but except it be regulated by the word, and by the Spirit of God, it produces absurd superstitions, or detestable idolatries. Or, at best, it quiets the sinner's conscience with unmeaning ceremonies. Infidels have often been remarkable for believing ridiculous falsehoods.

Verses 17-20

Ahaz put contempt upon the sabbath, and thus opened a wide inlet to all manner of sin. This he did for the king of Assyria. When those who have had a ready passage to the house of the Lord, turn it another way to please their neighbours, they are going down-hill apace to ruin.

Chapter 17

Chapter Outline

Captivity of the Israelites. (7–23)

The nations placed in the land of Israel. (24–41)

Verses 1-6

When the measure of sin is filled up, the Lord will forbear no longer. The inhabitants of Samaria must have endured great affliction. Some of the poor Israelites were left in the land. Those who were carried captives to a great distance, were mostly lost among the nations.

Verses 7-23

Though the destruction of the kingdom of the ten tribes was but briefly related, it is in these verses largely commented upon, and the reasons of it given. It was destruction from the Almighty: the Assyrian was but the rod of his anger, Isa 10:5. Those that bring sin into a country or family, bring a plague into it, and will have to answer for all the mischief that follows. And vast as the outward wickedness of the world is, the secret sins, evil thoughts, desires, and purposes of mankind are much greater. There are outward sins which are marked by infamy; but ingratitude, neglect, and enmity to God, and the idolatry and impiety which proceed therefrom, are far more malignant. Without turning from every evil way, and keeping God's statutes, there can be no true godliness; but this must spring from belief of his testimony, as to wrath against all ungodliness and unrighteousness, and his mercy in Christ Jesus.

Verses 24-41

The terror of the Almighty will sometimes produce a forced or feigned submission in unconverted men; like those brought from different countries to inhabit Israel. But such will form unworthy thoughts of God, will expect to please him by outward forms, and will vainly try to reconcile his service with the love of the world and the indulgence of their lusts. May that fear of the Lord, which is the beginning of wisdom, possess our hearts, and influence our conduct, that we may be ready for every change. Wordly settlements are uncertain; we know not whither we may be driven before we die, and we must soon leave the world; but the righteous hath chosen that good part which shall not be taken from him.

Chapter 18

Chapter Outline

Good reign of Hezekiah in Judah, Idolatry. (1–8)

Sennacherib invades Judah. (9–16)

Rabshakeh's blasphemies. (17–37)

Verses 1-8

Hezekiah was a true son of David. Some others did that which was right, but not like David. Let us not suppose that when times and men are bad, they must needs grow worse and worse; that does not follow: after many bad kings, God raised one up like David himself. The brazen serpent had been carefully preserved, as a memorial of God's goodness to their fathers in the wilderness; but it was idle and wicked to burn incense to it. All helps to devotion, not warranted by the word of God, interrupt the exercise of faith; they always lead to superstition and other dangerous evils. Human nature perverts every thing of this kind. True faith needs not such aids; the word of God, daily thought upon and prayed over, is all the outward help we need.

Verses 9-16

The descent Sennacherib made upon Judah, was a great calamity to that kingdom, by which God would try the faith of Hezekiah, and chastise the people. The secret dislike, the hypocrisy, and lukewarmness of numbers, require correction; such trials purify the faith and hope of the upright, and bring them to simple dependence on God.

Verses 17-37

Rabshakeh tries to convince the Jews, that it was to no purpose for them to stand it out. What confidence is this wherein thou trustest? It were well if sinners would submit to the force of this argument, in seeking peace with God. It is, therefore, our wisdom to yield to him, because it is in vain to contend with him: what confidence is that which those trust in who stand out against him? A great deal of art there is in this speech of Rabshakeh; but a great deal of pride, malice, falsehood, and blasphemy. Hezekiah's nobles held their peace. There is a time to keep silence, as well as a time to speak; and there are those to whom to offer any thing religious or rational, is to cast pearls before swine. Their silence made Rabshakeh yet more proud and secure. It is often best to leave such persons to rail and blaspheme; a decided expression of abhorrence is the best testimony against them. The matter must be left to the Lord, who has all hearts in his hands, committing ourselves unto him in humble submission, believing hope, and fervent prayer.

Chapter 19

Chapter Outline

The Assyrian army destroyed, Sennacherib slain.

Verses 1-7

Hezekiah discovered deep concern at the dishonour done to God by Rabshakeh's blasphemy. Those who speak from God to us, we should in a particular manner desire to speak to God for us. The great Prophet is the great Intercessor. Those are likely to prevail with God, who lift up their hearts in prayer. Man's extremity is God's opportunity. While his servants can speak nothing but terror to the profane, the proud, and the hypocritical, they have comfortable words for the discouraged believer.

Verses 8-19

Prayer is the never-failing resource of the tempted Christian, whether struggling with outward difficulties or inward foes. At the mercy-seat of his almighty Friend he opens his heart, spreads his case, like Hezekiah, and makes his appeal. When he can discern that the glory of God is engaged on his side, faith gains the victory, and he rejoices that he shall never be moved. The best pleas in prayer are taken from God's honour. (2Ki 19:20-34)

Verses 20-34

All Sennacherib's motions were under the Divine cognizance. God himself undertakes to defend the city; and that person, that place, cannot but be safe, which he undertakes to protect. The invasion of the Assyrians probably had prevented the land from being sown that year. The next is supposed to have been the sabbatical year, but the Lord engaged that the produce of the land should be sufficient for their support during those two years. As the performance of this promise was to be after the destruction of Sennacherib's army, it was a sign to Hezekiah's faith, assuring him of that present deliverance, as an earnest of the Lord's future care of the kingdom of Judah. This the Lord would perform, not for their righteousness, but his own glory. May our hearts be as good ground, that his word may strike root therein, and bring forth fruit in our lives.

Verses 35-37

That night which followed the sending of this message to Hezekiah, the main body of their army was slain. See how weak the mightiest men are before Almighty God. Who ever hardened himself against Him and prospered? The king of Assyria's own sons became his murderers. Those whose children are undutiful, ought to consider whether they have not been so to their Father in heaven? This history exhibits a strong proof of the good of firm trust and confidence in God. He will afflict, but not forsake his people. It is well when our troubles drive us to our knees. But does it not reprove our unbelief? How unwilling are we to rest on the declaration of Jehovah! How desirous to know in what way he will save us! How impatient when relief is delayed! But we must wait for the fulfilling of his word. Lord, help our unbelief.

Chapter 20

Chapter Outline

Hezekiah's sickness, His recovery in answer
to prayer.

(1–11)

Hezekiah shows his treasures to the
ambassadors from Babylon, His death.

(12–21)

Verses 1-11

Hezekiah was sick unto death, in the same year in which the king of Assyria besieged Jerusalem. A warning to prepare for death was brought to Hezekiah by Isaiah. Prayer is one of the best preparations for death, because by it we fetch in strength and grace from God, to enable us to finish well. He wept sorely: some gather from hence that he was unwilling to die; it is in the nature of man to dread the separation of soul and body. There was also something peculiar in Hezekiah's case; he was now in the midst of his usefulness. Let Hezekiah's prayer, see Isa 38. interpret his tears; in that is nothing which is like his having been under that fear of death, which has bondage or torment. Hezekiah's piety made his sick-bed easy. "O Lord, remember now;" he does not speak as if God needed to be put in mind of any thing by us; nor, as if the reward might be demanded as due; it is Christ's righteousness only that is the purchase of mercy and grace. Hezekiah does not pray, Lord, spare me; but, Lord, remember me; whether I live or die, let me be thine. God always hears the prayers of the broken in heart, and will give health, length of days, and temporal deliverances, as much and as long as is truly good for them. Means were to be used for Hezekiah's recovery; yet, considering to what a height the disease was come, and how suddenly it was checked, the cure was miraculous. It is our duty, when sick, to use such means as are proper to help nature, else we do not trust God, but tempt him. For the confirmation of his faith, the shadow of the sun was carried back, and the light was continued longer than usual, in a miraculous manner. This work of wonder shows the power of God in heaven as well as on earth, the great notice he takes of prayer, and the great favour he bears to his chosen.

Verses 12-21

The king of Babylon was at this time independent of the king of Assyria, though shortly after subdued by him. Hezekiah showed his treasures and armour, and other proofs of his wealth and power. This was the effect of pride and ostentation, and departing from simple reliance on God. He also seems to have missed the opportunity of speaking to the Chaldeans, about Him who had wrought the miracles which excited their attention, and of pointing out to them the absurdity and evil of idolatry. What is more common than to show our friends our houses and possessions? But if we do this in the pride of ours hearts, to gain applause from men, not giving praise to God, it becomes sin in us, as it did in Hezekiah. We may expect vexation from every object with which we are unduly pleased. Isaiah, who had often been Hezekiah's comforter, is now is reprover. The blessed Spirit is both, Joh 16:7, 8. Ministers must be both, as there is occasion. Hezekiah allowed the justice of the sentence, and God's goodness in the respite. Yet the prospect respecting his family and nation must have given him many painful feelings. Hezekiah was indeed humbled for the pride of his heart. And blessed are the dead who die in the Lord; for they rest from their labours, and their works do follow them.

Chapter 21

Chapter Outline

Wicked reign of Manasseh.   (1–9)

The prophetic denunciations against Judah.   (10–18)

Wicked reign and death of Amon.   (19–26)

Verses 1-9

Young persons generally desire to become their own masters, and to have early possession of riches and power. But this, for the most part, ruins their future comfort, and causes mischief to others. It is much happier when young persons are sheltered under the care of parents or guardians, till age gives experience and discretion. Though such young persons are less indulged, they will afterwards be thankful. Manasseh wrought much wickedness in the sight of the Lord, as if on purpose to provoke him to anger; he did more evil than the nations whom the Lord destroyed. Manasseh went on from bad to worse, till carried captive to Babylon. The people were ready to comply with his wishes, to obtain his favour and because it suited their depraved inclinations. In the reformation of large bodies, numbers are mere time-servers, and in temptation fall away.

Verses 10-18

Here is the doom of Judah and Jerusalem. The words used represent the city emptied and utterly desolate, yet not destroyed thereby, but cleansed, and to be kept for the future dwelling of the Jews: forsaken, yet not finally, and only as to outward privileges, for individual believers were preserved in that visitation. The Lord will cast off any professing people who dishonour him by their crimes, but never will desert his cause on earth. In the book of Chronicles we read of Manasseh's repentance, and acceptance with God; thus we may learn not to despair of the recovery of the greatest sinners. But let none dare to persist in sin, presuming that they may repent and reform when they please. There are a few instances of the conversion of notorious sinners, that none may despair; and but few, that none may presume.

Verses 19-26

Amon profaned God's house with his idols; and God suffered his house to be polluted with his blood. How unrighteous soever they were that did it, God was righteous who suffered it to be done. Now was a happy change from one of the worst, to one of the best of the kings of Judah. Once more Judah was tried with a reformation. Whether the Lord bears long with presumptuous offenders, or speedily cuts them off in their sins, all must perish who persist in refusing to walk in his ways.

Chapter 22

Chapter Outline

Josiah's good reign, His care for repairing   (1–10)
the temple, The book of the law found.

Josiah consults Huldah the prophetess.   (11–20)

Verses 1-10

The different event of Josiah's early succession from that of Manasseh, must be ascribed to the distinguishing grace of God; yet probably the persons that trained him up were instruments in producing this difference. His character was most excellent. Had the people joined in the reformation as heartily as he persevered in it, blessed effects would have followed. But they were wicked, and had become fools in idolatry. We do not obtain full knowledge of the state of Judah from the historical records, unless we refer to the writings of the prophets who lived at the time. In repairing the temple, the book of the law was found, and brought to the king. It seems, this book of the law was lost and missing; carelessly mislaid and neglected, as some throw their Bibles into corners, or maliciously concealed by some of the idolaters. God's care of the Bible plainly shows his interest in it. Whether this was the only copy in being or not, the things contained in it were new, both to the king and to the high priest. No summaries, extracts, or collections out of the Bible, can convey and preserve the knowledge of God and his will, like the Bible itself. It was no marvel that the people were so corrupt, when the book of the law was so scarce; they that corrupted them, no doubt, used arts to get that book out of their hands. The abundance of Bibles we possess aggravates our national sins; for what greater contempt of God can we show, than to refuse to read his word when put into our hands, or, reading it, not to believe and obey it? By the holy law is the knowledge of sin, and by the blessed gospel is the knowledge of salvation. When the former is understood in its strictness and excellence, the sinner begins to inquire, What must I do to be saved? And the ministers of the gospel point out to him Jesus Christ, as the end of the law for righteousness to every one that believeth.

Verses 11-20

The book of the law is read before the king. Those best honour their Bibles, who study them; daily feed on that bread, and walk by that light. Convictions of sin and wrath should put us upon this inquiry, What shall we do to be saved? Also, what we may expect, and must provide for. Those who are truly apprehensive of the weight of God's wrath, cannot but be very anxious how they may be saved. Huldah let Josiah know what judgments God had in store for Judah and Jerusalem. The generality of the people were hardened, and their hearts unhumbled, but Josiah's heart was tender.

This is tenderness of heart, and thus he humbled himself before the Lord. Those who most fear God's wrath, are least likely to feel it. Though Josiah was mortally wounded in battle, yet he died in peace with God, and went to glory. Whatever such persons suffer or witness, they are gathered to the grave in peace, and shall enter into the rest which remaineth for the people of God.

Chapter 23

Chapter Outline

Verses 1-3

Josiah had received a message from God, that there was no preventing the ruin of Jerusalem, but that he should only deliver his own soul; yet he does his duty, and leaves the event to God. He engaged the people in the most solemn manner to abolish idolatry, and to serve God in righteousness and true holiness. Though most were formal or hypocritical herein, yet much outward wickedness would be prevented, and they were accountable to God for their own conduct.

Verses 4-14

What abundance of wickedness in Judah and Jerusalem! One would not have believed it possible, that in Judah, where God was known, in Israel, where his name was great, in Salem, in Zion, where his dwelling-place was, such abominations should be found. Josiah had reigned eighteen years, and had himself set the people a good example, and kept up religion according to the Divine law; yet, when he came to search for idolatry, the depth and extent were very great. Both common history, and the records of God's word, teach, that all the real godliness or goodness ever found on earth, is derived from the new-creating Spirit of Jesus Christ.

Verses 15-24

Josiah's zeal extended to the cities of Israel within his reach. He carefully preserved the sepulchre of that man of God, who came from Judah to foretell the throwing down of Jeroboam's altar. When they had cleared the country of the old leaven of idolatry, then they applied themselves to the keeping of the feast. There was not holden such a passover in any of the foregoing reigns. The revival of a long-neglected ordinance, filled them with holy joy; and God recompensed their zeal in destroying idolatry with uncommon tokens of his presence and favour. We have reason to think that during the remainder of Josiah's reign, religion flourished.

Verses 25-30

Upon reading these verses, we must say, Lord, though thy righteousness be as the great mountains, evident, plainly to be seen, and past dispute; yet thy judgments are a great deep, unfathomable, and past finding out. The reforming king is cut off in the midst of his usefulness, in mercy to him, that he might not see the evil coming upon his kingdom: but in wrath to his people, for his death was an inlet to their desolations. (2Ki 23:31-37)

Verses 31-37

After Josiah was laid in his grave, one trouble came on another, till, in twenty-two years, Jerusalem was destroyed. The wicked perished in great numbers, the remnant were purified, and Josiah's reformation had raised up some to join the few who were the precious seed of their future church and nation. A little time, and slender abilities, often suffice to undo the good which pious men have, for a course of years, been labouring to effect. But, blessed be God, the good work which he begins by his regenerating Spirit, cannot be done away, but withstands all changes and temptations.

Chapter 24

Chapter Outline

Jehoiakim subdued by Nebuchadnezzar.   (1–7)

Jehoiachim captive in Babylon.   (8–20)

Verses 1-7

If Jehoiakim had served the Lord, he had not been servant to Nebuchadnezzar. If he had been content with his servitude, and true to his word, his condition had been no worse; but, rebelling against Babylon, he plunged himself into more trouble. See what need nations have to lament the sins of their fathers, lest they smart for them. Threatenings will be fulfilled as certainly as promises, if the sinner's repentance prevent not. (2Ki 24:8-20)

Verses 8-20

Jehoiachin reigned but three months, yet long enough to show that he justly smarted for his fathers' sins, for he trod in their steps. His uncle was intrusted with the government. This Zedekiah was the last of the kings of Judah. Though the judgments of God upon the three kings before him might have warned him, he did that which was evil, like them. When those intrusted with the counsels of a nation act unwisely, and against their true interest, we ought to notice the displeasure of God in it. It is for the sins of a people that God hides from them the things that belong to the public peace. And in fulfilling the secret purposes of his justice, the Lord needs only leave men to the blindness of their own minds, or to the lusts of their own hearts. The gradual approach of Divine judgments affords sinners space for repentance, and believers leisure to prepare for meeting the calamity, while it shows the obstinacy of those who will not forsake their sins.

Chapter 25

Chapter Outline

Verses 1-7

Jerusalem was so fortified, that it could not be taken till famine rendered the besieged unable to resist. In the prophecy and Lamentations of Jeremiah, we find more of this event; here it suffices to say, that the impiety and misery of the besieged were very great. At length the city was taken by storm. The king, his family, and his great men escaped in the night, by secret passages. But those deceive themselves who think to escape God's judgments, as much as those who think to brave them. By what befell Zedekiah, two prophecies, which seemed to contradict each other, were both fulfilled. Jeremiah prophesied that Zedekiah should be brought to Babylon, Jer 32:5; 34:3; Ezekiel, that he should not see Babylon, Eze 12:13. He was brought thither, but his eyes being put out, he did not see it.

Verses 8-21

The city and temple were burnt, and, it is probable, the ark in it. By this, God showed how little he cares for the outward pomp of his worship, when the life and power of religion are neglected. The walls of Jerusalem were thrown down, and the people carried captive to Babylon. The vessels of the temple were carried away. When the things signified were sinned away, what should the signs stand there for? It was righteous with God to deprive those of the benefit of his worship, who had preferred false worships before it; those that would have many altars, now shall have none. As the Lord spared not the angels that sinned, as he doomed the whole race of fallen men to the grave, and all unbelievers to hell, and as he spared not his own Son, but delivered him up for us all, we need not wonder at any miseries he may bring upon guilty nations, churches, or persons.

Verses 22-30

The king of Babylon appointed Gedaliah to be the governor and protector of the Jews left their land. But the things of their peace were so hidden from their eyes, that they knew not when they were well off. Ishmael basely slew him and all his friends, and, against the counsel of Jeremiah, the rest went to Egypt. Thus was a full end made of them by their own folly and disobedience; see Jeremiah chap. 40 to 45 Jehoiachin was released out of prison, where he had been kept 37 years. Let none say that they shall never see good again, because they have long seen little but evil: the most miserable know not what turn Providence may yet give to their affairs, nor what comforts they are reserved for, according to the days wherein they have been afflicted. Even in this world the Saviour brings a release from bondage to the distressed sinner who seeks him, bestowing foretastes of the pleasures which are at his right hand for evermore. Sin alone can hurt us; Jesus alone can do good to sinners.

1 Chronicles

The books of Chronicles are, in a great measure, repetitions of what is in the books of Samuel and of the Kings, yet there are some excellent useful things in them which we find not elsewhere. The FIRST BOOK traces the rise of the Jewish people from Adam, and afterward gives an account of the reign of David. In the SECOND BOOK the narrative is continued, and relates the progress and end of the kingdom of Judah; also it notices the return of the Jews from the Babylonish captivity. Jerome says, that whoever supposes himself to have knowledge of the Scriptures without being acquainted with the books of Chronicles, deceives himself. Historical facts passed over elsewhere, names, and the connexion of passages are to be found here, and many questions concerning the gospel are explained.

Chapter 1

Chapter Outline

Genealogies, Adam to Abraham.   (1–27)

The descendants of Abraham.   (28–54)

Verses 1-27

This chapter, and many that follow, repeat the genealogies, or lists of fathers and children in the Bible history, and put them together, with many added. When compared with other places, there are some differences found; yet we must not therefore stumble at the word, but bless God that the things necessary to salvation are plain enough. The original of the Jewish nation is here traced from the first man that God created, and is thereby distinguished from the obscure, fabulous, and absurd origins assigned to other nations. But the nations now are all so mingled with one another, that no one nation, nor the greatest part of any, is descended entirely from any of one nation, nor the greatest part of any, is descended entirely from any of these fountains. Only this we are sure of, that God has created of one blood all nations of men; they are all descended from one Adam, one Noah. Have we not all one father? Has not one God created us? Mal 2:10.

Verses 28-54

The genealogy is from hence confined to the posterity of Abraham. Let us take occasion from reading these lists of names, to think of the multitudes that have gone through this world, have done their parts in it, and then quitted it. As one generation, even of sinful men, passes away, another comes. Ec 1:4; Nu 32:14, and will do so while the earth remains. Short is our passage through time into eternity. May we be distinguished as the Lord's people.

Chapter 2

Genealogies.

—We are now come to the register of the children of Israel, that distinguished people, who were to dwell alone, and not be reckoned among the nations. But now, in Christ, all are welcome to his salvation who come to him; all have equal privileges according to their faith in him, their love and devotedness to him. All that is truly valuable consists in the favour, peace, and image of God, and a life spent to his glory, in promoting the welfare of our fellow-creatures.

Chapter 3

Genealogies.

—Of all the families of Israel, none were so illustrious as the family of David: here we have a full account of it. From this family, as concerning the flesh, Christ came. The attentive observer will perceive that the children of the righteous enjoy many advantages.

Chapter 4

Genealogies.

—In this chapter we have a further account of Judah, the most numerous and most famous of all the tribes; also an account of Simeon. The most remarkable person in this chapter is Jabez. We are not told upon what account Jabez was more honourable than his brethren; but we find that he was a praying man. The way to be truly great, is to seek to do God's will, and to pray earnestly. Here is the prayer he made. Jabez prayed to the living and true God, who alone can hear and answer prayer; and, in prayer he regarded him as a God in covenant with his people. He does not express his promise, but leaves it to be understood; he was afraid to promise in his own strength, and resolved to devote himself entirely to God. Lord, if thou wilt bless me and keep me, do what thou wilt with me; I will be at thy command and disposal for ever. As the text reads it, this was the language of a most ardent and affectionate desire, Oh that thou wouldest bless me! Four things Jabez prayed for. 1. That God would bless him indeed. Spiritual blessings are the best blessings: God's blessings are real things, and produce real effects. 2. That He would enlarge his coast. That God would enlarge our hearts, and so enlarge our portion in himself, and in the heavenly Canaan, ought to be our desire and prayer. 3. That God's hand might be with him. God's hand with us, to lead us, protect us, strengthen us, and to work all our works in us and for us, is a hand all-sufficient for us. 4. That he would keep him from evil, the evil of sin, the evil of trouble, all the evil designs of his enemies, that they might not hurt, nor make him a Jabez indeed, a man of sorrow. God granted that which he requested. God is ever ready to hear prayer: his ear is not now heavy.

Chapter 5

Genealogies.

—This chapter gives some account of the two tribes and a half seated on the east side of Jordan. They were made captives by the king of Assyria, because they had forsaken the Lord. Only two things are here recorded concerning these tribes. 1. They all shared in a victory. Happy is that people who live in harmony together, who assist each other against the common enemies of their souls, trusting in the Lord, and calling upon him. 2. They shared in captivity. They would have the best land, not considering that it lay most exposed. The desire of earthly objects draws to a distance from God's ordinances, and prepares men for destruction.

Chapter 6

Genealogies.

—We have an account of Levi in this chapter. The priests and Levites were more concerned than any other Israelites, to preserve their descent clear, and to be able to prove it; because all the honours and privileges of their office depended upon their descent. Now, the Spirit of God calls ministers to their work, without any limit as to the families they came from; and then, as now, though believers and ministers may be very useful to the church, none but our great High Priest can make atonement for sin, nor can any be accepted but through his atonement.

Chapter 7

Genealogies.

—Here is no account either of Zebulun or Dan. We can assign no reason why they only should be omitted; but it is the disgrace of the tribe of Dan, that idolatry began in that colony which fixed in Laish, and called it Dan, Jud 18 and there one of the golden calves was set up by Jeroboam. Dan is omitted, Re 7. Men become abominable when they forsake the worship of the true God, for any creature object.

Chapter 8

Genealogies.

—Here is a larger list of Benjamin's tribe. We may suppose that many things in these genealogies, which to us seem difficult, abrupt, and perplexed, were plain and easy at that time, and fully answered the intention for which they were published. Many great and mighty nations then were in being upon earth, and many illustrious men, whose names are now wholly forgotten; while the names of multitudes of the Israel of God are here kept in everlasting remembrance. The memory of the just is blessed.

Chapter 9

Genealogies.

—This chapter expresses that one end of recording all these genealogies was, to direct the Jews, when they returned out of captivity, with whom to unite, and where to reside. Here is an account of the good state into which the affairs of religion were put, on the return from Babylon. Every one knew his charge. Work is likely to be done well when every one knows the duty of his place, and makes a business of it. God is the God of order. Thus was the temple a figure of the heavenly one, where they rest not day nor night from praising God, Re 4:8. Blessed be His name, believers there shall, not in turn, but all together, without interruption, praise him night and day: may the Lord make each of us fit for the inheritance of the saints in light.

Chapter 10

The death of Saul.

—The design chiefly in view in these books of the Chronicles, appears to be to preserve the records of the house of David. Therefore the writer repeats not the history of Saul's reign, but only of his death, by which a way was made for David to the throne. And from the ruin of Saul, we may learn, 1. That the sin of sinners will certainly find them out, sooner or later; Saul died for his transgression. 2. That no man's greatness can exempt him from the judgments of God. 3. Disobedience is a killing thing. Saul died for not keeping the word of the Lord. May be delivered from unbelief, impatience, and despair. By waiting on the Lord we shall obtain a kingdom that cannot be moved.

Chapter 11

Chapter Outline

Verses 1-9

David was brought to possess the throne of Israel after he had reigned seven years in Hebron, over Judah only. God's counsels will be fulfilled at last, whatever difficulties lie in the way. The way to be truly great, is to be really useful, to devote all our talents to the Lord.

Verses 10-47

An account is given of David's worthies, the great men who served him. Yet David reckoned his success, not as from the mighty men that were with him, but from the mighty God, whose presence is all in all. In strengthening him, they strengthened themselves and their own interest, for his advancement was theirs. We shall gain by what we do in our places for the support of the kingdom of the Son of David; and those that are faithful to Him, shall find their names registered much more to their honour, than these are in the records of fame.

Chapter 12

Chapter Outline

Verses 1-22

Here is an account of those who appeared and acted as David's friends, while he was persecuted. No difficulties or dangers should keep the sinner from coming to the Savior, nor drive the believer from the path of duty. Those who break through, and overcome in these attempts, will find abundant recompence. From the words of Amasai we may learn how to testify our affection and allegiance to the Lord Jesus; his we must be throughly; on his side we must be forward to appear and act. If we are under the influence of the Spirit, we shall desire to have our lot among them, and to declare ourselves on their side; if in faith and love we embrace the cause of Christ, he will receive, employ, and advance us.

Verses 23-40

When the throne of Christ is set up in a soul, there is, or ought to be, great joy in that soul; and provision is made, not as here, for a few days, but for the whole life, and for eternity. Happy are those who wisely perceive it to be their duty and interest, to submit to the Saviour Jesus Christ, the Son of David; who renounce for his sake all that is not consistent; whose earnest endeavours to do good are directed by the wisdom that God giveth, through acquaintance with his word, experience, and observation. If any man lack this wisdom, let him ask it of God, who giveth to all men liberally, and upbraideth not, and it shall be given him.

Chapter 13

Chapter Outline

David consults about the ark. (1–5)

The removal of the ark. (6–14)

Verses 1-5

David said not, What magnificent thing shall I do now? or, What pleasant thing? but, What pious thing? that he might have the comfort and benefit of that sacred oracle. Let us bring the ark to us, that it may be a blessing to us. Those who honour God, profit themselves. It is the wisdom of those setting out in the world, to take God's ark with them. Those are likely to go on in the favour of God, who begin in the fear of God. (1Ch 13:6-14)

Verses 6-14

Let the sin of Uzza warn all to take heed of presumption, rashness, and irreverence, in dealing with holy things; and let none think that a good design will justify a bad action. Let the punishment of Uzza teach us not to dare to trifle with God in our approaches to him; yet let us, through Christ, come boldly to the throne of grace. If the gospel be to some a savour of death unto death, as the ark was to Uzza, yet let us receive it in the love of it, and it will be to us a savour of life unto life.

Chapter 14

David's victories.

—In this chapter we have an account of, 1. David's kingdom established. 2. His family built up. 3. His enemies defeated. This is repeated from 2Sa 5. Let the fame of David be looked upon as a type and figure of the exalted honour of the Son of David.

Chapter 15

Chapter Outline

Preparations for the removal of the ark. (1–24)

The removal of the ark. (25–29)

Verses 1-24

Wise and good men may be guilty of oversights, which they will correct, as soon as they are aware of them. David does not try to justify what had been done amiss, nor to lay the blame on others; but he owns himself guilty, with others, of not seeking God in due order

Verses 25-29

It is good to notice the assistance of Divine Providence, even in things which fall within the compass of our natural powers; if God did not help us, we could not stir a step. If we do our religious duties in any degree aright, we must own it was God that helped us; had we been left to ourselves, we should have been guilty of some fatal errors. And every thing in which we engage, must be done in dependence on the mercy of God through the sacrifice of the Redeemer.

Chapter 16

Chapter Outline

Verses 1-6

Though God's word and ordinances may be clouded and eclipsed for a time, they shall shine out of obscurity. This was but a tent, a humble dwelling, yet this was the tabernacle which David, in his psalms, often speaks of with so much affection. David showed himself generous to his subjects, as he had found God gracious to him. Those whose hearts are enlarged with holy joy, should show it by being open-handed.

Verses 7-36

Let God be glorified in our praises. Let others be edified and taught, that strangers to him may be led to adore him. Let us ourselves triumph and trust in God. Those that give glory to God's name are allowed to glory in it. Let the everlasting covenant be the great matter of our joy his people of old, be remembered by us with thankfulness to him. Show forth from day to day his salvation, his promised salvation by Christ. We have reason to celebrate that from day to day; for we daily receive the benefit, and it is a subject that can never be exhausted. In the midst of praises, we must not forget to pray for the servants of God in distress.

Verses 37-43

The worship of God ought to be the work of every day. David put it into order. At Jerusalem, where the ark was, Asaph and his brethren were to minister before the ark continually, with songs of praise. No sacrifices were offered there, nor incense burnt, because the altars were not there; but David's prayers were directed as incense, and the lifting up of his hands as the evening sacrifice. So early did spiritual worship take place of ceremonial. Yet the ceremonial worship, being of Divine institution, must by no means be omitted; therefore at Gibeon, at the altars, the priests attended; for their work was to sacrifice and burn incense; and that they did continually, morning and evening, according to the law of Moses. As the ceremonies were types of the mediation of Christ, the observance of them was of great consequence. The attendance of his appointed ministers is right in itself, and encourages the people.

Chapter 17

David's purposes; God's gracious promises.
—This chapter is the same as 2Sa 7. See what is there said upon it. It is very observable that what in Samuel is said to be, "for thy word's sake," is here said to be, "for thy servant's sake," ver. #(19). Jesus Christ is both the Word of God, Re 19:13, and the Servant of God, Isa 42:1; and it is for his sake, upon account of his mediation, that the promises are made good to all believers; it is in him, that they are yea and amen. For His sake it is done, for his sake it is made known; to him we owe all this greatness, from him we are to expect all these great things. They are the unsearchable riches of Christ, which, if by faith we see in themselves, and see in the Lord Jesus, we cannot but magnify as the only true greatness, and speak honourably of them. For this blessedness may we look amidst the trials of life, and when we feel the hand of death upon us; and seek it for our children after us.

Chapter 18

David's victories.
—This chapter is the same as 2Sa 8. Our good fight of faith, under the Captain of our salvation, will end in everlasting triumph and peace. The happiness of Israel, through David's victories, and just government, faintly shadowed forth the happiness of the redeemed in the realms above.

Chapter 19

David's wars.
—The history is here repeated which we read 2Sa 10. The only safety of sinners consists in submitting to the Lord, seeking peace with him, and becoming his servants. Let us assist each other in a good cause; but let us fear lest, while made instruments of good to others, we should come short of salvation, through unbelief and sin.

Chapter 20

David's wars.

—Though the Lord will severely correct the sins of his believing people, he will not leave them in the hands of their enemies. His assistance will overcome all advantages of number and strength of those that defy his Israel. All that trust in Christ, shall be made more than conquerors through him that loveth them.

Chapter 21

David's numbering the people.

—No mention is made in this book of David's sin in the matter of Uriah, neither of the troubles that followed it: they had no needful connexion with the subjects here noted. But David's sin, in numbering the people, is related: in the atonement made for that sin, there was notice of the place on which the temple should be built. The command to David to build an altar, was a blessed token of reconciliation. God testified his acceptance of David's offerings on this altar. Thus Christ was made sin, and a curse for us; it pleased the Lord to bruise him, that through him, God might be to us, not a consuming Fire, but a reconciled God. It is good to continue attendance on those ordinances in which we have experienced the tokens of God's presence, and have found that he is with us of a truth. Here God graciously met me, therefore I will still expect to meet him.

Chapter 22

Chapter Outline

David's preparations for the temple.	(1–5)
David's instructions to Solomon.	(6–16)
The prices commanded to assist.	(17–19)

Verses 1-5

On occasion of the terrible judgment inflicted on Israel for the sin of David, God pointed out the place where he would have the temple built; upon which, David was excited to make preparations for the great work. David must not build, but he would do all he could; he prepared abundantly before his death. What our hands find to do for God, and our souls, and those round us, let us do it with all our might, before our death; for after death there is no device nor working. And when the Lord refuses to employ us in those services which we desired, we must not be discouraged or idle, but do what we can, though in a humbler sphere.

Verses 6-16

David gives Solomon the reason why he should build the temple. Because God named him. Nothing is more powerful to engage us in any service for God, than to know that we are appointed thereto. Because he would have leisure and opportunity to do it. He should have peace and quietness. Where God gives rest, he expects work. Because God had promised to establish his kingdom. God's gracious promises should quicken and strengthen our religious service. David delivered to Solomon an account of the vast preparations he had made for this building; not from pride and vain-glory, but to encourage Solomon to engage cheerfully in the great work. He must not think, by building the temple, to purchase a dispensation to sin; on the contrary, his doing that would not be accepted, if he did not take heed to fulfil the statutes of the Lord. In our spiritual work, as well as in our spiritual warfare, we have need of courage and resolution. (1Ch 22:17-19)

Verses 17-19

Whatever is done towards rendering the word of God generally known and attended to, is like bringing a stone, or an ingot of gold, towards erecting the temple. This should encourage us when we grieve that we do not see more fruit of our labours; much good may appear after our death, which we never thought of. Let us not then be weary of well doing. The work is in the hands of the Prince of peace. As he, the Author and Finisher of the work, is pleased to employ us as his instruments, let us arise and be doing, encouraging and helping one another; working by his rule, after his example, in dependence on his grace, assured that he will be with us, and that our labour shall not be in vain in the Lord.

Chapter 23

Chapter Outline

Verses 1-23

David, having given charge concerning the building of the temple, settles the method of the temple service, and orders the officers of it. When those of the same family were employed together, it would engage them to love and assist one another.

Verses 24-32

Now the people of Israel were so many, there should be more employed in the temple service, that every Israelite who brought an offering might find a Levite ready to help him. When more work is to be done, it is pity but there should be more workmen. A new heart, a spiritual mind, which delights greatly in God's commandments, and can find a refreshing feast in his ordinances, forms the great distinction between the true Christian and all other men in the world. To the spiritual man every service will yield satisfaction. He will be ever abounding in the work of the Lord; being never so happy as when employed for such a good Master, in so pleasant a service. He will not regard whether he is called to take the lead, or to keep the charge of others who are placed over him. May we seek and serve the Lord uprightly, and leave all the rest to his disposal, by faith in his word.

Chapter 24

The divisions of the priests and Levites.

—When every one has, knows, and keeps his place and work, the more there are the better. In the mystical body of Christ, every member has its use, for the good of the whole. Christ is High Priest over the house of God, to whom all believers, being made priests, are to be in subjection. In Christ, no difference is made between bond and free, elder and younger. The younger brethren, if faithful and sincere, shall be no less acceptable to Christ than the fathers. May we all be children of the Lord, fitted to sing his praises for ever in his temple above.

Chapter 25

The singers and musicians.

—David put those in order who were appointed to be singers and musicians in the temple. To prophesy, in this place, means praising God with great earnestness and devout affections, under the influences of the Holy Spirit. In raising these affections, poetry and music were employed. If the Spirit of God do not put life and fervour into our devotions, they will, however ordered, be a lifeless, worthless form.

Chapter 26

The offices of the Levites.

—The porters and treasurers of the temple, had occasion for strength and valour to oppose those who wrongly attempted to enter the sanctuary, and to guard the sacred treasures. Much was expended daily upon the altar; flour, wine, oil, salt, fuel, beside the lamps; quantities of these were kept beforehand, besides the sacred vestments and utensils. These were the treasures of the house of God. These treasures typified the plenty there is in our heavenly Father's house, enough and to spare. From those sacred treasuries, the unsearchable riches of Christ, all our wants are supplied;

and receiving from his fulness, we must give him the glory, and endeavour to dispose of our abilities and substance according to his will. We have an account of those employed as officers and judges. The magistracy is an ordinance of God for the good of the church, as truly as the ministry, and must not be neglected. None of the Levites who were employed in the service of the sanctuary, none of the singers or porters, were concerned in this outward business; one duty was enough to engage the whole man. Wisdom, courage, strength of faith, holy affections, and constancy of mind in doing our duty, are requisite or useful for every station.

Chapter 27

Chapter Outline

David's military force.	(1–15)
Princes and officers.	(16–34)

Verses 1-15

In the kingdoms of this world readiness for war forms a security for peace; in like manner, nothing so much encourages Satan's assaults as to be unwatchful. So long as we stand armed with the whole armour of God, in the exercise of faith, and preparation of heart for the conflict, we shall certainly be safe, and probably enjoy inward peace.

Verses 16-34

The officers of the court, or the rulers of the king's substance, had the oversight and charge of the king's tillage, his vineyards, his herds, his flocks, which formed the wealth of eastern kings. Much of the wisdom of princes is seen in the choice of their ministry, and common persons show it in the choice of their advisers. David, though he had all these about him, preferred the word of God before them all. Thy testimonies are my delight and my counsellors.

Chapter 28

Chapter Outline

David exhorts the people to the fear of the Lord.	(1–10)
He gives instructions for the temple.	(11–21)

Verses 1-10

During David's last sickness, many chief priests and Levites were at Jerusalem. Finding himself able, David spoke of his purpose to build a temple for God, and of God's disallowing that purpose. He opened to them God's gracious purposes concerning Solomon. David charged them to cleave stedfastly to God and their duty. We cannot do our work as we should, unless we put on resolution, and fetch in strength from Divine grace. Religion or piety has two distinct parts. The first is knowledge of God, the second is worship of God. David says, Know thou the God of thy father, and serve him with a perfect heart and a willing mind. God is made known by his works and word. Revelation alone shows the whole character of God, in his providence, his holy law, his condemnation of sinners, his blessed gospel, and the ministration of the Spirit to all true believers. The natural man cannot receive this knowledge of God. But thus we learn the value of the Saviour's atonement, and of the sanctification of the Holy Spirit, and are influenced to walk in all his commandments. It brings a sinner to his proper place at the foot of the cross, as a poor, guilty, helpless worm, deserving wrath, yet expecting every thing needful from the free mercy and grace of God our Father, and the Lord Jesus Christ. Having been forgiven much, the pardoned sinner learns to love much.

Verses 11-21

The temple must be a sacred thing, and a type of Christ; it must be framed by Divine teaching. Christ is the true temple, the church is the gospel temple, and heaven the everlasting temple; all are framed according to the Divine counsels, and the plan laid in the Divine wisdom, ordained before the world, for God's glory and our good. David gave this pattern to Solomon, that he might go by rule. Materials were provided for the most costly utensils of the temple. Directions were given which way to look for help in this great undertaking. Be not dismayed; God will help thee, and thou must look up to him in the first place. We may be sure that God, who owned our fathers, and carried them through the services of their day, will, in like manner, never leave us, while he has any work to do in us, or by us. Good work is likely to go on, when all concerned are hearty in furthering it. Let us hope in God's mercy; if we seek him, he will be found of us.

Chapter 29

Chapter Outline

David induces the princes and people to offer willingly.	(1–9)
His thanksgiving and prayer.	(10–19)
Solomon enthroned.	(20–25)
David's reign and death.	(26–30)

Verses 1-9

What is done in works of piety and charity, should be done willingly, not by constraint; for God loves a cheerful giver. David set a good example. This David offered, not from constraint, or for show; but because he had set his affection to the house of God, and thought he could never do enough towards promoting that good work. Those who would draw others to good, must lead the way themselves.

Verses 10-19

We cannot form a right idea of the magnificence of the temple, and the buildings around it, about which such quantities of gold and silver were employed. But the unsearchable riches of Christ exceed the splendour of the temple, infinitely more than that surpassed the meanest cottage on earth. Instead of boasting of these large oblations, David gave solemn thanks to the Lord. All they gave for the Lord's temple was his own; if they attempted to keep it, death would soon have removed them from it. They only use they could make of it to their real advantage, was, to consecrate it to the service of Him who gave it.

Verses 20-25

This great assembly joined with David in adoring God. Whoever is the mouth of the congregation, those only have the benefit who join him, not by bowing down the head, so much as by lifting up the soul. Solomon sat on the throne of the Lord. Solomon's kingdom typified the kingdom of the Messiah, whose throne is the throne of the Lord.

Verses 26-30

When we read the second book of Samuel, we could scarcely have expected to behold David appear so illustrious in his closing scene. But his repentance had been as remarkable as his sin; and his conduct during his afflictions, and towards the end of his life, appears to have had a good effect on his subjects. Blessed be God, even the chief of sinners may hope for a glorious departure, when brought to repent and flee for refuge to the Saviour's atoning blood. Let us mark the difference between the spirit and character of the man after God's own heart, living and dying, and those of worthless professors, who resemble him in nothing but their sins, and who wickedly try to excuse their crimes by his sins. Let us watch and pray, lest we be overcome by temptation, and overtaken by sin, to the dishonour of God, and the wounding of our own consciences. When we feel that we have offended, let us follow David's example of repentance and patience, looking for a glorious resurrection, through our Lord Jesus Christ.

2 Chronicles

Solomon's choice of wisdom, His strength and wealth.

—SOLOMON began his reign with a pious, public visit to God's altar. Those that pursue present things most eagerly, are likely to be disappointed; while those that refer themselves to the providence of God, if they have not the most, have the most comfort. Those that make this world their end, come short of the other, and are disappointed in this also; but those that make the other world their end, shall not only obtain that, and full satisfaction in it, but shall have as much of this world as is good for them, in their way. Let us then be contented, without those great things which men generally covet, but which commonly prove fatal snares to the soul.

Chapter 2

Solomon's message to Huram respecting the temple, His treaty with Huram.

—Solomon informs Huram of the particular services to be performed in the temple. The mysteries of the true religion, unlike those of the Gentile superstitions, sought not concealment. Solomon endeavoured to possess Huram with great and high thoughts of the God of Israel. We should not be afraid or ashamed to embrace every opportunity to speak of God, and to impress others with a deep sense of the importance of his favour and service. Now that the people of Israel kept close to the law and worship of God, the neighbouring nations were willing to be taught by them in the true religion, as the Israelites had been willing in the days of their apostacy, to be infected with the idolatries and superstitions of their neighbours. A wise and pious king is an evidence of the Lord's special love for his people. How great then was God's love to his believing people, in giving his only-begotten Son to be their Prince and their Saviour.

Chapter 3

The building of the temple.

—There is a more particular account of the building of the temple in 1Ki 6. It must be in the place David had prepared, not only which he had purchased, but which he had fixed on by Divine direction. Full instructions enable us to go about our work with certainty and to proceed therein with comfort. Blessed be God, the Scriptures are enough to render the man of God thoroughly furnished for every good work. Let us search the Scriptures daily, beseeching the Lord to enable us to understand, believe, and obey his word, that our work and our way may be made plain, and that all may be begun, continued, and ended in him. Beholding God, in Christ, his true Temple, more glorious than that of Solomon's, may we become a spiritual house, a habitation of God through the Spirit.

Chapter 4

The furniture of the temple.

—Here is a further account of the furniture of God's house. Both without doors and within, there was that which typified the grace of the gospel, and shadowed out good things to come, of which the substance is Christ. There was the brazen altar. The making of this was not mentioned in the book of Kings. On this all the sacrifices were offered, and it sanctified the gift. The people who worshipped in the courts might see the sacrifices burned. They might thus be led to consider the great Sacrifice, to be offered in the fulness of time, to take away sin, and put an end to death, which the blood of bulls and goats could not possibly do. And, with the smoke of the sacrifices, their hearts might ascend to heaven, in holy desires towards God and his favour. In all our devotions we must keep the eye of faith fixed upon Christ. The furniture of the temple, compared with that of the tabernacle, showed that God's church would be enlarged, and his worshippers multiplied. Blessed be God, there is enough in Christ for all.

Chapter 5

Chapter Outline

Verses 1-10

The ark was a type of Christ, and, as such, a token of the presence of God. That gracious promise, Lo, I am with you alway, even unto the end of the world, does, in effect, bring the ark into our religious assemblies, if we by faith and prayer plead that promise; and this we should be most earnest for. When Christ is formed in a soul, the law written in the heart, the ark of the covenant settled there, so that it becomes the temple of the Holy Ghost, there is true satisfaction in that soul.

Verses 11-14

God took possession of the temple; he filled it with a cloud. Thus he signified his acceptance of this temple, to be the same to him that the tabernacle of Moses was, and assured his people that he would be the same in it. Would we have God dwell in our hearts, we must leave room for him; every thing else must give way. The Word was made flesh; and when he comes to his temple, like a refiner's fire, who may abide the day of his coming? May he prepare us for that day.

Chapter 6

Solomon's prayer at the dedication of the temple.

—The order of Solomon's prayer is to be observed. First and chiefly, he prays for repentance and forgiveness, which is the chief blessing, and the only solid foundation of other mercies: he then prays for temporal mercies; thereby teaching us what things to mind and desire most in our prayers. This also Christ hath taught us in his perfect pattern and form of prayer, where there is but one prayer for outward, and all the rest are for spiritual blessings. The temple typified the human nature of Christ, in whom dwelleth all the fulness of the Godhead bodily. The ark typified his obedience and sufferings, by which repenting sinners have access to a reconciled God, and communion with him. Jehovah has made our nature his resting-place for ever, in the person of Emmanuel, and through him he dwells with, and delights in his church of redeemed sinners. May our hearts become his resting-place; may Christ dwell therein by faith, consecrating them as his temples, and shedding abroad his love therein. May the Father look upon us in and through his Anointed; and may he remember and bless us in all things, according to his mercy to sinners, in and through Christ.

Chapter 7

God's answer to Solomon's prayer.

—God gave a gracious answer to Solomon's prayer. The mercies of God to sinners are made known in a manner well suited to impress all who receive them, with his majesty and holiness. The people worshipped and praised God. When he manifests himself as a consuming Fire to sinners, his people can rejoice in him as their Light. Nay, they had reason to say, that God was good in this. It is of the Lord's mercies we are not consumed, but the sacrifice in our stead, for which we should be very thankful. And whoever beholds with true faith, the Saviour agonizing and dying for man's sin, will, by that view, find his godly sorrow enlarged, his hatred of sin increased, his soul made more watchful, and his life more holy. Solomon prosperously effected all he designed, for adorning both God's house and his own. Those who begin with the service of God, are likely to go on successfully in their own affairs. It was Solomon's praise, that what he undertook, he went through with; it was by the grace of God that he prospered in it. Let us then stand in awe, and sin not. Let us fear the Lord's displeasure, hope in his mercy, and walk in his commandments.

Chapter 8

Solomon's buildings and trade.

—It sometimes requires more wisdom and resolution to govern a family in the fear of God, than to govern a kingdom with reputation. The difficulty is increased, when a man has a hinderance instead of a help meet in the wife of his bosom. Solomon kept up the holy sacrifices, according to the law of Moses. In vain had the altar been built, in vain had fire come down from heaven, if sacrifices had not been constantly brought. Spiritual sacrifices are required of us, which we are to bring daily and weekly; it is good to be in a settled method of devotion. When the service of the temple was put into good order, it is said, The house of the Lord was perfected. The work was the main matter, not the place; the temple was unfinished till all this was done. Canaan was a rich country, and yet must send to Ophir for gold The Israelites were a wise people, but must be beholden to the king of Tyre for men that had knowledge of the seas. Grace, and not gold, is the best riches, and acquaintance with God and his law, the best knowledge. Leaving the children of this world to scramble for the toys of this world, may we, as the children of God, lay up our treasure in heaven, that where our treasure is, our hearts also may be.

Chapter 9

Chapter Outline

The queen of Sheba.   (1–12)

Solomon's riches, and his death.   (13–31)

Verses 1-12

This history has been considered, 1Ki 10; yet because our Saviour has proposed it as an example in seeking after him, Mt 12:42, we must not pass it over without observing, that those who know the worth of true wisdom will grudge no pains or cost to obtain it. The queen of Sheba put herself to a great deal of trouble and expense to hear the wisdom of Solomon; and yet, learning from him to serve God, and do her duty, she thought herself well paid for her pains. Heavenly wisdom is that pearl of great price, for which, if we part with all, we make a good bargain.

Verses 13-31

The imports here mentioned, would show that prosperity drew the minds of Solomon and his subjects to the love of things curious and uncommon, though useless in themselves. True wisdom and happiness are always united together; but no such alliance exists between wealth and the enjoyment of the things of this life. Let us then acquaint ourselves with the Saviour, that we may find rest for our souls. Here is Solomon reigning in wealth and power, in ease and fulness, the like of which could never since be found; for the most known of the great princes of the earth were famed for their wars; whereas Solomon reigned forty years in profound peace. The promise was fulfilled, that God would give him riches and honour, such as no kings have had or shall have. The lustre wherein he appeared, was typical of the spiritual glory of the kingdom of the Messiah, and but a faint representation of His throne, which is above every throne. Here is Solomon dying, and leaving all his wealth and power to one who he knew would be a fool! Ec 2:18, 19. This was not only vanity, but vexation of spirit. Neither power, wealth, nor wisdom, can ward off or prepare for the stroke of death. But thanks be to God who giveth the victory to the true believer, even over this dreaded enemy, through Jesus Christ our Lord.

Chapter 10

The ten tribes revolt from Rehoboam.
—Moderate counsels are wisest and best. Gentleness will do what violence will not do. Most people like to be accosted mildly. Good words cost only a little self-denial, yet they purchase great things. No more needs to be done to ruin men, than to leave them to their own pride and passion. Thus, whatever are the devices of men, God is doing his own work by all, and fulfilling the word which he has spoken. No man can bequeath his prosperity to his heirs any more than his wisdom; though our children will generally be affected by our conduct, whether good or bad. Let us then seek those good things which will be our own for ever; and crave the blessing of God upon our posterity, in preference to wealth or worldly exaltation.

Chapter 11

Chapter Outline

Rehoboam forbidden to war against Israel.   (1–12)

The priests and Levites find refuge in Judah.   (13–23)

Verses 1-12

A few good words might have prevented the rebellion of Rehoboam's subjects; but all the force of his kingdom cannot bring them back. And it is in vain to contend with the purpose of God, when it is made known to us. Even those who are destitute of true faith, will at times pay some regard to the word of God, and be kept by it from wrong actions, to which they are prone by nature.

Verses 13-23

When the priests and Levites came to Jerusalem, the devout, pious Israelites followed them. Such as set their hearts to seek the Lord God of Israel, left the inheritance of their fathers, and went to Jerusalem, that they might have free access to the altar of God, and be out of the temptation to worship the calves. That is best for us, which is best for our souls; in all our choices, religious advantages must be sought before all outward conveniences. Where God's faithful priests are, his faithful people should be. And when it has been proved that we are willing to renounce our worldly interests, so far as we are called to do so for the sake of Christ and his gospel, we have good evidence that we are truly his disciples. And it is the interest of a nation to protect religion and religious people.

Chapter 12

Rehoboam, forsaking the Lord, is punished.

—When Rehoboam was so strong that he supposed he had nothing to fear from Jeroboam, he cast off his outward profession of godliness. It is very common, but very lamentable, that men, who in distress or danger, or near death, seem much engaged in seeking and serving God, throw aside all their religion when they have received a merciful deliverance. God quickly brought troubles upon Judah, to awaken the people to repentance, before their hearts were hardened. Thus it becomes us, when we are under the rebukes of Providence, to justify God, and to judge ourselves. If we have humbled hearts under humbling providences, the affliction has done its work; it shall be removed, or the property of it be altered. The more God's service is compared with other services, the more reasonable and easy it will appear. Are the laws of temperance thought hard? The effects of intemperance will be found much harder. The service of God is perfect liberty; the service of our lusts is complete slavery. Rehoboam was never rightly fixed in his religion. He never quite cast off God; yet he engaged not his heart to seek the Lord. See what his fault was; he did not serve the Lord, because he did not seek the Lord. He did not pray, as Solomon, for wisdom and grace; he did not consult the word of God, did not seek to that as his oracle, nor follow its directions. He made nothing of his religion, because he did not set his heart to it, nor ever came up to a steady resolution in it. He did evil, because he never was determined for good.

Chapter 13

Abijah overcomes Jeroboam.

—Jeroboam and his people, by apostacy and idolatry, merited the severe punishment Abijah was permitted to execute upon them. It appears from the character of Abijah, 1Ki 15:3, that he was not himself truly religious, yet he encouraged himself from the religion of his people. It is common for those that deny the power of godliness, to boast of the form of it. Many that have little religion themselves, value it in others. But it was true that there were numbers of pious worshippers in Judah, and that theirs was the more righteous cause. In their distress, when danger was on every side, which way should they look for deliverance unless upward? It is an unspeakable comfort, that our way thither is always open. They cried unto the Lord. Earnest prayer is crying. To the cry of prayer they added the shout of faith, and became more than conquerors. Jeroboam escaped the sword of Abijah, but God struck him; there is no escaping his sword.

Chapter 14

Asa's piety, He strengthens his kingdom.

—Asa aimed at pleasing God, and studied to approve himself to him. Happy those that walk by this rule, not to do that which is right in their own eyes, or in the eye of the world, but which is so in God's sight. We find by experience that it is good to seek the Lord; it gives us rest; while we pursue the world, we meet with nothing but vexation. Asa consulted with his people how to make a good use of the peace they enjoyed; and concluded with them that they must not be idle, nor secure. A formidable army of Ethiopians invaded Asa's kingdom. This evil came upon them, that their faith in God might be tried. Asa's prayer is short, but it is the real language of faith and expectation from God. When we go forth in God's name, we cannot but prosper, and all things work together for the good of those whom he favours.

Chapter 15

The people make a solemn covenant with God.

—The work of complete reformation appeared so difficult, that Asa had not courage to attempt it, till assured of Divine assistance and acceptance. He and his people offered sacrifices to God; thanksgiving for the favours they had received, and supplication for further favours. Prayers and praises are now our spiritual sacrifices. The people, of their own will, covenanted to seek the Lord, each for himself, with earnestness. What is religion but seeking God, inquiring after him, applying to him upon all occasions? We make nothing of our religion, if we do not make heart-work of it; God will have all the heart, or none. Our devotedness to God our Saviour, should be avowed and shown in the most solemn and public manner. What is done in hypocrisy is a mere drudgery.

Chapter 16

Asa seeks the aid of the Syrians, His death.

—A plain and faithful reproof was given to Asa by a prophet of the Lord, for making a league with Syria. God is displeased when he is distrusted, and when an arm of flesh is relied on, more than his power and goodness. It is foolish to lean on a broken reed, when we have the Rock of ages to rely upon. To convince Asa of his folly, the prophet shows that he, of all men, had no reason to distrust God, who had found him such a powerful Helper. The many experiences we have had of the goodness of God to us, aggravate our distrust of him. But see how deceitful our hearts are! we trust in God when we have nothing else to trust to, when need drives us to him; but when we have other things to stay on, we are apt to depend too much on them. Observe Asa's displeasure at this reproof. What is man, when God leaves him to himself! He that abused his power for persecuting God's prophet, was left to himself, to abuse it further for crushing his own subjects. Two years before he died, Asa was diseased in his feet. Making use of physicians was his duty; but trusting to them, and expecting that from them which was to be had from God only, were his sin and folly. In all conflicts and sufferings we need especially to look to our own hearts, that they may be perfect towards God, by faith, patience, and obedience.

Chapter 17

Jehoshaphat promotes religion in Judah, His prosperity.

—Jehoshaphat found his people generally very ignorant, and therefore endeavoured to have them well taught. The public teaching of the word of God forms, in all ages, the great method of promoting the power of godliness. Thereby the understanding is informed, the conscience is awakened and directed. We have a particular account of Jehoshaphat's prosperity. But it was not his formidable army that restrained the neighbouring nations from attempting any thing against Israel, but the fear of God which fell upon them, when Jehoshaphat reformed his country, and set up a preaching ministry in it. The ordinances of God are more the strength and safety of a kingdom, than soldiers and weapons of war. The Bible requires use to notice the hand of God in every event, yet this is little regarded. But let all employ the talents they have: be faithful, even in that which is little. Set up the worship of God in your houses. The charge of a family is important. Why should you not instruct them as Jehoshaphat did his subjects, in the book of the law of the Lord. But be consistent. Do not recommend one thing, and practise another. Begin with yourselves. Seek to the Lord God of Israel, then call upon children and servants to follow your example.

Chapter 18

Jehoshaphat's alliance with Ahab.

—This history we read in 1Ki 22. Abundant riches and honour give large opportunities of doing good, but they are attended with many snares and temptations. Men do not know much of the artifices of Satan and the deceitfulness of their own hearts, when they covet riches with the idea of being able to do good with them. What can hurt those whom God will protect? What can shelter those whom God will destroy? Jehoshaphat is safe in his robes, Ahab killed in his armour; for the race is not to the swift, nor the battle to the strong. We should be cautious of entangling ourselves in the worldly undertakings of evil men; and still more we should avoid engaging in their sinful projects. But, when they call upon him, God can and will bring his faithful people out of the difficulties and dangers into which they have sinfully run themselves. He has all hearts in his hand, so that he easily rescues them. Blessed is the man that putteth his trust in the Lord.

Chapter 19

Jehoshaphat visits his kingdom.

—Whenever we return in peace to our houses, we ought to acknowledge God's providence in preserving our going out and coming in. And if we have been kept through more than common dangers, we are, in a special manner, bound to be thankful. Distinguishing mercies lay us under strong obligations. The prophet tells Jehoshaphat he had done very ill in joining Ahab. He took the reproof well. See the effect the reproof had upon him. He strictly searched his own kingdom. By what the prophet said, Jehoshaphat perceived that his former attempts for reformation were well-pleasing to God; therefore he did what was then left undone. It is good when commendations quicken us to our duty. There are diversities of gifts and operations, but all from the same Spirit, and for the public good; and as every one has received the gift, so let him minister the same. Blessed be God for magistrates and ministers, scribes and statesmen, men of books, and men of business. Observe the charge the king gave. They must do all in the fear of the Lord, with a perfect, upright heart. And they must make it their constant care to prevent sin, as an offence to God, and what would bring wrath on the people.

Chapter 20

Chapter Outline

Verses 1-13

In all dangers, public or personal, our first business should be to seek help from God. Hence the advantage of days for national fasting and prayer. From the first to the last of our seeking the Lord, we must approach him with humiliation for our sins, trusting only in his mercy and power. Jehoshaphat acknowledges the sovereign dominion of the Divine Providence. Lord, exert it on our behalf. Whom should we seek to, whom should we trust to for relief, but the God we have chosen and served. Those that use what they have for God, may comfortably hope he will secure it to them. Every true believer is a son of Abraham, a friend of God; with such the everlasting covenant is established, to such every promise belongs. We are assured of God's love, by his dwelling in human nature in the person of the Saviour. Jehoshaphat mentions the temple, as a token of God's favourable presence. He pleads the injustice of his enemies. We may well appeal to God against those that render us evil for good. Though he had a great army, he said, We have no might without thee; we rely upon thee.

Verses 14-19

The Spirit of prophecy came upon a Levite in the midst of the congregation. The Spirit, like the wind, blows where and on whom He listeth. He encouraged them to trust in God. Let the Christian soldier go out against his spiritual enemies, and the God of peace will make him more than a conqueror. Our trials will prove our gain. The advantage will be all our own, but the whole glory must be given to God.

Verses 20-30

Jehoshaphat exhorted his troops to firm faith in God. Faith inspires a man with true courage; nor will any thing help more to the establishing of the heart in shaking times, than a firm belief of the power, and mercy, and promise of God. In all our trust in the Lord, and our praises of him, let us especially look at his everlasting mercy to sinners through Jesus Christ. Never was an army so destroyed as that of the enemy. Thus God often makes wicked people destroy one another. And never was a victory celebrated with more solemn thanksgivings.

Verses 31-37

Jehoshaphat kept close to the worship of God, and did what he could to keep his people close to it. But after God had done such great things for him, given him not only victory, but wealth; after this, to go and join himself with a wicked king, was very ungrateful. What could he expect but that God would be angry with him? Yet it seems, he took the warning; for when Ahaziah afterward pressed him to join him, he would not, 1Ki 22:49. Thus the alliance was broken, and the Divine rebuke had its effect, at least for a season. Let us be thankful for any losses which may have prevented the loss of our immortal souls. Let us praise the Lord, who sought after us, and left us not to perish in our sins.

Chapter 21

Chapter Outline

Verses 1-11

Jehoram hated his brethren, and slew them, for the same reason that Cain hated Abel, and slew him, because their piety condemned his impiety. In the mystery of Providence such men sometimes prosper for a time; but the Lord has righteous purposes in permitting such events, part of which may now be made out, and the rest will be seen hereafter.

Verses 12-20

A warning from God was sent to Jehoram. The Spirit of prophecy might direct Elijah to prepare this writing in the foresight of Jehoram's crimes. He is plainly told that his sin should certainly ruin him. But no marvel that sinners are not frightened from sin, and to repentance, by the threatenings of misery in another world, when the certainty of misery in this world, the sinking of their estates, and the ruin of their health, will not restrain them from vicious courses. See Jehoram here stripped of all his comforts. Thus God plainly showed that the controversy was with him, and his house. He had slain all his brethren to strengthen himself; now, all his sons are slain but one. David's house must not be wholly destroyed, like those of Israel's kings, because a blessing was in it; that of the Messiah. Good men may be afflicted with diseases; but to them they are fatherly chastisements, and by the support of Divine consolations the soul may dwell at ease, even when the body lies in pain. To be sick and poor, sick and solitary, but especially to be sick and in sin, sick and under the curse of God, sick and without grace to bear it, is a most deplorable case. Wickedness and profaneness make men despicable, even in the eyes of those who have but little religion.

Chapter 22

The reign of Ahaziah, Athaliah destroys the royal family.
—The counsel of the ungodly ruins many young persons when they are setting out in the world. Ahaziah gave himself up to be led by evil men. Those who advise us to do wickedly, counsel us to our destruction; while they pretend to be friends, they are our worst enemies. See and dread the mischief of bad company. If not the infection, yet let the destruction be feared, Re 18:4. We have here, a wicked woman endeavouring to destroy the house of David, and a good woman preserving it. No word of God shall fall to the ground. The whole truth of the prophecies that the Messiah was to come from David, and thereby the salvation of the world, appeared to be now hung upon the brittle thread of the life of a single infant, to destroy whom was the interest of the reigning power. But God had purposed, and vain were the efforts of earth and hell.

Chapter 23

Joash crowned, and Athaliah slain.
—To look upon ourselves and each other as the Lord's people, should make us earnest in the discharge of our duty both to God and man. Thus was this happy revolution brought about, and the people rejoiced. When the Son of David is enthroned in the soul, all is quiet, and joyful. See 2Ki 11.

Chapter 24

Chapter Outline

Joash, of Judah, The temple repaired.   (1–14)

Joash falls into idolatry, He is slain by his   (15–27)
servants.

Verses 1-14

Joash is more zealous about the repair of the temple than Jehoiada himself. It is easier to build temples, than to be temples to God. But the repairing of places for public worship is a good work, which all should promote. And many a good work would be done that now lies undone, if active men would put it forward.

Verses 15-27

See what a great judgment on any prince or people, the death of godly, zealous, useful men is. See how necessary it is that we act in religion from inward principle. Then the loss of a parent, a minister, or a friend, will not be losing our religion. Often both princes and inferior people have been flattered to their ruin. True grace alone will enable a man to bring forth fruit unto the end. Zechariah, the son of Jehoiada, being filled with the Spirit of prophecy, stood up, and told the people of their sin. This is the work of ministers, by the word of God, as a lamp and a light, to discover the sin of men, and expound the providences of God. They stoned Zechariah to death in the court of the house of the Lord. Observe the dying martyr's words: The Lord look upon it, and require it! This came not from a spirit of revenge, but a spirit of prophecy. God smote Joash with great diseases, of body, or mind, or both, before the Syrians departed from him. If vengeance pursue men, the end of one trouble will be but the beginning of another. His own servants slew him. These judgments are called the burdens laid upon him, for the wrath of God is a heavy burden, too heavy for any man to bear. May God help us to take warning, to be upright in heart, and to persevere in his ways to the end.

Chapter 25

Chapter Outline

Amaziah, king of Judah.   (1–13)

Amaziah worships the idols of Edom.   (14–16)

Amaziah's rash challenge.   (17–28)

Verses 1-13

Amaziah was no enemy to religion, but cool and indifferent friend. Many do what is good, but not with a perfect heart. Rashness makes work for repentance. But Amaziah's obedience to the command of God was to his honour. A firm belief of God's all-sufficiency to bear us out in our duty, and to make up all the loss and damage was sustain in his service, will make his yoke very easy, and his burden very light. When we are called to part with any thing for God and our religion, it should satisfy us, that God is able to give us much more than this. Convinced sinners, who have not true faith, always object to self-denying obedience. They are like Amaziah; they say, But what shall we do for the hundred talents? What shall we do if by keeping the sabbath holy we lose so many good customers? What shall we do without this gain? What shall we do if we lose the friendship of the world? Many endeavour to quiet their consciences by the pretence that forbidden practices are necessary. The answer is, as here, The Lord is able to give thee much more than this. He makes up, even in this world, for all that is given up for his sake.

Verses 14-16

To worship the gods of those whom Amaziah had conquered, who could not help their own worshippers, was the greatest absurdity. If men would consider how unable all those things are to help them, to which they look whenever they forsake God, they would not be such enemies to themselves. The reproof God sent by a prophet was too just to be answered; themselves. The reproof God sent by a prophet was too just to be answered; but he was bidden not to say a word more. The secure sinner rejoices to have silenced his reprovers and monitors; but what comes of it? Those that are deaf to reproof, are ripening for destruction.

Verses 17-28

Never was a proud prince more thoroughly mortified than Amaziah by Joash king of Israel. A man's pride will bring him low, Pr 29:23; it goes before his destruction, and deservedly brings it on. He that exalteth himself shall be abased. He that goes forth hastily to strive, will not know what he shall do in the end thereof, when his neighbour has put him to shame, Pr 25:8. And what are we when we offer to establish our own righteousness, or presume to justify ourselves before the Most High God, but despicable thistles, that fancy themselves stately cedars? And are not various temptations, is not every corruption, a wild beast of the desert, which will trample on the wretched boaster, and tread his haughty pretensions to the dust? A man's pride shall bring him low; his ruin may be dated from his turning from the Lord.

Chapter 26

Chapter Outline

Uzziah's good reign in Judah.   (1–15)

Uzziah's attempt to burn incense.   (16–23)

Verses 1-15

As long as Uzziah sought the Lord, and minded religion, God made him to prosper. Those only prosper whom God makes to prosper; for prosperity is his gift. Many have owned, that as long as they sought the Lord, and kept close to their duty, they prospered; but when they forsook God, every thing went cross. God never continues either to bless the indolent or to withhold his blessing from the diligent. He will never suffer any to seek his face in vain. Uzziah's name was famed throughout all the neighbouring countries. A name with God and good people makes truly honourable. He did not delight in war, nor addict himself to sports, but delighted in husbandry.

Verses 16-23

The transgression of the kings before Uzziah was, forsaking the temple of the Lord, and burning incense upon idolatrous altars. But his transgression was, going into the holy place, and attempting to burn incense upon the altar of God. See how hard it is to avoid one extreme, and not run into another. Pride of heart was at the bottom of his sin; a lust that ruins many. Instead of lifting up the name God in gratitude to him who had done so much for him, his heart was lifted up to his hurt. Men's pretending to forbidden knowledge, and seeking things too high for them, are owing to pride of heart. The incense of our prayers must be, by faith, put into the hands of our Lord Jesus, the great High Priest of our profession, else we cannot expect it to be accepted by God, Re 8:3. Though Uzziah strove with the priests, he would not strive with his Maker. But he was punished for his transgression; he continued a leper to his death, shut out from society. The punishment answered the sin as face to face in a glass. Pride was at the bottom of his transgression, and thus God humbled him, and put dishonour upon him. Those that covet forbidden honours, forfeit allowed ones. Adam, by catching at the trcc of knowledge which he might not eat of, debarred himself of the tree of life which he might have eaten of. Let all that read say, The Lord is righteous. And when the Lord sees good to throw prosperous and useful men aside, as broken vessels, if he raises up others to fill their places, they may rejoice to renounce all worldly concerns, and employ their remaining days in preparation for death.

Chapter 27

Jotham's reign in Judah.

—The people did corruptly. Perhaps Jotham was wanting towards the reformation of the land. Men may be very good, and yet not have courage and zeal to do what they might. It certainly casts blame upon the people. Jotham prospered, and became mighty. The more stedfast we are in religion, the more mighty we are, both to resist evil, and to do good. The Lord often removes wise and pious rulers, and sends others, whose follies and vices punish a people that valued not their mercies.

Chapter 28

The wicked reign of Ahaz in Judah.

—Israel gained this victory because God was wroth with Judah, and made them the rod of his indignation. He reminds them of their own sins. It ill becomes sinners to be cruel. Could they hope for the mercy of God, if they neither showed mercy nor justice to their brethren? Let it be remembered, that every man is our neighbour, our brother, our fellow man, if not our fellow Christian. And no man who is acquainted with the word of God, need fear to maintain that slavery is against the law of love and the gospel of grace. Who can hold his brother in bondage, without breaking the rule of doing to others as he would they should do unto him? But when sinners are left to their own heart's lusts, they grow more desperate in wickedness. God commands them to release the prisoners, and they obeyed. The Lord brought Judah low. Those who will not humble themselves under the word of God, will justly be humbled by his judgments. It is often found, that wicked men themselves have no real affection for those that revolt to them, nor do they care to do them a kindness. This is that king Ahaz! that wretched man! Those are wicked and vile indeed, that are made worse by their afflictions, instead of being made better by them; who, in their distress, trespass yet more, and have their hearts more fully set in them to do evil. But no marvel that men's affections and devotions are misplaced, when they mistake the author of their trouble and of their help. The progress of wickedness and misery is often rapid; and it is awful to reflect upon a sinner's being driven away in his wickedness into the eternal world.

Chapter 29

Chapter Outline

Verses 1-19

When Hezekiah came to the crown, he applied at once to work reform. Those who begin with God, begin at the right end of their work, and it will prosper accordingly. Those that turn their backs upon God's ordinances, may truly be said to forsake God himself. There are still such neglects, if the word be not duly read and opened, for that was signified by the lighting the lamps, and also if prayers and praise be not offered up, for that was signified by the burning incense. Neglect of God's worship was the cause of the calamities they had lain under. The Lord alone can prepare the heart of man for vital godliness: when much good is done in a little time, the glory must be ascribed to him; and all who love him or the souls of men, will rejoice therein. Let those that do good work, learn to do it well.

Verses 20-36

As soon as Hezekiah heard that the temple was ready, he lost no time. Atonement must be made for the sins of the last reign. It was not enough to lament and forsake those sins; they brought a sin-offering. Our repentance and reformation will not obtain pardon but in and through Christ, who was made sin, that is, a sin-offering for us. While the offerings were on the altar, the Levites sang. Sorrow for sin must not prevent us from praising God. The king and the congregation gave their consent to all that was done. It is not enough for us to be where God is worshipped, if we do not ourselves worship with the heart. And we should offer up our spiritual sacrifices of praise and thanksgiving, and devote ourselves and all we have, as sacrifices, acceptable to the Father only through the Redeemer.

Chapter 30

Chapter Outline

Hezekiah's passover.	(1–12)
The passover celebrated.	(13–20)
The feast of unleavened bread.	(21–27)

Verses 1-12

Hezekiah made Israel as welcome to the passover, as any of his own subjects. Let us yield ourselves unto the Lord. Say not, you will do what you please, but resolve to do what he pleases. We perceive in the carnal mind a stiffness, an obstinacy, an unaptness to compel with God; we have it from our fathers: this must be overcome. Those who, through grace, have turned to God themselves, should do all they can to bring others to him. Numbers will be scorners, but some will be humbled and benefited; perhaps where least expected. The rich mercy of God is the great argument by which to enforce repentance; the vilest who submit and yield themselves to the Lord, seek his grace, and give themselves to his service, shall certainly be saved. Oh that messengers were sent forth to carry these glad tidings to every city and every village, through every land!

Verses 13-20

The great thing needful in attendance upon God in solemn ordinances, is, that we make heart-work of it; all is nothing without this. Where this sincerity and fixedness of heart are, there may yet be many things short of the purification of the sanctuary. These defects need pardoning, healing grace; for omissions in duty are sins, as well as omissions of duty. If God should deal with us in strict justice, even as to the very best of our doings, we should be undone. The way to obtain pardon, is to seek it of God by prayer; it must be gotten by petition through the blood of Christ.

Yet every defect is sin, and needs forgiveness; and should be matter to humble, but not to discourage us, though nothing can make up for the want of a heart prepared to seek the Lord.

Verses 21-27

Many prayers were put up to God with the peace-offerings. In these Israel looked to God as the God of their fathers, a God in covenant with them. There was also abundance of good preaching. The Levites read and explained the Scriptures. Faith cometh by hearing, and true religion preaching has abounded. They sang psalms every day: praising God should be much of our work in religious assemblies. Having kept the seven days of the feast in this religious manner, they had so much comfort in it, that they kept other seven days also. This they did with gladness. Holy duties should be done with holy gladness. And when sinners humble themselves before the Lord, they may expect gladness in his ordinances. Those who taste this happiness will not soon grow weary of it, but will be glad to prolong their enjoyment.

Chapter 31

Hezekiah destroys idolatry.
—After the passover, the people of Israel applied with vigour to destroy the monuments of idolatry. Public ordinances should stir us up to cleanse our hearts, our houses, and shops, from the filth of sin, and the idolatry of covetousness, and to excite others to do the same. The after-improvement of solemn ordinances, is of the greatest importance to personal, family, and public religion. When they had tasted the sweetness of God's ordinance in the late passover, they were free in maintaining the temple service. Those who enjoy the benefit of a settled ministry, will not grudge the expense of it. In all that Hezekiah attempted in God's service, he was earnest and single in his aim and dependence, and was prospered accordingly. Whether we have few or many talents intrusted to us, may we thus seek to improve them, and encourage others to do the same. What is undertaken with a sincere regard to the glory of God, will succeed to our own honour and comfort at last.

Chapter 32

Chapter Outline

Verses 1-23

Those who trust God with their safety, must use proper means, else they tempt him. God will provide, but so must we also. Hezekiah gathered his people together, and spake comfortably to them. A believing confidence in God, will raise us above the prevailing fear of man. Let the good subjects and soldiers of Jesus Christ, rest upon his word, and boldly say, Since God is for us, who can be against us? By the favour of God, enemies are lost, and friends gained.

Verses 24-33

God left Hezekiah to himself, that, by this trial and his weakness in it, what was in his heart might be known; that he was not so perfect in grace as he thought he was. It is good for us to know ourselves, and our own weakness and sinfulness, that we may not be conceited, or self-confident, but may always live in dependence upon Divine grace. We know not the corruption of our own hearts, nor what we shall do if God leaves us to ourselves. His sin was, that his heart was lifted up. What need have great men, and good men, and useful men, to study their own infirmities and follies, and their obligations to free grace, that they may never think highly of themselves; but beg earnestly of God, that he will always keep them humble! Hezekiah made a bad return to God for his favours, by making even those favours the food and fuel of his pride. Let us shun the occasions of sin: let us avoid the company, the amusements, the books, yea, the very sights that may administer to sin. Let us commit ourselves continually to God's care and protection; and beg of him never to leave us nor forsake us. Blessed be God, death will soon end the believer's conflict; then pride and every sin will be abolished. He will no more be tempted to withhold the praise which belongs to the God of his salvation.

Chapter 33

Chapter Outline

Manasseh's and repentance.	(1–20)
Amon's wicked reign in Judah.	(21–25)

Verses 1-20

We have seen Manasseh's wickedness; here we have his repentance, and a memorable instance it is of the riches of God's pardoning mercy, and the power of his renewing grace. Deprived of his liberty, separated from his evil counsellors and companions, without any prospect but of ending his days in a wretched prison, Manasseh thought upon what had passed; he began to cry for mercy and deliverance. He confessed his sins, condemned himself, was humbled before God, loathing himself as a monster of impiety and wickedness. Yet he hoped to be pardoned through the abundant mercy of the Lord. Then Manasseh knew that Jehovah was God, able to deliver. He knew him as a God of salvation; he learned to fear, trust in, love, and obey him. From this time he bore a new character, and walked in newness of life. Who can tell what tortures of conscience, what pangs of grief, what fears of wrath, what agonizing remorse he endured, when he looked back on his many years of apostacy and rebellion against God; on his having led thousands into sin and perdition; and on his blood-guiltiness in the persecution of a number of God's children? And who can complain that the way of heaven is blocked up, when he sees such a sinner enter? Say the worst against thyself, here is one as bad who finds the way to repentance. Deny not to thyself that which God hath not denied to thee; it is not thy sin, but thy impenitence, that bars heaven against thee. (2Ch 33:21-25)

Verses 21-25

Amon's father did ill, but he did worse. Whatever warnings or convictions he had, he never humbled himself. He was soon cut off in his sins, and made a warning for all men not to abuse the example of God's patience and mercy to Manasseh, as an encouragement to continue in sin. May God help us to be honest to ourselves, and to think aright respecting our own character, before death fixes us in an unchangeable state.

Chapter 34

Josiah's good reign in Judah.
—As the years of infancy cannot be useful to our fellow-creatures, our earliest youth should be dedicated to God, that we may not waste any of the remaining short space of life. Happy and wise are those who seek the Lord and prepare for usefulness at an early age, when others are pursuing sinful pleasures, contracting bad habits, and forming ruinous connexions. Who can express the anguish prevented by early piety, and its blessed effects? Diligent self-examination and watchfulness will convince us of the deceitfulness and wickedness of our own hearts, and the sinfulness of our lives. We are here encouraged to humble ourselves before God, and to seek unto him, as Josiah did. And believers are here taught, not to fear death, but to welcome it, when it takes them away from the evil to come. Nothing hastens the ruin of a people, nor ripens them for it, more than their disregard of the attempts made for their reformation. Be not deceived, God is not mocked. The current and tide of affections only turns at the command of Him who raises up those that are dead in trespasses and sins. We behold peculiar loveliness, in the grace the Lord bestows on those, who in tender years seek to know and to love the Saviour. Hath Jesus, the Day-spring from on high, visited you? Can you trace your knowledge of this light and life of man, like Josiah, from your youth? Oh the unspeakable happiness of becoming acquainted with Jesus from our earliest years!

Chapter 35

Chapter Outline

The passover kept by Josiah.   (1–19)

Josiah slain in battle.   (20–27)

Verses 1-19

The destruction Josiah made of idolatry, was more largely related in the book of Kings. His solemnizing the passover is related here. The Lord's supper resembles the passover more than any other of the Jewish festivals; and the due observance of that ordinance, is a proof of growing piety and devotion. God alone can truly make our hearts holy, and prepare them for his holy services; but there are duties belonging to us, in doing which we obtain this blessing from the Lord.

Verses 20-27

The Scripture does not condemn Josiah's conduct in opposing Pharaoh. Yet Josiah seems to deserve blame for not inquiring of the Lord after he was warned; his death might be a rebuke for his rashness, but it was a judgment on a hypocritical and wicked people. He that lives a life of repentance, faith, and obedience, cannot be affected by the sudden manner in which he is removed. The people lamented him. Many mourn over sufferings, who will not forsake the sins that caused God to send them. Yet this alone can turn away judgments. If we blame Josiah's conduct, we should be watchful, lest we be cut down in a way dishonourable to our profession.

Chapter 36

Chapter Outline

The destruction of Jerusalem.   (1–21)

The proclamation of Cyrus.   (22, 23)

Verses 1-21

The ruin of Judah and Jerusalem came on by degrees. The methods God takes to call back sinners by his word, by ministers, by conscience, by providences, are all instances of his compassion toward them, and his unwillingness that any should perish. See here what woful havoc sin makes, and, as we value the comfort and continuance of our earthly blessings, let us keep that worm from the root of them. They had many times ploughed and sowed their land in the seventh year, when it should have rested, and now it lay unploughed and unsown for ten times seven years. God will be no loser in his glory at last, by the disobedience of men. If they refused to let the land rest, God would make it rest. What place, O God, shall thy justice spare, if Jerusalem has perished? If that delight of thine were cut off for wickedness, let us not be high-minded, but fear.

Verses 22, 23

God had promised the restoring of the captives, and the rebuilding of Jerusalem, at the end of seventy years; and that time to favour Zion, that set time, came at last. Though God's church be cast down, it is not cast off; though his people be corrected, they are not abandoned; though thrown into the furnace, they are not lost there, nor left there any longer than till the dross be separated. Though God contend long, he will not contend always. Before we close the books of the Chronicles, which contain a faithful register of events, think what desolation sin introduced into the world, nay, even into the church of God. Let us tremble at what is here recorded, while in the character of some few gracious souls, we discover that the Lord left not himself without witness. And when we have looked at this faithful portrait of man by nature, let us contrast with it that same nature, when recovered by Almighty grace, through the justifying and soul-adorning righteousness of Christ our Saviour.

Ezra

The history of this book is the accomplishment of Jeremiah's prophecy concerning the return of the Jews out of Babylon. From its contents we especially learn, that every good work will meet with opposition from enemies, and be hurt by the misconduct of friends; but that God will make his cause to prevail, notwithstanding all obstacles and adversaries. The restoration of the Jews was an event of the highest consequence, tending to preserve religion in the world, and preparing the way for the appearance of the Great Deliverer, the Lord Jesus Christ.

Chapter 1

Chapter Outline

The proclamation of Cyrus for the rebuilding of the temple.   (1–4)

The people provide for their return.   (5–11)

Verses 1-4

The Lord stirred up the spirit of Cyrus. The hearts of kings are in the hand of the Lord. God governs the world by his influence on the spirits of men; whatever good they do, God stirs up their spirits to do it. It was during the captivity of the Jews, that God principally employed them as the means of calling the attention of the heathen to him. Cyrus took it for granted, that those among the Jews who were able, would offer free-will offerings for the house of God. He would also have them supplied out of his kingdom. Well-wishers to the temple should be well-doers for it.

Verses 5-11

The same God that raised up the spirit of Cyrus to proclaim liberty to the Jews, raised up their spirits to take the benefit. The temptation was to some to stay in Babylon; but some feared not to return, and they were those whose spirits God raised, by his Spirit and grace. Whatever good we do, is owing to the grace of God. Our spirits naturally bow down to this earth and the things of it; if they move upward in any good affections or good actions, it is God who raises them. The calls and offers of the gospel are like the proclamation of Cyrus. Those bound under the power of sin, may be made free by Jesus Christ. Whosoever will, by repentance and faith, return to God, Jesus Christ has opened the way for him, and raises him out of the slavery of sin into the glorious liberty of the children of God. Many that hear this joyful sound, choose to sit still in Babylon, are in love with their sins, and will not venture upon a holy life; but some break through all discouragements, whatever it cost them; they are those whose spirit God has raised above the world and the flesh, whom he has made willing. Thus will the heavenly Canaan be filled, though many perish in Babylon; and the gospel offer will not have been made in vain. The bringing back the Jews from captivity, represents the redemption of sinners by Jesus Christ.

Chapter 2

Chapter Outline

Verses 1-35

An account was kept of the families that came up out of captivity. See how sin lowers a nation, which righteousness would exalt!

Verses 36-63

Those who undervalue their relation to the Lord in times of reproach, persecution, or distress, will have no benefit from it when it becomes honourable or profitable. Those who have no evidence that they are, by the new birth, spiritual priests unto God, through Jesus Christ, have no right to the comforts and privileges of Christians.

Verses 64-70

Let none complain of the needful expenses of their religion. Seek first the kingdom of God, his favour and his glory, then will all other things be added unto them. Their offerings were nothing, compared with the offerings of the princes in David's time; yet, being according to their ability, were as acceptable to God. The Lord will carry us through all undertakings entered on according to his will, with an aim to his glory, and dependence on his assistance. Those who, at the call of the gospel, renounce sin and return to the Lord, shall be guarded and guided through all perils of the way, and arrive safely at the mansions provided in the holy city of God.

Chapter 3

Chapter Outline

Verses 1-7

From the proceedings of the Jews on their arrival, let us learn to begin with God, and to do what we can in the worship of God, when we cannot do what we would. They could not at once have a temple, but they would not be without an altar. Fear of danger should stir us to our duty. Have we many enemies? Then it is good to have God our Friend, and to keep up communion with him. Our fears should drive us to our knees. The sacrifices for all these solemnities were a heavy expense for so poor a company; yet besides those expressly appointed, many brought free-will offerings to the Lord. And they made preparation for the building of the temple without delay: whatever God calls us to do, we may depend upon his providence to furnish us with the needful means.

Verses 8-13

There was a remarkable mixture of affections upon laying the foundation of the temple. Those that only knew the misery of having no temple at all, praised the Lord with shouts of joy. To them, even this foundation seemed great. We ought to be thankful for the beginnings of mercy, though it be not yet perfect. But those who remembered the glory of the first temple, and considered how far inferior this was likely to be, wept with a loud voice. There was reason for it, and if they bewailed the sin that was the cause of this melancholy change, they did well. Yet it was wrong to cast a damp upon the common joys. They despised the day of small things, and were unthankful for the good they enjoyed. Let not the remembrance of former afflictions drown the sense of present mercies.

Chapter 4

Chapter Outline

Verses 1-5

Every attempt to revive true religion will stir up the opposition of Satan, and of those in whom he works. The adversaries were the Samaritans, who had been planted in the land of Israel, 2Ki 17. It was plain that they did not mean to unite in the worship of the Lord, according to his word. Let those who discourage a good work, and weaken them that are employed in it, see whose pattern they follow. (Ezr 4:6-24)

Verses 6-24

It is an old slander, that the prosperity of the church would be hurtful to kings and princes. Nothing can be more false, for true godliness teaches us to honour and obey our sovereign. But where the command of God requires one thing and the law of the land another, we must obey God rather than man, and patiently submit to the consequences. All who love the gospel should avoid all appearance of evil, lest they should encourage the adversaries of the church. The world is ever ready to believe any accusation against the people of God, and refuses to listen to them. The king suffered himself to be imposed upon by these frauds and falsehoods. Princes see and hear with other men's eyes and ears, and judge things as represented to them, which are often done falsely. But God's judgment is just; he sees things as they are.

Chapter 5

Chapter Outline

The leaders forward the building of the temple. (1, 2)

letter against the Jews. (3–17)

Verses 1, 2

The building of the temple was stopped about fifteen years. Then they had two good ministers, who urged them to go on with the work. It is a sign that God has mercy in store for a people, when he raises up prophets to be helpers in the way and work of God, as guides, overseers, and rulers. In Haggai, we see what great things God does by his word, which he magnifies above all his name, and by his Spirit working with it.

Verses 3-17

While employed in God's work, we are under his special protection; his eye is upon us for good. This should keep us to our duty, and encourage us therein, when difficulties are ever so discouraging. The elders of the Jews gave the Samaritans an account of their proceedings. Let us learn hence, with meekness and fear, to give a reason of the hope that is in us; let us rightly understand, and then readily declare, what we do in God's service, and why we do it. And while in this world, we always shall have to confess, that our sins have provoked the wrath of God. All our sufferings spring from thence, and all our comforts from his unmerited mercy. However the work may seem to be hindered, yet the Lord Jesus Christ is carrying it on, his people are growing unto a holy temple in the Lord, for a habitation of God through the Spirit.

Chapter 6

Chapter Outline

The decree for completing the temple. (1–12)

The temple is finished. (13–22)

Verses 1-12

When God's time is come for fulfilling his gracious purposes concerning his church, he will raise up instruments to do it, from whom such good service was not expected. While our thoughts are directed to this event, we are led by Zechariah to fix our regard on a nobler, a spiritual building. The Lord Jesus Christ continues to lay one stone upon another: let us assist the great design. Difficulties delay the progress of this sacred edifice. Yet let not opposition discourage us, for in due season it will be completed to his abundant praise. He shall bring forth the head-stone thereof with shoutings, crying, Grace, grace unto it.

Verses 13-22

The gospel church, that spiritual temple, is long in the building, but it will be finished at last, when the mystical body is completed. Every believer is a living temple, building up himself in his most holy faith: much opposition is given to this work by Satan and our own corruptions. We trifle, and proceed in it with many stops and pauses; but He that has begun the good work, will see it performed. Then spirits of just men will be made perfect. By getting their sins taken away, the Jews would free themselves from the sting of their late troubles. Their service was with joy. Let us welcome holy ordinances with joy, and serve the Lord with gladness.

Chapter 7

Chapter Outline

Ezra goes up to Jerusalem.	(1–10)
The commission to Ezra.	(11–26)
Ezra blesses God for his favour.	(27, 28)

Verses 1-10

Ezra went from Babylon to Jerusalem, for the good of his country. The king was kind to him; he granted all his requests, whatever Ezra desired to enable him to serve his country. When he went, many went with him; he obtained favour from his king, by the Divine favour. Every creature is that to us, which God makes it to be. We must see the hand of God in the events that befal us, and acknowledge him with thankfulness.

Verses 11-26

The liberality of heathen kings to support the worship of God, reproached the conduct of many kings of Judah, and will rise up in judgment against the covetousness of wealthy professed Christians, who will not promote the cause of God. But the weapons of Christian ministers are not carnal. Faithful preaching, holy lives, fervent prayers, and patient suffering when called to it, are the means to bring men into obedience to Christ.

Verses 27, 28

Two things Ezra blessed God for: 1. For his commission. If any good appear in our hearts, or in the hearts of others, we must own that God put it there, and bless him; it is he that worketh in us, both to will and to do that which is good. 2. For his encouragement: God has extended mercy to me. Ezra was a man of courage, yet he ascribed this not to his own heart, but to God's hand. If God give us his hand, we are bold and cheerful; if he withdraw it, we are weak as water. Whatever we are enabled to do for God and those around us, God must have all the glory.

Chapter 8

Chapter Outline

Verses 1-20

Ezra assembles the outcasts of Israel, and the dispersed of Judah. God raised up the spirits of a small remnant to accompany him. What a pity that good men should omit a good work, for want of being spoken to!

Verses 21-23

Ezra procured Levites to go with him; but what will that avail, unless he have God with him? Those who seek God, are safe under the shadow of his wings, even in their greatest dangers; but those who forsake him, are always exposed. When entering upon any new state of life, our care should be, to bring none of the guilt of the sins of our former condition into it. When we are in any peril, let us be at peace with God, and then nothing can do us any real hurt. All our concerns about ourselves, our families, and our estates, it is our wisdom and duty, by prayer to commit to God, and to leave the care of them with him. And, on some occasions, we should decline advantages which are within our reach, lest we should cause others to stumble, and so our God be dishonoured. Let us ask wisdom of God, that we may know how to use or to refuse lawful things. We shall be no losers by venturing, suffering, or giving up for the Lord's sake. Their prayers were answered, and the event declared it. Never have any that sought God in earnest, found that they sought him in vain. In times of difficulty and danger, to set a season apart for secret or for social prayer, is the best method for relief we can take.

Verses 24-30

Do we expect that God should, by his providence, keep that which belongs to us, let us, by his grace, keep that which belongs to him. Let God's honour and interest be our care; and then we may expect that our lives and comforts will be his.

Verses 31-36

Enemies laid wait for the Jews, but God protected them. Even the common perils of journeys, call us to go out with prayer, and to return with praise and thanksgiving. But what shall we render when the Lord has led us safely through the pilgrimage of life, through the gloomy vale of death, out of the reach of all our enemies, into everlasting happiness! Among their sacrifices they had a sin-offering. The atonement sweetens and secures every mercy to us, which will not be truly comfortable, unless sin be taken away, and our peace made with God. Then had the church rest. The expressions here used, direct us to the deliverance of sinners from spiritual bondage, and their pilgrimage to the heavenly Jerusalem, under the care and protection of their God and Saviour.

Chapter 9

Chapter Outline

Ezra mourns for the Jews' conduct.   (1–4)

Ezra's confession of sins.   (5–15)

Verses 1-4

Many corruptions lurk out of the view of the most careful rulers. Some of the people disobeyed the express command of God, which forbade all marriages with the heathen, De 7. Disbelief of God's all-sufficiency, is at the bottom of the sorry shifts we make to help ourselves. They exposed themselves and their children to the peril of idolatry, that had ruined their church and nation. Carnal professors may make light of such connexions, and try to explain away the exhortations to be separate; but those who are best acquainted with the word of God, will treat the subject in another manner. They must forebode the worst from such unions. The evils excused, and even pleaded for; by many professors, astonish and cause regret in the true believer. All who profess to be God's people, ought to strengthen those that appear and act against vice and profaneness.

Verses 5-15

The sacrifice, especially the evening sacrifice, was a type of the blessed Lamb of God, who in the evening of the world, was to take away sin by the sacrifice of himself. Ezra's address is a penitent confession of sin, the sin of his people. But let this be the comfort of true penitents, that though their sins reach to the heavens, God's mercy is in the heavens. Ezra, speaking of sin, speaks as one much ashamed. Holy shame is as necessary in true repentance as holy sorrow. Ezra speaks as much amazed. The discoveries of guilt cause amazement; the more we think of sin, the worse it looks. Say, God be merciful to me sinner. Ezra speaks as one much afraid. There is not a surer or saddler presage of ruin, than turning to sin, after great judgments, and great deliverances. Every one in the church of God, has to wonder that he has not wearied out the Lord's patience, and brought destruction upon himself. What then must be the case of the ungodly? But though the true penitent has nothing to plead in his own behalf, the heavenly Advocate pleads most powerfully for him.

Chapter 10

Chapter Outline

Verses 1-5

Shechaniah owned the national guilt. The case is sad, but it is not desperate; the disease threatening, but not incurable. Now that the people begin to lament, a spirit of repentance seems to be poured out; now there is hope that God will forgive, and have mercy. The sin that rightly troubles us, shall not ruin us. In melancholy times we must observe what makes for us, as well as against us. And there may be good hopes through grace, even where there is the sense of great guilt before God. The case is plain; what has been done amiss, must be undone again as far as possible; nothing less than this is true repentance. Sin must be put away, with a resolution never to have any thing more to do with it. What has been unjustly got, must be restored. Arise, be of good courage. Weeping, in this case, is good, but reforming is better. As to being unequally yoked with unbelievers, such marriages, it is certain, are sinful, and ought not to be made; but now they are not null, as they were before the gospel did away the separation between Jews and Gentiles.

Verses 6-14

There is hope concerning people, when they are convinced, not only that it is good to part with their sins, but that it is necessary; we must do it, or we are undone. So rich is the mercy, and so plenteous the redemption of God, that there is hope for the vilest who hear the gospel, and are willing to accept of free salvation. When sinners mourn for their sins, and tremble at the word of God, there is hope that they will forsake them. To affect others with godly sorrow or love to God, we must ourselves be affected. It was carefully agreed how this affair should be carried on. That which is hastily resolved on seldom proves lasting.

Verses 15-44

The best reformers can but do their endeavour; when the Redeemer himself shall come to Zion, he shall effectually turn away ungodliness from Jacob. And when sin is repented of and forsaken, God will forgive it; but the blood of Christ, our Sin-offering, is the only atonement which takes away our guilt. No seeming repentance or amendment will benefit those who reject Him, for self-dependence proves them still unhumbled. All the names written in the book of life, are those of penitent sinners, not of self-righteous persons, who think they have no need of repentance.

Nehemiah

The Old Testament history closes with the book of Nehemiah, wherein is recorded the workings of his heart, in the management of public affairs; with many devout reflections.

Chapter 1

Nehemiah's distress for the misery of Jerusalem, His prayer.

—Nehemiah was the Persian king's cup-bearer. When God has work to do, he will never want instruments to do it with. Nehemiah lived at ease, and in honour, but does not forget that he is an Israelite, and that his brethren are in distress. He was ready to do them all the good offices he could; and that he might know how best to do them a kindness, he makes inquiries about them. We should inquire especially concerning the state of the church and religion. Every Jerusalem on this side the heavenly one will have some defect, which will require the help and services of its friends. Nehemiah's first application was to God, that he might have the fuller confidence in his application to the king. Our best pleas in prayer are taken from the promise of God, the word on which he has caused us to hope. Other means must be used, but the effectual fervent prayer of a righteous man avails most. Communion with God will best prepare us for our dealings with men. When we have intrusted our concerns to God, the mind is set at liberty; it feels satisfaction and composure, and difficulties vanish. We know that if the affair be hurtful, he can easily hinder it; and if it be good for us, he can as easily forward it.

Chapter 2

Chapter Outline

Nehemiah's request to the king.	(1–8)
Nehemiah comes to Jerusalem.	(9–18)
The opposition of the adversaries.	(19, 20)

Verses 1-8

Our prayers must be seconded with serious endeavours, else we mock God. We are not limited to certain moments in our addresses to the King of kings, but have liberty to go to him at all times; approaches to the throne of grace are never out of season. But the sense of God's displeasure and the afflictions of his people, are causes of sorrow to the children of God, under which no earthly delights can comfort. The king encouraged Nehemiah to tell his mind. This gave him boldness to speak; much more may the invitation Christ has given us to pray, and the promise that we shall speed, encourage us to come boldly to the throne of grace. Nehemiah prayed to the God of heaven, as infinitely above even this mighty monarch. He lifted up his heart to that God who understands the language of the heart. Nor should we ever engage in any pursuit in which it would be wrong for us thus to seek and expect the Divine direction, assistance, and blessing. There was an immediate answer to his prayer; for the seed of Jacob never sought the God of Jacob in vain.

Verses 9-18

When Nehemiah had considered the matter, he told the Jews that God had put it into his heart to build the wall of Jerusalem. He does not undertake to do it without them. By stirring up ourselves and one another to that which is good, we strengthen ourselves and one another for it. We are weak in our duty, when we are cold and careless.

Verses 19, 20

The enmity of the serpent's seed against the cause of Christ is confined to no age or nation. The application to ourselves is plain. The church of God asks for our help. Is it not desolate, and exposed to assaults? Does the consideration of its low estate cause you any grief? Let not business, pleasure, or the support of a party so engage attention, as that Zion and her welfare shall be nothing to you.

Chapter 3

The rebuilding the walls of Jerusalem.

—The work was divided, so that every one might know what he had to do, and mind it, with a desire to excel; yet without contention, or separate interests. No strife appears among them, but which should do most for the public good. Every Israelite should lend a hand toward the building up of Jerusalem. Let not nobles think any thing below them, by which they may advance the good of their country. Even some females helped forward the work. Some repaired over against their houses, and one repaired over against his chamber. When a general good work is to be done, each should apply himself to that part which is within his reach. If every one will sweep before his own door, the street will be clean; if every one will mend one, we shall all be mended. Some that had first done helped their fellows. The walls of Jerusalem, in heaps of rubbish, represent the desperate state of the world around, while the number and malice of those who hindered the building, give some faint idea of the enemies we have to contend with, while executing the work of God. Every one must begin at home; for it is by getting the work of God advanced in our own souls that we shall best contribute to the good of the church of Christ. May the Lord thus stir up the hearts of his people, to lay aside their petty disputes, and to disregard their worldly interests, compared with building the walls of Jerusalem, and defending the cause of truth and godliness against the assaults of avowed enemies.

Chapter 4

Chapter Outline

Verses 1-6

Many a good work has been looked upon with contempt by proud and haughty scorners. Those who disagree in almost every thing, will unite in persecution. Nehemiah did not answer these fools according to their folly, but looked up to God by prayer. God's people have often been a despised people, but he hears all the slights that are put upon them, and it is their comfort that he does so. Nehemiah had reason to think that the hearts of those sinners were desperately hardened, else he would not have prayed that their sins might never be blotted out. Good work goes on well, when people have a mind to it. The reproaches of enemies should quicken us to our duty, not drive us from it.

Verses 7-15

The hindering good work is what bad men aim at, and promise themselves success in; but good work is God's work, and it shall prosper. God has many ways of bringing to light, and so of bringing to nought, the devices and designs of his church's enemies. If our enemies cannot frighten us from duty, or deceive us into sin, they cannot hurt us. Nehemiah put himself and his cause under the Divine protection. It was the way of this good man, and should be our way. All his cares, all his griefs, all his fears, he spread before God. Before he used any means, he made his prayer to God. Having prayed, he set a watch against the enemy. If we think to secure ourselves by prayer, without watchfulness, we are slothful, and tempt God; if by watchfulness, without prayer, we are proud, and slight God: either way, we forfeit his protection. God's care of our safety, should engage and encourage us to go on with vigour in our duty. As soon as a danger is over, let us return to our work, and trust God another time.

Verses 16-23

We must watch always against spiritual enemies, and not expect that our warfare will be over till our work is ended. The word of God is the sword of the Spirit, which we ought to have always at hand, and never to have to seek for it, either in our labours, or in our conflicts, as Christians. Every true Christian is both a labourer and a soldier, working with one hand, and fighting with the other. Good work is likely to go on with success, when those who labour in it, make a business of it. And Satan fears to assault the watchful Christian; or, if attacked, the Lord fights for him. Thus must we wait to the close of life, never putting off our armour till our work and warfare are ended; then we shall be welcomed to the rest and joy of our Lord.

Chapter 5

Chapter Outline

Verses 1-5

Men prey upon their fellow-creatures: by despising the poor they reproach their Maker. Such conduct is a disgrace to any, but who can sufficiently abhor it when adopted by professing Christians? With compassion for the oppressed, we should lament the hardships which many in the world are groaning under; putting our souls into their souls' stead, and remembering in our prayers and succours those who are burdened. But let those who show no mercy, expect judgment without mercy.

Verses 6-13

Nehemiah knew that, if he built Jerusalem's walls ever so high, so thick, or so strong, the city could not be safe while there were abuses. The right way to reform men's lives, is to convince their consciences. If you walk in the fear of God, you will not be either covetous of worldly gain, or cruel toward your brethren. Nothing exposes religion more to reproach, than the worldliness and hard-heartedness of the professors of it. Those that rigorously insist upon their right, with a very ill grace try to persuade others to give up theirs. In reasoning with selfish people, it is good to contrast their conduct with that of others who are liberal; but it is best to point to His example, who though he was rich, yet for our sakes became poor, that we, through his poverty, might be rich, 2Co 8:9. They did according to promise. Good promises are good things, but good performances are better.

Verses 14-19

Those who truly fear God, will not dare to do any thing cruel or unjust. Let all who are in public places remember that they are so placed to do good, not to enrich themselves. Nehemiah mentions it to God in prayer, not as if he had merited any favour from God, but to show that he depended upon God only, to make up to him what he had lost and laid out for his honour. Nehemiah evidently spake and acted as one that knew himself to be a sinner. He did not mean to claim a reward as of debt, but in the manner that the Lord rewards a cup of cold water given to a disciple for his sake. The fear and love of God in the heart, and true love of the brethren, will lead to every good work. These are proper evidences of justifying faith; and our reconciled God will look upon persons of this character for good, according to all they have done for his people.

Chapter 6

Chapter Outline

Verses 1-9

Let those who are tempted to idle merry meetings by vain companions, thus answer the temptation, We have work to do, and must not neglect it. We must never suffer ourselves to be overcome, by repeated urgency, to do anything sinful or imprudent; but when attacked with the same temptation, must resist it with the same reason and resolution. It is common for that which is desired only by the malicious, to be falsely represented by them as desired by the many. But Nehemiah knew at what they aimed, he not only denied that such things were true, but that they were reported; he was better known than to be thus suspected. We must never omit any known duty for fear it should be misconstrued; but, while we keep a good conscience, let us trust God with our good name. God's people, though loaded with reproach, are not really fallen so low in reputation as some would have them thought to be. Nehemiah lifted up his heart to Heaven in a short prayer. When, in our Christian work and warfare, we enter upon any service or conflict, this is a good prayer, I have such a duty to do, such a temptation to grapple with; now, therefore, O God, strengthen my hands. Every temptation to draw us from duty, should quicken us the more to duty.

Verses 10-14

The greatest mischief our enemies can do us, is, to frighten us from our duty, and to lead us to do what is sinful. Let us never decline a good work, never do a bad one. We ought to try all advice, and to reject what is contrary to the word of God. Every man should study to be consistent. Should I, a professed Christian, called to be a saint, a child of God, a member of Christ, a temple of the Holy Ghost, should I be covetous, sensual, proud, or envious? Should I yield to impatience, discontent, or anger? Should I be slothful, unbelieving, or unmerciful? What effects will such conduct have upon others? All that God has done for us, or by us, or given to us, should lead us to watchfulness, self-denial, and diligence. Next to the sinfulness of sin, we should dread the scandal.

Verses 15-19

The wall was begun and finished in fifty-two days, though they rested on the sabbaths. A great deal of work may be done in a little time, if we set about it in earnest, and keep close to it. See the mischief of marrying with strangers. When men once became akin to Tobiah, they soon became sworn to him. A sinful love leads to a sinful league. The enemy of souls employs many instruments, and forms many projects, to bring reproach on the active servants of God, or to take them from their work. But we should follow the example of Him who laid down his life for the sheep. Those that simply cleave to the Lord and his work will be supported.

Chapter 7

Chapter Outline

Verses 1-4

Nehemiah, having finished the wall, returned to the Persian court, and came to Jerusalem again with a new commission. The public safety depends on every one's care to guard himself and his family against sin.

Verses 5-73

Nehemiah knew that the safety of a city, under God, depends more upon the inhabitants than upon its walls. Every good gift and every good work are from above. God gives knowledge, he gives grace; all is of him, and therefore all must be to him. What is done by human prudence, must be ascribed to the direction of Divine Providence. But woe to those who turn back from the Lord, loving this present world! and happy those who dedicate themselves, and their substance, to his service and glory!

Chapter 8

Chapter Outline

Verses 1-8

Sacrifices were to be offered only at the door of the temple; but praying and preaching were, and are, services of religion, as acceptably performed in one place as in another. Masters of families should bring their families with them to the public worship of God. Women and children have souls to save, and are therefore to acquaint themselves with the word of God, and to attend on the means of grace. Little ones, as they come to reason, must be trained up in religion. Ministers when they go to the pulpit, should take their Bibles with them; Ezra did so. Thence they must fetch their knowledge; according to that rule they must speak, and must show that they do so. Reading the Scriptures in religious assemblies is an ordinance of God, whereby he is honoured, and his church edified. Those who hear the word, should understand it, else it is to them but an empty sound of words. It is therefore required of teachers that they explain the word, and give the sense of it. Reading is good, and preaching is good, but expounding makes reading the better understood, and preaching the more convincing. It has pleased God in almost every age of the church to raise up, not only those who have preached the gospel, but also those who have given their views of Divine truth in writing; and though many who have attempted to explain Scripture, have darkened counsel by words without knowledge, yet the labours of others are of excellent use. All that we hear must, however, be brought to the test of Scripture. They heard readily, and minded every word. The word of God demands attention. If through carelessness we let much slip in hearing, there is danger that through forgetfulness we shall let all slip after hearing.

Verses 9-12

It was a good sign that their hearts were tender, when they heard the words of the law. The people were to send portions to those for whom nothing was prepared. It is the duty of a religious feast, as well as of a religious fast, to draw out the soul to the hungry; God's bounty should make us bountiful. We must not only give to those that offer themselves, but send to those out of sight. Their strength consisted in joy in the Lord. The better we understand God's word, the more comfort we find in it; the darkness of trouble arises from the darkness of ignorance.

Verses 13-18

They found written in the law about the feast of tabernacles. Those who diligently search the Scriptures, find things written there which they have forgotten. This feast of tabernacles was a representation of the believer's tabernacle state in this world, and a type of the holy joy of the gospel church. The conversion of the nations to the faith of Christ, is foretold under the figure of this feast, Zec 14:16. True religion will render us strangers and pilgrims upon earth. We read and hear the word acceptably and profitably, when we do according to what is written therein; when what appears to be our duty is revived, after it has been neglected. They minded the substance; else the ceremony had been of no use. They did it, rejoicing in God and his goodness. These are the means which the Spirit of God crowns with success, in bringing the hearts of sinners to tremble and to become humbled before God. But those are enemies to their own growth in holiness, who always indulge sorrow, even for sin, and put away from them the consolations tendered by the word and Spirit of God.

Chapter 9

Chapter Outline

A solemn fast.   (1–3)

Prayer and confession of sin.   (4–38)

Verses 1-3

The word will direct and quicken prayer, for by it the Spirit helps our infirmities in prayer. The careful study of God's word will more and more discover to us our own sinfulness, and the plenteousness of his salvation; thus it calls us to mourn for sin, and to rejoice in him. Every discovery of the truth of God, should render us more unwearied in attendance on his sacred word, and on his worship.

Verses 4-38

The summary of their prayers we have here upon record. Much more, no doubt, was said. Whatever ability we have to do any thing in the way of duty, we are to serve and glorify God according to the utmost of it. When confessing our sins, it is good to notice the mercies of God, that we may be the more humbled and ashamed. The dealings of the Lord showed his goodness and long-suffering, and the hardness of their hearts. The testimony of the prophets was the testimony of the Spirit in the prophets, and it was the Spirit of Christ in them. They spake as they were moved by the Holy Ghost, and what they said is to be received accordingly. The result was, wonder at the Lord's mercies, and the feeling that sin had brought them to their present state, from which nothing but unmerited love could rescue them. And is not their conduct a specimen of human nature? Let us study the history of our land, and our own history. Let us recollect our advantages from childhood, and ask what were our first returns? Let us frequently do so, that we may be kept humble, thankful, and watchful. Let all remember that pride and obstinacy are sins which ruin the soul. But it is often as hard to persuade the broken-hearted to hope, as formerly it was to bring them to fear. Is this thy case? Behold this sweet promise, A God ready to pardon! Instead of keeping away from God under a sense of unworthiness, let us come boldly to the throne of grace, that we may obtain mercy, and find grace to help in time of need. He is a God ready to pardon.

Chapter 10

Chapter Outline

The covenant, Those who signed it.   (1–31)

Their engagement to sacred rites.   (32–39)

Verses 1-31

Conversion is separating from the course and custom of this world, devoting ourselves to the conduct directed by the word of God. When we bind ourselves to do the commandments of God, it is to do all his commandments, and to look to him as the Lord, and our Lord.

Verses 32-39

Having covenanted against the sins of which they had been guilty, they obliged themselves to observe the duties they had neglected. We must not only cease to do evil, but learn to do well. Let not any people expect the blessing of God, unless they keep up public worship. It is likely to go well with our houses, when care is taken that the work of God's house goes on well. When every one helps, and every one gives, though but little, toward a good work, the whole will come to be a large sum. We must do what we can in works of piety and charity; and whatever state we are placed in, cheerfully perform our duty to God, which will be the surest way to ease and liberty. As the ordinances of God are the appointed means of support to our souls, the believer will not grudge the expense; yet most people leave their souls to starve.

Chapter 11

The distribution of the people.
—In all ages, men have preferred their own ease and advantage to the public good. Even the professors of religion too commonly seek their own, and not the things of Christ. Few have had such attachment to holy things and holy places, as to renounce pleasure for their sake. Yet surely, our souls should delight to dwell where holy persons and opportunities of spiritual improvement most abound. If we have not this love to the city of our God, and to every thing that assists our communion with the Saviour, how shall we be willing to depart hence; to be absent from the body, that we may be present with the Lord? To the carnal-minded, the perfect holiness of the New Jerusalem would be still harder to bear than the holiness of God's church on earth. Let us seek first the favour of God, and his glory; let us study to be patient, contented, and useful in our several stations, and wait, with cheerful hope, for admission into the holy city of God.

Chapter 12

Chapter Outline

Verses 1-26

It is a debt we owe to faithful ministers, to remember our guides, who have spoken to us the word of God. It is good to know what our godly predecessors were, that we may learn what we should be.

Verses 27-43

All our cities, all our houses, must have holiness to the Lord written upon them. The believer should undertake nothing which he does not dedicate to the Lord. We are concerned to cleanse our hands, and purify our hearts, when any work for God is to pass through them. Those that would be employed to sanctify others, must sanctify themselves, and set themselves apart for God. To those who are sanctified, all their creature-comforts and enjoyments are made holy. The people greatly rejoiced. All that share in public mercies, ought to join in public thanksgivings.

Verses 44-47

When the solemnities of a thanksgiving day leave such impressions on ministers and people, that both are more careful and cheerful in doing their duty, they are indeed acceptable to the Lord, and turn to good account. And whatever we do, must be purified by the blood of sprinkling, and by the grace of the Holy Spirit, or it cannot be acceptable to God.

Chapter 13

Chapter Outline

Nehemiah turns out the mixed multitude.	(1–9)
Nehemiah's reform in the house of God.	(10–14)
Sabbath-breaking restrained.	(15–22)
The dismissal of strange wives.	(23–31)

Verses 1-9

Israel was a peculiar people, and not to mingle with the nations. See the benefit of publicly reading the word of God; when it is duly attended to, it discovers to us sin and duty, good and evil, and shows wherein we have erred. We profit, when we are thus wrought upon to separate from evil. Those that would drive sin out of their hearts, the living temples, must throw out its household stuff, and all the provision made for it; and take away all the things that are the food and fuel of lust; this is really to mortify it. When sin is cast out of the heart by repentance, let the blood of

Christ be applied to it by faith, then let it be furnished with the graces of God's Spirit, for every good work.

Verses 10-14

If a sacred character will not keep men from setting an evil example, it must not shelter any one from deserved blame and punishment. The Levites had been wronged; their portions had not been given them. They were gone to get livelihoods for themselves and their families, for their profession would not maintain them. A maintenance not sufficient, makes a poor ministry. The work is neglected, because the workmen are. Nehemiah laid the fault upon the rulers. Both ministers and people, who forsake religion and the services of it, and magistrates, who do not what they can to keep them to it, will have much to answer for. He delayed not to bring the Levites to their places again, and that just payment should be made. Nehemiah on every occasion looked up to God, and committed himself and all his affairs to Him. It pleased him to think that he had been of use to revive and support religion in his country. He here refers to God, not in pride, but with a humble appeal concerning his honest intention in what he had done. He prays, "Remember me;" not, Reward me. "Wipe not out my good deeds;" not, Publish them, or record them. Yet he was rewarded, and his good deeds recorded. God does more than we are able to ask.

Verses 15-22

The keeping holy the Lord's day forms an important object for their attention who would promote true godliness. Religion never prospers while sabbaths are trodden under foot. No wonder there was a general decay of religion, and corruption of manners among the Jews, when they forsook the sanctuary and profaned the sabbath. Those little consider what an evil they do, who profane the sabbath. We must answer for the sins others are led to commit by our example. Nehemiah charges it on them as an evil thing, for so it is, proceeding from contempt of God and our own souls. He shows that sabbath-breaking was one of the sins for which God had brought judgments upon them; and if they did not take warning, but returned to the same sins again, they had to expect further judgments. The courage, zeal, and prudence of Nehemiah in this matter, are recorded for us to do likewise; and we have reason to think, that the cure he wrought was lasting. He felt and confessed himself a sinner, who could demand nothing from God as justice, when he thus cried unto him for mercy.

Verses 23-31

If either parent be ungodly, corrupt nature will incline the children to take after that one; which is a strong reason why Christians should not be unequally yoked. In the education of children, great care should be taken about the government of their tongues; that they learn not the language of Ashdod, no impious or impure talk, no corrupt communication. Nehemiah showed the evil of these marriages. Some, more obstinate than the rest, he smote, that is, ordered them to be beaten by the officers according to the law, De 25:2, 3. Here are Nehemiah's prayers on this occasion He prays, "Remember them, O my God." Lord, convince and convert them; put them in mind of what they should be and do. The best services to the public have been forgotten by those for whom they were done, therefore Nehemiah refers himself to God, to recompense him. This may well be the summary of our petitions; we need no more to make us happy than this; Remember me, O my God, for good. We may humbly hope that the Lord will remember us and our services, although, after lives of unwearied activity and usefulness, we shall still see cause to abhor ourselves and repent in dust and ashes, and to cry out with Nehemiah, Spare me, O my God, according to the greatness of they mercy.

Esther

We find in this book, that even those Jews who were scattered in the province of the heathen, were taken care of, and were wonderfully preserved, when threatened with destruction. Though the name of God be not in this book, the finger of God is shown by minute events for the bringing about his people's deliverance. This history comes in between Ezr 6; 7.

Chapter 1

Chapter Outline

The royal feast of Ahasuerus.   (1–9)

Vashti's refusal to appear, The king's decree.   (10–22)

Verses 1-9

The pride of Ahasuerus's heart rising with the grandeur of his kingdom, he made an extravagant feast. This was vain glory. Better is a dinner of herbs with quietness, than this banquet of wine, with all the noise and tumult that must have attended it. But except grace prevails in the heart, self-exaltation and self-indulgence, in one form or another, will be the ruling principle. Yet none did compel; so that if any drank to excess, it was their own fault. This caution of a heathen prince, even when he would show his generosity, may shame many called Christians, who, under pretence of sending the health round, send sin round, and death with it. There is a woe to them that do so; let them read it, and tremble, Hab 2:15, 16.

Verses 10-22

Ahasuerus's feast ended in heaviness, by his own folly. Seasons of peculiar festivity often end in vexation. Superiors should be careful not to command what may reasonably be disobeyed. But when wine is in, men's reason departs from them. He that had rule over 127 provinces, had no rule over his own spirit. But whether the passion or the policy of the king was served by this decree, God's providence made way for Esther to the crown, and defeated Haman's wicked project, even before it had entered into his heart, and he arrived at his power. Let us rejoice that the Lord reigns, and will overrule the madness or folly of mankind to promote his own glory, and the safety and happiness of his people.

Chapter 2

Chapter Outline

Esther chosen queen.   (1–20)

Mordecai discovers a plot against the king.   (21–23)

Verses 1-20

We see to what absurd practices those came, who were destitute of Divine revelation, and what need there was of the gospel of Christ, to purify men from the lusts of the flesh, and to bring them back to the original institution of marriage. Esther was preferred as queen. Those who suggest that Esther committed sin to come at this dignity, do not consider the custom of those times and countries. Every one that the king took was married to him, and was his wife, though of a lower rank. But how low is human nature sunk, when such as these are the leading pursuits and highest worldly happiness of men! Disappointment and vexation must follow; and he most wisely consults his enjoyment, even in this present life, who most exactly obeys the precepts of the Divine law. But let us turn to consider the wise and merciful providence of God, carrying on his deep but holy designs in the midst of all this. And let no change in our condition be a pretext for forgetting our duties to parents, or the friends who have stood in their place.

Verses 21-23

Good subjects must not conceal any bad design they know of against the prince, or the public peace. Mordecai was not rewarded at the time, but a remembrance was written. Thus, with respect to those who serve Christ, though their recompence is not till the resurrection of the just, yet an account is kept of their work of faith and labour of love, which God is not unrighteous to forget. The servant of God must be faithful to every trust, and watchful for those who employ him. If he appear to be neglected now, he will be remembered hereafter. None of our actions can be forgotten; even our most secret thoughts are written in lasting registers, Re 20:12.

Chapter 3

Chapter Outline

Haman seeks to destroy the Jews.   (1–6)

He obtains a decree against the Jews.   (7–15)

Verses 1-6

Mordecai refused to reverence Haman. The religion of a Jew forbade him to give honours to any mortal man which savoured of idolatry, especially to so wicked a man as Haman. By nature all are idolaters; self is our favourite idol, we are pleased to be treated as if every thing were at our disposal. Though religion by no means destroys good manners, but teaches us to render honour to whom honour is due, yet by a citizen of Zion, not only in his heart, but in his eyes, such a vile person as Haman was, is contemned, Ps 15:4. The true believer cannot obey edicts, or conform to fashions, which break the law of God. He must obey God rather than man, and leave the consequences to him. Haman was full of wrath. His device was inspired by that wicked spirit, who has been a murderer from the beginning; whose enmity to Christ and his church, governs all his children.

Verses 7-15

Without some acquaintance with the human heart, and the history of mankind, we should not think that any prince could consent to a dreadful proposal, so hurtful to himself. Let us be thankful for mild and just government. Haman inquires, according to his own superstitions, how to find a lucky day for the designed massacre! God's wisdom serves its own purposes by men's folly. Haman has appealed to the lot, and the lot, by delaying the execution, gives judgment against him. The event explains the doctrine of a particular providence over all the affairs of men, and the care of God over his church. Haman was afraid lest the king's conscience should smite him for what he had done; to prevent which, he kept him drinking. This cursed method many often take to drown convictions, and to harden their own hearts, and the hearts of others, in sin. All appeared in a favourable train to accomplish the project. But though sinners are permitted to proceed to the point they aim at, an unseen but almighty Power turns them back. How vain and contemptible are the strongest assaults against Jehovah! Had Haman obtained his wish, and the Jewish nation perished, what must have become of all the promises? How could the prophecies concerning the great Redeemer of the world have been fulfilled? Thus the everlasting covenant itself must have failed, before this diabolical project could take place.

Chapter 4

Chapter Outline

The Jews lament their danger.	(1–4)
Esther undertakes to plead for the Jews.	(5–17)

Verses 1-4

Mordecai avowed his relation to the Jews. Public calamities, that oppress the church of God, should affect our hearts more than any private affliction, and it is peculiarly distressing to occasion sufferings to others. God will keep those that are exposed to evil by the tenderness of their consciences.

Verses 5-17

We are prone to shrink from services that are attended with peril or loss. But when the cause of Christ and his people demand it, we must take up our cross, and follow him. When Christians are disposed to consult their own ease or safety, rather than the public good, they should be blamed. The law was express, all knew it. It is not thus in the court of the King of kings: to the footstool of his throne of grace we may always come boldly, and may be sure of an answer of peace to the prayer of faith. We are welcome, even into the holiest, through the blood of Jesus. Providence so ordered it, that, just then, the king's affections had cooled toward Esther; her faith and courage thereby were the more tried; and God's goodness in the favour she now found with the king, thereby shone the brighter. Haman no doubt did what he could to set the king against her. Mordecai suggests, that it was a cause which, one way or other, would certainly be carried, and which therefore she might safely venture in. This was the language of strong faith, which staggered not at the promise when the danger was most threatening, but against hope believed in hope. He that by sinful devices will save his life, and will not trust God with it in the way of duty, shall lose it in the way of sin. Divine Providence had regard to this matter, in bringing Esther to be queen. Therefore thou art bound in gratitude to do this service for God and his church, else thou dost not answer the end of thy being raised up. There is wise counsel and design in all the providences of God, which will prove that they are all intended for the good of the church. We should, every one, consider for what end God has put us in the place where we are, and study to answer that end: and take care that we do not let it slip. Having solemnly commended our souls and our cause to God, we may venture upon his service. All dangers are trifling compared with the danger of losing our souls. But the trembling sinner is often as much afraid of casting himself, without reserve, upon the Lord's free mercy, as Esther was of coming before the king. Let him venture, as she did, with earnest prayer and supplication, and he shall fare as well and better than she did. The cause of God must prevail: we are safe in being united to it.

Chapter 5

Chapter Outline

Esther's application received.   (1–8)

Haman prepares to hang Mordecai.   (9–14)

Verses 1-8

Esther having had power with God, and prevailing, like Jacob, had power with men too. He that will lose his life for God, shall save it, or find it in a better life. The king encouraged her. Let us from this be encouraged to pray always to our God, and not to faint. Esther came to a proud, imperious man; but we come to the God of love and grace. She was not called, but we are; the Spirit says, Come, and the Bride says, Come. She had a law against her, we have a promise, many a promise, in favour of us; Ask, and it shall be given you. She had no friend to go with her, or to plead for her; on the contrary, he that was then the king's favourite, was her enemy; but we have an Advocate with the Father, in whom he is well pleased. Let us therefore come boldly to the throne of grace. God put it into Esther's heart to delay her petition a day longer; she knew not, but God did, what was to happen in that very night.

Verses 9-14

This account of Haman is a comment upon Pr 21:24. Self-admirers and self-flatterers are really self-deceivers. Haman, the higher he is lifted up, the more impatient he is of contempt, and the more enraged at it. The affront from Mordecai spoiled all. A slight affront, which a humble man would scarcely notice, will torment a proud man, even to madness, and will mar all his comforts. Those disposed to be uneasy, will never want something to be uneasy at. Such are proud men; though they have much to their mind, if they have not all to their mind, it is as nothing to them. Many call the proud happy, who display pomp and make a show; but this is a mistaken thought. Many poor cottagers feel far less uneasiness than the rich, with all their fancied advantages around them. The man who knows not Christ, is poor though he be rich, because he is utterly destitute of that which alone is true riches.

Chapter 6

Chapter Outline

Providence recommends Mordecai to the king's favour.	(1–3)
Haman's counsel honours Mordecai.	(4–11)
Haman's friends tell him of his danger.	(12–14)

Verses 1-3

The providence of God rules over the smallest concerns of men. Not a sparrow falls to the ground without him. Trace the steps which Providence took towards the advancement of Mordecai. The king could not sleep when Providence had a design to serve, in keeping him awake. We read of no illness that broke his sleep, but God, whose gift sleep is, withheld it from him. He who commanded a hundred and twenty-seven provinces, could not command one hour's sleep.

Verses 4-11

See how men's pride deceives them. The deceitfulness of our own hearts appears in nothing more than in the conceit we have of ourselves and our own performances: against which we should constantly watch and pray. Haman thought the king loved and valued no one but himself, but he was deceived. We should suspect that the esteem which others profess for us, is not so great as it seems to be, that we may not think too well of ourselves, nor trust too much in others. How Haman is struck, when the king bids him do honour to Mordecai the Jew, the very man whom he hated above all men, whose ruin he was now designing!

Verses 12-14

Mordecai was not puffed up with his honours, he returned to his place and the duty of it. Honour is well bestowed on those that do not think themselves above their business. But Haman could not bear it. What harm had it done him? But that will break a proud man's heart, which will not break a humble man's sleep. His doom was, out of this event, read to him by his wife and his friends. They plainly confessed that the Jews, though scattered through the nations, were special objects of Divine care. Miserable comforters are they all; they did not advise Haman to repent, but foretold his fate as unavoidable. The wisdom of God is seen, in timing the means of his church's deliverance, so as to manifest his own glory.

Chapter 7

Chapter Outline

Esther accuses Haman.   (1–6)

Haman hanged on his own gallows.   (7–10)

Verses 1-6

If the love of life causes earnest pleadings with those that can only kill the body, how fervent should our prayers be to Him, who is able to destroy both body and soul in hell! How should we pray for the salvation of our relatives, friends, and all around us! When we petition great men, we must be cautious not to give them offence; even just complaints must often be kept back. But when we approach the King of kings with reverence, we cannot ask or expect too much. Though nothing but wrath be our due, God is able and willing to do exceeding abundantly, even beyond all we can ask or think.

Verses 7-10

The king was angry: those that do things with self-will, reflect upon them afterward with self-reproach. When angry, we should pause before we come to any resolution, and thus rule our own spirits, and show that we are governed by reason. Those that are most haughty and insolent when in power and prosperity, commonly, like Haman, are the most abject and poor-spirited when brought down. The day is coming when those that hate and persecute God's chosen ones, would gladly be beholden to them. The king returns yet more angry against Haman. Those about him were ready to put his wrath into execution. How little can proud men be sure of the interest they think they have! The enemies of God's church have often been thus taken in their own craftiness. The Lord is known by such judgments. Then was the king's wrath pacified, and not till then. And who pities Haman hanged on his own gallows? who does not rather rejoice in the Divine righteousness displayed in the destruction his own art brought upon him? Let the workers of iniquity tremble, turn to the Lord, and seek pardon through the blood of Jesus.

Chapter 8

Chapter Outline

Mordecai is advanced.	(1, 2)
Esther makes suit for the Jews.	(3–14)
Mordecai honoured, The joy of the Jews.	(15–17)

Verses 1, 2

What Haman would have done mischief with, Esther will do good with. All the trust the king had reposed in Haman, he now placed in Mordecai: a happy change. See the vanity of laying up treasure upon earth; he that heapeth up riches, knoweth not who shall gather them. With what little pleasure, nay, with what constant vexation, would Haman have looked upon his estate, if he could have foreseen that Mordecai, the man he hated above all men in the world, should have rule over all that wherein he had laboured! It is our interest to make sure of those riches which will not be left behind, but which will go with us to another world.

Verses 3-14

It was time to be earnest, when the church of God was at stake. Esther, though safe herself, fell down and begged for the deliverance of her people. We read of no tears when she begged for her own life, but although she was sure of that, she wept for her people. Tears of pity and tenderness are the most Christ-like. According to the constitution of the Persian government, no law or decree could be repealed or recalled. This is so far from speaking to the wisdom and honour of the Medes and Persians, that it clearly shows their pride and folly. This savours of that old presumption which ruined all, We will be as gods! It is God's prerogative not to repent, or to say what can never be altered or unsaid. Yet a way was found, by another decree, to authorize the Jews to stand upon their defence. The decree was published in the languages of all the provinces. Shall all the subjects of an earthly prince have his decrees in languages they understand, and shall God's oracles and laws be locked up from any of his servants in an unknown tongue?

Verses 15-17

Mordecai's robes now were rich. These things are not worth notice, but as marks of the king's favour, and the fruit of God's favour to his church. It is well with a land, when ensigns of dignity are made the ornaments of serious piety. When the church prospers, many will join it, who will be shy of it when in trouble. When believers have rest, and walk in the fear of the Lord, and the comfort of the Holy Ghost, they will be multiplied. And the attempts of Satan to destroy the church, always tend to increase the number of true Christians.

Chapter 9

Chapter Outline

Verses 1-19

The enemies of the Jews hoped to have power over them by the former edict. If they had attempted nothing against the people of God, they would not themselves have suffered. The Jews, acting together, strengthened one another. Let us learn to stand fast in one spirit, and with one mind, striving together against the enemies of our souls, who endeavour to rob us of our faith, which is more precious than our lives. The Jews, to the honour of their religion, showed contempt of wordly wealth, that they might make it appear they desired nothing except their own preservation. In every case the people of God should manifest humanity and disinterestedness, frequently refusing advantages which might lawfully be obtained. The Jews celebrated their festival the day after they had finished their work. When we have received great mercies from God, we ought to be speedy in making thankful returns to him.

Verses 20-32

The observance of the Jewish feasts, is a public declaration of the truth of the Old Testament Scriptures. And as the Old Testament Scriptures are true, the Messiah expected by the Jews is come long ago; and none but Jesus of Nazareth can be that Messiah. The festival was appointed by authority, yet under the direction of the Spirit of God. It was called the feast of Purim, from a Persian word, which signifies a lot. The name of this festival would remind them of the almighty power of the God of Israel, who served his own purposes by the superstitions of the heathen. In reviewing our mercies, we should advert to former fears and distresses. When our mercies are personal, we should not by forgetfulness lose the comfort of them, or withhold from the Lord the glory due to his name. May the Lord teach us to rejoice, with that holy joy which anticipates and prepares for the blessedness of heaven. Every instance of Divine goodness to ourselves, is a new obligation laid on us to do good, to those especially who most need our bounty. Above all, redemption by Christ binds us to be merciful, 2Co 8:9.

Chapter 10

Greatness of Ahasuerus—Mordecai's advancement.

—Many instances of the grandeur of Ahasuerus might have been given: these were written in the Persian chronicles, which are long since lost, while the sacred writings will live till time shall be no more. The concerns of the despised worshippers of the Lord are deemed more important by the Holy Spirit, than the exploits of the most illustrious monarch on earth. Mordecai was truly great, and his greatness gave him opportunities of doing the more good. He did not disown his people the Jews, and no doubt kept to the true religion. He did not seek his own wealth, but the welfare of his people. Few have it in their power to do so much good as Mordecai; but all have it in their power to do hurt, and who has it not in his power to do some good? We are not required to do what is not in our power, or is unsuited to our station; but all are bound to live under the influence of the tempers displayed in the saints, whose examples are recorded in the Bible. If we live by the faith of Christ, we shall be active according to the ability and opportunities he gives us, in promoting his glory and the best interests of men. If our faith be genuine, it will work by love. Wait in faith and prayer, and the event will be safe and glorious; our salvation is sure, through our Lord Jesus Christ.

Job

This book is so called from Job, whose prosperity, afflictions, and restoration, are here recorded. He lived soon after Abraham, or perhaps before that patriarch. Most likely it was written by Job himself, and it is the most ancient book in existence. The instructions to be learned from the patience of Job, and from his trials, are as useful now, and as much needed as ever. We live under the same Providence, we have the same chastening Father, and there is the same need for correction unto righteousness. The fortitude and patience of Job, though not small, gave way in his severe troubles; but his faith was fixed upon the coming of his Redeemer, and this gave him stedfastness and constancy, though every other dependence, particularly the pride and boast of a self-righteous spirit, was tried and consumed. Another great doctrine of the faith, particularly set forth in the book of Job, is that of Providence. It is plain, from this history, that the Lord watched over his servant Job with the affection of a wise and loving father.

Chapter 1

Chapter Outline

The piety and prosperity of Job.	(1–5)
Satan obtains leave to try Job.	(6–12)
The loss of Job's property, and the death of his children.	(13–19)
Job's patience and piety.	(20–22)

Verses 1-5

Job was prosperous, and yet pious. Though it is hard and rare, it is not impossible for a rich man to enter into the kingdom of heaven. By God's grace the temptations of worldly wealth may be overcome. The account of Job's piety and prosperity comes before the history of his great afflictions, showing that neither will secure from troubles. While Job beheld the harmony and comforts of his sons with satisfaction, his knowledge of the human heart made him fearful for them. He sent and sanctified them, reminding them to examine themselves, to confess their sins, to seek forgiveness; and as one who hoped for acceptance with God through the promised Saviour, he offered a burnt-offering for each. We perceive his care for their souls, his knowledge of the sinful state of man, his entire dependence on God's mercy in the way he had appointed.

Verses 6-12

Job's afflictions began from the malice of Satan, by the Lord's permission, for wise and holy purposes. There is an evil spirit, the enemy of God, and of all righteousness, who is continually seeking to distress, to lead astray, and, if possible, to destroy those who love God. How far his influence may extend, we cannot say; but probably much unsteadiness and unhappiness in Christians may be ascribed to him. While we are on this earth we are within his reach. Hence it concerns us to be sober and vigilant, 1Pe 5:8. See how Satan censures Job. This is the common way of slanderers, to suggest that which they have no reason to think is true. But as there is nothing we should dread more than really being hypocrites, so there is nothing we need dread less than being called and counted so without cause. It is not wrong to look at the eternal recompence in our obedience; but it is wrong to aim at worldly advantages in our religion. God's people are taken under his special protection; they, and all that belong to them. The blessing of the Lord makes rich; Satan himself owns it. God suffered Job to be tried, as he suffered Peter to be sifted. It is our comfort that God has the devil in a chain, Re 20:1. He has no power to lead men to sin, but what they give him themselves; nor any power to afflict men, but what is given him from above. All this is here described to us after the manner of men. The Scripture speaks thus to teach us that God directs the affairs of the world.

Verses 13-19

Satan brought Job's troubles upon him on the day that his children began their course of feasting. The troubles all came upon Job at once; while one messenger of evil tidings was speaking, another followed. His dearest and most valuable possessions were his ten children; news is brought him that they are killed. They were taken away when he had most need of them to comfort him under other losses. In God only have we a help present at all times. (Job 1:20-22)

Verses 20-22

Job humbled himself under the hand of God. He reasons from the common state of human life, which he describes. We brought nothing of this world's goods into the world, but have them from others; and it is certain we can carry nothing out, but must leave them to others. Job, under all his losses, is but reduced to his first state. He is but where he must have been at last, and is only unclothed, or unloaded rather, a little sooner than he expected. If we put off our clothes before we go to bed, it is some inconvenience, but it may be the better borne when it is near bed-time. The same who gave hath taken away. See how Job looks above instruments, and keeps his eye upon the First Cause. Afflictions must not divert us from, but quicken us to religion. If in all our troubles we look to the Lord, he will support us. The Lord is righteous. All we have is from his gift; we have forfeited it by sin, and ought not to complain if he takes any part from us. Discontent and impatience charge God with folly. Against these Job carefully watched; and so must we, acknowledging that as God has done right, but we have done wickedly, so God has done wisely, but we have done very foolishly. And may the malice and power of Satan render that Saviour more precious to our souls, who came to destroy the works of the devil; who, for our salvation, suffered from that enemy far more than Job suffered, or we can think.

Chapter 2

Chapter Outline

Verses 1-6

How well is it for us, that neither men nor devils are to be our judges! but all our judgment comes from the Lord, who never errs. Job holds fast his integrity still, as his weapon. God speaks with pleasure of the power of his own grace. Self-love and self-preservation are powerful in the hearts of men. But Satan accuses Job, representing him as wholly selfish, and minding nothing but his own ease and safety. Thus are the ways and people of God often falsely blamed by the devil and his agents. Permission is granted to Satan to make trial, but with a limit. If God did not chain up the roaring lion, how soon would he devour us! Job, thus slandered by Satan, was a type of Christ, the first prophecy of whom was, that Satan should bruise his heel, and be foiled.

Verses 7-10

The devil tempts his own children, and draws them to sin, and afterwards torments, when he has brought them to ruin; but this child of God he tormented with affliction, and then tempted to make a bad use of his affliction. He provoked Job to curse God. The disease was very grievous. If at any time we are tried with sore and grievous distempers, let us not think ourselves dealt with otherwise than as God sometimes deals with the best of his saints and servants. Job humbled himself under the mighty hand of God, and brought his mind to his condition. His wife was spared to him, to be a troubler and tempter to him. Satan still endeavours to draw men from God, as he did our first parents, by suggesting hard thoughts of Him, than which nothing is more false. But Job resisted and overcame the temptation. Shall we, guilty, polluted, worthless creatures, receive so many unmerited blessings from a just and holy God, and shall we refuse to accept the punishment of our sins, when we suffer so much less than we deserve? Let murmuring, as well as boasting, be for ever done away. Thus far Job stood the trial, and appeared brightest in the furnace of affliction. There might be risings of corruption in his heart, but grace had the upper hand.

Verses 11-13

The friends of Job seem noted for their rank, as well as for wisdom and piety. Much of the comfort of this life lies in friendship with the prudent and virtuous. Coming to mourn with him, they vented grief which they really felt. Coming to comfort him, they sat down with him. It would appear that they suspected his unexampled troubles were judgments for some crimes, which he had vailed under his professions of godliness. Many look upon it only as a compliment to visit their friends in sorrow; we must look life. And if the example of Job's friends is not enough to lead us to pity the afflicted, let us seek the mind that was in Christ.

Chapter 3

Chapter Outline

Verses 1-10

For seven days Job's friends sat by him in silence, without offering consolation: at the same time Satan assaulted his mind to shake his confidence, and to fill him with hard thoughts of God. The permission seems to have extended to this, as well as to torturing the body. Job was an especial type of Christ, whose inward sufferings, both in the garden and on the cross, were the most dreadful; and arose in a great degree from the assaults of Satan in that hour of darkness. These inward trials show the reason of the change that took place in Job's conduct, from entire submission to the will of God, to the impatience which appears here, and in other parts of the book. The believer, who knows that a few drops of this bitter cup are more dreadful than the sharpest outward afflictions, while he is favoured with a sweet sense of the love and presence of God, will not be surprised to find that Job proved a man of like passions with others; but will rejoice that Satan was disappointed, and could not prove him a hypocrite; for though he cursed the day of his birth, he did not curse his God. Job doubtless was afterwards ashamed of these wishes, and we may suppose what must be his judgment of them now he is in everlasting happiness.

Verses 11-19

Job complained of those present at his birth, for their tender attention to him. No creature comes into the world so helpless as man. God's power and providence upheld our frail lives, and his pity and patience spared our forfeited lives. Natural affection is put into parents' hearts by God. To desire to die that we may be with Christ, that we may be free from sin, is the effect and evidence of grace; but to desire to die, only that we may be delivered from the troubles of this life, savours of corruption. It is our wisdom and duty to make the best of that which is, be it living or dying; and so to live to the Lord, and die to the Lord, as in both to be his, Ro 14:8. Observe how Job describes the repose of the grave; There the wicked cease from troubling. When persecutors die, they can no longer persecute. There the weary are at rest: in the grave they rest from all their labours. And a rest from sin, temptation, conflict, sorrows, and labours, remains in the presence and enjoyment of God. There believers rest in Jesus, nay, as far as we trust in the Lord Jesus and obey him, we here find rest to our souls, though in the world we have tribulation.

Verses 20-26

Job was like a man who had lost his way, and had no prospect of escape, or hope of better times. But surely he was in an ill frame for death when so unwilling to live. Let it be our constant care to get ready for another world, and then leave it to God to order our removal thither as he thinks fit. Grace teaches us in the midst of life's greatest comforts, to be willing to die, and in the midst of its greatest crosses, to be willing to live. Job's way was hid; he knew not wherefore God contended with him. The afflicted and tempted Christian knows something of this heaviness; when he has been looking too much at the things that are seen, some chastisement of his heavenly Father will give him a taste of this disgust of life, and a glance at these dark regions of despair. Nor is there any help until God shall restore to him the joys of his salvation. Blessed be God, the earth is full of his goodness, though full of man's wickedness. This life may be made tolerable if we attend to our duty. We look for eternal mercy, if willing to receive Christ as our Saviour.

Chapter 4

Chapter Outline

Verses 1-6

Satan undertook to prove Job a hypocrite by afflicting him; and his friends concluded him to be one because he was so afflicted, and showed impatience. This we must keep in mind if we would understand what passed. Eliphaz speaks of Job, and his afflicted condition, with tenderness; but charges him with weakness and faint-heartedness. Men make few allowances for those who have taught others. Even pious friends will count that only a touch which we feel as a wound. Learn from hence to draw off the mind of a sufferer from brooding over the affliction, to look at the God of mercies in the affliction. And how can this be done so well as by looking to Christ Jesus, in whose unequalled sorrows every child of God soonest learns to forget his own?

Verses 7-11

Eliphaz argues, 1. That good men were never thus ruined. But there is one event both to the righteous and to the wicked, Ec 9:2, both in life and death; the great and certain difference is after death. Our worst mistakes are occasioned by drawing wrong views from undeniable truths. 2. That wicked men were often thus ruined: for the proof of this, Eliphaz vouches his own observation. We may see the same every day.

Verses 12-21

Eliphaz relates a vision. When we are communing with our own hearts, and are still, Ps 4:4, then is a time for the Holy Spirit to commune with us. This vision put him into very great fear. Ever since man sinned, it has been terrible to him to receive communications from Heaven, conscious that he can expect no good tidings thence. Sinful man! shall he pretend to be more just, more pure, than God, who being his Maker, is his Lord and Owner? How dreadful, then, the pride and presumption of man! How great the patience of God! Look upon man in his life. The very foundation of that cottage of clay in which man dwells, is in the dust, and it will sink with its own weight. We stand but upon the dust. Some have a higher heap of dust to stand upon than others but still it is the earth that stays us up, and will shortly swallow us up. Man is soon crushed; or if some lingering distemper, which consumes like a moth, be sent to destroy him, he cannot resist it. Shall such a creature pretend to blame the appointments of God? Look upon man in his death. Life is short, and in a little time men are cut off. Beauty, strength, learning, not only cannot secure them from death, but these things die with them; nor shall their pomp, their wealth, or power, continue after them. Shall a weak, sinful, dying creature, pretend to be more just than God, and more pure than his Maker? No: instead of quarrelling with his afflictions, let him wonder that he is out of hell. Can a man be cleansed without his Maker? Will God justify sinful mortals, and clear them from guilt? or will he do so without their having an interest in the righteousness and gracious help of their promised Redeemer, when angels, once ministering spirits before his throne, receive the just recompence of their sins? Notwithstanding the seeming impunity of men for a short time, though living without God in the world, their doom is as certain as that of the fallen angels, and is continually overtaking them. Yet careless sinners note it so little, that they expect not the change, nor are wise to consider their latter end.

Chapter 5

Chapter Outline

Eliphaz urges that the sin of sinners in their ruin.	(1–5)
God is to be regarded in affliction.	(6–16)
The happy end of God's correction.	(17–27)

Verses 1-5

Eliphaz here calls upon Job to answer his arguments. Were any of the saints or servants of God visited with such Divine judgments as Job, or did they ever behave like him under their sufferings? The term, "saints," holy, or more strictly, consecrated ones, seems in all ages to have been applied to the people of God, through the Sacrifice slain in the covenant of their reconciliation. Eliphaz doubts not that the sin of sinners directly tends to their ruin. They kill themselves by some lust or other; therefore, no doubt, Job has done some foolish thing, by which he has brought himself into this condition. The allusion was plain to Job's former prosperity; but there was no evidence of Job's wickedness, and the application to him was unfair and severe.

Verses 6-16

Eliphaz reminds Job, that no affliction comes by chance, nor is to be placed to second causes. The difference between prosperity and adversity is not so exactly observed, as that between day and night, summer and winter; but it is according to the will and counsel of God. We must not attribute our afflictions to fortune, for they are from God; nor our sins to fate, for they are from ourselves. Man is born in sin, and therefore born to trouble. There is nothing in this world we are born to, and can truly call our own, but sin and trouble. Actual transgressions are sparks that fly out of the furnace of original corruption. Such is the frailty of our bodies, and the vanity of all our enjoyments, that our troubles arise thence as the sparks fly upward; so many are they, and so fast does one follow another. Eliphaz reproves Job for not seeking God, instead of quarrelling with him. Is any afflicted? let him pray. It is heart's ease, a salve for every sore. Eliphaz speaks of rain, which we are apt to look upon as a little thing; but if we consider how it is produced, and what is produced by it, we shall see it to be a great work of power and goodness. Too often the great Author of all our comforts, and the manner in which they are conveyed to us, are not noticed, because they are received as things of course. In the ways of Providence, the experiences of some are encouragements to others, to hope the best in the worst of times; for it is the glory of God to send help to the helpless, and hope to the hopeless. And daring sinners are confounded, and forced to acknowledge the justice of God's proceedings.

Verses 17-27

Eliphaz gives to Job a word of caution and exhortation: Despise not thou the chastening of the Almighty. Call it a chastening, which comes from the Father's love, and is for the child's good; and notice it as a messenger from Heaven. Eliphaz also encourages Job to submit to his condition. A good man is happy though he be afflicted, for he has not lost his enjoyment of God, nor his title to heaven; nay, he is happy because he is afflicted. Correction mortifies his corruptions, weans his heart from the world, draws him nearer to God, brings him to his Bible, brings him to his knees. Though God wounds, yet he supports his people under afflictions, and in due time delivers them. Making a wound is sometimes part of a cure. Eliphaz gives Job precious promises of what God would do for him, if he humbled himself. Whatever troubles good men may be in, they shall do them no real harm. Being kept from sin, they are kept from the evil of trouble. And if the servants of Christ are not delivered from outward troubles, they are delivered by them, and while overcome by one trouble, they conquer all. Whatever is maliciously said against them shall not hurt them. They shall have wisdom and grace to manage their concerns. The greatest blessing, both in our employments and in our enjoyments, is to be kept from sin. They shall finish their course with joy and honour. That man lives long enough who has done his work, and is fit for another world. It is a mercy to die seasonably, as the corn is cut and housed when fully ripe; not till then, but then not suffered to stand any longer. Our times are in God's hands; it is well they are so. Believers are not to expect great wealth, long life, or to be free from trials. But all will be ordered for the best. And remark from Job's history, that steadiness of mind and heart under trial, is one of the highest attainments of faith. There is little exercise for faith when all things go well. But if God raises a storm, permits the enemy to send wave after wave, and seemingly stands aloof from our prayers, then, still to hang on and trust God, when we cannot trace him, this is the patience of the saints. Blessed Saviour! how sweet it is to look unto thee, the Author and Finisher of faith, in such moments!

Chapter 6

Chapter Outline

Verses 1-7

Job still justifies himself in his complaints. In addition to outward troubles, the inward sense of God's wrath took away all his courage and resolution. The feeling sense of the wrath of God is harder to bear than any outward afflictions. What then did the Saviour endure in the garden and on the cross, when he bare our sins, and his soul was made a sacrifice to Divine justice for us! Whatever burden of affliction, in body or estate, God is pleased to lay upon us, we may well submit to it as long as he continues to us the use of our reason, and the peace of our conscience; but if either of these is disturbed, our case is very pitiable. Job reflects upon his friends for their censures. He complains he had nothing offered for his relief, but what was in itself tasteless, loathsome, and burdensome.

Verses 8-13

Job had desired death as the happy end of his miseries. For this, Eliphaz had reproved him, but he asks for it again with more vehemence than before. It was very rash to speak thus of God destroying him. Who, for one hour, could endure the wrath of the Almighty, if he let loose his hand against him? Let us rather say with David, O spare me a little. Job grounds his comfort upon the testimony of his conscience, that he had been, in some degree, serviceable to the glory of God. Those who have grace in them, who have the evidence of it, and have it in exercise, have wisdom in them, which will be their help in the worst of times.

Verses 14-30

In his prosperity Job formed great expectations from his friends, but now was disappointed. This he compares to the failing of brooks in summer. Those who rest their expectations on the creature, will find it fail when it should help them; whereas those who make God their confidence, have help in the time of need, Heb 4:16. Those who make gold their hope, sooner or later will be ashamed of it, and of their confidence in it. It is our wisdom to cease from man. Let us put all our confidence in the Rock of ages, not in broken reeds; in the Fountain of life, not in broken cisterns. The application is very close; "for now ye are nothing." It were well for us, if we had always such convictions of the vanity of the creature, as we have had, or shall have, on a sick-bed, a death-bed, or in trouble of conscience. Job upbraids his friends with their hard usage. Though in want, he desired no more from them than a good look and a good word. It often happens that, even when we expect little from man, we have less; but from God, even when we expect much, we have more. Though Job differed from them, yet he was ready to yield as soon as it was made to appear that he was in error. Though Job had been in fault, yet they ought not to have given him such hard usage. His righteousness he holds fast, and will not let it go. He felt that there had not been such iniquity in him as they supposed. But it is best to commit our characters to Him who keeps our souls; in the great day every upright believer shall have praise of God.

Chapter 7

Chapter Outline

Verses 1-6

Job here excuses what he could not justify, his desire of death. Observe man's present place: he is upon earth. He is yet on earth, not in hell. Is there not a time appointed for his abode here? yes, certainly, and the appointment is made by Him who made us and sent us here. During that, man's life is a warfare, and as day-labourers, who have the work of the day to do in its day, and must make up their account at night. Job had as much reason, he thought, to wish for death, as a poor servant that is tired with his work, has to wish for the shadows of the evening, when he shall go to rest. The sleep of the labouring man is sweet; nor can any rich man take so much satisfaction in his wealth, as the hireling in his day's wages. The comparison is plain; hear his complaint: His days were useless, and had long been so; but when we are not able to work for God, if we sit still quietly for him, we shall be accepted. His nights were restless. Whatever is grievous, it is good to see it appointed for us, and as designed for some holy end. When we have comfortable nights, we must see them also appointed to us, and be thankful for them. His body was noisome. See what vile bodies we have. His life was hastening apace. While we are living, every day, like the shuttle, leaves a thread behind: many weave the spider's web, which will fail, ch. 8:14. But if, while we live, we live unto the Lord, in works of faith and labours of love, we shall have the benefit, for every man shall reap as he sowed, and wear as he wove.

Verses 7-16

Plain truths as to the shortness and vanity of man's life, and the certainty of death, do us good, when we think and speak of them with application to ourselves. Dying is done but once, and therefore it had need be well done. An error here is past retrieve. Other clouds arise, but the same cloud never returns: so a new generation of men is raised up, but the former generation vanishes away. Glorified saints shall return no more to the cares and sorrows of their houses; nor condemned sinners to the gaieties and pleasures of their houses. It concerns us to secure a better place when we die. From these reasons Job might have drawn a better conclusion than this, I will complain. When we have but a few breaths to draw, we should spend them in the holy, gracious breathings of faith and prayer; not in the noisome, noxious breathings of sin and corruption. We have much reason to pray, that He who keeps Israel, and neither slumbers nor sleeps, may keep us when we slumber and sleep. Job covets to rest in his grave. Doubtless, this was his infirmity; for though a good man would choose death rather than sin, yet he should be content to live as long as God pleases, because life is our opportunity of glorifying him, and preparing for heaven.

Verses 17-21

Job reasons with God concerning his dealings with man. But in the midst of this discourse, Job seems to have lifted up his thoughts to God with some faith and hope. Observe the concern he is in about his sins. The best men have to complain of sin; and the better they are, the more they will complain of it. God is the Preserver of our lives, and the Saviour of the souls of all that believe; but probably Job meant the Observer of men, whose eyes are upon the ways and hearts of all men. We can hide nothing from Him; let us plead guilty before his throne of grace, that we may not be condemned at his judgment-seat. Job maintained, against his friends, that he was not a hypocrite, not a wicked man, yet he owns to his God, that he had sinned. The best must so acknowledge, before the Lord. He seriously inquires how he might be at peace with God, and earnestly begs forgiveness of his sins. He means more than the removing of his outward trouble, and is earnest for the return of God's favour. Wherever the Lord removes the guilt of sin, he breaks the power of sin. To strengthen his prayer for pardon, Job pleads the prospect he had of dying quickly. If my sins be not pardoned while I live, I am lost and undone for ever. How wretched is sinful man without a knowledge of the Saviour!

Chapter 8

Chapter Outline

Bildad reproves Job.	(1–7)
Hypocrites will be destroyed.	(8–19)
Bildad applies God's just dealing to Job.	(20–22)

Verses 1-7

Job spake much to the purpose; but Bildad, like an eager, angry disputant, turns it all off with this, How long wilt thou speak these things? Men's meaning is not taken aright, and then they are rebuked, as if they were evil-doers. Even in disputes on religion, it is too common to treat others with sharpness, and their arguments with contempt. Bildad's discourse shows that he had not a favourable opinion of Job's character. Job owned that God did not pervert judgment; yet it did not therefore follow that his children were cast-aways, or that they did for some great transgression. Extraordinary afflictions are not always the punishment of extraordinary sins, sometimes they are the trials of extraordinary graces: in judging of another's case, we ought to take the favorable side. Bildad puts Job in hope, that if he were indeed upright, he should yet see a good end of his present troubles. This is God's way of enriching the souls of his people with graces and comforts. The beginning is small, but the progress is to perfection. Dawning light grows to noon-day.

Verses 8-19

Bildad discourses well of hypocrites and evil-doers, and the fatal end of all their hopes and joys. He proves this truth of the destruction of the hopes and joys of hypocrites, by an appeal to former times. Bildad refers to the testimony of the ancients. Those teach best that utter words out of their heart, that speak from an experience of spiritual and divine things. A rush growing in fenny ground, looking very green, but withering in dry weather, represents the hypocrite's profession, which is maintained only in times of prosperity. The spider's web, spun with great skill, but easily swept away, represents a man's pretensions to religion when without the grace of God in his heart. A formal professor flatters himself in his own eyes, doubts not of his salvation, is secure, and cheats the world with his vain confidences. The flourishing of the tree, planted in the garden, striking root to the rock, yet after a time cut down and thrown aside, represents wicked men, when most firmly established, suddenly thrown down and forgotten. This doctrine of the vanity of a hypocrite's confidence, or the prosperity of a wicked man, is sound; but it was not applicable to the case of Job, if confined to the present world.

Verses 20-22

Bildad here assures Job, that as he was so he should fare; therefore they concluded, that as he fared so he was. God will not cast away an upright man; he may be cast down for a time, but he shall not be cast away for ever. Sin brings ruin on persons and families. Yet to argue, that Job was an ungodly, wicked man, was unjust and uncharitable. The mistake in these reasonings arose from Job's friends not distinguishing between the present state of trial and discipline, and the future state of final judgment. May we choose the portion, possess the confidence, bear the cross, and die the death of the righteous; and, in the mean time, be careful neither to wound others by rash judgments, nor to distress ourselves needlessly about the opinions of our fellow-creatures.

Chapter 9

Chapter Outline

Job acknowledges God's justice.   (1–13)

He is not able to contend with God.   (14–21)

Men not to be judged by outward condition.   (22–24)

Verses 1-13

In this answer Job declared that he did not doubt the justice of God, when he denied himself to be a hypocrite; for how should man be just with God? Before him he pleaded guilty of sins more than could be counted; and if God should contend with him in judgment, he could not justify one out of a thousand, of all the thoughts, words, and actions of his life; therefore he deserved worse than all his present sufferings. When Job mentions the wisdom and power of God, he forgets his complaints. We are unfit to judge of God's proceedings, because we know not what he does, or what he designs. God acts with power which no creature can resist. Those who think they have strength enough to help others, will not be able to help themselves against it.

Verses 14-21

Job is still righteous in his own eyes, ch. 32:1, and this answer, though it sets forth the power and majesty of God, implies that the question between the afflicted and the Lord of providence, is a question of might, and not of right; and we begin to discover the evil fruits of pride and of a self-righteous spirit. Job begins to manifest a disposition to condemn God, that he may justify himself, for which he is afterwards reproved. Still Job knew so much of himself, that he durst not stand a trial. If we say, We have no sin, we not only deceive ourselves, but we affront God; for we sin in saying so, and give the lie to the Scripture. But Job reflected on God's goodness and justice in saying his affliction was without cause.

Verses 22-24

Job touches briefly upon the main point now in dispute. His friends maintained that those who are righteous and good, always prosper in this world, and that none but the wicked are in misery and distress: he said, on the contrary, that it is a common thing for the wicked to prosper, and the righteous to be greatly afflicted. Yet there is too much passion in what Job here says, for God doth not afflict willingly. When the spirit is heated with dispute or with discontent, we have need to set a watch before our lips.

Verses 25-35

What little need have we of pastimes, and what great need to redeem time, when it runs on so fast towards eternity! How vain the enjoyments of time, which we may quite lose while yet time continues! The remembrance of having done our duty will be pleasing afterwards; so will not the remembrance of having got worldly wealth, when it is all lost and gone. Job's complaint of God, as one that could not be appeased and would not relent, was the language of his corruption. There is a Mediator, a Daysman, or Umpire, for us, even God's own beloved Son, who has purchased peace for us with the blood of his cross, who is able to save to the uttermost all who come unto God through him. If we trust in his name, our sins will be buried in the depths of the sea, we shall be washed from all our filthiness, and made whiter than snow, so that none can lay any thing to our charge. We shall be clothed with the robes of righteousness and salvation, adorned with the graces of the Holy Spirit, and presented faultless before the presence of his glory with exceeding joy. May we learn the difference between justifying ourselves, and being thus justified by God himself. Let the tempest-tossed soul consider Job, and notice that others have passed this dreadful gulf; and though they found it hard to believe that God would hear or deliver them, yet he rebuked the storm, and brought them to the desired haven. Resist the devil; give not place to hard thoughts of God, or desperate conclusions about thyself. Come to Him who invites the weary and heavy laden; who promises in nowise to cast them out.

Chapter 10

Chapter Outline

Job complains of his hardships.	(1–7)
He pleads with God as his Maker.	(8–13)
He complains of God's severity.	(14–22)

Verses 1-7

Job, being weary of his life, resolves to complain, but he will not charge God with unrighteousness. Here is a prayer that he might be delivered from the sting of his afflictions, which is sin. When God afflicts us, he contends with us; when he contends with us, there is always a reason; and it is desirable to know the reason, that we may repent of and forsake the sin for which God has a controversy with us. But when, like Job, we speak in the bitterness of our souls, we increase guilt and vexation. Let us harbour no hard thoughts of God; we shall hereafter see there was no cause for them. Job is sure that God does not discover things, nor judge of them, as men do; therefore he thinks it strange that God continues him under affliction, as if he must take time to inquire into his sin.

Verses 8-13

Job seems to argue with God, as if he only formed and preserved him for misery. God made us, not we ourselves. How sad that those bodies should be instruments of unrighteousness, which are capable of being temples of the Holy Ghost! But the soul is the life, the soul is the man, and this is the gift of God. If we plead with ourselves as an inducement to duty, God made me and maintains me, we may plead as an argument for mercy, Thou hast made me, do thou new-make me; I am thine, save me.

Verses 14-22

Job did not deny that as a sinner he deserved his sufferings; but he thought that justice was executed upon him with peculiar rigour. His gloom, unbelief, and hard thoughts of God, were as much to be ascribed to Satan's inward temptations, and his anguish of soul, under the sense of God's displeasure, as to his outward trials, and remaining depravity. Our Creator, become in Christ our Redeemer also, will not destroy the work of his hands in any humble believer; but will renew him unto holiness, that he may enjoy eternal life. If anguish on earth renders the grave a desirable refuge, what will be their condition who are condemned to the blackness of darkness for ever? Let every sinner seek deliverance from that dreadful state, and every believer be thankful to Jesus, who delivereth from the wrath to come.

Chapter 11

Chapter Outline

Zophar reproves Job.   (1–6)

God's perfections and almighty power.   (7–12)

Zophar assures Job of blessings if he   (13–20)
repented.

Verses 1-6

Zophar attacked Job with great vehemence. He represented him as a man that loved to hear himself speak, though he could say nothing to the purpose, and as a man that maintained falsehoods. He desired God would show Job that less punishment was exacted than he deserved. We are ready, with much assurance, to call God to act in our quarrels, and to think that if he would but speak, he would take our part. We ought to leave all disputes to the judgment of God, which we are sure is according to truth; but those are not always right who are most forward to appeal to the Divine judgment.

Verses 7-12

Zophar speaks well concerning God and his greatness and glory, concerning man and his vanity and folly. See here what man is; and let him be humbled. God sees this concerning vain man, that he would be wise, would be thought so, though he is born like a wild ass's colt, so unteachable and untameable. Man is a vain creature; empty, so the word is. Yet he is a proud creature, and self-conceited. He would be wise, would be thought so, though he will not submit to the laws of wisdom. He would be wise, he reaches after forbidden wisdom, and, like his first parents, aiming to be wise above what is written, loses the tree of life for the tree of knowledge. Is such a creature as this fit to contend with God?

Verses 13-20

Zophar exhorts Job to repentance, and gives him encouragement, yet mixed with hard thoughts of him. He thought that worldly prosperity was always the lot of the righteous, and that Job was to be deemed a hypocrite unless his prosperity was restored. Then shalt thou lift up thy face without spot; that is, thou mayst come boldly to the throne of grace, and not with the terror and amazement expressed in ch. 9:34. If we are looked upon in the face of the Anointed, our faces that were cast down may be lifted up; though polluted, being now washed with the blood of Christ, they may be lifted up without spot. We may draw near in full assurance of faith, when we are sprinkled from an evil conscience, Heb 10:22.

Chapter 12

Chapter Outline

Job reproves his friends.	(1–5)
The wicked often prosper.	(6–11)
Job speaks of the wisdom and power of God.	(12–25)

Verses 1-5

Job upbraids his friends with the good opinion they had of their own wisdom compared with his. We are apt to call reproofs reproaches, and to think ourselves mocked when advised and admonished; this is our folly; yet here was colour for this charge. He suspected the true cause of their conduct to be, that they despised him who was fallen into poverty. It is the way of the world. Even the just, upright man, if he comes under a cloud, is looked upon with contempt.

Verses 6-11

Job appeals to facts. The most audacious robbers, oppressors, and impious wretches, often prosper. Yet this is not by fortune or chance; the Lord orders these things. Worldly prosperity is of small value in his sight: he has better things for his children. Job resolves all into the absolute proprietorship which God has in all the creatures. He demands from his friends liberty to judge of what they had said; he appeals to any fair judgment. (Job 12:12-25)

Verses 12-25

This is a noble discourse of Job concerning the wisdom, power, and sovereignty of God, in ordering all the affairs of the children of men, according to the counsel of His own will, which none can resist. It were well if wise and good men, who differ about lesser things, would see how it is for their honour and comfort, and the good of others, to dwell most upon the great things in which they agree. Here are no complaints, or reflections. He gives many instances of God's powerful management of the children of men, overruling all their counsels, and overcoming all their oppositions. Having all strength and wisdom, God knows how to make use, even of those who are foolish and bad; otherwise there is so little wisdom and so little honesty in the world, that all had been in confusion and ruin long ago. These important truths were suited to convince the disputants that they were out of their depth in attempting to assign the Lord's reasons for afflicting Job; his ways are unsearchable, and his judgments past finding out. Let us remark what beautiful illustrations there are in the word of God, confirming his sovereignty, and wisdom in that sovereignty: but the highest and infinitely the most important is, that the Lord Jesus was crucified by the malice of the Jews; and who but the Lord could have known that this one event was the salvation of the world?

Chapter 13

Chapter Outline

Verses 1-12

With self-preference, Job declared that he needed not to be taught by them. Those who dispute are tempted to magnify themselves, and lower their brethren, more than is fit. When dismayed or distressed with the fear of wrath, the force of temptation, or the weight of affliction, we should apply to the Physician of our souls, who never rejects any, never prescribes amiss, and never leaves any case uncured. To Him we may speak at all times. To broken hearts and wounded consciences, all creatures, without Christ, are physicians of no value. Job evidently speaks with a very angry spirit against his friends. They had advanced some truths which nearly concerned Job, but the heart unhumbled before God, never meekly receives the reproofs of men.

Verses 13-22

Job resolved to cleave to the testimony his own conscience gave of his uprightness. He depended upon God for justification and salvation, the two great things we hope for through Christ. Temporal salvation he little expected, but of his eternal salvation he was very confident; that God would not only be his Saviour to make him happy, but his salvation, in the sight and enjoyment of whom he should be happy. He knew himself not to be a hypocrite, and concluded that he should not be rejected. We should be well pleased with God as a Friend, even when he seems against us as an enemy. We must believe that all shall work for good to us, even when all seems to make against us. We must cleave to God, yea, though we cannot for the present find comfort in him. In a dying hour, we must derive from him living comforts; and this is to trust in him, though he slay us.

Verses 23-28

Job begs to have his sins discovered to him. A true penitent is willing to know the worst of himself; and we should all desire to know what our transgressions are, that we may confess them, and guard against them for the future. Job complains sorrowfully of God's severe dealings with him. Time does not wear out the guilt of sin. When God writes bitter things against us, his design is to make us bring forgotten sins to mind, and so to bring us to repent of them, as to break us off from them. Let young persons beware of indulging in sin. Even in this world they may so possess the sins of their youth, as to have months of sorrow for moments of pleasure. Their wisdom is to remember their Creator in their early days, that they may have assured hope, and sweet peace of conscience, as the solace of their declining years. Job also complains that his present mistakes are strictly noticed. So far from this, God deals not with us according to our deserts. This was the language of Job's melancholy views. If God marks our steps, and narrowly examines our paths, in judgment, both body and soul feel his righteous vengeance. This will be the awful case of unbelievers, yet there is salvation devised, provided, and made known in Christ.

Chapter 14

Chapter Outline

Job speaks of man's life.	(1–6)
Of man's death.	(7–15)
By sin man is subject to corruption.	(16–22)

Verses 1-6

Job enlarges upon the condition of man, addressing himself also to God. Every man of Adam's fallen race is short-lived. All his show of beauty, happiness, and splendour falls before the stroke of sickness or death, as the flower before the scythe; or passes away like the shadow. How is it possible for a man's conduct to be sinless, when his heart is by nature unclean? Here is a clear proof that Job understood and believed the doctrine of original sin. He seems to have intended it as a plea, why the Lord should not deal with him according to his own works, but according to His mercy and grace. It is determined, in the counsel and decree of God, how long we shall live. Our times are in his hands, the powers of nature act under him; in him we live and move. And it is very useful to reflect seriously on the shortness and uncertainty of human life, and the fading nature of all earthly enjoyments. But it is still more important to look at the cause, and remedy of these evils. Until we are born of the Spirit, no spiritually good thing dwells in us, or can proceed from us. Even the little good in the regenerate is defiled with sin. We should therefore humble ourselves before God, and cast ourselves wholly on the mercy of God, through our Divine Surety. We should daily seek the renewing of the Holy Ghost, and look to heaven as the only place of perfect holiness and happiness.

Verses 7-15

Though a tree is cut down, yet, in a moist situation, shoots come forth, and grow up as a newly planted tree. But when man is cut off by death, he is for ever removed from his place in this world.

The life of man may fitly be compared to the waters of a land flood, which spread far, but soon dry up. All Job's expressions here show his belief in the great doctrine of the resurrection. Job's friends proving miserable comforters, he pleases himself with the expectation of a change. If our sins are forgiven, and our hearts renewed to holiness, heaven will be the rest of our souls, while our bodies are hidden in the grave from the malice of our enemies, feeling no more pain from our corruptions, or our corrections.

Verses 16-22

Job's faith and hope spake, and grace appeared to revive; but depravity again prevailed. He represents God as carrying matters to extremity against him. The Lord must prevail against all who contend with him. God may send disease and pain, we may lose all comfort in those near and dear to us, every hope of earthly happiness may be destroyed, but God will receive the believer into realms of eternal happiness. But what a change awaits the prosperous unbeliever! How will he answer when God shall call him to his tribunal? The Lord is yet upon a mercy-seat, ready to be gracious. Oh that sinners would be wise, that they would consider their latter end! While man's flesh is upon him, that is, the body he is so loth to lay down, it shall have pain; and while his soul is within him, that is, the spirit he is so loth to resign, it shall mourn. Dying work is hard work; dying pangs often are sore pangs. It is folly for men to defer repentance to a death-bed, and to have that to do which is the one thing needful, when unfit to do anything.

Chapter 15

Chapter Outline

Eliphaz reproves Job.   (1–16)

The unquietness of wicked men.   (17–35)

Verses 1-16

Eliphaz begins a second attack upon Job, instead of being softened by his complaints. He unjustly charges Job with casting off the fear of God, and all regard to him, and restraining prayer. See in what religion is summed up, fearing God, and praying to him; the former the most needful principle, the latter the most needful practice. Eliphaz charges Job with self-conceit. He charges him with contempt of the counsels and comforts given him by his friends. We are apt to think that which we ourselves say is important, when others, with reason, think little of it. He charges him with opposition to God. Eliphaz ought not to have put harsh constructions upon the words of one well known for piety, and now in temptation. It is plain that these disputants were deeply convinced of the doctrine of original sin, and the total depravity of human nature. Shall we not admire the patience of God in bearing with us? and still more his love to us in the redemption of Christ Jesus his beloved Son?

Verses 17-35

Eliphaz maintains that the wicked are certainly miserable: whence he would infer, that the miserable are certainly wicked, and therefore Job was so. But because many of God's people have prospered in this world, it does not therefore follow that those who are crossed and made poor, as Job, are not God's people. Eliphaz shows also that wicked people, particularly oppressors, are subject to continual terror, live very uncomfortably, and perish very miserably. Will the prosperity of presumptuous sinners end miserably as here described? Then let the mischiefs which befal others, be our warnings. Though no chastening for the present seemeth to be joyous, but grievous, nevertheless, afterward it yieldeth the peaceable fruits of righteousness to them that are exercised thereby. No calamity, no trouble, however heavy, however severe, can rob a follower of the Lord of his favour. What shall separate him from the love of Christ?

Chapter 16

Chapter Outline

Verses 1-5

Eliphaz had represented Job's discourses as unprofitable, and nothing to the purpose; Job here gives his the same character. Those who pass censures, must expect to have them retorted; it is easy, it is endless, but what good does it do? Angry answers stir up men's passions, but never convince their judgments, nor set truth in a clear light. What Job says of his friends is true of all creatures, in comparison with God; one time or other we shall be made to see and own that miserable comforters are they all. When under convictions of sin, terrors of conscience, or the arrests of death, only the blessed Spirit can comfort effectually; all others, without him, do it miserably, and to no purpose. Whatever our brethren's sorrows are, we ought by sympathy to make them our own; they may soon be so.

Verses 6-16

Here is a doleful representation of Job's grievances. What reason we have to bless God, that we are not making such complaints! Even good men, when in great troubles, have much ado not to entertain hard thoughts of God. Eliphaz had represented Job as unhumbled under his affliction: No, says Job, I know better things; the dust is now the fittest place for me. In this he reminds us of Christ, who was a man of sorrows, and pronounced those blessed that mourn, for they shall be comforted.

Verses 17-22

Job's condition was very deplorable; but he had the testimony of his conscience for him, that he never allowed himself in any gross sin. No one was ever more ready to acknowledge sins of infirmity. Eliphaz had charged him with hypocrisy in religion, but he specifies prayer, the great act of religion, and professes that in this he was pure, though not from all infirmity. He had a God to go to, who he doubted not took full notice of all his sorrows. Those who pour out tears before God, though they cannot plead for themselves, by reason of their defects, have a Friend to plead for them, even the Son of man, and on him we must ground all our hopes of acceptance with God. To die, is to go the way whence we shall not return. We must all of us, very certainly, and very shortly, go this journey. Should not then the Saviour be precious to our souls? And ought we not to be ready to obey and to suffer for his sake? If our consciences are sprinkled with his atoning blood, and testify that we are not living in sin or hypocrisy, when we go the way whence we shall not return, it will be a release from prison, and an entrance into everlasting happiness.

Chapter 17

Chapter Outline

Job appeals from man to God.   (1–9)

His hope is not in life, but in death.   (10–16)

Verses 1-9

Job reflects upon the harsh censures his friends had passed upon him, and, looking on himself as a dying man, he appeals to God. Our time is ending. It concerns us carefully to redeem the days of time, and to spend them in getting ready for eternity. We see the good use the righteous should make of Job's afflictions from God, from enemies, and from friends. Instead of being discouraged in the service of God, by the hard usage this faithful servant of God met with, they should be made bold to proceed and persevere therein. Those who keep their eye upon heaven as their end, will keep their feet in the paths of religion as their way, whatever difficulties and discouragements they may meet with.

Verses 10-16

Job's friends had pretended to comfort him with the hope of his return to a prosperous estate; he here shows that those do not go wisely about the work of comforting the afflicted, who fetch their comforts from the possibility of recovery in this world. It is our wisdom to comfort ourselves, and others, in distress, with that which will not fail; the promise of God, his love and grace, and a well-grounded hope of eternal life. See how Job reconciles himself to the grave. Let this make believers willing to die; it is but going to bed; they are weary, and it is time that they were in their beds. Why should not they go willingly when their Father calls them? Let us remember our bodies are allied to corruption, the worm and the dust; and let us seek for that lively hope which shall be fulfilled, when the hope of the wicked shall be put out in darkness; that when our bodies are in the grave, our souls may enjoy the rest reserved for the people of God.

Chapter 18

Chapter Outline

Verses 1-4

Bildad had before given Job good advice and encouragement; here he used nothing but rebukes, and declared his ruin. And he concluded that Job shut out the providence of God from the management of human affairs, because he would not admit himself to be wicked.

Verses 5-10

Bildad describes the miserable condition of a wicked man; in which there is much certain truth, if we consider that a sinful condition is a sad condition, and that sin will be men's ruin, if they do not repent. Though Bildad thought the application of it to Job was easy, yet it was not safe nor just. It is common for angry disputants to rank their opponents among God's enemies, and to draw wrong conclusions from important truths. The destruction of the wicked is foretold. That destruction is represented under the similitude of a beast or bird caught in a snare, or a malefactor taken into custody. Satan, as he was a murderer, so he was a robber, from the beginning. He, the tempter, lays snares for sinners wherever they go. If he makes them sinful like himself, he will make them miserable like himself. Satan hunts for the precious life. In the transgression of an evil man there is a snare for himself, and God is preparing for his destruction. See here how the sinner runs himself into the snare.

Verses 11-21

Bildad describes the destruction wicked people are kept for, in the other world, and which in some degree, often seizes them in this world. The way of sin is the way of fear, and leads to everlasting confusion, of which the present terrors of an impure conscience are earnests, as in Cain and Judas. Miserable indeed is a wicked man's death, how secure soever his life was. See him dying; all that he trusts to for his support shall be taken from him. How happy are the saints, and how indebted to the lord Jesus, by whom death is so far done away and changed, that this king of terrors is become a friend and a servant! See the wicked man's family sunk and cut off. His children shall perish, either with him or after him. Those who consult the true honour of their family, and its welfare, will be afraid of withering all by sin. The judgments of God follow the wicked man after death in this world, as a proof of the misery his soul is in after death, and as an earnest of that everlasting shame and contempt to which he shall rise in the great day. The memory of the just is blessed, but the name of the wicked shall rot, Pr 10:7. It would be well if this report of wicked men would cause any to flee from the wrath to come, from which their power, policy, and riches cannot deliver them. But Jesus ever liveth to deliver all who trust in him. Bear up then, suffering believers. Ye shall for a little time have sorrow, but your Beloved, your Saviour, will see you again; your hearts shall rejoice, and your joy no man taketh away.

Chapter 19

Chapter Outline

Verses 1-7

Job's friends blamed him as a wicked man, because he was so afflicted; here he describes their unkindness, showing that what they condemned was capable of excuse. Harsh language from friends, greatly adds to the weight of afflictions: yet it is best not to lay it to heart, lest we harbour resentment. Rather let us look to Him who endured the contradiction of sinners against himself, and was treated with far more cruelty than Job was, or we can be. (Job 19:8-22)

Verses 8-22

How doleful are Job's complaints! What is the fire of hell but the wrath of God! Seared consciences will feel it hereafter, but do not fear it now: enlightened consciences fear it now, but shall not feel it hereafter. It is a very common mistake to think that those whom God afflicts he treats as his enemies. Every creature is that to us which God makes it to be; yet this does not excuse Job's relations and friends. How uncertain is the friendship of men! but if God be our Friend, he will not fail us in time of need. What little reason we have to indulge the body, which, after all our care, is consumed by diseases it has in itself. Job recommends himself to the compassion of his friends, and justly blames their harshness. It is very distressing to one who loves God, to be bereaved at once of outward comfort and of inward consolation; yet if this, and more, come upon a believer, it does not weaken the proof of his being a child of God and heir of glory.

Verses 23-29

The Spirit of God, at this time, seems to have powerfully wrought on the mind of Job. Here he witnessed a good confession; declared the soundness of his faith, and the assurance of his hope. Here is much of Christ and heaven; and he that said such things are these, declared plainly that he sought the better country, that is, the heavenly. Job was taught of God to believe in a living Redeemer; to look for the resurrection of the dead, and the life of the world to come; he comforted himself with the expectation of these. Job was assured, that this Redeemer of sinners from the yoke of Satan and the condemnation of sin, was his Redeemer, and expected salvation through him; and that he was a living Redeemer, though not yet come in the flesh; and that at the last day he would appear as the Judge of the world, to raise the dead, and complete the redemption of his people. With what pleasure holy Job enlarges upon this! May these faithful sayings be engraved by the Holy Spirit upon our hearts. We are all concerned to see that the root of the matter be in us. A living, quickening, commanding principle of grace in the heart, is the root of the matter; as necessary to our religion as the root of the tree, to which it owes both its fixedness and its fruitfulness. Job and his friends differed concerning the methods of Providence, but they agreed in the root of the matter, the belief of another world.

Chapter 20

Chapter Outline

Zophar speaks of the short joy of the wicked.	(1–9)
The ruin of the wicked.	(10–22)
The portion of the wicked.	(23–29)

Verses 1-9

Zophar's discourse is upon the certain misery of the wicked. The triumph of the wicked and the joy of the hypocrite are fleeting. The pleasures and gains of sin bring disease and pain; they end in remorse, anguish, and ruin. Dissembled piety is double iniquity, and the ruin that attends it will be accordingly.

Verses 10-22

The miserable condition of the wicked man in this world is fully set forth. The lusts of the flesh are here called the sins of his youth. His hiding it and keeping it under his tongue, denotes concealment of his beloved lust, and delight therein. But He who knows what is in the heart, knows what is under the tongue, and will discover it. The love of the world, and of the wealth of it, also is wickedness, and man sets his heart upon these. Also violence and injustice, these sins bring God's judgments upon nations and families. Observe the punishment of the wicked man for these things. Sin is turned into gall, than which nothing is more bitter; it will prove to him poison; so will all unlawful gains be. In his fulness he shall be in straits, through the anxieties of his own mind. To be led by the sanctifying grace of God to restore what was unjustly gotten, as Zaccheus was, is a great mercy. But to be forced to restore by the horrors of a despairing conscience, as Judas was, has no benefit and comfort attending it.

Verses 23-29

Zophar, having described the vexations which attend wicked practices, shows their ruin from God's wrath. There is no fence against this, but in Christ, who is the only Covert from the storm and tempest, Isa 32:2. Zophar concludes, "This is the portion of a wicked man from God;" it is allotted him. Never was any doctrine better explained, or worse applied, than this by Zophar, who intended to prove Job a hypocrite. Let us receive the good explanation, and make a better application, for warning to ourselves, to stand in awe and sin not. One view of Jesus, directed by the Holy Spirit, and by him suitably impressed upon our souls, will quell a thousand carnal reasonings about the suffering of the faithful.

Chapter 21

Chapter Outline

Job entreats attention.	(1–6)
The prosperity of the wicked.	(7–16)
The dealings of God's providence.	(17–26)
The judgement of the wicked is in the world to come.	(27–34)

Verses 1-6

Job comes closer to the question in dispute. This was, Whether outward prosperity is a mark of the true church, and the true members of it, so that ruin of a man's prosperity proves him a hypocrite? This they asserted, but Job denied. If they looked upon him, they might see misery enough to demand compassion, and their bold interpretations of this mysterious providence should be turned into silent wonder.

Verses 7-16

Job says, Remarkable judgments are sometimes brought upon notorious sinners, but not always. Wherefore is it so? This is the day of God's patience; and, in some way or other, he makes use of the prosperity of the wicked to serve his own counsels, while it ripens them for ruin; but the chief reason is, because he will make it appear there is another world. These prospering sinners make light of God and religion, as if because they have so much of this world, they had no need to look after another. But religion is not a vain thing. If it be so to us, we may thank ourselves for resting on the outside of it. Job shows their folly.

Verses 17-26

Job had described the prosperity of wicked people; in these verses he opposes this to what his friends had maintained about their certain ruin in this life. He reconciles this to the holiness and justice of God. Even while they prosper thus, they are light and worthless, of no account with God, or with wise men. In the height of their pomp and power, there is but a step between them and ruin. Job refers the difference Providence makes between one wicked man and another, into the wisdom of God. He is Judge of all the earth, and he will do right. So vast is the disproportion between time and eternity, that if hell be the lot of every sinner at last, it makes little difference if one goes singing thither, and another sighing. If one wicked man die in a palace, and another in a dungeon, the worm that dies not, and the fire that is not quenched, will be the same to them. Thus differences in this world are not worth perplexing ourselves about.

Verses 27-34

Job opposes the opinion of his friends, That the wicked are sure to fall into visible and remarkable ruin, and none but the wicked; upon which principle they condemned Job as wicked. Turn to whom you will, you will find that the punishment of sinners is designed more for the other world than for this, Jude 1:14, 15. The sinner is here supposed to live in a great deal of power. The sinner shall have a splendid funeral: a poor thing for any man to be proud of the prospect of. He shall have a stately monument. And a valley with springs of water to keep the turf green, was accounted an honourable burial place among eastern people; but such things are vain distinctions. Death closes his prosperity. It is but a poor encouragement to die, that others have died before us. That which makes a man die with true courage, is, with faith to remember that Jesus Christ died and was laid in the grave, not only before us, but for us. That He hath gone before us, and died for us, who is alive and liveth for us, is true consolation in the hour of death.

Chapter 22

Chapter Outline

Verses 1-4

Eliphaz considers that, because Job complained so much of his afflictions, he thought God was unjust in afflicting him; but Job was far from thinking so. What Eliphaz says, is unjustly applied to Job, but it is very true, that when God does us good it is not because he is indebted to us. Man's piety is no profit to God, no gain. The gains of religion to men are infinitely greater than the losses of it. God is a Sovereign, who gives no account of his conduct; but he is perfectly wise, just, faithful, good, and merciful. He approves the likeness of his own holiness, and delights in the fruits of his Spirit; he accepts the thankful services of the humble believer, while he rejects the proud claim of the self-confident.

Verses 5-14

Eliphaz brought heavy charges against Job, without reason for his accusations, except that Job was visited as he supposed God always visited every wicked man. He charges him with oppression, and that he did harm with his wealth and power in the time of his prosperity.

Verses 15-20

Eliphaz would have Job mark the old way that wicked men have trodden, and see what the end of their way was. It is good for us to mark it, that we may not walk therein. But if others are consumed, and we are not, instead of blaming them, and lifting up ourselves, as Eliphaz does here, we ought to be thankful to God, and take it for a warning.

Verses 21-30

The answer of Eliphaz wrongly implied that Job had hitherto not known God, and that prosperity in this life would follow his sincere conversion. The counsel Eliphaz here gives is good, though, as to Job, it was built upon a false supposition that he was a stranger and enemy to God. Let us beware of slandering our brethren; and if it be our lot to suffer in this manner, let us remember how Job was treated; yea, how Jesus was reviled, that we may be patient. Let us examine whether there may not be some colour for the slander, and walk watchfully, so as to be clear of all appearances of evil.

Chapter 23

Chapter Outline

Job complains that God has withdrawn.   (1–7)

He asserts his own integrity.   (8–12)

The Divine terrors.   (13–17)

Verses 1-7

Job appeals from his friends to the just judgement of God. He wants to have his cause tried quickly. Blessed be God, we may know where to find him. He is in Christ, reconciling the world unto himself; and upon a mercy-seat, waiting to be gracious. Thither the sinner may go; and there the believer may order his cause before Him, with arguments taken from his promises, his covenant, and his glory. A patient waiting for death and judgment is our wisdom and duty, and it cannot be without a holy fear and trembling. A passionate wishing for death or judgement is our sin and folly, and ill becomes us, as it did Job.

Verses 8-12

Job knew that the Lord was every where present; but his mind was in such confusion, that he could get no fixed view of God's merciful presence, so as to find comfort by spreading his case before him. His views were all gloomy. God seemed to stand at a distance, and frown upon him. Yet Job expressed his assurance that he should be brought forth, tried, and approved, for he had obeyed the precepts of God. He had relished and delighted in the truths and commandments of God. Here we should notice that Job justified himself rather than God, or in opposition to him, ch. 32:2. Job might feel that he was clear from the charges of his friends, but boldly to assert that, though visited by the hand of God, it was not a chastisement of sin, was his error. And he is guilty of a second, when he denies that there are dealings of Providence with men in this present life, wherein the injured find redress, and the evil are visited for their sins.

Verses 13-17

As Job does not once question but that his trials are from the hand of God, and that there is no such thing as chance, how does he account for them? The principle on which he views them is, that the hope and reward of the faithful servants of God are only laid up in another life; and he maintains that it is plain to all, that the wicked are not treated according to their deserts in this life, but often directly the reverse. But though the obtaining of mercy, the first-fruits of the Spirit of grace, pledges a God, who will certainly finish the work which he has began; yet the afflicted believer is not to conclude that all prayer and entreaty will be in vain, and that he should sink into despair, and faint when he is reproved of Him. He cannot tell but the intention of God in afflicting him may be to produce penitence and prayer in his heart. May we learn to obey and trust the Lord, even in tribulation; to live or die as he pleases: we know not for what good ends our lives may be shortened or prolonged.

Chapter 24

Chapter Outline

Verses 1-12

Job discourses further about the prosperity of the wicked. That many live at ease who are ungodly and profane, he had showed, ch. xxi. Here he shows that many who live in open defiance of all the laws of justice, succeed in wicked practices; and we do not see them reckoned with in this world. He notices those that do wrong under pretence of law and authority; and robbers, those that do wrong by force. He says, "God layeth not folly to them;" that is, he does not at once send his judgments, nor make them examples, and so manifest their folly to all the world. But he that gets riches, and not by right, at his end shall be a fool, Jer 17:11.

Verses 13-17

See what care and pains wicked men take to compass their wicked designs; let it shame our negligence and slothfulness in doing good. See what pains those take, who make provision for the flesh to fulfil the lusts of it: pains to compass, and then to hide that which will end in death and hell at last. Less pains would mortify and crucify the flesh, and be life and heaven at last. Shame came in with sin, and everlasting shame is at the end of it. See the misery of sinners; they are exposed to continual frights: yet see their folly; they are afraid of coming under the eye of men, but have no dread of God's eye, which is always upon them: they are not afraid of doing things which they are afraid of being known to do.

Verses 18-25

Sometimes how gradual is the decay, how quiet the departure of a wicked person, how is he honoured, and how soon are all his cruelties and oppressions forgotten! They are taken off with other men, as the harvestman gathers the ears of corn as they come to hand. There will often appear much to resemble the wrong view of Providence Job takes in this chapter. But we are taught by the word of inspiration, that these notions are formed in ignorance, from partial views. The providence of God, in the affairs of men, is in every thing a just and wise providence. Let us apply this whenever the Lord may try us. He cannot do wrong. The unequalled sorrows of the Son of God when on earth, unless looked at in this view, perplex the mind. But when we behold him, as the sinner's Surety, bearing the curse, we can explain why he should endure that wrath which was due to sin, that Divine justice might be satisfied, and his people saved.

Chapter 25

Bildad shows that man cannot be justified before God.

—Bildad drops the question concerning the prosperity of wicked men; but shows the infinite distance there is between God and man. He represents to Job some truths he had too much overlooked. Man's righteousness and holiness, at the best, are nothing in comparison with God's, Ps 89:6. As God is so great and glorious, how can man, who is guilty and impure, appear before him? We need to be born again of water and of the Holy Ghost, and to be bathed again and again in the blood of Christ, that Fountain opened, Zec 13:1. We should be humbled as mean, guilty, polluted creatures, and renounce self-dependence. But our vileness will commend Christ's condescension and love; the riches of his mercy and the power of his grace will be magnified to all eternity by every sinner he redeems.

Chapter 26

Chapter Outline

Verses 1-4

Job derided Bildad's answer; his words were a mixture of peevishness and self-preference. Bildad ought to have laid before Job the consolations, rather than the terrors of the Almighty. Christ knows how to speak what is proper for the weary, Isa 50:4; and his ministers should not grieve those whom God would not have made sad. We are often disappointed in our expectations from our friends who should comfort us; but the Comforter, the Holy Ghost, never mistakes, nor fails of his end.

Verses 5-14

Many striking instances are here given of the wisdom and power of God, in the creation and preservation of the world. If we look about us, to the earth and waters here below, we see his almighty power. If we consider hell beneath, though out of our sight, yet we may conceive the discoveries of God's power there. If we look up to heaven above, we see displays of God's almighty power. By his Spirit, the eternal Spirit that moved upon the face of the waters, the breath of his mouth, Ps 33:6, he has not only made the heavens, but beautified them. By redemption, all the other wonderful works of the Lord are eclipsed; and we may draw near, and taste his grace, learn to love him, and walk with delight in his ways. The ground of the controversy between Job and the other disputants was, that they unjustly thought from his afflictions that he must have been guilty of heinous crimes. They appear not to have duly considered the evil and just desert of original sin; nor did they take into account the gracious designs of God in purifying his people. Job also darkened counsel by words without knowledge. But his views were more distinct. He does not appear to have alleged his personal righteousness as the ground of his hope towards God. Yet what he admitted in a general view of his case, he in effect denied, while he complained of his sufferings as unmerited and severe; that very complaint proving the necessity for their being sent, in order to his being further humbled in the sight of God.

Chapter 27

Chapter Outline

Verses 1-6

Job's friends now suffered him to speak, and he proceeded in a grave and useful manner. Job had confidence in the goodness both of his cause and of his God; and cheerfully committed his cause to him. But Job had not due reverence when he spake of God as taking away his judgment, and vexing his soul. To resolve that our hearts shall not reproach us, while we hold fast our integrity, baffles the designs of the evil spirit.

Verses 7-10

Job looked upon the condition of a hypocrite and a wicked man, to be most miserable. If they gained through life by their profession, and kept up their presumptuous hope till death, what would that avail when God required their souls? The more comfort we find in our religion, the more closely we shall cleave to it. Those who have no delight in God, are easily drawn away by the pleasures, and easily overcome by the crosses of this life. (Job 27:11-23)

Verses 11-23

Job's friends, on the same subject, spoke of the misery of wicked men before death as proportioned to their crimes; Job considered that if it were not so, still the consequences of their death would be dreadful. Job undertook to set this matter in a true light. Death to a godly man, is like a fair gale of wind to convey him to the heavenly country; but, to a wicked man, it is like a storm, that hurries him away to destruction. While he lived, he had the benefit of sparing mercy; but now the day of God's patience is over, and he will pour out upon him his wrath. When God casts down a man, there is no flying from, nor bearing up under his anger. Those who will not now flee to the arms of Divine grace, which are stretched out to receive them, will not be able to flee from the arms of Divine wrath, which will shortly be stretched out to destroy them. And what is a man profited if he gain the whole world, and thus lose his own soul?

Chapter 28

Chapter Outline

Verses 1-11

Job maintained that the dispensations of Providence were regulated by the highest wisdom. To confirm this, he showed of what a great deal of knowledge and wealth men may make themselves masters. The caverns of the earth may be discovered, but not the counsels of Heaven. Go to the miners, thou sluggard in religion, consider their ways, and be wise. Let their courage and diligence in seeking the wealth that perishes, shame us out of slothfulness and faint-heartedness in labouring for the true riches. How much better is it to get wisdom than gold! How much easier, and safer! Yet gold is sought for, but grace neglected. Will the hopes of precious things out of the earth, so men call them, though really they are paltry and perishing, be such a spur to industry, and shall not the certain prospect of truly precious things in heaven be much more so?

Verses 12-19

Job here speaks of wisdom and understanding, the knowing and enjoying of God and ourselves. Its worth is infinitely more than all the riches in this world. It is a gift of the Holy Ghost which cannot be bought with money. Let that which is most precious in God's account, be so in ours. Job asks after it as one that truly desired to find it, and despaired of finding it any where but in God; any way but by Divine revelation. (Job 28:20-28)

Verses 20-28

There is a two-fold wisdom; one hid in God, which is secret, and belongs not to us; the other made known by him, and revealed to man. One day's events, and one man's affairs, have such reference to, and so hang one upon another, that He only, to whom all is open, and who sees the whole at one view, can rightly judge of every part. But the knowledge of God's revealed will is within our reach, and will do us good. Let man look upon this as his wisdom, To fear the Lord, and to depart from evil. Let him learn that, and he is learned enough. Where is this wisdom to be found? The treasures of it are hid in Christ, revealed by the word, received by faith, through the Holy Ghost. It will not feed pride or vanity, or amuse our vain curiosity. It teaches and encourages sinners to fear the Lord, and to depart from evil, in the exercise of repentance and faith, without desiring to solve all difficulties about the events of this life.

Chapter 29

Chapter Outline

Verses 1-6

Job proceeds to contrast his former prosperity with his present misery, through God's withdrawing from him. A gracious soul delights in God's smiles, not in the smiles of this world. Four things were then very pleasant to holy Job. 1. The confidence he had in the Divine protection. 2. The enjoyment he had of the Divine favour. 3. The communion he had with the Divine word. 4. The assurance he had of the Divine presence. God's presence with a man in his house, though it be but a cottage, makes it a castle and a palace. Then also he had comfort in his family. Riches and flourishing families, like a candle, may be soon extinguished. But when the mind is enlightened by the Holy Spirit, when a man walks in the light of God's countenance, every outward comfort is doubled, every trouble is diminished, and he may pass cheerfully by this light through life and through death. Yet the sensible comfort of this state is often withdrawn for a season; and commonly this arises from sinful neglect, and grieving the Holy Spirit: sometimes it may be a trial of a man's faith and grace. But it is needful to examine ourselves, to seek for the cause of such a change by fervent prayer, and to increase our watchfulness.

Verses 7-17

All sorts of people paid respect to Job, not only for the dignity of his rank, but for his personal merit, his prudence, integrity, and good management. Happy the men who are blessed with such gifts as these! They have great opportunities of honouring God and doing good, but have great need to watch against pride. Happy the people who are blessed with such men! it is a token for good to them. Here we see what Job valued himself by, in the day of his prosperity. It was by his usefulness. He valued himself by the check he gave to the violence of proud and evil men. Good magistrates must thus be a restraint to evil-doers, and protect the innocent; in order to this, they should arm themselves with zeal and resolution. Such men are public blessings, and resemble Him who rescues poor sinners from Satan. How many who were ready to perish, now are blessing Him! But who can show forth His praises? May we trust in His mercy, and seek to imitate His truth, justice, and love.

Verses 18-25

Being thus honoured and useful, Job had hoped to die in peace and honour, in a good old age. If such an expectation arise from lively faith in the providence and promise of God, it is well; but if from conceit of our own wisdom, and dependence on changeable, earthly things, it is ill grounded, and turns to sin. Every one that has the spirit of wisdom, has not the spirit of government; but Job had both. Yet he had the tenderness of a comforter. This he thought upon with pleasure, when he was himself a mourner. Our Lord Jesus is a King who hates iniquity, and upon whom the blessing of a world ready to perish comes. To Him let us give ear.

Chapter 30

Chapter Outline

Job's honour is turned into contempt.	(1–14)
Job a burden to himself.	(15–31)

Verses 1-14

Job contrasts his present condition with his former honour and authority. What little cause have men to be ambitious or proud of that which may be so easily lost, and what little confidence is to be put in it! We should not be cast down if we are despised, reviled, and hated by wicked men. We should look to Jesus, who endured the contradiction of sinners.

Verses 15-31

Job complains a great deal. Harbouring hard thoughts of God was the sin which did, at this time, most easily beset Job. When inward temptations join with outward calamities, the soul is hurried as in a tempest, and is filled with confusion. But woe be to those who really have God for an enemy! Compared with the awful state of ungodly men, what are all outward, or even inward temporal afflictions? There is something with which Job comforts himself, yet it is but a little. He foresees that death will be the end of all his troubles. God's wrath might bring him to death; but his soul would be safe and happy in the world of spirits. If none pity us, yet our God, who corrects, pities us, even as a father pitieth his own children. And let us look more to the things of eternity: then the believer will cease from mourning, and joyfully praise redeeming love.

Chapter 31

Chapter Outline

Job declares his uprightness.	(1–8)
His integrity.	(9–15)
Job merciful.	(16–23)
Job not guilty of covetousness or idolatry.	(24–32)

Job not guilty of hypocrisy and violence.   (33–40)

Verses 1-8

Job did not speak the things here recorded by way of boasting, but in answer to the charge of hypocrisy. He understood the spiritual nature of God's commandments, as reaching to the thoughts and intents of the heart. It is best to let our actions speak for us; but in some cases we owe it to ourselves and to the cause of God, solemnly to protest our innocence of the crimes of which we are falsely accused. The lusts of the flesh, and the love of the world, are two fatal rocks on which multitudes split; against these Job protests he was always careful to stand upon his guard. And God takes more exact notice of us than we do of ourselves; let us therefore walk circumspectly. He carefully avoided all sinful means of getting wealth. He dreaded all forbidden profit as much as all forbidden pleasure. What we have in the world may be used with comfort, or lost with comfort, if honestly gotten. Without strict honestly and faithfulness in all our dealings, we can have no good evidence of true godliness. Yet how many professors are unable to abide this touchstone!

Verses 9-15

All the defilements of the life come from a deceived heart. Lust is a fire in the soul: those that indulge it, are said to burn. It consumes all that is good there, and lays the conscience waste. It kindles the fire of God's wrath, which, if not quenched by the blood of Christ, will consume even to eternal destruction. It consumes the body; it consumes the substance. Burning lusts bring burning judgments. Job had a numerous household, and he managed it well. He considered that he had a Master in heaven; and as we are undone if God should be severe with us, we ought to be mild and gentle towards all with whom we have to do.

Verses 16-23

Job's conscience gave testimony concerning his just and charitable behaviour toward the poor. He is most large upon this head, because in this matter he was particularly accused. He was tender of all, and hurtful to none. Notice the principles by which Job was restrained from being uncharitable and unmerciful. He stood in awe of the Lord, as certainly against him, if he should wrong the poor. Regard to worldly interests may restrain a man from actual crimes; but the grace of God alone can make him hate, dread, and shun sinful thoughts and desires.

Verses 24-32

Job protests, 1. That he never set his heart upon the wealth of this world. How few prosperous professors can appeal to the Lord, that they have not rejoiced because their gains were great! Through the determination to be rich, numbers ruin their souls, or pierce themselves with many sorrows. 2. He never was guilty of idolatry. The source of idolatry is in the heart, and it corrupts men, and provokes God to send judgments upon a nation. 3. He neither desired nor delighted in the hurt of the worst enemy he had. If others bear malice to us, that will not justify us in bearing malice to them. 4. He had never been unkind to strangers. Hospitality is a Christian duty, 1Pe 4:9.

Verses 33-40

Job clears himself from the charge of hypocrisy. We are loth to confess our faults, willing to excuse them, and to lay the blame upon others. But he that thus covers his sins, shall not prosper, Pr 28:13. He speaks of his courage in what is good, as an evidence of his sincerity in it. When men get estates unjustly, they are justly deprived of comfort from them; it was sown wheat, but shall come up thistles. What men do not come honestly by, will never do them any good. The words of Job are ended. They end with a bold assertion, that, with respect to accusation against his moral and religious character as the cause for his sufferings, he could appeal to God. But, however confident Job was, we shall see he was mistaken, chap. 40:4, 5; 1Jo 1:8. Let us all judge ourselves; wherein we are guilty, let us seek forgiveness in that blood which cleanseth from all sin; and may the Lord have mercy upon us, and write his laws in our hearts!

Chapter 32

Chapter Outline

Verses 1-5

Job's friends were silenced, but not convinced. Others had been present. Elihu was justly displeased with Job, as more anxious to clear his own character than the justice and goodness of God. Elihu was displeased with Job's friends because they had not been candid to Job. Seldom is a quarrel begun, more seldom is a quarrel carried on, in which there are not faults on both sides. Those that seek for truth, must not reject what is true and good on either side, nor approve or defend what is wrong.

Verses 6-14

Elihu professes to speak by the inspiration of the Holy Spirit, and corrects both parties. He allowed that those who had the longest experience should speak first. But God gives wisdom as he pleases; this encouraged him to state his opinion. By attention to the word of God, and dependence upon the Holy Spirit, young men may become wiser than the aged; but this wisdom will render them swift to hear, slow to speak, and disposed to give others a patient hearing.

Verses 15-22

If we are sure that the Spirit of God suggested what we are about to say, still we ought to refrain, till it comes to our turn to speak. God is the God of order, not of confusion. It is great refreshment to a good man, to speak for the glory of the Lord, and to edify others. And the more we consider the majesty of God, as our Maker, and the more we dread his wrath and justice, the less shall we sinfully fear or flatter men. Could we set the wrath Lord always before us, in his mercies and his terrors, we should not be moved from doing our duty in whatever we are called to do.

Chapter 33

Chapter Outline

Verses 1-7

Job had desired a judge to decide his appeal. Elihu was one according to his wish, a man like himself. If we would rightly convince men, it must be by reason, not by terror; by fair argument, not by a heavy hand.

Verses 8-13

Elihu charges Job with reflecting upon the justice and goodness of God. When we hear any thing said to God's dishonour, we ought to bear our testimony against it. Job had represented God as severe in marking what he did amiss. Elihu urges that he had spoken wrong, and that he ought to humble himself before God, and by repentance to unsay it. God is not accountable to us. It is unreasonable for weak, sinful creatures, to strive with a God of infinite wisdom, power, and goodness. He acts with perfect justice, wisdom, and goodness, where we cannot perceive it.

Verses 14-18

God speaks to us by conscience, by providences, and by ministers; of all these Elihu discourses. There was not then, that we know of, any Divine revelation in writing, though now it is our principal guide. When God designs men's good, by the convictions and dictates of their own consciences, he opens the heart, as Lydia's, and opens the ears, so that conviction finds or forces its way in. The end and design of these admonitions are to keep men from sin, particularly the sin of pride. While sinners are pursuing evil purposes, and indulging their pride, their souls are hastening to destruction.

That which turns men from sin, saves them from hell. What a mercy it is to be under the restraints of an awakened conscience!

Verses 19-28

Job complained of his diseases, and judged by them that God was angry with him; his friends did so too: but Elihu shows that God often afflicts the body for good to the soul. This thought will be of great use for our getting good from sickness, in and by which God speaks to men. Pain is the fruit of sin; yet, by the grace of God, the pain of the body is often made a means of good to the soul. When afflictions have done their work, they shall be removed. A ransom or propitiation is found. Jesus Christ is the Messenger and the Ransom, so Elihu calls him, as Job had called him his Redeemer, for he is both the Purchaser and the Price, the Priest and the sacrifice. So high was the value of souls, that nothing less would redeem them; and so great the hurt done by sin, that nothing less would atone for it, than the blood of the Son of God, who gave his life a ransom for many. A blessed change follows. Recovery from sickness is a mercy indeed, when it proceeds from the remission of sin. All that truly repent of their sins, shall find mercy with God. The works of darkness are unfruitful works; all the gains of sin will come far short of the damage. We must, with a broken and contrite heart, confess our sins to God, 1Jo 1:9. We must confess the fact of sin; and not try to justify or excuse ourselves. We must confess the fault of sin; I have perverted that which was right. We must confess the folly of sin; So foolish have I been and ignorant. Is there not good reason why we should make such a confession?

Verses 29-33

Elihu shows that God's great and gracious design toward the children of men, is, to save them from being for ever miserable, and to bring them to be for ever happy. By whatever means we are kept back from the we shall bless the Lord for them at least, and should bless him for them though they be painful and distressing. Those that perish for ever are without excuse, for they would not be healed.

Chapter 34

Chapter Outline

Verses 1-9

Elihu calls upon those present to decide with him upon Job's words. The plainest Christian, whose mind is enlightened, whose heart is sanctified by the Spirit of God, and who is versed in the Scriptures, can say how far matters, words, or actions, agree with true religion, better than any that lean to their own understandings. Job had spoken as if he meant wholly to justify himself. He that say, I have cleansed my hands in vain, does not only offend against God's children, Ps 73:13–15, but gratifies his enemies, and says as they say.

Verses 10-15

Elihu had showed Job, that God meant him no hurt by afflicting him, but intended his spiritual benefit. Here he shows, that God did him no wrong by afflicting him. If the former did not satisfy him, this ought to silence him. God cannot do wickedness, nor the Almighty commit wrong. If services now go unrewarded, and sins now go unpunished, yet there is a day coming, when God will fully render to every man according to his works. Further, though the believer's final condemnation is done away through the Saviour's ransom, yet he has merited worse than any outward afflictions; so that no wrong is done to him, however he may be tried.

Verses 16-30

Elihu appeals directly to Job himself. Could he suppose that God was like those earthly princes, who hate right, who are unfit to rule, and prove the scourges of mankind? It is daring presumption to condemn God's proceedings, as Job had done by his discontents. Elihu suggests divers considerations to Job, to produce in him high thoughts of God, and so to persuade him to submit. Job had often wished to plead his cause before God. Elihu asks, To what purpose? All is well that God does, and will be found so. What can make those uneasy, whose souls dwell at ease in God? The smiles of all the world cannot quiet those on whom God frowns.

Verses 31-37

When we reprove for what is amiss, we must direct to what is good. Job's friends would have had him own himself a wicked man. Let will only oblige him to own that he spoke unadvisedly with his lips. Let us, in giving reproof, not make a matter worse than it is. Elihu directs Job to humble himself before God for his sins, and to accept the punishment. Also to pray to God to discover his sins to him. A good man is willing to know the worst of himself; particularly, under affliction, he desires to be told wherefore God contends with him. It is not enough to be sorry for our sins, but we must go and sin no more. And if we are affectionate children, we shall love to speak with our Father, and to tell him all our mind. Elihu reasons with Job concerning his discontent under affliction. We are ready to think every thing that concerns us should be just as we would have it; but it is not reasonable to expect this. Elihu asks whether there was not sin and folly in what Job said. God is righteous in all his ways, and holy in all his works, Ps 145:17. The believer saith, Let my Saviour, my wise and loving Lord, choose every thing for me. I am sure that will be wisest, and the best for his glory and my good.

Chapter 35

Chapter Outline

Elihu speaks of man's conduct.	(1–8)
Why those who cry out under afflictions are not regarded.	(9–13)
Elihu reproves Job's impatience.	(14–16)

Verses 1-8

Elihu reproves Job for justifying himself more than God, and called his attention to the heavens. They are far above us, and God is far above them; how much then is he out of the reach, either of our sins or of our services! We have no reason to complain if we have not what we expect, but should be thankful that we have better than we deserve.

Verses 9-13

Job complained that God did not regard the cries of the oppressed against their oppressors. This he knew not how to reconcile the justice of God and his government. Elihu solves the difficulty. Men do not notice the mercies they enjoy in and under their afflictions, nor are thankful for them, therefore they cannot expect that God should deliver them out of affliction. He gives songs in the night; when our condition is dark and melancholy, there is that in God's providence and promise, which is sufficient to support us, and to enable us even to rejoice in tribulation. When we only pore upon our afflictions, and neglect the consolations of God which are treasured up for us, it is just in God to reject our prayers. Even the things that will kill the body, cannot hurt the soul. If we cry to God for the removal of an affliction, and it is not removed, the reason is, not because the Lord's hand is shortened, or his ear heavy; but because we are not sufficiently humbled.

Verses 14-16

As in prosperity we are ready to think our mountain will never be brought low; so when in adversity, we are ready to think our valley will never be filled up. But to conclude that to-morrow must be as this day, is as absurd as to think that the weather, when either fair or foul, will be always so. When Job looked up to God, he had no reason to speak despairingly. There is a day of judgment, when all that seems amiss will be found to be right, and all that seems dark and difficult will be cleared up and set straight. And if there is Divine wrath in our troubles, it is because we quarrel with God, are fretful, and distrust Divine Providence. This was Job's case. Elihu was directed by God to humble Job, for as to some things he had both opened his mouth in vain, and had multiplied words without knowledge. Let us be admonished, in our afflictions, not so much to set forth the greatness of our suffering, as the greatness of the mercy of God.

Chapter 36

Chapter Outline

Verses 1-4

Elihu only maintained that the affliction was sent for his trial; and lengthened because Job was not yet thoroughly humbled under it. He sought to ascribe righteousness to his Maker; to clear this truth, that God is righteous in all his ways. Such knowledge must be learned from the word and Spirit of God, for naturally we are estranged from it. The fitness of Elihu's discourse to the dispute between Job and his friends is plain. It pointed out to Job the true reason of those trials with which he had been pointed out to Job the true reason of those trials with which he had been visited. It taught that God had acted in mercy towards him, and the spiritual benefit he was to derive from them. It corrected the mistake of his friends, and showed that Job's calamities were for good.

Verses 5-14

Elihu here shows that God acts as righteous Governor. He is always ready to defend those that are injured. If our eye is ever toward God in duty, his eye will be ever upon us in mercy, and, when we are at the lowest, will not overlook us. God intends, when he afflicts us, to discover past sins to us, and to bring them to our remembrance. Also, to dispose our hearts to be taught: affliction makes people willing to learn, through the grace of God working with and by it. And further, to deter us from sinning for the future. It is a command, to have no more to do with sin. If we faithfully serve God, we have the promise of the life that now is, and the comforts of it, as far as is for God's glory and our good: and who would desire them any further? We have the possession of inward pleasures, the great peace which those have that love God's law. If the affliction fail in its work, let men expect the furnace to be heated till they are consumed. Those that die without knowledge, die without grace, and are undone for ever. See the nature of hypocrisy; it lies in the heart: that is for the world and the flesh, while perhaps the outside seems to be for God and religion. Whether sinners die in youth, or live long to heap up wrath, their case is dreadful. The souls of the wicked live after death, but it is in everlasting misery.

Verses 15-23

Elihu shows that Job caused the continuance of his own trouble. He cautions him not to persist in frowardness. Even good men need to be kept to their duty by the fear of God's wrath; the wisest and best have enough in them to deserve his stroke. Let not Job continue his unjust quarrel with God and his providence. And let us never dare to think favourably of sin, never indulge it, nor allow ourselves in it. Elihu thinks Job needed this caution, he having chosen rather to gratify his pride and humour by contending with God, than to mortify them by submitting, and accepting the punishment. It is absurd for us to think to teach Him who is himself the Fountain of light, truth, knowledge, and instruction. He teaches by the Bible, and that is the best book; teaches by his Son, and he is the best Master. He is just in all proceedings.

Verses 24-33

Elihu endeavours to fill Job with high thought of God, and so to persuade him into cheerful submission to his providence. Man may see God's works, and is capable of discerning his hand in them, which the beasts are not, therefore they ought to give him the glory. But while the worker of iniquity ought to tremble, the true believer should rejoice. Children should hear with pleasure their Father's voice, even when he speaks in terror to his enemies. There is no light but there may be a cloud to intercept it. The light of the favour of God, the light of his countenance, the most blessed light of all, even that light has many a cloud. The clouds of our sins cause the Lord to his face, and hinder the light of his loving-kindness from shining on our souls.

Chapter 37

Chapter Outline

Elihu observes the power of God.	(1–13)
Job required to explain the works of nature.	(14–20)
God is great, and is to be feared.	(21–24)

Verses 1-13

The changes of the weather are the subject of a great deal of our thoughts and common talk; but how seldom do we think and speak of these things, as Elihu, with a regard to God, the director of them! We must notice the glory of God, not only in the thunder and lightning, but in the more common and less awful changes of the weather; as the snow and rain. Nature directs all creatures to shelter themselves from a storm; and shall man only be unprovided with a refuge? Oh that men would listen to the voice of God, who in many ways warns them to flee from the wrath to come; and invites them to accept his salvation, and to be happy. The ill opinion which men entertain of the Divine direction, peculiarly appears in their murmurs about the weather, though the whole result of the year proves the folly of their complaints. Believers should avoid this; no days are bad as God makes them, though we make many bad by our sins. (Job 37:14-20)

Verses 14-20

Due thoughts of the works of God will help to reconcile us to all his providences. As God has a powerful, freezing north wind, so he has a thawing, composing south wind: the Spirit is compared to both, because he both convinces and comforts, So 4:16. The best of men are much in the dark concerning the glorious perfections of the Divine nature and the Divine government. Those who, through grace, know much of God, know nothing, in comparison with what is to be known, and of what will be known, when that which is perfect is come.

Verses 21-24

Elihu concludes his discourse with some great sayings concerning the glory of God. Light always is, but is not always to be seen. When clouds come between, the sun is darkened in the clear day. The light of God's favour shines ever towards his faithful servants, though it be not always seen. Sins are clouds, and often hinder us from seeing that bright light which is in the face of God. Also, as to those thick clouds of sorrow which often darken our minds, the Lord hath a wind which passes and clears them away. What is that wind? It is his Holy Spirit. As the wind dispels and sweeps away the clouds which are gathered in the air, so the Spirit of God clears our souls from the clouds and fogs of ignorance and unbelief, of sin and lust. From all these clouds the Holy Spirit of God frees us in the work of regeneration. And from all the clouds which trouble our consciences, the Holy Spirit sets us free in the work of consolation. Now that God is about to speak, Elihu delivers a few words, as the sum of all his discourse. With God is terrible majesty. Sooner or later all men shall fear him.

Chapter 38

Chapter Outline

God calls upon Job to answer.	(1–3)
God questions Job.	(4–11)
Concerning the light and darkness.	(12–24)
Concerning other mighty works.	(25–41)

Verses 1-3

Job had silenced, but had not convinced his friends. Elihu had silenced Job, but had not brought him to admit his guilt before God. It pleased the Lord to interpose. The Lord, in this discourse, humbles Job, and brings him to repent of his passionate expressions concerning God's providential dealings with him; and this he does, by calling upon Job to compare God's being from everlasting to everlasting, with his own time; God's knowledge of all things, with his own ignorance; and God's almighty power, with his own weakness. Our darkening the counsels of God's wisdom with our folly, is a great provocation to God. Humble faith and sincere obedience see farthest and best into the will of the Lord.

Verses 4-11

For the humbling of Job, God here shows him his ignorance, even concerning the earth and the sea. As we cannot find fault with God's work, so we need not fear concerning it. The works of his providence, as well as the work of creation, never can be broken; and the work of redemption is no less firm, of which Christ himself is both the Foundation and the Corner-stone. The church stands as firm as the earth.

Verses 12-24

The Lord questions Job, to convince him of his ignorance, and shame him for his folly in prescribing to God. If we thus try ourselves, we shall soon be brought to own that what we know is nothing in comparison with what we know not. By the tender mercy of our God, the Day-spring from on high has visited us, to give light to those that sit in darkness, whose hearts are turned to it as clay to the seal, 2Co 4:6. God's way in the government of the world is said to be in the sea; this means, that it is hid from us. Let us make sure that the gates of heaven shall be opened to us on the other side of death, and then we need not fear the opening of the gates of death. It is presumptuous for us, who perceive not the breadth of the earth, to dive into the depth of God's counsels. We should neither in the brightest noon count upon perpetual day, nor in the darkest midnight despair of the return of the morning; and this applies to our inward as well as to our outward condition. What folly it is to strive against God! How much is it our interest to seek peace with him, and to keep in his love!

Verses 25-41

Hitherto God had put questions to Job to show him his ignorance; now God shows his weakness. As it is but little that he knows, he ought not to arraign the Divine counsels; it is but little he can do, therefore he ought not to oppose the ways of Providence. See the all-sufficiency of the Divine Providence; it has wherewithal to satisfy the desire of every living thing. And he that takes care of the young ravens, certainly will not be wanting to his people. This being but one instance of the Divine compassion out of many, gives us occasion to think how much good our God does, every day, beyond what we are aware of. Every view we take of his infinite perfections, should remind us of his right to our love, the evil of sinning against him, and our need of his mercy and salvation.

Chapter 39

God inquires of Job concerning several animals.

—In these questions the Lord continued to humble Job. In this chapter several animals are spoken of, whose nature or situation particularly show the power, wisdom, and manifold works of God. The wild ass. It is better to labour and be good for something, than to ramble and be good for nothing. From the untameableness of this and other creatures, we may see, how unfit we are to give law to Providence, who cannot give law even to a wild ass's colt. The unicorn, a strong, stately, proud creature. He is able to serve, but not willing; and God challenges Job to force him to it. It is a great mercy if, where God gives strength for service, he gives a heart; it is what we should pray for, and reason ourselves into, which the brutes cannot do. Those gifts are not always the most valuable that make the finest show. Who would not rather have the voice of the nightingale, than the tail of the peacock; the eye of the eagle and her soaring wing, and the natural affection of the stork, than the beautiful feathers of the ostrich, which can never rise above the earth, and is without natural affection? The description of the war-horse helps to explain the character of presumptuous sinners. Every one turneth to his course, as the horse rushes into the battle. When a man's heart is fully set in him to do evil, and he is carried on in a wicked way, by the violence of his appetites and passions, there is no making him fear the wrath of God, and the fatal consequences of sin. Secure sinners think themselves as safe in their sins as the eagle in her nest on high, in the clefts of the rocks; but I will bring thee down from thence, saith the Lord, Jer 49:16. All these beautiful references to the works of nature, should teach us a right view of the riches of the wisdom of Him who made and sustains all things. The want of right views concerning the wisdom of God, which is ever present in all things, led Job to think and speak unworthily of Providence.

Chapter 40

Chapter Outline

Job humbles himself to God.	(1–5)
The Lord reasons with Job to show his righteousness, power, and wisdom.	(6–14)
God's power shown in Behemoth.	(15–24)

Verses 1-5

Communion with the Lord effectually convinces and humbles a saint, and makes him glad to part with his most beloved sins. There is need to be thoroughly convinced and humbled, to prepare us for remarkable deliverances. After God had shown Job, by his manifest ignorance of the works of nature, how unable he was to judge of the methods and designs of Providence, he puts a convincing question to him; Shall he that contendeth with the Almighty instruct him? Now Job began to melt into godly sorrow: when his friends reasoned with him, he did not yield; but the voice of the Lord is powerful. When the Spirit of truth is come, he shall convince. Job yields himself to the grace of God. He owns himself an offender, and has nothing to say to justify himself. He is now sensible that he has sinned; and therefore he calls himself vile. Repentance changes men's opinion of themselves. Job is now convinced of his error. Those who are truly sensible of their own sinfulness and vileness, dare not justify themselves before God. He perceived that he was a poor, mean, foolish, and sinful creature, who ought not to have uttered one word against the Divine conduct. One glimpse of God's holy nature would appal the stoutest rebel. How, then will the wicked bear the sight of his glory at the day of judgment? But when we see this glory revealed in Jesus Christ, we shall be humbled without being terrified; self-abasement agrees with filial love. (Job 40:6-14)

Verses 6-14

Those who profit by what they have heard from God, shall hear more from him. And those who are truly convinced of sin, yet need to be more thoroughly convinced and more humbled. No doubt God, and he only, has power to humble and bring down proud men; he has wisdom to know when and how to do it, and it is not for us to teach him how to govern the world. Our own hands cannot save us by recommending us to God's grace, much less rescuing us from his justice; and therefore into his hand we must commit ourselves. The renewal of a believer proceeds in the same way of conviction, humbling, and watchfulness against remaining sin, as his first conversion. When convinced of many evils in our conduct, we still need convincing of many more.

Verses 15-24

God, for the further proving of his own power, describes two vast animals, far exceeding man in bulk and strength. Behemoth signifies beasts. Most understand it of an animal well known in Egypt, called the river-horse, or hippopotamus. This vast animal is noticed as an argument to humble ourselves before the great God; for he created this vast animal, which is so fearfully and wonderfully made. Whatever strength this or any other creature has, it is derived from God. He that made the soul of man, knows all the ways to it, and can make the sword of justice, his wrath, to approach and touch it. Every godly man has spiritual weapons, the whole armour of God, to resist, yea, to overcome the tempter, that his never-dying soul may be safe, whatever becomes of his frail flesh and mortal body.

Chapter 41

Concerning Leviathan.
—The description of the Leviathan, is yet further to convince Job of his own weakness, and of God's almighty power. Whether this Leviathan be a whale or a crocodile, is disputed. The Lord, having showed Job how unable he was to deal with the Leviathan, sets forth his own power in that mighty creature. If such language describes the terrible force of Leviathan, what words can express the power of God's wrath? Under a humbling sense of our own vileness, let us revere the Divine Majesty; take and fill our allotted place, cease from our own wisdom, and give all glory to our gracious God and Saviour. Remembering from whom every good gift cometh, and for what end it was given, let us walk humbly with the Lord.

Chapter 42

Chapter Outline

Verses 1-6

Job was now sensible of his guilt; he would no longer speak in his own excuse; he abhorred himself as a sinner in heart and life, especially for murmuring against God, and took shame to himself. When the understanding is enlightened by the Spirit of grace, our knowledge of Divine things as far exceeds what we had before, as the sight of the eyes excels report and common fame. By the teachings of men, God reveals his Son to us; but by the teachings of his Spirit he reveals his Son in us, Ga 1:16, and changes us into the same image, 2Co 3:18. It concerns us to be deeply humbled for the sins of which we are convinced. Self-loathing is ever the companion of true repentance. The Lord will bring those whom he loveth, to adore him in self-abasement; while true grace will always lead them to confess their sins without self-justifying.

Verses 7-9

After the Lord had convinced and humbled Job, and brought him to repentance, he owned him, comforted him, and put honour upon him. The devil had undertaken to prove Job a hypocrite, and his three friends had condemned him as a wicked man; but if God say, Well done, thou good and faithful servant, it is of little consequence who says otherwise. Job's friends had wronged God, by making prosperity a mark of the true church, and affliction a certain proof of God's wrath. Job had referred things to the future judgment and the future state, more than his friends, therefore he spake of God that which was right, better than his friends had done. And as Job prayed and offered sacrifice for those that had grieved and wounded his spirit, so Christ prayed for his persecutors, and ever lives, making intercession for the transgressors. Job's friends were good men, and belonged to God, and He would not let them be in their mistake any more than Job; but having humbled him by a discourse out of the whirlwind, he takes another way to humble them. They are not to argue the matter again, but they must agree in a sacrifice and a prayer, and that must reconcile them, Those who differ in judgment about lesser things, yet are one in Christ the great Sacrifice, and ought therefore to love and bear with one another. When God was angry with Job's friends, he put them in a way to make peace with him. Our quarrels with God always begin on our part, but the making peace begins on his. Peace with God is to be had only in his own way, and upon his own terms. These will never seem hard to those who know how to value this blessing: they will be glad of it, like Job's friends, upon any terms, though ever so humbling. Job did not insult over his friends, but God being graciously reconciled to him, he was easily reconciled to them. In all our prayers and services we should aim to be accepted of the Lord; not to have praise of men, but to please God. (Job 42:10-17)

Verses 10-17

In the beginning of this book we had Job's patience under his troubles, for an example; here, for our encouragement to follow that example, we have his happy end. His troubles began in Satan's malice, which God restrained; his restoration began in God's mercy, which Satan could not oppose. Mercy did not return when Job was disputing with his friends, but when he was praying for them. God is served and pleased with our warm devotions, not with our warm disputes. God doubled Job's possessions. We may lose much for the Lord, but we shall not lose any thing by him. Whether the Lord gives us health and temporal blessings or not, if we patiently suffer according to his will, in the end we shall be happy. Job's estate increased. The blessing of the Lord makes rich; it is he that gives us power to get wealth, and gives success in honest endeavours. The last days of a good man sometimes prove his best, his last works his best works, his last comforts his best comforts; for his path, like that of the morning light, shines more and more unto the perfect day.

Psalms

David was the penman of most of the psalms, but some evidently were composed by other writers, and the writers of some are doubtful. But all were written by the inspiration of the Holy Ghost; and no part of the Old Testament is more frequently quoted or referred to in the New. Every psalm either points directly to Christ, in his person, his character, and offices; or may lead the believer's thoughts to Him. And the psalms are the language of the believer's heart, whether mourning for sin, thirsting after God, or rejoicing in Him. Whether burdened with affliction, struggling with temptation, or triumphing in the hope or enjoyment of deliverance; whether admiring the Divine perfections, thanking God for his mercies, mediating on his truths, or delighting in his service; they form a Divinely appointed standard of experience, by which we may judge ourselves. Their value, in this view, is very great, and the use of them will increase with the growth of the power of true religion in the heart. By the psalmist's expressions, the Spirit helps us to pray. If we make the psalms familiar to us, whatever we have to ask at the throne of grace, by way of confession, petition, or thanksgiving, we may be assisted from thence. Whatever devout affection is working in us, holy desire or hope, sorrow or joy, we may here find words to clothe it; sound speech which cannot be condemned. In the language of this Divine book, the prayers and praises of the church have been offered up to the throne of grace from age to age.

Chapter 1

Chapter Outline

The holiness and happiness of a godly man.	(1–3)
The sinfulness and misery of a wicked man, The ground and reason of both.	(4–6)

Verses 1-3

To meditate in God's word, is to discourse with ourselves concerning the great things contained in it, with close application of mind and fixedness of thought. We must have constant regard to the word of God, as the rule of our actions, and the spring of our comforts; and have it in our thoughts night and day. For this purpose no time is amiss.

Verses 4-6

The ungodly are the reverse of the righteous, both in character and condition. The ungodly are not so, ver. 4; they are led by the counsel of the wicked, in the way of sinners, to the seat of the scornful; they have no delight in the law of God; they bring forth no fruit but what is evil. The righteous are like useful, fruitful trees: the ungodly are like the chaff which the wind drives away: the dust which the owner of the floor desires to have driven away, as not being of any use. They are of no worth in God's account, how highly soever they may value themselves. They are easily driven to and fro by every wind of temptation. The chaff may be, for a while, among the wheat, but He is coming, whose fan is in his hand, and who will thoroughly purge his floor. Those that, by their own sin and folly, make themselves as chaff, will be found so before the whirlwind and fire of Divine wrath. The doom of the ungodly is fixed, but whenever the sinner becomes sensible of this guilt and misery, he may be admitted into the company of the righteous by Christ the living way, and become in Christ a new creature. He has new desires, new pleasures, hopes, fears, sorrows, companions, and employments. His thoughts, words, and actions are changed. He enters on a new state, and bears a new character. Behold, all things are become new by Divine grace, which changes his soul into the image of the Redeemer. How different the character and end of the ungodly!

Chapter 2

Chapter Outline

Threatenings against the enemies of Christ's kingdom.	(1–6)
Promise to Christ as the Head of this kingdom.	(7–9)
Counsel to all, to espouse its interests.	(10–12)

Verses 1-6

We are here told who would appear as adversaries to Christ. As this world is the kingdom of Satan, unconverted men, of every rank, party, and character, are stirred up by him to oppose the cause of God. But the rulers of the earth generally have been most active. The truths and precepts of Christianity are against ambitious projects and worldly lusts. We are told what they aim at in this opposition. They would break asunder the bands of conscience, and the cords of God's commandments; they will not receive, but cast them away as far as they can. These enemies can show no good cause for opposing so just and holy a government, which, if received by all, would bring a heaven upon earth. They can hope for no success in so opposing so powerful a kingdom. The Lord Jesus has all power both in heaven and in earth, and is Head over all things to the church, notwithstanding the restless endeavours of his enemies. Christ's throne is set up in his church, that is, in the hearts of all believers.

Verses 7-9

The kingdom of the Messiah is founded upon an eternal decree of God the Father. This our Lord Jesus often referred to, as what he governed himself by. God hath said unto him, Thou art my Son, and it becomes each of us to say to him, Thou art my Lord, my Sovereign'. The Son, in asking the heathen for his inheritance, desires their happiness in him; so that he pleads for them, ever lives to do so, and is able to save to the uttermost, and he shall have multitudes of willing, loyal subjects, among them. Christians are the possession of the Lord Jesus; they are to him for a name and a praise. God the Father gives them to him, when, by his Spirit and grace, he works upon them to submit to the Lord Jesus.

Verses 10-12

Whatever we rejoice in, in this world, it must always be with trembling, because of the uncertainty of all things in it. To welcome Jesus Christ, and to submit to him, is our wisdom and interest. Let him be very dear and precious; love him above all, love him in sincerity, love him much, as she did, to whom much was forgiven, and, in token of it, kissed his feet, Lu 7:38. And with a kiss of loyalty take this yoke upon you, and give up yourselves to be governed by his laws, disposed of by his providence, and entirely devoted to his cause. Unbelief is a sin against the remedy. It will be utter destruction to yourselves; lest ye perish in the way of your sins, and from the way of your vain hopes; lest your way perish, lest you prove to have missed the way of happiness. Christ is the way; take heed lest ye be cut off from Him as your way to God. They thought themselves in the way; but neglecting Christ, they perish from it. Blessed will those be in the day of wrath, who, by trusting in Christ, have made him their Refuge.

Chapter 3

Chapter Outline

David complains to God of his enemies, and   (1–3)
confides in God.

He triumphs over his fears, and gives God   (4–8)
the glory, and takes to himself the comfort.

Verses 1-3

An active believer, the more he is beaten off from God, either by the rebukes of providence, or the reproaches of enemies, the faster hold he will take, and the closer will he cleave to him. A child of God startles at the very thought of despairing of help in God. See what God is to his people, what he will be, what they have found him, what David found in him. 1. Safety; a shield for me; which denotes the advantage of that protection. 2. Honour; those whom God owns for his, have true honour put upon them. 3. Joy and deliverance. If, in the worst of times, God's people can lift up their heads with joy, knowing that all shall work for good to them, they will own God as giving them both cause and hearts to rejoice.

Verses 4-8

Care and grief do us good, when they engage us to pray to God, as in earnest. David had always found God ready to answer his prayers. Nothing can fix a gulf between the communications of God's grace towards us, and the working of his grace in us; between his favour and our faith. He had always been very safe under the Divine protection. This is applicable to the common mercies of every night, for which we ought to give thanks every morning. Many lie down, and cannot sleep, through pain of body, or anguish of mind, or the continual alarms of fear in the night. But it seems here rather to be meant of the calmness of David's spirit, in the midst of his dangers. The Lord, by his grace and the consolations of his Spirit, made him easy. It is a great mercy, when we are in trouble, to have our minds stayed upon God. Behold the Son of David composing himself to his rest upon the cross, that bed of sorrows; commending his Spirit into the Father's hands in full confidence of a joyful resurrection. Behold this, O Christian: let faith teach thee how to sleep, and how to die; while it assures thee that as sleep is a short death, so death is only a longer sleep; the same God watches over thee, in thy bed and in thy grave. David's faith became triumphant. He began the psalm with complaints of the strength and malice of his enemies; but concludes with rejoicing in the power and grace of his God, and now sees more with him than against him. Salvation belongeth unto the Lord; he has power to save, be the danger ever so great. All that have the Lord for their God, are sure of salvation; for he who is their God, is the God of Salvation.

Chapter 4

Chapter Outline

The children of men proved, and the   (1–5)
happiness of godly people.

God's favour is happiness.   (6–8)

Verses 1-5

Hear me for thy mercy-sake, is our best plea. He who will not ask such blessings as pardon, and justifying righteousness, and eternal life, must perish for the want of them. Alas! that so many should make so fearful a choice. The psalmist warns against sin. Keep up holy reverence of the glory and majesty of God. You have a great deal to say to your hearts, they may be spoken with, let it not be unsaid. Examine them by serious self-reflection; let your thoughts fasten upon that which is good, and keep close to it. Consider your ways, and before you turn to sleep at night, examine your consciences with respect to what you have done in the day; particularly what you have done amiss, that you may repent of it. when you awake in the night, meditate upon God, and the things that belong to your peace. Upon a sick-bed, particularly, we should consider our ways. Be still. when you have asked conscience a question, be serious, be silent, wait for an answer. Open not the mouth to excuse sin. All confidence must be pan answer. Open not the mouth to excuse sin. All confidence only: therefore, after commanding the sacrifices of righteousness, the psalmist says, Put your trust in the Lord.

Verses 6-8

Wordly people inquire for good, not for the chief good; all they want is outward good, present good, partial good, good meat, good drink, a good trade, and a good estate; but what are all these worth? Any good will serve the turn of most men, but a gracious soul will not be put off so. Lord, let us have thy favour, and let us know that we have it, we desire no more; let us be satisfied of thy loving-kindness, and will be satisfied with it. Many inquire after happiness, but David had found it. When God puts grace in the heart, he puts gladness in the heart. Thus comforted, he pitied, but neither envied nor feared the most prosperous sinner. He commits all his affairs to God, and is prepared to welcome his holy will. But salvation is in Christ alone; where will those appear who despise him as their Mediator, and revile him in his disciples? May they stand in awe, and no longer sin against the only remedy.

Chapter 5

Chapter Outline

God will certainly hear prayer: David gives to God the glory, and takes to himself the comfort. (1–6)

He prayed for himself, that God would guide him, and for all the Lord's people, that God would give them joy, and keep them safe. (7–12)

Verses 1-6

God is a prayer-hearing God. Such he has always been, and he is still as ready to hear prayer as ever. The most encouraging principle of prayer, and the most powerful plea in prayer, is, to look upon him as our King and our God. David also prays to a sin-hating God. sin is folly, and sinners are the greatest of all fools; fools of their own making. Wicked people hate God; justly are they hated of him, and this will be their endless misery and ruin. Let us learn the importance of truth and sincerity, in all the affairs of life. Liars and murderers resemble the devil, and are his children, therefore it may well be expected that God should abhor them. These were the characters of David's enemies; and such as these are still the enemies of Christ and his people.

Verses 7-12

David prayed often alone, yet was very constant in attendance on public worship. The mercy of God should ever be the foundation both of our hope and of our joy, in every thing wherein we have to do with him. Let us learn to pray, not for ourselves only, but for others; grace be with all that love Christ in sincerity. The Divine blessing comes down upon us through Jesus Christ, the righteous or just One, as of old it did upon Israel through David, whom God protected, and placed upon the throne. Thou, O Christ, art the righteous Saviour, thou art the King of Israel, thou art the Fountain of blessing to all believers; thy favour is the defence and protection of thy church.

Chapter 6

Chapter Outline

The psalmist deprecates God's wrath, and begs for the return of his favour.   (1–7)

He assures himself of an answer of peace.   (8–10)

Verses 1-7

These verses speak the language of a heart truly humbled, of a broken and contrite spirit under great afflictions, sent to awaken conscience and mortify corruption. Sickness brought sin to his remembrance, and he looked upon it as a token of God's displeasure against him. The affliction of his body will be tolerable, if he has comfort in his soul. Christ's sorest complaint, in his sufferings, was of the trouble of his soul, and the want of his Father's smiles. Every page of Scripture proclaims the fact, that salvation is only of the Lord. Man is a sinner, his case can only be reached by mercy; and never is mercy more illustrious than in restoring backsliders. With good reason we may pray, that if it be the will of God, and he has any further work for us or our friends to do in this world, he will yet spare us or them to serve him. To depart and be with Christ is happiest for the saints; but for them to abide in the flesh is more profitable for the church.

Verses 8-10

What a sudden change is here! Having made his request known to God, the psalmist is confident that his sorrow will be turned into joy. By the workings of God's grace upon his heart, he knew his prayer was accepted, and did not doubt but it would, in due time, be answered. His prayers will be accepted, coming up out of the hands of Christ the Mediator. The word signifies prayer made to God, the righteous Judge, as the God of his righteousness, who would plead his cause, and right his wrongs. A believer, through the blood and righteousness of Christ, can go to God as a righteous God, and plead with him for pardon and cleansing, who is just and faithful to grant both. He prays for the conversion of his enemies, or foretells their ruin.

Chapter 7

Chapter Outline

The psalmist prays to God to plead his cause, and judge for him.   (1–9)

He expresses confidence in God, and will give him the glory of his deliverance.   (10–17)

Verses 1-9

David flees to God for succour. But Christ alone could call on Heaven to attest his uprightness in all things. All His works were wrought in righteousness; and the prince of this world found nothing whereof justly to accuse him. Yet for our sakes, submitting to be charged as guilty, he suffered all evils, but, being innocent, he triumphed over them all. The plea is, "For the righteous God trieth the hearts and the reins." He knows the secret wickedness of the wicked, and how to bring it to an end; he is witness to the secret sincerity of the just, and has ways of establishing it. When a man has made peace with God about all his sins, upon the terms of grace and mercy, through the sacrifice of the Mediator, he may, in comparison with his enemies, appeal to God's justice to decide.

Verses 10-17

David is confident that he shall find God his powerful Saviour. The destruction of sinners may be prevented by their conversion; for it is threatened, If he turn not from his evil way, let him expect it will be his ruin. But amidst the threatenings of wrath, we have a gracious offer of mercy. God gives sinners warning of their danger, and space to repent, and prevent it. He is slow to punish, and long-suffering to us-ward, not willing that any should perish. The sinner is described, ver. #(14–16), as taking more pains to ruin his soul than, if directed aright, would save it. This is true, in a sense, of all sinners. Let us look to the Saviour under all our trials. Blessed Lord, give us grace to look to thee in the path of tribulation, going before thy church and people, and marking the way by thine own spotless example. Under all the persecutions which in our lesser trials mark our way, let the looking to Jesus animate our minds and comfort our hearts.

Chapter 8

Chapter Outline

God is to be glorified, for making known himself to us.	(1, 2)
And for making even the heavenly bodies useful to man, thereby placing him but little lower than the angels.	(3–9)

Verses 1, 2

The psalmist seeks to give unto God the glory due to his name. How bright this glory shines even in this lower world! He is ours, for he made us, protects us, and takes special care of us. The birth, life, preaching, miracles, suffering, death, resurrection, and ascension of Jesus are known through the world. No name is so universal, no power and influence so generally felt, as those of the Saviour of mankind. But how much brighter it shines in the upper world! We, on this earth, only hear God's excellent name, and praise that; the angels and blessed spirits above, see his glory, and praise that; yet he is exalted far above even their blessing and praise. Sometimes the grace of God appears wonderfully in young children. Sometimes the power of God brings to pass great things in his church, by very weak and unlikely instruments, that the excellency of the power might the more evidently appear to be of God, and not of man. This he does, because of his enemies, that he may put them to silence.

Verses 3-9

We are to consider the heavens, that man thus may be directed to set his affections on things above. What is man, so mean a creature, that he should be thus honoured! so sinful a creature, that he should be thus favoured! Man has sovereign dominion over the inferior creatures, under God, and is appointed their lord. This refers to Christ. In Heb 2:6–8, the apostle, to prove the sovereign dominion of Christ, shows he is that Man, that Son of man, here spoken of, whom God has made to have dominion over the works of his hands. The greatest favour ever showed to the human race, and the greatest honour ever put upon human nature, were exemplified in the Lord Jesus. With good reason does the psalmist conclude as he began, Lord, how excellent is thy name in all the earth, which has been honoured with the presence of the Redeemer, and is still enlightened by his gospel, and governed by his wisdom and power! What words can reach his praises, who has a right to our obedience as our Redeemer?

Chapter 9

Chapter Outline

David praises God for protecting his people. (1–10)

And for cause to praise him. (11–20)

Verses 1-10

If we would praise God acceptably, we must praise him in sincerity, with our whole heart. When we give thanks for some one particular mercy, we should remember former mercies. Our joy must not be in the gift, so much as in the Giver. The triumphs of the Redeemer ought to be the triumphs of the redeemed. The almighty power of God is that which the strongest and stoutest of his enemies are no way able to stand before. We are sure that the judgment of God is according to truth, and that with him there is no unrighteousness. His people may, by faith, flee to him as their Refuge, and may depend on his power and promise for their safety, so that no real hurt shall be done to them. Those who know him to be a God of truth and faithfulness, will rejoice in his word of promise, and rest upon that. Those who know him to be an everlasting Father, will trust him with their souls as their main care, and trust in him at all times, even to the end; and by constant care seek to approve themselves to him in the whole course of their lives. Who is there that would not seek him, who never hath forsaken those that seek Him?

Verses 11-20

Those who believe that God is greatly to be praised, not only desire to praise him better themselves, but desire that others may join with them. There is a day coming, when it will appear that he has not forgotten the cry of the humble; neither the cry of their blood, or the cry of their prayers. We are never brought so low, so near to death, but God can raise us up. If he has saved us from spiritual and eternal death, we may thence hope, that in all our distresses he will be a very present help to us. The overruling providence of God frequently so orders it, that persecutors and oppressors are brought to ruin by the projects they formed to destroy the people of God. Drunkards kill themselves; prodigals beggar themselves; the contentious bring mischief upon themselves: thus men's sins may be read in their punishment, and it becomes plain to all, that the destruction of sinners is of themselves. All wickedness came originally with the wicked one from hell; and those who continue in sin, must go to that place of torment. The true state, both of nations and of individuals, may be correctly estimated by this one rule, whether in their doings they remember or forget God. David encourages the people of God to wait for his salvation, though it should be long deferred. God will make it appear that he never did forget them: it is not possible he should. Strange that man, dust in his and about him, should yet need some sharp affliction, some severe visitation from God, to bring him to the knowledge of himself, and make him feel who and what he is.

Chapter 10

Chapter Outline

The psalmist complains of the wickedness of the wicked.	(1–11)
He prays to God to appear for the relief of his people.	(12–18)

Verses 1-11

God's withdrawings are very grievous to his people, especially in times of trouble. We stand afar off from God by our unbelief, and then complain that God stands afar off from us. Passionate words against bad men do more hurt than good; if we speak of their badness, let it be to the Lord in prayer; he can make them better. The sinner proudly glories in his power and success. Wicked people will not seek after God, that is, will not call upon him. They live without prayer, and that is living without God. They have many thoughts, many objects and devices, but think not of the Lord in any of them; they have no submission to his will, nor aim for his glory. The cause of this is pride. Men think it below them to be religious. They could not break all the laws of justice and goodness toward man, if they had not first shaken off all sense of religion.

Verses 12-18

The psalmist speaks with astonishment, at the wickedness of the wicked, and at the patience and forbearance of God. God prepares the heart for prayer, by kindling holy desires, and strengthening our most holy faith, fixing the thoughts, and raising the affections, and then he graciously accepts the prayer. The preparation of the heart is from the Lord, and we must seek unto him for it. Let the poor, afflicted, persecuted, or tempted believer recollect, that Satan is the prince of this world, and that he is the father of all the ungodly. The children of God cannot expect kindness, truth, or justice from such persons as crucified the Lord of glory. But this once suffering Jesus, now reigns as King over all the earth, and of his dominion there shall be no end. Let us commit ourselves unto him, humbly trusting in his mercy. He will rescue the believer from every temptation, and break the arm of every wicked oppressor, and bruise Satan under our feet shortly. But in heaven alone will all sin and temptation be shut out, though in this life the believer has a foretaste of deliverance.

Chapter 11

David's struggle with, and triumph over a strong temptation to distrust God, and betake himself to indirect means for his own safety, in a time of danger.

—Those that truly fear God and serve him, are welcome to put their trust in him. The psalmist, before he gives an account of his temptation to distrust God, records his resolution to trust in Him, as that by which he was resolved to live and die. The believer, though not terrified by his enemies, may be tempted, by the fears of his friends, to desert his post, or neglect his work. They perceive his danger, but not his security; they give him counsel that savours of worldly policy, rather than of heavenly wisdom. The principles of religion are the foundations on which the faith and hope of the righteous are built. We are concerned to hold these fast against all temptations to unbelief; for believers would be undone, if they had not God to go to, God to trust in, and future bliss to hope for. The prosperity of wicked people in their wicked, evil ways, and the straits and distresses which the best men are sometimes brought into, tried David's faith. We need not say, Who shall go up to heaven, to fetch us thence a God to trust in? The word is nigh us, and God in the word; his Spirit is in his saints, those living temples, and the Lord is that Spirit. This God governs the world. We may know what men seem to be, but God knows what they are, as the refiner knows the value of gold when he has tried it. God is said to try with his eyes, because he cannot err, or be imposed upon. If he afflicts good people, it is for their trial, therefore for their good. However persecutors and oppressors may prosper awhile, they will for ever perish. God is a holy God, and therefore hates them. He is a righteous Judge, and will therefore punish them. In what a horrible tempest are the wicked hurried away at death! Every man has the portion of his cup assigned him. Impenitent sinner, mark your doom! The last call to repentance is about to be addressed to you, judgement is at hand; through the gloomy shade of death you pass into the region of eternal wrath. Hasten then, O sinner, to the cross of Christ. How stands the case between God and our souls? Is Christ our hope, our consolation, our security? Then, not otherwise, will the soul be carried through all its difficulties and conflicts.

Chapter 12

The psalmist begs help of God, because there were none among men whom he durst trust.
—This psalm furnishes good thoughts for bad times; a man may comfort himself with such meditations and prayers. Let us see what makes the times bad, and when they may be said to be so. Ask the children of this world, What makes the times bad? they will tell you, Scarcity of money, decay of trade, and the desolations of war, make the times bad: but the Scripture lays the badness of the times on causes of another nature, 2Ti 3:1, &c.: perilous times shall come, for sin shall abound; and of this David complains. When piety decays times really are bad. He who made man's mouth will call him to an account for his proud, profane, dissembling, or even useless words. When the poor and needy are oppressed, then the times are very bad. God himself takes notice of the oppression of the poor, and the sighing of the needy. When wickedness abounds, and is countenanced by those in authority, then the times are very bad. See with what good things we are here furnished for such bad times; and we cannot tell what times we may be reserved for. 1. We have a God to go to, from whom we may ask and expect the redress of all our grievances. 2. God will certainly punish and restrain false and proud men. 3. God will work deliverance for his oppressed people. His help is given in the fittest time. Though men are false, God is faithful; though they are not to be trusted, God is. The preciousness of God's word is compared to silver refined to the highest degree. How many proofs have been given of its power and truth! God will secure his chosen remnant, however bad the times are. As long as the world stands, there will be a generation of proud and wicked men. But all God's people are put into the hands of Christ our Saviour; there they are in safety, for none can pluck them thence; being built on Him, the Rock, they are safe, notwithstanding temptation or persecution come with ever so much force upon them.

Chapter 13

The psalmist complains that God had long withdrawn. He earnestly prays for comfort. He assures himself of an answer of peace.
—God sometimes hides his face, and leaves his own children in the dark concerning their interest in him: and this they lay to heart more than any outward trouble whatever. But anxious cares are heavy burdens with which believers often load themselves more than they need. The bread of sorrows is sometimes the saint's daily bread; our Master himself was a man of sorrows. It is a common temptation, when trouble lasts long, to think that it will last always. Those who have long been without joy, begin to be without hope. We should never allow ourselves to make any complaints but what drive us to our knees. Nothing is more killing to a soul than the want of God's favour; nothing more reviving than the return of it. The sudden, delightful changes in the book of Psalms,

are often very remarkable. We pass from depth of despondency to the height of religious confidence and joy. It is thus, ver. 5. All is gloomy dejection in ver. 4; but here the mind of the despondent worshipper rises above all its distressing fears, and throws itself, without reserve, on the mercy and care of its Divine Redeemer. See the power of faith, and how good it is to draw near to God. If we bring our cares and griefs to the throne of grace, and leave them there, we may go away like Hannah, and our countenances will be no more said, 1Sa 1:18. God's mercy is the support of the psalmist's faith. Finding I have that to trust to, I am comforted, though I have no merit of my own. His faith in God's mercy filled his heart with joy in his salvation; for joy and peace come by believing. He has dealt bountifully with me. By faith he was as confident of salvation, as if it had been completed already. In this way believers pour out their prayers, renouncing all hopes but in the mercy of God through the Saviour's blood: and sometimes suddenly, at others gradually, they will find their burdens removed, and their comforts restored; they then allow that their fears and complaints were unnecessary, and acknowledge that the Lord hath dealt bountifully with them.

Chapter 14

A description of the depravity of human nature, and the deplorable corruption of a great part of mankind.

—The fool hath said in his heart, There is no God. The sinner here described is an atheist, one that saith there is no Judge or Governor of the world, no Providence ruling over the affairs of men. He says this in his heart. He cannot satisfy himself that there is none, but wishes there were none, and pleases himself that it is possible there may be none; he is willing to think there is none. This sinner is a fool; he is simple and unwise, and this is evidence of it: he is wicked and profane, and this is the cause. The word of God is a discerner of these thoughts. No man will say, There is no God, till he is so hardened in sin, that it is become his interest that there should be none to call him to an account. The disease of sin has infected the whole race of mankind. They are all gone aside, there is none that doeth good, no, not one. Whatever good is in any of the children of men, or is done by them, it is not of themselves, it is God's work in them. They are gone aside from the right way of their duty, the way that leads to happiness, and are turned into the paths of the destroyer. Let us lament the corruption of our nature, and see what need we have of the grace of God: let us not marvel that we are told we must be born again. And we must not rest in any thing short of union with Christ, and a new creation to holiness by his Spirit. The psalmist endeavours to convince sinners of the evil and danger of their way, while they think themselves very wise, and good, and safe. Their wickedness is described. Those that care not for God's people, for God's poor, care not for God himself. People run into all manner of wickedness, because they do not call upon God for his grace. What good can be expected from those that live without prayer? But those that will not fear God, may be made to fear at the shaking of a leaf. All our knowledge of the depravity of human nature should endear to us salvation out of Zion. But in heaven alone shall the whole company of the redeemed rejoice fully, and for evermore. The world is bad; oh that the Messiah would come and change its character! There is universal corruption; oh for the times of reformation! The triumphs of Zion's King will be the joys of Zion's children. The second coming of Christ, finally to do away the dominion of sin and Satan, will be the completing of this salvation, which is the hope, and will be the joy of every Israelite indeed. With this assurance we should comfort ourselves and one another, under the sins of sinners and sufferings of saints.

Chapter 15

The way to heaven, if we would be happy, we must be holy. We are encouraged to walk in that way.

—Here is a very serious question concerning the character of a citizen of Zion. It is the happiness of glorified saints, that they dwell in the holy hill; they are at home there, they shall be for ever there. It concerns us to make it sure to ourselves that we have a place among them. A very plain and particular answer is here given. Those who desire to know their duty, will find the Scripture a very faithful director, and conscience a faithful monitor. A citizen of Zion is sincere in his religion. He is really what he professes to be, and endeavours to stand complete in all the will of God. He is just both to God and man; and, in speaking to both, speaks the truth in his heart. He scorns and abhors wrong and fraud; he cannot reckon that a good bargain, nor a saving one, which is made with a lie; and knows that he who wrongs his neighbour will prove, in the end, to have most injured himself. He is very careful to do hurt to no man. He speaks evil of no man, makes not others' faults the matter of his common talk; he makes the best of every body, and the worst of nobody. If an ill-natured story be told him, he will disprove it if he can; if not, it goes no further. He values men by their virtue and piety. Wicked people are vile people, worthless, and good for nothing; so the word signifies. He thinks the worse of no man's piety for his poverty and mean condition. He reckons that serious piety puts honour upon a man, more than wealth, or a great name. He honours such, desires their conversation and an interest in their prayers, is glad to show them respect, or do them a kindness. By this we may judge of ourselves in some measure. Even wise and good men may swear to their own hurt: but see how strong the obligation is, a man must rather suffer loss to himself and his family, than wrong his neighbour. He will not increase his estate by extortion, or by bribery. He will not, for any gain, or hope of it to himself, do any thing to hurt a righteous cause. Every true living member of the church, like the church itself, is built upon a Rock. He that doeth these things shall not be moved for ever. The grace of God shall always be sufficient for him. The union of these tempers and this conduct, can only spring from repentance for sin, faith in the Saviour, and love to him. In these respects let us examine and prove our own selves.

Chapter 16

This psalm begins with expressions of devotion, which may be applied to Christ; but ends with such confidence of a resurrection, as must be applied to Christ, and to him only.

—David flees to God's protection, with cheerful, believing confidence. Those who have avowed that the Lord is their Lord, should often put themselves in mind of what they have done, take the comfort of it, and live up to it. He devotes himself to the honour of God, in the service of the saints. Saints on earth we must be, or we shall never be saints in heaven. Those renewed by the grace of God, and devoted to the glory of God, are saints on earth. The saints in the earth are excellent ones, yet some of them so poor, that they needed to have David's goodness extended to them. David declares his resolution to have no fellowship with the works of darkness; he repeats the solemn choice he had made of God for his portion and happiness, takes to himself the comfort of the choice, and gives God the glory of it. This is the language of a devout and pious soul. Most take the world for their chief good, and place their happiness in the enjoyments of it; but how poor soever my condition is in this world, let me have the love and favour of God, and be accepted of him; let me have a title by promise to life and happiness in the future state; and I have enough. Heaven is an inheritance; we must take that for our home, our rest, our everlasting good, and look upon this world to be no more ours, than the country through which is our road to our Father's house. Those that have God for their portion, have a goodly heritage. Return unto thy rest, O my soul, and look no further. Gracious persons, though they still covet more of God, never covet more than God; but, being satisfied of his loving-kindness, are abundantly satisfied with it: they envy not any their carnal mirth and delights. But so ignorant and foolish are we, that if left to ourselves, we shall forsake our own mercies for lying vanities. God having given David counsel by his word and Spirit, his own thoughts taught him in the night season, and engaged him by faith to live to God. Verses #(8–11), are quoted by St. Peter in his first sermon, after the pouring out of the Spirit on the day of Pentecost, Ac 2:25–31; he declared that David in them speaks concerning Christ, and particularly of his resurrection. And Christ being the Head of the body, the church, these verses may be applied to all Christians, guided and animated by the Spirit of Christ; and we may hence learn, that it is our wisdom and duty to set the Lord always before us. And if our eyes are ever toward God, our hearts and tongues may ever rejoice in him. Death destroys the hope of man, but not the hope of a real Christian. Christ's resurrection is an earnest of the believer's resurrection. In this world sorrow is our lot, but in heaven there is joy, a fulness of joy; our pleasures here are for a moment, but those at God's right hand are pleasures for evermore. Through this thy beloved Son, and our dear Saviour, thou wilt show us, O Lord, the path of life; thou wilt justify our souls now, and raise our bodies by thy power at the last day; when earthly sorrow shall end in heavenly joy, pain in everlasting happiness.

Chapter 17

Chapter Outline

David's integrity.   (1–7)

The character of his enemies. His hope of   (8–15)
happiness.

Verses 1-7

This psalm is a prayer. Feigned prayers are fruitless; but if our hearts lead our prayers, God will meet them with his favour. The psalmist had been used to pray, so that it was not his distress and danger that now first brought him to his duty. And he was encouraged by his faith to expect God would notice his prayers. Constant resolution and watchfulness against sins of the tongue, will be a good evidence of our integrity. Aware of man's propensity to wicked works, and of his own peculiar temptations, David had made God's word his preservative from the paths of Satan, which lead to destruction. If we carefully avoid the paths of sin, it will be very lead to destruction. If we carefully avoid the paths of sin, it will be very comfortable in the reflection, when we are in trouble. Those that are, through grace, going in God's paths, should pray that their goings may be held up in those paths. David prays, Lord, still hold me up. Those who would proceed and persevere in the ways of God, must, by faith prayer, get daily fresh supplies of grace and strength from him. Show thy marvellous loving-kindness, distinguishing favours, not common mercies, but be gracious to me; do as thou usest to do to those who love thy name.

Verses 8-15

Being compassed with enemies, David prays to God to keep him in safety. This prayer is a prediction that Christ would be preserved, through all the hardships and difficulties of his humiliation, to the glories and joys of his exalted state, and is a pattern to Christians to commit the keeping of their souls to God, trusting him to preserve them to his heavenly kingdom. Those are our worst enemies, that are enemies to our souls. They are God's sword, which cannot move without him, and which he will sheathe when he has done his work with it. They are his hand, by which he chastises his people. There is no fleeing from God's hand, but by fleeing to it. It is very comfortable, when we are in fear of the power of man, to see it dependent upon, and in subjection to the power of God. Most men look on the things of this world as the best things; and they look no further, nor show any care to provide for another life. The things of this world are called treasures, they are so accounted; but to the soul, and when compared with eternal blessings, they are trash. The most afflicted Christian need not envy the most prosperous men of the world, who have their portion in this life. Clothed with Christ's righteousness, having through his grace a good heart and a good life, may we by faith behold God's face, and set him always before us. When we awake every morning, may we be satisfied with his likeness set before us in his word, and with his likeness stamped upon us by his renewing grace. Happiness in the other world is prepared only for those that are justified and sanctified: they shall be put in possession of it when the soul awakes, at death, out of its slumber in the body, and when the body awakes, at the resurrection, out of its slumber in the grave. There is no satisfaction for a soul but in God, and in his good will towards us, and his good work in us; yet that satisfaction will not be perfect till we come to heaven.

Chapter 18

Chapter Outline

David rejoices in the deliverances God   (1–19)
wrought for him.

He takes the comfort of his integrity, which   (20–28)
God had cleared up.

He gives to God the glory of all his mighty   (29–50)
deeds.

Verses 1-19

The first words, "I will love thee, O Lord, my strength," are the scope and contents of the psalm. Those that truly love God, may triumph in him as their Rock and Refuge, and may with confidence call upon him. It is good for us to observe all the circumstances of a mercy which magnify the power of God and his goodness to us in it. David was a praying man, and God was found a prayer-hearing God. If we pray as he did, we shall speed as he did. God's manifestation of his presence is very fully described, ver. #(7–15). Little appeared of man, but much of God, in these deliverances. It is not possible to apply to the history of the son of Jesse those awful, majestic, and stupendous words which are used through this description of the Divine manifestation. Every part of so solemn a scene of terrors tells us, a greater than David is here. God will not only deliver his people out of their troubles in due time, but he will bear them up under their troubles in the mean time. Can we meditate on ver. 18, without directing one thought to Gethsemane and Calvary? Can we forget that it was in the hour of Christ's deepest calamity, when Judas betrayed, when his friends forsook, when the multitude derided him, and the smiles of his Father's love were withheld, that the powers of darkness prevented him? The sorrows of death surrounded him, in his distress he prayed, Heb 5:7. God made the earth to shake and tremble, and the rocks to cleave, and brought him out, in his resurrection, because he delighted in him and in his undertaking.

Verses 20-28

Those that forsake the ways of the Lord, depart from their God. But though conscious to ourselves of many a false step, let there not be a wicked departure from our God. David kept his eye upon the rule of God's commands. Constant care to keep from that sin, whatever it be, which most easily besets us, proves that we are upright before God. Those who show mercy to others, even they need mercy. Those who are faithful to God, shall find him all that to them which he has promised to be. The words of the Lord are pure words, very sure to be depended on, and very sweet to be delighted in. Those who resist God, and walk contrary to him, shall find that he will walk contrary to them, Le 26:21–24. The gracious recompence of which David spoke, may generally be expected by those who act from right motives. Hence he speaks comfort to the humble, and terror to the proud; "Thou wilt bring down high looks." And he speaks encouragement to himself; "Thou wilt light my candle:" thou wilt revive and comfort my sorrowful spirit; thou wilt guide my way, that I may avoid the snares laid for me. Thou wilt light my candle to work by, and give me an opportunity of serving thee. Let those that walk in darkness, and labour under discouragements, take courage; God himself will be a Light to them.

Verses 29-50

When we praise for one mercy, we must observe the many more, with which we have been compassed all our days. Many things had contributed to David's advancement, and he owns the hand of God in them all, to teach us to do likewise. In verse #(32), and the following verses, are the gifts of God to the spiritual warrior, whereby he is prepared for the contest, after the example of his victorious Leader. Learn that we must seek release being made through Christ, shall be rejected. In David the type, we behold out of trouble through Christ. The prayer put up, without reconciliation Jesus our Redeemer, conflicting with enemies, compassed with sorrows and with floods of ungodly men, enduring not only the pains of death, but the wrath of God for us; yet calling upon the Father with strong cries and tears; rescued from the grave; proceeding to reconcile, or to put under his feet all other enemies, till death, the last enemy, shall be destroyed. We should love the Lord, our Strength, and our Salvation; we should call on him in every trouble, and praise him for every deliverance; we should aim to walk with him in all righteousness and true holiness, keeping from sin. If we belong to him, he conquers and reigns for us, and we shall conquer and reign through him, and partake of the mercy of our anointed King, which is promised to all his seed for evermore. Amen.

Chapter 19

Chapter Outline

The glory of God's works.	(1–6)
His holiness and grace as shown in his word.	(7–10)
Prayer for the benefit of them.	(11–14)

Verses 1-6

The heavens so declare the glory of God, and proclaim his wisdom, power, and goodness, that all ungodly men are left without excuse. They speak themselves to be works of God's hands; for they must have a Creator who is eternal, infinitely wise, powerful, and good. The counter-changing of day and night is a great proof of the power of God, and calls us to observe, that, as in the kingdom of nature, so in that of providence, he forms the light, and creates the darkness, Isa 45:7, and sets the one against the other. The sun in the firmament is an emblem of the Sun of righteousness, the Bridegroom of the church, and the Light of the world, diffusing Divine light and salvation by his gospel to the nations of the earth. He delights to bless his church, which he has espoused to himself; and his course will be unwearied as that of the sun, till the whole earth is filled with his light and salvation. Let us pray for the time when he shall enlighten, cheer, and make fruitful every nation on earth, with the blessed salvation. They have no speech or language, so some read it, and yet their voice is heard. All people may hear these preachers speak in their own tongue the wonderful works of God. Let us give God the glory of all the comfort and benefit we have by the lights of heaven, still looking above and beyond them to the Sun of righteousness.

Verses 7-10

The Holy Scripture is of much greater benefit to us than day or night, than the air we breathe, or the light of the sun. To recover man out of his fallen state, there is need of the word of God. The word translated "law," may be rendered doctrine, and be understood as meaning all that teaches us true religion. The whole is perfect; its tendency is to convert or turn the soul from sin and the world, to God and holiness. It shows our sinfulness and misery in departing from God, and the necessity of our return to him. This testimony is sure, to be fully depended on: the ignorant and unlearned believing what God saith, become wise unto salvation. It is a sure direction in the way of duty. It is a sure fountain of living comforts, and a sure foundation of lasting hopes. The statues of the Lord are right, just as they should be; and, because they are right, they rejoice the heart. The commandments of the Lord are pure, holy, just, and good. By them we discover our need of a Saviour; and then learn how to adorn his gospel. They are the means which the Holy Spirit uses in enlightening the eyes; they bring us to a sight and sense of our sin and misery, and direct us in the way of duty. The fear of the Lord, that is, true religion and godliness, is clean, it will cleanse our way; and it endureth for ever. The ceremonial law is long since done away, but the law concerning the fear of God is ever the same. The judgments of the Lord, his precepts, are true; they are righteous, and they are so altogether; there is no unrighteousness in any of them. Gold is only for the body, and the concerns of time; but grace is for the soul, and the concerns of eternity. The word of God, received by faith, is more precious than gold; it is sweet to the soul, sweeter than honey. The pleasure of sense soon surfeit, yet never satisfy; but those of religion are substantial and satisfying; there is no danger of excess.

Verses 11-14

God's word warns the wicked not to go on in his wicked way, and warns the righteous not to turn from his good way. There is a reward, not only after keeping, but in keeping God's commandments. Religion makes our comforts sweet, and our crosses easy, life truly valuable, and death itself truly desirable. David not only desired to be pardoned and cleansed from the sins he had discovered and confessed, but from those he had forgotten or overlooked. All discoveries of sin made to us by the law, should drive us to the throne of grace, there to pray. His dependence was the same with that of every Christian who says, Surely in the Lord Jesus have I righteousness and strength. No prayer can be acceptable before God which is not offered in the strength of our Redeemer or Divine Kinsman, through Him who took our nature upon him, that he might redeem us unto God, and restore the long-lost inheritance. May our hearts be much affected with the excellence of the word of God; and much affected with the evil of sin, and the danger we are in of it, and the danger we are in by it.

Chapter 20

This psalm is a prayer for the kings of Israel, but with relation to Christ.

—Even the greatest of men may be much in trouble. Neither the crown on the king's head, nor the grace in his heart, would make him free from trouble. Even the greatest of men must be much in prayer. Let none expect benefit by the prayers of the church, or their friends, who are capable of praying for themselves, yet neglect it. Pray that God would protect his person, and preserve his life. That God would enable him to go on in his undertakings for the public good. We may know that God accepts our spiritual sacrifices, if by his Spirit he kindles in our souls a holy fire of piety and love to God. Also, that the Lord would crown his enterprises with success. Our first step to victory in spiritual warfare is to trust only in the mercy and grace of God; all who trust in themselves will soon be cast down. Believers triumph in God, and his revelation of himself to them, by which they distinguish themselves from those that live without God in the world. Those who make God and his name their praise, may make God and his name their trust. This was the case when the pride and power of Jewish unbelief, and pagan idolatry, fell before the sermons and lives of the humble believers in Jesus. This is the case in every conflict with our spiritual enemies, when we engage them in the name, the spirit, and the power of Christ; and this will be the case at the last day, when the world, with the prince of it, shall be brought down and fall; but believers, risen-from the dead, through the resurrection of the Lord, shall stand, and sing his praises in heaven. In Christ's salvation let us rejoice; and set up our banners in the name of the Lord our God, assured that by the saving strength of his right hand we shall be conquerors over every enemy.

Chapter 21

Chapter Outline

Thanksgiving for victory.   (1–6)

Confidence of further success.   (7–13)

Verses 1-6

Happy the people whose king makes God's strength his confidence, and God's salvation his joy; who is pleased with all the advancements of God kingdom, and trusts God to support him in all he does for the service of it. All our blessings are blessings of goodness, and are owing, not to any merit of ours, but only to God's goodness. But when God's blessings come sooner, and prove richer than we imagine; when they are given before we prayed for them, before we were ready for them, nay, when we feared the contrary; then it may be truly said that he prevented, or went before us, with them. Nothing indeed prevented, or went before Christ, but to mankind never was any favour more preventing than our redemption by Christ. Thou hast made him to be a universal, everlasting blessing to the world, in whom the families of the earth are, and shall be blessed; and so thou hast made him exceeding glad with the countenance thou hast given to his undertaking, and to him in the prosecution of it. The Spirit of prophecy rises from what related to the king, to that which is peculiar to Christ; none other is blessed for ever, much less a blessing for ever.

Verses 7-13

The psalmist teaches to look forward with faith, and hope, and prayer upon what God would further do. The success with which God blessed David, was a type of the total overthrow of all Christ's enemies. Those who might have had Christ to rule and save them, but rejected him and fought against him, shall find the remembrance of it a worm that dies not. God makes sinners willing by his grace, receives them to his favour, and delivers them from the wrath to come. May he exalt himself, by his all-powerful grace, in our hearts, destroying all the strong-holds of sin and Satan. How great should be our joy and praise to behold our Brother and Friend upon the throne, and for all the blessings we may expect from him! yet he delights in his exalted state, as enabling him to confer happiness and glory on poor sinners, who are taught to love and trust in him.

Chapter 22

Chapter Outline

Verses 1-10

The Spirit of Christ, which was in the prophets, testifies in this psalm, clearly and fully, the sufferings of Christ, and the glory that should follow. We have a sorrowful complaint of God's withdrawings. This may be applied to any child of God, pressed down, overwhelmed with grief and terror. Spiritual desertions are the saints' sorest afflictions; but even their complaint of these burdens is a sign of spiritual life, and spiritual senses exercised. To cry our, My God, why am I sick? why am I poor? savours of discontent and worldliness. But, "Why hast thou forsaken me?" is the language of a heart binding up its happiness in God's favour. This must be applied to Christ. In the first words of this complaint, he poured out his soul before God when he was upon the cross, Mt 27:46. Being truly man, Christ felt a natural unwillingness to pass through such great sorrows, yet his zeal and love prevailed. Christ declared the holiness of God, his heavenly Father, in his sharpest sufferings; nay, declared them to be a proof of it, for which he would be continually praised by his Israel, more than for all other deliverances they received. Never any that hoped in thee, were made ashamed of their hope; never any that sought thee, sought thee in vain. Here is a complaint of the contempt and reproach of men. The Saviour here spoke of the abject state to which he was reduced. The history of Christ's sufferings, and of his birth, explains this prophecy.

Verses 11-21

In these verses we have Christ suffering, and Christ praying; by which we are directed to look for crosses, and to look up to God under them. The very manner of Christ's death is described, though not in use among the Jews. They pierced his hands and his feet, which were nailed to the accursed tree, and his whole body was left so to hang as to suffer the most severe pain and torture. His natural force failed, being wasted by the fire of Divine wrath preying upon his spirits. Who then can stand before God's anger? or who knows the power of it? The life of the sinner was forfeited, and the life of the Sacrifice must be the ransom for it. Our Lord Jesus was stripped, when he was crucified, that he might clothe us with the robe of his righteousness. Thus it was written, therefore thus it behoved Christ to suffer. Let all this confirm our faith in him as the true Messiah, and excite our love to him as the best of friends, who loved us, and suffered all this for us. Christ in his agony prayed, prayed earnestly, prayed that the cup might pass from him. When we cannot rejoice in God as our song, yet let us stay ourselves upon him as our strength; and take the comfort of spiritual supports, when we cannot have spiritual delights. He prays to be delivered from the Divine wrath. He that has delivered, doth deliver, and will do so. We should think upon the sufferings and resurrection of Christ, till we feel in our souls the power of his resurrection, and the fellowship of his sufferings.

Verses 22-31

The Saviour now speaks as risen from the dead. The first words of the complaint were used by Christ himself upon the cross; the first words of the triumph are expressly applied to him, Heb 2:12. All our praises must refer to the work of redemption. The suffering of the Redeemer was graciously accepted as a full satisfaction for sin. Though it was offered for sinful men, the Father did not despise or abhor it for our sakes. This ought to be the matter of our thanksgiving. All humble, gracious souls should have a full satisfaction and happiness in him. Those that hunger and thirst after righteousness in Christ, shall not labour for that which satisfies not. Those that are much in praying, will be much in thanksgiving. Those that turn to God, will make conscience of worshipping before him. Let every tongue confess that he is Lord. High and low, rich and poor, bond and free, meet in Christ. Seeing we cannot keep alive our own souls, it is our wisdom, by obedient faith, to commit our souls to Christ, who is able to save and keep them alive for ever. A seed shall serve him. God will have a church in the world to the end of time. They shall be accounted to him for a generation; he will be the same to them that he was to those who went before them. His righteousness, and not any of their own, they shall declare to be the foundation of all their hopes, and the fountain of all their joys. Redemption by Christ is the Lord's own doing. Here we see the free love and compassion of God the Father, and of our Lord Jesus Christ, for us wretched sinners, as the source of all grace and consolation; the example we are to follow, the treatment as Christians we are to expect, and the conduct under it we are to adopt. Every lesson may here be learned that can profit the humbled soul. Let those who go about to establish their own righteousness inquire, why the beloved Son of God should thus suffer, if their own doings could atone for sin? Let the ungodly professor consider whether the Saviour thus honoured the Divine law, to purchase him the privilege of despising it. Let the careless take warning to flee from the wrath to come, and the trembling rest their hopes upon this merciful Redeemer. Let the tempted and distressed believer cheerfully expect a happy end of every trial.

Chapter 23

Confidence in God's grace and care.
—"The Lord is my shepherd." In these words, the believer is taught to express his satisfaction in the care of the great Pastor of the universe, the Redeemer and Preserver of men. With joy he reflects that he has a shepherd, and that shepherd is Jehovah. A flock of sheep, gentle and harmless, feeding in verdant pastures, under the care of a skilful, watchful, and tender shepherd, forms an emblem of believers brought back to the Shepherd of their souls. The greatest abundance is but a dry pasture to a wicked man, who relishes in it only what pleases the senses; but to a godly man, who by faith tastes the goodness of God in all his enjoyments, though he has but little of the world, it is a green pasture. The Lord gives quiet and contentment in the mind, whatever the lot is. Are we blessed with the green pastures of the ordinances, let us not think it enough to pass through them, but let us abide in them. The consolations of the Holy Spirit are the still waters by which the saints are led; the streams which flow from the Fountain of living waters. Those only are led by the still waters of comfort, who walk in the paths of righteousness. The way of duty is the truly pleasant way. The work of righteousness in peace. In these paths we cannot walk, unless. God lead us into them, and lead us on in them. Discontent and distrust proceed from unbelief; an unsteady walk is the consequence: let us then simply trust our Shepherd's care, and hearken to his voice. The valley of the shadow of death may denote the most severe and terrible affliction, or dark dispensation of providence, that the psalmist ever could come under. Between the part of the flock on earth and that which is gone to heaven, death lies like a dark valley that must be passed in going from one to the other. But even in this there are words which lessen the terror. It is but the shadow of death: the shadow of a serpent will not sting, nor the shadow of a sword kill. It is a valley, deep indeed, and dark, and miry; but valleys are often fruitful, and so is death itself fruitful of comforts to God's people. It is a walk through it: they shall not be lost in this valley, but get safe to the mountain on the other side. Death is a king of terrors, but not to the sheep of Christ. When they come to die, God will rebuke the enemy; he will guide them with his rod, and sustain them with his staff. There is enough in the gospel to comfort the saints when dying, and underneath them are the everlasting arms. The Lord's people feast at his table, upon the provisions of his love. Satan and wicked men are not able to destroy their comforts, while they are anointed with the Holy Spirit, and drink of the cup of salvation which is ever full. Past experience teaches believers to trust that the goodness and mercy of God will follow them all the days of their lives, and it is their desire and determination, to seek their happiness in the service of God here, and they hope to enjoy his love for ever in heaven. While here, the Lord can make any situation pleasant, by the anointing of his Spirit and the joys of his salvation. But those that would be satisfied with the blessings of his house, must keep close to the duties of it.

Chapter 24

Chapter Outline

Verses 1-6

We ourselves are not our own; our bodies, our souls, are not. Even those of the children of men are God's, who know him not, nor own their relation to him. A soul that knows and considers its own nature, and that it must live for ever, when it has viewed the earth and the fulness thereof, will sit down unsatisfied. It will think of ascending toward God, and will ask, What shall I do, that I may abide in that happy, holy place, where he makes his people holy and happy? We make nothing of religion, if we do not make heart-work of it. We can only be cleansed from our sins, and renewed unto holiness, by the blood of Christ and the washing of the Holy Ghost. Thus we become his people; thus we receive blessing from the Lord, and righteousness from the God of our salvation. God's peculiar people shall be made truly and for ever happy. Where God gives righteousness, he designs salvation. Those that are made meet for heaven, shall be brought safe to heaven, and will find what they have been seeking.

Verses 7-10

The splendid entry here described, refers to the solemn bringing in of the ark into the tent David pitched for it, or the temple Solomon built for it. We may also apply it to the ascension of Christ into heaven, and the welcome given to him there. Our Redeemer found the gates of heaven shut, but having by his blood made atonement for sin, as one having authority, he demanded entrance. The angels were to worship him, Heb 1:6: they ask with wonder, Who is he? It is answered, that he is strong and mighty; mighty in battle to save his people, and to subdue his and their enemies. We may apply it to Christ's entrance into the souls of men by his word and Spirit, that they may be his temples. Behold, he stands at the door, and knocks, Rev 3:20. The gates and doors of the heart are to be opened to him, as possession is delivered to the rightful owner. We may apply it to his second coming with glorious power. Lord, open the everlasting door of our souls by thy grace, that we may now receive thee, and be wholly thine; and that, at length, we may be numbered with thy saints in glory.

Chapter 25

Chapter Outline

Verses 1-7

In worshipping God, we must lift up our souls to him. It is certain that none who, by a believing attendance, wait on God, and, by a believing hope, wait for him, shall be ashamed of it. The most advanced believer both needs and desires to be taught of God. If we sincerely desire to know our duty, with resolution to do it, we may be sure that God will direct us in it. The psalmist is earnest for the pardon of his sins. When God pardons sin, he is said to remember it no more, which denotes full remission. It is God's goodness, and not ours, his mercy, and not our merit, that must be our plea for the pardon of sin, and all the good we need. This plea we must rely upon, feeling our own unworthiness, and satisfied of the riches of God's mercy and grace. How boundless is that mercy which covers for ever the sins and follies of a youth spent without God and without hope! Blessed be the Lord, the blood of the great Sacrifice can wash away every stain.

Verses 8-14

We are all sinners; and Christ came into the world to save sinners, to teach sinners, to call sinners to repentance. We value a promise by the character of him that makes it; we therefore depend upon God's promises. All the paths of the Lord, that is, all his promises and all his providences, are mercy and truth. In all God's dealings his people may see his mercy displayed, and his word fulfilled, whatever afflictions they are now exercised with. All the paths of the Lord are mercy and truth; and so it will appear when they come to their journey's end. Those that are humble, that distrust themselves, and desire to be taught and to follow Divine guidance, these he will guide in judgment, that is, by the rule of the written word, to find rest for their souls in the Saviour. Even when the body is sick, and in pain, the soul may be at ease in God.

Verses 15-22

The psalmist concludes, as he began, with expressing dependence upon God, and desire toward him. It is good thus to hope, and quietly to wait for the salvation of the Lord. And if God turns to us, no matter who turns from us. He pleads his own integrity. Though guilty before God, yet, as to his enemies, he had the testimony of conscience that he had done them no wrong. God would, at length, give Israel rest from all their enemies round about. In heaven, God's Israel will be perfectly redeemed from all troubles. Blessed Saviour, thou hast graciously taught us that without thee we can do nothing. Do thou teach us how to pray, how to appear before thee in the way which thou shalt choose, and how to lift up our whole hearts and desires after thee, for thou art the Lord our righteousness.

Chapter 26

David, in this psalm, appeals to God touching his integrity.

—David here, by the Spirit of prophecy, speaks of himself as a type of Christ, of whom what he here says of his spotless innocence was fully and eminently true, and of Christ only, and to Him we may apply it. We are complete in him. The man that walks in his integrity, yet trusting wholly in the grace of God, is in a state of acceptance, according to the covenant of which Jesus was the Mediator, in virtue of his spotless obedience even unto death. This man desires to have his inmost soul searched and proved by the Lord. He is aware of the deceitfulness of his own heart; he desires to detect and mortify every sin; and he longs to be satisfied of his being a true believer, and to practise the holy commands of God. Great care to avoid bad company, is both a good evidence of our integrity, and a good means to keep us in it. Hypocrites and dissemblers may be found attending on God's ordinances; but it is a good sign of sincerity, if we attend upon them, as the psalmist here tells us he did, in the exercise of repentance and conscientious obedience. He feels his ground firm under him; and, as he delights in blessing the Lord with his congregations on earth, he trusts that shortly he shall join the great assembly in heaven, in singing praises to God and to the Lamb for evermore.

Chapter 27

Chapter Outline

The psalmist's faith.   (1–6)

His desire toward God, and expectation from   (7–14)
him.

Verses 1-6

The Lord, who is the believer's light, is the strength of his life; not only by whom, but in whom he lives and moves. In God let us strengthen ourselves. The gracious presence of God, his power, his promise, his readiness to hear prayer, the witness of his Spirit in the hearts of his people; these are the secret of his tabernacle, and in these the saints find cause for that holy security and peace of mind in which they dwell at ease. The psalmist prays for constant communion with God in holy ordinances. All God's children desire to dwell in their Father's house. Not to sojourn there as a wayfaring man, to tarry but for a night; or to dwell there for a time only, as the servant that abides not in the house for ever; but to dwell there all the days of their life, as children with a father. Do we hope that the praising of God will be the blessedness of our eternity? Surely then we ought to make it the business of our time. This he had at heart more than any thing. Whatever the Christian is as to this life, he considers the favour and service of God as the one thing needful. This he desires, prays for and seeks after, and in it he rejoices.

Verses 7-14

Wherever the believer is, he can find a way to the throne of grace by prayer. God calls us by his Spirit, by his word, by his worship, and by special providences, merciful and afflicting. When we are foolishly making court to lying vanities, God is, in love to us, calling us to seek our own mercies in him. The call is general, "Seek ye my face;" but we must apply it to ourselves, "I will seek it." The word does us no good, when we do not ourselves accept the exhortation: a gracious heart readily answers to the call of a gracious God, being made willing in the day of his power. The psalmist requests the favour of the Lord; the continuance of his presence with him; the benefit of Divine guidance, and the benefit of Divine protection. God's time to help those that trust in him, is, when all other helpers fail. He is a surer and better Friend than earthly parents are, or can be. What was the belief which supported the psalmist? That he should see the goodness of the Lord. There is nothing like the believing hope of eternal life, the foresights of that glory, and foretastes of those pleasures, to keep us from fainting under all calamities. In the mean time he should be strengthened to bear up under his burdens. Let us look unto the suffering Saviour, and pray in faith, not to be delivered into the hands of our enemies. Let us encourage each other to wait on the Lord, with patient expectation, and fervent prayer.

Chapter 28

Chapter Outline

Verses 1-5

David is very earnest in prayer. Observe his faith in prayer; God is my rock, on whom I build my hope. Believers should not rest till they have received some token that their prayers are heard. He prays that he may not be numbered with the wicked. Save me from being entangled in the snares they have laid for me. Save me from being infected with their sins, and from doing as they do. Lord, never leave me to use such arts of deceit and treachery for my safety, as they use for my ruin. Believers dread the way of sinners; the best are sensible of the danger they are in of being drawn aside: we should all pray earnestly to God for his grace to keep us. Those who are careful not to partake with sinners in their sins, have reason to hope that they shall not receive their plagues. He speaks of the just judgments of the Lord on the workers of iniquity, ver. #(4). This is not the language of passion or revenge. It is a prophecy that there will certainly come a day, when God will punish every man who persists in his evil deeds. Sinners shall be reckoned with, not only for the mischief they have done, but for the mischief they designed, and did what they could to effect. Disregard of the works of the Lord, is the cause of the sin of sinners, and becomes the cause of their ruin.

Verses 6-9

Has God heard our supplications? Let us then bless his name. The Lord is my strength, to support me, and carry me on through all my services and sufferings. The heart that truly believes, shall in due time greatly rejoice: we are to expect joy and peace in believing. God shall have the praise of it: thus must we express our gratitude. The saints rejoice in others' comfort as well as their own: we have the less benefit from the light of the sun, nor from the light of God's countenance, for others' sharing therein. The psalmist concludes with a short, but comprehensive prayer. God's people are his inheritance, and precious in his eyes. He prays that God would save them; that he would bless them with all good, especially the plenty of his ordinances, which are food to the soul. And direct their actions and overrule their affairs for good. Also, lift them up for ever; not only those of that age, but his people in every age to come; lift them up as high as heaven. There, and there only, will saints be lifted up for ever, never more to sink, or be depressed. Save us, Lord Jesus, from our sins; bless us, thou Son of Abraham, with the blessing of righteousness; feed us, thou good Shepherd of the sheep, and lift us up for ever from the dust, O thou, who art the Resurrection and the Life.

Chapter 29

Exhortation to give glory to God.
—The mighty and honourable of the earth are especially bound to honour and worship him; but, alas, few attempt to worship him in the beauty of holiness. When we come before him as the Redeemer of sinners, in repentance faith, and love, he will accept our defective services, pardon the sin that cleaves to them, and approve of that measure of holiness which the Holy Spirit enables us to exercise. We have here the nature of religious worship; it is giving to the Lord the glory due to his name. We must be holy in all our religious services, devoted to God, and to his will and glory. There is a beauty in holiness, and that puts beauty upon all acts of worship. The psalmist here sets forth God's dominion in the kingdom of nature. In the thunder, and lightning, and storm, we may see and hear his glory. Let our hearts be thereby filled with great, and high, and honourable thoughts of God, in the holy adoring of whom, the power of godliness so much consists. O Lord our God, thou art very great! The power of the lightning equals the terror of the thunder. The fear caused by these effects of the Divine power, should remind us of the mighty power of God, of man's weakness, and of the defenceless and desperate condition of the wicked in the day of judgment. But the effects of the Divine word upon the souls of men, under the power of the Holy Spirit, are far greater than those of thunder storms in the nature world. Thereby the stoutest are made to tremble, the proudest are cast down, the secrets of the heart are brought to light, sinners are converted, the savage, sensual, and unclean, become harmless, gentle, and pure. If we have heard God's voice, and have fled for refuge to the hope set before us, let us remember that children need not fear their Father's voice, when he speaks in anger to his enemies. While those tremble who are without shelter, let those who abide in his appointed refuge bless him for their security, looking forward to the day of judgment without dismay, safe as Noah in the ark.

Chapter 30

Chapter Outline

Praise to God for deliverance.   (1–5)

Others encouraged by his example.   (6–12)

Verses 1-5

The great things the Lord has done for us, both by his providence and by his grace, bind us in gratitude to do all we can to advance his kingdom among men, though the most we can do is but little. God's saints in heaven sing to him; why should not those on earth do the same? Not one of all God's perfections carries in it more terror to the wicked, or more comfort to the godly, than his holiness. It is a good sign that we are in some measure partakers of his holiness, if we can heartily rejoice at the remembrance of it. Our happiness is bound up in the Divine favour; if we have that, we have enough, whatever else we want; but as long as God's anger continues, so long the saints' weeping continues.

Verses 6-12

When things are well with us, we are very apt to think that they will always be so. When we see our mistake, it becomes us to think with shame upon our carnal security as our folly. If God hide his face, a good man is troubled, though no other calamity befal him. But if God, in wisdom and justice, turn from us, it will be the greatest folly if we turn from him. No; let us learn to pray in the dark. The sanctified spirit, which returns to God, shall praise him, shall be still praising him; but the services of God's house cannot be performed by the dust; it cannot praise him; there is none of that device or working in the grave, for it is the land of silence. We ask aright for life, when we do so that we may live to praise him. In due time God delivered the psalmist out of his troubles. Our tongue is our glory, and never more so than when employed in praising God. He would persevere to the end in praise, hoping that he should shortly be where this would be the everlasting work. But let all beware of carnal security. Neither outward prosperity, nor inward peace, here, are sure and lasting. The Lord, in his favour, has fixed the believer's safety firm as the deep-rooted mountains, but he must expect to meet with temptations and afflictions. When we grow careless, we fall into sin, the Lord hides his face, our comforts droop, and troubles assail us.

Chapter 31

Chapter Outline

Confidence in God.   (1–8)

Prayer in trouble.   (9–18)

Praise for God's goodness.   (19–24)

Verses 1-8

Faith and prayer must go together, for the prayer of faith is the prevailing prayer. David gave up his soul in a special manner to God. And with the words, ver. 5, our Lord Jesus yielded up his last breath on the cross, and made his soul a free-will offering for sin, laying down his life as a ransom. But David is here as a man in distress and trouble. And his great care is about his soul, his spirit, his better part. Many think that while perplexed about their worldly affairs, and their cares multiply, they may be excused if they neglect their souls; but we are the more concerned to look to our souls, that, though the outward man perish, the inward man may suffer no damage. The redemption of the soul is so precious, that it must have ceased for ever, if Christ had not undertaken it. Having relied on God's mercy, he will be glad and rejoice in it. God looks upon our souls, when we are in trouble, to see whether they are humbled for sin, and made better by the affliction. Every believer will meet with such dangers and deliverances, until he is delivered from death, his last enemy.

Verses 9-18

David's troubles made him a man of sorrows. Herein he was a type of Christ, who was acquainted with grief. David acknowledged that his afflictions were merited by his own sins, but Christ suffered for ours. David's friends durst not give him any assistance. Let us not think it strange if thus deserted, but make sure of a Friend in heaven who will not fail. God will be sure to order and dispose all for the best, to all those who commit their spirits also into his hand. The time of life is in God's hands, to lengthen or shorten, make bitter or sweet, according to the counsel of his will. The way of man is not in himself, nor in our friend's hands, nor in our enemies' hands, but in God's. In this faith and confidence he prays that the Lord would save him for his mercies's sake, and not for any merit of his own. He prophesies the silencing of those that reproach and speak evil of the people of God. There is a day coming, when the Lord will execute judgment upon them. In the mean time, we should engage ourselves by well-doing, if possible, to silence the ignorance of foolish men.

Verses 19-24

Instead of yielding to impatience or despondency under our troubles, we should turn our thoughts to the goodness of the Lord towards those who fear and trust in Him. All comes to sinners through the wondrous gift of the only-begotten Son of God, to be the atonement for their sins. Let not any yield to unbelief, or think, under discouraging circumstances, that they are cut off from before the eyes of the Lord, and left to the pride of men. Lord, pardon our complaints and fears; increase our faith, patience, love, and gratitude; teach us to rejoice in tribulation and in hope. The deliverance of Christ, with the destruction of his enemies, ought to strengthen and comfort the hearts of believers under all their afflictions here below, that having suffered courageously with their Master, they may triumphantly enter into his joy and glory.

Chapter 32

Chapter Outline

Verses 1, 2

Sin is the cause of our misery; but the true believer's transgressions of the Divine law are all forgiven, being covered with the atonement. Christ bare his sins, therefore they are not imputed to him. The righteousness of Christ being reckoned to us, and we being made the righteousness of God in him, our iniquity is not imputed, God having laid upon him the iniquity of us all, and made him a sin-offering for us. Not to impute sin, is God's act, for he is the Judge. It is God that justifies. Notice the character of him whose sins are pardoned; he is sincere, and seeks sanctification by the power of the Holy Ghost. He does not profess to repent, with an intention to indulge in sin, because the Lord is ready to forgive. He will not abuse the doctrine of free grace. And to the man whose iniquity is forgiven, all manner of blessings are promised.

Verses 3-7

It is very difficult to bring sinful man humbly to accept free mercy, with a full confession of his sins and self-condemnation. But the true and only way to peace of conscience, is, to confess our sins, that they may be forgiven; to declare them that we may be justified. Although repentance and confession do not merit the pardon of transgression, they are needful to the real enjoyment of forgiving mercy. And what tongue can tell the happiness of that hour, when the soul, oppressed by sin, is enabled freely to pour forth its sorrows before God, and to take hold of his covenanted mercy in Christ Jesus! Those that would speed in prayer, must seek the Lord, when, by his providence, he calls them to seek him, and, by his Spirit, stirs them up to seek him. In a time of finding, when the heart is softened with grief, and burdened with guilt; when all human refuge fails; when no rest can be found to the troubled mind, then it is that God applies the healing balm by his Spirit.

Verses 8-11

God teaches by his word, and guides with the secret intimations of his will. David gives a word of caution to sinners. The reason for this caution is, that the way of sin will certainly end in sorrow. Here is a word of comfort to saints. They may see that a life of communion with God is far the most pleasant and comfortable. Let us rejoice, O Lord Jesus, in thee, and in thy salvation; so shall we rejoice indeed.

Chapter 33

Chapter Outline

God to be praised.   (1–11)

His people encouraged by his power.   (12–22)

Verses 1-11

Holy joy is the heart and soul of praise, and that is here pressed upon the righteous. Thankful praise is the breath and language of holy joy. Religious songs are proper expressions of thankful praise. Every endowment we possess, should be employed with all our skill and earnestness in God's service. His promises are all wise and good. His word is right, and therefore we are only in the right when we agree with it. His works are all done in truth. He is the righteous Lord, therefore loveth righteousness. What a pity it is that this earth, which is so full of the proofs and instances of God's goodness, should be so empty of his praises; and that of the multitudes who live upon his bounty, there are so few who live to his glory! What the Lord does, he does to purpose; it stands fast. He overrules all the counsels of men, and makes them serve his counsels; even that is fulfilled, which to us is most surprising, the eternal counsel of God, nor can any thing prevent its coming to pass.

Verses 12-22

All the motions and operations of the souls of men, which no mortals know but themselves, God knows better than they do. Their hearts, as well as their times, are all in his hand; he formed the spirit of each man within him. All the powers of the creature depend upon him, and are of no account, of no avail at all, without him. If we make God's favour sure towards us, then we need not fear whatever is against us. We are to give to him the glory of his special grace. All human devices for the salvation of our souls are vain; but the Lord's watchful eye is over those whose conscientious fear of his name proceeds from a believing hope in his mercy. In difficulties they shall be helped; in dangers they shall not receive any real damage. Those that fear God and his wrath, must hope in God and his mercy; for there is no flying from him, but by flying to him. Let thy mercy, O Lord, be upon us; let us always have the comfort and benefit, not according to our merits, but according to the promise which thou hast in thy word given to us, and according to the faith thou hast by thy Spirit and grace wrought in us.

Chapter 34

Chapter Outline

David praises God, and encourages to trust   (1–10)
him.

He exhorts to fear.   (11–22)

Verses 1-10

If we hope to spend eternity in praising God, it is fit that we should spend much of our time here in this work. He never said to any one, Seek ye me in vain. David's prayers helped to silence his fears; many besides him have looked unto the Lord by faith and prayer, and it has wonderfully revived and comforted them. When we look to the world, we are perplexed, and at a loss. But on looking to Christ depends our whole salvation, and all things needful thereunto do so also. This poor man, whom no man looked upon with any respect, or looked after with any concern, was yet welcome to the throne of grace; the Lord heard him, and saved him out of all his troubles. The holy angels minister to the saints, and stand for them against the powers of darkness. All the glory be to the Lord of the angels. By taste and sight we both make discoveries, and have enjoyment; Taste and see God's goodness; take notice of it, and take the comfort of it. He makes all truly blessed that trust in him. As to the things of the other world, they shall have grace sufficient for the support of spiritual life. And as to this life, they shall have what is necessary from the hand of God. Paul had all, and abounded, because he was content, Php 4:11–18. Those who trust to themselves, and think their own efforts sufficient for them, shall want; but they shall be fed who trust in the Lord. Those shall not want, who with quietness work, and mind their own business.

Verses 11-22

Let young persons set out in life with learning the fear of the Lord, if they desire true comfort here, and eternal happiness hereafter. Those will be most happy who begin the soonest to serve so good a Master. All aim to be happy. Surely this must look further than the present world; for man's life on earth consists but of few days, and those full of trouble. What man is he that would see the good of that where all bliss is perfect? Alas! few have this good in their thoughts. That religion promises best which creates watchfulness over the heart and over the tongue. It is not enough not to do hurt, we must study to be useful, and to live to some purpose; we must seek peace and pursue it; be willing to deny ourselves a great deal for peace' sake. It is the constant practice of real believers, when in distress, to cry unto God, and it is their constant comfort that he hears them. The righteous are humbled for sin, and are low in their own eyes. Nothing is more needful to true godliness than a contrite heart, broken off from every self-confidence. In this soil every grace will flourish, and nothing can encourage such a one but the free, rich grace of the gospel of Jesus Christ. The righteous are taken under the special protection of the Lord, yet they have their share of crosses in this world, and there are those that hate them. Both from the mercy of Heaven, and the malice of hell, the afflictions of the righteous must be many. But whatever troubles befal them, shall not hurt their souls, for God keeps them from sinning in troubles. No man is desolate, but he whom God has forsaken.

Chapter 35

Chapter Outline

Verses 1-10

It is no new thing for the most righteous men, and the most righteous cause, to meet with enemies. This is a fruit of the old enmity in the seed of the serpent against the Seed of the woman. David in his afflictions, Christ in his sufferings, the church under persecution, and the Christian in the hour temptation, all beseech the Almighty to appear in their behalf, and to vindicate their cause. We are apt to justify uneasiness at the injuries men do us, by our never having given them cause to use us so ill; but this should make us easy, for then we may the more expect that God will plead our cause. David prayed to God to manifest himself in his trial. Let me have inward comfort under all outward troubles, to support my soul. If God, by his Spirit, witness to our spirits that he is our salvation, we need desire no more to make us happy. If God is our Friend, no matter who is our enemy. By the Spirit of prophecy, David foretells the just judgments of God that would come upon his enemies for their great wickedness. These are predictions, they look forward, and show the doom of the enemies of Christ and his kingdom. We must not desire or pray for the ruin of any enemies, except our lusts and the evil spirits that would compass our destruction. A traveller benighted in a bad road, is an expressive emblem of a sinner walking in the slippery and dangerous ways of temptation. But David having committed his cause to God, did not doubt of his own deliverance. The bones are the strongest parts of the body. The psalmist here proposes to serve and glorify God with all his strength. If such language may be applied to outward salvation, how much more will it apply to heavenly things in Christ Jesus!

Verses 11-16

Call a man ungrateful, and you can call him no worse: this was the character of David's enemies. Herein he was a type of Christ. David shows how tenderly he had behaved towards them in afflictions. We ought to mourn for the sins of those who do not mourn for themselves. We shall not lose by the good offices we do to any, how ungrateful soever they may be. Let us learn to possess our souls in patience and meekness like David, or rather after Christ's example.

Verses 17-28

Though the people of God are, and study to be, quiet, yet it has been common for their enemies to devise deceitful matters against them. David prays, My soul is in danger, Lord, rescue it; it belongs to thee the Father of spirits, therefore claim thine own; it is thine, save it! Lord, be not far from me, as if I were a stranger. He who exalted the once suffering Redeemer, will appear for all his people: the roaring lion shall not destroy their souls, any more than he could that of Christ, their Surety. They trust their souls in his hands, they are one with him by faith, are precious in his sight, and shall be rescued from destruction, that they may give thanks in heaven.

Chapter 36

Chapter Outline

The bad state of the wicked. (1–4)

The goodness of God. (5–12)

Verses 1-4

From this psalm our hearts should be duly affected with hatred of sin, and seek satisfaction in God's loving-kindness. Here is the root of bitterness, from which all the wickedness of wicked men comes. It takes rise from contempt of God, and the want of due regard to him. Also from the deceit they put upon their own souls. Let us daily beg of God to preserve us from self-flattery. Sin is very hurtful to the sinner himself, and therefore ought to be hateful; but it is not so. It is no marvel, if those that deceive themselves, seek to deceive all mankind; to whom will they be true, who are false to their own souls? It is bad to do mischief, but worse to devise it, to do it with plot and management. If we willingly banish holy meditations in our solitary hours, Satan will soon occupy our minds with sinful imaginations. Hardened sinners stand to what they have done, as though they could justify it before God himself.

Verses 5-12

Men may shut up their compassion, yet, with God we shall find mercy. This is great comfort to all believers, plainly to be seen, and not to be taken away. God does all wisely and well; but what he does we know not now, it is time enough to know hereafter. God's loving-kindness is precious to the saints. They put themselves under his protection, and then are safe and easy. Gracious souls, though still desiring more of God, never desire more than God. The gifts of Providence so far satisfy them, that they are content with such things as they have. The benefit of holy ordinances is sweet to a sanctified soul, and strengthening to the spiritual and Divine life. But full satisfaction is reserved for the future state. Their joys shall be constant. God not only works in them a gracious desire for these pleasures, but by his Spirit fills their souls with joy and peace in believing. He quickens whom he will; and whoever will, may come, and take from him of the waters of life freely. May we know, and love, and uprightly serve the Lord; then no proud enemy, on earth or from hell, shall separate us from his love. Faith calleth things that are not, as though they were. It carries us forward to the end of time; it shows us the Lord, on his throne of judgment; the empire of sin fallen to rise no more.

Chapter 37

David persuades to patience and confidence in God, by the state of the godly and of the wicked.

Verses 1-6

When we look abroad we see the world full of evil-doers, that flourish and live in ease. So it was seen of old, therefore let us not marvel at the matter. We are tempted to fret at this, to think them the only happy people, and so we are prone to do like them: but this we are warned against. Outward prosperity is fading. When we look forward, with an eye of faith, we shall see no reason to envy the wicked. Their weeping and wailing will be everlasting. The life of religion is a believing trust in the Lord, and diligent care to serve him according to his will. It is not trusting God, but tempting him, if we do not make conscience of our duty to him. A man's life consists not in abundance, but, Thou shalt have food convenient for thee. This is more than we deserve, and it is enough for one that is going to heaven. To delight in God is as much a privilege as a duty. He has not promised to gratify the appetites of the body, and the humours of the fancy, but the desires of the renewed, sanctified soul. What is the desire of the heart of a good man? It is this, to know, and love, and serve God. Commit thy way unto the Lord; roll thy way upon the Lord, so the margin reads it. Cast thy burden upon the Lord, the burden of thy care. We must roll it off ourselves, not afflict and perplex ourselves with thoughts about future events, but refer them to God. By prayer spread thy case and all thy cares before the Lord, and trust in him. We must do our duty, and then leave the event with God. The promise is very sweet: He shall bring that to pass, whatever it is, which thou has committed to him.

Verses 7-20

Let us be satisfied that God will make all to work for good to us. Let us not discompose ourselves at what we see in this world. A fretful, discontented spirit is open to many temptations. For, in all respects, the little which is allotted to the righteous, is more comfortable and more profitable than the ill-gotten and abused riches of ungodly men. It comes from a hand of special love. God provides plentifully and well, not only for his working servants, but for his waiting servants. They have that which is better than wealth, peace of mind, peace with God, and then peace in God; that peace which the world cannot give, and which the world cannot have. God knows the believer's days. Not one day's work shall go unrewarded. Their time on earth is reckoned by days, which will soon be numbered; but heavenly happiness shall be for ever. This will be a real support to believers in evil times. Those that rest on the Rock of ages, have no reason to envy the wicked the support of their broken reeds.

Verses 21-33

The Lord our God requires that we do justly, and render to all their due. It is a great sin for those that are able, to deny the payment of just debts; it is a great misery not to be able to pay them.

He that is truly merciful, will be ever merciful. We must leave our sins; learn to do well, and cleave to it. This is true religion. The blessing of God is the spring, sweetness, and security of all earthly enjoyments. And if we are sure of this, we are sure not to want any thing good for us in this world. By his grace and Holy Spirit, he directs the thoughts, affections, and designs of good men. By his providence he overrules events, so as to make their way plain. He does not always show them his way for a distance, but leads them step by step, as children are led. God will keep them from being ruined by their falls, either into sin or into trouble, though such as fall into sin will be sorely hurt. Few, if any, have known the consistent believer, or his children, reduced to abject, friendless want. God forsakes not his saints in affliction; and in heaven only the righteous shall dwell for ever; that will be their everlasting habitation. A good man may fall into the hands of a messenger of Satan, and be sorely buffeted, but God will not leave him in his enemy's hands.

Verses 34-40

Duty is ours, and we must mind it; but events are God's, we must refer the disposal of them to him. What a striking picture is in ver. #(35, 36), of many a prosperous enemy of God! But God remarkably blights the projects of the prosperous wicked, especially persecutors. None are perfect in themselves, but believers are so in Christ Jesus. If all the saint's days continue dark and cloudy, his dying day may prove comfortable, and his sun set bright; or, if it should set under a cloud, yet his future state will be everlasting peace. The salvation of the righteous will be the Lord's doing. He will help them to do their duties, to bear their burdens; help them to bear their troubles well, and get good by them, and, in due time, will deliver them out of their troubles. Let sinners then depart from evil, and do good; repent of and forsake sin, and trust in the mercy of God through Jesus Christ. Let them take his yoke upon them, and learn of him, that they may dwell for evermore in heaven. Let us mark the closing scenes of different characters, and always depend on God's mercy.

Chapter 38

Chapter Outline

God's displeasure at sin. (1–11)

The psalmist's sufferings and prayers. (12–22)

Verses 1-11

Nothing will disquiet the heart of a good man so much as the sense of God's anger. The way to keep the heart quiet, is to keep ourselves in the love of God. But a sense of guilt is too heavy to bear; and would sink men into despair and ruin, unless removed by the pardoning mercy of God. If there were not sin in our souls, there would be no pain in our bones, no illness in our bodies. The guilt of sin is a burden to the whole creation, which groans under it. It will be a burden to the sinners themselves, when they are heavy-laden under it, or a burden of ruin, when it sinks them to hell.

When we perceive our true condition, the Good Physician will be valued, sought, and obeyed. Yet many let their wounds rankle, because they delay to go to their merciful Friend. When, at any time, we are distempered in our bodies, we ought to remember how God has been dishonoured in and by our bodies. The groanings which cannot be uttered, are not hid from Him that searches the heart, and knows the mind of the Spirit. David, in his troubles, was a type of Christ in his agonies, of Christ on his cross, suffering and deserted.

Verses 12-22

Wicked men hate goodness, even when they benefit by it. David, in the complaints he makes of his enemies, seems to refer to Christ. But our enemies do us real mischief only when they drive us from God and our duty. The true believer's trouble will be made useful; he will learn to wait for his God, and will not seek relief from the world or himself. The less we notice the unkindness and injuries that are done us, the more we consult the quiet of our own minds. David's troubles were the chastisement and the consequence of his transgressions, whilst Christ suffered for our sins and ours only. What right can a sinner have to yield to impatience or anger, when mercifully corrected for his sins? David was very sensible of the present workings of corruption in him. Good men, by setting their sorrow continually before them, have been ready to fall; but by setting God always before them, they have kept their standing. If we are truly penitent for sin, that will make us patient under affliction. Nothing goes nearer to the heart of a believer when in affliction, than to be under the apprehension of God's deserting him; nor does any thing come more feelingly from his heart than this prayer, "Be not far from me." The Lord will hasten to help those who trust in him as their salvation.

Chapter 39

Chapter Outline

Verses 1-6

If an evil thought should arise in the mind, suppress it. Watchfulness in the habit, is the bridle upon the head; watchfulness in acts, is the hand upon the bridle. When not able to separate from wicked men, we should remember they will watch our words, and turn them, if they can, to our disadvantage. Sometimes it may be necessary to keep silence, even from good words; but in general we are wrong when backward to engage in edifying discourse. Impatience is a sin that has its cause within ourselves, and that is, musing; and its ill effects upon ourselves, and that is no less than burning. In our greatest health and prosperity, every man is altogether vanity, he cannot live long; he may die soon. This is an undoubted truth, but we are very unwilling to believe it. Therefore let us pray that God would enlighten our minds by his Holy Spirit, and fill our hearts with his grace, that we may be ready for death every day and hour.

Verses 7-13

There is no solid satisfaction to be had in the creature; but it is to be found in the Lord, and in communion with him; to him we should be driven by our disappointments. If the world be nothing but vanity, may God deliver us from having or seeking our portion in it. When creature-confidences fail, it is our comfort that we have a God to go to, a God to trust in. We may see a good God doing all, and ordering all events concerning us; and a good man, for that reason, says nothing against it. He desires the pardoning of his sin, and the preventing of his shame. We must both watch and pray against sin. When under the correcting hand of the Lord, we must look to God himself for relief, not to any other. Our ways and our doings bring us into trouble, and we are beaten with a rod of our own making. What a poor thing is beauty! and what fools are those that are proud of it, when it will certainly, and may quickly, be consumed! The body of man is as a garment to the soul. In this garment sin has lodged a moth, which wears away, first the beauty, then the strength, and finally the substance of its parts. Whoever has watched the progress of a lingering distemper, or the work of time alone, in the human frame, will feel at once the force of this comparison, and that, surely every man is vanity. Afflictions are sent to stir up prayer. If they have that effect, we may hope that God will hear our prayer. The believer expects weariness and ill treatment on his way to heaven; but he shall not stay here long : walking with God by faith, he goes forward on his journey, not diverted from his course, nor cast down by the difficulties he meets. How blessed it is to sit loose from things here below, that while going home to our Father's house, we may use the world as not abusing it! May we always look for that city, whose Builder and Maker is God.

Chapter 40

Chapter Outline

Verses 1-5

Doubts and fears about the eternal state, are a horrible pit and miry clay, and have been so to many a dear child of God. There is power enough in God to help the weakest, and grace enough to help the unworthiest of all that trust in him. The psalmist waited patiently; he continued believing, hoping, and praying. This is applicable to Christ. His agony, in the garden and on the cross, was a horrible pit and miry clay. But those that wait patiently for God do not wait in vain. Those that have been under religious melancholy, and by the grace of God have been relieved, may apply ver. #(2) very feelingly to themselves; they are brought up out of a horrible pit. Christ is the Rock on which a poor soul can alone stand fast. Where God has given stedfast hope, he expects there should be a steady, regular walk and conduct. God filled the psalmist with joy, as well as peace in believing. Multitudes, by faith beholding the sufferings and glory of Christ, have learned to fear the justice and trust in the mercy of God through Him. Many are the benefits with which we are daily loaded, both by the providence and by the grace of God.

Verses 6-10

The psalmist foretells that work of wonder, redemption by our Lord Jesus Christ. The Substance must come, which is Christ, who must bring that glory to God, and that grace to man, which it was impossible the sacrifices should ever do. Observe the setting apart of our Lord Jesus to the work and office of Mediator. In the volume, or roll, of the book it was written of him. In the close rolls of the Divine decrees and counsel, the covenant of redemption was recorded. Also, in all the volumes of the Old Testament something was written of him, Joh 19:28. Now the purchase of our salvation is made, the proclamation is sent forth, calling us to come and accept it. It was preached freely and openly. Whoever undertook to preach the gospel of Christ, would be under great temptation to conceal it; but Christ, and those he calls to that work, are carried on in it. May we believe his testimony, trust his promise, and submit to his authority.

Verses 11-17

The best saints see themselves undone, unless continually preserved by the grace of God. But see the frightful view the psalmist had of sin. This made the discovery of a Redeemer so welcome. In all his reflections upon each step of his life, he discovered something amiss. The sight and sense of our sins in their own colours, must distract us, if we have not at the same time some sight of a Saviour. If Christ has triumphed over our spiritual enemies, then we, through him, shall be more than conquerors. This may encourage all that seek God and love his salvation, to rejoice in him, and to praise him. No griefs nor poverty can render those miserable who fear the Lord. Their God, and all that he has or does, is the ground of their joy. The prayer of faith can unlock his fulness, which is adapted to all their wants. The promises are sure, the moment of fulfilment hastens forward. He who once came in great humility, shall come again in glorious majesty.

Chapter 41

Chapter Outline

God's care for his people.   (1–4)

The treachery of David's enemies.   (5–13)

Verses 1-4

The people of God are not free from poverty, sickness, or outward affliction, but the Lord will consider their case, and send due supplies. From his Lord's example the believer learns to consider his poor and afflicted brethren. This branch of godliness is usually recompensed with temporal blessings. But nothing is so distressing to the contrite believer, as a fear or sense of the Divine displeasure, or of sin in his heart. Sin is the sickness of the soul; pardoning mercy heals it, renewing grace heals it, and for this spiritual healing we should be more earnest than for bodily health.

Verses 5-13

We complain, and justly, of the want of sincerity, and that there is scarcely any true friendship to be found among men; but the former days were no better. One particularly, in whom David had reposed great confidence, took part with his enemies. And let us not think it strange, if we receive evil from those we suppose to be friends. Have not we ourselves thus broken our words toward God? We eat of his bread daily, yet lift up the heel against him. But though we may not take pleasure in the fall of our enemies, we may take pleasure in the making vain their designs. When we can discern the Lord's favour in any mercy, personal or public, that doubles it. If the grace of God did not take constant care of us, we should not be upheld. But let us, while on earth, give heartfelt assent to those praises which the redeemed on earth and in heaven render to their God and Saviour.

Chapter 42

The conflict in the soul of a believer.

Verses 1-5

The psalmist looked to the Lord as his chief good, and set his heart upon him accordingly; casting anchor thus at first, he rides out the storm. A gracious soul can take little satisfaction in God's courts, if it do not meet with God himself there. Living souls never can take up their rest any where short of a living God. To appear before the Lord is the desire of the upright, as it is the dread of the hypocrite. Nothing is more grievous to a gracious soul, than what is intended to shake its confidence in the Lord. It was not the remembrance of the pleasures of his court that afflicted David; but the remembrance of the free access he formerly had to God's house, and his pleasure in attending there. Those that commune much with their own hearts, will often have to chide them. See the cure of sorrow. When the soul rests on itself, it sinks; if it catches hold on the power and promise of God, the head is kept above the billows. And what is our support under present woes but this, that we shall have comfort in Him. We have great cause to mourn for sin; but being cast down springs from unbelief and a rebellious will; we should therefore strive and pray against it.

Verses 6-11

The way to forget our miseries, is to remember the God of our mercies. David saw troubles coming from God's wrath, and that discouraged him. But if one trouble follow hard after another, if all seem to combine for our ruin, let us remember they are all appointed and overruled by the Lord. David regards the Divine favour as the fountain of all the good he looked for. In the Saviour's name let us hope and pray. One word from him will calm every storm, and turn midnight darkness into the light of noon, the bitterest complaints into joyful praises. Our believing expectation of mercy must quicken our prayers for it. At length, is faith came off conqueror, by encouraging him to trust in the name of the Lord, and to stay himself upon his God. He adds, And my God; this thought enabled him to triumph over all his griefs and fears. Let us never think that the God of our life, and the Rock of our salvation, has forgotten us, if we have made his mercy, truth, and power, our refuge. Thus the psalmist strove against his despondency: at last his faith and hope obtained the victory. Let us learn to check all unbelieving doubts and fears. Apply the promise first to ourselves, and then plead it to God.

Chapter 43

David endeavours to still his spirit, with hope and confidence in God.

—As to the quarrel God had with David for sin, he prays, Enter not into judgment with me, if Thou doest so I shall be condemned; but as to the quarrel his enemies had with him, he prays, Lord, judge me, and in thy providence appear on my behalf. If we cannot comfort ourselves in God, we may stay ourselves upon him, and may have spiritual supports, when we want spiritual delights. He never cast off any that trusted in him, whatever fears they may have had of their own state. We need desire no more to make us happy, than the good that flow from God's favour, and is included in his promise. Those whom God leads, he leads to his holy hill; those, therefore, who pretend to be led by the Spirit, and yet turn their backs upon ordinance, deceive themselves. We are still to pray for the Spirit of light and truth, who supplies the want of Christ's bodily presence, to guide us in the way to heaven. Whatever we rejoice or triumph in, the Lord must be the joy of it. David applies to God as his never-failing hope. Let us pray earnestly, that the Lord would send forth the truth of his word, and the light of his Spirit, to guide us into the way of holiness, peace, and salvation. The desire of the Christian, like that of the prophet in distress, is to be saved from sin as well as sorrow; to be taught in the way of righteousness by the light of heavenly wisdom, shining in Jesus Christ, and to be led by this light and truth to the New Jerusalem.

Chapter 44

A petition for succour and relief.

Verses 1-8

Former experiences of God's power and goodness are strong supports to faith, and powerful pleas in prayer under present calamities. The many victories Israel obtained, were not by their own strength or merit, but by God's favour and free grace. The less praise this allows us, the more comfort it affords, that we may see all as coming from the favour of God. He fought for Israel, else they had fought in vain. This is applicable to the planting of the Christian church in the world, which was not by any human policy or power. Christ, by his Spirit, went forth conquering and to conquer; and he that planted a church for himself in the world, will support it by the same power and goodness. They trusted and triumphed in and through him. Let him that glories, glory in the Lord. But if they have the comfort of his name, let them give unto him the glory due unto it.

Verses 9-16

The believer must have times of temptation, affliction, and discouragement; the church must have seasons of persecution. At such times the people of God will be ready to fear that he has cast them off, and that his name and truth will be dishonoured. But they should look above the instruments of their trouble, to God, well knowing that their worst enemies have no power against them, but what is permitted from above.

Verses 17-26

In afflictions, we must not seek relief by any sinful compliance; but should continually meditate on the truth, purity, and knowledge of our heart-searching God. Hearts sins and secret sins are known to God, and must be reckoned for. He knows the secret of the heart, therefore judges of the words and actions. While our troubles do not drive us from our duty to God, we should not suffer them to drive us from our comfort in God. Let us take care that prosperity and ease do not render us careless and lukewarm. The church of God cannot be prevailed on by persecution to forget God; the believer's heart does not turn back from God. The Spirit of prophecy had reference to those who suffered unto death, for the testimony of Christ. Observe the pleas used, ver. #(25, 26). Not their own merit and righteousness, but the poor sinner's pleas. None that belong to Christ shall be cast off, but every one of them shall be saved, and that for ever. The mercy of God, purchased, promised, and constantly flowing forth, and offered to believers, does away every doubt arising from our sins; while we pray in faith, Redeem us for thy mercies' sake.

Chapter 45

This psalm is a prophecy of Messiah the Prince, and points to him as a Bridegroom espousing the church to himself, and as a King ruling in it, and for it.

Verses 1-5

The psalmist's tongue was guided by the Spirit of God, as the pen is by the hand of a ready writer. This psalm is touching the King Jesus, his kingdom and government. It is a shame that this good matter is not more the subject of our discourse. There is more in Christ to engage our love, than there is or can be in any creature. This world and its charms are ready to draw away our hearts from Christ; therefore we are concerned to understand how much more worthy he is of our love. By his word, his promise, his gospel, the good will of God is made known to us, and the good work of God is begun and carried on in us. The psalmist, ver. #(3–5), joyfully foretells the progress and success of the Messiah. The arrows of conviction are very terrible in the hearts of sinners, till they are humbled and reconciled; but the arrows of vengeance will be more so to his enemies who refuse to submit. All who have seen his glory and tasted his grace, rejoice to see him, by his word and Spirit, bring enemies and strangers under his dominion.

Verses 6-9

The throne of this almighty King is established for ever. While the Holy Spirit leads Christ's people to look to his cross, he teaches them to see the evil of sin and the beauty of holiness; so that none of them can feel encouragement to continue in sin. The Mediator is God, else he had been neither able to do the Mediator's work, nor fit to wear the Mediator's crown. God the Father, as his God in respect to his human nature and mediatorial offices, has given to him the Holy Spirit without measure. Thus anointed to be a Prophet, Priest, and King, Christ has pre-eminence in the gladdening gifts and graces of the spirit, and from his fulness communicates them to his brethren in human nature. The Spirit is called the oil of gladness, because of the delight wherewith Christ was filled, in carrying on his undertakings. The salvation of sinners is the joy of angels, much more of the Son. And in proportion as we are conformed to his holy image, we may expect the gladdening gifts influences of the Comforter. The excellences of the Messiah, the suitableness of his offices, and the sufficiency of his grace, seem to be intended by the fragrance of his garments. The church formed of true believers, is here compared to the queen, whom, by an everlasting covenant, the Lord Jesus has betrothed to himself. This is the bride, the Lamb's wife, whose graces are compared to fine linen, for their purity; to gold, for their costliness: for as we owe our redemption, so we owe our adorning, to the precious blood of the Son of God.

Verses 10-17

If we desire to share these blessings, we must hearken to Christ's word. We must forget our carnal and sinful attachments and pursuits. He must be our Lord as well as our Saviour; all idols must be thrown away, that we may give him our whole heart. And here is good encouragement, thus to break off from former alliances. The beauty of holiness, both on the church and on particular believers, is, in the sight of Christ, of great price, and very amiable. The work of grace is the workmanship of the Spirit, it is the image of Christ upon the soul, a partaking of the Divine nature. It is clear of all sin, there is none in it, nor any comes from it. There is nothing glorious in the old man or corrupt nature; but in the new man, or work of grace upon the soul, every thing is glorious. The robe of Christ's righteousness, which he has wrought out for his church, the Father imputes unto her, and bestows upon her. None are brought to Christ, but those whom the Father brings. This notes the conversion of souls to him. The robe of righteousness, and garments of salvation, the change of raiment Christ has put upon her. Such as strictly cleave to Christ, loving him in singleness of heart, are companions of the bride, who partake of the very same grace, enjoy the same privileges, and share in one common salvation. These, every one, shall be brought to the King; not one lost or left behind. Instead of the Old Testament church, there shall be a New

Testament church, a Gentile church. In the believing hope of our everlasting happiness in the other world, let us always keep up the remembrance of Christ, as our only way thither; and transmit the remembrance of him to succeeding generations, that his name may endure for ever.

Chapter 46

Chapter Outline

Confidence in God. (1–5)

An exhortation to behold it. (6–11)

Verses 1-5

This psalm encourages to hope and trust in God; in his power and providence, and his gracious presence with his church in the worst of times. We may apply it to spiritual enemies, and the encouragement we have that, through Christ, we shall be conquerors over them. He is a Help, a present Help, a Help found, one whom we have found to be so; a Help at hand, one that is always near; we cannot desire a better, nor shall we ever find the like in any creature. Let those be troubled at the troubling of the waters, who build their confidence on a floating foundation; but let not those be alarmed who are led to the Rock, and there find firm footing. Here is joy to the church, even in sorrowful times. The river alludes to the graces and consolations of the Holy Spirit, which flow through every part of the church, and through God's sacred ordinances, gladdening the heart of every believer. It is promised that the church shall not be moved. If God be in our hearts, by his word dwelling richly in us, we shall be established, we shall be helped; let us trust and not be afraid.

Verses 6-11

Come and see the effects of desolating judgments, and stand in awe of God. This shows the perfect security of the church, and is an assurance of lasting peace. Let us pray for the speedy approach of these glorious days, and in silent submission let us worship and trust in our almighty Sovereign. Let all believers triumph in this, that the Lord of hosts, the God of Jacob, has been, is, and will be with us; and will be our Refuge. Mark this, take the comfort, and say, If God be for us, who can be against us? With this, through life and in death, let us answer every fear.

Chapter 47

The people exhorted to praise God.

Verses 1-4

The God with whom we have to do, is a God of awful majesty. The universal and absolute sovereignty of a holy God would be too terrible for us even to think of, were it not exercised by his Son from a mercy-seat; but now it is only terrible to the workers of iniquity. While his people express confidence and joy, and animate each other in serving him, let sinners submit to his authority, and accept his salvation. Jesus Christ shall subdue the Gentiles; he shall bring them as sheep into the fold, not for slaughter, but for preservation. He shall subdue their affections, and make them a willing people in the day of his power. Also it speaks of his giving them rest and settlement. Apply this spiritually; the Lord himself has undertaken to be the inheritance of his people. It shows the faith and submission of the saints. This is the language of every gracious soul, The Lord shall choose my inheritance for me; he knows what is good for me better than I do.

Verses 5-9

Praise is a duty in which we ought to be frequent and abundant. But here is a needful rule; Sing ye praises with understanding. As those that understand why and for what reasons they praise God, and what is the meaning of the service. It is not an acceptable service, if it is not a reasonable service. We are never to forget the end of Messiah's exaltation, so continually do the prophets dwell upon the conversion of the nations to the gospel of Christ. Why do we vainly fancy that we belong to him, unless the Spirit reign in our hearts by faith? Lord, is it not thy glory and delight to give repentance to Israel and remission of sins, now that thou art exalted as a Prince and a Saviour? Set up thy kingdom in our hearts. Bring into captivity every thought to the obedience of Christ. And so sweetly constrain all the powers and faculties of the souls of thy redeemed, into holy love, fear, and delight in thee, that praise with the understanding may rise from every heart, both here and for ever, to Thee, our God.

Chapter 48

The glories of the church of Christ.

Verses 1-7

Jerusalem is the city of our God: none on earth render him due honour except the citizens of the spiritual Jerusalem. Happy the kingdom, the city, the family, the heart, in which God is great, in which he is all. There God is known. The clearer discoveries are made to us of the Lord and his greatness, the more it is expected that we should abound in his praises. The earth is, by sin, covered with deformity, therefore justly might that spot of ground, which was beautified with holiness, be called the joy of the whole earth; that which the whole earth has reason to rejoice in, that God would thus in very deed dwell with man upon the earth. The kings of the earth were afraid of it. Nothing in nature can more fitly represent the overthrow of heathenism by the Spirit of the gospel, than the wreck of a fleet in a storm. Both are by the mighty power of the Lord.

Verses 8-14

We have here the improvement which the people of God are to make of his glorious and gracious appearances for them. Let our faith in the word of God be hereby confirmed. Let our hope of the stability of the church be encouraged. Let our minds be filled with good thoughts of God. All the streams of mercy that flow down to us, must be traced to the fountain of His loving-kindness. Let us give to God the glory of the great things he has done for us. Let all the members of the church take comfort from what the Lord does for his church. Let us observe the beauty, strength, and safety of the church. Consider its strength; see it founded on Christ the Rock, fortified by the Divine power, guarded by Him who neither slumbers nor sleeps. See what precious ordinances are its palaces, what precious promises are its bulwarks, that you may be encouraged to join yourselves to it: and tell this to others. This God, who has now done such great things for us, is unchangeable in his love to us, and his care for us. If he is our God, he will lead and keep us even to the last. He will so guide us, as to set us above the reach of death, so that it shall not do us any real hurt. He will lead us to a life in which there shall be no more death.

Chapter 49

Chapter Outline

A call for attention.	(1–5)
Folly of worldlings.	(6–14)
Against fear of death.	(15–20)

Verses 1-5

We seldom meet with a more solemn introduction: there is no truth of greater importance. Let all hear this with application to ourselves. The poor are in danger from undue desire toward the wealth of the world, as rich people from undue delight in it. The psalmist begins with applying it to himself, and that is the right method in which to treat of Divine things. Before he sets down the folly of carnal security, he lays down, from his own experience, the benefit and comfort of a holy, gracious security, which they enjoy who trust in God, and not in their worldly wealth. In the day of judgment, the iniquity of our heels, or of our steps, our past sins, will compass us. In those days, worldly, wicked people will be afraid; but wherefore should a man fear death who has God with him?

Verses 6-14

Here is a description of the spirit and way of worldly people. A man may have wealth, and may have his heart enlarged in love, thankfulness, and obedience, and may do good with it. Therefore it is not men's having riches that proves them to be worldly, but their setting their hearts upon them as the best things. Worldly men have only some floating thoughts of the things of God, while their fixed thoughts, their inward thoughts, are about the world; that lies nearest the heart. But with all their wealth they cannot save the life of the dearest friend they have. This looks further, to the eternal redemption to be wrought out by the Messiah. The redemption of the soul shall cost very dear; but, being once wrought, it shall never need to be repeated. And he, the Redeemer, shall rise again before he sees corruption, and then shall live for evermore, Re 1:18. This likewise shows the folly of worldly people, who sell their souls for that which will never buy them. With all their wealth they cannot secure themselves from the stroke of death. Yet one generation after another applaud their maxims; and the character of a fool, as drawn by heavenly Wisdom itself, Lu 12:16–21, continues to be followed even among professed Christians. Death will ask the proud sinner, Where is thy wealth, thy pomp? And in the morning of the resurrection, when all that sleep in the dust shall awake, the upright shall be advanced to the highest honour, when the wicked shall be filled with everlasting shame and contempt, Da 12:2. Let us now judge of things as they will appear in that day. The beauty of holiness is that alone which the grave cannot touch, or damage.

Verses 15-20

Believers should not fear death. The distinction of men's outward conditions, how great soever in life, makes none at death; but the difference of men's spiritual states, though in this life it may seem of small account, yet at and after death is very great. The soul is often put for the life. The God of life, who was its Creator at first, can and will be its Redeemer at last. It includes the salvation of the soul from eternal ruin. Believers will be under strong temptation to envy the prosperity of sinners. Men will praise thee, and cry thee up, as having done well for thyself in raising an estate and family. But what will it avail to be approved of men, if God condemn us? Those that are rich in the graces and comforts of the Spirit, have something of which death cannot strip them, nay, which death will improve; but as for worldly possessions, as we brought nothing into the world, so it is certain that we shall carry nothing out; we must leave all to others. The sum of the whole matter is, that it can profit a man nothing to gain the whole world, to become possessed of all its wealth and all its power, if he lose his own soul, and is cast away for want of that holy and heavenly wisdom which distinguishes man from the brutes, in his life and at his death. And are there men who can prefer the lot of the rich sinner to that of poor Lazarus, in life and death, and to eternity? Assuredly there are. What need then we have of the teaching of the Holy Ghost; when, with all our boasted powers, we are prone to such folly in the most important of all concerns!

Chapter 50

Chapter Outline

The glory of God.	(1–6)
Sacrifices to be changed for prayers.	(7–15)
Sincere obedience required.	(16–23)

Verses 1-6

This psalm is a psalm of instruction. It tells of the coming of Christ and the day of judgment, in which God will call men to account; and the Holy Ghost is the Spirit of judgement. All the children of men are concerned to know the right way of worshipping the Lord, in spirit and in truth. In the great day, our God shall come, and make those hear his judgement who would not hearken to his law. Happy are those who come into the covenant of grace, by faith in the Redeemer's atoning sacrifice, and show the sincerity of their love by fruits of righteousness. When God rejects the services of those who rest in outside performances, he will graciously accept those who seek him aright. It is only by sacrifice, by Christ, the great Sacrifice, from whom the sacrifices of the law derived what value they had, that we can be accepted of God. True and righteous are his judgments; even sinners' own consciences will be forced to acknowledge the righteousness of God.

Verses 7-15

To obey is better than sacrifice, and to love God and our neighbour better than all burnt-offerings. We are here warned not to rest in these performances. And let us beware of resting in any form. God demands the heart, and how can human inventions please him, when repentance, faith, and holiness are neglected? In the day of distress we must apply to the Lord by fervent prayer. Our troubles, though we see them coming from God's hand, must drive us to him, not drive us from him. We must acknowledge him in all our ways, depend upon his wisdom, power, and goodness, and refer ourselves wholly to him, and so give him glory. Thus must we keep up communion with God; meeting him with prayers under trials, and with praises in deliverances. A believing supplicant shall not only be graciously answered as to his petition, and so have cause for praising God, but shall also have grace to praise him.

Verses 16-23

Hypocrisy is wickedness, which God will judge. And it is too common, for those who declare the Lord's statutes to others, to live in disobedience to them themselves. This delusion arises from the abuse of God's long-suffering, and a wilful mistake of his character and the intention of his gospel. The sins of sinners will be fully proved on them in the judgment of the great day. The day is coming when God will set their sins in order, sins of childhood and youth, of riper age and old age, to their everlasting shame and terror. Let those hitherto forgetful of God, given up to wickedness, or in any way negligent of salvation, consider their urgent danger. The patience of the Lord is very great. It is the more wonderful, because sinners make such ill use of it; but if they turn not, they shall be made to see their error when it is too late. Those that forget God, forget themselves; and it will never be right with them till they consider. Man's chief end is to glorify God: whoso offers praise, glorifies him, and his spiritual sacrifices shall be accepted. We must praise God, sacrifice praise, put it into the hands of the Priest, our Lord Jesus, who is also the altar: we must be fervent in spirit, praising the Lord. Let us thankfully accept God's mercy, and endeavour to glorify him in word and deed.

Chapter 51

Chapter Outline

Verses 1-6

David, being convinced of his sin, poured out his soul to God in prayer for mercy and grace. Whither should backsliding children return, but to the Lord their God, who alone can heal them? he drew up, by Divine teaching, an account of the workings of his heart toward God. Those that truly repent of their sins, will not be ashamed to own their repentance. Also, he instructs others what to do, and what to say. David had not only done much, but suffered much in the cause of God; yet he flees to God's infinite mercy, and depends upon that alone for pardon and peace. He begs the pardon of sin. The blood of Christ, sprinkled upon the conscience, blots out the transgression, and, having reconciled us to God, reconciles us to ourselves. The believer longs to have the whole debt of his sins blotted out, and every stain cleansed; he would be thoroughly washed from all his sins; but the hypocrite always has some secret reserve, and would have some favorite lust spared. David had such a deep sense of his sin, that he was continually thinking of it, with sorrow and shame. His sin was committed against God, whose truth we deny by wilful sin; with him we deal deceitfully. And the truly penitent will ever trace back the streams of actual sin to the fountain of original depravity. He confesses his original corruption. This is that foolishness which is bound in the heart of a child, that proneness to evil, and that backwardness to good, which is the burden of the regenerate, and the ruin of the unregenerate. He is encouraged, in his repentance, to hope that God would graciously accept him. Thou desirest truth in the inward part; to this God looks, in a returning sinner. Where there is truth, God will give wisdom. Those who sincerely endeavour to do their duty shall be taught their duty; but they will expect good only from Divine grace overcoming their corrupt nature.

Verses 7-15

Purge me with hyssop, with the blood of Christ applied to my soul by a lively faith, as the water of purification was sprinkled with a bunch of hyssop. The blood of Christ is called the blood of sprinkling, Heb 12:24. If this blood of Christ, which cleanses from all sin, cleanse us from our sin, then we shall be clean indeed, Heb 10:2. He asks not to be comforted, till he is first cleansed; if sin, the bitter root of sorrow, be taken away, he can pray in faith, Let me have a well-grounded peace, of thy creating, so that the bones broken by convictions may rejoice, may be comforted.

Hide thy face from my sins; blot out all mine iniquities out of thy book; blot them out, as a cloud is blotted out and dispelled by the beams of the sun. And the believer desires renewal to holiness as much as the joy of salvation. David now saw, more than ever, what an unclean heart he had, and sadly laments it; but he sees it is not in his own power to amend it, and therefore begs God would create in him a clean heart. When the sinner feels this change is necessary, and reads the promise of God to that purpose, he begins to ask it. He knew he had by his sin grieved the Holy Spirit, and provoked him to withdraw. This he dreads more than anything. He prays that Divine comforts may be restored to him. When we give ourselves cause to doubt our interest in salvation, how can we expect the joy of it? This had made him weak; he prays, I am ready to fall, either into sin or into despair, therefore uphold me with thy Spirit. Thy Spirit is a free Spirit, a free Agent himself, working freely. And the more cheerful we are in our duty, the more constant we shall be to it. What is this but the liberty wherewith Christ makes his people free, which is contrasted with the yoke of bondage? Ga 5:1. It is the Spirit of adoption spoken to the heart. Those to whom God is the God of salvation, he will deliver from guilt; for the salvation he is the God of, is salvation from sin. We may therefore plead with him, Lord, thou art the God of my salvation, therefore deliver me from the dominion of sin. And when the lips are opened, what should they speak but the praises of God for his forgiving mercy?

Verses 16-19

Those who are thoroughly convinced of their misery and danger by sin, would spare no cost to obtain the remission of it. But as they cannot make satisfaction for sin, so God cannot take any satisfaction in them, otherwise than as expressing love and duty to him. The good work wrought in every true penitent, is a broken spirit, a broken and a contrite heart, and sorrow for sin. It is a heart that is tender, and pliable to God's word. Oh that there were such a heart in every one of us! God is graciously pleased to accept this; it is instead of all burnt-offering and sacrifice. The broken heart is acceptable to God only through Jesus Christ; there is no true repentance without faith in him. Men despise that which is broken, but God will not. He will not overlook it, he will not refuse or reject it; though it makes God no satisfaction for the wrong done to him by sin. Those who have been in spiritual troubles, know how to pity and pray for others afflicted in like manner. David was afraid lest his sin should bring judgements upon the city and kingdom. No personal fears or troubles of conscience can make the soul, which has received grace, careless about the interests of the church of God. And let this be the continued joy of all the redeemed, that they have redemption through the blood of Christ, the forgiveness of sins according to the riches of his grace.

Chapter 52

Chapter Outline

582

Verses 1-5

Those that glory in sin, glory in their shame. The patience and forbearance of God are abused by sinners, to the hardening of their hearts in their wicked ways. But the enemies in vain boast in their mischief, while we have God's mercy to trust in. It will not save us from the guilt of lying, to be able to say, there was some truth in what we said, if we make it appear otherwise than it was. The more there is of craft and contrivance in any wickedness, the more there is of Satan in it. When good men die, they are transplanted from the land of the living on earth, to heaven, the garden of the Lord, where they shall take root for ever; but when wicked men die, they are rooted out, to perish for ever. The believer sees that God will destroy those who make not him their strength.

Verses 6-9

Those wretchedly deceive themselves, who think to support themselves in power and wealth without God. The wicked man trusted in the abundance of his riches; he thought his wickedness would help him to keep his wealth. Right or wrong, he would get what he could, and keep what he had, and ruin any one that stood in his way; this he thought would strengthen him; but see what it comes to! Those who by faith and love dwell in the house of God, shall be like green olive-trees there. And that we may be as green olive-trees, we must live a life of faith and holy confidence in God and his grace. It adds much to the beauty of our profession, and to fruitfulness in every grace, to be much in praising God; and we never can want matter for praise. His name alone can be our refuge and strong tower. It is very good for us to wait on that saving name; there is nothing better to calm and quiet our spirits, when disturbed, and to keep us in the way of duty, when tempted to use any crooked courses for our relief, than to hope, and quietly wait for the salvation of the Lord. None ever followed his guidance but it ended well.

Chapter 53

The corruption of man by nature.
—This psalm is almost the same as the 14th. The scope of it is to convince us of our sins. God, by the psalmist, here shows us how bad we are, and proves this by his own certain knowledge. He speaks terror to persecutors, the worst of sinners. He speaks encouragement to God's persecuted people. How comes it that men are so bad? Because there is no fear of God before their eyes. Men's bad practices flow from their bad principles; if they profess to know God, yet in works, because in thoughts, they deny him. See the folly of sin; he is a fool, in the account of God, whose judgment we are sure is right, that harbours such corrupt thoughts. And see the fruit of sin; to what it brings men, when their hearts are hardened through the deceitfulness of sin. See also the faith of the saints, and their hope and power as to the cure of this great evil. There will come a Saviour, a great salvation, a salvation from sin. God will save his church from its enemies. He will save all believers from their own sins, that they may not be led captive by them, which will be everlasting joy to them.

From this work the Redeemer had his name JESUS, for he shall save his people from their sins, Mt 1:21.

Chapter 54

Chapter Outline

David complains of the malice of his enemies.	(1–3)
Assurance of the Divine favour and protection.	(4–7)

Verses 1-3

God is faithful, though men are not to be trusted, and it is well for us it is so. David has no other plea to depend upon than God's name, no other power to depend upon than God's strength, and these he makes his refuge and confidence. This would be the effectual answer to his prayers. Looking unto David, betrayed by the men of Judah, and to Jesus, betrayed by one of his apostles, what can we expect from any who have not set God before them, save ingratitude, treachery, malice, and cruelty? What bonds of nature, or friendship, or gratitude, or covenant, will hold those that have broken through the fear of God? Selah; Mark this. Let us set God before us at all times; for if we do not, we are in danger of despair.

Verses 4-7

Behold, God is mine Helper. If we are for him, he is for us; and if he is for us, we need not fear. Every creature is that to us, and no more, which God makes it to be. The Lord will in due time save his people, and in the mean time he sustains them, and bears them up, so that the spirit he has made shall not fail. There is truth in God's threatenings, as well as in his promises; sinners that repent not, will find it so to their cost. David's present deliverance was an earnest of further deliverance. He speaks of the completion of his deliverance as a thing done, though he had as yet many troubles before him; because, having God's promise for it, he was as sure of it as if it was done already. The Lord would deliver him out of all his troubles. May he help us to bear our cross without repining, and at length bring us to share his victories and glory. Christians never should suffer the voice of praise and thanksgiving to cease in the church of the redeemed.

Chapter 55

Chapter Outline

Verses 1-8

In these verses we have, 1. David praying. Prayer is a salve for every sore, and a relief to the spirit under every burden. 2. David weeping. Griefs are thus, in some measure, lessened, while those increase that have no vent given them. David in great alarm. We may well suppose him to be so, upon the breaking out of Absalom's conspiracy, and the falling away of the people. Horror overwhelmed him. Probably the remembrance of his sin in the matter of Uriah added much to the terror. When under a guilty conscience we must mourn in our complaint, and even strong believers have for a time been filled with horror. But none ever was so overwhelmed as the holy Jesus, when it pleased the Lord to put him to grief, and to make his soul an offering for our sins. In his agony he prayed more earnestly, and was heard and delivered; trusting in him, and following him, we shall be supported under, and carried through all trials. See how David was weary of the treachery and ingratitude of men, and the cares and disappointments of his high station: he longed to hide himself in some desert from the fury and fickleness of his people. He aimed not at victory, but rest; a barren wilderness, so that he might be quiet. The wisest and best of men most earnestly covet peace and quietness, and the more when vexed and wearied with noise and clamour. This makes death desirable to a child of God, that it is a final escape from all the storms and tempests of this world, to perfect and everlasting rest.

Verses 9-15

No wickedness so distresses the believer, as that which he witnesses in those who profess to be of the church of God. Let us not be surprised at the corruptions and disorders of the church on earth, but long to see the New Jerusalem. He complains of one that had been very industrious against him. God often destroys the enemies of the church by dividing them. And an interest divided against itself cannot long stand. The true Christian must expect trials from professed friends, from those with whom he has been united; this will be very painful; but by looking unto Jesus we shall be enabled to bear it. Christ was betrayed by a companion, a disciple, an apostle, who resembled Ahithophel in his crimes and doom. Both were speedily overtaken by Divine vengeance. And this prayer is a prophecy of the utter, the everlasting ruin, of all who oppose and rebel against the Messiah.

Verses 16-23

In every trial let us call upon the Lord, and he will save us. He shall hear us, and not blame us for coming too often; the oftener the more welcome. David had thought all were against him; but now he sees there were many with him, more than he supposed; and the glory of this he gives to

God, for it is he that raises us up friends, and makes them faithful to us. There are more true Christians, and believers have more real friends, than in their gloomy hours they suppose. His enemies should be reckoned with, and brought down; they could not ease themselves of their fears, as David could, by faith in God. Mortal men, though ever so high and strong, will easily be crushed by an eternal God. Those who are not reclaimed by the rod of affliction, will certainly be brought down to the pit of destruction. The burden of afflictions is very heavy, especially when attended with the temptations of Satan; there is also the burden of sin and corruption. The only relief under it is, to look to Christ, who bore it. Whatever it is that thou desirest God should give thee, leave it to him to give it in his own way and time. Care is a burden, it makes the heart stoop. We must commit our ways and works to the Lord; let him do as seemeth him good, and let us be satisfied. To cast our burden upon God, is to rest upon his providence and promise. And if we do so, he will carry us in the arms of his power, as a nurse carries a child; and will strengthen our spirits by his Spirit, so that they shall sustain the trial. He will never suffer the righteous to be moved; to be so shaken by any troubles, as to quit their duty to God, or their comfort in him. He will not suffer them to be utterly cast down. He, who bore the burden of our sorrows, desires us to leave to him to bear the burden of our cares, that, as he knows what is best for us, he may provide it accordingly. Why do not we trust Christ to govern the world which he redeemed?

Chapter 56

Chapter Outline

David seeks mercy from God, amidst the malice of his enemies.	(1–7)
He rests his faith on God's promises, and declares his obligation to praise him for mercies.	(8–13)

Verses 1-7

Be merciful unto me, O God. This petition includes all the good for which we come to throne of grace. If we obtain mercy there, we need no more to make us happy. It implies likewise our best plea, not our merit, but God's mercy, his free, rich mercy. We may flee to, and trust the mercy of God, when surrounded on all sides by difficulties and dangers. His enemies were too hard for him, if God did not help him. He resolves to make God's promises the matter of his praises, and so we have reason to make them. As we must not trust an arm of flesh when engaged for us, so we must not be afraid of an arm of flesh when stretched out against us. The sin of sinners will never be their security. Who knows the power of God's anger; how high it can reach, how forcibly it can strike?

Verses 8-13

The heavy and continued trials through which many of the Lord's people have passed, should teach us to be silent and patient under lighter crosses. Yet we are often tempted to repine and despond under small sorrows. For this we should check ourselves. David comforts himself, in his distress and fear, that God noticed all his grievances and all his griefs. God has a bottle and a book for his people's tears, both the tears for their sins, and those for their afflictions. He observes them with tender concern. Every true believer may boldly say, The Lord is my helper, and then I will not fear what man shall do unto me; for man has no power but what is given him from above. Thy vows are upon me, O Lord; not as a burden, but as that by which I am known to be thy servant; as a bridle that restrains me from what would be hurtful, and directs me in the way of my duty. And vows of thankfulness properly accompany prayers for mercy. If God deliver us from sin, either from doing it, or by his pardoning mercy, he has delivered our souls from death, which is the wages of sin. Where the Lord has begun a good work he will carry it on and perfect it. David hopes that God would keep him even from the appearance of sin. We should aim in all our desires and expectations of deliverance, both from sin and trouble, that we may do the better service to the Lord; that we may serve him without fear. If his grace has delivered our souls from the death of sin, he will bring us to heaven, to walk before him for ever in light.

Chapter 57

Chapter Outline

Verses 1-6

All David's dependence is upon God. The most eminent believers need often repeat the publican's prayer, "God be merciful to me a sinner." But if our souls trust in the Lord, this may assure us, in our utmost dangers, that our calamities will at length be overpast, and in the mean time, by faith and prayer, we must make him our refuge. Though God be most high, yet he condescends so low, as to take care that all things are made to work for good to his people. This is a good reason why we should pray earnestly. Look which way we will on this earth, refuge fails, no help appears; but we may look for it from heaven. If we have fled from the wrath to come, unto Jesus Christ, he that performed all things needful to purchase the salvation of his people, will do for us and in us all things needful for our enjoyment of it. It made David droop to think there should be those that bore him so much ill-will. But the mischief they designed against him, returned on themselves. And when David was in the greatest distress and disgrace, he did not pray, Lord, exalt me, but, Lord, exalt thine own name. Our best encouragement in prayer, is taken from the glory of God, and to that, more than to our own comfort, we should have regard in all our petitions for mercy.

Verses 7-11

By lively faith, David's prayers and complaints are at once turned into praises. His heart is fixed; it is prepared for every event, being stayed upon God. If by the grace of God we are brought into this even, composed frame of mind, we have great reason to be thankful. Nothing is done to purpose, in religion, unless it is done with the heart. The heart must be fixed for the duty, put in frame for it; fixed in the duty by close attention. Our tongue is our glory, and never more so than when praising God; dull and sleepy devotions will never be acceptable to God. Let us awake early in the morning, to begin the day with God; early in the beginning of a mercy. When God comes toward us with his favours, let us go forth to meet him with our praises. David desired to bring others to join in praising God; and in his psalms, he is still praising God among the people, singing to Him among the nations. Let us seek to have our hearts fixed to praise his boundless mercy and unfailing faithfulness; and to glorify him with body, soul, and spirit, which are his. Let us earnestly pray that the blessings of the gospel may be sent through every land.

Chapter 58

Chapter Outline

Wicked judges described and reproved.   (1–5)

A prayer that they may be disabled, and their   (6–11)
ruin predicted.

Verses 1-5

When wrong is done under the form of law, it is worse than any other; especially it is grievous to behold those who profess to be children of God, joining together against any of his people. We should thank the Lord for merciful restraints; we should be more earnest in seeking renewing grace, more watchful over ourselves, and more patient under the effects of fallen nature in others. The corruption of their nature was the root of bitterness. We may see in children the wickedness of the world beginning. They go astray from God and their duty as soon as possibly they can. And how soon will little children tell lies! It is our duty to take pains to teach them, and above all, earnestly to pray for converting grace to make our children new creatures. Though the poison be within, much of it may be kept from breaking forth to injure others. When the Saviour's words are duly regarded, the serpent becomes harmless. But those who refuse to hear heavenly wisdom, must perish miserably, for ever.

Verses 6-11

David prayed that the enemies of God's church and people might be disabled to do further mischief. We may, in faith, pray against the designs of the enemies of the church. He foretells their ruin. And who knows the power of God's anger? The victories of the Just One, in his own person and that of his servants, over the enemies of man's salvation, produce a joy which springs not from revenge, but from a view of the Divine mercy, justice, and truth, shown in the redemption of the elect, the punishment of the ungodly, and the fulfilment of the promises. Whoever duly considers these things, will diligently seek the reward of righteousness, and adore the Providence which orders all thing aright in heaven and in earth.

Chapter 59

Chapter Outline

David prays for deliverance from his enemies. (1–7)

He foresees their destruction. (8–17)

Verses 1-7

In these words we hear the voice of David when a prisoner in his own house; the voice of Christ when surrounded by his merciless enemies; the voice of the church when under bondage in the world; and the voice of the Christian when under temptation, affliction, and persecution. And thus earnestly should we pray daily, to be defended and delivered from our spiritual enemies, the temptations of Satan, and the corruptions of our own hearts. We should fear suffering as evil-doers, but not be ashamed of the hatred of workers of iniquity. It is not strange, if those regard not what they themselves say, who have made themselves believe that God regards not what they say. And where there is no fear of God, there is nothing to secure proper regard to man.

Verses 8-17

It is our wisdom and duty, in times of danger and difficulty, to wait upon God; for he is our defence, in whom we shall be safe. It is very comfortable to us, in prayer, to look to God as the God of our mercy, the Author of all good in us, and the Giver of all good to us. The wicked can never be satisfied, which is the greatest misery in a poor condition. A contented man, if he has not what he would have, yet he does not quarrel with Providence, nor fret within himself. It is not poverty, but discontent that makes a man unhappy. David would praise God because he had many times, and all along, found Him his refuge in the day of trouble. He that is all this to us, is certainly worthy of our best affections, praises, and services. The trials of his people will end in joy and praise. When the night of affliction is over, they will sing of the Lord's power and mercy in the morning. Let believers now, in assured faith and hope, praise Him for those mercies, for which they will rejoice and praise him for ever.

Chapter 60

Chapter Outline

David prays for the deliverance of Israel   (1–5)
from their enemies.

He entreats God to carry on and complete   (6–12)
their victories.

Verses 1-5

David owns God's displeasure to be the cause of all the hardships he had undergone. And when God is turning his hand in our favour, it is good to remember our former troubles. In God's displeasure their troubles began, therefore in his favour their prosperity must begin. Those breaches and divisions which the folly and corruption of man make, nothing but the wisdom and grace of God can repair, by pouring out a spirit of love and peace, by which only a kingdom is saved from ruin. The anger of God against sin, is the only cause of all misery, private or public, that has been, is, or shall be. In all these cases there is no remedy, but by returning to the Lord with repentance, faith, and prayer; beseeching him to return to us. Christ, the Son of David, is given for a banner to those that fear God; in him they are gathered together in one, and take courage. In his name and strength they wage war with the powers of darkness.

Verses 6-12

If Christ be ours, all things, one way or another, shall be for our eternal good. The man who is a new creature in Christ, may rejoice in all the precious promises God has spoken in his holiness. His present privileges, and the sanctifying influences of the Spirit, are sure earnests of heavenly glory. David rejoices in conquering the neighbouring nations, which had been enemies to Israel. The Israel of God are through Christ more than conquerors. Though sometimes they think that the Lord has cast them off, yet he will bring them into the strong city at last. Faith in the promise will assure us that it is our Father's good pleasure to give us the kingdom: But we are not yet made complete conquerors, and no true believer will abuse these truths to indulge sloth, or vain confidence. Hope in God is the best principle of true courage, for what need those fear who have God on their side? All our victories are from him, and while those who willingly submit to our anointed King shall share his glories, all his foes shall be put under his feet.

Chapter 61

Chapter Outline

David seeks God upon former experience.   (1–4)

He vows to serve God.   (5–8)

Verses 1-4

David begins with prayers and tears, but ends with praise. Thus the soul, being lifted up to God, returns to the enjoyment of itself. Wherever we are, we have liberty to draw near to God, and may find a way open to the throne of grace. And that which separates us from other comforts, should drive us nearer to God, the fountain of all comfort. Though the heart is overwhelmed, yet it may be lifted up to God in prayer. Nay, I will cry unto thee, for by that means it will be supported and relieved. Weeping must quicken praying, and not deaden it. God's power and promise are a rock that is higher than we are. This rock is Christ. On the Divine mercy, as on a rock, David desired to rest his soul; but he was like a ship-wrecked sailor, exposed to the billows at the bottom of a rock too high for him to climb without help. David found that he could not be fixed on the Rock of salvation, unless the Lord placed him upon it. As there is safety in Him, and none in ourselves, let us pray to be led to and fixed upon Christ our Rock. The service of God shall be his constant work and business: all must make it so who expect to find God their shelter and strong tower. The grace of God shall be his constant comfort.

Verses 5-8

There is a people in the world that fear God's name. There is a heritage peculiar to that people; present comforts in the soul, earnests of future bliss. Those that fear God have enough in him, and must not complain. We need desire no better heritage than that of those who fear God. Those abide to good purpose in this world, who abide before God, serve him, and walk in his fear; those who do so, shall abide before him for ever. And these words are to be applied to Him of whom the angel said, the Lord shall give unto him the throne of his father David, and of his kingdom there shall be no end, Lu 1:32. God's promises, and our faith in them, are not to do away, but to encourage prayer. We need not desire to be better secured than under the protection of God's mercy and truth. And if we partake of that grace and truth which came by Jesus Christ, we may praise him, whatever be our outward circumstances. But renewed experience of God's mercy and truth towards his people in Christ, is the main matter of our joy in him, and our praise unto him.

Chapter 62

Chapter Outline

Verses 1-7

We are in the way both of duty and comfort, when our souls wait upon God; when we cheerfully give up ourselves, and all our affairs, to his will and wisdom; when we leave ourselves to all the ways of his providence, and patiently expect the event, with full satisfaction in his goodness. See the ground and reason of this dependence. By his grace he has supported me, and by his providence delivered me. He only can be my Rock and my salvation; creatures are nothing without him, therefore I will look above them to him. Trusting in God, the heart is fixed. If God be for us, we need not fear what man can do against us. David having put his confidence in God, foresees the overthrow of his enemies. We have found it good to wait upon the Lord, and should charge our souls to have such constant dependence upon him, as may make us always easy. If God will save my soul, I may well leave every thing else to his disposal, knowing all shall turn to my salvation. And as David's faith in God advances to an unshaken stedfastness, so his joy in God improves into a holy triumph. Meditation and prayer are blessed means of strengthening faith and hope.

Verses 8-12

Those who have found the comfort of the ways of God themselves, will invite others into those ways; we shall never have the less for others sharing with us. the good counsel given is, to trust wholly in God. We must so trust in him at all times, as not at any time to put that trust in ourselves, or in any creature, which is to be put in him only. Trust in him to guide us when in doubt, to protect us when in danger, to supply us when in want, to strengthen us for every good word and work. We must lay out wants and our wishes before him, and then patiently submit our wills to his: this is pouring out our hearts. God is a refuge for all, even for as many as will take shelter in him. The psalmist warns against trusting in men. The multitude, those of low degree, are changeable as the wind. The rich and noble seem to have much in their power, and lavish promises; but those that depend on them, are disappointed. Weighed in the balance of Scripture, all that man can do to make us happy is lighter than vanity itself. It is hard to have riches, and not to trust in them if they increase, though by lawful and honest means; but we must take heed, lest we set our affections unduly upon them. A smiling world is the most likely to draw the heart from God, on whom alone it should be set. The consistent believer receives all from God as a trust; and he seeks to use it to his glory, as a steward who must render an account. God hath spoken as it were once for all, that power belongs to him alone. He can punish and destroy. Mercy also belongs to him; and his recompensing the imperfect services of those that believe in him, blotting out their transgressions for the Redeemer's sake, is a proof of abundant mercy, and encourages us to trust in him. Let us trust in his mercy and grace, and abound in his work, expecting mercies from him alone.

Chapter 63

Chapter Outline

Verses 1, 2

Early will I seek thee. The true Christian devotes to God the morning hour. He opens the eyes of his understanding with those of his body, and awakes each morning to righteousness. He arises with a thirst after those comforts which the world cannot give, and has immediate recourse by prayer to the Fountain of the water of life. The true believer is convinced, that nothing in this sinful world can satisfy the wants and desires of his immortal soul; he expects his happiness from God, as his portion. When faith and hope are most in exercise, the world appears a weary desert, and the believer longs for the joys of heaven, of which he has some foretastes in the ordinances of God upon earth.

Verses 3-6

Even in affliction we need not want matter for praise. When this is the regular frame of a believer's mind, he values the loving-kindness of God more than life. God's loving-kindness is our spiritual life, and that is better than temporal life. We must praise God with joyful lips; we must address ourselves to the duties of religion with cheerfulness, and speak forth the praises of God from a principle of holy joy. Praising lips must be joyful lips. David was in continual danger; care and fear held his eyes waking, and gave him wearisome nights; but he comforted himself with thoughts of God. The mercies of God, when called to mind in the night watches, support the soul, making darkness cheerful. How happy will be that last morning, when the believer, awaking up after the Divine likeness, shall be satisfied with all the fulness of God, and praise him with joyful lips, where there is no night, and where sorrow and sighing flee away!

Verses 7-11

True Christians can, in some measure, and at some times, make use of the strong language of David, but too commonly our souls cleave to the dust. Having committed ourselves to God, we must be easy and pleased, and quiet from the fear of evil. Those that follow hard after God, would soon fail, if God's right hand did not uphold them. It is he that strengthens us and comforts us. The psalmist doubts not but that though now sowing in tears, he should reap in joy. Messiah the Prince shall rejoice in God; he is already entered into the joy set before him, and his glory will be completed at his second coming. Blessed Lord, let our desire towards thee increase every hour; let our love be always upon thee; let all our enjoyment be in thee, and all our satisfaction from thee. Be thou all in all to us while we remain in the present wilderness state, and bring us home to the everlasting enjoyment of thee for ever.

Chapter 64

Chapter Outline

Prayer for deliverance. (1–6)

The destruction of the wicked, (7–10)
encouragement to the righteous.

Verses 1-6

The psalmist earnestly begs of God to preserve him from disquieting fear. The tongue is a little member, but it boasts great things. The upright man is the mark at which the wicked aim, they cannot speak peaceably either of him or to him. There is no guard against a false tongue. It is bad to do wrong, but worse to encourage ourselves and one another in it. It is a sign that the heart is hardened to the greatest degree, when it is thus fully set to do evil. A practical disbelief of God's knowledge of all things, is at the bottom of every wickedness. The benefit of a good cause and a good conscience, appears most when nothing can help a man against his enemies, save God alone, who is always a present help.

Verses 7-10

When God brings upon men the mischiefs they have desired on others, it is weight enough to sink a man to the lowest hell. Those who love cursing, it shall come upon them. Those who behold this shall understand, and observe God's hand in all; unless we do so, we are not likely to profit by the dispensations of Providence. The righteous shall be glad in the Lord; not glad of the misery and ruin of their fellow-creatures, but glad that God is glorified, and his word fulfilled, and the cause of injured innocence pleaded effectually. They rejoice not in men, nor in themselves, nor in any creature, or creature enjoyments, nor in their wisdom, strength, riches, or righteousness; but in Christ, in whom all the seed of Israel are justified and glory, and in what he is to them, and has done for them.

Chapter 65

Chapter Outline

God is to be praised in the kingdom of (1–5)
grace.

In the kingdom of providence. (6–13)

Verses 1-5

All the praise the Lord receives from this earth is from Zion, being the fruit of the Spirit of Christ, and acceptable through him. Praise is silent unto thee, as wanting words to express the great goodness of God. He reveals himself upon a mercy-seat, ready to hear and answer the prayers of all who come unto him by faith in Jesus Christ. Our sins prevail against us; we cannot pretend to balance them with any righteousness of our own: yet, as for our transgressions, of thine own free mercy, and for the sake of a righteousness of thine own providing, we shall not come into condemnation for them. Observe what it is to come into communion with God in order to blessedness. It is to converse with him as one we love and value; it is to apply ourselves closely to religion as to the business of our dwelling-place. Observe how we come into communion with God; only by God's free choice. There is abundance of goodness in God's house, and what is satisfying to the soul; there is enough for all, enough for each: it is always ready; and all without money and without price. By faith and prayer we may keep up communion with God, and bring in comfort from him, wherever we are. But it is only through that blessed One, who approaches the Father as our Advocate and Surety, that sinners may expect or can find this happiness.

Verses 6-13

That Almighty strength which sets fast the mountains, upholds the believer. That word which stills the stormy ocean, and speaks it into a calm, can silence our enemies. How contrary soever light and darkness are to each other, it is hard to say which is most welcome. Does the watchman wait for the morning? so does the labourer earnestly desire the shades of evening. Some understand it of the morning and evening sacrifices. We are to look upon daily worship, both alone and with our families, to be the most needful of our daily occupations, the most delightful of our daily comforts. How much the fruitfulness of this lower part of the creation depends upon the influence of the upper, is easy to observe; every good and perfect gift is from above. He who enriches the earth, which is filled with man's sins, by his abundant and varied bounty, can neither want power nor will to feed the souls of his people. Temporal mercies to us unworthy creatures, shadow forth more important blessings. The rising of the Sun of righteousness, and the pouring forth of the influences of the Holy Spirit, that river of God, full of the waters of life and salvation, render the hard, barren, worthless hearts of sinners fruitful in every good work, and change the face of nations more than the sun and rain change the face of nature. Wherever the Lord passes, by his preached gospel, attended by his Holy Spirit, his paths drop fatness, and numbers are taught to rejoice in and praise him. They will descend upon the pastures of the wilderness, all the earth shall hear and embrace the gospel, and bring forth abundantly the fruits of righteousness which are, through Jesus Christ, to the glory of the Father. Manifold and marvellous, O Lord, are thy works, whether of nature or of grace; surely in loving-kindness hast thou made them all.

Chapter 66

Chapter Outline

Praise for God's sovereign power in the creation.　　　　　　　　　　　　　　　　　(1–7)

For his favour to his church.　　　　　　　　　　　　　　　　　(8–12)

And the psalmist's praise for his experience   (13–20)
of God's goodness.

Verses 1-7

The holy church throughout all the world lifts up her voice, to laud that Name which is above every name, to make the praise of Jesus glorious, both by word and deed; that others may be led to glorify him also. But nothing can bring men to do this aright, unless his effectual grace create their hearts anew unto holiness; and in the redemption by the death of Christ, and the glorious deliverances it effects, are more wondrous works than Israel's deliverance from Egyptian bondage.

Verses 8-12

The Lord not only preserves our temporal life, but maintains the spiritual life which he has given to believers. By afflictions we are proved, as silver in the fire. The troubles of the church will certainly end well. Through various conflicts and troubles, the slave of Satan escapes from his yoke, and obtains joy and peace in believing: through much tribulation the believer must enter into the kingdom of God.

Verses 13-20

We should declare unto those that fear God, what he has done for our souls, and how he has heard and answered our prayers, inviting them to join us in prayer and praise; this will turn to our mutual comfort, and to the glory of God. We cannot share these spiritual privileges, if we retain the love of sin in our hearts, though we refrain from the gross practice, Sin, regarded in the heart, will spoil the comfort and success of prayer; for the sacrifice of the wicked is an abomination of the Lord. But if the feeling of sin in the heart causes desires to be rid of it; if it be the presence of one urging a demand we know we must not, cannot comply with, this is an argument of sincerity. And when we pray in simplicity and godly sincerity, our prayers will be answered. This will excite gratitude to Him who hath not turned away our prayer nor his mercy from us. It was not prayer that fetched the deliverance, but his mercy that sent it. That is the foundation of our hopes, the fountain of our comforts; and ought to be the matter of our praises.

Chapter 67

A prayer for the enlargement of Christ's kingdom.
—All our happiness comes from God's mercy; therefore the first thing prayed for is, God be merciful to us, to us sinners, and pardon our sins. Pardon is conveyed by God's blessing, and secured in that. If we, by faith, walk with God, we may hope that his face will shine on us. The psalmist passes on to a prayer for the conversion of the Gentiles, which shows that the Old Testament saints desired that their advantages might also be enjoyed by others. And many Scripture prophecies and

promises are wrapped up in prayers: the answer to the prayer of the church is as sure as the performance of God's promises. The joy wished to the nations, is holy joy. Let them be glad that by his providence the Lord will overrule the affairs of kingdoms; that even the kingdoms of this world shall became the kingdom of the Lord, and of his Christ. Then is declared a joyful prospect of all good when God shall do this. The success of the gospel brings outward mercies with it; righteousness exalts a nation. The blessing of the Lord sweetens all our creature-comforts to us, and makes them comforts indeed. All the world shall be brought to worship Him. When the gospel begins to spread, it shall go forward more and more, till it reaches to the ends of the earth. It is good to cast in our lot with those that are the blessed of the Lord. If nothing had been spoken in Scripture respecting the conversion of the heathen, we might think it vain to attempt so hopeless a work. But when we see with what confidence it is declared in the Scriptures, we may engage in missionary labours, assured that God will fulfil his own word. And shall we be backward to make known to the heathen the knowledge with which we are favoured, and the salvation we profess to glory in? They cannot learn unless they are taught. Then let us go forward in the strength of the Lord, and look to him to accompany the word the Holy Ghost; then Satan's kingdom shall be destroyed, and the kingdom of our Redeemer established.

Chapter 68

Chapter Outline

Verses 1-6

None ever hardened his heart against God, and prospered. God is the joy of his people, then let them rejoice when they come before him. He who derives his being from none, but gives being to all, is engaged by promise and covenant to bless his people. He is to be praised as a God of mercy and tender compassion. He ever careth for the afflicted and oppressed: repenting sinners, who are helpless and exposed more than any fatherless children, are admitted into his family, and share all their blessings.

Verses 7-14

Fresh mercies should put us in mind of former mercies. If God bring his people into a wilderness, he will be sure to go before them in it, and to bring them out of it. He provided for them, both in the wilderness and in Canaan. The daily manna seems here meant. And it looks to the spiritual provision for God's Israel. The Spirit of grace and the gospel of grace are the plentiful rain, with which God confirms his inheritance, and from which their fruit is found. Christ shall come as showers that water the earth. The account of Israel's victories is to be applied to the victories over death and hell, by the exalted Redeemer, for those that are his. Israel in Egypt among the kilns appeared wretched, but possessed of Canaan, during the reigns of David and Solomon, appeared glorious. Thus the slaves of Satan, when converted to Christ, when justified and sanctified by him, look honourable. When they reach heaven, all remains of their sinful state disappear, they shall be as the wings of the dove, covered with silver, and her feathers as gold. Full salvation will render those white as snow, who were vile and loathsome through the guilt and defilement of sin.

Verses 15-21

The ascension of Christ must here be meant, and thereto it is applied, Eph 4:8. He received as the purchase of his death, the gifts needful for the conversion of sinners, and the salvation of believers. These he continually bestows, even on rebellious men, that the Lord God might dwell among them, as their Friend and Father. He gave gifts to men. Having received power to give eternal life, the Lord Jesus bestows it on as many as were given him, Joh 17:2. Christ came to a rebellious world, not to condemn it, but that through him it might be saved. The glory of Zion's King is, that he is a Saviour and Benefactor to all his willing people, and a consuming fire to all that persist in rebellion against him. So many, so weighty are the gifts of God's bounty, that he may be truly said to load us with them. He will not put us off with present things for a portion, but will be the God of our salvation. The Lord Jesus has authority and power to rescue his people from the dominion of death, by taking away the sting of it from them when they die, and giving them complete victory over it when they rise again. The crown of the head, the chief pride and glory of the enemy, shall be smitten; Christ shall crush the head of the serpent.

Verses 22-28

The victories with which God blessed David over the enemies of Israel, are types of Christ's victory, for himself and for all believers. Those who take him for theirs, may see him acting as their God, as their King, for their good, and in answer to their prayers; especially in and by his word and ordinances. The kingdom of the Messiah shall be submitted to by all the rulers and learned in the world. The people seem to address the king, ver. #(28). But the words are applicable to the Redeemer, to his church, and every true believer. We pray, that thou, O God the Son, wilt complete thine undertaking for us, by finishing thy good work in us.

Verses 29-31

A powerful invitation is given to those that are without, to join the church. Some shall submit from fear; overcome by their consciences, and the checks of Providence, they are brought to make peace with the church. Others will submit willingly, ver. #(29, 31). There is that beauty and benefit in the service of God, and in the gospel of Christ which went forth from Jerusalem, which is enough to invite sinners out of all nations.

Verses 32-35

God is to be admired and adored with reverence and godly fear, by all that attend in his holy places. The God of Israel gives strength and power unto his people. Through Christ strengthening us we can do all things, not otherwise; therefore he must have the glory of all we do, with our humble thanks for enabling us to do it, and for accepting the work of his hands in us.

Chapter 69

Chapter Outline

Verses 1-12

We should frequently consider the person of the Sufferer here spoken of, and ask why, as well as what he suffered, that, meditating thereon, we may be more humbled for sin, and more convinced of our danger, so that we may feel more gratitude and love, constraining us to live to His glory who died for our salvation. Hence we learn, when in affliction, to commit the keeping of our souls to God, that we may not be soured with discontent, or sink into despair. David was hated wrongfully, but the words far more fully apply to Christ. In a world where unrighteousness reigns so much, we must not wonder if we meet with those that are our enemies wrongfully. Let us take care that we never do wrong; then if we receive wrong, we may the better bear it. By the satisfaction Christ made to God for our sin by his blood, he restored that which he took not away, he paid our debt, suffered for our offences. Even when we can plead Not guilty, as to men's unjust accusations, yet before God we must acknowledge ourselves to deserve all that is brought upon us. All our sins take rise from our foolishness. They are all done in God's sight. David complains of the unkindness of friends and relations. This was fulfilled in Christ, whose brethren did not believe on him, and who was forsaken by his disciples. Christ made satisfaction for us, not only by putting off the honours due to God, but by submitting to the greatest dishonours that could be done to any man. We need not be discouraged if our zeal for the truths, precepts, and worship of God, should provoke some, and cause others to mock our godly sorrow and deadness to the world.

Verses 13-21

Whatever deep waters of affliction or temptation we sink into, whatever floods of trouble or ungodly men seem ready to overwhelm us, let us persevere in prayer to our Lord to save us. The tokens of God's favour to us are enough to keep our spirits from sinking in the deepest outward troubles. If we think well of God, and continue to do so under the greatest hardships, we need not fear but he will do well for us. And if at any time we are called on to suffer reproach and shame, for Christ's sake, this may be our comfort, that he knows it. It bears hard on one that knows the worth of a good name, to be oppressed with a bad one; but when we consider what a favour it is to be accounted worthy to suffer shame for the name of Jesus, we shall see that there is no reason why it should be heart-breaking to us. The sufferings of Christ were here particularly foretold, which proves the Scripture to be the word of God; and how exactly these predictions were fulfilled in Jesus Christ, which proves him to be the true Messiah. The vinegar and the gall given to him, were a faint emblem of that bitter cup which he drank up, that we might drink the cup of salvation. We cannot expect too little from men, miserable comforters are they all; nor can we expect too much from the God of all comfort and consolation.

Verses 22-29

These are prophecies of the destruction of Christ's persecutors. Verses #(22, 23), are applied to the judgments of God upon the unbelieving Jews, in Ro 11:9, 10. When the supports of life and delights of sense, through the corruption of our nature, are made the food and fuel of sin, then our table is a snare. Their sin was, that they would not see, but shut their eyes against the light, loving darkness rather; their punishment was, that they should not see, but should be given up to their own hearts' lusts which hardened them. Those who reject God's great salvation proffered to them, may justly fear that his indignation will be poured out upon them. If men will sin, the Lord will reckon for it. But those that have multiplied to sin, may yet find mercy, through the righteousness of the Mediator. God shuts not out any from that righteousness; the gospel excludes none who do not, by unbelief, shut themselves out. But those who are proud and self-willed, so that they will not come in to God's righteousness, shall have their doom accordingly; they themselves decide it. Let those not expect any benefit thereby, who are not glad to be beholden to it. It is better to be poor and sorrowful, with the blessing of the Lord, than rich and jovial, and under his curse. This may be applied to Christ. He was, when on earth, a man of sorrows that had not where to lay his head; but God exalted him. Let us call upon the Lord, and though poor and sorrowful, guilty and defiled, his salvation will set us up on high.

Verses 30-36

The psalmist concludes the psalm with holy joy and praise, which he began with complaints of his grief. It is a great comfort to us, that humble and thankful praises are more pleasing to God than the most costly, pompous sacrifices. The humble shall look to him, and be glad; those that seek him through Christ shall live and be comforted. God will do great things for the gospel church, in which let all who wish well to it rejoice. A seed shall serve him on earth, and his servants shall inherit his heavenly kingdom. Those that love his name shall dwell before him for ever. He that spared not his own Son, but delivered him up for us all, how shall he not with him also freely give us all things? Arise, thou great Restorer of the ancient places to dwell in, and turn away ungodliness from thy people.

Chapter 70

The speedy destruction of the wicked, and the preservation of the godly.
—This psalm is almost the same as the last five verses of Ps 40. While here we behold Jesus Christ set forth in poverty and distress, we also see him denouncing just and fearful punishment on his Jewish, heathen, and antichristian enemies; and pleading for the joy and happiness of his friends, to his Father's honour. Let us apply these things to our own troubled circumstances, and in a believing manner bring them, and the sinful causes thereof, to our remembrance. Urgent trials should always awake fervent prayers.

Chapter 71

Chapter Outline

Prayers that God would deliver and save.   (1–13)

Believing praises.   (14–24)

Verses 1-13

David prays that he might never be made ashamed of dependence upon God. With this petition every true believer may come boldly to the throne of grace. The gracious care of Divine providence in our birth and infancy, should engage us to early piety. He that was our Help from our birth, ought to be our Hope from our youth. Let none expect ease or comfort from the world. Those who love the Lord, often are hated and persecuted; men wondered at for their principles and conduct; but the Lord has been their strong refuge. The faithful servants of God may be assured that he will not cast them off in old age, nor forsake them when their strength fails.

Verses 14-24

The psalmist declares that the righteousness of Christ, and the great salvation obtained thereby, shall be the chosen subject of his discourse. Not on a sabbath only, but on every day of the week, of the year, of his life. Not merely at stated returns of solemn devotion, but on every occasion, all the day long. Why will he always dwell on this? Because he knew not the numbers thereof. It is impossible to measure the value or the fulness of these blessings. The righteousness is unspeakable, the salvation everlasting. God will not cast off his grey-headed servants when no longer capable of labouring as they have done. The Lord often strengthens his people in their souls, when nature is sinking into decay. And it is a debt which the old disciples of Christ owe to succeeding generations, to leave behind them a solemn testimony to the advantage of religion, and the truth of God's promises; and especially to the everlasting righteousness of the Redeemer. Assured of deliverance and victory, let us spend our days, while waiting the approach of death, in praising the Holy One of Israel with all our powers. And while speaking of his righteousness, and singing his praises, we shall rise above fears and infirmities, and have earnests of the joys of heaven. The work of redemption ought, above all God's works, to be spoken of by us in our praises. The Lamb that was slain, and has redeemed us to God, is worthy of all blessing and praise.

Chapter 72

Chapter Outline

David begins with a prayer for Solomon.	(1)
He passes into a prophecy of the glories of his reign, and of Christ's kingdom.	(2–17)
Praise to God.	(18–20)

Verse 1

This psalm belongs to Solomon in part, but to Christ more fully and clearly. Solomon was both the king and the king's son, and his pious father desired that the wisdom of God might be in him, that his reign might be a remembrance of the kingdom of the Messiah. It is the prayer of a father for his child; a dying blessing. The best we can ask of God for our children is, that God would give them wisdom and grace to know and to do their duty.

Verses 2-17

This is a prophecy of the kingdom of Christ; many passages in it cannot be applied to the reign of Solomon. There were righteousness and peace at first in the administration of his government; but, before the end of his reign, there were troubles and unrighteousness. The kingdom here spoken of is to last as long as the sun, but Solomon's was soon at an end. Even the Jewish expositors understood it of the kingdom of the Messiah. Observe many great and precious promises here made, which were to have full accomplishment only in the kingdom of Christ. As far as his kingdom is set up, discord and contentions cease, in families, churches, and nations. The law of Christ, written in the heart, disposes men to be honest and just, and to render to all their due; it likewise disposes men to live in love, and so produces abundance of peace. Holiness and love shall be lasting in Christ's kingdom. Through all the changes of the world, and all the changes of life, Christ's kingdom will support itself. And he shall, by the graces and comforts of his Spirit, come down like rain upon the mown grass; not on that cut down, but that which is left growing, that it may spring again. His gospel has been, or shall be, preached to all nations. Though he needs not the services of any, yet he must be served with the best. Those that have the wealth of this world, must serve Christ with it, do good with it. Prayer shall be made through him, or for his sake; whatever we ask of the Father, should be in his name. Praises shall be offered to him: we are under the highest obligations to him. Christ only shall be feared throughout all generations. To the end of time, and to eternity, his name shall be praised. All nations shall call HIM blessed.

Verses 18-20

We are taught to bless God in Christ, for all he has done for us by him. David is earnest in prayer for the fulfilment of this prophecy and promise. It is sad to think how empty the earth is of the glory of God, how little service and honour he has from a world to which he is so bountiful. May we, like David, submit to Christ's authority, and partake of his righteousness and peace. May we bless him for the wonders of redeeming love. May we spend our days, and end our lives, praying for the spread of his gospel.

Made in the USA
Coppell, TX
22 July 2022